To Mary
with love,
April

Dreams of the Soul

The Poetry Guild

Dreams of the Soul
Copyright © 1997 by The Poetry Guild

Rights to individual poems reside with the submitting artists.
All rights reserved under international copyright conventions. No part of this
book may be reproduced, stored in a retrieval system or transmitted in any form,
electronic, mechanical, or by other means, without the written permission of the publisher.
Address all inquiries to Publisher.

Library of Congress
Cataloging in Publication Data

ISBN 1-888680-22-9

Printed in the United States of America by
The Poetry Guild
Finalist Publishing Center
3687 Ira Road · Bath, OH 44210

Editor's Acknowledgment

In conducting its poetry competitions, The Poetry Guild has received and evaluated poems written by poets from all walks of life. The collected works of *Dreams of the Soul* consist of a wide range of sounds and styles: free verse, traditional verse, narrative, lyric, dramatic, avant-garde and even experimental.

As the Editor of this book, the hardest part of my job was going through all the poems and making choices about which ones to use. All of the poems featured in this anthology deserve to be celebrated in the form of publication. And all beginning poets should especially be cheered.

Of course, our panel of judges assumed the most difficult task in choosing the prize winners. Because so many of the poems exhibited a powerful voice, it was even harder to pick the Grand Prize Winner. But one poem did succeed. You will find this poem, entitled "A Country Road," by Robert Collins featured on page 3.

One of the traits that makes this anthology unique is that it gives newcomers a chance to write and be read, and by doing so brings poetry back to the people. After all, art is meant to be appreciated.

The real beauty of this anthology is its inspiration. In some ways, all of us can relate to the topics and themes expressed in these poems, which address important and often timely issues that we might otherwise ignore or suppress. Each poem conveys its own message, and provides a vehicle of expression for diverse attitudes and fresh insights.

I would like to congratulate each and every poet on their inclusion in this special anthology. In addition, I am grateful to the editors, book designers, production assistants and countless others for their efforts in creating this important work. Most of all, a special thanks goes out to those of you who chose to share your poetry with us and the world!

Terence Troon, Editor

"Poetry is life distilled."

—Gwendolyn Brooks

Welcome to the Poetry Guild's heralded edition of *Dreams of the Soul!* This unique anthology contains a collection of selected poems composed by a variety of individuals.

When the idea for this anthology surfaced, its main purpose was to create an ongoing resource for those interested in publishing their own poetry and, more than anything else, to showcase the best original work.

Members of our staff have been hard at work creating this special edition. Our judges vigorously critiqued thousands of poems in order to select only the most praiseworthy of verse. Each poem in this prize anthology has been chosen based on its merit.

You will find featured the work of 1,774 contributors whose poems deal with a wide range of subjects. The selected poems focus on the reflective power of words to inform the public and create awareness about significant issues through frequently meaningful observations and vastly different poetic styles.

We are happy to say that we have a number of prize winning poems featured in the book as well, including the Grand Prize Winner and a number of honourable mention awards. (The winning entries are presented in Chapter One.) We are also delighted to publish those poets who were not prize recipients, but whose work we feel is definitely worthy of publication.

As communicators in the literary field, we all want to reach the widest possible audience. This anthology appeals to a broad spectrum of poetry lovers. By having a poem published in this anthology, you will be gaining exposure and sharing your work with many others in the poetry community.

In addition to poems, this anthology also features special dedications and a most interesting chapter of "Personal Profiles." This book encourages you to browse. In reading it, we hope that you will come away with new understandings and shared realizations of our world and experiences.

Table of Contents

Chapter One	**The Winners' Forum**	1
	Winners' Announcement Page	2
	The Winning Poems	3
Chapter Two	**Noteworthy Works**	21
	The Anthology of Poems	22
Chapter Three	**Personal Profiles**	309
	The Biographies	310
Appendix	**Index of Poets**	329

CHAPTER ONE

The Winners' Forum

It is with great pleasure that we proudly present to you this year's National Poetry Competition winners.

The poems featured in this chapter are notable not only for the masterful way in which they convey the poets' ideas, but also because they challenge the reader to reinterpret significant subject matters. It is truly amazing to see the variety of styles among the poems submitted. All have received honourable mentions from our judges. Robert Collin's "A Country Road" stands out with its superb style, craft and the poet's ability to make his poem "live and breathe."

EDITOR'S NOTE: *You will find that some of the works represented in this and the following chapter are dedicated to people who perhaps influenced or inspired the individual authors. All special dedications are composed by the poets at their personal request.*

Grand Prize

"A Country Road"
— Robert Collins

Honourable Mention

Sheila Allen–*Journey*
Meredith Allison–*Echoes Call...*
Josephine M. Ansumana–*Nemesis*
Chris Antoniou–*The Soldier*
Karen Ashjian–*If We Were Strangers*
Robin Austin–*The Bubble In The Honey*
Stephen O. Bisset–*Snowfall*
Denise Blohm/Beauregard–*In Me*
Sasha A. Bluvshteyn–*Untitled*
Andrea C. Boucher–*The Boxy Bee*
E. N. Bryant–*Autumn Song*
Ethel M. Burch–*Don't Laugh At Me*
Renate Buxton–*My Fallen Comrades*
Gary Cairns–*Love Apart*
Faith Campbell–*Untitled*
Denise Chamberlain–*Sleepless*
Wanda Cook–*Underneath My Mama's Feet In The Kitchen*
Amanda M. Coots–*Loved Me*
W. Maurice Crook–*Until...*
Vivian Davis–*Remembered Pleasures*
Joanne D. Denko–*A Small Boy's Bedtime*
Sharon Dennis–*A Symphony Of Words*
Joseph M. DiPerna, Jr.–*Adoption*
Katherine Divolis–*A Different Time*
Clayton Drysdale–*Someday*
Robert Evans–*I Wish I'd Known When I Was Young*
Lana J. Farley–*Baby Boomer Blues*
Helen Farris–*No Clear Path*
David Fleming–*It Reminds Me*
Lynda Fraser–*Ice Mist*
Sherri A. Fulton–*It Is*
Gary Gaines–*The Gladstone In Parkdale*
Jeannie Giordano–*Mourning Hunger*

Patti Goodwin–*Untitled*
Shirley Goulden–*Enchantment*
Roberta L. Hagen–*To My Former English Lover*
Sue Harding–*Suicide*
Kathryn Emilie Harris–*Armistice Joy*
Anne Herbig–*Dawn Song*
Elizabeth Herreid–*Evening Magic*
Barbara Hetzel–*Untitled*
C. Lincoln Humes–*Rhythmic Feet*
Laura Isaacson–*Winter Wind*
Conni Jackson–*Safe?*
F. M. Johnson–*What Goes On*
Jason Jones–*Punch–Drunk*
Cynthia M. Kadow–*Tiny Tears*
Cezar Khursigara–*My Last Lover*
Linda King–*The Headwaters*
Donald Lashley–*Rainstorm*
Vincent LoPresto–*Tide Of Life*
Sharon Loyd–*The Other Side*
Grace Wheeler Luby–*Gramma's House*
P. Marcotulio–*Questions For A Day Lily*
Stephen Martin–*Caged*
Elizabeth McDonald–*First Love*
Jerry McGinley–*Dream Of Flying*
Valerie McNeilis–*The Jogger*
Marie McNulty–*Dancing Skaters*
Valerie Meadows–*Windows*
Chris Moat–*The Mole*
Joey Neggers–*No One Wins*
Bob Neil–*The Gift*
J. C. Old–*Autumnal Thoughts*
Joseph Parker–*A Tribute To A Mentor*
Anita L. Pederson–*My Garden Of Poetry*

Jenifer Rajkumar–*Luna And Lunatic*
Veronica W. Reeves–*Rule Of Love*
Jodi A. Richardson–*Vibrations*
S. K. Rickwood–*Let Me Be*
Jenny Terrero Rivera–*Not Of This World*
Sabrina Rogers–*Shadows And Shade*
Patricia G. Rourke–*Another Set of Ears*
Barbara R. Sawtelle–*Intimacy*
Linda Schoppe–*The Best Of Time*
Ruth A. Scott–*My Summer*
Wednesday A. Scott–*Regarding Fear*
Ellen Sims–*Country Lanes*
Audrey Nadine Smith–*Hush*
Richard Smith–*Seasons*
Troyce Solley–*Taciturn*
Kristina Stecco–*My Solo*
Amanda Anne Stirn–*The Daisies In The Field*
Freyda E. Strackeljahn–*All*
Mary D. Strahler–*Resurrection*
P. Swambo–*Untitled*
C. Robert Swanbeck–*Autumn's Glory*
Marcie Swank-Kolb–*Layers*
Lisa Muer Tanner–*Dream Catcher*
Beckie Taylor–*Scattered*
Marie Ann Tenny–*The Willow's Children*
Diana Tiernan–*The Twenty–Ninth Of August*
Stephanie L. Wallace–*Nocturnal*
Heather Weeks–*The Storm*
Joyce Wilkinson–*New Friends*
Gerald D. Williams–*Coal*
Elaine Wong–*The Ice Princess*
Patrica Woodley–*The Surrender*
Lesley Woodward–*Full Circle*

A Country Road

by Robert Collins

Once I walked along a country road
lined with trees for shade
I stood for just a moment
leaning against an old log–split fence
That time had painted with the strokes
of wind and rain
Baked by the sun to ashy shades
of black and gray
I listened to the wild flowers
swaying in the breeze
Their sweet fragrances soothing
to my untapped senses
So serene it was
there alone with nature
It could have been
any time in history.

Dreams of the Soul

It Is
Sherri A. Fulton
It is the fresh aroma of a tender rain.
The sight of a warm, sunlight, illumination piercing the heart.

And the butterfly flutters,
Flickering its delicate illusive wings.

Children chase and aspire,
Running after this keeper of youthful fire.
Yet in contemplative stillness it descends up a hand.

Who dare rip its translucent filmy wings?
Flier and Dreamer, Hope and never Fear.
Dare you cage or pin these wings?
Kill and destroy this priceless gift from our God?!

It is the virginal meadow,
Purest with paper thin blades of green.
It is the warm wet earth nurturing a multitude of fresh children.
Inspiration of music, poetry, and artful expression...

And the butterfly flutters,
And the butterfly flutters.

For you see the sacred and delicate wings
have flickered against the edges of my soul,

Its gentle understanding completes all that is whole.

The Headwaters
Linda King
He is a circular stream; a continuous, natural flow that feels no need for deviation,
Carrying past to present while seeking his future which lies in the Headwaters.
Rules for life, within his banks, remain true; they sing the songs of the Headwaters.
Life sways in the wind anchored only by love.
He protects the cloudy waters of the past, shielding them as He is dredged by the present.
His goal; his destined future, is to serve the Headwaters

She is a restless river, liberating or oppressing the ripples of turbulence within;
Feeling the need to deviate while journeying to her future which lies in the Headwaters.
Rules for life, within her banks, alter, they sing new songs of the Headwaters.
Life is uprooted and blown into exile.
She can protect or reject her cloudy waters; She can stretch the boundary of the present.
Her goal; her intended future, is to become the Headwaters.

This is the future He expected: life abiding by the rules, created by the Headwaters.
But, what if the rules for life changed and life rebelled, as rebels do?
Bubbles bursting on the surface cause gentle ripples to gather in speed and go with the flow.
He becomes then a tributary of She.

Is this the future she expected: life abiding by the rules which are hers; the Headwaters?
But, what of the undercurrents, sucking at life as eddies do?
Agitated waters become rapids which burst the banks; exiling and destroying life in vain.
All life that's left is one life; She.

Dedication: My dad; my circular stream

Loved Me
Amanda M. Coots
I was younger, less experienced in life.
You were carefree—
but you took care of me.
You taught me to drive, to fly kites,
to love.

I loved your arms,
tanned to their elbows and white to their shoulders,
the brilliant whiskers of your jaw,
and the hole in the right pocket of all of your jeans.

You loved me for me.
I loved being yours;
even your jealousy flattered me.

The day before I moved
you acted like nothing was wrong.
The day I moved
you wouldn't look at me or touch me
or say good–bye.

You stood in front my house
until we left and probably a while after.

Why don't you write?

The Willow's Children
Marie Ann Tenny
I wonder if the willow tree
Is weeping down with sorrow
With pain all the way to his inner core
From the memories of the children
Who once swung in his branches
But too soon grew away.
And does he wish they
Would come back for one more day of play?

Dawn Song
Anne Herbig
I wake and hear your voice, the sound of a star calling me out into the darkness
I speak my prayers into the cool morning stillness, while the hearths of women are yet cold
You dance among the reeds, hooves splashing in the grass under the pale moonlight
A child of the Morning Star, she guides you in from the fields to forage in my pockets for warm milk

Your sides heave and I feel the pounding of your heart
Soft muzzle tugging at the bottle, gulping warm milk
A trickle runs down my arm as I lift the bottle higher, and you calm
Brushing my face against your soft coat I see the mark of Morning Star Woman on your throat

I listen to the rhythm of your breathing as the sun rises over the eastern hills
And draw warm milk from the nanny goat in streams that sing against the
sides of the metal bucket:
Sun rises, steam rises
Moon is beautiful, star is beautiful
Dawn is beautiful, woman is beautiful
Graceful is the dance of a paint horse in the moonlight
I am Morning Star
I am your Dawn Song

Winners' Forum

No One Wins
Joey Neggers
No one wins,
The two sides battle,
Guns fire,
Bombs drop,
Men scream,
Armies die,
Until no soldiers are left,
And the war is through,
No one wins.

Enchantment
Shirley Goulden
The rising sun cast its rays across the meadows,
Awoke a sleepy lark and it began to trill.
It's song carried over the dew—glistened fields
Right into an old farmhouse behind the hill.

A heavy—eyed lad lazily tossed back the sheets,
Blinked crossly at the brilliant, golden light,
Talked to himself as he donned blue dungarees,
Visioning proud glances, if the fish did bite.

The sun smiled teasingly at the white lilies,
Turned on more heat as they stretched and yawned;
Tickled a bushy—tailed squirrel behind his wee ear,
Touched the whole, dopey world with it's magic wand.

The morning glories peaked shyly into the kitchen,
Grinned at the young lady eating breakfast there,
Nodded their tiny, sweet faces in greeting,
At the little grandma with the silvery hair.

Out in the barnyard, the chipmunks scurried about.
Farmer Brown sang a lyric as he milked peaceful Nell,
"What's the cause of such enchanted bliss?" he asked.
But the sun who knew the answer, whispered, "Won't tell, won't tell!"

Untitled
Faith Campbell
I walked into the sunlight hoping to see the day before me
But I saw only the clouds that hung overhead; their weight upon my
  shoulders
Holding me down and causing tears to well inside
I walked along further, hoping that it was only shade
But again I was in despair at the realization that I was wrong
  once more
Remote memories circled around me
As the burden became more of days in childhood buried beneath
  cobwebs of stone
Sadness consuming the losses I suffered; the days since that I recalled
  such tragedies
Wishing brings nothing back and the clouds darken
I am falling under the weight of guilt and sorrow that haunts me;
Breaking, tearing apart at the seams
My soul cries for help but alone I carry the load and blame no
  one for the hurt inside
I no longer deny and what light can I see but that I search for
But empty handed as I am now, what is left of my sanity
I cannot hide in the shadows of self pity for there is nowhere that this
  world will find me
I want the light so that I can bask in its glory to feel its heat warm my
  skin
Set on fire my withering soul and into this entity I will wallow
And death come to my sorrow as the weight I carry upon my back be removed
And my stature returned, I mourn no more

All
Freyda E. Strackeljahn
A cup is all I hold, in it...
warm tea and memories,
a romance changed by the season...
sadness, fills my heart.

My hands carefully embrace the warm cup,
I cleave to it,
the warm tea, the memories...
the aroma of memories gently touch my lips... as I sip.

This is all that is left,
after the talks of you and me,
after... all...
can this be all?... life... so callous.

From here... where to?,
etched memories of what was, cannot be erased.
What never came to fruition, like the flower that never blossomed,
... cut before its time.

perhaps...
the painted roses on the cup will never fade,
its vibrant red colors will bring back...
ardent memories... of what once... was.

Intimacy
Barbara R. Sawtelle
It's been said No Man is an Island,
But I disagree.
Each being has a world of its own—
An inner sanctity
Of thoughts and feelings
Inaccessible but by invitation.
And each creature,
With its idiosyncratic preferences,
Holds peculiar things precious
Unto itself

Country Lanes
Ellen Sims
As I walked beside a field of new—mown hay,
And inhaled the sweet aroma as it lay
In rows fresh cut this early dew—filled morn,
My spirit was transported to the place where I was born.

I felt again the dreamy summer days,
Fog bound morns off by noontime haze,
Billowy white clouds of sunny afternoon,
Warm lazy days when school let out in June.

Vacation time stretched endlessly it seemed,
A child then, I played and worked and dreamed
Of glamorous city life and fortune gained,
Bright lights and movie stars and fame.

For little did I know the value of
Rolling fields with sky stretched wide above,
The glow of sunshine filtering through the trees
On sparkling water shimmering in a soft warm breeze.

Rich heritage instilled in childhood days will be
Eternally a treasured part of me,
And in sweet memory every now and then
I'll travel back to country lanes again.

Dreams of the Soul

I Wish I'd Known When I Was Young
Robert Evans

Dad's new cutter came in a box
body sleek and graceful as a fox
teeth as sharp as a butcher's hook;
Dad winked and fixed me with a knowing look

He said, Watch me trim this hedge in record time, son
and laughing, ran the cable out, switched on
I listened open–mouthed to the motor's dreadful roar
and crouched in lonely dread behind the door

Dad went on chuckling while he worked
till the thing quite suddenly, extraordinarily, jerked;
scarcely a sign betrayed his agony, not a sound, no groan
as it slashed his fingers clean through to the bone

inside he shrugged it off with a laugh, a wink
while I watched the water redden in the sink
Mum ushered me away with a reprimand
about homework or something equally as bland

I wish they'd been honest with me then
I wish they'd told me why it was we men
must always put on such a false brave face
as if to show emotion was a crime, a fall from grace

Underneath My Mama's Feet In The Kitchen
Wanda Cook

Underneath my mama's feet in the kitchen—
Where pots boiled and simmered
And hope rarely glimmered—
Seven hungry cries assaulted her ears.
Never mindful of her tears
We'd query, "Is it ready yet?"
Unaware that her regrets
Boiled harder than the food awaited,
We'd squirm, our hunger unabated,
Underneath my mama's feet in the kitchen.

Seasons
Richard Smith

Spring's sweet rhythm fills my head,
Like newly–blooming flowers, I rise from the dead;
A breath of fresh air – she entered my life,
Bringing an end to the coldness and strife.

Passions rise with the summer heat,
I eagerly await each time we're to meet;
I can't believe I have found such bliss,
No longer fated to the same old hit–and–miss.

We walk hand in hand through the autumn leaves,
But the temperature seems to drop between her and me;
I search myself, yet no answers can I find,
And so I assume that it's all in my mind.

The ground starts to freeze as winter sets in,
And I feel a chill as well from within;
I never expected that we'd ever part–
Now I'm here, alone, with a hole in my heart.

Spring's sweet rhythm fills my mind,
And just like the flowers, I'm beginning again;
Seeking some solace to enter my soul,
I've realized that, by myself, I can still be whole.

Journey
Sheila Allen

Hey don't wake me up!
The air is cold, I pull towards my warm bed.
Mystery, darkness, voices. What's going on?
Being carried downstairs!

Out into the pitch black
This isn't fair.
The slam of a car door;
Moving off, a shoulder comes near my cheek.
An arm holds me close.
Questioning, wonder, sleep overcomes me.

A guard's whistle, a shunting train;
Moving left and then right. A voice calls out
"Be still!"
The rhythm of movement lulls me to sleep once more.

Bodies – moving, jostling, reaching, stretching
Something is thrust into my hand
A smiling face looks down: "We're here!"
A large hand reaches for mine: "Hold tight!"
A voice shouts, "There's the sea!"

Dedication: In memory of my parents

Hush
Audrey Nadine Smith

Tasting the bittersweet milk from my heavy breasts
You have found comfort and sustenance
Like our newborn in that white crib in the corner
I will rock you to sleep after we are spent from sex
And in the hush of the night
I watch the moonlight scatter white patterns on the floor
And listen to the two of you breathe
Evenly, gently
And if one of you finds discomfort in sleep
I will be there to slay imaginary dragons or demons
Quickly hushing fears

Full Circle
Lesley Woodward

Turning, ever turning, season following season,
Do we ever take the time to wonder at the reason?
The wheel of life continues, we cannot change its course,
The miracles of nature are a strong, yet gentle, force.

In spring, the winter's cold gives way to days of gentle mildness,
Leaves and flowers emerge from buds, enjoying nature's kindness.
All the birds and animals awaken from their slumbers,
Choose their mates, select their homes, and slowly swell their numbers.

In summer, spring's cool, breezy, days give way to long hot hours,
Birdsong and young animal cries, lush grass and pretty flowers.
Children play, their happy laughter echoing all around,
Whilst frogs jump into garden ponds, what a mysterious sound.

In autumn, summer's sun grows cool, days grow shorter now,
Flower heads begin to droop, brown leaves fall from the bough.
Squirrels start to forage for their food supplies to store,
Children, birds and animals aren't heard much any more.

In winter, autumn's blustery days give way to a dark, cold freeze,
Holly, pine, ivy, yew show green through tall, bare trees.
Icicles form, snow falls, creating a wondrous view,
A buried land, in wait for spring, to start its life anew.

Winners' Forum

Echoes Call...
Meredith Allison

Echoes call despairingly,
remembering a long distant past
hearing again the heartbroken laments
of two souls as love perished,
life blood flowing across the point of a blade.

Echoes call searchingly,
drifting through the ages
hoping – yearning
longing to find the love which died
too soon, too young, so long ago.

Echoes call triumphantly,
two strangers lock gazes
passed flows to present
twin souls remember love
rejoice in finding and rebinding.

Echoes fall silent.
lovers joined once more –
lost souls blend together as one
cosmic balance restored
Their search complete.

No Clear Path
Helen Farris

So you are facing another
mountain, that seems much to
high for you to climb. The
thorns and thistles have grown
so tall. It seems there is no
clear path, but if you will
remember who's in charge,
you will find another path,
where others have already
crossed the mountain,
and so can you!

Resurrection
Mary D. Strahler

After crimson flowers faded
and foliage turned brown and dead
I put the bulb in a small paper bag
just as the florist had said.

I tucked it all in a tomb–like place
underneath the stair,
Forgot about the captured life
stored in the bulb resting there.

Days were filled with other concerns
until again it was time to plant.
I sought the bulb in the brown paper bag
in that tomb where the light was scant.

The sight I saw surprised me.
Broken through the brown bag jail,
Yearning for life, was a flower,
strong, yet pink and pale.

Potted and placed in the sunlight
the amaryllis blushed brilliant red,
Proclaiming full life and wonder
to the faithless whose hopes were dead.

My Solo
Kristina Stecco

When I step outside in the middle of the night.
The full moon becomes my spotlight,
The stars my audience, the Earth my stage.

On this stage hidden from everything but the moon.
I can find the solitude that makes my heart swoon.
On this stage I am also far from the facade of the day.
Alone on the stage to be me and not what others say.
It is here during my solo that my audience listens to me
Not for who I am but for me.

Under the soft spotlight I shed the mask of day
Wishing the night would never go away.
It is here during my soliloquy
That my audience disappears at the break of day.
The mask goes back on,
My spotlight, the moon, is gone.

Until the sun will set
Then my mask I can forget.
It is then that I step outside in the middle of the night,
The full moon becomes my spotlight,
The stars my audience, the Earth my stage.

Taciturn
Troyce Solley

I'm closed
cut off
some say secretive
Until
someone reaches me
showing compassion
and warmth
Then
we bond
share love
and trust

The Boxy Bee
Andrea C. Boucher

Driving home from work one day, I had the bad luck of getting
Stuck behind a school bus. Grumbling softly, I eased up as the
Giant, pregnant bee brought herself to a halt, red lights flashing,
Warning of her stop. The doors swung open, and three small
Children were birthed. A trio of girls, most likely sisters, raced
Up the driveway, anxious to be the first to buzz about the
Adventures of recess, the lessons, even that day's lunch.
The smells, sounds, and memories of the bus came rushing
Back, flooding my mind in my little grown–up car:
— Our bus driver, stomping on squirt guns unfortunately misaimed —
Rock music blaring from the back of the bus (that's where the big kids
    sat) —
And my sisters and me, seated somewhere in the middle,
    crammed together in
One green seat, giggling as we bounced impossibly high
    (or so we thought)
As the bus roared over the potholes that dotted the country roads —
An hour–long trek each way, every day, once taken for granted
But now cherished as a precious, realized memory.
The school bus: an orange–yellow, boxy bee
Oozing swarms of sweet, young life,
Blank slates cohabiting in a world
Contained completely within itself.

Dreams of the Soul

Vibrations
Jodi A. Richardson
Hollow frames
Animal skin stretched
Interwoven with twine
Stimulates my spirit
Yes, the titillating rhythm of the drum
Awakens the senses and physical movements of the body
An invaluable symbol of history
From tribal ceremonies to survival communications
The message in the beat
Echoes in one's soul
Crossing bridges of generations

Sleepless
Denise Chamberlain
Digital white sheen cuts through the gloom,
highlighting my form camouflaged in quilt.
Radio plays its lullaby,
searing notes stirring subconscious souvenirs,
marauding memories.

Recollections trigger recriminations and regrets.
Wounds open, eyes burn,
despair, like a sniper, lies in wait.

Tired of surrender to torture of self,
the whipping boy raises it's willful head.

Putting thoughts in order
on optimistic lines
of cool, calm paper,
Faith and Fortitude combine forces.

Assured of the advent of inevitable joy,
the quelling of hope allayed,
the mind declares a cease–fire;
longed–for sleep is granted.

Questions For A Day Lily
P. Marcotulio
Day Lily... Born anew new each morn.
Glowing orange, swaying green, graceful bobbing in the breeze.

Do you count the minutes of dawn? Or envy the tall trees?
You have no eyes to see how the sun goes,
but you follow its track across the skies.

No built– in second hands to warn you of their passing,
no ears to overhear the time of day. The "Dance of the Hours" flies!

I watch you closely, What will you do when the sun leaves
my windowsill to
drop behind the nearby hill.

You droop and wilt in spite of my concern. What tells you to
fold your petals
and let go? I yearn to know!

This day is over. I am sad, But not too sad!

A new bud waits... it knows exactly when to unfold and to it's life be true.
Who tells it to?

The Bubble In The Honey
Robin Austin
The spirit in matter is like
the bubble in the honey
that is carried into the coffee,
tasting neither the sweet of the honey,
nor the bitter of the coffee.
It enters sheltered by what is cool and sweet
to be set free by melting in what is hot and bitter.
—Tasting neither—
It rises again to be reunited
with the infinitely greater atmosphere...
Which always was
its true nature.

Suicide
Sue Harding
When they bring you back from the edge of despair
from the brink of the end of everything
and they pronounce you "resting quietly now"
and they pull the whispering screens from around your bed
and tiptoe softly away
the world intrudes once more.

And the old lady in the next bed asks "better now, dearie?"
and the library trolley squeaks by
and it's pureed peas again on the menu
and the vicar and your family stay forever
and you wish they'd go away
and "you be a good girl and you'll be out in ten days".

Out?
Out there?

When they bring you back from the edge of despair
from the brink of the end of everything
they commit you to Everlasting Hell

Until the next time...

The Storm
Heather Weeks
The world around me is dark and silent.
The earth itself seems to hold its breath.
And then in the silence, a whisper is heard
as the wind begins to blow.
Harder, and harder, and harder still
blows the sharp and biting wind.
The trees bend as if to touch the ground.
Before this awesome force, they bow.
The earth shakes as thunder rolls in the sky above.
A lightening flash turns night to day, and back to night again.
Again and again the cycle repeats,
as the wind howls and the rain pounds the ground.
Suddenly, all is still
and the earth is silent again.
The storm is over as fast as it began,
and by morning few signs of it remain.
The birds sing in their trees,
and the grass is fresh with dew.
All the earth smells fresh,
for it has been washed anew.

Dedication: All those who encouraged me

Winners' Forum

My Garden Of Poetry
Anita L. Pederson
I gathered seeds of poetry
A metaphor here, a choice phrase there.
I planted them in nice neat rows;
Placing each word with gentle care.
I watered them with tender tears
Of joy, of fear, of love, and pain;
And then I helped them grow and bloom
Into my very own hybrid strain.
I shared with all my garden fair
Inviting them to come and see
In hopes that they'd enjoy the flowers
I grew from the seeds of poetry.

The Surrender
Patrica Woodley
Sam was going to be a Brother,
And with swelling manly chest
He proudly told his Father
He'd be better than the rest!
He'd teach the baby fishing;
And football in the park:
Then at night, beneath the bedclothes
They'd be Spacemen, in the dark —
But looking at the cradle,
His heart began to Sink!
For the babe beneath the counterpane
Was clad in shades of Pink!...

He felt an Angel touch upon his hand–
He gave a little sigh;
Her tiny fingers 'round his, curled;
She gazed with dewy eye! —
'Twas then that Sam surrendered:
Down fell the Hero Brave
For she was his little Angel——
And he, her willing Slave!

To My Former English Lover
Roberta L. Hagen
You talked to me on your cell–phone
through the streets of Manchester
about Coco's and One–legged Pigeons.

We walked in Jackson Square
rode around Nawlins in a carriage.
We made love at the Airport Hilton
while dreaming of tomorrow.

We shared tea and scones and
wandered through bookstores in love.
I believed what you said.

When you left, you took your love with you.
You couldn't call, Wendy would get mad about the bill.
Your e–mails sounded false.
You wouldn't answer your cell–phone anymore.

When we met in August you said,
"Right people, wrong time."
I don't know if I believed you?
Maybe I never did.

Safe?
Conni Jackson
Is it safe where you are?
You seem to think so, but I do not
There is much danger where you are!
Emotions are not your enemy
nor is intimacy
nor am I

Emotions can cause pain...
and often do
Maybe some pain is the price
of feeling
of caring
of being connected
of loving
of being truly alive

What may, to you, feel warm and safe
can, instead, be a place that slowly grows cold
And when you, in the end, die alone
Who will know that you are gone?
Who will care?

Tide Of Life
Vincent LoPresto
As I sit on the lawn and
gaze out to sea,
I can lose myself in daydreams.
With the roaring tide of life
that lie,
and the drifting of the stars.
For in the vastness of space,
and the infinity of time.
Each wave that pounds the beach,
there seems to be a note
of sadness.
After all, we must know the
proper limits of our own farewell.

Mourning Hunger
Jeannie Giordano
The seams split open
anguish and lace intertwined
jutting forward, sailing back
So long I waited
to hear your voice.
When I woke up
that morning
acid noise, your voice
chewed at my soul
sweet butter
spread softly
with a serrated knife

I knew I would not
be satisfied.
Your taste,
still on the tip
of my tongue
slipped back and digested
into the belly
of loneliness

Dreams of the Soul

What Goes On
F. M. Johnson

When waning days of summer
Slide into foundling days of fall –
When flowers dim,
Sunlight grows thin,
And grass turns brown and dull –
Then trees explode with color
And tart air energizes.
Creatures hurry,
Wild things scurry,
Each chore list compromised.

Animals and folk
Harvest food and fashion shelter –
Cozy space here,
Storage out there –
Bring life at last to order.
For winter swoops upon us
Sooner than we think best.
Man gets older,
Wild life, bolder,
And plants draw God's seventh day for rest.

In Me
Denise Blohm/Beauregard

In a drawing, there is more than lines and the form they design.
In a sculpture, there is more than stone and the chisel carving.
In a painting, there is more than color and the strokes of a brush.
In a book, there is more than pages and the words upon them.
In a poem, there is more than rhyme and the rhythm that moves it.
In a life, there is more than flesh and the blood beating in it.
In me, there is more than sleep and the waking each day.
There is fear and the courage to face it,
there is envy and admiration to replace it,
there is hate and the love that destroys it,
there is pain and the healing that relieves it,
there is sorrow and the joy that erases it,
there is emotion and the logic that rebukes it!

Punch–Drunk
Jason Jones

I peek through the wire mesh screen, alert
though my eyes are vacant.
The sun in September lends fact to the mythical world
I have engineered, giving me moments of clarity.
I nudge open the door to let the tropical air accommodate me.
It has recorded a squall in the Atlantic—one that hit beyond the gulf
where the ocean starts to curve around the Earth.
The ivory mist of dawn burns away—
my cotton gauze perspective is gone.
Soon it will be back to non–fiction, again.
So let me browse the Cadillac pinks and mail truck blues,
and sample the Popsicle greens and candy–apple reds
a while longer—before daylight adds more tonic to my drink...
And when the sun begins its reign,
I want to sink into a conscious state, without getting too comfortable.
Because I might miss the transition: when sterling blue gives way to
    alabaster,
silver shine to October gold,
mango to rich lavender,
blue smoke to deep navy,
diamond–studded black to sleep.

Don't Laugh At Me
Ethel M. Burch

Don't laugh at me as I totter by
Nor mock me when I pass,
But understand
The way you are now
I once was——
Young, smooth, beautiful,
Straight, thin, tall,
With a sharp eye, a quick look,
A strong hand, flashing teeth,
A sure step,
The World at my feet.
The way I am now
You will be——
Old, wrinkled, ugly,
Bent, weak, bald,
With a shaky hand, snaggled teeth,
A dull eye, a slow look,
A faltering step,
The grave at your feet.

Dedication: Those many, many wonderful students

It Reminds Me
David Fleming

I walk the beach in the daylight hours
The winds race across the dunes
The surf beats relentlessly on the eroding sands
And it reminds me of the troubled times in my life
When there seemed no hope, no escape
No peace from the daily trials and tribulations of life

I walk the same beach in the twilight hours
But the winds have calmed
The water now gently laps at the sand's edge
There is peace and tranquility
The days cares seem to somehow vanish
And it reminds me of you.

Gramma's House
Grace Wheeler Luby

On Sunny Days –
We stretched the bands and bands of dandelions
and dangled them on the chestnut tree.
We tied the knots and made the wreaths
and played our childish games
of hide–and–seek, kick the can, and iffer tag.
We counted cars and stars
on her front porch
in a quiet time ago
at Gramma's House.

On Rainy Days –
We rummaged through the dirt floor cellars
believing hidden ghosts spied on us
as we practiced words from our spellers.
We found diamond dust in the coal bin
and monsters in the canning closet.
We had so little — we had so much.
Even the witches under the stairs
knew. We had no cares
in Gramma's House.

Winners' Forum

A Tribute To A Mentor
Joseph Parker

In an overgrown patch in the middle of a field,
Stood a tender sapling withering away.
The sun threatened to dry it up completely,
Every breeze shook it violently.

A master cultivator nurtured this young tree,
Replanted it in a protected environment,
Shaded it from the sun and watered it often,
Then watched it grow and take on new life.

Years have passed and now standing in the forest
A tall tree, robust with many branches.
At times gusty winds blow through its dense foliage,
Yet it stands upright; for it has developed healthy roots.
Yes I stand upright! for I have developed healthy roots.

Dancing Skaters
Marie McNulty

Two graceful bodies,
Move as one,
Forgotten are the crowds,
The heartbeat quickens,
Gliding, curving, arching,
A symphony of their own,
Soars through the well –
toned limbs,
So graceful, so fluid,
Like a hymn,
A majesty,
Traversing, skirts swirling,
Blades flashing across
the ice.
A move, a union,
Ascending, descending,
Revolving.
Involved with each other.
A harmony, a delight,
Artistry on a winter's night.

Caged
Stephen Martin

The fire burned cold that night,
its flames unable to ward the chill night air,
my bones protested the cold,
yet I sat there boldly, without care.
Upon my lap a book rested,
its broad–leafed pages yellow with age,
I sighed, sipped cognac and considered,
how my life became a cage.
One minute to mid–night the time,
the fire ebbed– flames dying low,
my cognac spilled upon the floor,
face pale in the hearth's dull glow.
Now look, its the stroke of midnight,
death stares me in the face,
he beckons with a skeletal hand,
leading me away with haste.
I look back and see the light dim,
"Goodbye" I said to the cage,
death bears me in his doleful grip,
no more turning of the page.

A Different Time
Katherine Divolis

Nothing about you seems
familiar anymore. Not your face,
not your eyes, not the girl in your
arms... Absolutely nothing.

I vaguely remember, a time
so long ago, where your face
was more familiar to me than my very
own... And your eyes reflected into mine
every morning, when you used to be my
sunshine.

Your skin, so soft, so well matched
to my velvet touch, a different time
so long ago, when I loved you so very much.

Autumn's Glory
C. Robert Swanbeck

When summer fields turn beige and lean
And the oaks and poplars are no longer green
When autumn leaves come upon the scene
And the woodland trees stand bare and clean
Splashing hills with red and gold,
A dazzling, beautiful picture to behold
The age–old story oft retold,
Of how we watch the earth turn cold,
The gypsy leaves come tumbling down
Too soon their tints have turned to brown
Walnuts and hickories carpet the ground
Clusters of orange pumpkins also abound
It's time for bobbing apples
A time for shucking the corn
It's time to gather the walnuts
Early in the morn
Flocks of geese in V formation
Wing to a sun–warmed destination
No other journey is quite so grand
As when autumn takes us by the hand.

Untitled
Patti Goodwin

Down to the Bones
of the Fire
The river holds reflection
– so accurate
I cannot decipher
– which way is up
despite the positioning
of my feet
Slowly I forget
the panic of my life
I find comfort in the vertigo
I may fall
I may fly
Always a surprise...
There is a crackle
and a snap
Still – no answers
but it is quiet enough to find them
Down here
in the Bones of the Fire.

Dreams of the Soul

Love Apart
Gary Cairns
How sweet the pain of love seems
at dusk when the spirit
has had its day
How deeply mysterious are
the strings which tug at a restless heart
and yet amidst the despair of
separation from my love
I bask in glorious retreat into
that sweet state which is sleep
to taste once more the painless mists
of deep slumber
Where no man can challenge
Nor maiden beguile
Until with sun's first rays
The hurt begins again.

New Friends
Joyce Wilkinson
He lives a few doors down.
We met through another neighbor and got to talking.
I was surprised by how many interests and experiences
we shared. One thing we agreed on from the first—
Lovers come and go, so friends are better.
We're two human beings trying to make a connection.
We lower our defenses and release a little at a time,
But this can still be painful and misunderstood.
Our words don't always have the same meanings.
Our interests, beliefs, and egos sometimes conflict.
Discussing hurts without hurting more is difficult.
What we learn about each other is filtered through
our own past experiences and momentary emotions.
Are we capable of seeing another person clearly?
I don't know yet, but we're attempting to find out.
Accepting differences increases our understanding.
Exploring each other's lives expands our own.
We're slowly building a solid foundation of trust.
We're two separate worlds mixing, clashing, discovering,
Each growing fuller and stronger because we are friends.

The Ice Princess
Elaine Wong
There she stands
In a dramatic stance
She is slightly shaking
Awaiting her music.

The melody sings itself onto the ice,
The skater sweeps herself into motion.
The tune speeds up, her style quickens
She twirls around, then one! two! three! jumps.
Then, tucked tightly, does a sit spin.
Axles, Lutzes, leaps and more spins are done in turn.
The judges seem very impressed

Roses from the crowd shower the floor when she stops.
The panel of judges show... perfect marks!
She steps onto her position on the podium
A diamond tiara set with pearls is on her head.
Roses are in her arms and a gold medal around her neck,
Yes, she is reigning and will forever rule as
The Ice Princess.

The Best Of Time
Linda Schoppe
When I was a little girl,
And my Mother dressed my hair in curls,
And lay her hand upon my brow,
The best of time in life is now... I thought.

When through my teenage years I ran,
And then married a fine young man,
How great life was then to me,
Any better it just couldn't be... I thought.

When first a Mother I became,
I knew I'd never again be the same,
I had never known such love before,
Life could never offer anything more... I thought.

Now I have hair that is turning gray,
And a few more aches and pains each day,
But I also have grandchildren —
with the purest love that God allows,
The best of time in life is now... I know.

The Daisies In The Field
Amanda Anne Stirn
I remember the days when the daisies bloomed
and in the fields they did sway.
Walking down a wilderness trail,
I noticed the beauty of a bird
and the brilliant colors seemingly painted on its tail.
Sometimes before the sun would set,
I would wonder through these woods
on that vestige where the daisies and grove met.
There I would lay in this bright pasture of beauty
and observe the clouds aloft.
Knowing I must be departing soon,
I yet would lay there with the daisies in the field
and watch the rising of the new moon.

Dedication: God and Michael, my inspiration

First Love
Elizabeth McDonald
Dreary day, dark clouds, drizzle.
Passing by, the connections of
The chain link fence blur together.
On the field, unknown faces, unknown players;
The crack of the bat, the red stitches contrasted on white;
The driven ball,
Brings me back to innocence.
The crisp air, the swaying trees,
The rays of the sun resting upon the grass
Sprinkled with dew at eight in the morning.
The faint smell of leather mixed with dirt.
So familiar, yet so distant.
The yells, the cheers, the fury of excitement
As he is safe.
The inexperienced feeling of my first crush.
When he smiles and winks, time is frozen.
At ten years old, feeling one.
Memories thrown back and caught,
Like the last play of the Championship Game,
Never to be forgotten.

Nocturnal
Stephanie L. Wallace

I wait for the night song to greet me each evening.
The lullaby of solitude
hums me into a blissful state.

The image of you greets me with the cool evening air.
I reach out to grasp a space devoted to your being.
I need the brief shadow that evening brings.

I rattle my cage.
Shake the dust loose.
It has been a long time since I've felt touched.
The projection in front of me.
The worn film of memory produces a soundtrack
that I play every evening.

I revel at evening.
It is my chance to be.
I love the promise that each dark fall makes.
Like dusk, I too can fall back to Earth.
A pillow of down, and a lullaby, of solitude.

Nemesis
Josephine M. Ansumana

You are imprinted on my mind, like a macabre verse
Inscribed on a tablet of stone.
Constantly flashing like amber in a traffic jam.
You are that part of my life I wish to forget.
That old wound that never heals,
The scar that never fades.
That page in my history I pretend was never written... never happened.
Yet, you invade my life and cloud my mind.
You change the tempo of my heartbeat
Every time you pop into my head.
You take away my sanity, and make me vulnerable.
I loose myself just thinking of you.
Why do you have to be my undoing?
My Misery...
My Nemesis...

Untitled
Barbara Hetzel

The earth rises
over the
Sea of Tranquility
on the
moon's surface
as I float
in the suspended
weightlessness
of peace.

It is a buoyancy
a light-heartedness,
that reminds me
of laying on the grass
as a child
and feeling myself
part of
the passing clouds.

Time, has stood still.

Someday
Clayton Drysdale

Someday all doubt and mystery,
will be made clear.
The threatened clouds which now we see,
will disappear.
Someday what seems a punishment,
or loss, or pain,
will prove to be God's blessing sent,
for every gain.
Someday our weary feet will rest,
in sweet content.
And we will know how we were blest,
By what was sent.
And looking back with clearer eyes,
o'er life's short span,
will see with wondering, glad surprise
God's perfect plan.
And knowing that the way we went,
was God's own way.
will understand His wise intent,
Someday — someday.

Rhythmic Feet
C. Lincoln Humes

I hear the feet of the pallbearers
of our love
as they walk you to the door,
taking you to the other side of town.
Nail after cruel nail
are hammered into the coffin
as they gave you reasons
to stuff
our love in the sarcophagus
of division and hate.
Now that you and your love are gone
I can still hear the patting
of those feet as they walk away
killing the life
we had made.

Luna And Lunatic
Jenifer Rajkumar

What if all sense of hunger were lost?
Then to keep from growing emaciated,
Would we wear hung-o-meters
Around our necks,
As reminders of the need for food?

Would the loss of hunger
Free one from desire,
And create a healthy being?
Or would hunger's loss create laziness,
And failure to eat?

Why should I ponder hunger's existence,
If I know it will always exist?

The moon seems to give me
This wild, insensible, thought,
And often we sit together, the bright light and I,
Marveling at the consequences
Of impossible situations.

Dreams of the Soul

Layers
Marcie Swank–Kolb
Slowly it blooms,
Variable layers of delicate life unfold.
Once opened, all its grandeur is exposed.
Intricate patterns,
Brilliant hues,
And mysterious workings
Reveal the true treasures
That lie deep within its layers.

Few recognize this
and only gaze upon the blossom.
Not bothering to really look at
the beautiful,
the delicate
core
Beneath
the layers.

Windows
Valerie Meadows
Row on row these winter windows
burn from within, spilling
red–glow circles
to the white streets and the men
who linger there.
They beckon inward, teasing,
taunting; lace curtains wide open exposing
warmth and laughter, carelessly
inviting hungry stares
from hollow–faced voyeurs,
these men
who stand and watch dumbly
recalling vague childhood's spent
at hearth and kitchen.
Ancient times and days long
dead, as ashes cold and heaped
on sidewalks, called forth
and remembered now, outsiders
looking in.

My Summer
Ruth A. Scott
Oh, my summer, do not leave me,
I know you're getting older and
it's your absence that I dread.
It's you who'll always keep me
in the arms of your tomorrows
But it's winter's white head looming
that will call
A tear
To trickle, down my brown and wrinkled cheek.
Oh my darling, don't deceive me
When I ask if you are leaving,
For it's you, and you alone who holds
My heart inside your head.
When I see those blue eyes closing,
and your blonde hair turning grey
I smile a smile of sadness, for
I know I'll be alone.
Once my summer; — My lovely
summer, has slipped away.

Coal
Gerald D. Williams
They never saw the sun
Those coal dust blackened men
Burrowing like moles
In a dark dank desperate hole
Deep, deep ever deeper dig
To win the prize of coal
The swinging pick flashes bright
In the dim lamp light
Choking dust filled lungs
Gasp for air
To sing bawdy songs
In this starless never ending night
Coal hewn from an unforgiving pit
Won with blood touches all our lives
Aberfan the scar on a nation's soul
A generation in innocence lost
This is the price of coal

My Fallen Comrades
Renate Buxton
The quiet of dawn is breaking,
to sleep — is now only a dream.
We trudge through the endless night,
to yet another battlefield of bloodshed.

The soles of our boots are worn bare,
as the wicked cold has crippled many.
We find the strength to march again,
to yet another battlefield of bloodshed.

Young lads have lost their precious youth,
they cry in darkness for their Mothers.
Their innocent eyes have seen the horrors,
to yet another battlefield of bloodshed.

Our vast numbers have dwindled to few,
lifeless around me — lay Fathers and sons.
God — when will this hellish dream end?
To yet another battlefield of bloodshed.

My Last Lover
Cezar Khursigara
Somebody hit repeat...
What could I do to extort passions
As bodies twist like vines with thorns,
We kept our distance.

With sweet whisper never heard
Like too much bad taste in music
We listened to the same songs
About desire on demand.

And disassociated dispositions
Filled dry conversation with impassive
Gestures, suggesting something which could
Not even walk in the shadow of love.

And yet, we filled our nights
With a wild and delicious course
Without once looking into each other's eyes
And without ever being lost.

Alabama

Winners' Forum

Snowfall
Stephen O. Bisset

I had forgotten your magic
until I paused in deep woods
to feel your silence sweep
across my face.
You have power
to bring this world by the nose
to the temple of silence.
Still, it is lost if there
are no ears to hear... no eyes to see
the wonders of this moment.
But I will enter the holy shrine
to pay homage to your splendor!
And in my reverence,
you touch me with the
holy power of your presence,
and seal in memory's vault
the pictures of the silence.

Dream Catcher
Lisa Muer Tanner

My son made an Indian dream catcher in school
woven like a basket with white yarn spreading
outward in a circle
he said the bad dreams fall through the spaces
while the good dreams are held within its orb
to be savored in the morning

The other night I had a dream that
my son was an Indian prince
and he held his dream catcher up to a full moon
fingers splayed against a backdrop of stars
while wolves howled soulfully in the distance

And in the dream we met
our dream selves spinning fierce in the moonlit sky
mouths open wide in sudden recognition
falling downward
head to toe, Mother to son
in the warm winds of another dimension

Rule Of Love
Veronica W. Reeves

Reassure me when I'm afraid, miss me when I'm away,
believe in what I say. Laugh with me when I'm happy,
cry with me when I'm blue, and when you love me, really
love me, prove your love is true. Correct me when I'm
wrong, stand by me when I'm right, think of me in the
morning, dream of me at night. Comfort me when I'm
lonely have faith in what I do. Follow me to the end of
the of the earth, as I would follow you. Kiss me softly
and gently, hold me tenderly but tight. If I should lose
my temper, please don't let us fight. When you say you love
me, mean it with all your heart, and if you really mean it,
even Death can't make us part. Forgive me when I'm
not myself, try to understand, just put your arms around
me, and tightly hold my hand. God bless you when you
say yours, the way I pray for you, and tell him with all
your soul to keep our (young) love true. Keep these rules
of love with everything you have to give, Though rules were
made to be broken our love was meant to
Live

Armistice Joy
Kathryn Emilie Harris

The train comes clattering in
And joyous calls ring out
To welcome heroes home.
One woman stands alone as the doors slide open
And amidst the kissing, jostling, and laughter,
A pine box is lowered to the platform.
The woman walks to stand beside it
With proud head held high.
Her reserve and control cannot stop
The single tear that slides beneath
The scalloped trim of her veil.
The gaiety fades around her
And dwindles to silence
As one by one, all hats are removed.
This final gesture of respect,
Given with the same reverence
As the neatly folded Stars and Stripes,
Is the only consolation for a Mother
Whose baby boy is home at last.

The Other Side
Sharon Loyd

Sweet notes of melody float out
over the night. The candles
cast shadows from a radiant light.

All is peaceful.
All is right, but

Half a world away...

A child cries for hunger.
A woman draws her thin
shawl about her for warmth.

All is wrong.
The night is long

Half a world away.

Let Me Be
S. K. Rickwood

Let me be, those men
Who love and caress my body
With their minds.
Don't patronize me please
With your loving desires
That seem so sexual.

Don't you see, you're eating away
My heart and my mind.
You're making the struggle for the
Quest of Love
So hard for me to find.

So let me be, to find my own love.
My heart, and my mind must be clear
Don't put shadows in my way.
For when the day comes, that I
Give up my heart
I want it to be forever.

Dreams of the Soul

Baby Boomer Blues
Lana J. Farley
Once she wore dresses with organdy sashes;
Now she wears girdles and suffers hot flashes.

Her high school sweetheart lies beside her, snoring;
Though decades have passed, nonetheless, he's adoring.

They sometimes hold hands when taking long walks,
And always share secrets and jokes when they talk.

He seems not to care that her waistline has thickened;
Her soft, gentle touch always makes his heart quicken.

It seems very strange how fast time has flown;
Their children are married with kids of their own.

The cool rock 'n roller with a cute little fanny,
Who was once called "babe", now answers to "granny".
Dedication: Richard Farley... forever my sweetheart

Not Of This World
Jenny Terrero Rivera
Sing oh strings unto me
Melodious tunes
Remedy my wounded soul
Elevate my mournful spirit

Oh trombone, oh piano keys
Violins do sing for me.
I'll fall asleep in the arms
Of a cellos hum

Oh blessed Mozart
Blessed Bach, blessed Beethoven
Anointed hands ears and heart
Anointed with Angelic melodies
Of another world
Perhaps a little taste of the
Heavenly choirs.

Dream Of Flying
Jerry McGinley
I dream again tonight of flying;
my arms sprout soft gray down for hair
and stiff silver quills; my black arrow
head slashes a path through autumn air.

I lift above lights, a plumed kite
towed by invisible magnetic thread,
eyes keen for landmarks and stars,
forty miles an hour, me in the lead.

I am bull–goose pulling a slipstream
wedge of feathered brothers south.
My haunting voice leads a honking choir:
"Come, we are heading for the Gulf!"

All night we glide over checkerboard fields,
then drop at dawn. My nimble wingtips stir
the mist, then whiffle like a maple leaf
and skid to rest on egg–shell icy water.

Untitled
P. Swambo
Sometimes, I glance across a room and see your smile
And catch my breath with loving you so much.
Sometimes, your fingers trace the contours of my face
And all the warmth of all my life and yours is centred in your touch.
Sometimes, when I'm away from you it seems
The darkness closes in from all around
And I am lost, bewildered, empty now
Just living to remember how it was
When you were here.
Sometimes I feel I've loved you all my life,
Through all my childish years and mis–spent youth,
That you were all the laughter, all the tears,
The beauty, sadness, pathos, fears and truth.
If all I had with you was just a day
To love you to the very depths of love,
Sometimes, I feel that it could be enough
To keep me from the cold of all the empty years
When you are gone, but only sometimes.

The Gift
Bob Neil
A place in time has come and gone, I did not see it pass.

I was too busy then enjoying life to think it might not last.

Now I look back with clarity at what young eyes had failed to see,
because just being there consumed me. I get the scent of burning
leaves on cool crisp autumn air, it mingles with the chimney smoke of
winter.
Soon crystal trees will melt to bring the buds that turn to
fields of spring, then die, to live again in autumn splendor.

It seems I spent my childhood as a blind man.
Not seeing though my eyes were open wide. The beauty of
life's seasons passed before them through the years,
I saw it, but it never came inside.

I missed it then, but see it now, for God has given me
a gift that time cannot erase, a precious memory.

Untitled
Sasha A. Bluvshteyn
The planks of rotten woods
and orchards so long forgotten
the crows sit in the lavender fields
where last spring
the cherry tomatoes took over at first
then the rabbits ate them
you would drag in the tomato's pulp
when you walked through there
scaring the rabbits
the pillows of cotton wood
under the white broken fences stale
as the green takes over
capturing the wrinkles and folds
of the blackening trees
how tall they stood once
proud and erect
but now only the seedlings begin to show
their fleshy tops breaking through
the earth's skin.

Winners' Forum

Winter Wind
Laura Isaacson

It tugs thin clouds with silver spider threads,
Across the moon's dull glow of solemn trance.
It is the silent symphony that leads
All nature in a rhythmic shadow dance.
But winter wind is freezing, cold, and bites.
Wisps of snow scamper across the frozen ground
like ghosts of midnight chased by morning light.
Crystal crusted ice and sculpted snow drifts mound.
It chokes out breath and nips the flesh that bears
stinging, chasing all warm feeling away
Yet I have wandered far from such a care,
and now am one of frost; in shadow stay
and dance with gusts of ice; to night prolong
the winter wind, the echo to my silent song.

Regarding Fear
Wednesday A. Scott

Not afraid to try
Just afraid to fail
Not afraid to be alone
Just afraid to be lonely
Not afraid to be loved
Just afraid love will end
Not afraid to ask
Just afraid of rejection
Not afraid to feel
Just afraid of feelings
Not afraid to die
Just afraid to live

The Mole
Chris Moat

The mole our sacred sod
has marred, and undermined
smooth turf so free of weeds.
He, guileless, beguiling,
laughs up small volcanoes
and with underground nose
knows earth's winter planting,
seeks out her secret seeds.
He sees, where eyes are blind,
the darker face of God.

Dedication: Diana Metcalfe, for early encouragement

Another Set of Ears
Patricia G. Rourke

I heard her tell a story about me
It was not the way it happened—
but it is how she wanted to remember it.

On another day, I would have
entered into it without permission,
protesting her detail with my set of facts.

But now I want to listen to what
She has believed over the years.
It may be closer to the truth.

It may tell me what she
always wanted to be for me but
could never quite get reality
to match her dream.

A Symphony Of Words
Sharon Dennis

Poetry is a word song,
a lyrical muse,
a melody of syllables of different hues.
It's the rhythms of emotions:
elation, fears, and tears;
a metronome of mutterings and harmonious rhymes;
or rhythmic, cacophonous, discordant lines;
solos of monologues, cadences of phrases;
applauded by intellectuals
and appreciated by the common man;
remembered by everyone for recitations
long after the composer is dead.
Poetry is a symphony of words
scored by the poet and conducted by the pen.

Evening Magic
Elizabeth Herreid

A summer night,
made for youth and love.
The heat of the day gives way
to evening coolness.
The shadows lengthen.
Magic is in the air —
tonight, anything can happen.

As night approaches,
all grows still.
A man and woman walk together,
speaking softly under the spell of twilight.
At the brink of the hill,
they pause,
hands and hearts entwined,
to gaze at the sunset
framed in the darkness
of the yet to be.

A Small Boy's Bedtime
Joanne D. Denko

Brilliant silver light
Of August night
Portraits your face.
And you, my child, reveal to me
"Moon lives in sycamore tree."

Before I sing how angels keep
Their watches o'er you while you sleep,
You stage your evening rite.

"Good night, Moon," you say,
And for my time–dulled ears
Repeat her answer,
"Good night, Boy. . . . Sleep tight."

Dreams of the Soul

Scattered
Beckie Taylor

The farmhouse teetered.
Its beams moaning
Like a Grandmother in a groaning chair,
Spinning memories.

Un–flowered pots cry for water
By the door that hangs like a loose tooth.
The dust has moved in,
Eating of broken dishes and
Sleeping on musty beds.
Where wallpaper crackles the toil
When prosperity covered the soil.

This is the West, the great frontier.
Brought to us by rusted iron ties
Taken away by steel.

Autumn Song
E. N. Bryant

Our "spring" and "summer" songs are sung and flown
Their laughter and tears, echo down the fleeting years
the page is turned

And in due season our "winter"
May beckon with icy finger beyond the distant bend
But have no fear,
Together, we'll weather those twilight years.
But for now!
With crimson sunsets and warm mellow hues
of flame and russet
Our "autumn time" unfolds...
Come stay by my side
And together let us walk
Hand in hand,
Into the golden years.

Adoption
Joseph M. DiPerna, Jr.

I hold the door open for an elderly lady
walking behind me in a neighborhood store.
Imagine if she was related to me
but I was adopted and can't be sure.
People talk about who they look like.
Who has moms nose and dad's eyes.
I offer nothing to the conversation.
Feeling left out, my emotions, I disguise.
My ties to humanity are a mystery.
I ponder daily about why I was let go.
If someone could just come forward
and say "it is me in case you want to know."
I can ask the questions "What did I do? And
why, after birth, did you sever our nine month bond?"
I am afraid to meet this person and ask these questions
because I don't know how she'll respond.

Dedication: My fiancee, Barbara Blum

The Jogger
Valerie McNeilis

'There she goes' he quietly said.
The one who's dressed all in red.
With shining hair and carefree smile,
She beats the others by a mile.
I cannot blink for fear I might
Lose her from my blurring sight.
What a girl, a lovely thing
She really makes my old heart sing.
I memorize her every move
Hoping that she might approve,
Of me appraising her each day
As she jogs along the way.
But she only shouts as she runs by.
"Good morning granddad" and "goodbye".

Dedication: For all my beautiful family

Ice Mist
Lynda Fraser

The ice mist hangs
in the air.
It covers the trees.
It fills my lungs.
The ice mist hangs
in the air
Making it hard to see
The downtown skyline.
Only the tallest buildings
(Their bright neon signs)
Poking out the top.
The ice mist hangs
in the air
Hiding the river valley
And the homeless
Who live there.

Autumnal Thoughts
J. C. Old

The sun rises to a frosty day, illuminating the countryside
Reflecting the shades of the falling leaves, autumn has arrived.
The spider spinning her cobwebs in the early morning dew
Sees her delicate threads shimmering in the pale light anew.
The squirrel, acorn clutched in tiny trembling paw
Senses winter coming, and hurries to replenish it's food store.
A generous abundance of chilly early morning mists
Surrounds the forest, as the distant hills are kissed
By a cold incandescent condensed mass of thin low cloud.
The forest fox is glad to be with a warm fur coat endowed.
Leaves tumbling down in the freshening autumnal breeze
Mark the change in the season as they drift from the trees.
Field mice twitch their whiskers, and look for somewhere warm
And rabbits secure their warrens against the winter storms.
The inimical wind scatters the carpet of leaves around.
Winter begins in earnest as snow falls, muffling all sound.

Winners' Forum

Shadows And Shade
Sabrina Rogers
Upon the darkened entry stair
I saw the shadows dancing there
Hiding from the bright sunlight
Waiting for the starlit night
So there I stayed throughout the day
And watched the deepening shadows play
Into the peace that darkness brings
They flew on newly sprouted wings
I crept back to my empty loft
And tried to sleep 'neath silken cloth
Yet through the night I heard their choices
As they debated in shadow voices
Dancing and talking in whispers and shade
Until the dawn light from which they fade
To return again to the entry stair
And dance with joy in the darkness there

The Twenty-Ninth Of August
Diana Tiernan
Tonight I knew it was the end of summer.
Not by dead or dying leaves,
or ghostly fragrance of long dead, sun baked, herb or rose,
but sharp and clean upon the air –
the taste of frost.
Startled, as any stag, I turned scenting the breeze,
to search, in the echoes of my memory,
for the smell of autumn bonfires.
But it was too soon.
Carried on that faint wind,
came only the rich, moist smell, of dew soaked soil
and the full leaf rustle of trees.
There was no time for haunting melancholy
at that first autumn tingle,
for through the mist grey, smoke blue, twilight of the garden,
a simple yellow fruit seemed turned to gold,
a gold of promise –
the promise of the harvest.

The Soldier
Chris Antoniou
Young men sign on the dotted line
to become mentally and physically fit,
to become brave men,
to protect this great Nation.

They become men of rank, number and of great tolerance.
In battle, they see fellow soldiers and friends fall upon the earth.
They feel the pain of wounds,
but they bravely soldier on.

The memories of battle and the smell
of death haunt them for all eternity.
In any era, in any generation these brave men
must never ever be forgotten by us all.

Never forgotten.

Tiny Tears
Cynthia M. Kadow
Tiny tears falling from the sky,
why is it, that you cry?
Is it for the helpless children abandoned and abused,
and the little ones neglected and misused?
Little hearts so full of pain,
shed tears, like falling rain.
A childhood shadowed with so many fears,
saddened faces stained with tears.
Children feeling lost and alone,
dealing with the hurt and pain on their own.
Grasping for a ray of hope,
Lord, give them strength to cope.
Struggling to survive, what ever the cost,
young innocence forever lost.
Living a life that is so unfair,
Lord, take them in your loving care.
Tiny tears falling from the sky.
Shower blessings on the children that cry.

Remembered Pleasures
Vivian Davis
Like the hope of spring
on a long winter's eve,
unbidden,
you wander in and out
of the dreams I weave.
In almost forgotten agony
my silent heart still
prays
that you will come again,
someday.
Yet, in my waking thoughts I know
the past is gone,
and so,
only in my deepest dreams
I find,
remembered pleasures in my mind.

The Gladestone In Parkdale
Gary Gaines
The hotel is old. Grey as clouds of smoke dancing on parched faces, and dancing to idols. Its ghosts breathing their foul air into my naked flesh. The eyes of fate cast their demonic gaze, killing everything they touch. We rejoice by raising our cup of draft, and listen to our prayers: Why GOD! Why? The sound of music has already passed on; though, if you stay quiet, you can hear it in the

souls of the living. The laughter of a child, a flight of a sea gull; this is what an eternity really is—nothing more. Life is like a perfect rose that fades and dies before its time—loved more in death than life. We are just as guilty; we wanted to see the expression on her face, before she died. We all are children of the gutter, but some of us are reaching for the stars.

Dreams of the Soul

If We Were Strangers
Karen Ashjian
Like cars
racing passed an abandoned house
at midnight
You walk by me
everyday
and while others have stared
deep into my eyes
and seen my soul
You won't even turn your head
to acknowledge me.

And I know
it wouldn't hurt half as much
or so damn bad
if we were strangers
but we aren't
and it does.

Until...
W. Maurice Crook
.... then Autumn came, and with their golden leaves
majestic trees succumbed to earth's endowed authority.
Yet had not Summer's crown of green been worn with regal dignity!
Now bowed and well asway, the chilling wind caressing
and enfolding branch and limb – the crown is seized,
to flutter bird–like to the hungry earth,
fulfilling it's creator's wondrous symmetry.

Were I not mortal, and of clay bespoke,
would that a tree's crude bark my outer garb did form;
for then, all Summer long I'd proudly stand,
accepting servile homage from both flower and reed.
Till once again at Summer's end, the call 'Divest thyself of crown
and stately power' were whispered on the wind throughout the land.
Then gladly would I abdicate to berried evergreen and Larch.
For had I not for one bright Summer ruled my kingdom well!
The earth about my feet would sated rest... until the Spring.

Rainstorm
Donald Lashley
Winding bridges weaving
stretching into the lining
finding secret channels
streaming overflowing ledges
outside opening panels
hidden inside spreading
through the vast emptiness
stranded distance of silence

The infinite search begins
into the flooded night
a lost unknown plight
deceived by delusions
received reflections
dreams imagined sight
beside the water alone
shadow on the sky of stone

CHAPTER TWO

Noteworthy Works

Ben Johnson once said, "A good poet's made as well as born." These are words of encouragement to all of us who aspire to the craft. The following collection of poems is wonderfully varied and draws from the talents of numerous individuals. Although the poems featured in this chapter did not receive any awards, they should nevertheless serve as an inspiration. This chapter is devoted to those poets whose work shows true promise.

Dreams of the Soul

A Dawn Of Thanksgivings
Diane M. Valand
As the sun is rising
in the early morning dawn,
I subside into my pillow,
thinking on the things above.
My heart is guarded with
a deep inner peace,
a fruit of the spirit, my
mind is also at ease.
My gracious Father, who
gives me all things,
to Him only, his praises
I sing.
With humbleness of heart,
I lift up to Him, a
prayer of thanksgiving,
as this new day begins.

Dedication: My dear, special friend, Katie

The White Rose Of Sickness
Stephanie M. Jacoby
I take off my clothes
and say I look fat
I rush to the bathroom
and make myself sick
I rush back again
I scream at myself
"I look fat"
I pull out a knife
I try
I can't
I'm scared
I look at the rose
I touch myself
I feel strong
but I'm weak
I try not to feel sick
but I am sick
I am sick just like the rose
I need a new body
I need a new life
I'm scared to live
and want to die
I pick up the knife
I press it against the hot flesh on my wrist
and faint in my own arms
I lay on the ground as I wake up
I thought I was dead
the only word that comes to my mind is damn
I see the blood
I thank the so-called god
I thank hell
I thank myself for being brave
I feel sorry
I want to turn back
I know it's too late
I look in the mirror
I scream
I lay awake in death
I whisper to the world
"I feel free"
I have no more fearful nightmares
I have strength
I have no more pain
I rest in silence

Dedication: In memory of Danielle Jones

Apart
Jean H. Sparrock
My nights are long and empty
Since we've been apart
My mind just doesn't comprehend
What's already in my heart
My life just like an empty void
That I must learn to fill
But all I seem to want to do
Is sit or stand quite still
I cannot come to terms right now
With things the way they are
It can't be over I tell myself
It hasn't gone that far
My heart knows its over
And tries to tell my head
Its finished its over
The life we lived is dead
I've got to come to terms with it
Or I'll drive myself insane
But life is just an empty void
of memories and pain.

Memories From A Time Forgotten
Tanner Harris
Memories of the Pledge of Allegiance and the Hokey Poky on soft foam puzzle floors,
my feet sunken in plush red "a" bordered by blue. Memories of a lush yard stretching
out over vast ground covered with rocks and grass like small jungles, perfect forts for
Sergeant Savage, King Cobra, Luke, Darth Vader or little one piece robots looking for
protection against the enemies lurking in the deep jungle abound. Memories of walking
down an empty hall in a boundless school, to the second-grade math class, leaving all
the others behind to toil over their easy math, so proud was I, sitting with the other kids
so much larger and more intelligent. Memories of sweltering days crouched beneath
Large leaves and branches placed in the sandbox, our only weapons, long metal batons
with bright plastic caps on end. Glitter swirling round and round with each swipe.
Memories of a Grandmother's lap amongst jungles of tall grass bordered by lovely flower
beds, the chicken coop Continuously clucking, and the cornfield pressed tight against
the old barn, playing in the damp basement, its shelves brimming with preserves,
strawberry and rhubarb, green beans and corn, and jams galore. Memories of a porch
encased in vines, small bugs crawling up the towering screen protected from any
predator that might lay abound, jumping from the huge tree, plastic bags for parachutes.
Tough it never worked I always tried. Memories of walking across open fields with a tall
slender old man, topped with strands of silver and white, placing coins on the tracks,
waiting for the train to pass by, searching for the flat nickels and pennies scattered
everywhere by the brute force of the train. Memories of days long gone. Wishing for
them not to be memories of a past life, but of yesterday And days to come. Memories.

Dedication: M. A. Hoffaker

Noteworthy Works

Untitled
Valene Green

There is a place
A place of darkness and of peace
Where feelings are lost,
like bird song on the wind
And there is warmth, unyielding and embracing
penetrating body and soul, until they are one
And it is calm.
Darkness rules in this place
an engulfing, drowning darkness
There is no up or down, no forward or back
But there is movement, without direction
never ceasing or slowing
like a leaf caught on a gentle breeze.
And it is calm.
There is no love in this place, nor is there hate
No lust or greed or passion; no happiness or sorrow
No fear, regret or envy
Only existence
And it is calm
And it is home.

The World War Soldier
Jonathan Swift

They spread out among the territory on enemy lines
Terror floods their heart they move, stagnancy means death

They run, hearts beat fast with adrenaline and nervousness
Questions, so many question of just what is going on

A silent prayer is muttered out in the mind, reaching high above
That of the whistles of ammunition

Artillery sounds as thunder through hills, sounds of men falling
All around, some dive in cool waters others to barren earth for
refuge

They march on, with a constant drive, teams of men streaming
On as swarms of insects

Wales and sounds of pain and horror blend with the other ravenous
Tones of men's fates.

As they near closer to the enemy, there's an explosion, men in
The vicinity fly as toys from a now flaming ravine

Shouts of God help me! And cries of distress are muttered in
A situation that tries men's faith

They advance, reaching their destination, yells of attack!, and
Fight! Can be heard above the crowd

Valor takes over good judgement, as more men are killed and
Wounded, they keep on for their country

They battle for days until 3/4 of an infantry lay dead, those
Left feel a since of gratefulness and humbleness

Some gave their lives, others risked theirs, their gallantry
Made forth away for all Americans

As day nears end in the west, those still standing move on to
A new battle, and challenge

One day their prayers will be answered, the war will end and
The world war solider will get to go home

Dedication: To grandfather, my inspiration, love Jonathan

Between Me And You
Adriana Villarreal

The other night that I saw you
Just proved that my feelings were still true!
I only wish you knew,
The pain that I am going through!
Do you feel for me, what I feel for you?
Or do you not think of me, now that you've found someone new?
So many times I think, and wonder why?
I think so much I start to cry.
People tell me that life goes on,
But how can I live my life with you gone?
They say it's just a phase that I am going through.
I guess that is why I am always sad and blue!
Maybe they know what's best for me...
All I can do is go on with my life and let it be...
I must find someone to heal my heart,
Now that you have broken it apart!
Day by day my wounds will heal,
I want you to know that my pain for you was real!
You will always have a special place within me,
But please just keep it between me and you!!!

Teachers Thank You
Mildred Bridges

In the lines printed here before us
Our "Thanks" go out to you
For so many years of teaching
God's Word in love so true.

We appreciate your kindness
For all that you have done
In teaching us the lessons
That were taught by God's own Son.

For through your voice, God speaks to us,
And helps each strive to be
A better person every day
With friends and family.

If God had no one here on earth
To teach his Message great,
It makes us wonder if our lives
Might not have been at stake.

So Christmas seems the proper time
For us to let you know;
Our heartfelt Thanks and Love
We hope to you to show.

We realize the hours involved
Have taken lots of time;
But what a joy when He shall say,
"Well done—you're one of Mine."

So Thanks to each of you again.
Please know we really care.
We appreciate, respect, and welcome you
Each week you come to share.

May our Good Lord always bless you
As you teach us every week.
And may He be there for you
As His presence you do seek.

If we fail to show you
Or thank you now and then,
Forgive us, always knowing
We appreciate you, our friend.

Dreams of the Soul

Saying Goodbye
Donna J. Zuk
The sandstones quickly fall to our
departure in life. How quickly brown hair
turns gray. I look back at the days of my
youth noticing I didn't have any.
I look at the present
only to find sadness
and fear of living...
I look again. I see
nothing I could
have done better
than to serve the
beautiful graying
and wrinkled bodies
that I care for every day.
I make a friend, create a smile.
So as they leave me one by one, I
say goodbye to my loved ones, knowing
I will meet them again, someday. Knowing
happily, that they will be in a place
where they don't need me.
Dedication: My daughter, Melonie Howarth–Valley

Snowball Man
Helen Rebecca Rodney
Here in the rural town, there is snow all around,
the geese flying southward bound.

The leaves are covered with snow, as they lay there below,
the tall barren trees looking down.

Yes, Old Man Winter has finally come,
when he does, it's a job well done.

He brings icy flakes and a billowing chill,
he blows such a gust, it's hard to be still.

Better announce the news:
Button Boots!, Bears Snooze!, Snuggle to Someone You Love!

It will be a cold winter, light the coals and the splinter,
lest you think the almanac lied.

I'm afraid my dear friend it was right once again,
for the truth is glistening outside.

The innkeepers are stirring their grogs and
the fireplaces are stacked with lumberjack logs

The merchant, he cries, "Pay lest ye die!",
and his register rings, Cling, a cling, Cling

But it won't be long for spring to be sprung,
and with that, I'll sing me a song—

Hurray, Hurray for the canoe on the lake
hurray for the money I'll make

Selling my snowballs in the hot blazing sun,
for my job begins when Old Winter Man's done.

Cling, a cling, Clang, my wagon wheels roll,
snowballs for sale

At the days end—All Sold!
Dedication: Grandmother, Clara Cooper Rasin

Something Special
Mark Amatelli
Something I always wanted, I've always kept aside
Never really shared it, something deep inside
Too bad I could not have it, it's really sad to say
With all my heart I wish and wish, it will never be the day.

I guess you're wondering what it is, a dog is what I wish
A friendly dog to be my buddy make me laugh and be real muddy
But still that day will never come, I will never be with one
Then another day passes by, I wish all over again but why.

I still cannot tell a single soul because of what they might say
Other days I say oh well who cares what they may think
Why oh why should I try so hard to get something special from my heart
If it's so special it should be there, in my arms for me to care.

There are so many types of dogs running all about
Then there is a special one that's mine standing tall and stout
After thinking real hard I finally chose one
Though I won't get, it still was very fun.

The dog I found was a Chihuahua
I know they may be nasty but I don't agree
The bulging eyes, the squeaky voice why can't I be with thee
Since I was little I always wanted one... Always wanted one to love.

Bernie
Anna E. Enarson
Bernie was a Saint Bernard, with
large floppy ears,
With eyes so sad, they looked like
they had tears,
She was sweet, and friendly, and
lovable too,
But as time went on, she grew
and grew
She was 105 pounds, when fully
grown
When brushed her long silky hair
shone
She was a true companion, always
at my side
I loved my Bernie, and one morning
she died
I stroked her lovingly, and lay
down I said
She did as I asked, and I patted
her head
One hour later, I awoke to start
the day
And still my Bernie beside my bed
lay
Bounding to the kitchen, she never
came
I finally looked around and called
her by name
She always came and couldn't wait
to be fed
Went back to the bedroom, and found
my Bernie dead
At 5:30, in the morning, she pawed
me so softly
She woke me to say goodbye ever
so gently
Knowing Bernie this truly was the
way she would go
She was a true friend, and the best
dog I will ever know

Lost Time
Jason Forget

Daylight Savings
You waste another year.
You don't know what you've got
Until it disappears.

If it were me
there would be no time.
But looking through an hourglass
You have to draw the line.

You don't know what you've got until it disappears.

I don't want to go now
I've just begun to understand
How the world turns
And works the other hand.

The wrath of Old Man Time
Has filled me up with fright
But if he's taught me one thing,
He's taught me to hold on and fight!

I know what I've got and I won't pass it up!
Dedication: My grandmother and Aunt Jane

Our Purpose
Katie Willis

Sometimes I can hear them
Can you hear them my love
the bells that chime softly
from the clouds up above

They are calling my name
in a soft gentle tone
telling me of my purpose
and when I'll return home

My job is not done yet
I shall not leave
I have more still to do
I must make you believe.

Learn from me now
hear what I say
you will once again love
without fear of betray.

One day we shall lie
together as one
But first you shall know
What you're here to become

For you have a purpose
Just as important as mine
You having love
gracious and kind.

For love is life's greatest miracle
Our eyes shall ever see
When I fill my purpose here
then you will live on through me

And if one day it shall be
that we might have to part
look not in the world around you
for you will find me in your heart.

My Feelings About Our Daddy
Lisa Hoback

I remember only pieces just fragments of the past
Though time our torment eases the memories surely last

Bitter scenes hurl me like a whirlwind in despair
With grown–up eyes I look back and find them hidden there

I wonder how he came to be a man that I should fear
Now I've seen him broken down he's suffered now for years

With age I've come to realize the pain he must have felt
Knowledge of his childhood home helped my anger melt

We're products of our families though we cannot see
As children we will forge our ways yet like our parents be

There's value in his legacy his life's lesson taught
He gave us all that he could give in truth it was a lot

He gave us goals and strength and pride and set our standards high
He gave us opportunity to spread our wings and fly.

I know he was a tortured man who could not show us love
He was a man with faith in God now he's gone above

Let us look back and share the pain together we can feel
We need to learn and grow and love together we can heal

What You lose
Courtney Huston

You don't let me love you
You'll never know quite how that makes me feel

To want to be with someone
Who pushes you away
To want the best for them

To want them to want the best for you
To tell them that you love them
Only to never hear it said

It takes a toll
Thinking you know
Yet not knowing
Living in a mystery that one day you understand – the next you don't
Having to guess someone's feelings
Having to tell yourself– "their actions show they care"

When all you really want is to hear them say– "I care"
So, all will finally be clear – the mystery solved

I've told myself be strong
Let your feelings be known
Risk the possibility of rejection

After all I convince myself – "What do I have to lose?"
A little part of myself–
Never to return

What you gain

To love without expecting
Reliance on the Lord
To live without selfishness
To not demand your needs be met
To not be bitter, but better
To love again

Dreams of the Soul

A Fair Fight
Darce Glaze

"Dine ye now," I silently snub
As a great length of spider wire
Baited with the fattest of grub
Fades into the thick lily pads

Patience now, I've met with you here
Even though you've fought a fair fight
Now for the last five or six years
Oh please don't disappoint me now

To spar with you is true passion
An unquenchable thirst in me
Like many girls show for fashion
Pity, I'm not one of those girls

The hot adrenaline doth flow
Through dungaree-clad, wobbly knees
The slick adversary arose
Flailing airborne to be set free

I see the smirk in amber eyes
You enjoyed this fight, sly dog
But you are far too great a prize
My conscience won't allow me lunch

Dedication: Rosa Lee Whitney (beloved grandmother)

Why Me
William F. Crowe, Jr.

This question we often ask ourselves
with things we don't understand
We become overwhelmed with situations
and all that life demands.

Just when you see the light
it becomes dim and fades away
Your left in a tunnel of darkness
feeling helpless and left astray

WHY ME? WHY ME?

It has to be a good reason
for I know it's not all in vain
I just wish someone would answer
or at least be there to explain

My days seem longer and more tiring
as I awaken and face the sun
I guess the hard part is not knowing
when my boss will consider my job done

WHY ME? WHY ME?

Everything in life has a reason
what mine is I'm not sure
I feel the Lord has chosen me
because he knows only the strongest endure

I hope that through my struggle
knowledge and wisdom will be gained
So that someone else in this world
Won't have to endure my pain

I believe I understand my task
for the light is so bright too see
I know that answer to my question
The Lord knows I'm Special, that's WHY ME!

Earlene, Barbara-Jean And Me
Beverly R. Thompson

The days were always too short to get in all we wanted to do;
There were red apples on the tree that had to come off, but who would climb the tree
Earlene, Barbara-Jean and me

The pear tree was full with pears but hardly ever fell; guess who would bump against the tree,
Earlene, Barbara-Jean and me

There were strawberries, and blackberries, and walnuts to pick, so tasty for our tea parties
under the pine tree playhouse carpeted with fallen pine needles.
There was always Earlene, Barbara-Jean and me.

We had church some days, Earlene preached and prayed the way you were supposed to; we also had weddings, and one day we had a funeral, we buried our dolls and after a short while dug them up and started over again. Earlene was the preacher Barbara-Jean and me would sit, watch and listen while Earlene held service, we said amen at the appropriate time, sang our songs, had prayer and even shouted.

Some days we just rode our bikes, jumped rope, or simply played with our dolls.

It was rare Earlene did not come to play. I am so glad I have these wonderful memories of Earlene, Barbara-Jean and me.

If Only It Could Be
Kathy A. Yarbrough

I walked in, you looked so fine
My adrenaline was flowing, how I wished you were mine
When you looked back and I saw you see
I hoped and prayed if only it could be

You played, you smiled, you winked
I know I turned several shades of pink
I couldn't believe that it was all happening to me
I hoped and I prayed if only it could be

I was so excited, my heart beat so fast
Here it was – my chance at last
You stopped at my table, you looked down at me
I hoped and prayed if only it could be

"Hello pretty lady", you said with a smile
I pictured the red carpet stretched out in the aisle
I was so happy, my emptiness now filled
I could not believe that you were for real

You walked me out, you held me so tight
You said "Kathy why does it feel so right?"
You looked at me so sincere, gently kissing me
My prayers were answered, I knew it could be

Now it's been weeks since I've seen your face
But I remember exactly how sweet your lips did taste
Your gentle touch, the sincerity in your eyes
when I'm with you, I'm a natural high

So much has happened since that first night
When you genuinely love it feels so right
With no other, have I ever felt this way
But to this giant among men I can say
I Love You —

Dedication: Elvis Presley (The King)

Noteworthy Works

Sensible Shoes
Mary Paula G. Wheeler
When he was a boy, his mother, in sensible shoes,
would walk around the kitchen, baking cookies, oatmeal–raisin.
Once, he heard the click of her heels as she danced,
down the hall and out the door, leaving behind a cloud of perfume,
only once, sensible shoes don't dance out doors.

Then he began to notice, the girl next door, she was dancing in red cowboy boots,
laughter hanging in the air, she danced, in red boots, bare feet, white sandals, and
pearl–bedecked wedding shoes. Two years later, she carried their daughter
into his world, and he admired the tiny feet and was enchanted
by the soon–to–be–bronzed booties of ribbon and lace, he did not see on
her mother, sensible shoes.

His daughter grew up to laugh and dance in puddles on the driveway,
where oil once spilled. She dances on rainbows, he smiled, and she danced,
in ballet slippers, bare feet, and Mother's old boots. She danced her way into the heart
of the boy down the street, and danced away with the golden ring, never
wearing, sensible shoes.

Four years later, his little girl who danced on rainbows had a new partner,
and he had a new grandson. As he looked, with pride, his eyes glanced
down, sensible shoes.

SENSIBLE SHOES CAN'T DANCE ON RAINBOWS.

Butterflies
J. A. Bygrave
Butterflies scooting like ants
Afraid that someone might detect
their existence.
They cower and flutter
hoping this will be a deterrent to intruders

Does not work

they have been spotted.
The sinking feeling is real
No plan of action is prepared
They thought the barrage of flapping
was enough.

Too late.

Their hue has gone,
their innocence of life oozing,
A sense of suffocation
envelopes them.

Now been seen

The large expanse of flesh is looming,
shading the light,
As it makes its descent
the butterflies squeal in terror

All is darkness

This inner world is unreal.
No familiarity is available
They form a pact, one that
can never
be
met.

The Reason
Kimberlee Schmader
Why don't I ever say to you
You mean more than the world to me?
That without you in my life
There would be no reason to be.

That if there ever came a day
I didn't wake and see your eyes,
Dawn may as well never come
For I have no reason to rise.

If I could never hold your hand
Savor the sweetness of your kiss,
See your beautiful smile
Hear laughter from your tender lips.

Forget the bright stars in the sky
Take away the warmth of the sun,
Don't listen to falling rain
Or taste its cool drops on my tongue.

For without you there's no reason
To live or to love or to breathe,
You not only mean the world –
Because you ARE the world to me.

Dedication: My husband, Timothy—my reason

Lost
Lynn Jorgensen
One day I saw my star.
A star so bright and
shiny
like the one I knew.

I felt alive and well,
so well I forgot to tell
exactly what it was
that fell.

Deep within my soul
a hole
so deep I couldn't
control
the hold
on so much... life.

Escaped... where I don't know
but not here
where? somewhere
somehow
Now—when?

My soul is burning
turning—in deep
desire of the face
The face of love
that's safe, secure,
obscure.

My heart is vacant,
sacred lost and found
upon the ground.
My face is pinned
no grin
no friend
The End.

Dreams of the Soul

An Angel's Joy
Lisa G. Gawel
My sadness comes from her joy unseen,
To see a child, to see a dream.

She waited patiently for me to grow,
To learn the lessons that life will show.

I made it through college and learned about life,
Met a wonderful man, now I'm his wife.

A life inside me began to form,
She couldn't wait for him to be born.

But, she waited patiently for him to grow,
To see her first great–grandchild, to hold and to show.

But an angel came and took her away,
Five weeks to the day of his birthing day.

So my sadness comes from this tale of time,
She never got to hold the dream that was hers and mine.

But, in the eyes of an angel, I know she can see,
God's wonderful gift to my Grandmother and me.

A little boy, so innocent and sweet,
Through the eyes of two angels they finally meet.
Dedication: My grandmother – Wilma Keziah

Heaven's Grocery Store
Gregory P. Alston
I was walking down life's highway a long time ago, when one
day I saw a sign that read, "Heaven's Grocery Store".

On the inside, I saw a host of angels, they were standing everywhere,
one handed me a basket and said, "My friend, shop with care".

First I got some "Patience" and I got some "Love" that was in the same
row. Further down the aisle was "Understanding", you need that
everywhere you go.

I got a bag or two of "Wisdom" and "Faith", and I couldn't miss the
"Holy Spirit" for it filled the entire place.

I stopped to get some "Strength and Courage" to help me run this race.
By then the basket was getting full, but I remembered some "Grace".

Then I started towards the counter to pay my grocery bill, for I thought
I had everything I needed to do the "Master's Will".

As I went up the aisle I saw "Prayer" and I just had to squeeze it in,
'cause I knew when I
stepped outside, I would run right into "Old man Satan and Sin".

Then I said to the Angel, "Now tell me, how much do I owe"? He
smiled and said, "If you
will just keep these treasures in your heart always, simply take them
and go".

Looking at the blessings in my basket warmed my heart so, again I
smiled and said, "No really, how much do I pay, what is it owe"?

The Angel looked at me with his face all aglow, replying, "My child,
Jesus paid your bill
on the "Cross at Calvary" a long, long time ago".
Dedication: To my loving mother, Gregory

Fishing In Majuro
Dianne Eisen
Blue skies, Ocean grey
Endless Horizon,
What a beautiful day.

To the reef Waves make their way
Our boat riding their crest,
What a beautiful day.

Lures bobbing, Men at Play
Fish aren't biting,
But what a beautiful day.

Dolphins jumping, Join us in Play.
Guiding our bow,
What a beautiful day.

Sun is shining, Patience they say
Is needed to catch a fish,
What a beautiful day.

Light breeze blowing, Palm trees sway
Fish now biting,
What a beautiful day.

Engines roaring, Lines bay
Fish landed, success, O what a beautiful day.
Dedication: My father and love of fishing

My Mother Wears Many Hats
Meredith Edwards–Bardecker
My Mother has a life
So full and complete
Her vocabulary doesn't contain
The word... Defeat!!!!!!

She has a hat of determination
Wearing it high upon her head
And doesn't fall short
In any direction she is led.

Another hat of accomplishment
In her closet can be found
A single Mom that raised two children
And showered them with love all around.

Another hat to be mentioned
Is the one full of love
Its color is pure white
Like that of a graceful dove.

Her closet holds yet another
She continues to push aside
This hat represents fear
And it's totally black inside.

My Mom is always thankful
For she knows she has been blessed
Therefore, the green hat of envy
Is one she doesn't possess.

I completely admire my Mother
And I thank God he gave her to me
For I will honor her throughout my life
For the whole world to see.
Dedication: Julia, my wonderful mother and friend

Noteworthy Works

On Wings Of Prayer
Gail Wilkerson Saunders
My restless soul takes quiet flight.
On wings of prayer I'll spend the night.

It's been a long day with its toils and worry.
So I'm off to the Master in the greatest of hurry.

Jesus bids "enter", there's room at His feet
For me to relax, and my heart skips a beat.

He soothes my anguish; calms my doubt.
I find peace within; no more fears without.

He sends me forth to the very next day,
But never alone, by my side He'll stay.

Towards that new morning I rapidly soar.
There! I've just made it as day opens her door.

I awake with joy and a song in my heart,
Traces of love that only God could impart.

When life overwhelms and you can't see the light
Stop! send your soul on a much needed flight.

In the blink of an eye, it's but a brief visit
Yet like me, you wouldn't have missed it.
Dedication: To Tommy, husband and friend

Give Me A Chance
Marga Fernandez
American, American, give me a chance.
I want to work, I want to thrive,
I want to live in peace and love.

I don't want anything free;
I have two arms to work, a heart to love,
And a strong spirit to fight.

I would like to help build up this nation.
I would like this country to be a great nation.
One that is truly "God's Town."

What are the differences between you and I?
Is it the color of your eyes?
Is it the color of my skin?

You have the strength of the sky in your eyes.
I have the power of the sun in my skin.
We most join them both together
To rise above our differences.

I dream the same as you, I sing the same as you,
I cry the same as you, I feel the same as you,
And also, I love the same as you.

Let me know you, let me learn from you,
Let me teach you, let's go to talk.
If we work together we will be able to make
A better World.

We have the same body, we have the same mind,
We have the same soul, we have the same Father.
Our Father, God, who sent Jesus to die for us.

We can live all together forever and ever.
Just... give me a chance.

My Mother's Love
Becky Doemel
As the years went by I have
grown to see,

Why a Mother in your life just
has to be,

She knows what to say when
times are bad,

She feels for you when you are
sad,

Together forever till death do
us part,

I love you my Mother with all
of my heart,

As the years went by it's sad to say
I wish we were together every
night and day.

Time mends all wounds but
The scars are still there,

For give me my Mother for
I really did care

Stray Dog
J. A. McCrea
old, broken, breed mixture;
i read the rings
around your eyes,
estimating your age.

favoring your right hind,
those apathetic eyes
dimly illuminate some inner battle of wills.
misery becomes the opponent of desire.

an instinctive need for human contact
justifies the necessity of worldly temptations.

reaching forth my hand
to stroke your head,
you cringe at the ready,
resigned to either kindness or cruelty—
braced for the latter.

touching coarse fur, i make contact
with that suffocated trust within you.

leaning heavily into my strokes,
you sigh an honest, tired, canine breath.

tail twitches.
tongue probes my palm.

i move slowly away...

you follow... two or three paces behind...

each step a possibility
that you may finally be going home...
Dedication: Donna Welch, "Rescuer" and Friend

Dreams of the Soul

The Beautiful, Mysterious Ocean
Eva Frost
I love to go for walks, along the ocean, in any kind of season.
I find it to be soothing, and I don't need a particular reason.

If I watch the ocean long enough, I can become mesmerized.
Getting lost in my thoughts, with the sound of the tide.

I can sit for hours, listening to the crashing of the waves.
As they hit against the rocks, creating an enormous spray.

It's amazing to watch the waves form and curl, with such a roar.
Then they turn into foam, as they break, and wash upon the shore.

Leaving behind seaweed, driftwood, smooth rocks, and shells.
Each item having its own story, that only, the ocean can tell!

I always make the time, to walk to the very end of the pier.
As I look out at the horizon, I watch the sun slowly disappear.

If I look directly behind me, there's a beautiful mountain range.
The peacefulness I feel at that moment, I hope will never change.

Far off in the distance, I can hear the rumble of a train.
Then, just as I look up, I see a cloud that looks full of rain.

Sailboats become faint images, as they're guided by the wind.
Then as I feel a chill, I see the fog is rapidly rolling in.

Every time I go there, I experience a different kind of emotion.
It thank God, for creating such a beautiful, mysterious ocean!

I Am The Dream My Mother Dreamed Of
Theresa Costanzo
I am the dream my Mother dreamed of... I am their most precious
blessing and Gift from God above.
I am the most wonderful Love that my Father could give – I have
a special reason to come to them now, and to live.
I am the only Gift that they can truly share and treasure – the
purpose of their Love and their lifetime together.
I am the joy that shines from within my Mother's heart – all my
Father saw inside her soul – right from the very start.
I am the Gift that God created to show – that their unconditional
Love – was all they ever really needed to know.
I am the most perfect Gift of my parent's life – their treasure to
behold as a Husband and Wife.
I am the most fortunate child to be given these two as my own
I am the truth in their Love, and in Love I have grown.
I am their most wonderful hope for today and tomorrow, their
brightest joy in place of their sorrows.
I am the reason why these two souls have become one – God has
chosen their hearts as the place I'll call home.
I am proof of their faith, that prayers of the heart – can come true, a
bond to keep them together in all that they do.
I was their dream, their hope, and a much wanted blessing; They
have shown their Love and Faith in all their life lessons.
I am the most special one that they could have envisioned in their
minds – I am everything they've wanted and all the Love they
ever needed to find.
God knows everything they will ever need, and will ever feel – I
was sent from above to show them his Love is so real.
They prayed for ME, and God heard their prayers – so He sent me
"His Special Angel" and let me come here.
God chose Me – "His Angel" – I am his child; a most precious one
He heard their prayers and through him it's been done.
I am the dream that my Mother dreamed of... I will be their joy and
happiness and proof of God's most precious Love.

Dedication: Sibyl– from her dream– Samantha

No One
Jill D. Weidman
How often I have listened to you recall memories of
our childhood. You say, "no one knew of the horror,
or joy."

So thin the line, I live between them as if they
were going to mesh, like beautiful sadness.

You say, "no one" was there to hear your cries, to
quiet the deafening madness of all that encircled
you, holding you prisoner in your fear.

You say, "no one" understood the flood of emotions
that nearly drowned you at times, the terror that
left you frozen, the anger that blurred your vision
the hurt, too painful to speak of.

I sit, and let you speak, even when your lips are
still, I read what is in your eyes, I see what is in your
heart, and I hear what you cannot explain.

You say "if only someone was there", and you end with,
"no one was".

Dear heart, recall this, if you can.

In all your agony, in the dark when you were
crying, I was there, remember me?,

I'm no one.

Full Moon Raccoon
Janinka E. Walulik
In the middle of the month of June, on a hot, hot night, with a big full
moon
I sat and watched re–run TV, my cat was sleeping, close to me

I think we both had heard the sound, we jumped and quickly turned around,
"There's something there!" I said out loud, and as I slowly stood, I
found,

My cat was standing nose–to–nose, Thank goodness the screen door was
closed,
It made that noise, the one we'd heard, not a peep, like from a bird,

It kind of growled, or hissed, at first, and then the noise got much, much
worse
I've never heard a sound like that, not like a dog, or mouse, or cat

It wasn't like a pig, or cow, I strained to see with knitted brow,
It moved around into the light, then there it was, could I be right?

The light was bright, that night in June, it must be from that big full
moon
He wore a mask, to hide his face, and slowly sneaked around the place

He had a coat of heavy fur, all brown with black stripes, yes, I'm sure
My cat jumped up onto the chair, and on her back, stood up her hair

She arched way up, and made a hiss, I wasn't quite as scared as this
I tried to tell her what it was, and where it lives and what it does,

She was so scared, she'd never seen, its eyes were shining, bright and
green
He's looking for something to eat, a nut, or fruit or garbage treat

I'd better calm her down real soon, too bad he didn't come at noon
I named him "Rocky" from that old tune, he's just a hungry, young Raccoon

Stan's Smile
Madeline J. Carlson

I've been reflecting dear, on the Christmas we met
It was the most wonderful day, I'll never forget

We didn't converse much, your winning smile said it all
Your personality made you seem at least ten feet tall

You had a jovial smile that won my heart
I knew it was true love from the very start

When you became physically disabled, you didn't ask why
You smiled and faced the challenge eye to eye

"The world won't stop" you declared, "I must keep on going"
You ventured forward full speed, your smile always showing

You always smiled even when things got tough
Doing things half way, for you, wasn't enough

You encouraged others around you with your smile
Dealing with your own adversity all the while

The Eagle you admire because it's brave, strong and free;
These are only a few of the qualities in you I see

Stan, you're my hero, my confidant
You are all I'll ever need or want

My love, always keep that jovial smile on your handsome face;
You'll make our little corner of the world a much happier place.

The Parsley Garden
Sebastian Darrel Simon Sears

Between the wind, Under the sky, There is no being, Greater than I!
I need no belongings! I need no affection! For as you can see, I am perfection!
In the parsley garden, I work today, Minding my purpose, Of cutting away,
To make each cut perfect, In cut and size, For perfection is what, I won't compromise!
The Sun is shining, Onto my skin. My life is perfect! Now she comes in.
She's as pretty as light, And as fresh as the sea, But not quite perfect.
Not good enough for me!
I thus turn away, Showing my rejection. She is quite good, But not like perfection!
I'm the perfect being, More perfect than God! She asks. "Do you like me?" I give her a nod.
A negative nod! For she cannot see, That she's not perfect! Not good enough for me!
Only another I, Is good enough for me! Since none exist it's an, Impossibility!
But her eyes are lost, Blind to my perfection, Rejecting my reason. Those eyes are a weapon.
She says. "I love you." And now tells me why. "You are different," "Under this sky."
She must now know, All others are worse! I am one of a kind, In the whole Universe!
But I will cut some more, For an hour or so, Until she can see, The answer is no!
I show her a bit, Of perfection to see. And now she laughs, Challenging me!
I now turn around, Displaying contention, To prove to her, I am perfection!
I now cry out, For all kind to see! I shall display for all, The perfection in me!
I reach to within, And pour it all out! She laughs even more, As if to doubt.
But I cannot fail! And I try once more, Right to the heart, Bearing its core!
She takes no notice, That leaves one question. I ask of you, Am I perfection!

Dream Angel
Emily J. Bergman

Do you sleep tonight while
I slumber?

Do you whisper soft nothings
in my ear while I dream?

Do you make my sleep a
peaceful quest or ships
a sail in roaring waves of
pain I fear?

Are you my dream maker
of a sort?
Do you sit to guide my nitly
ship to harbors unknown;
That I awake with sudden
jolts of lighting flashes, with
earthquake clashes to twist
my soul; of mysteries lurking
in my mind in daytime thoughts
of night time horrors or
Better yet a quest at best
to caress an old time lover
once more.

Dream angel give me peace
within my sleep; give me
love from up above and
lead me home, Dream
Angel.

The First Chapter
Angela Vassar

A story so simple
Yet so expressive

Our love is like...

The many pages of a diary
Revealing our thoughts
Our dreams
Our desires

A schoolbook...
We read to learn
We learn to teach

A mystery novel...
Venturing into the unknown
Finding us both guilty
of love in the first degree

An unfinished journal...
Filled with memories we've made
and memories yet to be made

So when you're lost
and can't find your way...
You must remember to
keep the book open

Read me... read the pages of my soul

For this is the First Chapter of our lives
And this is a story that never ends

Dedication: My husband, Ken, with love

Dreams of the Soul

The Night GOD Decided To Take A Walk (Hurricane Fran)
Villa Kelly Gaddy
As the night approached God decided it was time to take a walk.
He spoke to the stars and they put out their lights. He spoke to the clouds and they all
turned black. He spoke to the world and this time we listened.

We could not see Him for this was His mission. No moon, no stars just the dark, dark clouds. You could feel God as He moved along the path,
Because the wind was blowing to move all the trash.

You could not see Him as He walked.
The wind was blowing and the trees bowed down for Him to pass.
It was a dark, dark night when God decided to take a walk.

He looked at catastrophe, devastation, and destruction.
He looked at deception, desolation, and treachery.
He looked at divorce, condemnation, corruption, abomination, and damnation.

God looked back at the trail he walked, then... He smiled when he saw:
Benevolence, ambition, discern, hope, joy, love, praise, righteousness, and redemption.

When He finished His walk, He spoke to the sun, the moon, the stars, and the clouds.
Go back to work God commanded.

It was a dark land for days and the trees no longer waved. Neighbors helping neighbors. Such a Spiritual gain. But...
The trees are still bowed because... God Decided to Take a Walk.

Dedication: Lee, Kristen, Simon, my family

I Remember Not So Long Ago
Chiva
I remember not so long ago— I rejoiced when you were born...
The bond of Mother to daughter never seemed so strong.

I remember not so long ago— your 1st day of school... You wore
Size 3 and believe me— you were the tiniest in the class, but you
Sure moved fast!

I remember not so long ago— you graduated from school... In
Your red cap and gown, I know you felt real "cool".

I remember not so long ago— you walked down the aisle... With
The biggest smile.

I remember not so long ago— you gave birth to your 1st child...
Gone were the days of being "wild".

I remember not so long ago— you gave birth to your little
Boy... With the glow of total joy.

I remember not so long ago your daughter started school...
Petite and pretty and shy, a replica of you.

I remember not so long ago— watching your son... Intent on a
Project and full of fun.

I remember not so long ago— watching these children growing
Into caring and loving people—a tribute to their parents and
The joy that they do bring.

I remember not so long ago— my Mother's supportive stand...
With tears in her eyes as she held your tiny hand.

Life goes full circle— hand in hand— in hand again... Mother to
Daughter and Mother to daughter again.

The Face Of Hunger
Jewel M. Norderud
Amongst the passersby, unseeingly or no mind seem to take
Whence on my ears the sobs of a child, those of hunger and cold, for not a wrap on her back.

I observed the Mother's pain–etched face, as if in a trance she did appear

Seemingly un–noticing of the muddy tattered–clothed child at her side, so near...

Gazing at me she asked not for a pence...

I most wanted to give a pound...

But speeded my gait, as encouraged by my companions...

Regretful since.

I carry not a heaviness in my heart so great, for the woman who stood penniless, as it appeared to be...

It's the cries of the child; which fails my soul to free.

A victim of circumstance one may contend,

Or failure to try... Please... how is it all explained,

To the stomach of a "Hungry Child?"

Dedication: My husband, Vincent Norderud

The Rose At His Feet
Rebecca N. Dyer
As the crucial sharp nails were
hammered into His hands,
And the crown of thorns was slammed
onto His head,
Everyone knew He'd be back, that He
couldn't be beat,
His soul and His blood sank into the rose
at His feet.

As the people cried below His cross,
They accepted Him into their hearts.
Everyone knew that He did not know
defeat,
And His mind and His love sank
into the rose at His feet.

As they all whispered His name below
their breath.
He filled their lives with His forgiveness,
Then out came a shout, from a man
with a sheep,
As the shepherd knelt by the rose at
His feet.

"Jesus shall live on!" cried another
man,
As the people formed a circle
and held each other's hands,
Then out came a bright light with
great belief.
His spirit arose from the rose
at His feet.

Dedication: Those who inspire me

Noteworthy Works

Mother Earth
Iva Clark

Here is to the rising sun, the sun rises up
and our day has began!
Chirping birds are singing, for what they feast
is what Mother of Earth brings!
The buzzing of bees, going to work, they gather the
pollen of flowers and trees, they know their job so well,
Mother Nature doesn't have to whisper or tell!
All so beautiful, from flowers and trees, to birds
and bees! All animals in flocks or herds, or alone
ya see, the fresh waters and ocean's salty seas!
these are all treasures of Mother Nature's needs !
So why do I, tear up her land? So why do I,
think I can? So why did I, take her treasures and
return her, with trash on holy land! So why
do I, no longer follow her footsteps in the sand?
So why do, the things we do? why deny and try and lie?
So what on land, or in the air, in the rivers
or ocean's sands, what part of Mother Nature do we
not understand! To Mother Nature we have
been, so unfair! Our children are the ones who
pay for our mistakes!
Have you answered the prayer of a mantas?
or understood roaring lion's Hiss!
She gave us all life, why do we throw it away!
we better all try and do something today?
The falling sun, falls into night, darkness
falls, over the mountain tops, leaped the moon
our coldest light!

Dedication: All the mothers of the earth

Complex Simplicity
Barbara J. Sedor

The world comes down around me
Shrouding me like a veil

The complicity I call life
Is a multifaceted orb

Awake I search the pathways
Finding solutions and release

In sleep I wonder in and out
Dark places hidden from the light

I search for the simplicity
Which eludes me

My solitude and peace
Seem ever from my grasp

Listening to serenity of the basics
on earth
Withdrawal from confusion and
turmoil

Seek your own life
Everyone has their own life to live

It's time to break away from the
confusion of minds
Finding my own way home to
my basic self and repose

Among my inner thoughts and
instincts
Happiness is a natural again

Around The Clock
John E. Jones

Changing to light,
Across the horizon spreading bright;
While awakening at dawn,
As the rising sun.

Coming into view,
When the weather brings new;
While energy flowing,
As nature continue growing.

When daily starting fresh,
Of a peaceful night rest;
While reaching places among time,
With a different purpose in mind.

While moving upon land,
With a distance to understand;
As life carry for more,
When following steps, and having a chore.

While feelings turn within all,
With hunger out comes a call;
As relieving when receiving,
Of a routine perceiving.

While your will leaves unlocked,
Of a part through,
Around the clock.

Dedication: The world over

Momma, Why?
Susan J. Feltner

Momma,
Why did you leave?
Where did you go?
Why did you leave us children all alone?

We looked everywhere,
That we knew.
But Momma,
We couldn't find you.

There was no one to feed us,
Or give us a bath.
The babies,
They started crying,
So I put them on my lap.

I guess they knew Momma,
That you wouldn't be back.

Why didn't you leave us a note?
Didn't you know that we would be scared?
You didn't even say goodbye,
Or try to make us understand.

Momma,
What did we do wrong?
We'll try to make it right.
Don't be mad Momma,
We promise not to fight.

Oh Momma,
Why did you leave?
Won't you please come home?
Please don't leave us all alone.

Dreams of the Soul

??????
F. K. Youe
Barbed wire fences
Brick walls

Fog
Open spaces

Curtains
Windows

Money
Intelligence

Talent
Beauty

Authority
Superiority

Busyness
Nonchalance

False smiles
Corny jokes

Constant chatter
Silence

Memories and cobwebs

What is a barrier?

Alone
Monica Isle
I would like to learn to laugh again
To feel the wind, blow gently through my hair,
Walk by rippling streams, or golden beaches
To be a child and sleep without a care.

I would like someone to share my dreams
To love, and hold my hand.
To climb a rugged mountain
Or walk bare foot in the sand.

I would like to fill a rucksack
Say goodbye, and to walk out the door
To leave behind all material things
For they're not important anymore

I need to cry, cry and cry
Until all my tears run dry.
And then and only then I'd smile
Smile until the day I die.

I feel I've lived a lifetime
And have witnessed so much pain,
I would like the chance to laugh
The chance to love again.

I would like so many things
Things that money cannot buy,
I feel I'm locked within myself
And I don't know the reason why.

I just don't have the answer
I only have the pain,
And my laughter turns to sadness
Like sunshine turns to rain.

Hope
Joseph A. Tartaglia III
In this world so dark and cold I am walking in an endless desert of mist and

uncertainty. I look around to see that I am standing alone in a vast land

of hatred, violence, and loneliness. I can't help but feel desperation,

complete and total abandonment of hope. Death is a welcomed friend, a

friend I forever long for. It is a walk towards my own damnation.

I can see a warm, bright, welcoming light at the end of all this depression.

A light that will end my hurt, my loneliness, my broken heart.

I quicken my step only to increase the distance between me and my salvation.

I'm running in a furious frenzy, but the light only continues to recede deeper into

the surrounding darkness. I yearn for the light. To feel its warmth and

unconditional love but I can't not yet. It's not my time.

The light is my hope and I only need to find my future, to find myself.
Until then
I must search in all of this mist, this desert, this loneliness – for my path of inner peace.

Jeremiah
Virginia R. Davis
A time to weep, and a time to mourn
Into times like these, Jeremiah was born.

Jeremiah, the prophet, who wrote Lamentations,
Was called by God, to speak to the nations.

Turning from God, Israel began to stray,
For without hope, they saw no need to pray.

God gave Jeremiah a vision of things to be;
But, how do you reach people, who cannot see?

How could anyone as depressed as he;
Foretell what the future of Jerusalem would be?

Times were hard, and patience began to fray,
When Babylon came to carry Jerusalem away.

Quitting on God; O, what a shame!
It's never God, who is the blame.

This is never the Christian's way;
Each new tomorrow, brings a fresh new day.

Out of great suffering, came the thorn.
Out of despair – new hope was born.

With Jerusalem's problems, he couldn't contend.
But, his words to us, seem heaven sent.

Jeremiah speaks loud and clear.
It is not a plan to do us harm,
But a plan to call us near.
God has a plan – can't you hear?

Omnipresent Love
David Marshall

The mere thought of you brings out the best in me

When a feeling of melancholic surrounds me, a beautiful
Picture of you turns my entire universe upside down

I am always in a mode of exaltation when I discern you
Blooming into a world of freshness

You make my world extremely felicitate just knowing that
You will never purposely abandon me

I hold and cherish you when others think that you are
Not relevant

Even in your mode of somnolence, my feelings for you
Explode into a loveable nuclear reaction

When I cogitate about what you have meant to me over the
Passage of time, my whole environment transforms into a
Consistent rhythm of enjoyment

The sprinkle of water resurrects your physical state into a
High level of human satisfaction and wild imagination

When I receive a hint of your demise, my world of mental
Collectedness becomes a big struggle for my destination
Of tomorrow

As the clouds melt into their own area of relaxation, I
Will always hold you close in my busy world of endeavors

In The Hospital, The Day The Staff Struck
Dorothy E. Smith

'Twas Wednesday the 13th December, when the domestic staff all struck,
The day I shall always remember, 'cos it brought all us patients good luck.

Instead of the usual bustle and rushing to and fro, the day went by just like clockwork,
A strike on? Well we did not know.

The morning was quiet and calmly arranged washes, temps taken and pressures,
Everything seemed to be so changed, life once more had its pleasures.

Our meal's were really super, roast pork, vegetables, applesauce all hot,
Ice cream and jelly and a gorgeous cuppa, we really enjoyed the lot.

Supper was tomatoes, ham salad and potatoes, creamed, of course.
They even found all the trimmings, right down to the mayonnaise sauce.

The loving experience was shown, infused right through the young nursing staff;
maybe some of them were confused, for to see them jump to it made us laugh.

There was an air of influence all around, efficiency, thoroughness and calm.
Truly these wonderful Volunteers had retained their old Nurse Nightingale charm.

Never had such loving care been given to the making of beds before.
We even got washed and gently rubbed on the places where one gets sore.

Well I give my thanks to the Volunteers for such dedication I may never again see the like
nor to have experienced such devotion.

I'm glad the Domestics had their strikes.

Inside The Forest
Todd Shindledecker

Inside the forest of the mind's perception
Grows the trees of experienced direction

Where the water flows of a special kind
Leaving leaves of common sense to find

Paths lead to here and there
You stick to the path from which you hold dear
In the realm of consciousness
Asking God to bless

Along the stream you'll find some dreams
Where everything's real or so it seems

Within the forest you find a lake which
Helps the trees to remain awake

The moon reflects off the lake
Reflections of chances you want to take

The path you have chosen has been cleared
Now you can go places that were once feared

Now the decision has to be made
The path must be laid

All of my fears have begun to subside
Inside the forest I have found my guide

Dedication: Harmony of Hearts

Six Of Me
Rose Hayes

If there could be six more of me
How fantastic life would be
One to shop and cook the food
and to cater for my every mood

One to look after all the pets
and make those journey's to the vets
The cat to groom the dog to walk
She might even teach the budgie to talk

One the house to clean and dust
To polish and Hoover now that's a must
Windows to clean both inside and out
That she'll be kept busy there is no doubt

One to be my husband's mate
To fetch and carry and on him wait
and go behind him with a broom
as the chores get done room by room

One the clothes to wash and to press
From anorak's to evening dress
and if there should be time to spare
There's always things that need repair

The last one can be just for me
To run my bath and make the tea
To paint my nails and wash my hair
and plump the cushions in my chair

But I know it's a dream
and just cannot be
For he can only afford
Just one of me

Dreams of the Soul

Untitled
Elana Payne

In our sadness and grief today
as the silent teardrops fall
We have to stop and thank the Lord
for giving us Mother at all.

He must have known how much we'd need
her tender loving way
The prayers she'd send, the care she'd give
as she nurtured us day by day.

The endless bumps and bruises she'd kiss
with genuine care and concern
The tears that she'd dry over the years
While in her own eyes they'd burn.

He must have known right from the start
the sacrifices she'd willingly make
To see that we had everything that we'd need
upon our own life's journey to take.

She gave us love, laughter, and fun
in her own heartwarming style
She taught us faith and gave us the strength
to walk that extra mile.

Some children never know the joy
of having a Mother to care
So even in grief, we thank you God
for giving us one so RARE!

Dedication: My mother, "The wind beneath my wings"

The Dragon Slayer
Clare S. Marder

She emerged from the cave an unsightly gray mass
She flaunted her pain as a newfound sexuality
Shameless, exposed, naked... raw...
Waiting to be admired for her courage...
her vulnerability... her naturalness
But they were shocked at her nakedness; and they were
ashamed for her; and they were repulsed by her
lack of pride
She told them how she wrestled the dragon, and the dragon
singed her hair and skin so only what was once beneath
was now inside out
They turned away from the ugliness and the stench
And when she told of making love with the beast as it whipped
her with its long tail
They shrieked in horror at her insanity
And it made them tremble and quake to the very core
For they always wondered what it was like to make love
to a beast
And they wanted to know if the beast was tamed, but they dared
not ask for that would show their own curiosity with the
beast and their envy for what she knew
So she bathed and swabbed her wounds and put on her dressing
and made herself pretty for the others
And they gathered 'round her again
And she laughed as she told them it was not a dragon at all
"I took a great fall," she said. "And some bumps and
bruises."
And the others stood agape——
Then they were angered for feeling duped
Or was it disappointed...
After all, dragons are but a myth.

Dedication: To my sons, Jeffrey and David

My Appalachian Mule
Mel Johnson

Early to rise, and early to shine
you lazy mule, you lazy swine
you're just a beast of burden.
God's servant to man. A four-legged
creature, long eared funny kind.
For 18 long hot, cold, and dry
seasons, you have been a faithful mule,
and friend of mine;
helping me plant, and raise a poor
man's crop at harvest time.
From sunrise to sunset;
We both have marched a million miles
thru those hills, and valleys;
tilling soil, rocks, and roots,
and over mountain tops with
plow, and muddy boots.
But now our life's journey, and
work is nearing an end;
because we are now both old, and gray,
and nearly blind.
"Oh!! how I curse Father Time."
So lift up your eyes, and ears
to heaven mule;
can you hear the Master's voice,
calling us home to that beautiful
garden in the sky.
Where faithful old mules, and poor
dirt farmers come to rest in the great
by–and–by.

Dedication: The hardworking farmers and coalminers and Native Appalachia

---

Wanting A Lasting Love
Elma L. Greer

I have always wanted
Someone sweet and kind
One who knows what's on
his mind.

I thought I found that
Special one. Who made me
Feel as though I was
Not just the one. But the
only one.

But as weeks passed I
dropped more tears only
to discover my fears were
near.

Yet I lust for more, I
Could not find him at his
door.

My desire is strong and
Maybe wrong But I sure
would be happy if this
lasting love could last on
and on,

My needs are deep. But I
won't weep. I'll just rely
On that special one. Not
To take this lasting love
So cheap

Dedication: Roy, whom I love and respect

Noteworthy Works

A Dream
Anita Elliott

I saw a woman walking by and I noticed the anguish in her face. I looked again but she was gone and instead I saw an angel.

Though the sky was bleak and the rain was softly falling, I saw the illuminance of the halo.

And, oh, what a glorious view I thought.

She wiped my tears. I saw her smile and it was then I heard the sound. I looked again and I saw more angels.

No, I said, "This cannot be."

I saw a great ensemble. Oh, so many angels smiling as they sang.

Their gowns were softly flowing and iridescent, rainbow–like, in color.

I watch amazed at such a sight

An angel said to me, "It's all right, do not worry."
"We leave you peace, serenity, hope, faith, and much love to last forever."

And then I woke and it was but a dream.

Dedication: My beloved mother, Victoria

Hand In Hand
Gerri Simon

Hand in hand we set out on a beautiful summer day
We just wanted from the daily routine to get away

Walking down the lane we hardly spoke at all
We were admiring the beautiful trees standing so tall

We sat and watched the squirrels gathering food for their young
We just sat in silence, no words flowing from our tongues

We slowly moved along and passed by a small graveyard
We commented about how on the families it must be so hard

There was a freshly dug grave covered with flowers and wreaths
It made us both want to sit down and weep

We came upon an old man sitting all alone on his steps
We stopped to see if he needed any help

He just needed someone to talk, so we sat down for awhile
It did our hearts good to see this old man smile

We passed a small church with the windows boarded and the steeple torn down
They had built a modern larger building and moved into town

We passed an old couple and stopped for awhile to talk
We wished them well and continued on with our walk

We then decided to head home as the sun was beginning to go down
Hand in hand we said a silent prayer for the peace of mind this day we had found

Dedication: My mom, whom I love

A Wakeup For My Psyche
Debra F. Golden

I have My rules; they must be obeyed. I have My expectations; they must be exceeded.
I demand respect; after all I give you life.
Because I am disappointed with my own existence–I live through you, but on My terms.
I cannot see My flaws, because that would admit I am not superhuman; but I expand on your flaws–you are to blame for MY failures.
My dreams, I force to be your dreams, or nightmares; My desires I push on to you.
Because I feel inadequate–I make you give me worthiness, a sense of being, but I took
your identity–I killed your spirit attempting to make ME OMNIPOTENT.
Now I am forced to face my own dysfunctionality. I must let you go, against my heart's
desire and against my soul's covet. I stand here in flesh and watch, but cannot see.
My beloved child leaves me forever. I may never apologizes, touch your hair or hold your
hand.
You are gone from me eternally to a 3 by 6 dirt environment–I could never bear even ice
cream on your face.
For some reason, the words from the doctor—SUICIDE—cannot reach my ears but
shatter my hear, soul, and psyche.
I only wish that time would let me have one more opportunity, so you and I could patch
what was broken with me and I might not have broken you.
I cannot say goodbye–it was not your time to die–it was MINE!

Dedication: Don Golden and Patrick Headrick

The Lighthouse
Edith Gattilia

He stands ever so tall,
As a mighty warrior

He has no hands, no feet,
no arms, no fear,
There is no limit to how
the forces of nature,
his body did smear

While far out. From the
shore!

Sailors, sleep in a peaceful
sleep.

They know his mighty
Warrior of stone
and brick

Will bring them
Safe to shore

They love his bright
beam
Forever more will
gleam

Shine on mighty
Warrior –

You are supreme.

Dedication: Tara Lisa Gragg

Dreams of the Soul

Cony
Elizabeth M. Bente

A friend of mine is named Cony, whose antics are not phony, gets himself into places
Where he can see faces. He explores with delight anything shiny and bright.
You start to read the morning paper, and he finds another caper, he'll wander in and out of the pages
Seemingly as though he gauges each turn of the sheet as a challenge for his feet.
He'll hang upside down on a mirror with no sign of fear. He's up and he's down
Just like a circus clown, so active he is, most of the day, then around eight he hits the hay.
HE'S HAD THE RUN OF THE HOUSE, JUST LIKE A LITTLE MOUSE, though he's seldom on the floor
Or, for that matter– never near a door
White is quite an attraction, he goes into action, he'll chew a tissue to shreds.
You should see what he does to threads. If I ask, "Cony, want some?" You'd see how fast he will come
For a celery leaf or a piece of bread, you can be sure he will not go to bed. He'll sit on my hand
Or my head, when I want him to be quiet instead. The other day I was painting and gluin', sounded
Like he asked, "What's ya doin'," Seems like he's been around for years. I know when he dies,
I'll be in tears. When he sits on my shoulder and pecks at my nose, it thrills me right down to my toes
His cooing and chatter– could that be a form of flatter? All he wants is a little attention.
I'll oblige– without mention. He has a plastic bird in his cage. If I bother it he goes into a rage
I enjoy watching my little parakeet, for entertainment he can't be beat.

A Rose And Wine
Troy E. Taylor

Look at the figure standing
What do you see
This is a shadow of a man
Whose life was not to be

Now look deep into his eyes
There's a beauty and softness within

Sometimes bitter and sweet
Flavorful yet delicate to begin

He touches you like a flower

Is smooth as a soothing drink

Yet he can hurt you like a thorn

But you still smile at his wink

Someday he will wilt and die

Or grow empty as a bottle... how subtle

Fades away into your memory

In your heart he is still there to cuddle

No this is not a man
For I live my life this way

I will touch you forever
I am... A ROSE AND WINE

Memories
J. Lilley

"Oh!" What a joy it is to see,
my sibling; with son upon his knee
It is with a pride that cannot compare,
When viewing my cherished ones upon that chair

A Grandmother's lot is so different from that,
of the Mother she once was surrounded by brats!
For now, when the going gets really tough,
She can take a back seat, and say, "I've had enough!"

Raising a family is no easy feat, and I say this
when recalling the times they just wouldn't sleep
The furrowed lines upon my brow,
tell yet another story of how, through sickness
and accidents you pull them through,
reliable as always and resilient too

The joys of Motherhood are next to none,
only fully appreciated once the job has been done.
Through a Grandmother's eyes you can put right those mistakes,
that now seem so trivial, but at the time appeared great

I remember the tears that so often I shed,
when sitting alone; the children in bed.
There were those tears of excitement when
achievements were made,
but none so traumatic as when they finally strayed.

So now they are parents retracing my steps,
raising my grandchildren with their various pets.
I will treasure these memories for use when I feel low,
and I'll never forget, it was "my" leading role.

Who am I
Ruth Eubanks

I once was dainty and fair
As I sat in my chair
With make-up on my face
And not a hair out of place
Now here in bed I lay
With face unmade and hair in disarray

Who am I?

I once could run and walk just about anywhere
Now I have to depend on hands to push my chair
My legs that once moved so fast – no one knew where I went
Are now all twisted and bent

Who am I?

I used to be on the go
Then something happened and my pace got slow
Now it's taking its toll and I have no control
I can hear but I can't speak and I ask myself, "Why?"
Now all I can do is cry

Who am I?

Remember we were once just like you
We could do the things you do
Someday you may be where we're at
Take time and think about that

Who are we?

Dedication: Residents of Toomsboro Nursing Center

Noteworthy Works

Old Betsy
Xina Michelle Renata

I loved my Old Betsy, my first car.
Me and my Old Betsy, we went far.

With many memories, of so fine.
$500 or best offer, was the sign.

A 1962 Ford Falcon, baby blue,
Her license plate, stuck on with glue.

She had this loud squeak.
And took a quart of oil, once a week.

A bedroom pillow sat so neat,
to hide her springs on the seat.

We went for miles on bald tires.
And sang to AM radio, while I held the wires.

With no reverse to go back,
I sailed ahead though her windshield cracked.

My Betsy Blue was so fine,
We'd valet park when we would dine.

Then one sad day, Old Betsy died.
Her last 40 mile an hour car ride.

There's a boom now – instead of a squeak.
And a gallon a day now for the oil leak.

She is now parked with this sign,
"Free to anyone, who'll call her mine".

Destroy
Phillip Brown

Dew rises from the meadows, sunlight sweeps fog away
Distant rainbow close to me, a pot of gold where children play
The sky shines behind me, beauty has faded through the years
Now life is war – and war is life, thunder rumbles – no one hears

Silence is gold melted down, defend yourself or ours is lost
Someone is knocking at nature's door, not preparing to accept the cost
Whispers echo in my head, who is right, who is wrong
Satellites sparkle above the clouds no one's weak – no one's strong

Destiny is written, it's nature's way, it's our testament of life and war
Who's in command – who's got control, what exactly are we fighting for?
We are what we are so the war began, they signaled the warning of one last kiss
Never condemned or too late to pray, who would have thought it'd come to this

The ground trembled from my tiny hole, it's not thunder with death so near
What have we done will we ever know, will it all just disappear?
Fire bombs explode, I am insane, hope you've warned us what to do
Telegraph the pope so he will know, that our threat was carried through

When the battle is over, the game will be done, presidents will unite and politically pray,
We followed you, yet you followed them, you'll accuse each other for blowing it away
Within the ash and eventual shame, there is no trace of us above the clay
No loser, no winner, no parade, and no one home to put the toys away.

A Quiet Day's Night
P. Vincent Nee

Night had closed to a shaded dawn:
LIGHT skimmed in opulent colors along the waking shores last YAWN!

BORN again these endless days grow in sensing living SOUNDS;
HORNS blared to duties' call on ships that make endless seaing ROUNDS!

HIGH overhead birds dance on a shifting WIND;
WHY we ask 1000 times why must SUMMER pass and begin to END!

DAYLIGHT frolics in SUNNING new raying BEAMS;
WEIGH each golden ray in worship before they end in a lightless STREAM!

RAINBOWS bind in spectrums of change as breezes GENTLE;
TRAINS BLOW along rivers that breathe in each new changing trees LENTIL!

LATE noon finds a swallow shifting in growing SEEDS;
WAIT now here again it happens on NATURE'S SHORE a pelting fall of BEADS!

ALWAYS this turning from night to day or yet is it day to NIGHT;
CRUSADE on open fields that blend into horizons of bluing LIGHT!

LEAVE darkness to voidless faces for in shapeless shadows they EXCEL;
WEAVE into beauty SUNLIGHT for in its warmth none need feel REPELLED!

NOW again the shaded shadows shift to curtain the day's amber LIGHT;
BOW if you feel you must to night's intemperance for me I'll take "A QUIET DAYS NIGHT"!

Average Man
Brian Rysdale

He would never be an household name
Didn't seek honour, glory, or fame
All he was, was an average man one of the
boys, one of the gang
No words of valour of him would be spoke
or a gallant tale of him wrote
As with others he crouched as in a trance
In a muddy trench somewhere in France,
His heart was heavy filled with sadness
For all this futility, all this madness
Was this justice, was this right, that man
Should arm, that man should fight
Couldn't he settle his wants, his needs, without
wars and evil deeds
But his not to say the reason why, all
he must do is to fight and to die
Soon would come to order somewhere in France,
fix bayonets, begin the advance
Hypnotized, he would grip his gun somewhere in
France, a poor Mother's son
Soon would come the time her heart would dream
as by bullet or bayonet he'd lie dead
Soon an obituary notice would be written, for
one of the fallen, one of the smitten
No more for him a rosy dawn, frosty night
or a sun kissed morn.
Just a plain white cross on a foreign shore
there to lie forevermore
For wars are fought and battles are won
and innocents must fall to the ways of the gun
So humbly I offer a prayer at least,
May you and your kind always R. I. P.

Dreams of the Soul

A Fading Light
Rita Harris

A star bursts forth from the sky.
It soars to anchor itself upon the ground to lie.

A streak of light glows in the heavens.
As it declines, its size shortens.

Slowly but surely it fizzles out.
For years before it had hung about.

Then so hard it struggled to survive.
Now 'tis gone to never revive.

Who will miss the light of one?
Will anyone notice that it hath gone?

A star among the heavens, a life that hath been born.
Not many will notice, not many will mourn.

To be loved, to be known by only one.
Never death will destroy, the life shall still live on.

As a leaf among a bundled pile.
'Tis lost but for only a little while.

Each life is stored in a file by name.
Once pulled, once read, thou shalt be known of in the same.

A child of God, a child of the earth.
Both as one – thou show thy worth.

Dedication: My foundation of strength – Daddy

Remember
Isobel Sherrard

I stand and gaze out at the sea deep dangerous and beautiful,
I think of thee and remember.
The golden grains of sand waiting to be caressed by the wild
white foam of the waves
breaking on the shore. I think of thee and remember.
High rise the waves, whipping against the rocks to make
their way back to the body of the ocean, the sun glistening
on its skin.
I think of thee and remember.
I see a rainbow as the sky moves down to mate with its master
the sea and the clouds
move across the sky in no hurry, no hurry. I think of thee
and remember.
I look to the horizon as the colours of the sky, blue and red join
the sea and the rays
of the sun create threads of gold like a carpet.
I think of thee and remember.
Is there anywhere on this earth a more beautiful place than this?
I feel I am at the
beginning of time. The waves are flirting and dancing with the sands,
sands of time.
I think of thee and remember.
I am happy with my thoughts and I feel you close, for you and I
have a bond of body
mind and spirit so strong it is silent and can never be broken. You are
the rose
between the pages of the book of my life. You are my story, and
when we are apart
I know you think of me and remember.

Dedication: Love; I will never forget

Grandma's Gifts Grandma's Toys
Alice Pike

Allison– My beautiful white Dove–
my precious gift from God above.

Adam – My shining Star–
the brightest star by far.

Eric– My spectacular Sunset–
how beautiful Eric can get.

Tiffany– My Rainbow and Pot of Gold–
Thank You God for Tiffany to hold.

Cory– My Sky so blue–
I'll keep on loving you.

Amanda– My Sunshine–
I'm so glad you're mine.

Katelyn– My beautiful big Red Rose–
as beautiful as the flower that grows.

Marissa– My Angel– my beautiful gift from God above–
an Angel sent for me to Love.

All of these gifts God gave to me–
and all of them were free.

My five pretty girls and my three beautiful boys.
the grandest of all of Grandma's grand toys.

Dedication: My eight beautiful grandchildren

Ode To A Nigerian
Patricia Williams

We are a nation – Africa's honor you must defend.
Mother told you to walk straight not to stoop or bend:

"The family" was embedded in your hearts at an early age,
The curtains are down, cut the act, you're not on stage.
Education has made thee mad–whoring after other gods–cultivating a wicked device,
Mother Africa's spirit is wounded please take this advice

Stop destroying the dream with lies and deceit,
Blaming your blue–eyed brothers for your many defeats.
You've forgotten from whence thou came – no future direction not
appreciation of the past;
The march to freedom is a steady one, it's not fast
Grab honor reality and wisdom along with grace.

Meet challenges as a brave warrior face to face.
Open your eyes so you may see,
There is much strength in unity.
The Indians lost their birthrights – yet they maintained their culture,
dignity and respect;

African values and principles – must we continue to neglect?
Mother Africa mourns because her most prized sons have divided the spoil,
We weren't nurtured by her tender breast – yet each trodded on her rich soil:

You've shown America a caste system among each other,
You've lost integrity and forgotten your m–o–t–h–e–r.

Dedication: Dan, Estelle and City–Parish

Noteworthy Works

Birth, Life And Death
Helena Miszta–Lane

Birth is a miracle song,
It inceptions from conception,
From dark to light,
From dependency to independence,
From weakness to strength,
It starts a new journey in life.

Life is a beautiful song,
Sometimes good,
Sometimes bad,
Sometimes happy,
Sometimes sad,
Sometimes short,
Sometimes long,
Sometimes weak,
Sometimes strong,

Death is an unknown, secret song,
From light to dark,
From known to unknown,
From problems to lack of them,
Sometimes happy,
Sometimes sad,
Sometimes sudden,
Sometimes long,
But always with hope,
That one day everybody will be together in a new journey,
Life after death.

Dedication: Roberta and Ross Lane

A. C. T. Holiday Home
June Whitehouse

The Black Country Museum has put in a bid,
for the place that I work, for quite a few quid.
The equipment and buildings are so antique,
To show the public would be unique.

The staff will be safe, without any doubt,
We'll kept them all on, no one will be out.
Maureen and Val, are put in charge,
Of lottery! Trips! And all gambling cards.

Gill and Iris take over P. A.
We know they will keep, tight control of our pay.
Velma and Di, will see to the launch,
they're always happy to have a good munch.

As for Val! well what can I say,
She'll find a breeze on a very calm day.
Sheila's on the hot line, so are James and Sue,
All of them work so hard, they will pull us through.

We must not forget, Helen our mate,
Although she's the boss, we get on just great.
KEEP THE NOISE DOWN, Put your phones on,
The callbacks are growing, a hundred to one.

There's one thing for sure, without any doubt,
Each one of them is the best workmate out.
the bosses don't know, that they have the best,
They're "considerate" "caring" they all pass the test.

Dedication: Friends, staff, management at A. C. T.

It's Okay To Be... Just Me!
Colleen Fillmore

When I was a little girl... probably about five years old...
For every birthday and Christmas I got a doll to love and hold...
I really loved my dollies, and named them every one...
But sometimes I thought a truck or car would be an awfully lot of fun.

I had a younger brother and he would always get
Baseball mitts and footballs... And once he got a jet.
And one time when he was playing— in my room with no one around...
I saw him grab a dolly and he didn't make a sound.

He kissed and loved and hugged her, and rocked her fast asleep...
He said he wished he had a doll that was his alone to keep.
So the next time that we were playing, I told him he was in luck...
I'd give him one of my dollies if he'd give me a great big truck.

I don't know who was happier — whether it was him or me
We both had something we wanted, and never thought we'd get, you see.
So girls should play with baseball bats and stuff my brother's got...
You never know, I might grow up to be an astronaut.

And boys can play with baby dolls and learn to cook and bake...
Cuz they may need to know those things when they're dads... for heaven's sake.
So why do parents think that kids should only like one thing...
My Mom likes to fish and golf... sometimes she likes to sing.

And dad, he likes to barbecue and can really bake a pie...
And I've seen him cuddle a baby when that baby starts to cry.
So if we share our toys and such and play with a doll or a car...
It's because we want to be like you because that's exactly how you are!

You Can Go...
Rachel Gillon

You can go, I wish you'd stay
I, the Lord whispers to your soul every day.

My love holds you with open arms
Promising to keep from all harm

But, should you return to whence you came

I will still cry out my love
In a gentle rain

Display it, in brilliance
The rising sun

Whisper it, the wind's
Soothing breeze

Hoping you see
My love forever and it's free

So, no matter where you are and
Should have a need

Don't forget, call on me
I'm never far

On the darkest of nights
I am the stars!

Dedication: Anthony Stallworth, always my blessing

Dreams of the Soul

God's Love
Cliff J. Latham
To see a loved one, lying there
Full of pain, in their chair,
Feeling helpless, no words to tell
Only their pain, their living hell.
You know they won't, get any better
But friends give you hope in a letter,
How much longer, no one knows
Life has dealt you heavy blows,
You pray and pray for a swift release
To give your loved one, a real peace,
Feeling helpless, what more can be said,
This is worse than them being dead
How can you face another day?
No more can be done, no more to say
Only with love, to ease them through
Their love for YOU still so true,
Wanting them, here, fearing them going
What's beyond death, there's no way of knowing,
You can only pray to ease their pain
For GOD has told us again and again
He will only let us bear so much
And he will give his loving touch,
The time will come to call them home
Their earthly body in a tomb,
But peace at last, will come one day
When GOD is ready, you will hear him say
I have your loved one, by my side,
No more pain now, they have died
A quietness, then, will come to you
YOUR love of GOD has pulled you through.

Forbidden Fruit
Jack Kelly
Now falls the autumn
Recall how we
Roved and plundered
Life's high seas,
Launched for spoils
Betwixt earth and heaven,
Like apple–piratical boys:
– From yon baleful tree
Since morn,
Crow's nest mariners
Forlorn,
Louring skies espied
Rainstorms, by and by.
Winds rising bleak,
Grey as slate,
Ruffled,
We remember late,
That Great Bird impaled
On the orchard gate
East of Eden; Nod's foreboding – landfall
Ho! For those that depredate.
O but still, farewell's
Fair Way, when souls do deprecate.
The time–honoured harvester appears
The Ancient, Days cease beckoning.
– Hearken then, O Christ! Haven – hove – to ark, bark
Our dead reckonings
Ebb across,
Orient
Carcass of albatross.

A Landscape In America
Muriel Huxtable
A man named Dennis Fronrath
Has bought a huge silk flag
All glorious stars and stripes.
It flies over his car lot,
Rippling against the Florida sky.
Red stripes, blue sky, bright sunshine,
And clouds.

The clouds, puffy as white cotton balls,
Or like grey smears superimposed on high, mighty rain clouds,
Clouds low on the horizon,
Great black clouds ready to spill torrents of rain,
So many kinds of clouds
In the sky, all together.
Nothing happens.
The flag flips against the mixed up sky.
The cars all shine in the slanting sun.
It's the Fourth of July.

Henry Flagler's house (the biggest house in the world when
he had it built)
Has a wide porch they're using for a stage this year.
A girl with a voice like a bell sings Rosina.
Birds on the roof sing along with her,
They've been listening at rehearsal.
The violins are sweet.
The birds trill, the grass is rich.
Little parties are eating fried chicken, French bread, and
Chablis wine
In their shorts.

Me In She
Shannon M. Ballenger
I suppose I would be considered her daughter's offspring.
but then again wouldn't I be considered one of
hers as well?

With her olive skin and mystical eyes
gleaming every time I stop by.
She comforts me every time I come to cry.

Where would I be without my Grandma?
Oh how I love her loving ways.
As she loves mine as well
We bring sunshine to each other's days.

When I look into the mirror, she is all I see.
So much beauty that would make the devil shed a tear.
With innocence and purity like a whisper to the ear.

A gay yet melancholy twist of life
bringing an angelic air to her being.
Taking care of all the souls, putting them
before herself.
It is oh so plain to see that she is me.

For I am glad that I have my grandma's ways,
an exact replica of her soul and grace,
Comforting arms, soft kisses, and an
extraordinarily beautiful face that takes me
away to a better place.

I love you Grandma!

Life
Jon K. Culp
A rocky dreamscape
Floating in a glass box; a
Snow-globe full of sand.

The Secret Room
Mildred Supe
When I was a little girl, many years ago,
my sister and I went to school, through rain, ice and snow.
Our rental house stood high on a hill, with two big ponds below.
Now if the dam were to overflow, there simply was no way to go.

We could not go one rainy day, the two miles seemed so far away.
there was no bus to pick us up, far different from today.
Now up in the attic, there was a room where we were forbidden to play,
what better chance for us to explore, than on this rainy, dismal day.

Up the steps we did go, the boards did creak as they were old.
"you go in first" my sister said and I did as I was told.

Gently we walked into that room; what a beautiful surprise,
it must have looked like heaven to our little eyes.

There were Bibles and egrets and glass domes galore,
old watches and wedding veils and much, much more.

We played there for hours, my older sister and I,
until the sun started to set in the sky.

Quietly we went down those stairs.
surely no one would ever know we were there.

This was our secret till this very day,
as it belonged to another, who lived far away.

My Own Tree
J. W. E. Douglas
If in my life no future I can see,
Which sometimes I confess disheartens me,
At once I hasten to a secret place
To soothe my fears and contemplate my case.

This secret spot is shaded by a tree,
A mighty friend but only known to me;
It has been mine since I was very small
And, whilst I live, cannot decay or fall.

Its branches shade a place where I can rest
On softest grass without a fear of pest,
A couch where Heaven itself might be
Could I but take my love along with me.

Yet, if I stand and reach above my head
My feet now firm upon the former bed,
The first branch makes an easy step for me
To find my way towards the canopy.

Through all my years of trying I have spent
dreams without number on this long ascent,
Lulled by scented bark and leaves and flowers,
A chance to bury fears and recoup powers.

I do not know how much the branches shade
Nor yet how tall my lovely tree is made,
Because our world is not the same to me
For, unlike you, I have not seen a tree.

Untitled
Douglas Koenig
Without despair
the quiet sun
gives rise
to daylight

My Dream World
Lori Wade Rice
There's a place I want to take you
Where no one else has been
It's called my special dream world
Come on, I'll let you in

Now inside my dream world
Where no one else can be
I open my heart and show you things
That only you can see

Now you know I freely give
All my heart to you
It's not easy, as with yours
It's been broken a time or two

I want us to forget the hurt
And be happy once again
I wish we could turn back time
To when our hurt began

I can't turn back the time
But you can come along with me
We'll enter my special dream world
Where only we will be

Dedication: To William Rice, my husband

Home
Jodi Anne Abbott
The frail fish foamed,
like an embryo out of womb.
Yearned to swim,
but couldn't get back to where it first grew.
Among the weeds,
a little flash of life.

No use left for scales.
Leave them behind for the earth to filet.

cold, heavy, wet

I gasped,
lungs ill-adapted to air.
My turn for longing of lucidity.

Were my lungs bleeding for you?

Home—
No memory of getting there.
He knows the way.

Can I leave my scales and come with you?

We
all saw you drown.
I
know you were just swimming home.

Dreams of the Soul

The Rape Fields
Y. Beadle
Yellow fields delight the eye
It seems that they are filled
With sunshine yellow paint
That was accidentally spilled

High School Graduation
Geoffrey Persten
You have spent the last 13 years in school:
Living and learning by the golden rule:

Now as an adult you are ready to leave the nest:
Off to college to do your best:

It's graduation day, you and your parents are thrilled,
But it's not all fun:
You see your parents sort of feel that their job is done:

As you are called up on stage and they sit below:
The swell of tears begins to flow:

As you ready yourself to walk away:
There's a split second that you turn back, cause you want to stay

There is a kind of sadness, because you and your parents know:
That you reached the point when it's time to go:

And go you will as there are seeds you must sow:
It's part of life, it's the next plateau:

You wipe back the tears, you're an adult and must leave the nest:
Off to college to do your best.
Dedication: My sons, Scott and Brian

Linda's Recipe For Health and Happiness
Linda L. Simon
1 Cup of All Purpose Family
1 16 oz. Can of Good Health
1 1/2 Cups of Grated Laughter
6 Tbsp. Human Touches
1/4 tsp. each of Gardening,
Painting, and Music
1/2 Cup Whipped Organization

2/3 Cup of Unchopped Time With Spouse
1 Cup of Old–Fashioned "Free Time"
1 Dozen Hugs and Kisses
2 Cloves of Uncooked – Undrained
Peace of Mind
A Pinch of Attention
A Dab of Money

In a large bowl combine Family, Health, Laughter, and Human Touches. Stir gently until
well blended. Slowly add the Gardening, Painting, and Music to flavor. Knead to make a smooth dough. Let sit for awhile.

Roll mixture out on flat surface and blend in the Whipped Organization. Sprinkle on the
Unchopped Time With Spouse. Spread on the Old–Fashioned Free Time. Top this with
Hugs and Kisses. Let mixture sit for awhile to soak in...
Finally, add Peace of Mind, Attention, and just a Dab of Money for spice. Let all stand for
a few minutes and serve at room temperature.

Untitled
Laura Preston
School, school
Boring, school
I'd rather play
At the swimming pool!

This Person Inside Of Me
Karen Lester
There's but one thing I'm pondering
And that one thing is I'm wondering
Who's this person inside of me!

I've been wandering place to place
Trying to find the person in back of my face.
No superficiality, I cried,
Let me be me, my soul replied!

Though warm–hearted, kind and free
I'm still trying to find me.
I wonder what people think of me—
Too noisy? Too dumb?
Too quiet? A bum?
Just what do people think of me?

I've been opening door to door
Just to find what's in store!
From thin to fat
What do you think of that?

From latch hook to ceramics
From music to a dog
From Community Support Program to church
I hoping to search
To find this person inside of me!

Ah, But Your Land Is Beautiful
Kira Stewart
To realise the inner beauty of this land is half the battle, is half the
victory.
To acknowledge what lies in its hand culminates in understanding,
culminates in love.

Dust–pink glow the Three Sisters
How majestic do they stand
Who would think that South Africa blisters
Under this blood–red sky?

What demon states this land is cursed?
Land of sugar, fruit and maize
See, the colourful people dispersed
Under one roof, under one gaze.

South Africa learns from its mistakes
And this the universe must recognise.
We will rectify for as long as it takes
To dress the wounds and heal the heart.

Who leaves without a farewell?
Do you seek for your soul elsewhere?
Will you know when rings the bell
And the mountains that beckon your return.

Yes, we see that war continues but combat is a well–known phase,
The spirit of South Africa renews and follows us out of grace.

Dedication: South Africa, our vulnerable nation

Untitled
James R. Hepburn
True friendship can be a treasure
to give a wealth of pleasure
can help to clear your blues away
like a sunny summers day.

Untitled
Carol A. Cusick
When we first met
You wanted more than friendship
But I was too young
and you were much older

Then years went by
yet nothing brought us closer
Then that special kiss
And I knew it was all over

I'd be in love forever
nothing would break us up
you were my Prince Charming
my best friend and now my lover

Over time your feelings changed
and your love for me faded
slowly my world fell apart
I no longer was in your heart

It's funny how things change
From the beginning till the end
now I'm the one who wants more than friendship
but your feelings remain the same.
Dedication: My one true love, Steven

I Once Had A Friend
Ernesto Loredo, Jr.
I once had a friend who I thought I knew well,
I once had a friend who my secrets I'd tell.

I once had a friend who would laugh at my jokes,
I once had a friend who was loved by my folks.

I once had a friend whose things I'd borrow,
I once had a friend whose footsteps I thought I'd follow.

I once had a friend who I thought was cool,
I once had a friend who I thought was no fool.

I once had a friend who was always there,
I once had a friend who I thought really cared.

I once had a friend who broke all the rules,
I once had a friend who dropped out of school.

I once had a friend who drank. beer by the mugs,
I once had a friend who did all types of drugs.

I once had a friend who committed all sorts of crimes,
I once had a friend who thought fights were good times.

I once had a friend who'd always look for trouble,
I once had a friend who'd run on the double.

I once had a friend who spray painted every wall,
I once had a friend who was "no friend at all".

Untitled
J. L. Anderson
When two people touch,
however briefly,
Ripples spread
eternally.

God's Own Creation
Elaine Cincotta
More than one thinks one is –
More than one knows one can be –

Capable of much,
Conditioned to less,
Sparked to try,
Enabled to do.

Always becoming,
Never knowing.
Free will in motion;
Love securing.

A speck in the Cosmos;
A Universe in the speck.

Who knows, can.
Who feels, does.
Who loves, conquers.
Who flees, dies.

Time measures wind, snow,
God's planets, mankind and music.
God's metronome is the beat of constant BEAUTY.
Dedication: Lovers of righteousness

Ode To My Granddaughter – Codi
Sandi Kahn
When I see her face,
My heart smiles
When I hear her speak
She touches my soul
I need time to contain myself
A moment, a while

Her honey hair
Her blue, blue eyes
Her laughing voice, the way that she sighs
She touches my soul
Is she good, is she bad, who cares

She stumbles, she falls
She looks for my help
I laugh, she reaches, she calls
She touches my soul

She's funny, she's sad
She's smells like sunshine
She's a brat, sometimes she's bad
She touches my soul

How lucky can I be
I have her to hold and love
To play with, to teach, so you see why...
She touches my soul
Dedication: To Codi

Dreams of the Soul

Rainbows
Melanie Hall
Rainbows rainbows big and bright
Shining on the warm spring day
Beautiful and colorful
Special in every way

You And Me
Sheri Setzer
I am yours
You are mine
from now on
'Til the end of time

We were meant to be
Deep in our heart
Just you and me
Never to part

You are there
When I'm gone
You always share
When I get home

No matter what
You help me to be
Everything I want
And everything I need

We help each other
In work or play
And by your side
Is where I stay
Dedication: My love, Amando

Love Lives On ↗
Carlo J. Villena
Tanya, please don't cry,
Don't worry, I shall not die.

I shall die when it's time,
But not now, while I'm in my prime.

I'll die old,
When my body is worn and my soul is sold.

I don't want to see you held, but instead be free,
Like an eagle flying above a tree.

I never believed your love for me was strong and true
Until I saw your side of being blue.

You are my first true love,
Together, we are an angel and a dove.

So please don't drown yourself to sleep,
I don't like watching you weep.

I will always be around so you definitely
Know where to find me.

Love Lives Long
Big And Strong
Forever
Dedication: Carlo N. Villena for helping write it.

North Carolina Mountains
Erma Jean Merrill
I have traveled a long way
from sea to sea
the North Carolina Mountains
are the best place to be

Love In Bloom
Mary E. Dixon
'Twas a golden day of autumn
When he walked into my life.
He brought the music that I thought
was gone.
He brought the sunshine back to
this heart of mine.
He brought the happiness that had
evaded me so long.
Our lives are so entwined in a pattern
only by fates hand.
We walk together hand in hand as we
travel along.

It was the hands of fate that brought
us together.
The sounds of music made our hearts glad.
The happiness we share; that special under—
standing, which shows we care.
We are swift to give praise; but slow to complain.
God gives us sunshine and rain.
He gives happiness and pain.
We ask not for wealth or fame.
Our needs He will provide;
As we walk side by side.
Dedication: Mr. Max Mazzarella

Tranquillity
B. Wright
I stood one day beside a stream
And pinched myself – Was it a dream?

The murmuring water greeted me
Saying softly – "Here's tranquillity"

Beyond the stream a cottage smiled
As much to say – "You are beguiled"

I was! I had to stand and stare
And say "How wonderful to live just there"

Ten long years passed time to retire
But where to find my heart's desire?

I searched and searched but could not find
The sort of place I had in mind

Till quite by chance – out for a drive
My old dream suddenly was alive

The stream, the cottage, a "For Sale" sign
The perfect place – could it be mine?

It is! I've been here just a year
And every day it gets more dear

It's warmth and peace enfolding me
Saying softly – "Here's tranquillity"

Masquerade
Daniel Lammers

If you see a twinkle in my eye,
It is only the sun,
Reflecting off pain-filled tears.

If you see a smile upon my face,
It is only physics,
Playing tricks upon your eyes.

If you see a bounce in my step,
It is only the ground,
Springing back from underfoot.

If you hear laughter from me,
It is only an echo,
Bouncing back from days gone by.

If you see life within me,
It is only a shadow,
Reaching out from yesterday.

If you see me,
I am only a ghost,
Rattling in the chains of a life lost.

If you see me you are blind to reality,
For I live only in fantasy.

The Estranged
Allison Still

I am not bound, but am not free
The chains I wear cannot be seen;
My jailer left so suddenly
He didn't think to leave the key!

Papa
Margarita Clement

Evening shadows advance with approaching night;
I begin my vigil while you sleep 'til morning light.

My hand in yours is there to say,
I will stay nearby and never go away.

I can see that Time has left its trace;
Weariness gently lines your face.

And I see the glisten of your silent tears,
From eyes dimmed by the passing years.

In memory, I direct my mind
To the happy days we left behind.

In times of crisis, you were my guide;
In a sea of troubles, you turned the tide.

Now the shadows, like fingers of a velvet glove,
Caress your face as gently as this daughter's love.

In a peaceful dream, sleep comes for you;
I will remain here to watch o'er you

And when the light of dawn sends the shadows away,
I will be here so you will hear me say,
"I love you, Papa..."

Dedication: John C. Cosgrove

True Love
Robert Aleksinski

A love we started out with
A love that lets us change
A love that has no boundaries
A love that will remain.

A love that must be shared
A love that takes just two
A love that lets me be me
A love that lets you be you.

A love that has its troubles
A love that lets us part
A love that heals all wounds
A love that has a new start.

A love that gives us courage
A love that gives us strength
A love that lets us suffer
A love at any length.

A love that is a gift
A love given from above
A love that's never-ending
A love we call "true love."

Dedication: Melanie A.

Untitled
Paulette Woodard

In the early hours of the morn
Just before the day is born
Lift up your eyes to God and pray,
For the strength to face this day.

Quiet Hours
Mildred Barnhill

I love to wake in the early dawn
When everything is still.

And faintly hear the far-off call
Of a lonely whippoorwill.

And then to rise and feel the sun
As it warms the moving air.

And watch the birds as they flutter about
Without a single care.

Or listen to the whispering wind
As it rustle through the trees.

And watch a leaf flutter to the ground
Move gently with the breeze.

To smell the scent of fresh-cut hay
And watch the flowers bloom.

To see the sunlight filter in
And spread across a room.

To watch as children roam about
Busy with their play.

And be able to thank our Lord above
For such a beautiful day.

Dreams of the Soul

Untitled
Helen V. Ruth

The same is changed. Her time is stopped. We are still watching.
Warm hugs are done. We look through the mist to find a ray, a
Beam of light, but the same is changed.
We go on, we go. A brief pause and we go. The light is made
Brighter by her and the same is changed.

Magic Dream
Kiran Shah

In my magic dream,
Fill the black room,
Whiter than white.
Star shine glowing bright white.
Universe expand black and white.
New creation created by its form.
Dancer dancing fanatically every where.
Filling empty spaces with his grace.
Creating the internal peace.
His form in glory glows bright.
Expanding in his wake,
New stars in its glory,
With every steps in black and white.
Like never ending story,
Of the thousand nights,
In my magic dream.
I stare with hypnotic trance,
Get pulled in his creation.
Dancing with the creators form,
Till sweat drops from my body.
Onto creation created,
Creating a new life.
Filling internal being with pride,
Sharing his dream with mine,
Creating in my magic dream.

My Daddy
Millie O'Daniel

I love my daddy,
He's the best
There's no one like him
Out of all the rest

He thinks I'm silly,
Cause I make him smile
He goes for me
That extra army mile

And when he's in his uniform,
He's got quite a job to do.
It makes me proud, yep, he's my hero,
How he takes care of our ol' red, white and blue.

I know sometimes at night I'll cry,
Cause he's gotta be away.
But still I ask my mama why,
As she wipes our tears away.

I made a promise to him,
And it was to be strong,
But I made him promise in return,
That he'd be back before too long.

I know my daddy's gotta go away,
But why does he have to be so far away?

Dedication: My wonderful husband and children

Creative Evolution
Veronica Free

A pinata of ideas burst in my head.
A river of emotion overflows from my heart.
Firecracker thoughts explode in my mind.
Confined feelings escape through my pen.
A poem evolves.

Promises
Melissa S. Thompson

Cry Mother
Tell me your promise
Tell me hardships of raising a child
Call me burden, not a beloved gift
What promise can you give me?

Scold Father
Chide me for wrongs already done
For past that is already lived
Bring up things already forgotten
From you, what promise can you give me?

Preach My Lord
Preach to me of your way
Tell me wrong from right
Show me your powers
Are you there?
If so, what promise can you give me?

Eternal life with no hardships?
My life is already lived
No gifts promised, no expectations created
Don't promise, just do for me what I do for you

What I can

Sadness
Pamela Fiedler

I am walking towards you—
but You cannot see
My soul is a mirror
of Blue, enigmatic dreams...

Haunting the silence,
to tremble
from Fear—

Truth is an apparition
of who was crucified
Here...

No one gives an answer—
Why do you not care?

Michaelangelo Screamed for you to listen
Rodin Sculpted his heart so clear

Sadness,
it whispers come closer—hear
Truth is just an illusion
where Doves embrace
Invisible Light

And die,
with no fear...

Dedication: Erica Radil, Barry Brownlee and Claudine Wofford

Noteworthy Works

Rainbows end
Brett A. Dotson

The pot of gold
Is yours to keep
Yet don't disturb
The spell that holds
The little leprechaun asleep!

My Inspiration
Kristina Oakes

It's been four months since you went away, I think about you every hour, minute, second, of each and every day. Even though we are far apart, you are always in my mind and heart.

Whenever I was down and wore a frown, you knew just what to say to bring a smile to my face. Now you are in a very special place where I know you are being taken care of and where you are very safe.

You changed my life in a way that is very hard to explain, and even though I have asked myself a lot why you left me, I know now that no one is to blame. You always knew the right things to say to brighten up my day. Even on rainy days, you were my light of sunshine shining through the dark clouds and skies with a beam of rays. You accepted me for me and who I wanted to be. You have been and still are my inspiration.

I have come to a realization that no matter what problems we face in life, you have shown me to live life to its fullest and to be thankful for each and every day that we are given. Even though you are gone, you are not really because your memory is still here with me. You were a great friend and you touched everybody's life that knew you. Especially mine.

Dedication: Charles Leslie Cooper

To a Fallen Comrade
Marvin J. Philips

Where have you gone Johnny my boy?
Where are you now, dear John?

I wish you could tell me, buddy of mine.
What it is like there, dear John.

You are missed by me and by your friends,
Life's not the same now, dear John.

I want to hear your voice and see your face.
I wish you could come back, dear John.

What's it like on the other side?
I wish you could tell us, dear John.

It's been a long time since you've gone away.
We miss you so much, dear John.

We are proud of all that you have done
And the country is proud of you too.

What must you think of those who won't fight
For the honor of the red, white and blue?

Traitors like that deserve no praise
Nor the right to be there with you.

We know you'll never come marching home,
But we'll love you forever, dear John.

Waiting For Christmas
Laura Thomas

Waiting for Christmas with twinkling eyes,
Watching for Santa to come down from the skies,
Soon he'll come down our chimney so big
with his roly–poly belly
goin' jig, jig, jig

Ye Old Hanging Tree
Alda R. Powell

I was once a proud oak tree,
standing tall for all to see; with branches full of bright green leaves.

I was admired for my beauty and my strength; and home to many of my woodland friends.

My branches were high and strong enough to be of use I heard them say:
To me that was my saddest day.

My branches were used to settle scores of crime and abuse; I cried; no; it's hopeless! no use.

Now I know the sound of death.

Over the years my appearance has changed, I am no longer a proud oak tree my beauty and strength have gone to seed.

My branches bare; my friends have gone; I stand alone outside of town.

They will come in the morning to chop me down, I heard them say; they're building a mall; and I'm in the way.

I will no longer be a sad sight to see; it will be the death of the hanging tree.

Memories
Janis A. Johnson

Memories give us glimpses of life that has passed.
We cling to them, share them, try to make them last.

Memories give us freedom to return to "remember when"
Picking out special events to recall from now and then.

Memories are glimpses and pictures of what has been.
Nostalgia prompts us to pull them up again and again

Every day of life creates still another "memory" page.
Pages of time that can never be obliterated with age.

Though memories recall strife and hard fought tears,
reflection shows that time has since calmed those fears.

Memories give us more time spent with loved ones gone.
How pleased they'd be... memories shared help them yet belong.

How beautiful to pull up a page of time from our book,
and allow ourselves the privilege of still another look.

Granny's hug, parents' reassuring smiles, friendships shared
What empty memories, if we had no reflection of those who cared.

How beautiful to look at our life that has since passed
and to look ahead to a plan that long ago was cast.

If we touched one life then how fortunate the paths we took.
Perhaps one day we too will be part of someone's memory book.

Dreams of the Soul

Why Rats Are Never Friends With Cats
Jennifer Sanders
There was a big eared rat
who talked to the curious cat.
He wanted a friend
but got eaten instead
that's why rats are never friends with cats.

One Lost Soul
Cheryl A. Wilson
As I watched her approach,
I tried not to stare, but stare I must.

She carried a suitcase, that looked like all the burdens of
the world were locked up inside,
She had not a coat, gloves, or hat to chase away the bitter
ocean breezes.

As she drew nearer, I could see her eyes, not a sign of
happiness could I see, they were full of pain and sorrow,
She walked as though, the world's problems were weighing
her down, with no sign of relief in her step.

As I watched her walk on by, I wondered why,
She had passed my way, and then I knew.
She was the image of this world today, loaded down with worry,
No smiles left, they had been used up years ago, friends were
something she had to do without, looking out for herself,
Was all she could manage.

Yes this one poor soul, was sent my way,
For me to see, all is not well in God's world,
For we need to reach out and touch all our friends yet to be.

Dedication: Our homeless friends

Untitled
Phyllis M. Coates
Old age can be a happy time.
When you dream of days gone by,
Remember the dances we went to,
The bicycle rides we enjoyed.
Rainy days by the seaside
The long ride home for tea

The babies we knew, are grown
up now.
Remember the laughter and tears
The girls came to cling to you
As you soothed away their fears

The boys were always so brave
and strong.
Giving Gran and Granddad a helping
hand,
When they met them walking along.
Along by the river, and through
the farm,
Always there to lend an arm.

All the picnics and parties
Easter and Christmas time,
Birthdays and weddings, buying new
clothes.
Hearing the wedding bells chime.
Sitting and dreaming in the sun
Remembering the sadness and the fun

Reflection
Katy Kabata
Raindrops on the window pane
teardrops in her eyes
as he walks down the lane
he'll be gone for a time
is it really drops of rain?

Together Let's Make Brighter Days And Happier Moments
Phyllis Weeks
I'll hold you close to my
heart;
In the letters you wrote
on the day we met,
We pulled the weeds, threw away
the tares,
to make a more beautiful garden
to see
One day the scent of roses will
spring through the open
windows to make my heart to
sing
We will share the fruit the soil
did bring up the seed. God placed
two in the garden of Eden. Then
by his command and grace, the
world blossomed into this most
beautiful place. Forever rainbows
after the clouds and rain. Flowers
and butterflies gather there now
which was once void in a space.
We filled the gap and chose his way
for now there is no darkness, for
love is the light that shines
on faces of every one.

Strangers
Mike Douse
I see the Romanies are back on Marlpit Lane. Perhaps it's opportune
To summon up my caravan of migrant memory (now parked unscholarly
Beside the Tud, asquat the fractured prams and way beyond the long—gone
Cattle pens) and call to mind those sombre visages who peddled our fresh
Lintels then, unflawed by all the war-year verities, with little timber
implements
That might, in simple faith, affix damp linens onto slack, inevitable
lines. Had I
Sufficient enterprise, I should have crossed with sixpences her grubby palm
and bid
That gypsy dowager to cast my fortune instantly, avoiding culpability along
the way.

I'd rather like to carry out that old transaction now, accept the tendered
pegs,
Entwine my well—washed recollections on the twirling strand, while she
incants
The hidden clause that conjures back two children, skipping over Rabbit
Hill, beyond
The tangled grasp of taunt and time (and soft, reluctant vagrancies, for
dark decades
Have hobbled by since I could outrun any mortal thing — excluding all my
self—indulgent
Fantasies, of course!). I fear the travellers' sphere has gone full circle
while such solid,
Anchored denizens as you and I, weighed down with maps and certainties
(and, albeit,
Lurching ideologies), have somehow been misplaced in our own avenues,
estranged.

Noteworthy Works

A Riddle
Deedle Storms
It lives It dies.
When darkness falls, it rests its weary soul
Where strong winds blow.
When dawn is born, it lives again
And sets the whole wide world aglow.

Given Strength
Maureen Green
As I lay in remorse
The moon overhead
It shines deep in the night
To give me light
His presence I feel

He has come down to heal
My pain will subside
As he laid down beside
I gaze at the stars
Answers to find

Trusting my God will somehow be kind
Sorrows and tears
Are for the past years
As I look to tomorrow
Forgetting my sorrows

The rain will sustain me
As it taps on my window
Morning did come
God's will be done
On earth as in heaven

Dedication: My foster mother, Mrs. Edith Ellerton

My Daddy
Shirley Taylor
You used to be my daddy, you held me when I cried
You told me that you loved me Oh! daddy how you lied
You used to tell me stories you sat me on your knee
You told me I was everything, you were everything to me

You said that I was perfect, your little pride and joy
You said that I would always be your daddy's little boy
You used to give me cuddles, you tucked me up in bed
And now I lie thinking of you and all the lies you said

You said you'd always be there at times when I was down
You said you'd never leave me you'd always be around
So where are you now daddy now that I'm needing you?
I think of all those promises, were they all untrue!

So was it something I said was it something that I've done?
To make you go and hurt us both especially my mum
My mummy loves you so much, more than words can say
I wish that you would come back, why did you go away?

I cry myself to sleep each night, I miss your loving touch
Oh daddy! how I need you, I miss you oh so much
I think it must be my fault, whatever I have done
If you can't forgive me daddy! please forgive my mum

One day I'll maybe understand why you had to go
But that might take forever, I'll maybe never know
I'll always love you daddy I'll always think of you
The tears I'll cry forever, I dedicate this poem to you.

The Dove Of Love
Alanna Holder–Riches
The Dove of Love
Who flies above
Just rests it's wings to see
If perhaps two singles mingle
Who perhaps don't want to be.

My Dream
Marcella Morey
While strolling through the garden on a bright and sunny day
The flowers seemed to turn to me as if they were to say,
Please come and join us in Paradise and happy you will be.

The daisies with bright and shining faces,
The sunflowers reaching high above
The orange blossoms and lilacs with their sweet perfume
All beckoned to me with love.

As I walked among the flowers
I saw this faint but glowing light
And then I heard the familiar call
"Marcella, here I am, just a little to your right.
I knew you'd come, I've missed you so."

I sat with him and he told me how wonderful it was
to be surrounded by all these angels,
friends and family in this heavenly garden of love.

No wars, no hunger, just glorious peace
The hurt, the pain, it has all ceased.
"I'm home with my Lord at last," he said.

And then I awakened only to find
It was just a beautiful dream.

A Child's Wish
Lisa Foucht
No blood testing,
no more sick days,
no more resting,
while other kids are playing;

Let's eat ice cream,
and birthday cake,
we are just kids,
for goodness sake;

No more blindness,
and kidney failure,
no infections,
that need looked after;

We're just some kids,
with diabetes,
we're sick of shots,
that just divide us;

People look and stare in pity,
we never quiet fit in,
even in an informed city,
the disease feels like a sin;

Won't someone help us find a cure,
to stop all these injections,
and maybe we could all learn more.
about this life's rejections

Dreams of the Soul

Life!
Josh Howard
Life is good
Life is sweet,
Life has a lot of feats,
Beat them all,
Life is neat!

A Child's Smile
Elizabeth Cotton
A child's smile can send universal love throughout the world. Children
are the future, they're the hope of the new generation. They're
the builders of tomorrow and the molders of life. There's nothing
like a child's smile.

Good examples must be set, respect must be earned and love must
be given.
Individuality should be taught, integrity should be within each heart.
Give them freedom to grow, have faith in them and their abilities.
There's nothing like a child's smile.

Show them right path to follow, faith lights the way. Samantha, Polly,
Stephanie, Chase, Colton, little Baylee. What was your destiny in life,
to touch the hearts of people throughout the world? There's nothing like
a child's smile.

Such a bright light flowed through you and continues to flow. Let
your life stand for peace and goodwill. Awareness among the
people of the world to preserve their universe and to protect our
children.

Your spirit will always live on and your bright lights will never dim.
Our angels of love, our ambassadors of peace. Michelle, Michael,
Jessica, Joe, Ryan and Tara there's nothing like a child's smile. A
child's smile, a child's smile. There's nothing like a child's smile.

The Face In The Mirror
Constance O'Banyoun
Dear Lord, open my eyes that I may see
The kind of person you'd like me to be.

Do my eyes see the wonders for which you have paid,
Or do they see me so wise, so shrewd, so self–made?

The ears, are they ready to listen to your word,
Or is it only my own gripes that will be heard?

Is this the face that my loved ones can admire,
When others look at it, does it seem to inspire?

Is it a face that meets you, without shame or fear,
Does it show what's in my heart, is it sincere?

My mouth could speak wisdom, or sound like a fool,
Does it lie, hurting others, am I the devil's tool?

Do I have to worry about what I might have said,
For my tongue is a weapon and easily misled?

Am I the type of Christian who can't control my wicked tongue –
Is it a profane, evil part of me poisoning my example to the young?

Am I so vain that I want more than what I need,
Quick to boast, words sharp as swords accompanying my greed?

Mirror, mirror, tell me please – as in this life I've trod–
Am I, or am I not, a loving child of God?

Untitled
Cindy Boudreaux
When I look at her sometimes I don't know her, she has changed
and yet she is the same. She
looks at me with sad eyes, and yet I can see happiness. Sometimes
she looks so frail and weak
and yet I see strength. Although I am sure how old she is, some
say she has had many life times,
some times I think she is in her twenties other times I am sure she
is in her late forties. She has
had many tragedies in her life, yet she smiles. When I am sad and
lonely she tells me all the
good things I need to hear. I pray for her heart and soul every day
and she prays for mine...
She does not have much money but is very wealthy with friends.
She has been told by some that she
is beautiful, I think she is plain. People say what a good person
she is, she is well liked. She
enjoys the simple things in life, she doesn't need or want fancy
things. When I feel sorry for her
and my tears fall because of all that she has gone through, she
reminds me that those are the
things that have shaped her into who she is today. When people
ask me about her and I tell them
just a few things they always respond the same way, with admiration.
Sometimes I like her, some
times I hate her each day I see her in my mirror.

Late Regret
Betty M. Hiscock
The fruit of my womb a tangled mess laid there,
A human life destroyed, I felt no despair.
I did not want a babe, I was too young.
Abortion, now I scream, was it my only choice?
God screams at me, I heeded not the still small voice.

Christmas Of The Heart
Verva M. Johnson
Every year the feeling starts
And then is blown away.
Who knows to where it flies,
I'd only like to find it.

Has Christmas always been this way,
A touch, a tear away?
I know the warmth in my heart
Should be there from the start.

Who said it was all love,
And mistletoe and holly?
When there's nothing way down
So very deep inside you.

The presents are wrapped, the lights are hung,
Of course there's Santa in the mall.
Gimme, Gimme, Get me.
But what happened to the giving?

Peace on Earth, Goodwill to men,
Is this just a joke?
There's hunger everywhere
And hearts so full of sadness.

I'd like to make it up
To those I see around me.
But it's so very hard to do,
When there's nothing deep inside me.

Noteworthy Works

Day Dreaming
Karen Johnson

I
Often wonder about the beauty of life
There is still beauty in life with
All it's problems and deep despair —
I am glad I can still see the beauty,
Yet still there.

Blind Sight
Lois Moussally

You say that I am blind, therefore, I cannot see —— But you are wrong.
I see beyond surface to substance,
I see beyond prejudice, for lacking sight, I know not that your skin
is red, yellow, black or white,
I see beyond ugliness, for lacking sight, I picture you as beautiful.
You destroy my vision of you only by the way you act.
If you use language softly, melodious of voice, you rest my
soul and become lovely.
If you destroy your words with gutter talk and words that
paint mankind with hate, you become ugly.
Are you fat or thin? I do not know. I do know if you have a
gentle touch, laughter as you speak, a hug that shows me
that you care.
You say that I am blind, therefore I cannot see — But you are wrong.
Graffiti on a wall I do not see, a slum I do not know
from paradise.
I only know you by the way you act. You say that I am
handicapped because I cannot see, but I say you are
handicapped because you see the surface of a man and
you make judgments with your eyes, not with your soul.
Only God knows if I am lacking sight because I see
not through my eyes but through my soul.
I am not blind —— I see the good in all mankind

Dedication: Peter, my love, my friend

Our Mother, Dying Young
Andrew Joseph Kos

O grave, you cannot catch her—
You are too slow.
Sometime ago, she was here,
Saw your gloom and fled,
Sped from earth;
Quick, on silver–wings
Fleet in her joy, she flew.

Fret not. Death, too, is dumb;
Yesterday, he came for her,
But she was gone.
She could not wait for him,
But left these tokens for his troubles:
These earthly clothes she wore, the while.
And this is all that you can have of her.

For naked, and still in love with life,
She has run ahead of you.
Far out of reach now.
She who was once our Mother,
Has made foolish all worldly suitors.

Even we, her children, who look for her,
Moping about this ground for clues,
Must brood no more at our loss,
And instead chase on, marvel at her speed,
And wonder if we shall be as quick as she was
To catch the wind blowing heavenward.

Day Into Night
Katherine Lightner

Waves into a song,
Stardust into magic,
As life becomes a fairy tale
And flowers become the sea.
The day turns into night
And I turn into me.

Brenda's 23rd Psalm
Brenda Faye Chalk

My shepherd is the Lord
I shall not be afraid
I will one day lay to rest
in Green Pastures, The water's
will be still for "Me, "
"My Soul" will also be Restored
He touched my heart to
Know, to walk only in his
Light, and read his words–
He is the way – I am walking
Daily in my shadow, of "Death"
I shall "fear" only God,
I do not "fear" Evil Doers
Because God is with me,
He is my shield, And my
Source, I am at Peace
with "my soul. "
My table I sit daily
with my "enemies"
"The Lord's Armor is
put on me, my heart
And spirit are with the
Lord – I am anointed. "
With goodness and mercy on my
life

From God With Love
Rachelle Mosier

I am with thee no matter what
wrong thou hast done

I will forgive thee tho
thou continue to sin

It is in my heart to send
special blessings to my child

Because thy faith is so strong in me

Ask me to hold your hand
and I will not deny you the privilege

For I myself once went thru
agony of sin – wanted none at all
to look for comfort and find not open arms

But darkness and a Father's back

I suffered just as much that day
as you ever could – but for that
I now offer you good graces and
fulfillment of needs

My arms will ever welcome you
my child – Forgiveness
is not a forbidden word

Dreams of the Soul

My Voice
Victor Charles Buffery

When I lay me down to sleep,
my voice it only says "cheep–cheep"!
but, when I wake again each morn,
it always sounds like a fog–horn.
When, at last, I'm old and grey
I've no idea what it will say!

Untitled
Lois M. Nyffeler

There's a little boy in my life today,
He's special–he's my grandson.
And people I know get tired of me.
Telling what Kevin has done.

When asked if he'd like to ride in a plane
He looked up with eyes big and round,
And said "Oh no I couldn't go, my whole
self would be off the ground."

Today I know he loves me,
I want everyone to see,
When told to bring his best friend to church
He asked if he could bring me!

What better way to show me, of his
life I have a real part.
To know I'm someone special,
It nearly breaks my heart.

I pray I live a long, long time,
and he feels like this to life's end.
To be your grandson's best friend.

Dedication: To my special grandson, Kevin Lindquist

Windows
Aaron Reese

The mansion is lovely in the spring
Except there are too many windows to open halfway each
morning and to close halfway each night
There is a constant twisting of the inner conscience
and the nonstop foreplay of souls between the four bare walls
The battle between the darkness and the light is a great one
But it is silent, so silent that all you can do is scream
A sound is heard in the back room
The kind of sound that puts you in a downward spiral into the deepest
depths of your emotions I hate being alone
I hate being alone with an exclamation on the amount of space that I have
to fill
The emptiness sneaks up on you quickly and quietly and the quietness is as
heavy as a mastodon around my neck
But being alone makes me feel free
Free to do anything I want, like jump on all the beds only in my underwear
I love it here
I love the warm air, I love it when it taps me on my cheeks and runs
through my hair to wake me up
The night breeze here is just as beautiful
The starry night seems endless while the moonlight fills me with a
romantic warmth
The warmth is more powerful when I can share it with a pretty face who
smiles when the breeze shifts her long brown hair

The mansion is lovely in the spring
Except there are too many windows to open halfway each morning
and to close halfway each night

Times Are A Changin'
Nancy Durnell

Purple pansy pot holders,
Yellow monochrome – in 3 D
Tiny stitches, musty, packed away
in cedar HOPE chest.
Gosh! They sure don't make MOTHERS
like they used to.

Untitled
Paul R. Thornton

You and I wind and rain, wind and rain earth
and sky. These wings I grow help me to
fly in your sky. These eyes of the earth
help thee to see, a place of love to you
from me.

A ship I build for you and I, as friends
we sail together. A heaven's sky in a
desert's July, whispers of a kiss upon
thy lips.

The look upon your face I hold near.
Forever in a day, I wait for thee my dear.
The look upon your face my mind can't
replace. I long to see that face again
in summer's rain.

Upon your return to my eyes, a place
among time's table awaits us. A love in
affinity's name we will share. So take my
hand my lady fair, for all of this we must
try. You and I wind and rain, wind and rain
Earth and sky

Dedication: My Sunflower in the desert

The Bright Side Of The Route
Juan Ernesto Gil

I know there's anger and violence at any time out there,
and I see lonely faces with no hope everywhere,
but I wanna feel the bright side of the route.

I know people lost control in matters of gold,
and many smiling faces are sometimes simply a bluff,
but I wanna see the bright side of the route.

Because living in shining my life's abounded in faith,
and I'm helping this dwelling to be a better common place,
that's why I wanna live in the side of the hope.

And hope is a brightening feeling of
helping each other for an only reason of love
giving ourselves a place to care and fight for,
so let's make all together the bright side of this route.

A route in this Earth
with no distance at all,
made up with our hands,
and inside of our souls
a day by day poetry
a feeling of love...
so let's live in the bright side of the route,
so let's give love a chance all thru this route,
so let's make all together the bright side become true.

Dedication: My dear nephew, Leo

Noteworthy Works

Untitled
A. Thomas
If love comes knocking at your door
Let it in and ask no more
If in doubt, don't let it in
And your one sad once it has been
Don't be sad, if love is true
It will come knocking back for you.

A Friendship Of Love
Kimberly Anne Douthart
The world flashes by.
Your whole life changes.
Never give up.
Never give in.

Those who are there.
Those who did not care.

Living on love.
Dying on hate.

I will never leave.
You will never stay.

A shoulder to cry on.
A tear to live on.

Listening to sorrow.
Loving your smile.

Giving you life.
Giving you love.
Remember it always,

A friendship of love.

That's My Dad
Carolyn Mae Joiner
That's my dad,
That's him, wearing blue

Sworn to duty,
Patience runs out with every fury,

To uphold the law, protect the weak,
Justice is done, in and out on the street,

See his badge and name tag,
He's not one, who thinks he's bad,

His life on the line,
As each day passes by,

Just a man, who cares too much,
Hoping someday, his heart will touch,

The ones gone bad,
The ones who are sad,

Who want that second chance,
To learn to live and dance,

But, cross him once, and never change,
He'll never forget, you'll always be the same.
Dedication: My beloved father, Wayne Joiner

The Bank
Patrick Vincent Clough
I told my Mother,
I had put my money
In the Bank:
She said "Lord, Lord
You have lost the
Lot now"

Untitled
Julie C. Kelly
Thinking back to yesteryear, peer through fragile glass
Memories of days gone by, glimpses of the past

A look, her touch, a fleeting smile
Things left unsaid, but yet we knew
Within her heart, held tender there
Love for us like wildflowers grew.

Sweet visions pass, we wander back,
To childhood we once knew
Worn Bible held there in her lap,
In her, its wisdom grew.

We knew she'd go, though now at hand
We long for one last chance
To thank her for her guidance
As we've stumbled through life's dance.

Heaven lies but just a breath away,
Draw comfort from His words
We'll meet again, up in the air, on angel's wings, unheard.

Until that day, sweet mem'ries share, watch over one another,
Remember well, inside those pearly gates,
Dwells our beloved godly Mother.

A Baby Girl
Sheila Beaty
Nine months goes by and the suspense subsides
A baby girl is born, Mom and Dad at her side

The planning begins, so much to do
All the baby girl can do is smile and coo

Mom brushes the long curly hair
Dad looks on with love and care

The hurt of the bumps can be kissed away
But you realize she's growing up every day

You remember the planning so long ago
You were supposed to do, where did the time go

She walks into the room with something to say
A boy friend she says, no way

More planning to do and so little time
An outdoors wedding in the sunshine

She walks down the isle, with Dad at her side
You can't believe your baby girl is now a bride

Nine months goes by and the suspense subsides
A baby girl is born, Mom and Dad at her side

Dedication: My daughters, Tabitha and Brittney

Dreams of the Soul

Untitled
Carla Longenberger
We'll forever remember the good times that we shared,
Your beautiful smiling face and how much you cared.
We'll always carry a part of you with us wherever we go,
We'll love you forever, and miss you so...
Dedication: My sister, my friend, Maureen Anne Longenberger

You Mean So Much To Me
Jeannie Stone
In life, there are seldom few, who fill our hearts as you do.

In your heart the Lord does dwell, it is no secret, for all can tell.

You've always been so sweet to me, you are all that we could be.

You were like a Father to me, as understanding as you could be.

In a life wrought with despair, through much of life I just didn't care.

But on your ranch I was worlds away, from life's true tragic grueling ways.

You always had a special way, to plan our visits when we'd stay.

And when we went out on your boat, on dreams each day we would float.

The Lord is surely there with you, you can see him in all you do.

The things you did, you thought were small, and didn't mean that much at all,
were some of my life's greatest treasures, and of them there is no measure.
Dedication: My uncle, John Smith

The Last Good–bye
Jim Hunter
I remember the day of our last good–bye, Mom standing there with tears in her eye.
The bus loaded and ready to go, still angry and upset because she moved so slow.
She stretched out her arms for a hug and a kiss, but this time I thought, "you're going to miss."
On my face written with disgust and hate, all I could say was "You made me late."

I pushed away and didn't look back as they loaded my bags she had carefully packed.
She said, "I love you son," as she waved good–bye. I just shook my head to make her cry.
The roar of the engine as the bus pulled away, I never thought this would be our last day.
The news came quickly, "Your Mother is dead", as a flood of emotions rushed through my head.

If God would grant me one wish with His power, I'd turn back the clock to that final hour.
I would take you in my arms and never let go and I'd be the one moving so slow.
Please forgive me for acting so tough. The words "I love you" just don't seem enough.
Mom the pain is still strong as I think back to that day when I broke your heart as I pulled away.

I miss you mom... your son Jim.

That Special Place
Carmen M. Cassette
Jesus found a garden
where He,
planted my soul,
for eternity.
Dedication: My Godmother, Carmelle Coussard, Canada

Memories Of West Virginia
Helen Dye
Where the wind bends the
willow, and the fog shrouds
the valley below.
Where the butterflies dance
in the meadow, and
the tall green grasses
grow
There the whippoorwill
calls in the evening as
the lavender hills cast a
spell
Where the May apples
bloom in the springtime
And the brook flows
fresh through the
dell
Where the frogs lie
moist on a Lily pad
And the tall reeds
grow in the pond
Where the fragrance of
spring, makes the
heart glad
And memories of
lovers now gone

The Joy Of Hunting (Revenge Of The Fox)
J. Lucock
I hear the recoat gentleman's hunting horn, shatter the
peace of nature's morn... and lift my head
to take the scent,
Of his hounds... a–yapping—baying... hellwood bent.
Time to rise and give them sight,
Of famous broom, so they can start in early morning light
towards the doom.
The stirrup cup is drained on frosty lips, and dashed
to icy cobbled stone,
And now, its time to go... tally–ho tally–ho.
Again with hunting horn and raucous baying
They charge in pursuit, in the name of sport
And not of slaying... and like the infantry on that
Balaclava day... horse and hounds obey.
Time I think to make use of my well known cunning
to zig... to zag across the field, confuse the hound
with uncoordinated running.
Fleet of foot, swift of brain I lead them all across the plain
Toward a favoured place of man
And here my plan, will now unfold
The hounds close in... They've not been told
about the trap man lays for hare,
"I know it isn't fair"... but I'm a fox... and I don't care
The baying, yapping hound now screams
His leg is torn and this hound will surely die...
But I'm a fox... and so will I.
The huntsman urges hounds to kill and just before my end
I wonder... how unlike am I... of man's best friend?

Noteworthy Works

How Could They?
Donna Hahn

How could they close their eyes and let the murders at
AUSCHWITZ, DACHAU, BELSEN
happen?
How could we close our eyes and let the murders of
KING, EVERS, CHANEY
happen?

Through The Eyes Of A Child
Dolores Bulthuis

Through the eyes of a child, the world comes to life,
As I watch my heart fills with delight.
The wind in the trees sings a song through its leaves
While he listens his eyes shine so bright.
He flaps his wee arms as he chases the birds
And he thinks maybe he too can fly.
But his feet just won't do, what his heart wants him to,
No matter how hard he may try.
The beauty he sees in the flowers and weeds, is a memory I lost long ago

Each day through his eyes my heart fairly cries, for I know I've rekindled a glow.
In the mid–morning sun — he runs cross the lawn, yelling,
"Oh Mom come see, please come see?"
and crushed in his fists were but two dandelions,
that he proudly presented to me
No rose ever grown will ever compare to the beauty of this loving gift
I've tucked it away in the back of a book for whenever my heart needs a lift.
For this I hold true — the sky will turn blue
If I see through the eyes of a child.

Dedication: To Jacob, with sweet memories

Marion
M. C. Dowie

In this year of nineteen fifty
You began your first decade
Born upon a September morn
Around the crack of dawn
In this year of my second decade
A daughter fair was born
Her name shall be Marion, born this day
22 September nineteen fifty
I grant you this reward

Now you are about to enter those
Difficult adolescent years
Some with tears and many cheers
'Tis only the child growing up, to know
The rights from wrongs
I grant you this reward

You grew you blossomed
You did so well
Your character it was formed
Your life, your own you made
For this I grant you the reward
It was I myself who gave you life
I thank you, for my reward
A dutiful daughter

Happy Fortieth Birthday
You Mum

Attention Please
Amanda I. Roller

Through a pane of glass
I finally saw him.
Inches close,
But years away.
His profound sadness hidden
By his smiling face.

The Maverick Spirit Lives On
Janet Middleton

Where can our maverick spirit find its place
in this modern world, Away from city dust. Longing
to be free, Casting off the shackles that bind
you and me. The Maverick Spirit Lives On.

Our maverick spirit lives on, It does not die,
It lives on, In the green fields and meadows
with gurgling stream, Where wildflowers in
in profusion grow, With clover green, With
you my love by my side the heavenly fields
will ring to the song, The Maverick Spirit
Lives On.

Free to roam wherever we wander, Our maverick
spirits free you and I together over green
fields and meadows roving together The Maverick
Spirit Lives On.

The maverick spirit cannot die, Its wandering way
is the centre of adventure, finding anew a love
of nature, You and I together over fields of green
the scent of the wildflower's perfume, in the air
It's a maverick spirit born, Two lovers in each
other's arms A song ringing in tune with nature's
song The Maverick Spirit Lives On.

What Is A Mom
Bev Gutzeit

A Mom is a girl who grows into a lady
She's pretty, curvaceous, with naught a malady,
She dates all the men and wishes for him
There's flirting and fun and a whole bunch of whims,
And then there's the day she meets her man
All of a sudden there are secret plans,
They date and they wait for that special time
When they'll be happy together and totally sublime,
So they wed and take part of the specials in life
Especially with babies, there's joy and there's strife,
A Mom is the strong one who's there everyday
To feed you and bathe you and see that you lay,
She's sweet and she's loving, whether it be day or night
And sometimes it's awful and a horrible sight,
But she smiles and gives you everything of herself
She seems always there when you needed her help,
A Mom is a giant among all that could be
She's the best of God's creatures for all to see,
It's not to say that a Daddy's not there
It's just that he's busy with little time to spare,
He works hard for the family and hopes that they know
That they all need his working to bring in the dough,
He too can be loving if he wishes to be
A little bit different because he's a he,
But Moms are the ultimate a family can have
So remember to cherish your Mom and your Dad,
I haven't yet found the words that define
This wonderful Mom that I can call mine!!!!

Dreams of the Soul

Life's Cornerstones
Hubert D. Williams
Some love roses while others fear their thorns.
Some convey love and others only scorn.
In all of God's creations each is unto its own.
Each has its own reason for being but does not stand alone.
All things are different and each other's cornerstones.

Light is to dark as love is to hate.
All are related in mysterious twists of fate.
All seem so separate they appear to stand alone.
But one is to the other life's cornerstone.

Living is for learning and wisdom to behold.
Through mistakes and forgiving God's love unfolds,
The mind is to the spirit what God is to the soul,
All things are related as a continuum of the celestial whole,
Even the seemingly insignificant are life's cornerstones,

All events that happen and all words that are said,
lay obscure foundations to all that lies ahead.
The potter's hands never stop creating from different pieces of clay,
always and forever amending mistakes of yesterday.
And even though all seem so separate and unrelated tones,
God knows all are to each other life's cornerstones.

Dedication: All my people, with love

Listen To A Child
Sandra Niemi
Did you ever really listen to a little child's prayer?
Knowing in his heart – God is really there.
Did you ever stop and wonder what your life could be?
If at this very moment, you saw what a child did see.

Dedication: Justin

Looking For God Through One Small Window
Doris Hancock
Looking For God Through One Small Window

One sad day when things seemed blue,
I walked to the window as I frequently do.

Gazed at the sights that aroused my thoughts,
to see so much beauty that God has brought.

Suddenly, I was no longer sad
because each day our life on earth is one day less.
But do not worry over this.

Go to your window, and find God on the dewdrops
That cling to the flower petals that only God can make.

Look how he made the bulbs push out of the earth!
After being sprinkled with sunshine and rain.

Oh! And look at the face of the small child,
As he walks with his Mother,

A smile of happiness, not a care in the world
As his Mother shows him all the places that God dwells.

So don't worry about tomorrow, and life being one day shorter.

For you are now one day closer to God's heaven,
When you may have full view of eternity.

The Rose
Laurie Ann Walker
Inside this little vase
I found a little place,

To set a pretty flower
that had gently brushed
my face.

I watched it bloom completely,
with its colors full of cheer
dancing off the glistening sunlight,
until the dark drew near.

With each mornings daybreak,
I saw my flowers smile,
until one day my flower quietly
wilted and died.

I carefully removed the flower
from it's little vase,
then simply pressed the petals between
some pages to remember the
smile it gave, and how it gently
brushed my face.

Dedication: To my Mom, with love...

Beauty Forever
Ronnie Duncan
Clouds in the sky
Catch my eye
My heart beats fast
Till I gasp
Beauty like that forever
Will last.

When Jesus Comes
Kelly Rosemarie Cavanaugh
I think when Jesus comes the sky will turn to gold,
all righteousness behold.

Trumpets will sound, horns will blow;
Everyone that is saved will go.

Angels obey, what God will say;
Love will overcome hate, joy over sadness.

Cars will crash, trains will thrash;
Heaven or Hell, only God can tell.

He'll pick us up, with his blood–stained hands;
people from different lands.

Lights will flash, people will dash;
People will fall, Jesus will call.

The sun and stars will disappear;
Everyone knows that Jesus is near.

Now and then, till the end;
Once again, a new begin.

Everyday, in every way;
Loving God.

WHEN JESUS COMES

Untitled
Joel W. Ellis
Poor, as church mice
This was back, in the early thirties
Then people were poor, like church mice
Most would eat water bread, and gravy
Pay then, a dollar a day, wasn't paradise

Boiled clothes in a pot, with lye soap
Cigarettes and snuff, nickel a pack
Mother cried, but never gave up hope
Daddy, worked for railroad, fixing track

Comparing today, to those of yesteryear
Washing clothes in tubs, and rubboards
Today about the same, lot less tears
There were good times, but still hard

The late thirties, brought out new stuff
First washing machine, with gas engine
Mother's work was easier, not so rough
Today, it's more than you, can imagine

After eating, nothing left, not a crumb
Everything you do, you pay the price
Few folks then, had more than some
Were so poor, we had no mice.

Daydream
Becky Sue Knopp
A day to dream
Dream a day
Past, Present, Future
No matter
Just dream
A daydream.

Elsie, I Presume
D. F. Mullins
If I could walk to where you are
Since you left us, just last June.
Then by tonight, by a lonely fire
I'd be camping on the moon.

Then next morning I'd set off
Headed for some distant star
I would use the stars as stepping stones
To be just where you are.

As I close in on angel land
I note the footprints in the sand,
And as I follow, my vision blurs,
As I pass the places
Where He carried her.

I wish that I the task was given
To carry the one I love to heaven
To save her those anxious backward
Glances
Looking for me as night advances.
She'll look no more, I'm at her door
She runs to meet me as I enter her
Room,
I clasp her to my heart and whisper
"My wife Elsie, I presume."

Dedication: My beloved daughter, Kay

Garden Of Hope
Patty Rotert
Out in the garden my Mother plays,
Roses and lilies make her smile,
Her days are filled with pleasure now,
She has waited for this awhile,

It won't be long before her pains will heal,
There is no one to harm her anymore,
An end to her lifelong fight,
She can now close that old door,

Looking in the mirror she sees a woman she once knew,
She sees she is something to behold,
No more bruises or scars to hide under,
She knows the truth must be told,

All women whether too meek or too proud,
Please find that you are strong,
For there is help an ask away,
When you know the road is too long,

With only beautiful days ahead,
You will be filled with hope and calm,
Follow my footsteps into the garden,
Life is worth living to see the dawn.

Dedication: To my angel Mother...

Untitled
Donna Howland
Time is a state of mind...
Distance is just a measure of steps...
The heart knows true love lasts a lifetime.
The heart holds that love close for all time.

Dedication: My family and friends

Now
Yvonne A. Mijares
Now that I am in heaven
I am looking down
I am laughing at what I see
Now I see you at my resting place
Now you bring me flowers
Now you talk and laugh with me
Now you have time to see me on holidays
Now you show me pictures
Now you make it a point to
Stop at my resting place

Now you have time for me
Now I am laughing at what I see
You are talking to a head stone
When you could have talked to me
Now you bring flowers to a head stone
When you could have brought them to me
We could have hugged and kissed on holidays
Instead you hug and kiss a head stone
Now you bring flowers to a head stone
when you could have brought them to me
Now you have time for me
Now that I am in heaven
I am looking down
I am laughing at what I see

Dedication: My brother, Daniel S. Aguilar

Dreams of the Soul

Final Plea
Sheila A. Hite

I wish someone could hear me.
I cry a voiceless cry,
That echoes in this unknown place
Where safety is implied.

I live in this enchanted world
Untouched my human sin;
Created by the love of God...
Then ensconced within.

Listen to me crying –
This unnamed, unheard soul.
I have a voice which can't be heard
By all those hearts grown cold.

I want to live! It is my right!
But, the decision has been made.
And this day I shall be no more,
The heartless have been paid.

I wish someone could hear me.
I scream a voiceless scream.
But I know as darkness settles in,
I am,
I was,
I dream...

Endless War
Annoria Lynn Shah

I have this endless war within myself.
When I have to complete something, and rather be doing anything else.
To make myself accomplish much is the hardest task.
I'd rather run away, and hide behind a concealing mask.
But, when I finish what I set out to do.
Finally, I realize this endless war its through.

Tourist Traveler
Eugene Skazinski

When on tour the Tourist chanced
upon this Delphic scene
Overcome by mythic feelings–sought
in rapturous wonder the advice of Muses Nine:
"What's wrong with modern man whose
nature seems to have gone astray?"

"Politically correct dictums debase man's glorious past, "
spoke Cilo; and Calliope in sonorous tones bemoaned the
lack of eloquence in heroes; Urania uttered a contempt
at man's delusion in virtual reality.

Then screamed Euterpe: "Your music is attuned to the
jingle of coins; " while Terpsichore lamented that dance
plummeted into a senseless gyration. "Confusion,
ambiguity, and pompous rhetoric are oration's fashion, "
snickered Polymnia.

Thalia grieved and groaned that poetry lost its sense of humor;
Erato bellowed, "poetry of lyricism and love slipped into a
jargon of lust; " and Melpomene shrieked that "tragedy became
abstract and gratuitous. "

Then the Tourist–Traveler in epiphanies of enlightenment
began to unravel this Delphic mystery
"Nowhere to be found were Truth, Beauty and Goodness"
only physical splendor exuded from the arts of man.

Untitled
Patricia A. Desrosiers

Imagine a parent watching a child grow up.
The joys the sorrows
The will to look for what might happen tomorrow.
The surprise that they bring in everything they
say and do.
As you look at them what you see is really
a part of you.

The Reasons I Teach
Kay Surles

The reasons I teach are as numerous as
the stars.
Like the beautiful expression on their face
when they learn about the planet, Mars.

Maybe it's the flowers in a paper cup
Or the cards that they just make up.

Eating a flattened piece of cake
That their Mom worked so hard to bake.

A child bringing in a bug,
Or the one who needs a constant hug.

Getting a magical Band–Aid out of my
first aid kit.
Drying up their tears when they get hit.

They reach out for your hand,
Because they know you understand.

I guess the main reason I teach those twenty–three
Is all the ways they show their love for me.

Dedication: My great teacher, Mom

Disappointments
Michelle Capella

When I look in the mirror I see rain that falls endlessly,
Like tear drops from the eyes of a person who's had their heart broken.
I see a blue and black sky that looks bruised,
Clouds that are of different shapes and sizes, and lightning that strikes
the unknowing.

When I look in the mirror I see mountains that stretch more than the
eye can see.
All filled with knowledge, strength, and accomplishments.
They are covered with snow which hides their beauty,
At times they are luscious green and full of life, but not now.

When I look in the mirror I see an ocean that extends to the horizon,
With sea gulls flying free,
The waters bluest of blue, so clear you can see the ground floor.
An ocean that acts with affection one minute, then with retribution.

When I look in the mirror I see a meadow that has no color.
No feeling, life, or soul,
Like its last bit of energy has been torn from it.
You can tell that once this meadow had vitality, and it held such
beauty when it existed.

When I look in the mirror I see a world that holds beauty.
Yet this beauty is muted, dull.
It does not shine like you think it would,
It looks dirty, almost poisoned, and has no strength to gleam.

Noteworthy Works

Friendship
Lisa McManus

Can I trust you with my heart?
Will you hold it close and near?
Never let it feel unsafe, out-of-place or insecure
Be its only true protector, in a cold and
cruel world.
Then and only then, can you be its trusted
friend!

Listen For The Whisper
Cynthia K. Kidder

It spoke quietly, but firmly,
the voice that whispered to my soul.
In the ordinariness of my days it spoke to me
in whispers I could not ignore.

It spoke of potential and of promise.
Of direction and purpose, and of a spirit set free
to explore the possibilities that had been held captive
for so very long.

It spoke of revelation and discovery.
Of embracing freedom and living the joy that life has to offer
without fear of ridicule and without the blame
so long attached to pursuing my own desires.

As I listened.
it spoke words of encouragement, of pride and dignity
and I knew that these were words I should have
heard long ago, but I didn't. Or couldn't.

And so, I have learned to listen, and to follow,
the voice that speaks so softly to my soul, and
I have come to know, and to trust in, its goodness.

I have learned to listen to the wisdom of the whispers of my heart.

Our Precious Child
Randall M. Dockery

As the morning sun did rise,
our Lord's, he did take.
Our precious little child,
long before she wake.

Last night, we were at its bedside,
a smile, a kiss goodnight.
The laughter was the assurance,
that everything would be all right.

For the short time they are with us,
our lives they do fulfill.
Our precious little child,
during the night she caught a chill.

While everyone was sleeping,
the angels they did come.
From heaven they descended,
and return to kingdom come.

My Lord's, our prayers are many,
each and every day.
Take care of our precious child,
for us to hold someday.

Dedication: To my girls, Amber and Kelsee

Untitled
Clara L. Morgan

Some are old and some are new,
None are borrowed and none are blue,
Just some quarters for you two.

Before they are spent,
Reminisce an event,
One for each year, they represent.

Cyber Dancing
Carrie Somerton

Memory fades to a dance... thru the cyber... on a chance...
Of a whim and a wisp... then up the steps of heaven...
He could dance – he could sing – and music he did bring
In a fog and on a cloud... it was light but heady–loud and senses he did
leaven

She was merely there – a lone thought in the air
'Til he swept to the outer realms of grace;
He projected utter charm as he held her in his arm
And gave her but a fleeting sight of face.

Time was immortal in the universal portal
And he stepped with fleeting wings of times gone by;
Yet the music was so right – ever gentle – ever light;
And he led her in the dances of the flight.

He held her hand – he held her close... He held her in a trance
And he held her in an utter state of glee –
While they danced away the hour in a rainbow sea of flower
And her eyes awakened soft and merrily.

He returned her to her place with a smile upon her face
Kissing her pinkened cheek of blushing trace
Then with a grin upon his chin and a hand that fluttered soft
Turned and quickly was cyberly aloft.

Eyes And Faces
Joanna Jones

The Mystical America
Within our reach...

Medieval Carnivals...
drum, drum, drum
Fire Throwers...
drum, Drum, drum
Bells of Fancy...
Drum, Drum, Drum
Gathering, Feel the Beat
And Men of Emerald Nights
rap with
Maidens of Courage and Truth and Right,
who
Repair Sweet Innocents of Might
while
Charming Sirens Chant Praises of Delight.

But through the Rainbow Haze,
to my eyes, becomes visible

Jesus and Buddha and Muhammad ibn Abdullah
Articulating, Radiating, Creating,

Light.

Dedication: To my beloved Lewis

Dreams of the Soul

Celebrating Accessibility
Helen Sherman
Alas, a time hardly anyone listens
Thru dedication
Friends here, there listen
Understanding enhances the action
As friends began to listen
Times are better thru dedication
From the heart that listens

Fascination In Desert
Ivan Mirosevic
The mirage is just a beast,
the thirst is overwhelming,
the forgotten beads of images,
escalating to place of hare,
hiding under the Joshua tree.

Touching the beard of cacti, razor dry tips.
Your inner being is conquered by the day,
the happiness appears within,
the melody echoes, wind song of the desert.
The walk of Sangueros, seen at distance,
recognized to be the Father and his Son.

The liquids of life are rare, hidden deep,
gushing to surface, somewhere, between poplar trees.
The explosion of petals appears,
eruption of color faint to be remembered,
to those of large crimson red, blended in pastels,
born to last for a few days, like in ecstasy
of spring.

The fertility, held in genes, of secluded turtle,
the champion, friend of my dream, to remember.
Dedication: My stars: Karenza, Melaina and Mireille

Dear God
Linda DeJesus
When I sit in wonder and awe
about the beauty which you have created

I smile to myself to know
how wonderful you are

With your never–ending love
and forgiveness

I'm proud to have been
told about you

And grateful that you always loved me

Even when I was very low and
couldn't seem to get up

You believed in me and were always
there to give a tender shove in the
right direction

you always listened to my problems
and were patient with my tears

I just want to thank you God
In heaven above for believing in me
Even when I didn't believe in myself

Untitled
Joan C. Lipin
Slip into the dawn
and let it speak
of radiant hues with softness peak
the water's ripple reflects an inner calm
of thoughts that go on and on
Dedication: My father, Dr. Theodore Lipin

My Dream Date
Akia Knight
One day soon, I wish to be
Going on my dream date,
Someone who is very popular,
A person that I know will
love me for me,
Wishing one day I can be,
With that person I admire most,
Wishing someday I can be,
In his arms,
hoping that the time will come,
For me to be with my dream date,
He has a great smile,
With lips I wish that soon
I'll be kissing,
Wishing that he loves me as much
as I love him,
Having his shoulder to lean on,
Giving my full attention to his needs,
Always being filled with affection and
passion,
For the one that I love most,
For the day when I can be,
In his arms.
Dedication: Marques Barrett Houston, with love

Of Me, And Of You
R. F. Thompson
A score and less than ten is where Hope finds her end.
No more laughter. No more tears. No more sadness, dreams, or fears.
We are the Found, and need no cues.
This is the tale of me, and of You.

A Lady stands stiff and tall, a torch gripped in her paw.
Vacant her eyes. Doused her fire. She is the whore of Hope's quagmire.
But we are the Found, and Blissful too.
This is the tale of me, and of You.

A great man stands beneath a dome, writing words to build Us a home.
Listless his pen. Useless his words. Myth and rhetoric play the louder chords.
But We are the Found and gawk at tricolor hues.
This is the tale of me, and of You.

Behind the glass and against the wood, lies Hope's Constitution.
Babble Babble. All's Babble Babble. Promises promises that flatter the rabble.
But We are the Found, and nod at such sweet woos.
This is the tale of me, and of You.

Gone are the dreams, washed away by polluted streams.
Imagination flounders. Minds lay bare. For knowledge is lost, forgotten or pared
But the Found stand tall and never perplexed
'Cause Hope is dead for the ones labeled X.

Kids
T. Williams

They go to school and back for tea
Early to bed no life for me.
That's all they shout on going out
I hope someday they have places to play
Far away from dirt around the streets.
New friends to meet places to see
That's the hope I want for thee

Ode To Reverend King
Henry M. Ortiz

The expressions on his face told a story,
of his losses and his glory.
Just when it seemed as though a wall in front
of him was built,
He'd think of all his people... and his heart
would fill with guilt.
He fought the struggle in his youth, until the
man that he became,
He held his head up high... when all others
would hide and bow in shame.
He led the march across the south, brothers and
sisters at his side,
He promised the bell of freedom for them
would ring,
As the people – his people would hear the angels
sing.
He had a vision of all the races standing proud,
together true,
The bell did ring proud brother, the bell of
freedom,
But not for us... it rang for you.
That bullet took your life dear Reverend,
But not your dream so true.

Dedication: Joseph and Joanna, follow your dreams

The End
Steve Kauffman

Now
You've been rejected
Once too often
And hurt
Once too deep
Cry till you're done
Knowing
This time
you
can't
bounce
back

Showing
This time
there's
no
more
slack

Cry all you want
Foolish one
The line stretched true
What you have lost
Is nothing
What you have found
Is you

God's Signature
Brenda G. Whitaker

Some treat it as an heirloom
Just an old antique
Its pages go unread
When placed on a shelf to keep.

Its words are like a deep, deep mine
Deeper than the sea, like a treasure chest
Hidden in its mighty depths
Are messages for you to read.

Learn from it, drown your sorrows
Feed upon its words – live by it
Listen to every word
As you learn of your tomorrows
For God's children know of its history;
But to many, it's still a mystery.

So don't neglect it, read it, obey and believe
It's the Good Book
For never be deceived
It bears God's Signature
THE BIBLE
—Only Believe!—

Dedication: George, whom I love

Grandpa
Stacy Ryan

Caring, generous,

Funny, loving, friendly, forgiving,

Kind–hearted, remembered,

Person

All Eternity Will Be Too Short! ✈
Evelyn Terry

To live, with certainty, in opening the door,
To love, with finality, now I can do no more.
To savor, with breathless anticipating, love's fulfilling
dream, to awaken, with ecstasy, a new love supreme!

To smile, with knowing pleasure, in advance of reality,
To accept, with gratitude, a touch of immortality!
To laugh, with full assurance, already living your future
Destiny,
To muse, with uplifting, in love–filled ascendancy.

To offer, with outstretched arms, his waiting arms to fill
To test, with quiet heart, understanding is ever so still
To dare, with absolute conviction, this union is right,
To perceive, with keen insight, "recognition at first sight"

To joy, with each day's passing, bringing him ever nearer
To drink, with soul's delight, his presence dearer and
dearer.
To pray, with fervency, swiftly for time to pass,
To whisper, with urgency, "I love you!", at last.

To long, with his longing, always in my heart,
To find, with him love forever, ne'er to part;
To soothe, with full comprehending, each and every hurt,
Then to realize... with ALL ETERNITY... TIME WILL BE TOO
SHORT.

Dreams of the Soul

Uncle Mike
Bobbie Jo Rutterbush
When the wind blows, I know
your spirit is soaring through
the winds.

When the sun shines, I know it's
you smiling.

When the sky is clear, the clouds
are gone. It's hot out, I know,
It's a day you would enjoy.

When I think of you I'll think
of your jokes and imitations.
Your overwhelming personality.

I'll think about your laughter.
How special you are to me.
Your nice strong loving hugs,
you gave me.

The conversations we had.

I'll think of you!

I love you Uncle Mike!

Untitled
Kevin B. Parsons
How wonderful is our lovely dance
when you give me a romantic glance
Maryjane you are so sweet
I will lift you off your feet
Our dance brings everlasting romance
Dedication: To my sweetheart, M. J.

Daddy
Megan Kelly
Daddy and little girl on his knee,
these memories are not of me!
You left me when I was young,
my life now has begun!

Not a card or a call did I receive,
Somehow, I think all dads leave!

So little memories already fading away,
this year on dad's day, I beg and plead,
that you try to find me!

I need someone to walk me down the aisle.
I need a strong hand to help me up with a smile!

Do you wonder or even care?
Oh my God, are you even out there?

I shudder at the things you have done,
but "forgive and forget" is my motto,
and I have won!

I got up the courage to say,
Dear Daddy,
Happy Father's Day!

Dedication: Nanny and Poppa, my loving grandparents

A New Day
Sam Mabry
Another day is about to dawn.
But what about yesterday, where has it gone?

For the less–than–brilliant – the average Joe,
The whole pattern is amazing – the Master's
show,

Or the need for a reason seems of no concern
Too many who just watch, enjoy, live, and learn.

The amazing beauty – the miraculous
panacea of fresh light.
Illuminates, invigorates, and clears away
the all–pervasive dark of night.

Then in the evening as the sun moves west,
The light begins to fade in another
glorious display – it's time to rest.

Can we – no, how can we say it other than
a divine plan
Created, implemented, and orchestrated
beyond the comprehension of man.

Dedication: Jeanne Mabry– my precious wife

Mirror Images
Lorraine Brown
Look through my eyes what do you see
Do you see who I am or what you want
me to be
If so,
You need to know, I cannot be what
you want me to be, but who I am not
just any, but me.

Perplexity
Jennifer A. Mackenzie
This temple of shaped plains and valleys of flesh,
edged in feathery fronds, this flesh–toned armoury
of my soul, with visual points for all to see.

My one cryptic edge, to choose or not to choose,
to induce, or not to induce, the search of my
obscurity.

Will you, won't you discover, discern, and having
done so, have the wit to unlock the hidden doors,
and persist in probing my elaborate camouflage?

Will your progress continue unimpeded by rocky
pathways; or will you stumble? And slipping perilously,
missing signposts arrive in that cul–de–sac reserved
for the unimaginative. But on arrival, allow your
acclamation to wallow in its narrow prosperity?

Rarely few complete the journey; portals remain
barred against the chosen few. Their success! Their failure!
Their contentment becomes my painful imprecation, like a
refugee at heart.

Dejected I exist; whilst we endure on different levels.
Until my intellectual pathways scream overdrive again.

Dedication: Especially for Rebecca and Giles

Neglected and Abused
Katherine Barragato

Stricken by the hands,
that used to hold me as a babe.

Shut out by the heart,
where just beneath it I was made.

Glared at by the eyes,
that at one time, could see no wrong.

Turned on by the back,
that once I sat so high upon.

Why is it you can't see,
that I am still the same inside?

Have you become immune,
from all the million tears I've cried?

Right now I am too small,
to hold the hands that hurt me so.

I hope the hate I live with,
doesn't follow as I grow.

Dedication: Dianna Isaac, for never-ending support

The Lord's Play
Ian DeLorean

Forever and a day
I will see you
I will speak to you
I will hear you
Although I cannot touch you
I will be with you
There is no finale in the Lord's play.

When I was 83
Florence Halvorson

Today Dear Lord, I'm 83.
There are so many things I still wish to see.
With all the changes and so much in store,
I'd like to live until I'm 84.

Dear Lord, I'm enjoying to be alive.
I'd like to be around until I'm 85.

With all the pollution, war, and still no end to government tricks,
I'd like to see what happens when I'm 86.

I know Dear Lord, it is nice in Heaven,
But! I'd like to stay here until I'm 87.

I know I'm slowing down and sometimes I'll be late,
But! I'd like to see what happens when I'm 88.

I've seen so many changes from scrub boards to electric machines,
And now I can relax and have a wonderful time,
Even tho' I'm almost 89.

Dear Lord, you know I have no fear, that 90 is now near,
Health and happiness go a long way,
Perhaps, I'll still make it to 100 one day.

If this should happen and I'll be fine,
Cuz, I'll be ready for Heaven anytime.

A Thought
Emily Miller

What is yesterday? What is tomorrow?
Was not today a tomorrow yesterday?
Was not yesterday, today just a day ago?
And why do some look to the yesterday to warm them,
while others look towards the thought of a bright tomorrow?
I believe we should all be brightened by the today while
it is here. For yesterday ended a day ago, and tomorrow doesn't
always go the way you plan.

I Would Like To Go Back
Ruby M. Merritt

I would like to go back, to see the old place again
Pretty flowers all around, so much beauty to be found
I would like to go back, to see the rolling hills again
The hills I used to climb, way back then

Mama would read the Bible, as we gathered at her feet
Dad would pray, that we would never stray
Jesus Christ the Lord, we heard his name each day
I would like to go back, to see the old place again

Brothers and sisters, standing in a row
Ready to go worship, at the church by the road
Times were hard, but there was food to eat
Grown in the fields, the soil was rich and deep

Dad went first, leaving Mama behind
Mama tried hard, to keep the family together
She did her best, telling about Christ
The children soon were grown, had lives of their own

Mama is now gone too
There's not much to hold on too
Mom and Dad loved the land, taught us to love it too
We have good memories, still I would like to go back.

Across The Road
Bernice Phillips

I love spring, I love summer,
I love fall, But I love winter
most of all.
There are no houses to block our
view, cars and trucks are very few.
Across the road.

Spring has sprung, grass is growing,
trees are budding, all new life is
showing.
Summer is games and fun
playing ball, and flowers reaching
for the sun.
Across the road.

The pumpkins are ripening,
The leaves are falling.
Can this mean, that next ol'
man winter is calling.

I wake up in the morning cold,
what a sight to behold.
The trees are glistening, shimmering,
sparkling in the morning sun.
Oh, my! Just look what God has
done.
Across the road.

Dreams of the Soul

Untitled
Darlene Espinoza
I've longed to write poems like Robert Frost.
Most of my attempts I merely tossed.

Some folks' poems I have read I didn't think stood a chance.
Maybe I should give my poems a second glance.

If I continue my endeavor,
perhaps someone to might find me clever.

My Shining Star
Louise Davis
My big brother means a lot to me
He's kind and thoughtful as anyone can see
Looking after other people and especially our Mother
He's the patriarch of the family and he's like no other

Raising a good family was first on the list
A church service on Sunday he'll never miss
Going on a mission for his beloved church
Salt Lake City was where he did his research

He's faced many challenges in his life
And he was always supported by his wife
She waited for him when he went to war
He delivered fuel to ships on the seas and shores

When I need someone special to show me the way
My shining star knows just what to say
Our Father, my hero used to fill this spot
His opinion and counseling I often sought

When my brother was sick the other day
I knew there were some things I needed to say
I'll love you forever, so let's not fuss
Get well and take care of yourself, for all of us

Life Without Sam
Pauline Russell
No more will I see your
snowy white fur,
Your gleaming bright,
amber eyes,
Hear your heavy tread
on the stairs,
Your faint meow and
furs,
No more will I feel your heavy
thump of your body on my bed,
Nor will I feel your pawing
at my bed clothes,
Or feel your wet nose against
my cheek,
Your friendly welcome
as I arrive home,
Your fixed stare to let me know
you are there,
I will miss you more than
words can tell,
And I thank you Sam
for your appealing nature,
So full of fun and love,
Your company, friendship
and loyalty
Was absolutely priceless
Dearest Sam.

The Love I Have
Jon Paul Emmanual Jones
The love I have for
you just always has
Been and just always
will be there is no
beginning and there
Is no end the love
I have has just
always been

The Ocean
Dafni Chrysostomou
One thing I know that is changing
Is how my heart feels inside.
Something is moving and twisting,
Rolling along on a tide.

Flowing through the emotions,
Dancing along on the shore.
Wondering where the sand's going,
Must not want me anymore.

The surface can't stay unbroken,
Must continue along on its path.
The depths of the water are shaky
Churned by the winds aftermath.

The tow pulls in my vision.
The mind begins to go down.
Pulling along all my reason,
Love makes me want to drown.

Preservers are scarce in the ocean.
Enter at your own risk.
Expect it to be without mercy.
I warn you, the pace there is brisk.

To Lillian
Darla Chevalier
As the buds appear
awakening the slumbering limbs
from their winter sleep;

As the flowers bloom along the roads,
and the garden path;

And the creek bubbles and gurgles happily on its way
After emerging from its icy winter shield;

The birds cheerfully welcome each new day; and
The wild flowers sprinkle the fields;

We bid farewell to you
And wish you well
On your journey new.

And we await the day
When we will meet again; on the other side
To live in joy and peace;

With no more tears or sorrow,
From our troubles and cares
We at last find release;

And no more have to
Wait and watch —for tomorrow.

Noteworthy Works

Love Crazy
Mia Bianco
I ran up the door
Opened the stairs
Said my pajamas
And put on my prayers
Turned off my bed
Tumbled into my light
and all because...
He kissed me good–night!

I'd Rather Not!
Laura Sampley
Take out the trash, I'd rather not do!
Stinky old rolls and pantyhose too!
It's not that I am lazy or don't want to!
It's just that taking our the trash is
Something I'd rather not do!

The garbage can is full of nasty old things like,
Banana peelings and pie fillings,
Molded macaroni and spaghetti too,
Dried up playdough and fried mushrooms!

I'll wash the dishes, paint the walls!
Clean out the cobwebs!
And scrub the halls!

And besides, there are other things to be done,
Like going to Grandma's
And getting errands done!

Oh, by the way, I forgot,
I have to read my book "Lillian Potts"!
So, I have got to go now, see ya soon!
Because taking out the trash is something
I'D RATHER NOT DO!!!!!!!!!!!!!!!!!!!!

Dream
Craig Hetherington
I dream in colour.

I dreamt of a prophet
staring into a clear pool
seeing his failed future
and crying real tears,
disturbing the water
and breaking the reflection of his sad face.

I dreamt of a guardian
guarding stone statues of ancient men
standing tall in parallel lines
sneering at each others faces,
no peace in their angry eyes
he wonders why.

I dreamt of a visionary
sitting amongst flowerbeds,
listening to the trees breathe
watching as the sun sets,
blowing his horn to the four winds
without a care in the world.

I wake up with the suddenness
of a sharp slap from an icy hand
and remember everything or nothing,
I wonder why that is?

Hunter
Cody Johns
Early one morning he awakes from his bed
still tired from his toes to his head
he opens the door to see a deer
He pulls up the gun without any fear
The deer is alert like his pet dog
Boom! he shoots but the bullets lost in the fog
When the fog clears away he sees a dead deer
He's full of glory but still he sheds a tear

The Fourth Way
April Finocchio
Life is given us from the start
A gift so precious... misunderstood.
We begin our journey to the heart
Our guide is seeing the true good.

With light to show us the way
As we labor to gain insight,
There's a dawning of a new day
For a willing heart sees no night.

Our guide is the Lord from above
Who loves us so much shares all,
And we become harmless as a dove
Redeeming us from the fall.

For his precious love forgives all:
Now seeing, sin has passed away
Releasing all from the fall
Only joy remains it's a new day.

The fourth way has come at last...
Last has become first, it's all one.
Life, light, Lord and love amassed
We really see we are the son.

It's Nice To Hear I Love You
Karen Maddox
I love you in the morning as I open my eyes.
I love you in the evening hours when the owl softly hoots his message so wise.

I'll love you anytime when the mood hits at any hour—
with soft caresses and sweet tender kisses, joyfully with succulent passion, you I will shower.

I'll love you gently.
I'll love you hard.
I'll love you so long and deep
you'll shout "Oh my Lord!"

I love you when it's hot.
I love you when it's cold.
I'll love you for as long as I can—
even when we're old.

I love you wealthy.
I love you poor
(because that's when you're truly all there is
so, I'd love you even more.)

Whether it's one–sided and romanticized
or "two–way" and real,
this is what is in my heart—
and just the way I feel.

Dreams of the Soul

Trust
Amanda Layton
Trust... Trust is like a chain,
Each link takes time to gain.
With every true friend the chain gets longer,
But only you can truly make it stronger.
One weak link and the whole chain can be torn apart.
To pick a strong link you must trust your heart.
You can't let one person break you down,
Because true trust can be found!

To Be Me
Jammey Kovaschetz
Not fighting,
Not getting hurt,
Being smart,
Not a flirt.

Afraid of dying,
Afraid to live,
Afraid of the world,
And how we live.

Not being here,
Not being there,
And really not being,
Anywhere.

So who I am,
and how I am,
Is what I am,
I am man.

So what I want to be,
Is something,
very important to me,
I want to be... Me!

Sarah
Evelyn M. Borden
August 28, 1996, the day you came to us.
Not in the way we wanted, not the way we preferred.
You came to us without our hearing a cry.
You came without life.

I sit, cry, wonder, and imagine.
What would you have been like in life.
Had you breathed and cried.
Had you stretched and moved.

Would you have grown to be short or tall.
Would you have brown eyes or blue.
Would your hair have been dark or light.
Would you have been shy or outgoing.

Would you have been a frilly, little girl or an athletic tomboy.
Would you have been a Girl Scout, a ballerina, a ballplayer, or a pianist.
Whatever your destiny in life, I'm sure you would have been capable of
accomplishing anything.

No, we did not get to carry you in our arms as we would have liked,
Or walk beside you as you held our hands.
But, please know, Sarah, we'll always carry you in our hearts.
You'll always be tucked away in a special spot.
While you enjoy the presence of Jesus.

Dedication: Allen and Lisa, with love

Enjoy Life
Tiffany Ellington
Enjoy life
it is beautiful
life is precious
but always remember
that to live life is a decision
we must all make alone
but remember— life is beautiful
so choose to live it or rest in it

Our World
Dovie Akin
When you look at a map of the
world
What comes to your mind
Do you think of all the beautiful
places you could go and see
or do you think about Mars and
Jupiter
places we may never get to see

Places in the United States
Can almost blow our minds
Such beauty and splendor
If we can't see their beauty
Then we know that we are blind

Such beautiful places in this old
world
Beautiful rivers, lakes, mountains
waterfalls
Large towns, small towns
The country and farms
If you wouldn't like to see all of
these
You should become alarmed

What You've Given Me!
Cuba Hagans
You hold my heart so precious and dear,
What's your intent?... (And be sincere)!

You've given me your love
Please don't ask for it back

This is my way of saying I'm sorry
This is for real, IT IS NOT AN ACT!

I play no games
when it comes to your heart,
I never want us to grow
further and further apart.

I know what I said
had you in tears,
I was only trying to be honest,
yet somewhat sincere.

You seem to be so intuitive in knowing my ways
What can I offer you?, What do you want me to say?

Let's work together on building our dreams
Let's take it slow, make it last, without all the extremes!

Without hesitation, broken promises or any further delays,
Let's strive for a lifetime full of love for the rest of our days!

Noteworthy Works

Spring
Susie Rempel

The sun is shining so clear and bright
And trees in their spring green, delight.
The beauty of flowers everywhere
Say cheery hellos as they fragrance the air.
Squirrels are scampering here and there
As birdsong fills the air.
Oh spring, how beautiful you can be,
You are such a joy to me.

A Dream
Elizabeth E. Ginnevan

I would like to hear the clouds pass by,
And ants, scramble across, my path.

I would like to hear the green grass grow,
And paint, a young child's laugh.

I would like to touch the stars at night,
And the love, a Mother, shows.

I would like to hear the sound of silence,
And ice melt, when it snows.

I would like to hear the flutter, of a beautiful butterfly's wings,

And touch the sound of a hummingbird, as it gently sings.

I would like to paint a young child's dream,
Quietly as they sleep.

But most of all, I'd like to paint,
The joy, when two friends meet!

Dedication: My dear mother, Nina Lawrence

The Wind Keeps Blowing
Jeanna Brink

The wind blowing all around. Pulling me into one circle and another. Until I am so dizzy I have to sit down and cry myself to sleep.

Once in awhile there is hope. Every day it is there when I awake. But by the end of the day that hope has turned into fear, doubt and confusion.

Putting up so many facades so no one can guess. Not answering questions pulls me farther away from the truth.

Which is hard enough to find when the truth is blocked by others and your own lies.

So many people telling me which way to go I cannot live in the past or present but I can live in the future where no one is yet.

So much going on inside, so many different feelings and thoughts I just want to discard them. As I always have, but I cannot.

And, so...
The wind just keeps blowing.

Dedication: Carl, my love and inspiration

There Once Was a Little Baby Child
Elizabeth A. Jackson

There once was a little baby child in a sweet yellow dress
Her tiny spirit was crushed for making an innocent mess
The grandparents tore her baby clothes and slapped her in the face
With stinky, smelly training pants for causing such disgrace

While Grandma held down the tiny child
Grandpa the virgin baby defiled
The brother screamed and the baby cried
A little girl's spirit almost died

Mother heard and ran quickly up the stair
For years she covered up the horror she saw there
Now baby is a lady who had a hard time remembering the truth
God blessed her with the memories, her crushed spirit to soothe

For the thirty nine year old lady's spirit is very sick indeed
Her faith is just a little speck, the size of a flower seed
But as she heals, the beautiful flower of her faith does bloom
This lovely flower will never be cut, never wither, never face a terrible doom

In the winter of her earthly life, she'll leave this traveling place
She'll be old and gray when she sees her Savior face to face
But in her heart it will always be a beautiful, perpetual spring
For her little baby heart has finally been allowed to sing.

Unity
Melvin D. Brewer

Make the world a place to be,
Not like the tourist, the things you want to see.
Brotherhood is not a thing of the past,
So Americans get together and make it last.
Your fellow man is something to treasure,
By all means we are not the one to measure.
Let your conscience be your guide, and friend...
Let's always stand side by side.

Dimensions Of Thought
Stephen J. Bradbury

Mountain spring spawns a new way
Ray of hope of natural means
This small brook winds then schemes
Offerings in temperamental dreams

One wonders how the mystic charms
How friends uncertain life does cease
This brook gains strength as speeds increase
She casts her coat like fallen fleece

Wider she doth grows in splendour
Life runs through now stronger veins
Creatures of the water gains
Hidden, driven by those eternal flames

Prepares her bed with sand then stone
Guides natural creatures to her treasure
Saunters slowly at her leisure
Dances to the tunes of pleasure

Waters deepen all through the river
Born in to this translucent life
Swirling, hurling boulders strife
She behaves like any truly loving wife.

Dedication: My loving wife, Joy

Dreams of the Soul

Go To Hell My Dearest!
Christine Buchman
Set out my supper dear
Clear the dishes again
Set the alarm for five
Bring me a water glass
Put it away my dearest
Turn the covers down I
am rather warm tonight
Fetch me warm slippers
Bring my warmest robes
Cook me some breakfast
Clear the dishes again
Clean this house today
I'll be home for twelve
So have my lunch ready
For I set out for town
As soon as we have ate
When I get back at two
We have to milk my cow
But gather eggs you do
Then when you are done
With all I have you do
Fix my supper dearest!
Clear the dishes again
Set the alarm for five
What is that you said?

Untitled
Cassandra A. Andrews
Playing ring around the rosie with our passion
Watching it Wanting it knowing it
And still and yet
like stealthy elfin thieves with conscience
we skip engaged with our own fire
He and Me

Dedication: My love

New Age Millennium
Doreene Hanks
I will walk living my century
into the "New Age" millennium.

A God–like man walked here two ages past.
He induced the will of time
In commencing with future.

I go into this turn of time having been
witness to all that was before.
I am of new age history.

i. e. color TV rock n' roll. Naivete of sins.
Vietnam. Helter skelter. AIDS. Space junk.
Cyber space. Repo by China. Big Brother's
Reality, had grandkids. Clones to freeze.

History will note that we occupied this
Planet for a few ages. And during our
Stay we exhumed from it her life.

I am content knowing I'll not survive
Another millennium.
Form, the quality of time, in time may
Become extinct.

Dedication: Alice, my best friend– my mentor– my teacher–my sister

---

This Land
Adalyn Keefe
This land, this earth, our planet
here,
Our land that's so sublime,
How can we not attempt to hear
your cry to all mankind?

To preserve your beauty that is ours,
To be gentle and be kind,
unto the land that gave us birth
How can we be so blind
That we cannot hear the fateful
cry
of our land so bright and fair,
Awaken to the fearful call
of destruction that is near.

Our lakes, our rivers and our trees
We must preserve them all.
Our forests and our mountains
We must listen to their call,
The call of anguish and
despair
From the very depths of earth
To make our planet livable
And give it new rebirth.

Untitled
Karen Soares
If you heed this simple creed
And let nothing intercede,
That with Godspeed you'll succeed.
Share your love, implant the seed
Bring to life a joyous breed
Teach of giving, not of greed.
Do the world this thoughtful deed
Then may all our hearts be freed.

Untitled
Tammy J. Hock
With the passing time
who can tell,
what tomorrow will bring.

All we have,
is here and now,
to make the best of things.

Each day,
brings something new,
something unexpected

Should it be exciting
and hopeful,
or the sadness of being
rejected.

Whatever it is,
time will come,
this we cannot stop.

This is why,
we live for here and
now,
because today is all
we've got.

Noteworthy Works

Untitled
Wolf Woman

Many moons ago, on my journey
I encountered a quiet man of great strength.

The words he spoke came from his heart
They were words of truth, integrity and honesty.

His presence was very powerful and he led his
people with a reverence that was respectful
to all.

His first kiss on my lips sent me into dizzy euphonia
His touch was so gentle and caring it was like
being brushed lightly with feathers.

I had waited so long for him to return.

Time passed and many lessons were to be
learned as we slowly began to know and
love one another.

There was a sacred place, sleeping, waiting
for our arrival.

In honour of our union the great bird
of the sky blessed our paths.

Mother's Day Poem
Susan L. Green

M   M is for Mother who is so sweet
O   O is for other things she does so neat
T   T is for time that she gives to us all
H   H is for her hands so busy yet small
E   E is for everything... her kind and understanding way
R   R is for roses, which I give to her on Mother's Day.

Dedication: Mom, who is my inspiration

Memories Of The Heart
Vickie Maryon

As the summer days grow cooler
I feel the autumn of my life
Slowly moving in around me
Like fog: on a moonlight night

Moonlight casts its silvery shadow
On the picture in my mind
Those memories fading cameos
Of someone I left behind

Those glimpses from my childhood
First dance, the graduate, the bride
Moments frozen in infinity
As we follow life's endless tides

There's something in the fog
You can't see and can't forget
Your Mother's touch, your baby's sweet smell
Those moments so clear; and yet

The mind holds not those memories
as the fog clears and moonlight departs
I find the sweetest comfort
In the memories of my heart

Dedication: Everyone in my heart; love

A Chance Encounter
Mary E. Bridges

When Michael came into my life
My mind was in turmoil and strife
I tried so hard to avoid him
But, now, things would be dull without him

As we dance to the music, I'm happy
He's so tall, thoughtful and charming
Now I know, my heart could be warming
To this man with a passion for building

I've found my man, and, he's willing
To dance, romance, it's so thrilling
We laugh, we chat, as he charms
Oh! My! I could melt in his arms

I have so much love and affection
Could there be some little attraction
For a woman who'd be genuine and caring
To the man who deserves a companion, if
Only to keep him from erring

We are country born naturals
No need for bilaterals
And just as there's heaven above
The language of music is love

Untitled
L. Lightkep

Did you know I was listening,
I heard what you said.
The names that you called me,
they hurt.
I was trying to help the best
that I could.
In spite of the pain, I'd do it again
I love you. Always.

America Is In Need
Angelia B. Tingle

When we read the paper or watch the news on TV
Disaster fills the headlines and sorrow is what we see
We suffer from such heartache, across this promised land
This is the time to reach out and lend a helping hand

There's drugs that tempt our children, to try them at free will
They're in our schools and on the streets, of every neighborhood
We're living in a drug war and so many have been killed
Please lend a hand to free this land, from the death of drugs for good

There's weapons in this country, that are meant to keep the peace
From the guns we own, in our homes, to the missiles that fill each base
But, when they're in the wrong hands, it's innocent lives that cease
Let's join the ranks together and stop this star wars race

There's an illness in this country, that's causing so much grief
It strikes you without warning, and takes you like a thief
Its victims are all treated, as if they are to blame
It has a tragic ending, and it's sweeping the terrain

Please open up your hearts, America is in need
We owe it to our country, to listen to her pleas
We owe it to our kids, their future is in our hands
We owe it to our God above, who gave us this great land

Dedication: Eddie, my love

Dreams of the Soul

Life's Choices
Maureen Ryan Doyle
The sun just touched the crib's soft edge,
And my heart has leapt as if a wedge
Has been set by stronger hands than mine.

I marvel at this stranger
Who stretches and cries and knows no danger
In this home made ready
By busy hearts and hands.

There are those before me who profess
This babe brings struggle, not happiness.
It's the pursuit of gold and silver
That deserve my time,
Not her runny nose and nursery rhymes.

They bemoan my fate with talk so glum.
I shake my head and bite my tongue.
They indulge themselves and fail to see.
For my career's not over
It's just begun!

I will teach and guide and pray and play,
For all our fates will be in HER hands one day.

Explain to me a more important job.

Mountains, Animals And Water
Jeffrey L. Mitchell
The condors are gone, maybe soon even the bears,
Humans are not concerned, they say "Who the hell cares"?
But when the Mountains, Animals and Water have all passed away,
Mankind will have certainly created his own doomsday.
So mark my words Brother, for we cannot survive,
Without the Mountains, Animals and Water to keep us alive.
The time is now my friends to open your eyes and get it together
And read the writing on the wall – before MOTHER EARTH DIES!!!

Mommy Kisses, Too
Lauren Lewis
I carried you inside me for all of forty weeks,
All I could see at first of you was hair and rounded cheeks.
Holding such a miracle in my long-awaiting arms,
I counted your toes and fingers and all your many charms.

I've waited for so long for you, nearly thirty-eight years,
Now my precious boy is here and it brings me to tears.
I cherish each and every moment that we have to spend together,
I will be here for you any day, any time and any weather.

I watch you as you're sleeping, so peaceful in your bed,
Dreaming the sweetest dreams that float into your head.
When you wake up in the morning and I see your smiling face,
Nothing could shine brighter in my heart or any other place.

When I hold you in my arms to feed you at bedtime,
The closeness that I feel to you is a feeling so sublime.
I hold your tiny hand in mine and press it to my heart,
A bond has grown between us no one can pull apart.

Most every night before bedtime you take a bath with daddy,
You love the water so much, you kick and become quite chatty.
As I lay you down in your bed at night and say that we love you,
I give you Eskimo kisses, butterfly kisses and mommy kisses, too.

Dedication: My husband and my son

Dream Time
D. T. Beahan
Close your sleepy eyes my baby, while I sing a lullaby;
Let the sandman sprinkle stardust gathered from the
evening sky.
Let the cradle that you lie in be a boat at your
command,
Gathering dreams along its journey to the shores of
Slumberland.

I will gently rock your cradle, as the angels watch
from high,
Angel voices that are carried on the breeze that
wanders by.
Sighing softly like the wind that billows in your
dreamboat sails,
Drifting like the thistledown along the starry,
moonlit trails.

Dream your dreams my precious babe, for soon the
golden sun will rise,
And all the world of make-believe will fade into the
morning skies,
And so too will the days of my childhood, lost forever
in the past;
Forgive me then, If I should try to make this
hallowed moment last!

Rain On Earth
Jonathon Cooper
It had happened before, that just a few drops of rain had fallen.
But this was an ongoing thing.
Green grass shoots began to glisten, delicate blades grew high,
The brightly coloured petals sparkled high and mighty
around the nectar and pollen.
A faint fragrance slowly and surely becoming stronger.
The oaks began to tower high above the small life on Earth.
Rain on Earth had fallen.

The Desert Flower
James A. Traynor
On land that wouldn't grow a living thing,
A desert flower bloomed.
Its blossoms cheered the bright yellow sun.
Then rested later to greet the moon,

One day, a little tear had formed,
Resting on a beautiful leaf,
A little tear that marked a sadness,
The sadness before a weep.

The sun and moon kept a vigil,
Through out the day and night,
Watching gently and tenderly listening,
And waiting for a sound or sight.

The wind and rain stayed ever nearby,
Always gentle and always caring,
Waiting for a sign of hope,
like the kind that they were sharing.

One morning, tears of joy were wept by the four, –
And tears not a few,
For what they saw in the little tear's place,
Was a beautiful droplet of dew.

Dedication: Lynne, one in a million

A Little Bit Of Old England
Brian Ridd

There's a little bit of Old England in Norfolk, at Felbrigg Hall;
A touch of magic in the air as you pass through the boundary wall,
To a scene of such tranquility where you step right back in time,
Recalling the days of yesteryear when rural England was at its prime.

At the site of the old majestic hall, you will linger for a while;
For Tudor, Gothic and Jacobean features combine in splendid style,
To give the place an air of grandeur while its parapets proudly stand
Surveying the rich green pastures of many a past squire's land.

Across the fields Saint Margaret's Church stands quiet and serene;
With the Great Wood and the lakeside, backcloths to an idyllic scene:
And right throughout the whole estate some wonderful names abound,
As quaint little cottages, Marble Hills and a Gothic Ice House can be found.

The blacksmith's forge still stands nearby, though its not so busy now,
As when casting shoes for the horses of the huntsman and the plough.
There are acres and acres of yeoman's farms where sheep and cattle grazed;
Just part of the pageantry of history that leaves one feeling so amazed.

Then as the evening shadows slowly lengthen and the sun begins to set,
All the features of this time—warp are thrown up in silhouette;
Adding a further touch of mystery as the darkness begins to fall
On this little bit of Old England that is known as Felbrigg Hall.

Alive
Kimberly A. Sheetz

In memories we sleep
In dreams we are alive
In our future we are both,
Asleep and alive
Let us never forget our memories or
our dreams
For they are who and what we
are.

Once
Becky Hedrick

I once was happy and full of LOVE
My heart all a flutter like a DOVE.
You walked in and gave my life a SPIN
Never will I be fooled by man, AGAIN.

I once was radiant and so full of LIFE
You tore me down, with cuts of a KNIFE.
My love for you, will ever be TRUE
My life without you, is now sad and BLUE.

I once gave you my all, to show my CARE
Now, to love another, I couldn't DARE.
My heart is broken, my pillow wet with TEARS
Because of what you allowed others to put in your EARS.

Once my love was unconditional and TRUE
And I lived from day to day for YOU.
Are you now happy and have life FULFILLED
Knowing my heart, and my love you KILLED.

I once dreamed about you and your sweet FACE
But I can't win, this love RACE
Know that I'll love you now and FOREVER
Without you and your love, I won't be happy again NEVER

Dedication: Wade Perry – with love

My Moon
Wendy Cronin

My moon cascading peacefully into
My eyes,
Like a desert rose swoons as it sweetly
Lies,
Singing, floating endlessly into my
Beckoning arms of silence.

My moon graces over a golden lit river,
Floats into my eyes with beauty as a
Giver,
Smiling, floating silently into my
Awakened soul.

To sweep over unconscious valleys of
A wandering soul,
Soothing me with a tempting light as
Fiery as coal,
To grasp in my deep floating silence.

My moon sighs and bows to float
Back into my spirit held,
Breathing in the sun and air of my dreaming
World,
Smiling, whispering peace into my
Floating silence.

The Ending
Joy Dent

The finality of death,
The rushing waters of life moving
forever onwards.

The fear, anger, helplessness, sadness
and acceptance

for the loss of a friend.

My Second Daughter
Elaine Overton Bulger

A beautiful little girl
Came into my life.
She came to me unselfishly
When I became her Dad's wife.

I often wondered
Just how all this would be.
Could we all be together
And be one big family?

She made this new adjustment
So very easy you see.
A little girl! What was I thinking
And she made this clear to me.

The sleepy voice I hear each morning
As her Dad wakes her from her sleep.
I love you baby, I love you daddy.
Those are the sweetest words to me.

This beautiful little girl is a woman now.
With a path of her own to choose.
But just remember that this is your home
And your Dad and I will always love you.

Dedication: My stepdaughter Donna, the inspiration for this poem

Dreams of the Soul

Sounds In The Night
Reya J. Gaines
A kiss in the dark
A helpless cry at night
A man steals for his family
A child dies of hunger tonight

These are the sounds of the night

A Mother's sorrowful cry
Her pain from a son's addiction
The breaking of glass
A burglar's soft footsteps

The shattering of heart
The cry of a child
His Mother has died
A victim of his Father's shame and anger

These are the sounds of the night

The burning of flames
The sirens of the heroes
The burning of a family's hopes and dreams
To live surrounded by these sounds
In your neighborhood, in mine
And I ask how do you sleep at night?

Untitled
Danielle Marty
Two stars shining brightly,
in a summer's midnight sky.
All's quiet,
then you hear a sudden cry.
Fierce as a mountain lions,
as sad as a lone wolf's howl.
The cry of my heart,
as one star slowly fades out.

Destination
Marlene K. Schirrmacher
Bitter lifeless being
Have forsaken all others.
In a closed shell,
Isolation.

With a liquid lover
Standing all alone.
Pain is overwhelming,
Desperation.

Reaching out in darkness
No hands there.
Knees on the floor,
Illumination.

Pain, past, sorrow—be gone,
No room here.
An empty soul of loneliness,
Restoration.

Light fades in and out
Touch of another.
Overcoming fear of truths,
Destination.

Dedication: To Hatsy... A special teacher

I Wonder
Christine Kinzer
Today as I look out my window at a city awakening;
The cars, trucks, vans, and buses filled with people going every which way.
My mind fills with questions and,
I WONDER.

What is the purpose for this day?
Are the people going to their place of work to accomplish a good day?
Are they returning home from a night of decision making?
Perhaps they are students on their way to learn;
Or people going to play for the day.
I WONDER.

And what will be my purpose today?
Will I help someone along the way?
Will I be the person God has sent to put cheer in someone's heart,
to encourage and build up, not put down?
Will I see the good in others first and not their faults?
Hold someone's hand or just listen to what they say?
I WONDER.

So today as I look out my window and WONDER,
Please dear God, let me know
So I will NOT WONDER.

Untitled
Mary Leona Grafton
Come and dry my tears for me
The usual is not the key
Why go to a dance where alone you'll be found
Why pretend to be worship when
your value is half a penny per pound
Such sweet words are pain and sorrow
Will you be lost or will you be found the
Answer lies within tomorrow

Defining Normal
Pamela L. Rapport
I used to live a Normal life
Free from worry, free from strife
Then one day a storm came about
And Normal took the first flight out

I regret that I just let It go,
I was naive, and I didn't know
But what is Normal? Those in distress will ask
Allow me to accept the task

I still have a glimpse of Normal, you see
Where Contentment reigns, and its subjects are free
Where Innocence is a comfortable state
And Acceptance never soils the slate

Normal always has a routine
Rituals of life that are safe and serene
Differences between people are like day and night
But we all know our zone, unless we lose sight

We may stray from Normal in an effort to rebel
But we always go back for we cannot expel
Those values ever so deeply ingrained
That which is at our core can never be changed

Dedication: Jana and Shelley

Noteworthy Works

What Does It Matter
Daisy E. Jones
What does it matter
if you have no claim to fame,
What does it matter
If you have never won a game,
If your voice was never loud
to be heard above the crowd,
What does it matter!

What does it matter,
That you never made the grade,
You could not make the top
of your chosen trade—

Somewhere in the middle
of that rocky road
You stopped to help another
with his heavy load,
So what does it matter
That you never reached the top,
To be a celebrity was not to be you lot.

But it did matter that what you did
what you tried to do, well
And found yourself still standing
When the others fell...

People
Naomi Wynn
People love you some times,
But sometimes it is bitter limes.
And some people dump you too.
The fear is so bitter to you people,
But are you going to the steeple.
So do you go and fear the end.
You go to sleep and wake and seeing the light,
And the truth is all of a sudden bright.

The Gift That Makes Me Free
Rebecca Atkinson
My love lives above the sky
In a beautiful loving place
He is the one I'll always love
My love, time can't erase

I get so peaceful inside myself
When I write these poems of love
I know, in my heart, my darling
You know, I'm sending my love, to you, above

These poems are meant to be happy
They're meant to be uplifting and loving too
They are meant to show everyone
That love really can be true

I'm so happy inside, my dear
That these poems come out of me
I'm praising the heavenly Father
For the gift that makes me free

I love you, my sweet darling
I always will my dear
Now, even though you are in Heaven
I don't always want to shed a tear

Dedication: My sweet love in Heaven

To Fly
L. F. Harris
I have always wondered how it would feel to fly, where you feel lighter
than air and soar above the clouds.
Now I know, for I seem to fly every time I'm in your arms.

I float on pillows of clouds and drift among the stars too finally
touch down with a feeling of awe.

Dedication: Jim, keeper of my heart

Glowing Light
Patricia Bratcher
Sleep came upon me one warm
summer night,
When I was awakened by a beautiful
glowing light.

Approaching each window with wide
open eyes,
This light formed a circle coming from
the skies

It was shining on roof tops and near
the hill,
Out of breath I was as I stood
so still.

The sight of this light asked me
to stay,
For He is the light that shows us
the way.

With all that is in me I wanted
to sing,
As angels carried me above on
their wings.

These Tiny Hands
L. B. Corbett
These tiny hands I hold in mine
DEAR LORD I claim, but are really thine.
Sent down to me from heaven above,
To brighten my life, to hold and to love

They're not like mine, so big and strong,
They're yet too young to know right from wrong.
They must be taught, and it's up to me.
That's why Dear Lord I have come to thee.

May they never learn the art to fight,
But humbly fold in prayer each night.
May they never hold any hate or greed,
But always be ready to help those in need.

Give me strength and the courage I need,
So along the right path these hands I might lead.
They must be taught, or they will never know,
The right from the wrong, or which way to go.

God help me as a Father to do my part,
To give these tiny hands the right kind of start.
When from this life someday I depart,
These precious little hands will know they held my Heart.

Dedication: My wife of 52 years

Dreams of the Soul

Moment
Marcia Jean Grzywacz
God sent me a daughter to love and nurture
Her smile, her eyes of understanding I care
With fondness of music, and her achievements
brought tenderness everywhere
The moment of passing brings me great tears
But what counts I was there.

Dedication: To my sweet angel, Shannon

God's Child
Susan L. Cupari
Don't hurt the child
Why must you go wild
Please refrain from inflicting pain
Are you completely insane

Thou shall not kill
It was never God's will
What gives you the right
To inflict such fright

For every child is a gift
That can be erased just as swift
The emotional scars that live on in a child
Are often repeated on their own child

Please break the chain
Just lean on God's cane
He will show you the way
Then no child will pay

There are many forms of abuse
None of which have a good excuse
So before hurting any child
Remember you too... are God's child!

A Homeless Family
Patricia Werdebaugh
Today I saw a homeless family, and I
wondered, what is their destiny?
No place to live, tattered clothes, and
worn shoes on their feet, and the
children saying, I'm hungry, can I
have something to eat?
A lump was in my throat, the
sight was more than I could take.
And my heart felt like it would break.
As I fought back tears, and I felt
so sad, I ask God, why do they
have to have it so bad?
I wished that I was a millionaire,
so I could help all the people in despair.
I'd help all I could, to give them
a nice warm place to stay, and
new clothes on their backs, and new
shoes on their feet, and plenty of food
for them to eat.
But I knew there was nothing I
could do, or say. So then I decided to
pray. Please God help all the homeless,
and let them find a way, keep them
safe on their journey today, and every day.

Dedication: My husband, my love, Dave

Untitled
Theresa M. D'Amato Perkins
Flowers appear upon the land,
Sunlight greets them hand to hand,
The voice of the wind throttles by,
And the birds from the trees fly by real high,
Now, the sun is going down,
The flowers are sleeping, the wind makes no sound,
The birds are all cuddled up in their nests,
Thanking GOD for letting them rest.

Words of Wisdom
Diane R. Stigen
Whenever you're unhappy
Whenever you're in doubt
There's someone up in heaven
Who's moving all about

He'll take your hand and hold it
He'll wipe away your tears
He'll tell you that he loves you
He'll take away your fears.

He'll teach you how to trust
And get that faith again
He'll never ever leave you
From beginning to the end.

He'll also be there daily
Watching over you
He's always there to help
In whatever you have to do

Just take his hand and hold it
You'll feel the love flow through
and never, ever wonder
Why the Lord loves you

In Hopes Of Love
Heidi R. Woods
Every morning I awake to meet the morning sun.
Every evening I lay down my head, to prove my day is done.
And even though I live my life in hopes of something new.
There's one thing that I'd never change and that's my love for you.

You greet me with a pleasing eye that never sees my wrong.
You complete me with your loving touch I feel the whole day long.
Your precious smile and thoughtfulness on bad days see me through,
The hardest times I don't feel I could get through without you.

There's special things about you that could only be your charm,
Your ability to shelter me and keep me safe from harm.
Your heart, your sensitivity, your strong but soft caress.
Your ability to give yet still uphold your thankfulness.

You never once would bat an eye, but catch me when I fall.
You're always standing idly by in case I ever call.
And yet you wonder why I stay so deep in love with you.
Though not a man on God's green earth has ever proved as true.

So believe me when I say the words.
As they're from deep within my soul.
There has never been another man,
That's made me feel so whole.

I love you...

Noteworthy Works

The Robin
Annette Gordon

Little robin red–breast
Your waist–coat shining bright
Amidst the winter foliage
Is a joyful sight.

We love to share our garden
With our feathered friends all year
And you brighten up our winter days
When they're wet and cold and drear.

Then in the summer evenings
Your sweet wee piping song
Gives thanks for all the good times
When the summer days are long.

You've raised another little brood
Who have all just flown away,
It really took a lot of work
To find them food each day

But now like us you can relax
And enjoy the evening sun,
And looking back on working days
Say—it was a job well done.

Nothing Bad Will Ever Stay
Scot Saracco

I say to you,
Nothing bad will ever stay.
Bad things come and go,
Just like night comes over day,
I say to you
Nothing bad will ever stay.

Dedication: My mother, Susan Lewis

Afraid
Amie Mann

Why are you afraid of facing the truth?
You have to face it and get it through.
Sometime you did not realize what you did wrong,
You need to talk out, so you could be strong.
I know that you are in fear.
Talk to me, so you can always be near.
Don't ever run away from the pain,
Or else you are not the same person again.
No matter how hard you try,
I know that you are doing just fine.
If you keep on hiding to yourself,
No one will ever know what your fear is all about.
Talk to me one more time,
Or you will never hear from me again.
I want to get to know you better,
But you just keep on trying to ignore.
You will become useless,
If you are not responsible for your fearfulness.
You used to tell me about everyday life and how people are,
If you can't face the truth, what is the use to live for?
Try to give our relationship one more chance,
I know deep in your heart that you can.
Please take good care of yourself whatever you do,
Remember... I care very deeply for you!

Dedication: The one I love, life

The Critics
Etta Lewis

THEY talk of talent, ability.
Whichever word they use.
Forgetting the need for opportunity.
Which is often refused.

From a lofty perch, they criticise.
Unseeing, without understanding.
Circumstances they despise.
Confidence is hard to find.

Such disparagement is unhelpful.
For those who seek to fulfil
An urge for expression
By means so uphill.

Creative writing classes.
Mixing old and new.
Show beginners and aspirers
What they can do.

Critics should attend.
To see to what end.
Talent and ability can descend.
And end without opportunity.

Forever
Kayann Hawkins

We are growing more mature
My love for you shall endure
Forever...
You for me...
Me for you...
That's how we will see life
Through...
Forever

Excuse Me
Shonette Roberts

Excuse me brother man, but you must be confused
'Cause God didn't put women here for you to use
Excuse me brother man, but I am not your maid
'Cause God didn't put me here to be your slave.

So brother if you look in the Bible, Genesis I believe
You will see that in the beginning there was "Adam and Eve"
God took a bone from Adam's side, and he didn't leave a scar that Adam had to hide
He took a bone from the side you see
So that women could have equality.

I'm sorry brother man; do you not like what I say?
Do you think I should be beaten if I disobey?
Well, maybe it's time you figured out what my purpose on this earth is to do
And it sure ain't spending my time pleasing you
I'm a woman, can't you see? I don't need you to rule me.

Pardon me brother man, I know you don't like what I say
You might even kill me before the end of the day
But death to me is a part of life
And it's also a way to get out of all this misery and strife.
But before you kill me let me just say, God made women to be a comfort and companion to men
To help them through any problem they are in.

Dreams of the Soul

Autumn Harvest
Marje Kaena Mizzi
The seeds of the Maiden's spontaneity are sown...
It's time to harvest my freedom,
end old patterns of emotional behavior,
reclaim and honor the child in myself — the child self needs to emerge!
Balance, harmonize, and blend all the elements of my personality,
set priorities,
re–create the "wahine" (woman),
and go forward quietly soaring like the eagle
over the Garden of Life.

The Moor Behind Loch Riaghain/Tiree
Georgina Henderson
Wandering spirits unfold dreams
of nature's beauty so vast and supreme
The windswept moors so wild and bare
have hidden beauty lying there
Raggin robin, buttercups,
orchids so rare
gurgling hillside river, water so clear
flanked by the iris
sentinels to guard
fledglings of the skylark, lapwing — hare,
Suddenly!
The sky abounds with an alien sound
When the snipe drives
distracting all around
from the grasses wherein her young lie hidden
To searching the sky
as she further flies
Further along the river in the blackness of the moor
paths of silvery cotton gleam
waving and fluttering along the stream
Then crops of grass move like waves
when the unseen wind its power displays
Which like the power of God unseen
alters man's ways by gentle means.

Dear Dad, Farewell
Sophia Garwood
It was a day, but not in May,
It was the month of June...

With whom, I must say,
You took him away...

But with us he stays,
For all our days,
Even though it's like a maze...

At peace he lies, way up in the skies,
But never far away...

Four young ladies in his life,
Oh! What trouble and strife,
And not forgetting his loving wife...

One happy little boy,
He was his pride and joy,
One sweet little girl,
She was his shining pearl...

What more can I say?
As I know one day,
You'll say to me, so happily,
One!... Two!... Three!...

A Magical Flight
Lorraine S. Norris
Through the air with the breeze so free, the smell of Autumn comes over the trees.
Orange, green, yellow and brown covers the entire ground. With a circular flight, he spreads his wings. The magical flight begins to sing. With all the
colors blending all over the ground, the whole world is mixing with a beautiful
sound. Today the magical flight goes smooth, for the hawk soars closer to the moon.

Raindrops
Trina S. Brown
Oh, little raindrop just fallen from the sky
Dropped upon my brow
A trickle of water so pure indeed
So natural, we don't know how

The cloud that holds this raindrop
A mass of grey and black
A merge of silvery balls of fluff
That somehow can't hold back

Rain falls from the heaven high above
It falls soft upon our skins
And this trickle wet and tender
Holds such peace and calm within

As we stand and look to the trees
So still, green and droplet moist
We see a vision so natural – yet
Unable to speak – no voice

Raindrop as you break from the sky
Making rhythmic lashing sound
We stomp and walk all over you
As you fall and retire to the ground

Celebrate The Future
Annita Aube
It seemed the applause would never end
At the high point of an award ceremony
Tree branches rhythmic clapping of hands
with the leave's heads bowed. Rise!

O grand rejoicing fans through the lands
Rejoice! Rejoice! Come celebrate the
Future, at this particular hour. Rise!
Wake–up Brethrens Rejoice! Rejoice!

Believe it's the signs of time. Rise!
Raise your hands! Come celebrate the
future. In reading the signs of nature,
What's the future?

Angelic Hosts offer great talents
As the trumpets sound Rejoice!
O Lord can they bring down the clouds?
Witness it, Heaven and Earth!

The dead shall raise among the first
with Praise. Rise! Rejoice!
Celebrate! Celebrate the future!
Clap your hands!

Dedication: My only son, Paul Henrick

Noteworthy Works

Together Forever
Maureen O'Brien
When you hold me close to you
I feel as though we're no longer two
as though we're joined one at the heart
to forever be together and never apart

When you wistfully gaze into my eyes that way
it's as though we're together somewhere far away
never to be found by our family and friends
just you and I together, ALONE, till the end

Come On In!
Betty Harris
If today was all you had
And God you'd face tomorrow
Could you stand before Him calmly?
Or would there be some sorrow?

People think because they've been good
The gates of Heaven will open wide.
But God will open the "Book of Life"
And your name won't be inside.

It tells us in the Bible
It's not how good you've been.
It's if you have accepted Jesus
As to whether or not you'll enter in!

So if you go through life being good
And the streets of gold you plan to trod.
Just being good will not get you there
You must surrender all to God.

You must accept Him as your Saviour
Then being good will crowns for you win.
Then you will one day walk on streets of gold,
For Jesus will bid you, "Come On In!"

Never Alone
Nancy Carol Mascaro
As I sat alone in that tiny room
I began to wonder why –
Why they would leave me all alone
And so I began to cry.

With no one to talk to
And no one to care –
All I could do
Was say a little prayer.

It was then out the window I saw it
It was high above a tree –
From way up on a hill top
A cross was staring at me.

At night when I looked out
That cross was lit up bright –
And I knew right at that moment
We are always in his sight.

That cross, it was my savior
Calling out to me –
To let me know he'd be there
Alone I'd never be.

Dedication: My husband–with love

For Today And Tomorrow
Maxine Smith
My eyes are the gateway to my heart and soul –
And you have to deserve a place in each of them –
As I do yours.
Without the equilibrium, there is no stability.
Appreciation – from you to me, from me to you,
Not necessarily at the same time, just on a regular basis.
Leave the familiarity on my doorstep
Alongside your muddy boots.
Please, never take me for granted...

Worm
Monica Williams
It worms its way
Into your brain
And wraps itself around
Your consciousness
Where it sits and waits
For your guard to fall—
As it must eventually.

And then it can feed.

And it sends images and feelings
To keep you off guard
So the barriers stay down
And thoughts continue
Until all that is left
Is an empty husk.

A shell that once contained
The entirety but now has
Nothing.

Empty.

Dead.

An Antidote For Mourning
Hannah Sexton
Ask not "How long will mourning last?"
Why try to limit the time,
Be content in savoring moments past,
The joyous, bittersweet, prime.

Those pictures of him at different ages:
A baby, a toddler, a teen,
Are part of your life in all his stages,
Relive each moment and scene.

His language paper from the third grade
In a box of old photos you've found,
Remember his pride when a compliment was paid
To his writing neatly cursive and round.

Let the pictures, etceteras find some space
In your depth of loss so grim,
To reflect and mirror his smiling face
And keep you close to him.

Forget not during his hospital stay
His patient bearing in pain,
Can anything mar that brave display
As long as your memories remain.

Dedication: Denis

Dreams of the Soul

Remembering
Debbie A. Barker
So cold, yet the wind did not blow
And it feels like the waiting is the hardest thing to do
But wherever you are how near or how far
I'll always love you, no matter how many tears you make me
cry my love for you will never die
The ocean softly whispers your name
You slip through the waves, unnoticed
I touch, I'm touching, for a moment to remember you
So cold, yet warmer than the sun

Precious Are My Memories
Shirley Jones
I was down, my spirits were low
You came by and said let's go
You took me away from it all
and said that if I need you to just call.

We laughed together and had some fun
My heart said stay my head said run
I knew in time that this would pass
But I couldn't help hoping that it might last.

We made some memories, good and bad
But now we must part, and that's so sad
You were here and now you're gone
Tell me why I feel so alone.

I see your smile, I feel your touch
No one knows how I miss you so much
You say you can't miss what is still there
But when I look around, I don't see you anywhere.

My memories are precious, my memories are few
I will always smile when I think of you.
Once again I had a happy face
You gave me something that no one can replace.

Frustration
Cashel Mack
Could be the cause of a death;
or maybe
just a scab rubbed off by a state
equally free
from an inner struggle
sparked by a conflict caught between
emotions

Thus, frustration
can kill a mind. Always struggling
with that inner force over which
one has no control. Rubbing
a wound created by contention
until a small trickle of relief
flows from the raw, irritated flesh.
A soothing word, a kind thought
or maybe a remedy, a gush of blood.

Face it. Frustration
the cause of suicide, insanity,
misunderstandings, destroyed relationships,
and the ultimate result of its
causes; one of man's worst enemies.
Something to be avoided, except
Life is frustrating
Life is special.

The Pathfinder Spacecraft
Linda Smathers
So much attention focused on me shot from Earth
like a cannonball, so much force that carries me away.

Up, up and away I landed on the red planet
Mars; Caught a glimpse of a few stars.

So much work to do, Sojourner Rover with me too.

Why we're here I haven't a clue.

He That Doeth Truth
Raymond E. Nielsen
By night, Nicodemus onto Jesus did seekingly come,
Professing Him as a great teacher; and by God sent;
Desirous of quick and easy answers about God's Kingdom;
Even yet, unprepared for the answer Jesus did present.

A Pharisee and a ruler of the Jews; yet, he understood not.
Jesus answered: a man must be born again, to see the kingdom;
He reasoned: a man reentering his Mother's womb, is naught!
Missing the point, relying solely on his worldly wisdom.

Clearly, he was not in tune with the Spirit of the Lord,
His mind blinded. The rebirth through baptism, to be done!
A spiritual ordinance he could not of himself reach accord;
His worldly domain clouded; following not, the Begotten Son.

Further He said: "Whosoever believeth in Him shall perish not, "
"Those who believeth not are already condemned by evil deed. "
"The Light came into the world. " He lovingly taught:
But, "men so love the darkness, " they fail to follow His lead.

Explaining further, "Those who doeth evil hateth the Light, "
"Neither do they cometh unto the Light; " Choosing to avoid it;
"But, he that doeth truth cometh unto the Light. "
"These are they who Eternal Life shall faithfully inherit. "

Keep The Lighthouses Open
Thomas E. Radcliffe
I know, as the lighthouses grow older,
And the need for them slowly recedes,
That we forget about the lives they've saved,
So shipping could bring our needs.

The keepers sorrows had a purpose,
How much they suffered is unguessed;
We do know what they've accomplished,
And that they gave their very best.

I know that we should never forget,
The many sacrifices that were made,
To keep our sailors from rock and reef;
But sometimes memories do fade.

By keeping these lighthouses open,
These keepers shall be remembered,
But many are being severely neglected,
Forgotten, lost and dismembered.

They add beauty to our coastline,
These lighthouses that sit by the sea,
There they should be kept forever,
So our children's children may see.

Dedication: My wonderful wife, Betty

Noteworthy Works

Clouds
Karen Joyce Green

White fluffy clouds go sailing by,
White fluffy clouds in a beautiful blue sky.
I lie on the grass,
So I can look up high
At the faces and pictures in the clouds
That go rolling by,
And I think to myself,
How lucky I am, that the Lord loved me
That He gave me eyes to see His artistry

Untitled
Mabel W. Phang

Oh, Winnetka! Oh, Winnetka!
Our Mother of education.
Through you we learn,
Through you we strive,
For a better future.

We are a gam of whales
With a great heart to learn.
Knowledge in mind,
We will swim all over the oceans –
Proud and unafraid.

Oh, Winnetka! Oh, Winnetka!
Teachers guidance here and there.
True friends playmates are not rare.
In a loving environment we learn and grow;
Form the character of a righteous role.

Thank you teachers for all your love.
Thank you all staffs for your care.
We will work hard.
We will improve.
We will spread Winnetka's goodwill
everywhere.

Hey Sport
Rilla Paige

In plush green meadow, sparkling with dew
The wild Shasta daisies, welcome you
But you do not see them, their beauty goes in rain
... For your purpose is to hunt!, a more exciting game

Oiled and polished, your gun in your hand
You kill with delight, you ravage the land

— Quick! lift your gun, toward beauteous sky above
With rapid fire bring down, the snow–white done

The cry for lost mate, ... pierces the air
With broken heart, circling back, for his lady fair

Ahh your eyes are quick, with precision and skill
... Steady now... aim... — make another kill

Go home now (insensitive man), your head up high and proud
Be welcomed by loved ones, when spy you sing loud

But look closely big sport, at little girl just turned three
Through tear–filled eyes, what does she see?

Broken and blood–stained, well tied on a tether
From your hand is hanging, the snow–white splendor
That God created... and sent forth from heaven

Whicky
P. C. Moindroti

God's little pussycat
So wild and playful for just
Two years to see.
A one–man cat only loveable
And cuddly to me.
Covered in white and even
More black.
But sad to say, God took,
His little pussycat back.

One
Henry J. Falcone

There is a oneness more sweeter than wine,
It is a love that flows through a heavenly vine.
It pours like a river, majestic and true,
His life is His source and flows freely to you.

There is a oneness more glorious than gold,
It is His constraining love of which I've been told.
How wonderful it is to live in his love,
It carries me higher on wings of a dove.

As we are united in Love, anchored in grace,
We look in your eyes and see you face to face.
A holy marriage for all who will abide
For eternity is birthing your pure spotless Bride.

Already the calling draws to its end,
The Spirit is lifting us to our eternal send.
A table awaits for all that are one,
Those who heard the knock of God's glorious Son.

There is a oneness more sweeter than wine,
It's the love of our Father flowing through his vine.

Dedication: To Donna, my best friend

Cravings
Jean A. Hogan

I have "cravings" from time to time,
A firm, young body I see
In my mind's eye, so prime...
And thoughts like hunger run through my brain
Similar, but not quite what you would describe as pain;
A heat, a tasting – a memory of what was done
The floor upon... with an energy that again
Returns, as if never gone...

You call it karma, I call it hunger
This craving from within and withunder.
And memory has a fast and furious recall
The energy within, it feels like storm and thunder
The memory so strong, akin to hunger...
Like a light switch, you turn it on.
Returns, as if never gone...

And over the distance, what amazes me...
Is the craving in your voice is what I hear
That's all it can be... your echo of me.
My tone, my hunger ignites your pain
And magically rises... like a golden cane
The energy over the distance
Returns, as if never gone...

Dedication: To my husband, my soulmate

Dreams of the Soul

Arrival
Don Woolums
I feel a completeness inside
but yet
I feel an emptiness of a book
that will end before the whole story is told

I am not depressed
nor of negative direction
I just have a feeling
of time passing before I arrive

The Wind In My Soul
Barbara L. Abel
The wind calls your name.
And nothing will remain
Of what was
The past is only that
If you let it go
You're free and
More happy than you dreamed you'd ever be
Then the sun will be reflected
In your eyes
Every time you smile

The moon creates the magic
When the world is dark
And Love's Cupids dance across the parks
The stars produce the glow
Then the rest is just for
Those in love to know

The storms subside
After racing across the sky
Leaving us to wonder
Why we were passed by

Dedication: In memory of John Lennon

Goodbye, My Glass Menagerie
Meleah Stout
My glass cage, it holds many memories
Good and bad, all shaped me, all hurt me
It stands as the reminder of what I was
And where I'm going

It started as a way to escape my world of torture,
Extended in to my reality, until reality was overrun
The garden paths so tangled that going back was
impossible

Consumed in the fear of humiliation, I ran
Troubled with the perception I gave, I ran
Back to my menagerie I ran
To hide from the world

But Jim came along, he told me to stop
Stop hiding, stop running, just stop
He helped me see, helped me break free
Free from my glass cage

I'm ready now, to let go completely
I don't need my cage anymore,
Not even as a crutch. It used to hold me
Now it just sits there empty, waiting

Waiting for my goodbye.

Tomorrows
Bruce Albrechtsen
I can see the tomorrows
that could have been.
But shudder the thought;
by what I've seen.

For all those tomorrows,
that would have been;
still can be:
what I've dreamed.

The Tears I Cry
Abbey Arwood
I hope you see why,
Things like that make me cry,
Just remember whatever you do,
I cried these tears out of my love for you.

You are a very big piece of my heart,
The saddest day will be the day we part.
Whenever you go, whatever you do,
I'll cry these tears out of my love for you.

You treat me nice and act like you care,
I didn't know there were guys like that out there.
Tears of happiness and tears that are sad too,
I cried these tears all because of you.

Sometimes I don't understand why,
But I will just sit and cry,
My tears are cried, but for who,
I know, my tears are cried for you.

One thing I don't understand why,
Is why you say that you don't cry.
Just so you know,
I cry my tears because you don't let yours go.

Indiana Autumn
Jean G. O'Brien
The deep green leaves of summer are now a thing of the past
And the many colors of fall are too beautiful to last.
Bright blue skies glow through red and yellow leaves,
While the warm sunny days give way to a cool evening breeze.

The sweet corn and big red tomatoes are gone.
Cool crisp apples are here.
Pumpkins smile from many porches,
Announcing that Halloween is near.

When we were young, we lay on haystacks
And gazed at a big friendly moon.
We counted the stars and planned our holidays –
They just couldn't come too soon!

With a hint of burning leaves in the air,
We walked the country roads still warm at night
Lined with fading fireflies,
Too fragile now to take flight.

All these natural wonders
Seldom appreciated before,
Are gathered in the fall
Right outside our door.

Dedication: To my children, with love

A Lover's Walk
Mary MacPhee
The wonder of my woodland walk,
Where birds and bees and insects talk,
And in the tarn upon a frond,
Swims a toad in his little pond.

While branches stir in a gentle breeze,
And lovers trample fallen leaves,
Where time goes by, But Oh! So fast,
Dear God! Please make this moment last.

The Soul Is Not Willing
Krysta Hill
Flying through the sky,
Carried on a breeze,
A last calling cry
Is heard through the trees.

A soul now departs
Upon the winds of change,
Whose constant shifting course
Remains puzzled and strange.

But the soul is not willing,
For strong is his tie
To the body on the ground
Not wanting to die.

But the breeze does not stop
For the soul who is torn
Between his rightful place
And where he was born.

Condemned to travel
A desolate land,
By a force he knows,
But has yet to understand.

Jumping The Moon
Revena M. Pollard
When I was just a little girl
a long, long time ago.
I lived out in the big old woods
in a house of just four rooms.

I thought I could do most anything,
and some I dared to try,
but the thing I wanted the most to do
was jump that moon in the sky.

When I was just a little girl,
I played out in the woods.
I ran and jumped most everything
just to see if I could.

When the sun went down, and the moon came up
I wondered if I tried–
I could jump that big old moon
hanging up in that sky.

As years went by and I grew up,
I came to realize
there's other ways to reach that moon
than jumping it in the sky.

Dedication: To my sister, Wanda

Grandma
Denise A. Bowser
Going places that are fun
Reading books when day is done
Always there no matter when
Never too busy for hugs and grins
Dear to all who are lucky to know
My wonderful grandma who always shows
A place where love forever grows

Dedication: My wonderful grandma, love Carly

The Lost
Jacquelyn Danks
Never without emptiness, floating on a lake of fire,
I'm consumed by loneliness and fear.
No one knows my world, for there is no way in or out
Everyone recalls the story of the boy who called wolf
They say I cry wolf too often, myself.
I wish my life were so easy as to make people rush to my aid.

The storm within me slips out, now and again,
I am always in trouble that one cannot see.
People's ears are full, and I am but a fly
Making noises no one cares to hear.
So, I weep for my losses alone, quietly
So no one will hear if I call "wolf".

No one touches the pain, the flame that consumes fiercely.
Without hope, without dreams, once again, I am alone.
"WOLF!"
See, it doesn't work, none rush to my aid, no one cares
about a pesky, old fly, buzzing around heedlessly
Life nor death holds comfort,
I am invisible, the unwanted soul
I am lost!.

Dedication: Harry Lenhart, a true friend

Faces In Life
Pamela J. Weaver
Many kinds of pain, in life you may feel
Much anger, disappointments, that are real
Joys in life come and go, but there's one thing I know
You can count on Jesus, all your life through

Can you see the baby crying, hear a Mother's sweet lullaby
Hear the soldiers fighting, see them go down
Hear the cries and anger, see the sadness all around
And do you see the funny–face clown

He is with you and hears your many cries
He can comfort you like a soft lullaby
He will carry your many burdens, as he did from the start
The love of Jesus will never depart

Happy go lucky funny–face clown
He always knows, whenever you're feeling down
He understands your heartache, pain and fears
He can comfort you now and all through the years

He will show you the path, in which to take
He lightens the heart, whenever it breaks
You can count on Jesus, through life's ups and downs
He sees the frown on the funny face clown

Dedication: Janet, Dana, Jade, Gary, Joshua

Dreams of the Soul

The Poem Coretta Found In Her Head
Coretta Rybeck
Far away where stardust swirls
in giant whirls
And fairies dance
on unicorns' backs
And magic is very common
The future lies in
children's dreams.
Could our two worlds
walk hand in hand?

A Drive in Springtime
Isabel Reed
Comfortable car, seat belts adjusted.
Car driven through country scenes.

Towering trees, birds' nests,
Maintained hedgerows, occasional tractor.
Bird song fills the air.
Sheep grazing in grassy fields with frisky young lambs.
A village in bloom.

Blossoming almond, lilac and forsythia.
Attractive shops, flower displays.
Daffodils, delphiniums, and pansies.
Thatched cottages, Tudor style houses.
A Norman church nearby.

Joyful wedding bells,
bride and bridegroom at the door.
Well wishers throw confetti,
Couple walk to the lych gate
Where the open landau is waiting.

Our journey continues
Through quiet country roads,
Heading for home and afternoon tea.

Beauty With Age
Anne Coldiron
Beauty is not
the color of my eyes,
The color of my hair or
the clothes I wear.

Beauty is within my skin
Being able to lose as well as win.
Being able to give as well as receive
Trust in God
in all I believe.

The wrinkled skin, the sagging chin
are life's rewards for growing within.
Without them there would be no way
to define the beauty
of our passing time.

Goodbye yesterday.
Hello! for today.
Don't question time
It's gone away.
But there you are for another day.

Wake up in the morning look within
You're a beautiful woman
underneath all that skin.

An Epitaph
Patricia Miller
The flowers are blooming
And life must go on;
Her memories are looming
Through the dusk and the dawn;
No more to laugh
No more to weep;
For she shall have eternal sleep.

Dedication: Memory of Linda Faye Huff

How Come?
Minor Busby
How come! You till the earth and plant the seed
Because your family has a need
But unless you cultivate just so
Your plants will just refuse to grow.

And if good weather doesn't hold
Or turns too dry or hot or cold
They'll simply not cooperate
and so for veggies you'll have to wait.

But if they grow and look all right
Then bugs will eat them overnight
But what about those awful weeds?
You didn't even plant the seeds.

But grow they will no matter why
and it never gets too hot or dry
It seems they grow to aggravate
and brother will they proliferate.

And not a bug in his right mind
Would on a weed commence to dine
Without one bit of tilling done
They'll grow so lush, please sir! How come?

Faith
Thomas S. Holliday
When I look upon the trials that come,
the toils that come in other's lives;
I wonder if I would so strive
to trust in Thee as they have done.

An easier thing it is to say;
to speak of faith, of how I run;
than peer through clouds that hide the sun
to smile with joy, and know Thy peace.

God grant that I when trials smite,
that I may pray as these others can
with faith in Thee, and Thy great might;
with heaven before me, and eternal day.

Though countless times I've mouthed the words,
the thoughts that should by words ensue
are absent, thrust out,
burned off like dew.

Yet when sight is clear, and heart is right;
when thoughts that should by words ensue
come rushing, burning in
rekindling my faith anew.

Dedication: Pat Gates

Ferns
Kathryn Johnson
Ferns grow like us,
Sheltered by the elder, bigger trees.
They stay inverted in their own thoughts
Until they learn
Enough to extend silently outward
Into the world.
And though they're old enough, wise enough
They like best the shade of the trees
Where they never fully leave the shelter of their roots.

Power Of Positive Thinking
Laurabelle Martin
Try this exceptional skill of achievement,
Very simple and easy to master.
It can be learned at a very young age
And over time helps to prevent disaster.

Take pride in whatever you've accomplished
And you'll build a sense of self-worth.
This growing power within you
Will ensure success to come forth.

You'll learn its powers are awesome
When confronting the most difficult work.
But, so amazing can be the outcome
You won't have to feel like a jerk.

Learn to be optimistic in the beginning
And the world will seem brighter and gay.
Many more things can be accomplished
Making you happier with each new day.

Always think of yourself succeeding
In whatever you set out to do.
This power of positive thinking
Will bring out the very best in you.

Bond Of Friendship
Robin Collins
There is a special feeling
Inside my heart for you
This precious bond of friendship
Happens to so very few.

Such a sweet relationship
Upon us now descends
As we share our hopes and dreams
And even some things mend.

This special bond of friendship
Grows a little more each day
Its having someone to count on
When things aren't going your way.

It's someone you can count on
In good times and in bad
To help your share your joy
And even share your sad.

It's someone you can count on
To have a listening ear
It's someone you can trust
To be there through the years.

Dedication: My children, Amy and Andrew

Fluffie
J. Granger
Gone the little padding paws, the gentle sweet meow,
My dainty ball of fluffy fur, I wish I had you Know,
The joy you gave, with love sincere, as much as you were able,
To think we only called you Cat, an unrealistic label!

To me you were the strings of love of a heavenly guitar,
Now you are so far away as the highest star.
All that I have to remember you is just a tiny cross.
And nothing in this whole wide world can compensate my loss.

Little Things
Ruth E. Steepy
Little things you say and do,
show me that you care.
Maybe you don't realize,
But you've begun to stare.

And when I raise my eyes to yours,
I feel I'm hypnotized,
Your eyes say many things to me.
They simply mesmerize.

You truly fascinate me,
Of that I can't deny.
You're different than the others,
On you, I can rely,

To say kind things about me
And never let me down,
When I need picking up again,
You seem to be around,

To keep my spirits soaring high,
To keep me going strong.
I can always count on you, it's true.
It's the little things you say and do.

Peace
Katherine Kindred
Make peace not war
Be peaceable all the time
Let's be peace makers
And not peace breakers

Let peace be our motto we carry
With us through the day
Wish peace and good will to
Everyone who comes your way

Let's stop this madness
Of hating because of color
Let's start loving each other

It's never too late
To turn things around
Let's put all these weapons
Of hate down

Think peace not hate
Hold your peace
Live in peace
Go and Come in Peace
Go and Come in Peace

Dedication: James Douglass Moore, Sr.

Dreams of the Soul

Love Is
Erica Ortiz
love is like a flower
if you water it
and care for it,
it will grow,
but if you leave it
without water it
will die.
Dedication: Lisa Baker and Tara Trujillo

My Little Embryo
Christine Diana
Oh, little embryo, How I loved you so!
Why God let me let you go,
I will never know.

People say you weren't a baby just a seed,
Like that will make me feel better,
In my moment of need.

Though I never knew if you were a boy or girl,
Not that it would make a difference,
All I know I would have loved you so,
And that I will always miss you.

When you passed through my womb,
I could not stand the pain
It wasn't for the physical; it was
the mental strain, of never knowing
What you may have looked like, or
holding you in my arms.

So little embryo your angel has come,
And one day we will meet,
Just know that I love you, even
though I never got to know you.

Clowns
Edith Foster
Different faces – and different names,
But my family of clowns
Are all still the same.

Set in a place of honor to see
After all they are all family to me!

I watch them with wonder, what do they see
Behind all the masks that they show me

Does a smile mean they're happy or just hiding a tea
Do they change their expressions whenever we're near

the mask of a clown – can cover up pain
make a child full of joy
make the world smile again
the show must go on, but without the clown
the cares of the world
would keep us all down.

A clown brings on smiles
When heartaches come round
But God pity a world
Without laughter of clowns
Dedication: Staff of Rock Creek Center

Untitled
Amanda Muffett
Life is but an illusion,
Something that's not real.
Something you can't see or touch,
Something you can't steal.

Dreams are a reality,
Lasting only a day.
Then like a life, it vanishes,
It slowly fades away.

War
Karen Tioran
A dissent between someone and their adherents,
Causes many struggles in human history,
To make things better is their cry,
But peace, my friend, you cannot buy.

They disagree about how it is being done,
But their voices will not be heard,
Stand up and speak for yourself,
But mark my word, war is not the only way out.

Off the innocent go to fight,
Wondering if what they are doing is right,
They leave all they own behind them,
Family, love, possessions and reality.

They fight and struggle day after day,
Seeing blood being shed along the way,
Dead bodies piling up beside one another,
And messages being sent home to their loved ones.

The corpse they place in the bier,
To be carried to the grave,
And lowered beneath the broken ground,
To be forever in its sleeping place.

Take My Hand
Brenda L. Peterson
Take my hand my love.
Walk with me side by
side.
Letting our hearts be
the guide.
We can face any hardships
that come along.
Because together we are
Strong.
I for you and you for me.
That is what was meant to be.
Shield me my Love from my
Heartaches and fears.
With just your touch, I'll
make it through the day.
Letting your smile light my
way.
With just a touch and a smile,
I can face whatever comes my way.
Believe in me my love, as I believe
in you.
I see your strengths.
In me you can see tomorrow,
with what it can be.
You and I can make this a better
Place, together hand in hand.

Noteworthy Works

It Is Time
Mary Rozanna Allensworth

There will come a time,
When all the world will know,
That Jesus is coming,
Because the Bible says it's so.

So tell all the doubters,
Spread the word,
Jesus Christ is coming,
Because the Bible says it's so.

What If?
Mary R. Ward

What if I'm a frowny face and you're a
big, big smile?
I hope you'll come and live with me — and
stay a long, long while.

What if I was a rain cloud — and you
were a drop of rain?
We'd sail the sky and passing by, we'd
cool the hot, dry plain!

What if I was a little bird — and you were
a big, big tree?
I'd light on you and sing my songs. How
happy we would be!

What if I was the big, blue moon — and you
were a shining star?
Then we could always see our friends —
no matter where they are!

What if I was this little book – and you
were my best friend?
You'd turn right back and read me —
Again, again, again!!

School Days
Delroy Henry

On Monday morning I was late,
At dinner time someone threw a plate.
In the afternoon it began to rain,
And everybody was a pain.

On Tuesday morning after swimming,
I joined the choir to do some singing.
I was so loud I broke all the glass,
I thought the teacher would kick me up the a**.

On Wednesday morning I was ill,
My mum called a doctor who gave me a pill,
He told me I had got the flu,
Before I got up and ran to the loo.

On Thursday morning I did some Art,
But my friend laughed so hard he began to fa**.
I tried to ignore him as I noticed a cute girl,
But the smell was so bad I just wanted to hurl.

On Friday I felt totally drained,
My back hurt and my neck pained.
I thought about Tuesday swimming in the pool,
I'm glad today is the last day of school.

Dedication: *Mum, Gran and H. G. S. – Cheers!*

A Visiting Painter
Deborah Rohan

From the cool and misty dark
Each morn the flame does rise.
His rays of light provide the paint
His canvas, open skies.

As if to say "Just look at me!"
He rises, claiming all
And watching over all of us,
Becomes a brilliant ball.

He then proceeds to paint a base
Of blue for the work called "Day".
Then deftly adds strange shapes in white
That quickly shift and play.

The cozy sphere must leave us now
It seems like we've just met.
He gives us one last work of his,
The painting called "Sunset".

The warmth is gone, the canvas blank.
No color, paint, or fun.
But in our dreams we see the return
Of the painter we call sun.

The School Of Hard Knocks
Jeanette Harrington

The school of hard knocks is a place
Where we all at some time must go;
But the lessons we learn stick with us
While the winds of adversity blow.

Our character is craftily molded
By the God of mercy and love;
He's the Author and Finisher of our faith
To make us like Jesus above.

The Song Of The Wheel
Vivian Stratton

Many the miles I rolled – rough and rugged
the trail–
Up to the peaks and down – then through a
quiet vale.
Fording the rushing streams, resting
by campfire's glow,
Rolling a gain with the dawn, creaking,
protesting and slow.

Heavy the load that I bore–valued by men
very dearly,
For it, they struggled and died–why, I could
never see clearly.
Sweat and tears was the cost– and often,
even their blood
All for those chunks of rock, that bogged
me down in the mud

Now, I am resting at last, glad to be through
with my task.
Gone is the noise and the strife, this peak
is all that I ask.
Here by the side of the trail, this boulder
my only companion.
I wait out the long, quiet years, in the
solitude of the canyon.

Dreams of the Soul

Young Mother's Prayer
Bill Wietrick

Help us Lord, oh this we pray
This child our love, has borne today
To watch her grow so straight and strong
To teach her both what's right and wrong

To guide her through each bright new day
And help and teach and show the way
To show the beauty in all things
And the wonders each new day brings

Although this baby was not planned
We'll watch her crawl—then she will stand
She'll grow up strong—straight as a rod
This newborn babe—our gift from God

The things she learns will always be
From both her Father and from me
We'll show the flowers and the birds
And teach the comfort of your words

And remember each and every night
When we love and hold her tight
And when drowsy, she begins to nod
How special is—our gift from God

Self-Portrait
Ashley Dunnigan

My hair is like leaves on a spring tree
that sways back and forth in the wind,
My eyes are like the brownness of tree's bark.
My teeth are as white as snow,
My body is as tall as a one-year-old tree.
My heart holds great wonders and fear.
My thoughts are as blue as the sky.

Dedication: To my family, with love

Father's Day
Billy D. Rains, Jr.

I'm grateful on this Father's Day,
As my children stand before me.
I'm proud of each and I can say,
They are my true immortality.

My first-born gift is almost a woman now,
She's so beautiful and smart.
We don't always agree, but anyhow,
She holds a deep spot in my heart.

My middle gift is my only son.
He's smart, handsome and strong.
He'll carry our name to the next generation,
He'll be a man before too long.

My youngest gift is the most like me.
She's strong-willed and independent.
Pretty and smart with a touch of tomboy,
A purer flower... God never sent.

Yes, I appreciate God's gifts to me,
On this glorious Father's Day.
All good things in life are truly free,
I love them all in a special way.

Dedication: My loving wife, Diane

Consider Prayer
Cleve Cullers

All prayers should address "Sovereign Lord",
In whom we praise, honor and look toward
Living with, when earth–life is o'er,
And all the saints who have gone before.

The renowned Supreme power of all times
Will listen to us confess our crimes.
He forgives and forgets the same
He even erases sin and blame.

How great an honor we are awarded
When we submit to his holy order.
The throne room is available to one and all
Every twenty-four hours to receive our call.

We ask for wisdom without boycott
He answers all and upbraideth not,
Total forgiveness and not just once.
Is freely given in abundance.

To be a Christian is truly divine
Better than all riches combined.
More rewarding than love of a Mother
Is to know that Christ as elder brother.

The Maze
Elizabeth A. Cyr

I'm alone trapped in this maze
Created by my own heartache
The leaves crackled underneath my feet as I walk
I stop to listen to the ringing in my ears caused by the silence
My voice calls out to the shadows of the dark
I began to cry
I realized I was stuck here with the maze and along with its silence

Dedication: My mom who inspired me (Aunt Sandy)

The Soul
Yvonne Highfield

True, honest, forever love comes from the deepest
and most holiest part of your heart.

It is the most vulnerable part for it lays itself
open to you and puts its trust in you not to
hurt it... ever.

This most honest of loves has no walls of
coldness for protection.
It's gentle, loving and trusting soul makes it
vulnerable to the diseases of life.

The most contagious disease for honest love
is the cancer of lies... lies... lies.

Lies eat at this gentle soul and coldness
creeps across to protect it from the cancer.

Coldness covers the warmth and tries to heal
its wounds, to repair this gentle love and return
it to its once grand appearance.
for all the heart loves this section the most.
It is the soul of the being and must be guarded.

Lies kill the loving soul.
Coldness protects the warm soul.

Big Black Spider
William B. Jones

Hey there big black spider
you're trapped in your now web
no, you're not stuck to it
but without it, you'd be dead

Hey there big black spider
you never venture very far
you build your web, your web of life
you wait and there you are

Hey there big black spider
a prisoner to your own devices
without a web, you can't live
when it's torn, you have a crisis

Hey there big black spider
do you think that you're not free
does it bother you, the least bit
that you can't leave like me

Hey there big black spider
be careful of the net you cast
for if by chance, the wrong bug's caught
you'll find he'll be your last

Earthly Trait
Mary Lou Cole

Tiny flowers beckon from the shadows
Enhancing my woodland retreat
With anxious hand did set your seed
To huddle by my path and greet

Essence exposed, and trusting face
You yield to your earthly fate
To renew, to sprout, to floreate
Unaware of your rueful trait

Our Cat Bimbo
Ellen Chiasson

We have a big old tom cat as cute as he can be.
His head is big, his belly fat and he cuddles on our knees.

He wakes us at four–twenty, oh, so early in the morn.
His food is not so plenty so he "meows" with such scorn.

Bimbo's such a saucy kitty, why do we love him so?
You'd think he is a preacher the way he "growls" so low!

Pampers his favorite cat food, smacks his lips with glee.
This pussy cats' so greedy he'd even eat a flea!

Bimbo likes to play outside and roll upon the grass,
Every time he hears a noise, he jumps up in a flash!

The Smith's cat is his best friend, he too is big and fat.
How can they spend all their time just lying on their backs?

The King's next door don't like him, he litters on their lawn.
If he was a person, he'd have to use the "john".

Garfield might be famous, but, Bimbo make no mistake,
Could make a mint in show biz if he wasn't such a fake.

Enough, about our tom cat there's more to life than this.
It's time to clean up cat hairs and fill his empty dish!

By Nature
Sonia Vallabh

Slowly I crawl
for that is my way
night by night
day by day.
I crawl
peacefully
over a flower
minute by minute
hour by hour
for that is a ladybug's way.

The Lady's Chair
R. Albert Canger

It was a massive thing, all carved of woods from distant lands.
"With attic dust, its velvet seat and polished arms, should not covered be.
Pray bring it down for me."

A sense of doing good, with muscles strong as steel, so I said "Yes".
Up I flew, two flights of steep and twisting stairs.
With it upon my back, I started down, free handed, with a flair.
It weighed a ton!

The sweat began to flow, my breath grew short, I gulped for air,
My eyes began to bulge, I groaned beneath the load,
I clung for life onto the shaky balustrade, my legs were bowed.

It tried to toss me headlong down the stairs.
At last the end. Exhausted, aching, worn, I sat me down.
"Not there!" "You're fat!" "Your weight's too much to bear!"
How dare I sit me down in that sweet lady's chair.

Those Hard Times
Barbara Ann Hartley

It was hard work in those days
digging shoveling grafting away
get up at five pick up me snap
Light a cig and walk two miles

When I got to pit to my locker
I would go to change my clothes
To go down below.

Get working hard lads the
Boss would say, then you'll get
extra money in your wage Friday

I hope the next shift works as
hard as us. Then I'll be able
to buy some snuff.

Up the shaft and back on land
To smell the air, boy it's grand.

Off to baths at the pit stop
good afternoon is that you pop.

There's plenty of coal at your
seam. I'm off home now
To my wife and family.

Dreams of the Soul

The Question Left Behind
Dianne Cummings
You're in our hearts forever, no matter what they say.
It will never be "Goodbye my Dad", just "Goodnight and have a nice day".
You're up there with your Father and resting all the time,
but, you left a question here behind for us to make up our minds.
"Will this be Goodnight my Child or shall we say Goodbye?
Only you will know the answer if the Lord is on your side".
"I want to see you once again and sit there by your side. So please don't let this be Goodbye, for you only have a short time to make up your minds".

Fighting Me
Maria J. Imperiale
Deny it as you only can.
Cover your eyes for as long as you want.
I will not go away.

I can't make this easy for you because
It's too hard for me.
I won't let you win.

I don't know who is more blind.
So little time you have for me.
So much more you spend with her.

You ask me for my one and most precious gift.
How, when you are not mine?
You will leave me once I give you what you want.

I will always be on your mind.
You can't erase me.

I am a fantasy in your worst nightmare
and nothing but a dream.

Dedication: Carmella Decola– my guardian angel

Beauty Endures
James Sabo
To love a beautiful woman
Is hardly a difficult chore
Especially when thought word and action
Enhance that beauty still more

When years erode outer beauty
And time starts to lessen her grace
A mature woman's true attraction
Does not yield to the rush of the pace

For the beauty that lies in her person
Is not glamour that gladdens the eye
But the glow of it shines from within her
And its radiance refuses to die

Personality ripened by wisdom
Lends spice that is better than par
And the smile that once was so fetching
Is much lovelier now by far

Men who are loved by such women
Have been wondrously blessed by fate
And the greatest of all life's adventures
Is to be chosen by one as a mate

Dedication: Dorothy, my wife and inspiration

Dark Thoughts
Gary F. Leonard
From nowhere thoughts,
dark as a winter night.
Peace disappears,
like a bat in blackness.
A past love gone.
A future tainted,
by a simian touch.
Oh to be back,
on the south side of Sumeru,
where a crystal tree shines.

TV Guide – Please Read As – My Holy Bible
Sorrow Julian
I turned the television off an hour ago.
Can't remember the last time I tuned out.
I guess it must have been about three months ago.
That's the nearest I can figure it.
That's when you left and the silence and loneliness became unbearable.
I turned on my softly glowing companion and it's taken all this time to turn off again.
I sit paralysed by the blackness.
I can feel the electrical charge sucking out of the room.
The static settling as the molecules de–charge.
I believe the withdrawal is starting.
My soporific brain is tingling with the fear of having to think for itself.
Can't cope.
Won't cope!
If I can just make it through the night without tuning in again then maybe I'll be OK.
If not then I know for sure I'm never making it out of this room again.
My hands are twitching for something to do.
Before I notice I've scratched my arm so badly the old scars are open and flowing again.
Anything to pass the suddenly endless time.
What did I used to do all day?
Pray for me Mr. TV.

Happiness
Eloise Wilson
As difficult to grasp and hold,
As feathers in a breeze.
As "fleeting" in its time with us,
As sunset on the seas.

Capricious "twinklings" out of time,
From whence? Oh! here and there!
So precious in its rarity,
It's yearned for everywhere.

Prized by men around the world,
To make this life worth living.
Without a price, untouchable,
Within us for the giving.

HAPPINESS unshared is lost,
Regained by many trials.
Lest we forget! Of all God's things!
It's only man, who smiles!

'Tis only those like unto Him,
Who weep for love of others.
Only man knows "HAPPINESS",
And shares it with his brothers!

Dedication: My precious daughter, Ronda

My Guiding Light
Glenda Louise Lucero

The Lord above is my guiding light.
He'll keep my angels in his sight.
He'll give me love with leaps and bounds;
No matter where I am journey bound.
He'll wrap me in his loving arms.
And protect me from the world's harm.
He'll comfort me in my hours of need;
And I will not even have to plead.
And when night falls and it is dark;
The Lord above will remain within my heart.

Pain!
Helen L. Strom

Out there... the sun is shining;
But my soul is pining, whining;
Evil thoughts in mind entwining;
On pain and grief, always dining;
My will to live... oft declining.
I wish to live... Nevermore.

Life is bleak, I'm a freak;
An antique, grown weak.
Peace I seek, soul doth shriek;
I cannot speak; I only squeak... Evermore.

Tired of feeling, mind is reeling;
Is there healing?... Nevermore.
Night comes stealing, darkness revealing
Pain I'm concealing... Evermore.

Soft, slinky shadows, slip into my soul;
Thoughts straying, body swaying;
Torment staying, voice saying,
I must live... Nevermore.

Dedication: My beloved son "Tracy–Bird"

Mutton Man
M. F. Russell

They lived in the mountains, way up in the hills,
No 'lectricity, piped water, or telephone bills,
But once every month that old mutton man came,
To visit the Russells, they know not his name.

But young Phillip Russell was so much impressed,
By that mutton man, though his folks never guessed,
'Til one day their Phillip stood on the front step,
And knocked on that door with such vigor and pep:

"Mutton Man," he said in his best salesman voice,
"Would you like to buy some, I have a good choice."
Those make–believe goodies he had in a sack,
Were tied to a tree branch slung over his back.

So from that day on Phillip's nickname was Mutt,
Named for the man by whom he was so struck,
'Cause that mutton man sold them good things to eat,
And his monthly visits were really a treat.

It's been a long time since he lived in those hills,
Now there's power, and water and telephone bills,
But to all his kinfolk, he's still Mutton Man,
And they still adore him, that whole Russell clan!

Dedication: Phillip and Lucky; Mom's inspirations

Sleeping Beauty
Arnold Leuenberger, Jr.

Amidst the quiescent pulchritude, a putrescent
carcass lay; the majestic form of a maiden, fair, dead
since the previous day.
Her eyes lay open but cannot see that my heart is
broken. The query rested on her lips, forever now
unspoken.
"Had she known my love for her, then this would
not have happened. But, I, the introvert, could not
commit a morganatic sin. By not revealing my love for
her, it was I that did her in."

Creation
LoriLee Litman

Part One: Anticipation
The anticipation of one kiss, One...
The hours, days had gradually lengthened.
Time seemed endless, until...
Finally. ... the touch of his sweet lips
Under the bright, full moon,
Replenished my soul with essence.
All the iniquities of the world had become antiquated.
Time, had taken possession of–
Tranquility...

Part Two: Desire

Serenity appears in chosen forms.
Waiting to share stolen moments...
It seemed time could disguise minutes from days.
When his arms were around me.
It felt as if I had always been there.
Then, out of desire... life was created.
Love's incessant force will now–
Possess no boundaries...

Dedication: To my daughter, with love...

Once More With Feelings
Luisangel De Ramirez

I didn't question you were dead, for I knew that to be true.
You just seem a little tired, not really well or ill... yet your
gracefulness and beauty slightly tinged by sorrow and
expectation, which produced upon your face a thoughtful
heartfelt grace.

But, even in my dream I thought you were out, perhaps
at work: or experiencing a great time, almost energized.
We seemed to be going away from an old house we've
lived. Everything was in disarray... there were boxes
everywhere.

Even asleep I was violently out of focus by your face,
the physical recognition of your face inches away from
mine, smiling lovingly and very alert. It was difficult
remembering your actual look without exertion.

Therefore when I saw your reliable face, your unmistakable
gaze generating all that warmth and clarity of you; we embrace
each other for the time my dream allowed us.

Sincerely you have come back to me, so I could gaze
at you once more, so I'll be able to hold you tenderly...
without feeling that this happiness would undoubtedly
depreciate anything or without thinking you were alive
once more.

Dreams of the Soul

Darling Fred
Hilda Barnes
I love you wait for me
please bear the pain,
That's selfish of me
Please my love wait for me
I love you so, I won't be
long.
I'll come with you
we must be together
Just you and me
For ever

A Best Friend
Wanda Perkins
A best friend is someone I can share anything with...
My thoughts, my dreams—
Whether silly or sweet,
happy or sad.
My hopes, my fears,
my triumphs, my failures,
will be easier with you standing behind me,
never sitting in judgement, just encouraging me to try again.

The wonderful memories between us are in abundance—
unhappy are so few.
There is no one in the world like you,
who believes in me,
more than I believe in myself sometimes.
Who has confidence that I'll do the right thing.
Who has high moral standards and abides by them.
Who follows the rules and encourages me to do the same.
What more could you ask for in friend?

Nothing at all...

Thank you God for sending me this special gift—
My best friend.

Nature's Sign
Lisa G. Newell
I can see the rain falling down
From the window nearby,
As the birds take shelter,
From the storm in the sky.
The trees appear bare,
With their slick winter glare,
From the moisture they hold
Within the air.

And the leaves have fallen to
the ground,
From the wind that rustled them
With its whistling sound.

Patiently I wait for the rainbow to appear,
It's the sign from above telling us
The storm is all clear.

I'd like to feel the warmth from the sun,
Breathing down from the Atmosphere.
Then I'll know the rain has
stopped,
And the sunny day
is finally here.

Dedication: Michael, Chris, Brian, Keith, Newell

The Pleasure Seekers
E. C. Tyler
Pine trees swaying in time with breaking waves, slapping
gently on the shore as if applauding nature's handicraft.
The two blues, of deep, distant and shallow, shoreland sea.
Crystal clear, reflecting the glow of azure sky into eyes
of city dwellers reaping their reward for months of toil.

Careworn sluggish, grey white bodies of newcomers slowly
assuming a golden ambience.
Moving awkwardly at first, then more freely as if they
realised that this should be their earned inheritance.

My Hero
Judith A. Ross
You're my knight
in shining armor –
The man that I adore...

You're everything
I dreamed of
And a whole lot more...

Although I'm less
than perfect –
You've never put me down.

If you were a king...
You'd be worthy
of your crown.

You're a very special person –
Sent to me...
from above.

God was watching over me,
And blesses me
With your Love...

The Smell Of Nature
Mary J. Jarbeau
As I gaze over the valley, crystal clear
The smell of God's earth, is very near
The swaying flowers, they smell so sweetly
God in his wisdom, has arranged so neatly.
The hills and the valleys, they meander along
The trees and the shrubs, here they belong.
The sky with its billowy clouds in the air
The sun shining through, this day is so fair.
The breeze touching softly on each child's face
As they play along, stop, and tie their shoelaces
The stream babbles along, aside of the hill
As I gaze to my left, I see a sawmill
The birds are all singing a sweet lullaby
To their young in the nest, who can't yet fly
The bees are all busy, collecting their honey
Then out from a bush, hops a little gray bunny
The ants are busy, building their mounds
Bringing back home, the food that they've found
Even the flies, belong here on earth
But to us humans they have really no worth
A dog runs on by, carrying his bone
He barks at the kids, saying it's time to go home
As I turn around, with the children to leave
This isn't the time, or the place to grieve
For as you look around, God's precious earth
If you look very closely, there's always a new birth.

Noteworthy Works

Clashing Personalities
Christine Thompson

Dear little sister –
Its been four long years
Since we last spoke.
Little do you realise,
With those harsh words,
My heart you broke.

How I wish we could make amends
and once again,
become sisters and friends

Wondering Mind
Brigit Kibunguchi

On the chair I sit with my eyes open.
Staring at the screen, which cannot communicate
My mind wondering around like a lost lamb,
On the blank screen know not what to convey
Is it love or a nightmare.

Nites and days pass by like directionless wind
It is that pigeon I dreamt of
The one that had flown from the east
Making my mind scattered as grass
Is it love or a nightmare.

Strong feeling I never experienced
Know not how to define it
It feels like slow dancing dolphins in the sea
Wondering to myself
Is it love or a nightmare

I thought will dream not like this
In my mind it clicks, my soul it rests,
In my body it tickles like an itch
How long is it to last
I hope it is love not a nightmare.

A Perception Of Love
Kristine Emerson

Love is like a River
feeding into an Ocean
so deep and Beautiful.

Love is like a newborn Baby
taking their first breath of Life.

Love is like a child's Laughter
filling the Air
with Warmth and Delight.

Love is like a Family
being Together
for the Night.

Love is like Nature
so mysterious yet it Echoes
through the Land.

Love is Precious
for all of us
no matter how
it may be perceived.

For the Lord is Love
and our everlasting light to see.

TV Widow
Alice Jane Tally

He calls it his baby,
He calls it his toy,
From this darn old thing
He seems to get his joy.
He has no time for anything
Else that is plain to see,
So one of these days I'm going
To break that blasted old TV.

Dedication: To wives everywhere who lost their husbands to TV

The Light
Susan Hoffman

On that day with the sun, I basked in the solace of the light,
Delighted in the warmth as I inhaled the perfumed essence.
I felt my soul caressed with comfort,
But on this day I forgot its source
And the care required to appreciate its presence.

On that day the sun did not appear
And my myopic vision searched for the light
To ease my strife.
On that day I could not focus
And felt little comfort from the dull glimmer.
It could not supply me with the warmth
For I closed the doors to my heart.

On that day the searching began
And I felt no longer abandoned.
The path of my journey let to an opening in the sky
And the light that had never neglected my spirit

On this day I plant the seeds in my heart
That with tender nurturing
Will blossom into a garden where the light will always
Shine with me.

Memories
Jim Marshall

Nostalgically, I often think
Of years long, long ago
When I, like many millions more
Left home to fight the foe

Our nation's life was threatened
Freedom's flame was burning dim
Against the foe, we stood alone
With survival looking grim.

Streets were dark, food was short
Sleep disturbed as sirens sounded
Our cities blitzed, our people killed
Our island home surrounded.

For six long years we battled
On sea, land, and in the air
Through Europe, desert and jungle
'Til victory, peace, the last 'all clear'.

I'll never forget those war–time years
And Britain's courageous stand
I'm proud perhaps my little part
Helped save our precious land.

Dedication: My wife Bette – Joyce and Carole

Dreams of the Soul

A Walk With Grandad
Jean Stevenson
As I walk through the meadows
Wild flowers all around
Memories come flooding back of many years ago
Walking hand in hand with Grandad
On how I loved him so.
His suntanned face brow creased with age
A life spent toiling on the land.
He'd always time to listen
And seemed to understand
Yes, my Grandad was just grand!

The Rubaiyat Of A Galway Donkey
Katie Kent
My donkey, "Hairy Engine",
Was sharp, swift and intelligent,
The loveliest donkey ever
To graze in a Galway field.

We grew up together in an Irish village;
I could catch, harness and yoke her to her trap
For the weekly shopping trip.
"Hairy Engine" was 12 hands of chestnut sweetness;
She was of no breeding, but I had seen
The countryside on her back.

She was gentle and knowing,
Did a perfect trot, her lovely mane
Weaving as she trotted along.
Perfect was her animal highway code.

The years rolled on,
No more quick movements to her stride.
Her unconquerable spirit
Met the end she would have desired:
A peaceful death in her own Galway cabin.
"Hairy Engine" was a lucky, happy donkey.

Easter Morning
F. Hannah
"All of one mind; let us be."
Appalachian violins, tapping feet.
Sing with me; I sing with you:
this day is new.

Easter Hallelujah
come from the Bose radio,
whizzing coffee grinder,
whining can opener left by Sam;
from old Cat squalling in the garage,
"Feed Me, Now!"

Hallelujah from the crack of my back;
the creak of my chair, soft
whistle sigh of my breath; pad
pad of my sandaled heels on bricks.

Violins from Appalachia: alto ratchet
ripples; lute, flute and laughter.
Murky morning, thick silver and wet.
No sunrise. Dayenu! Dayenu! Daylight!

Tap the beat, tap down feet.
Raise the cup. Black Bitter brew.
I choose to Hum: to crack with Smiles.
Dancing, Dancing for You.

Harbinger Of Spring
Marion E. Plaus
Welcome back, little bird
It is a joy to hear you sing
Your lovely melody is a harbinger of spring
Sunny skies, green grass and flowers
A welcome respite from cold, wind and
icy showers
Build your nest in a nearby tree
Let your song awaken me
When you leave again in the fall
I shall await your springtime call

Ode To T. L. (Red) Morris Of Taffy Three
W. Lee Andrus
No stone marker o'er Red's grave,
Fate chose his wet enclave,
He bravely fought the evil knave,
Now he lies beneath the wave,
Red, who died of Taffy Three.

Red's apt reward is justly paid,
He seeks no holiday's parade,
Nor impassioned accolade,
But a debt was surely made,
By Red's deeds with Taffy Three.

No field where poppies grow,
Nor white crosses row on row,
No sad tomb for all to mourn,
Excepting aching hearts forlorn,
For Red's loss in Taffy Three.

As you ply the Philippine Sea,
And the oceans blue and free,
Where Red surely died for thee,
Pass o'er his grave solemnly,
You are here with Taffy Three.

The Wait
Craig Sernotti
One, two, ten fifteen
energetic children playing as children do
in an open field. Freeze tag or chasing
butterflies or picking wildflowers in the
calm summer breeze.

Mama oh mama may I go out and join them?
May I go please? But of course not. Don't you
remember
what the children will say? Don't you
remember:
Excuse me, but is your Mother your sister,
alien boy?

And the encephalocele child remembered.
And he went to his dark room.
And he stared out the single window.
And oh how he wished he could join the ones in the park.
And he stared into the mirror.
And he saw the embossed flesh
between his eyes and the upper portion of his nose.
And he cried a thousand tears like he did so many times before.
And he prayed to God for the operation he was promised
to come soon.
And then he could join the children and play in an open field
as children do.

Noteworthy Works

Summer Morn
Joe Nolan

The honeysuckle fragrance permeated so sweet the air,
Rose bushes of deep red hue as if
dancing amongst the new morning dew.
Summertime,
Butterflies and humming birds, they were there too.
The dogwood and cherry trees reaching for the sun,
Bees dancing like lovers looking for their fill.
I remember my boyhood home up on the hill,
With daffodils and lilacs swelling with glee,
And I in this midst of heaven's tranquility.

Stormy Nights
Tammy W. Rue

Pouring out like there's a leak in
the sky.
Thunder up above, sounds like a war
aground.
Everything's so still, you can feel it in the
air.
No signs of any kind, can't find my way.
Feels like a force racing through my
blood.
Raining so hard as if it's washing away
the world.
My brain is bursting against my skull.
My heart is ripped, beyond repair.
The pain I feel, I hide so well.
Sweat dripping from my body, feels
like I'm drowning,
Gasping for air like there's no
tomorrow.
The world could come to an end.
Wondering if it's right around the
bend.

Dedication: Mary Winecoff Thies, love you!

If Tonight I Kiss You
Johnny Lee Madden

If tonight I kiss you under the illuminating rays of the
Moonlight, will you still love and favor me at the coming
Of morning's first light dawning.

If tonight I kiss you under the enchanting beams of the
Moonlight, will you still love and embrace me at the
Coming of morning's first light dawning.

If tonight I kiss you under the spellbinding glow of the
Moonlight, will you still love and desire me at the
Coming of morning's first light dawning.

If tonight I kiss you under the mystifying radiance of the
Moonlight, will you still love and encourage me at the
Coming of morning's first light dawning.

If tonight I kiss you under the captivating luminance of
The moonlight, will you still love and keep faith with me
At the coming of morning's first light dawning.

If tonight I kiss you under the resonating waves of the
Moonlight, will you still love and remember me, hold warm
And endearing memories of me and often recall and

Picture me in your mind with the passing days, weeks,
Months and years at the coming of morning's first light dawning.

Raining
Ben Robertson

The rain comes in sheets,
Sweeping the streets –
Here,
Here,
And here,
And umbrellas appear
Like mushrooms
And flowers
That bloom
In the showers.

Lonely
Linda L. Brechan

Only the lonely know for sure
The quiet, non-ringing phone.
The lack of invites one receives
To visit someone's home.

Where are those friends one used to have?
How come they seem so busy?
And relatives that used to call
In numbers that made one dizzy!

Only the lonely know it's true,
That when one's spouse is gone,
People stray from the one left alone
From guilt for the one that moved on.

Is this really what life's all about
After school, work, kids and taxes?
Aging alone in the scheme of things
A memory one greets and passes.

Only the lonely know what it takes
To wake up and face each new day
Filled with the same as the day before
With no plans for change to the fray.

Counting Stars
Donald Bishop

A breach among the trees,
Far beyond cities and cars,
Listening to rustling leaves,
All alone... counting stars.

Gazing into a moonless sky,
Whiskey obscures the pain,
Silence broken, a mournful cry,
Sounds of a distant train.

Unforeseen a brighter morrow
For hearts with many scars,
Love bequeaths sullen sorrow,
All alone... counting stars.

Guilt burdened by notoriety,
A flask of blended scotch,
Squelching somber sobriety,
Life nothingness a botch.

Night drifts listlessly away
Hopelessness finally at par,
Myself, I shall never betray,
All alone... counting stars.

Dreams of the Soul

Over And Over
Crede M. Kissell

Over and over I shout and sing.
Over and over the joy bells ring
Life got its start deep in my heart
When Jesus saved me from sin,

He keeps me singing along the way
He bears my burdens from day to day.

Jesus is mine Savior divine, forever
more.

Sun
Ella Johnson–Bentley

The golden sun streaks 'cross the sky,
on molten mercury feet,
Sending shafts of light into the dark,
to pierce the ebon deep.

Look yonder at that fiery orb,
As it binds and casts aside,
that black and fretful darkness drear,
A drape of light flung wide.

Behold the fiery spears cast down,
At dawn to birth the day,
Blazing, flowing ever on,
in life's eternal play.

Speed on thru strange uncharted deeps,
A cosmic race to run,
A blue white beacon in the sky,
A wilderness is won.

Thru comet tails and old star trails,
the sun sweeps on along,
to join the symphony of stars,
in a mystic lovely song.

The Fall
A. L. W. Berry

A season full of many things, of fresh and
bitter winds.
Of sun and showers that bring elation –
with slow and subtle transformation.
It is the loveliest season, there is no doubt,
atmospheric colour is what it is all about.
Red, gold and burnished brown steal the scene,
from fading shades of green.
And a beautiful tapestry unfolds before your
eyes,
Capturing the heart and imagination with ever
changing scenes.
Alas, before the picture is complete, leaves
trickle –
they fall and lay spent at your feet.
The winds that shake the boughs around, shed
nature's glory to the ground.
Leaves lie in heaps amid the shuffling sound.
Their short lives beauty soon forgotten by all
around.

And perish into dust.
The wonder of it all is Autumn and of course,
the Fall...

Our Special Gary
Celia Axe

O Gary I do love you and miss you very much
If only I could see you or just to feel your touch
My heart has been broken and broken in two
I just hope my other half is very much with you
The day that you did leave me
My life's not been the same
I will only feel much better
When I meet you once again
I just want to say I love you very dear
Would just love to hug you and feel you very near

In Praise Of Receptionists
J. Stevens

The front line of the company,
The first one seen and heard,
Men rarely look as pretty,
So women are preferred.

Everybody needs you,
Visitors want your time,
You're on the phone and at your desk,
Doing the post and all the rest.

Where would we be without you?
Our queries, requests and needs,
You have to keep it cheerful,
Or the customer becomes aggrieved.

The bossman can be crafty,
He has a special little line,
"Just do this before you go,
It doesn't take much time".

The Job is done and home you go
Always later than you think,
Staying late was all worthwhile
It pays the gas and rent.

Happy Mother's Day
Pamela C. Wilbur

Our baby is having a baby,
We're as happy as can be.
A brand new life to love,
"so tenderly."

Congratulations to Heather and Mike
on this their "Special Time."
May the Lord bless both of you
with love, happiness, and joy sublime.

We'll always be here to love and guide you,
and offer our support.
Please do not forget to give us every
"new baby" report.

Babies are a blessing, no matter what the sex,
so please share him or her with us,
in this do not neglect.

Here's our hugs (OOO)
and kisses (XXX) too,
sent with love from us to you!!!!

Dedication: Heather and family, love Mom

Have I Any Dreams
Sylvia F. Gause Gurganious
I would like to sell
I will do what I must
To help and give to others
For my dreams are not for sale
For what good is anyone
Without a dream
And great pride! And love,
American way, Dreams

Dedication: My mother, brothers, sisters and family

Suburban Living
Pearl E. McCray
The grass, the bushes,
The birds, and bees,
The squirrels, the snakes,
The flowers and trees.

The plants, the ivory,
The ants and bugs,
The spiders, the mosquitoes,
The gnats and slugs.

The roaches and termites,
That hide like fleas,
Under the house, around the house,
And under the leaves.

Don't forget the silverfish, crickets
And birds that sing,
The wasps and bumble bees,
That sometimes sting.

The firebrats, centipedes,
Moths and beetles,
Millipedes, earwigs,
And little rice weasels.

Fireflies
Lawrence Edward Notestine
As children we played while the summer days waned,
And the flicker of fireflies was always a thing
That challenged to catch them while they were bright,
Thinking a lot of them would make a greater light.

We looked the next morning, their light had gone,
Their search for each other was not for the dawn.
The lesson we learned, we each have a place
To shine like a firefly by God's infinite grace.

How nice it would be if we could hold time
Still at the place where life is sublime.
When destiny favors and things seem so right,
But, alas, they fade like fireflies at night.

Our family leaves us one by one,
Their allotment of time over and done.
Memories of years spent vivid and bright,
Just a gleam in the darkness like fireflies at night.

When our spirits are bright, it's the time to do
All the good things in life God wants us to.
Time and opportunity come to us each day,
The light of the firefly fades quickly away.

Untitled
Erin Barrett
I close my eyes and wish
I wish for hundreds of thousands of butterflies
beautiful, shimmering, carefree butterflies.
I want them to fill every speck of air
between me and the sky.
I want to breathe in the air from
under their wings – as they flutter
endlessly in my existence
I want to be free—
I want to be beautiful!

Forbidden Love
Jacqueline Ludlow
River deep, mountain high
A million stars up in the sky
A tender kiss, a warm embrace
Special moments, lost in space

Our love a kiss upon the wind
Forgive us now, for we have sinned
The magic in this love we share
Will they know, or even care?

Two hearts right now they beat as one
Above the clouds, above the sun
No one knows, and no one sees
I need him, as he needs me

Could this magic in our touch
Cause us pain, we dread so much?
The honesty these two hearts share
Bring love together, beyond compare

There's no one else, just him and I
Underneath this starry sky
Two hearts in love, as you can see
from now until eternity

Whooooo's On Court
Shirley Poppenga
She mixes her potions
And comes out at night
Hovering, sailing
In the eerie moonlight

Her broom wields its magic
As she moves 'round the court
For tennis, my dear
Is her favorite sport

Lobbing and smashing
She darts to and fro
Criss–crossing paths
With her partner, the crow

The cats, their opponents
Are grinning to here
Two Cheshires perhaps
But that could be a leer

The wise one looks down
On this midnight ballet
As it silently fades
At the new light of day

Dreams of the Soul

Plastic World
Richard Lee McVay III
Why are we so deceived,
pessimistic in our ways;
Is this the way it should be,
man killing countries,
feasting on young blood,
killed by the silent gun,
living in a daze...
A Plastic World

Dedication: Jenny, and beloved son Alex

I Am A Tree
Anne M. Chyten
I am a tree, with roots that should have sustained me, helping me grow
Tall, strong, proud
But, without nourishment, even the strongest of trees withers and dies
You were supposed to be my roots, where was my nourishment?
The pain, the cruelty, the hatred of your cold winds
How was I supposed to grow and be fruitful?
Your winds tore my leaves, your storms broke my branches
Where was the gentle rain, the warm loving rays of the sun?
Dark clouds were all I ever saw
But, this tree flourished, growing stronger despite the storms
For this tree found that its strength was not in its roots, but, in its
seeds
As I watch my saplings grow, I use my leaves to hold the moisture they need
when they are thirsty
My branches shield them from the storms
My shadow moves out of their way
So they can bathe in the warmth of the sunshine I never knew
Standing before me are the fruits of my labor
Tall, strong, proud
Reaching higher than my branches ever could
With roots that go much deeper than I ever thought possible
For they were planted and raised in love

Dedication: Arte, Jennifer, Danielle and Aaron

Peaks And Piques
Doris Helba
Fragrant and melodious, our
mountains
Pleasing our senses, enticing
our day.
Constant and bounteous, our
mountains
Firming our choices, embroidering
our way.
Peaceful and resplendent,
our mountains
Easing our hurts, delighting
our eyes.
Rugged and extensive,
our mountains
Testing our bodies, increasing
our highs.
Fruitful and prolific,
our mountains
Piquing our thoughts,
expanding our lore.
Tranquil and majestic,
our mountains
Resting our minds, teaching
our souls to soar!

Untitled
Mary Montgomery
bale of turtles,
bevy of quail, brood
CHICKY, CHICKY
care to try American crocodile this
fine evening, with thick
Cajun Tongue.
She lost a limb by moving in on them, I
read, I obliged her and dug in.
mob of kangaroos,
muster of peacocks, murder of crows.

Dear Grandma
Christopher Sampson
I love you.

You had a happy smile
that said "I love you Chris".

I remember your soft brown hair
and your loving blue eyes.

I remember how happy you were
when I made stuff for you.

You gave me long warm hugs
that made me feel happy and safe.

I love you
and I loved taking care of you.

You called me "your baby"
in your soft gentle voice.

I will miss you Grandma,
but most of all...

I will miss loving you.

Day of the Electric Leg
Grace Buller
An innocent encounter
The day my leg brushed yours.
Voltage shot up from my knee
You felt the jolt, I'm sure.

Day of the electric leg.
Had you known before?
Why I always longed to stay
You felt the jolt, I'm sure.

You got busy on the phone
But couldn't concentrate.
In anger you sent me out
Cheshire grin on my face.

Try as I may, I couldn't
Wipe that grin off my face.
I wanted to fly banners
And took giant steps all day.

Now as we sit together
And start to reminisce
"Day of the electric leg"
From you I get a kiss.

Noteworthy Works

Untitled
Kimberly Hoff
I hold your hand,
Even when we are not together.
And we soar to that place
Where our fingers brush the stars,
And our hearts are filled with all the
Mysteries of the sun and the moon,
And those who came to this place
Before us.
Dedication: My parents and Pamela Gardner

Prairie Wind
Lynda Rae Nelson
If you've ever heard a howling force,
A thundering horse
On a twisting course,
You've heard the prairie wind.

If you've ever seen the cottonwood trees
With fluttering leaves,
Or wheat in the breeze,
You've seen the prairie wind.

If you've ever sniffed the scent of dust
Whirled round in a gust
And then skyward thrust,
You've smelled the prairie wind.

If you've ever felt the icy chill,
The blustery thrill
Of winter's wild will,
You've felt the prairie wind.

If you've ever known the whimsical ways
Of soft, gentle sways
To tempestuous days,
You truly have known the prairie wind.

The Painter
Rebecca Lilley
At dawn I shall rise to the melody
Of emerald blades moist in dew and moonlight
Inhaling the aroma of a dazzling sunrise,
I will seize its beauty with a fervent sweep
Of copper, amber, and flaxen.

Pallidity burdens my heart; waiting, waiting—
Until it is broken again, and I bleed the tears
Of surreal, flamboyant madness,
Spilling onto ivory, a prism of emotions.

My stage is white canvas,
My palette: A mistress of color and texture
And I make love to her drama
In every detail, every stroke.

As I graze the surface with crimson and
amethyst,
I taste validity fit for a king!
Oh, beloved passion, stay true!
Seek refuge in loyalty
Fashion my altered visions,
And bathe my existence in rich hues—
A portrait for eternity.

For Sarah
Geraldine Lester
Away I go down the street
and who do I chance to meet?
A sweet little girl who
says "Grandma I Love You."
No other words can sound
so Sweet,
Or be so neat,
as "Grandma, I Love You."
Dedication: My granddaughter, Sarah

Ode To A Wandering Sailor
W. H. Bassett
Our thoughts travel on far over the sea,
To friends far away wherever they may be,
And they in their turn think of us just the same,
But always wishing to call us by name.

May the time pass quickly through thick and thin,
With never a thought of giving in,
No doubt at times you feel that way,
But carry on friend, till the distant day.

We each have our part to play that's plain,
Some on the high seas, while others sow grain,
But the parts fit in to a larger plan,
As we try for the best to benefit man.

False hopes are raised no doubt sometimes,
As the ship speeds on to different climes,
And when you're heading on towards Rome,
There's just that thought "you wish it were home".

May these few words help wherever you go,
That's just a thought I would like you to know,
As the time speeds along when you're homeward bound,
And you catch the first glimpse of Plymouth Sound.

A Need For Your Love
Barbara Marie Chesteen
I reach out to you but am pushed
away
I'll try again another day

Without you I feel so dejected
abandoned, abused and rejected

I tell you I love you but your heart
it never seems to reach
I try to talk to you but I'm no good
with speech

I try to tell you with my words
but they don't enter your ears
I tell myself it will be ok
but here come the tears

I try to show you in the things I do
only needing an I love you too

All I have ever wanted was a little of
your time
Mom please forgive me if loving you
is a crime

Dreams of the Soul

Another Fork In The Road
Rachel Badovinatz

It seems every day is different it has a new sight, feel, and sound—
And everywhere you walk is a new path, and every footstep marks a new place in the ground,
Every person has a new face, and every voice is new but seems old—
But every choice you make that day is just another fork in the road.

Every bird has its last song, like every leaf has its last dance—
But every bad thing can be good, 'cause we always have a second chance,
Like every sun rises and sets, like every wind has its' warmth and cold—
And every day winds and turns just like another fork in the road.

Dad
Miriam Viner

Where have all my words gone
We buried Dad today.
Mum, sis and Grandchildren
Their voices all raised in song.

Many friends of long ago
Filled the tiny chapel.
Still all reeling from the blow
That Dad had lost the battle

His love of music and his trees
Were all a well–known fact.
Square–topped Churches a surprise
And a wee dram used to please.

Three men's lives were saved by him
And he fought for wages and conditions
At the airport for years and years
Times ahead now seem very grim

Heavy clouds cried their tears
on this really sad, sad day
A willow tree his resting place
peace at last with no more fears

Jessica
David R. Jacks

Taking time and tracking wild in the jungle of the garth,
Measured paw steps rehearsed in twitching dreams by human hearth,
A million years of instinct bristle in white and ginger hair,
A tooled–up urban serial killer surveys her dreadful lair.

Her domain this is, defended with yowls and bitter rage,
Only the wizened vixen dares trespass upon her stage.
Jess teases screaming frogs then dispatches them with greed,
Pond–stained hide spews forth flesh she does not need.

The remnants of moonlit hunting offend her snooty nose:
Rude pellets crushed and stinking, encased in bony clothes,
Discarded by the owl, despised by creatures in his hour;
Therein lies his trademark of lust and bloody power.

Hunter's laser eyes spot a rodent's ill–judged dart,
She is still and silent as the death she would impart,
Comic book–like, double–take mouse, glazed and frozen in fright,
Wills himself to feel no pain as she bids him sweet goodnight.

She strikes with guile and stealth and feline ferocity,
Sneering at our disgust with primitive precocity.
The half–witted, blundering dog, craving hospitality,
Can only gawk and admire such sensual savagery.

The Great Hunt
Joan Gallagher

She pauses – then she runs.
She jumps, turns, dives, rolls over –
Lying on her back, tummy offered to the air,
Or to anyone passing with a willingness to give it a rub.
Short rest over, she begins again –
Pouncing on acquiescent ball, pawing at catnip mouse;
At times stalking a fray invisible to everyone but herself.

When it's all over, she curls up like an abalone in its shell,
And softly drifts into sleep, dreaming still of the "great hunt."

A Country Walk
Lachlan Taylor

The sun shone brightly in the sky
the birds were singing sweetly,
The colouring of the flowers around
stole the show completely.

As I walked along this woodland path
on this shining summer's day
I gazed at the wonders all around
they took the breath away.

You could scent the blossoms from the trees
and from the flowers in the dell,
It seemed that nature with her wand,
had wove a magic spell.

There was no pollution in the air
no smoke or any fumes,
All there was, was the perfumed scent
from off the flowering blooms.

There's naught that beats a country walk
to view the rural scene,
and spot the wild–woods at their best
so peaceful and serene.

Is It Me Or Is It You
C. Elson

I stand and stare at your picture there
You stare back eyes so blue.
You were my life. I thought complete
But soon time told, tales untold.
Deceit, lies and false good–byes
I paid you back or so I thought
But more lies and hurt
My anger grew and so I festered
I trusted you not, my thoughts not rested
I wanted to hurt you so much.
The way I feel the deep, deep rot.
No deeper could I go, the darker side showed.
It's not real, its not for good.
I know that now my heart's not wood.
My eyes do cry, but for who
It is me or is it you.
I've memories bitter and so sweet
Creep in my mind while I sleep.
I said goodbye, so it's my doing
I've lost my life, it's in ruins
You can guess, I think you know
What I say, cannot show
Read my mind and my heart
Then read again from the start.

Noteworthy Works

Midnight Tears
Charmaine Heimes
As the hours pass into the night,
Crickets sing, stars become bright.
Another day has come to an end,
No longer do you have to pretend.
The confidence and strength displayed all day,
Somehow, some way, just slipped away.
Your mind and thoughts begin to drift,
Feeling scared and alone comes very swift.
Darkness brings out many fears,
Eventually turning into midnight tears.

Dear Patti
Kay Halter
I said a prayer for you today,
That God wouldn't take you away.
Although my wish didn't come true.
I knew God would take good care of you.

Your pain and suffering is gone away,
Now with God you will stay.
The short time of life you did live,
It was in your heart to offer and give.

All the fun and memories as sisters we have shared,
No matter what happened you always cared.
You weren't only a sister but a friend,
From the beginning up till now, "the end".

I'll keep you daily in thought and prayer,
This will be something I'll learn to bear.
I'll help your family to keep their strength,
As you'd do for me up to great length.

Now until we meet again,
In my heart is where I keep you my friend.
Dedication: The Smokey Amsden family

Footsteps
Amanda Young
Why is it that you haunt me so?
Each time I think I've let you go.
I hear your footsteps sure and slow
Again.

It seems so strange that we should meet,
So often on the crowded street,
I hear your footsteps measured beat
Again.

I feel I can't take any more,
I'm running as I hit the floor
I hear your footsteps at my door
Again.

I know now that I cannot flee,
You simply will not let me be,
I hear your footsteps come for me
Again.

It's been a perfect, blissful day,
And yet I know you cannot stay,
I hear your footsteps fade away
Again.

The Swaying Of The Trees
Jennifer M. Jaichner
The swaying of the trees
on a warm summerday!
Expressing themselves freely;
glistening in the wind.
Green grass with an occasional
blue seeping through the
swaying trees.
The trees are calm now—oh
but wait!
The trees have begun to dance.

Volunteer
Luretta Elston
America, I will work for thee
Thank God I am free
I am proud to live in this great country
I will face each day with courage and dignity.

Everywhere I look I see
The beauty of this great country
The beautiful streams and hills
the singing whippoorwills
From the top of the mountain, to the deepest sea
Thank God for Liberty.

For this land many great soldiers have died
So that I could live and work with pride
On every mountainside I will do great things.

I will volunteer to spread goodwill
I will help build homes for the homeless
And care for those who are ill.

I will listen for those who cannot hear.
Make footsteps for those who cannot walk.
I will have a vision for those who cannot see.
I will inspire others to be a voice for Liberty.

Friend
Justin Mierzejewski
A day without shadows, a day without the cool breeze
A day without the birds' songs echoing through the trees
A day without a sunrise, a day the sun forgets to set
The stars never woken and a night never met

While others cast away their dreams and let their hopes all slip away
At times like these my mind's at ease and will not be led astray
For even the day the earth stands still and the seas all lose their tides
There will be no fear or doubt in me as long as you're there by my side

A friend like you who lifts me up when all the others fall
Who stays until the trouble is gone who's there without a call
A friend like you who shines so bright... so bright she outshines the sun
That if I were granted a million wishes I'd need but only one

I'd wish for you the best in life
In love, in all you do
And that the support and love you've given me
I could somehow give back to you

For all the power, glory or riches in the world
Not one could begin to compare
To the joy that you have brought to my life
Just by being there

Dreams of the Soul

Between Here And There
George Alberts
In this world, between here and there
Flesh will come together.
Binding and entwining itself,
In high ecstasy and pleasure.
Moments of sheer intimacy,
That seal man and wife.
A commitment of love,
A promise of new life.

Dedication: Robert E. Selland, Sr. (my loving husband)

The Winds of Time
Leonora Lewis–Stratford
The winds of time are wafting by,
they gently touch my cheek.
The joys of life's adventures lie
for me to search and seek.

The winds of time are breezing by,
they tousle up my hair.
The fun of living makes time fly,
I do not have a care

The winds of time are blowing by,
they fill my eyes with dust.
I try to reach the moon on high
because I know I must.

The winds of time are gusting by,
they dry and chap my face
Now I begin to wonder why
I can't keep up the pace.

The winds of time – a gale now,
have taken all my strength.
To old man Father Time I bow
I know I've run the length.

Country Candles
Grace A. Lyons
We are candles burning bright
Through the day and through the night
Flames that reach high, darting and dancing
Dripping great sculptures to tell of our prancing

Some proud and strong, happy as a lark
Burning with hope, passion and heart
The wax of their life taking shape, taking form
Each one unique, never a norm

Loving life with the high and the low
Needing only a spark to make it glow... Yet
Some flicker so faintly, their glow hard to see
Casting small shadows unseen by you and me

Their wax drips slowly, hardly leaving a trace
Rolling ever so slowly like tears down a face
The flame flickers and flutters, floundering in a pool
Spitting and sputtering, feeling like a fool

With a tip of fate the stagnation is released
The flame grows brighter, inner glow is increased
What's needed is a spark, the match of creation
Each candle burns bright in this, our great nation

We Two Are One
Clayton Hobart Fox
Those silken bonds of love
That with gentle strength caress
Hold us close so tenderly
With ties of happiness

True love is so special
it blossoms when it's shared
A gentle touch, a loving smile
Little things that show we care

A whispered word of love
Or perhaps a secret wink
Are the stuff of real happiness
That forge the strongest link

There's not a thing on earth
We know this well enough
that can offer greater riches
Than a life that's filled with love

So as we stroll life's pathways
Forever joined as one
Our lives will be complete
Our search for happiness is done.

Imagine
Elizabeth Kittrell
The air is flawless, crisp, and cool,
An Icy creek has melted to a gentle pool,
Pearly clouds are thin pieces of silk, floating through the sky,
I reach out and touch them, embrace them, one can when they're this high,
I am on the top of a wondrous, majestic mountain,
It's a beautiful place you may have never been,
As I look around me, I see a baby goat on a nearby peak,
The little one clings to its Mother, it is very young and meek,
Mother Nature watches over Earth on every winter day,
Through the frost, she whispers that soon, she'll send spring on its way.

Danny M. Anderson, Jr. M. D.
Margie Ruth Melone
A boy called Dan, Danny or Junior.
Who had many desires and ambitions.
To become a doctor, lawyer, and athlete,
His choice was to become a physician.

This physician, husband, Father and man
Is appreciated, but many times is never told.
Your concern, sincerity, and dedication is real.
It radiates warmth, and you do want to heal.

This shows each time you walk into the room.
Your caring and giving is sometimes hard to find.
To name all you've shown to all of my family,
"Danny Boy, you are one of a kind!!!"

Your work is long, hard and very tiring.
At times there seems to be no rest.
Somewhere inside your inner strength does emerge,
And God above knows you have given you best.

I know you will continue caring for all of them.
Your reward will just have to be great.
So great that the good Lord above—
Could be? May even make you a saint!!!

Noteworthy Works

When We Were Young
Theresa L. Miner
Our Mom did the laundry on an
old washboard.
And Dad drove a Chevy instead of
a ford.
Mom hung out the laundry, in the
sun to dry.
Under a beautiful, blue, blue
sky.
We'd play all day in an old
fruit room.
Mom chased away the dog from
the porch with a broom.
All six of us girls, slept in one
bedroom.
Eat a bowl of oats, and watch
Mr. Moon.
We couldn't ride the bus to school
at all.
But walking to school, made us feel
so tall.
Our life was full, in that tiny
little town.
Thank God for the love, we all
found.

Identity
Kamni Verma
Encumbered in grandness.
The tree stood.
Its leaves of autumn, of spring, of summer.
And its empty branches of winter.
Beneath still is the ground.
Above the sky and all around...
all around the surrounding of a fortress.
Pity the life of the grand victor
that breathes amidst this exilement.
——Yet the tree stands.

Untitled
Myeisha Jacobs
Never, Never, Never, Never, close your eyes,
Never, Never, Never, Never, hold your breath,
Never, Never, Never, Never close your ears,

If you do you'll miss the feelings down deep inside
Loneliness rains down upon you as the mind's door
will slam hard, hard, hard, hard, lock you in and lose the key

Does a dark cloud need to envelop your thoughts
Introverted, spaced away, a star in the night's sky
The morning dew that drops
Will you too dissipate like it
Let the sun's rays dry you up
till you no longer exist

Rise then like the clouds way up high
Move freely with the winds blow
Touch the rays of the sun
Then glide away with open vents

Feel the brush of the air
Open wide to exhale
Hear the rustle of the sounds
See the wide, wide, wide, wide space you surround

My Soul Friend
Chastity N. Roberts
I smiled when you were happy.
I cried when you were sad.
I prayed when you couldn't.
I dealt when you thought you shouldn't.

When I needed a friend,
I conversed with your soul.
No words were required.
By your spirit was I consoled,
As I sought freedom from a feeling undesired.

The connection we have surpasses nature.
It's not something one can simply find.
I understand you as I myself.
It's almost as if our spirits are intertwined.

I was liberated through your deliverance.
I looked forward as you moved ahead.
Euphoria erupted as I acknowledged your bliss.
No feelings of not you, but me instead.

I see me through you, past and future.
It's an intimacy deeper than a kiss.
You are a part of me, you're my soul friend.

A Valentine Wish
Jean M. Freeman
There was a time when love wasn't much
Then a year came especially for us
As time went by, my love for you grew
And our family became more than just two
This valentine wish is to let you know
That my love for you will grow and grow
For Valentine's day is a reminder to me
My promises to you were meant to be
To love, to cherish all the days of my life
Were given to you when I became your wife.

My Special Place
Colette M. O'Reilly
I open my eyes, how do I feel, am I ready for this day.
I close my eyes and take a deep breath
to chase negative thoughts away.

The sun is rising the sky is blue
the day should bring a smile.
But my heart is heavy and my spirit is weak
I must meditate for awhile.

I need to laugh, I need to love.
There must be a purpose to this day.
So I think nice thoughts and make some plans
and hope they are not too far away.

I think of a place, a special place
where we are all one under the sun.
We care, we share, we laugh, we smile.
We hurt, We cry once in a while.
But the love we give and the bonds we make
will never be undone.

This special place I talk about is only in my mind.
That doesn't mean there is no such place,
you seek and you shall find...

Dreams of the Soul

Hush Little Child
E. Middleston
Hush little child don't you cry
Come wipe the teardrops from
Your eyes. Even though you're
Sad and blue come little
Child let me comfort you

I know your mammy's gone away
And you cry teardrops every day
But Jesus needed her you see
Now she's in heaven a spirit free

So time will heal your broken
Heart. And you will never really
Be apart for you have your
Memories to see you through
The days that you feel sad
And blue.

So when your time does come
To part and Jesus takes
You to his heart. With your
Mammy once again you'll
Be two spirits together
For eternity.

Going Home
Rosa M. Cousins
We know you were tired and needed your rest,
But God always knows what's best.
We know you are in your heavenly home,
And you will never again be alone.
It hurts so bad when someone you love dies,
We can't help but weep and cry.
We pray we will see you again someday,
And that God will guide us along the way.
We say goodbye dear Mother, goodbye,
We know you had to go and don't question why.

Love
Wayne E. Pearson
Love is a very special bond
Going far beyond just being fond.
It seems too complex to state
Happens, succeeds or fails, by fate.

True love simply requires a trust,
Not very complex, but always just.
Holding a very simple belief,
Brings life's greatest joy, relief.

Oft' mystical, unclear, beset by flaw,
True love seems out-of-phase with law.
And oft' times it seems fate's whim
Sets off forces with results quite grim.

How then can true love survive?
By what route does it arrive?
What is the trick, where the wand
To attain the ultimate trust and bond?

There is a simple rule or way
To maintain it day by day.
To have a trust that is royal
Requires only that one love and be loyal.

Curious Kitten
Kathy Wakeland
Curiosity is a funny thing;
At times it may bring a bumble-bee sting.
I watched a kitten one day at play,
Nosing flowers, then he ran away.

He jumped around, then rubbed his nose;
A big, red bump, on his face grows.
He licked and rubbed to ease the pain,
But all his efforts seemed in vain.

Then rubbed his face upon the ground;
It seemed no comfort could be found.
He rolled around from side to side,
I think it also hurt his pride.

He rubbed his nose a little more;
Seemed to be getting very sore.
He soon got up and went on his way,
Left the flowers for another day.

A lesson, the kitten, must have learned;
To the flowers, he has not returned.
He seems quite timid, even shy,
Runs away when a bee flies by.

Tactile
Elizabeth Ann Ellis
What is tactile? To touch, to feel.
Touch splintered glass, and feel pain
Touch the cheek of a newborn baby,
And feel heaven
Touch tousled locks, and feel happy
Caress a standing stone, and feel cold and amazed
Splash your face in a cool stream,
And feel refreshed.
Touch a hand, feel the warmth of
Another human being, and feel content.

The Scar
Pearl L. Elmer
The scar is a memory
The healing took place
Of aches of by-gone days
Wounds from life's race.

But here is a deeper wound
Death has dug deep
Plummet, perilous pain
Surging in my heart, steep.

Somehow the hurt pangs
Upheaving cries flow
Dirgeous and sick
Unbury themselves so.

And then comes sweet healing
God lessens the pain
He places his dressings
But a scar still remains.

Each year comes and goes
But the scar still remains
The scar keeps me still
To remember God's gains.

Noteworthy Works

The Fox Hunt
Lydia Webster

Puir, quivering, russet–coated Tod,
Nae doubt they've chased ye lang an' hard.
Until ye've won intae ma yard, a'maist hauf deid.
Tak hairt! I'll ower ye staun' guard, as lang's the need!

An, here they are! They've a' come speerin;
Hounds intae neuk an' cran are peerin;
Wi' huntsmen, pokin; interferin; wi' whip an' lash.
I tell ye, I just feel like sweerin; at this stramash!

Awa! ye rascal, murderin' crew,
Wee Tod is in ma care the noo,
So turn ye roon' an' bid adieu tae this your quarry.
Puir chiels, your day has gone askew? Weel, I'm no' sorry.

Just pit yoursels in Toddy's place.
Wad ye no' think it a disgrace
If ye were object o' the chase, an run tae death?
Ye'd soon misca' the human race, wi' every breath!

It gars me greet that men should kill
And mutilate the fox at will,
In name o' SPORT? an' just tae fill their hours o' leesure?
I thank the Lord that nae sic thrill wad gie me pleesure.

Who Cares
Lewis T. Bebble

Rooti–toot–toot, Rooti–toot–toot,
I am a lad from the institute,
I don't smoke, I don't chew,
I don't go out with girls that do,
I won't curse, I won't drink,
Most people don't know what to think,
This is my story; sad but true,
I hope it doesn't bother you,
Rooti–toot–toot, Rooti–toot–toot,
Does anyone really give–a–hoot!

Saint Alban
G. A. Van De Voorde

Is this the causeway by the lake
Where once the martyr Alban walked
And did the saviour meet him there
Was he the Roman Jesus sought

Did he become a Christian
And denounce the heathen ways
Because the Lord had spoken
In those bygone days

And why was Alban taken
To the hill above
To become Saint Alban
And die for the cause he loved

So when we walk this pathway
Should we turn and look back
Could we also meet the Saviour
If faith we do not lack

And now today upon the hill
A mighty Church doth stand
To the memory of a Roman
Who gave the Lord his hand

To Jherilyne
Christine Ann Manges

It's a blessed individual
who's found the rare gem
of a kindred spirit
a bosom friend

A person you can count on
to stand there by your side
to listen to your problems
And take them all in stride

Never to condemn you,
even when they could
but rather they up–build you
just like you knew they would

A friend like this is rare indeed,
they're far between and few
but I've been blessed with the best
because my best friend is you.

So when the others turn away
and you feel you can't get through,
just remember you can call on me
and I'll be your friend too.

If
Rosemary Postlethwaite

If only God's will could be understood
So families of all species, could live in peaceful mood.
Without any horrors, to upset or scare,
When all life it would be fair.
The time it nears, when that shall be.
After waiting so long in futility.
do not give up hope, as inhumanity and perdition shall end
For God's light of divinity, has nearly stopped evil,
On that you can depend

Kindred Overture
Rhonda Shiffman

I worked very late one night
It was 2:00 a. m. the last time I checked the clock
Walking outside to catch the train
I noticed how ancient the evening was without stars
Happily exhausted I entered the train that would return me to my warm bed
Miles and miles later I realized
I was out of gasoline

I exited the train with a dark–skinned woman who worked with me
and followed her into the rhythmic neighborhood
First she stopped by a burning lamp in front of an all night donut shop
While I took in the aroma of black coffee, sinkers and pomade
she embraced a friend, making sure he knew about his ill cousin
On our way again she flowed into a smoke–puffing bar
where she shot pool and amused a middle–aged man with slick black hair
"You need to be home with your woman, " I heard her say

When we finally came out of the bar
the sky was twenty shades of pink
and there were no surprises
I woke to the sound of Vivaldi's four seasons
and there were no lies

Dedication: Kathryn, guardian of my heart

Dreams of the Soul

The Sun Will Rise Again
Thomas L. Haines

Hi, What's up it's me again
Welcome to the story of my life
Once my future was promising and bright
Now it's filled with trouble and strife

I can hear voices
When I kneel in prayer
Who're you talking to
there's no one there.

I had a fiancee
Who was also my best friend
Now that she's gone
My life came to an end.

My friends were there with me
putting up with my moans.
They stayed with me
Never leaving me alone.

There's one thing I know now
That I wish I did know then
When doubts turn to faith, sorrow turns to joy,
And the Sun Will Rise Again.

The Simple Optimist
Mary Kate Bennett

They think she's light
And spry for her years
Forever young
Through bodily age
I know she can be heavy
But prefers to never tire
For our adversity
Not always old
Not always a child
Forever alive.

Did I Close My Eyes Too Soon?
Misty M. Carroll

Did I close my eyes too soon?
Is that why you walked away?
Did I open up my heart to you
And leave you with nothing to say?

Did the echoes of my heartbeat find your soul?
Did your emptiness burn in the dark?
If I took part of you would you be whole?
And would you let me take you that far?

Have I caused you unspeakable pain
Like a mountain eroded by time?
Or have I just caused a drizzling rain
In the corners of your mind?

I have left no stone unturned
Save the one I could not lift
Reach for the fire and you will be burned
But the fire is God's greatest gift

If I could change a thing or two
And start where time began
I wouldn't have closed my eyes too soon
And you would still be my friend.

Majesty
Kathleen Pierre

Great, great are the rolling waves
As they dash against the shore.
Small, small are the ripples –
Brushing against the sand.

Loud, loud are the breakers
As they crash upon the rocks.
Quiet, quiet the incoming tide –
The sea meeting up with the land.

High, high comes in the tide –
It reaches the old sea wall.
Low, low it will come again
Barely the coast to meet.

Blue, blue is the sky above
And down it descends to enjoin
The green, green of the ocean
As up it swells to greet.

I gaze and stare in wonder –
And joy and awe to see
The mighty works of God above –
Then look down in humility.

Perils Of Self Pity
Bonnie Shaulis

Self–pity, oh, what a terrible sin its a path to destruction
When it first begins, it's a way of life where you never can win
It robs you of self–worth takes away your dignity and friends
It thrives on the negative side keeps you in such misery all you
Want to do is run and hide, it leads you to self–destruction of
The worst kind destroys you body soul and mind, to continue
This path would be a tragic mistake 'cause sooner or later
Its toll will take and finally you will learn that your self–
Pity must come to an end because you will realize it's your enemy
And not your friend

These Are Your Children
Jackie Browning

These are your children, you gave them to me
from 7:45 until a quarter after three.
You entrusted them with me, you put them in my care,
My knowledge and my love with them did I share.

These are your children, you gave them to me.
Some given freely, some more reluctantly.
I took what you gave and molded and shaped.
Sometimes I scolded, but mostly I praised.

Each one is different, unique and refined.
Each one is precious, lovable, and kind.
I have watched them change in ways you did not see.
I have watched them grow from a seedling into a young tree.

These are your children, I'm returning them to you.
I have taught them academics and values, too.
But these are only small things, the rest must come from you.
So love them and guide them and show them the right way
For you will have to answer for their lives one day.

These are your children, I'm returning them to you.
I have done my best, I have done my part.
I have taught them and loved them with all of my heart.

Two Loves
Jack E. Spry

Your love means more to me,
Than anything you see;
For you are always there,
To love, to hold, and care.

To me, we'll always be,
Two loves for those to see;
You are my life, my love,
Brought together, from above.

I just want you to know,
That I do love you so;
So tender and so sweet,
Our love shall be complete.

One day in time some place,
I'd love to see your face;
I see you night and day,
In my dreams so far away.

You are my life, my love,
Forever and ever true;
For you are the one my dear,
No one else for me but you.

Grandpa
Gina Davis

He's gone they say
I do not wish to hear
Sounds of collapse, fear
Hands to my ears
Closing out a pain
No chance to say what was true
A hero within my life
I cry at the thought of you
No chance to say good–byes
Or no I love you

The Perfect Dream
Linda Fox

Perhaps one day it won't matter...
The color of one's skin.
And people won't look just outside,
But will see what lies within.

Perhaps someday we will learn,
That we all are like one another.
For I am much the same as you,
We are all sisters and brothers.

Perhaps I am but a dreamer,
But there are more than just a few,
Who do their part to make a start
To make the dream come true.

So let us move together,
Not divide and drift apart.
And extend our hand to our fellow man,
With the love that is within our heart.

Perhaps one day in the future,
We will all play on one team,
And leave behind this nightmare
To live the perfect dream.

Wings Of Snowy White Velvet
Jessica Bryanne Crawford

Wings of snowy white velvet
Soar high above the starry sky
Wings of snowy white velvet
Sitting on the soft, fluffy clouds

Wings of snowy white velvet
Angels wear on their backs
Wings of snowy white velvet
And play harps of golden strings

Wings of snowy white velvet
My Grandma wears
Wings of snowy white velvet
At the top of Heaven's stairs

Wings of snowy white velvet
Are in the kingdom of God
Wings of snowy white velvet
And the choir of Angel's voices

Wings of snowy white velvet
Soar high above the starry sky
Wings of snowy white velvet
Sitting on soft, fluffy clouds.

You Heard Me Lord
Delores Brown–Harding

Heavenly Father, Heavenly Father, I adore you
Oh dear Savior You're the answer to my prayer
I was living in the world in sinful pleasure
You heard my cry, did not deny
You heard my call.
I was in the world and of the world dear Master
With Your love You picked me up and set me free.
I'm so glad, so glad, so glad,
That I'm your child, Lord
And it is You I know who cares for me.

A Question of Meaning
Dennis Martin

Imagine, if you will, nothing;
Absolute nothingness, only you;
How then would you answer,
"Who am I?" without a single clue

The question is in error,
For one "I" alone cannot be;
Multiple "me's; simultaneous selves";
And infinite "I's, all can see"

Stepping twice into the same river
Is impossible, cannot be done;
Stepping twice into the same "me"
Is likewise unreal; a black sun

If a film, my single identity,
Many individual images would scroll;
Each different "me" a valid "I";
Situationally unique, but quite whole

"Who am I?", is a question of meaning;
Like mirrored images in mirrors of doubt;
I am the smallest particle within,
And the ultimate universe without

Dreams of the Soul

I Met Him In The Chapel
Andrew Zamal
I went to the old country chapel
In the stillness of the night;
When the world was a—dreaming
Under the moonbeams soft and bright.

I walked along the lonely aisle
And knelt down to pray;
Before the Holy Altar
Where He waits night and day.

I said, "My heart is troubled, Lord,
My mind is worried, too;
I am so sad and bitter
I know not what to do."

"Let not your heart be troubled, Friend".
He gently said to me;
"I'll still the tempest in your life
And make your sorrows flee."

I left the chapel, warm and bright
Beneath the moonlit sky;
A greater joy I never felt
I knew He heard my cry!

Sounds Like
Diane Nichols
The sound of the
moving wheels.
They sound almost
god—like. They're
going somewhere,
and I feel like
I'm just standing
still. Oh how I wish
I could be a train
for a day.

The Mask—Erade
Julie Smith
As a child I adorned a mask
to play part in an amusing game —
As an adult I have shed my mask,
hoping my friend would do the same.

But I never know quite what to believe,
in all the words he may say —
His substance crumbles from stories he tells,
his mask slowly falls away.

For underneath there is a man
who no longer feels the same —
"I've never meant to hurt you," he says;
although he's played the game.

My face is no longer hidden
by the mask I once displayed —
Although I shared feelings more freely then,
I am now so much more afraid.

When I next hope to win the prize of love,
will a friend shed his mask and be true?
Or will his substance remain to be,
only that of paper and glue?

Heavenly Father
June V. Chandler
Dear Heavenly Father
Gracious and True,
Help Me This Day
And My Family Too.
Please Give Us The Blessings
That You Want To Give,
Let Us Be Grateful
As Long As We Live.

For We Love And Revere
Your Glorious Name,
Let Us Share In
Your Wonderful Fame.

When Your Son Jesus
Returns With His Grace,
We Will Be Ready To
Look Upon His Face.
And Live In His Kingdom
That Has No End,
We Will Love And Serve
You Forever, Dear Father—Amen.
Dedication: Our daughter, Michele Dawn Chandler

A Thought
Richard Goodman
If life was a nightmare we wouldn't begin,
If life was easy there wouldn't be sin,
If cruelness was kindness there wouldn't be death,
If living were dreadful we wouldn't draw breath,
If we are so brave then why do we cry,
If life is so great then why do we die,
If time is of the essence then why is there so much,
If life is such a bore then why onto it do we clutch,
If we were made to die then why do we cry with pain,
If we hate to kill then why do we kill again.

Lost and Found
Ruth J. Alwine
I thought I'd go crazy
With worry and fear
I needed to find her
And get her back here.

I needed to see her
To know she's okay
I needed to near her
To brighten my day.

Then the news came
It happened so fast
Her voice on the phone
Brought her back from the past

First came the anger
Then our souls we did bare
Then the tears flowed
God had answered my prayer

What could be better
Than seeing her face
To reach out and touch her
And feel her embrace

To My Dearest Mother
Kathleen Flibotte

Have I told you lately just how much I love you?
Have I told you just how much I care?
Then let me take a moment, as this I want to share.

Ever since I was a child, a Mother's love you gave.
Even when I got out of line, and sometimes misbehaved.
You offered me guidance in a loving, yet caring way.
You nurtured me and helped me grow to who I am today.

Reflecting on the years gone by, the memories we share,
I had to take this time to tell you, just how much I care.
When I think of our times together, recent and in the past,
a smile creeps upon my face, it almost makes me laugh.

My heart fills with warmth and love when thoughts of you occur.
There is no doubt in my mind, no of this I am not unsure.
I love you my dear Mom, more than words could ever say.
Mom you are more than special, to me in many a way.

While I know you know I love you, and just how much I care,
I had to tell my feelings, yes this I had to share.

I thank the Lord that you are my Mom and, I, your little girl.
But you are the best out of all the Moms in the entire world!

Lovely Day
Van L. Meigs

On a lovely day in springtime,
Not by reading poem or prose,
I met face to face with loveliness,
That I likened to a rose!
For the days we've been acquainted,
I have known this fact was true,
Only God himself has painted
The loveliness of you!

Dedication: Dearest Kara, my inspiration

Reaching Out To God
Lillie Maude Deffenbaugh Massey

As I was flying, high up in the sky,
I knew I wanted to go to heaven, when I die.
The clouds were so soft and white
And I reached out to God with all my might.

My thoughts began to ponder,
As I started to wonder,
Why so many people are discontented
And why they have not consented.

To let Jesus come into their hearts
And begin their life, with a brand new start
There are so many who do not know
That Christ can wash them white as snow.

They do not know that Jesus died
Or even why he was crucified
When all the while,
Jesus is reaching out with a smile,

Saying come unto Me
And I will make you free
I will give you peace that lasts
And happiness that will never pass.

The Mirror
William R. Reynolds II

The mirror stands tall,
while the cracks disjoin
the image
of the ominous figure.

Through the looking glass
he looks inside
of himself
with childlike curiosity.

He is set adrift
on a sea of blood,
with his pale face
and his cold, vacant stare.

He hears a voice
much like his own,
it sounds agitated and envenomed
but unintelligible.

When he looks again
his fingers meet on the glass,
his condensating breath takes form,
And he turns away unanswered.

Tomorrow
Katrena Langdon

Do you ever wonder what will
happen tomorrow? I don't, I
wonder what will happen today. I
can't think of tomorrow for tomorrow
is not here yet. You never really
know if there will be a tomorrow.
So, I say, look for what's next.
It just might surprise you. But,
if you look for tomorrow you'll never
find it. You'll just find today.

My Daddy
Nellie M. Johnston

My daddy always read his Bible
And asked blessings for each meal he took
He did this every morning
Before he went to work.

He never failed a morning
While we were growing up
To start the day with Jesus with him
Deep within his heart.

When momma was called home
Daddy was never alone
And he knew he'd see her again
When Jesus says, "Well done."

Now, daddy will see momma
That day when Christ returns
And then they'll be together
Holding hands with Christ the Lord.

O I'll be glad to see them
And sit on my daddy's knee
With momma and my brothers, too
Alongside that heavenly sea.

Dreams of the Soul

What A Sight
Theresa Adams
Both day and night,
Rippling waters, splendid
Delight
What a sight,
The ocean's cold,
With rainbow colors of
Blue, and gold —
Rippling waters
Gently sway, holds
Hope and promises for
Today

Wishes
Joyce Stanway
I wish the people of the world
Would learn to love each other
To live in peace and harmony
Like sister and like brother

I wish all colours and all creeds
Could be as one together
Give out love instead of hate
In fair and stormy weather

I wish that everyone on earth
All God's creatures too
Could live in happiness and love
All their whole life through

I wish I could right all wrongs
In this world today
Give everyone a helping hand
To guide them on their way

I wish to end this poem now
I've nothing else to say
May the dear Lord bless and keep you
Today and every day

Dear Anyone
Paul Hicks
I find it very hard to see
The little squirrels in the tree,
The easier animals I have found
Are those that live upon the ground.

Wouldn't it be funny, for just one day,
To see things live the other way.
The ones from the ground could go way up high,
And all of the little ones come down from the sky.

A horse perched way up in a tree,
Would be such an easy thing to see,
And robins galloping over the ground,
For once, could now be easily found.

I'm sure they'd like living the other way,
After all, it's only for just one day,
And I do miss meeting the ones up high,
As they very rarely come down from the sky.

I find it very hard to see.

Yours Sincerely,
Mr. Mole

Incredible
Duan Howard
You turned and looked at me
Suddenly, all that I could see
All that I could feel
The magical wonder, the joy of my emotions
Flooded my soul
I'm so happy, so full inside that
I am in awe of what I feel
And I stood there bathing in
This incredible feeling of you and me
Two stars, two hearts
One spectacular beat...

Mr. Wet Tail
Glen Hanington
I've got a kitty in the shower
Where he'll sit for about an hour
Because he likes to watch
The drippies as they drop!

He likes to listen to the tinkle
Of each drop and little sprinkle
As it crashes down
And splashes with a plop!

As each drop flows to the drain
He will pat and paw in vain
As he tries to make
The flow of water stop!

He will sit and wait for more
Although there's water on the floor
Quite unaware
He's standing in that slop!

When there are no more drops to see
He'll come out to rub on me
But his tail's all wet
And feels just like a mop!

The Flowering Splendour Of The Seasons
G. J. Stubbs
Springtime with its flowers so beautiful and so rare
Colourful daffodils and tulips, that are simply beyond compare,
The air is performed with such a delightful scent
From the blossoms in abundance, and surely heaven meant.

Then summer with its pastel roses, and clustered floribundas too
A time to relish, and a wonderful sight to view;
The warmth of halcyon days and the glorious August moon
Ripened corn and fruits, harvest–time is with us soon.

Autumn arrives with splendour and its pleasant golden hues
The leaves on the trees, show splendid rustic views;
And dahlias and asters they are in full bloom
Fresh walnuts and chestnuts, will be with us soon.

Winter cometh with its cold frost, ice and snow
But the fireside gives off, a warming rich glow;
Snowdrops, crocuses, primroses, they all will shortly be here
After the season of goodwill, and every good cheer.

Such lovely flowers which abound throughout all of the seasons
That Mother Nature shows and gives us so many reasons;
Why we all should appreciate this precious gift of life
And do our best to overcome, all this stupid strife.

The Sun
Chad Miller

The Sun is Bright,
But not at night.

When it rises it makes,
a beautiful sight,
For all the people,
and animals, after
the long dark night.
When it sets before,
The night, it makes
a very beautiful sight.

Your Position In Life
Sylvia Carraud

The icy cold glance that came from your eyes,
froze the love that was once in my heart,
The look on your face more than words ever could
told the truth I should have known from the start.

As an unknown stranger you came to this land,
Seeking your fortune and your position in life.
All this you greedily hoped you would gain.
By taking a well–connected girl for your wife.

You cleverly used me by pretending to care,
And I was so naive not to realise it before,
But I wanted so much to believe in your love,
That I unwittingly opened opportunity's door

My life was so lonely and lacking in love,
That I fell hopelessly under your spell,
But once I was trapped and unable to flee,
You stopped bothering to care, I could tell.

It seemed then that you no longer needed me,
You had achieved all you had set out to do.
Your money, your possessions, your position in life.
Were all that ever mattered to you.

The Disappointment
Eric Stanley

The little boy was happy as he walked down the village street,
His Dad was due to visit, and his train he had to meet,
He hadn't seen his Dad for months, and his mum he never knew,
His Father couldn't cope alone, so he'd found pastures new.

He'd found kindness in the village, and lots more good than bad,
But for all the kindness shown to him, his Dad was still his Dad,
So he'd started out quite early, he thought that would be best,
As the station was some distance, and halfway he'd have to rest.

He stood upon the platform, which was deserted but for the lad,
Just waiting, hoping, praying that the train would bring his Dad,
He saw the signal arm come down, the gates then opened wide,
And as the coaches passed him, he tried to peep inside.

The train was almost empty, there was lots and lots of space,
But the boy was quite excited, as he searched for his Dad's face,
But no passengers alighted, and as the train went on its way,
The boy was left in disbelief, and his face pained in dismay.

He'd been let down, a bitter blow, it really hit quite hard,
And his lip began to tremble, as he left the station yard.
But he'd be brave, he wouldn't cry although he felt a fool,
His Dad didn't come for he was ill, he'd tell the kids at school.

Cats
Elizabeth Brewer

The song of cats goes on. Just
one of a kind; not different.

I stroke her fur, so soft. Her
big blue eyes glossy, but, as
clear as a window's wind.

I see right through her. I see
her every dream, every point,
every move, but
in my heart I love her.

Joan
Leah Allen Russell

The most beautiful woman
I've ever known
Was my minister's wife
Her name was Joan

She was here on a mission
She had a message to share
To love others
And their pain she would bear

So many times
I think of Joan
The way she touched my life
Only here on loan

There are many nights
When I bow on my knees
"Lord God, Please use me, "
I ask, "As you please"

My greatest blessing
Will be to hear Him say
"You're a lot like Joan,
I like my servants that way"

The Dusty Trail
Hayden Gomes

The dusty trail,
miles wide,
with birds singing in the sky.
My brothers and me talking as we ride.

We talk about stories and legends,
about animals and Indians and nature.

When we find a place to camp we help Ma cook, good old Grandma clean,
and then watch Dad shave the lather off his face,
while dusk gathers over the looming mountains in the distance.

As I sleep,
I dream about the big journey ahead and the loved ones left behind.

I dream about meadows
and forests
and streams.
I dream about this new land we are going to and the land we are leaving.

When I wake up I hear the cry of life passing by.
Good old Grandma died.

Dedication: My grandfather, Joe Sconce

Dreams of the Soul

Dogs
Kristen Romanyschyn
Dogs are friendly,
Dogs are nice,
Dogs are sweeter than sugar and spice,
They have tails that wag all day long,
And if you say speak, they'll sing you
a little song.
Dogs will make you happy, when your
feeling blue,
And when you come in at night,
You know you have a friend that is
true to you.

Pardon?
Jan Lambert
"Do you have the time, please?" asked Philamon O'Grady
"What do you mean? How could you, Sir?" replied the young man, gravely.
"I only asked...!" "No, don't go on, your meaning is quite clear!
For after all you're standing there and I am standing here!"

"I need to know..." "I do not care to hear your petty fears!"
"But, really Sir. I only want..." "I can't believe my ears!
If two was three and one was four, d'you think today would be?
No, mark my words, the Kremlin would call in the cavalry!"

Philamon O'Grady looked above and shook his head,
"I asked..." "And do you think that I would be up out of bed
If oranges were whistles and bananas sang a song?
No, my hippocrocoscrewcomoose would end up far too long!"

"But if you listen carefully..." "Sir, I shall call a tree
If you don't stop with your tirade and stop harassing me!
I've had enough, can take no more of your procrastination
Someone would think you'd never thought about a blue Dalmatian!"

The young man turned away, a twinkle gleaming in his eye.
He chuckled to himself and shrugged, and then let out a sigh.
He waved around a photograph of something not quite there
And with a flash he disappeared... was gone into thin air!

Little Boy Lost...
Barbara A. Patterson
Little Boy Lost, my heart weeps for you,
Where are you now? I sure wish I knew.
Deep in my thoughts, I can still see,
How your eyes danced when you smiled at me.

You were so small and seemed very frail,
Skin like the snow, soft and so pale.
When I would hold you, sing you to sleep,
Off into dreamland, slumbering deep.

Your memories twinkle and shine in my heart,
Little Boy Lost, my love's where you are.
The roads might be long, it might be years,
My heart aches in silence in an ocean of tears.

The sun and the stars, and even the moon,
Help me believe you're coming home soon.
They shine with power, from distances high,
They know where you are when my heart starts to cry.

I pray for wisdom to endure through this test,
but each day that passes I feel more distress.
Little Boy Lost, you know if I could,
Bring you back home, you must know I would.

The Ship Of Time
D. J. Smith
As I sail a cloudless sky
My limbs do ache
As we pass through time
Lost souls do cry out
From the sea of dreams
Shivering, screeching, set us free
Swirling mists, so dark and grey
Rising, falling with salty spray
My eyes do sting
As I chart my course
To my makers keep.

A New Beginning
Ann R. Misenhimer
Morning had begun and he left me——
To go into the arms of another;
Morpheus had to take him for awhile,
For his eyes were closing, as we said goodnight.

It was a new day, a new beginning,
And yet—a beginning for what purpose!
Our live are patterned like the sand
Rushing into the sea.
Back and forth–washing away troubles one day,
Bringing them back at morning tide...

Yes, it was a new day, a happiness that enraptured me,
For I will help him try and wash away his fears... of emotion,
That rush in and leave a pattern in his mind, but perhaps,

One new day, a new beginning will come to him.
He will be so proud and will come to me and say... "Thank you,
The sands of time have sifted through my mind filled with turmoil,
And I now know I can say what I have deeply felt for so long..."

His fear is gone. He is complete.

My life will now start a new day: Another new beginning.

Someday
W. Izzard
A warm sensation fills my heart
Just to think of you
But it's tearing me apart to know
You don't feel the way I do

For so long now I've felt as if
My world will crumble away
I wish I could tell of the way I feel
But I'm scared that you won't stay

Hopefully one day you'll notice me
As more than just your friend
But till then I'll hope and pray
That you'll see me in the end

Then today you told me of your new found love
I acted pleased for you
You told me of her long red hair
And that her eyes were blue

But even though you're now with her
Still I hope and pray
That soon you will notice me
You'll notice me someday

Noteworthy Works

Porch Swings
Rachel Ann Smith

What happened to the porch swings?
A place where families sat and chat for hours.
A place that filled the need for quality time.
A place to sit and watch the rain fall.
A place to relax and drink lemonade.

Now we barely have enough time to say two words.
Now we need to plan a date for quality time.
Now the rain has become a nuisance in our busy lives.
Now you can forget about relaxing.
What happened to the porch swings.

Tramp
Angus Richmond

He sauntered in, a lonely tramp,
A cat abandoned in the street
Beneath a lowly wayside ramp,
A–shivering with cold feet.

Why, Tramp? We named him thus
Because against the odds, it seemed,
He'd come by cunning wiles to us
In hope; from a kind of poverty redeemed.

Shy at first, he shrank from human touch,
Afraid to give himself too trustingly
To anyone, a friend perhaps, who so much
As tried to woo him lovingly.

We are his foster–parents true;
He a child of nature needing direction.
We raised him from a kitten's mew
To a grown cat's occupation.

Mice, the soul of caution, know to beware
And not, fool–hardy, to venture out.
A glance from Tramp's enough to scare
The boldest rodent put to rout.

My Guardian Angel
Teresa Hill

There's hands touching me,
They are invisible to see.
I shiver from the thought,
As a mystery is brought.

Am I sharing life's ride,
With someone by my side?
Through it all I find,
My decisions are mine.

I may so freely talk,
But never alone do I walk.
Suddenly I hear my name,
It was so clearly it came.

Over my shoulder I look,
It was a chance I took.
Do I even need to dare,
Question who is there?

It's my guardian angel there,
Making me of her presence aware,
Though not seen at all is she,
Always by my side she'll be!

Youth Of The Morning
Helen B. Lisney

They who say you're too old, don't listen
You who have the youth of the morning!

Youth does not stop at twenty, thirty or even forty
It is here, so long as the world is here

We are the world – we, the youth of the morning
As vital as the sun, the moon and sea

Youth does not end, nor ever
It is part of eternity

Love On The Line
Robert Christopher

A journey of love started back in time
God's house St. Paul's is first on the line,
We thunder through tunnels black as night
fighting for space with all our might.

Under the city we surface at Bank
fighting our way, no people to thank,
Doors close, more treading on feet
suddenly its empty, must be Liverpool Street.

Still underground, Bethnal Green in the east
now Mile End where darkness and daylight meet,
Back to back houses, streets, people and cars
into the depths of Stratford we begin to see grass.

Through Leyton and Leytonstone now above ground
I see children playing, recreation parks abound,
Swings, slides, even coloured seesaws a few.
On to Wanstead Flats, Redbridge, and Gant's Hill too.

Newbury Park, Barkingside, near my journey's end
at last Fairlop, one more field just around the bend.
Will she be there this special endless love of mine
to meet and greet me, her love, who travelled the line.

Virtual Normality
Linda Hayes

No more crying, no more tears,
No more anxiety, worry or fears.
No more heartache, no more pain,
No more doubts, am I insane?

No more rights, no more wrongs,
No more memories, of sad old songs.
No more days, out of touch,
No more nights, suffering so much!

No more anger, just be glad,
No more unhappiness, don't be sad.
No more hopelessness, the end is near,
No more despair, everything is so clear!

No more depression, just peace of mind,
No more "Ifs and whys", I'm just one of a kind.
No more questions, let's just rest,
No more prayers, "GOD" knows best!

I will be happy, no thoughts of going mad,
I will be with my dear old dad.
I will be humble, wise, heed "HIS" word,
I will be quiet, content and with our "LORD"!

Dreams of the Soul

Shining Light
Sheryl Saxby

Do not walk in a room and think I am not there, because I am because I care. I had to leave you, I wanted to stay. But my learning was over, so I was called away.

I gently walk one step ahead, I found the shining light that lie ahead. Then I knew that the time was right, so I silently walked on into that beautiful light.

Do not miss me, now that I have gone. Because love in our hearts it just goes on and on. And then one day when the time is right you will walk into the shining light.

To My Wife ✈
Travis C. Forsberg

The look on your face, on our day of grace is a beautiful thing to see.
Everyone knowing today is for you and me.
We combine together at last, today we are as one.
The joy in my life is undenounced.
I love you!

Your long nine months of pain finally bring, to us a bundle of joy.
You wanted a girl, I wanted a boy.
We both got our wish, beautiful twins Tim and Trish.

The kids grew up, we grew old still together 25 years.
My love for you is greater now, than all of our passed years.
Each morning that I wake, a cleansing breath I take,
and your beautiful face I see.

Tim and Trisha called to celebrate with us,
our 50 years of joy.
"We love you!" they said. We said "Love you too!"

Now as we look down, friends and relatives frown.
We died together, it couldn't be better being with you for eternity
over half a century we were together, best of friends to the end
Our souls will rest in peace together walking on clouds
Until we get to Heaven. I Love You!

Don't Burn Our Flag
Katharine G. Leipold

Don't let them burn our flag, America,
The symbol of our land and of the free.
Our armed forces, soldiers, sailors and marines —
Have fought and shed their blood, for you and me.

It's precious as it flies in all its glory;
We pledge allegiance with our hands and hearts, to be —
Ever steadfast in reverence —— that's our story;
Don't desecrate our flag — let it fly free.

We're privileged just to live here in America,
Where justice and democracy, is the key;
So honor and revere our precious symbol —
For that's the way it really has to be

Let all who would oppose its desecration,
Sing out their voices for democracy;
And let this "God Protected" symbol of our country —
Forevermore, proclaim its liberty.

If prohibiting the burning of our flag, is unconstitutional
Then, God help us, — our hopes and dreams, we'll never see,
We'll need no morals, Supreme Courts or Justices —
Ruled by ignorance, unjustly, we'll just cease to be.

Untitled
Alfred Reynolds

Bluebells were ringing
The mavis was singing
Heather was blooming on valley and hill
The sun was shining and I was reclining
At peace with myself
Then I felt a chill.
This beautiful planet is fast disappearing
War and pollution are taking their toll
Before it's too late
Let's find a solution
Mankind is in danger of losing its soul.

Promise
Joyce French–Coleman

I am always near —
in the whisper of a prayer
in a lovely smile
or the sadness of a tear
in the scent of damp mossy
woodland trees
in the wind as it rustles
through the leaves
in sunbeams that dance on
forest and vale
in raindrops that fall on
your window pane
in the twinkle of stars that
shine at night
in the glow of the moon as
it sheds God's light
in the solitude of music you
love to hear
in peaceful moments we will
always share
in the surf as it resounds
on the shore
Remember, I will love you
forever more.

Ages
William L. Vasquez

Today, I'm forty–two,
questions ensue,
so much to do,
sometimes blue.

Today, I'm fifty–three,
longing to be free,
can't wait to see,
the retired me.

Today, I'm sixty–one,
so much fun,
not nearly as old,
as I was told.

Today, I'm seventy–five,
still drive,
needed by older friends,
day never ends.

Today, I'm eighty–four,
muscles sore,
trying to keep score,
don't really expect much...

Noteworthy Works

Untitled
F. Saxton
I took my collie dog for his early run,
The weather was very windy,
A gust of wind blew my hat off in the park,
I walked down the path for 200 yards,
There I met a fella with his dog,
Your dog seems to be enjoying chewing,
It looks like my hat, why didn't you pick it up,
It's not my hat he's chewing its your hat,
"I don't like your attitude" I said,
He said, "it's not my hat he chewed it's
Your hat he chewed."

Dad
Jaya Thomas Mulligan
When I think about my Dad it really breaks my heart,
I am so sorry that we had to part.
A man in my life I did truly adore,
As each day goes by I love him more.

Sweet memories are all I have got,
And Photographs I treasure the lot.
Life without him, I always feel lost,
I would have him back at any cost.

The little taffy I hold so dear
He looked so funny in his pit gear
He liked a pint at the local bar
No one denied him his frothy jar.

From the Rhonda valley my Dad came
David Glynowr was his name.
A Dad amongst dad's he was great
Until life took its unescaping fate.

Although I cannot see him I know he is near,
Looking out, protecting me I have nothing to fear
One day we will meet again, I know this in my heart
Then we will be together, and never have to part.

To My Love, My Wife
James C. Price
I leave this thought with you my love
If I should go away...
From time to time drift into dreams
About our bygone days...
Think of wonderful hours we share,
A fond embrace.
And if you do,
Somehow I know,
A smile will light your face.
Dwell for awhile,
Of our tender times,
Aglow with our happy times...
Then close your eyes and you will feel
The warmth of my love and caress.

Death can never erase true love,
Only makes it stronger.
So roam the land of reverie,
And I will linger longer.
Inside your heart,
I'll always be remembered.
I leave this thought with you my love
That says...
"Oh! please remember my love."

Paranoid
N. Palmer
Excuse me, were you just talking about me,
you were, that's alright then you see,
I thought I was just paranoid,
I thought my brain was just a void,
So people like you I tend to avoid,
Did I just say that, or am I paranoid.
What's wrong, are you confused,
the use of words have you abused,
I know the words I used are fused,
If you combined your brain to shoes,
Keep track my time, my wit, you lose.

With Or Without You
C. Richmond
Good times, bad times,
memories always last.
Happy days it used to be,
but now they're in the past.
Suffering in silence.
What have I to gain?
I'm feeling low, so deeply low.
I cannot shift my pain.
I can't go on much longer,
you've had the best of me.
So many ultimatums,
yet still you cannot see.
We're going round in circles,
my life is one big game.
I used to laugh, but now I cry,
for we'll never be the same.
My head is full of answers.
but will I make that choice,
to rock the boat or stay afloat
are you listening to my voice?
Decisions to be made
have I the strength to follow through?
My world's about to change
With or without you.

Dark Shade Of Love
Lynda Goodship
Your lips shower with kisses,
Your love is better than wine,
There is a fragrance about you,
Which is madly divine.

How your eyes shine with love,
let me hear that enchanting voice,
Oh, your lips are a scarlet ribbon,
What an amazing device.

But please don't look down on me,
Because of my colour,
I am the same person,
Despite the gala.

If you heard my voice and saw my eyes,
But not the colour of my skin,
Then you would give us a chance,
To hold our dreams within.

While I sleep, my heart is awake,
I dream of you knocking at my door,
I don't know what is so wonderful about you,
But I have never met anyone like you before.

Dreams of the Soul

Perspective
James Cater
She is rape,
For she holds my heart against my will,
Her icy clutch
Freezing me from inside.
Her playful mind is warped
Like a lioness toying with her prey.
She sees my pain as nothing,
When her own life is desolate
My joys will never excite her,
Though with my self–destruction
She grows strong enough to fade away.

Crawl Into My Silent World
M. McNeil
When I crawl into my silent world I feel like I'm your only
girl, I love you more than diamond and pearl, being with you
I'm on top of the world, you fill me with joy which directs
my pride, you make me feel good whenever I walk by your side.

Those tender loving moments, you are one of a kind oh darling
tell me why can't you be mine, when I crawl out of my silent
world it is like a nightmare to face the outside world panicking
in anguish, you were my best wish.

Why is life so bumpy there is always a twist, I know that I
miss you but do you miss me too, to tell you the truth I don't
know what I'm gonna do, your words were persuasive and your
actions seemed pure how can I predict when you'll come back home.

When you are in your silent world do you remember the way we
were, I always followed you like a shadow in every weather
my love for you could not be measured, though jealousy may make me
act immature, it was because I was feeling insecure.

Your love makes me feel so mature, please do not ignore me
anymore, welcome into my silent world, come share my passion
and appreciation, please rescue me, come set me free my
silent world is my mind.

A Remembrance Day Hymn
Mary M. Jenkins
O Lord, look down with favour
And listen to our prayer
As we recall our heroes
Of land and sea and air.

In ditches and in airplanes
And on the rolling sea
They shed their blood for England
For king and liberty.

The air with smoke was riven,
The mud was coloured red,
When millions lately living
Joined honour'd ranks of dead.

The Fathers, sons and brothers,
The husbands, daughters, wives,
Thru charity for others
Laid down their precious lives.

O Lord, may we be worthy
Of such a sacrifice,
And join that honour'd company
One day beyond the skies.

Norn
D. J. Smith
Circle of stones, rich in puce
why do you glow for me
In shades of mediocrity
Is not the traitors gate
To ruminate in the lands
Which tie our fate
If I be Norse from northern skies
Then to rule I must be wise
Oh, answer me, runes of time
So that you may
Guide my earthly state.

Wall Of Names (Vietnam Memorial)
Leon Sutherland
Oh America! Cry soft in sackcloth and ashes.
Touch gentle this wall of names.
Hear the silent voices all about you,
Feel too, the hurt in death's cold rain.

Pass the bitter cup from lips to lips,
Grasp it firmly in red stained hands,
Let not this symbol of weak leadership
Fade from the memory of a once–proud land.

Weakness in leadership is never a virtue.
Only the disease of a deadly plague.
A caisson of youth–filled coffins, empty voices,
All draped in America's flag.

What say you America and where to now!
Will you pull up bootstraps and play the game
Or will you play hide and seek with courage
And build more walls with rows of names.

Oh may our remembering be forever
Of this silent, marching throng,
And may our tributes touch the mountains
When we sing sweet freedom's song.

Complicatedly Torn
Karen Amy LaPoint
Halfway up a misty mountain top,
halfway drowning in seas of pain...
all I can see is what could have been and I am left too blinded by
what I wanted from you.
I have waited so long for you,
I have cried so many unshed tears.
The sky is growing grayer with each passing moment,
The tide is getting too high for me to make it back home,
The running away of a heart, the running away of memory...
all I can do now to save my torn soul, is to run away.
All that's left is emotions unknown for you,
I took all that I could hold, I wanted to take all that I need
But the walls are re–growing faster and stronger now...
And I now know that escaping from you
and your barbed wire prison, is best for me.
So long, farewell is all I can say,
So long, farewell I have had it with these games.
We could have had it all and I know,
we could have made it through our years of tangled webs.
We could have had what we yearned for, especially this time around
But now comes the time, just when it would be right,
That we must take our separate paths – – –
and leave our past behind, even though I have,
and still love you.

Noteworthy Works

Pathways Thru Life
Sylvia VanderFord
As we look back on life's changing patterns
No rhyme or reason
has made things happen
on our way.

We have lived life to its fullest
Merrily skipping along
as the final curtain
is coming down.

In Springtime, we were young and gay
Summertime we learned
to live and laugh
our path thru life.

Fall was very special to our loving hearts
Middle age has arrived.
Wintertime comes too soon
We've only begun.

Life is forever changing its pattern
as we continually
challenge its inspiring
Pathways Thru Life.

Another Summer
Joy Dorman Frederick
When nighttime came
The sweet scent of honeysuckle
Perfumed through my window screen
I lazily sprawled
Across my bed to dream
Thoughts of love
Once brand new
Another summer, another June
The scent lingered
The memories did too
Of another summer, another June

My Friend
Faith Palubinski
When I was little, I asked God to make me a friend;
one who could love me for me so I didn't have to pretend.

He told me of his great creation and left me with reminders;
so no matter where my friend may be I'll always be able to find her.

He said look into the sky above, the sky that is so deep blue;
there you will find the eyes of your friend filled with love and truth.

He said look up at the radiant sun, the sun that warms and comforts too;
there you will find the smile of your friend waiting to welcome you.

He said pay attention to the colorful flowers, all the flowers as they begin to bloom;
there you will find the gentle heart of your friend with kindness that fills up a room.

He said listen to the whistling wind, the wind that tickles your spirit;
there you will find the laughter of your friend that's contagious when you hear it.

Finally God said look deep my child, deep into your soul;
there you will find the acceptance of your friend, and the love for you she holds.

Me And Poetry
Liana Falaleeff
The Poetry Guild advertised
It read "YOUR POEM COULD WIN"
So I thought I'd get creative,
And wrote this ditty to send in.

My poems are not written
about love, pets, or the nations,
but the verses start to flow
in real life situations!

My poems are usually fairly short
and sometimes full of humour.
People say I've missed my calling
(And that's not just a rumour)!

When I've got the reason
and the words begin to flow
These poems I'll keep on writing
and go from amateur to PRO!

So here to you I do submit
the poetry that's "me".
Thought I'd chance to send it in
'cuz there's "NO ENTRY FEE"!!

My Holy Lord
Regina Jenkins
O' Holy Lord
You are my Holy Lord
I love you Lord
And I adore you my Lord
You are my Holy Lord

I praise you o' Lord
I worship you o' Lord
I exalt you o' Lord
You are my only Lord
You are my Holy Lord

Prisoner Of Pain
Merri Lee Culbert–Slute
She sits all alone in the darkness
and fights her constant war
while she thinks of the one she lost long ago;
he's all that matters anymore.

The pain of what she experienced
stays with her and haunts her every day
while she lives with the guilt and the love she has
for the son that she gave away.

She blamed everyone else in her life
for the decision that was made
and stood by and watched helplessly
as her life began to fade.

She was taken prisoner by her pain
and felt that no one understood,
so she put her trust in the uncertain hands
of the only thing that would.

It promised to soothe her broken heart
and to help make the time pass,
but it made her lose sight of the person within
while she watched life through the bottom of her empty glass.

Dreams of the Soul

The Love Of My Life
Grace G. Keeter
You're the love of my life
I shall always remember
The bond that we share
In Life's December

First it was friendship
Deep and abiding
Then love developed
In our hearts residing

You make me Laugh
And I really like that
Or we cry together
When we are sad

You're my very best friend
My Dad and my lover
You're also my darling
I have no other

You're the love of my life
I shall always remember
The bond that we share
In life's December

Sixteen
Olivia Deering
It's everything I felt on sunny days—
laughter, cokes, and bubble gum ways;

It's Ferriswheels and dizzy rides...
guys who wink with flirty eyes.

It's stars exploding in space—
A corner in my heart where memories
are placed.
Dedication: Bennie and Patrick McClendon

The Flooded Years of Yesterday
Gabriel Gerber
Looking back on yesterday
Time sure flies just like they say
We all have dreams to have it made
But staying high those dreams will fade

Feeling a little sad, a little undone
Mothers worry of what's become
Buying the years, having fun
The world is dwindling, I'm not the one.

Staying high and running away,
Wasting time you'll wash away,
You'll wash away
The flooded years of yesterday

Alone and quiet for a long time
Will there be someone to call mine
Waiting love is hard to find
Pictures of you always on my mind

Sometimes got to watch just what you say
It takes time that's how you play
And only the strong can make a stay
The flooded years of yesterday.

The Journey
Shirley O'Reilly
Horizontal lines through blinds awaken me to another day.
I begin my journey into the morning, down the hall
past framed synchronized memories.
From the wall my children stare gap–toothed happy
grins, baseball caps...

I progress onward past high school proms and
uniformed buff–shouldered patriotic men and finally
pictures of good husbands and fathers.
So it continues on through the living room
surrounded by the faces of all my grandchildren.
Pausing to straighten the frame that's always
crooked, I stare into a face that definitely
resembles mine. I smile.

Now in my empty kitchen, I sit sipping
coffee from my "World's Greatest Mom"
cup, staring through the window at unchanged
scenery.

Sighing and smiling I make my way
back down my hallway of memories
forward to my room to dress and re–invent
myself.

Foundation Of Maturity
Georgeta Srbu
There is no moonbeam tonight to dance around
your pillow, to kiss your cheek and stroke your
hair and walk along the window.

The breeze has gone to a far and distant land and
whispers to a stranger of pale white skin and
golden locks and a heart that is so tender.

The innocence has fled on a gentle rolling wave
on the dark, dark sea. A tear–stained face
awaits, awaits for its return she shall never see.

Untitled
Deborah S. Klingensmith
Bluebird in flight
Hummingbird on vine
Butterfly a–flutter
Springtime sign

Cows in the pasture
Fawns in the field
Warm sunny days
Winter does yield

A breath of dew
A blossomed flower
This is nature's
Finest hour

Babes in the woods
Chicks in the trees
Wonders of nature
Are all of these

Thank you O Lord
For the birds and bees
Thank you O Lord
For all of these

Noteworthy Works

The Birthday Toast
Rose McNamara

With glasses charged the revellers shouted.
Good luck, good health, live long, die young,
I wondered as I raised my glass,
what did it mean?

To live a life of many years.
One must grow old, and yet die young?
Throughout my youth this toast I pondered.
How could this be?

Every year the toast got longer.
Good luck, good health, much cheer, much wealth.
Live long die young.
Can this be done?

My youth has flown on fleeting wings.
A happy life is what I've had With wife, and table,
roof, and bed.
A sanctuary to lay my head.

Now I am old and soon to rest.
The toast is clear. Live long, die young. It can be done.
Put on my stone for all to see.
Here lies a young man of 93.

The Book
Andrea Wersyn

I opened a book that was big and blue
to take a look at the world's view.

I was disappointed to see that the water's not clean
and the only monkey can't be seen.

I took a look at this fragile world that is breaking
and made a list of things that are not for peoples' taking.

They were here first before our birth
so leave them alone — they belong to the earth.

Story Weaver
Andrea Evers

In ages past, the Story Weaver
spun a tale for young and old.
Words of wisdom, words of beauty,
tales which now are rarely told.

Few remain who know the wisdom,
Few who hear the Weaver's call.
We must learn again to listen
to the One who saved us all.

Weaver, Master, tell Your story
Life, Creation, Death and Hell.
Years will pass yet men remember
all the stories that You tell.

Journeys long and fraught with hardship,
prayers and off'rings, death and tears;
speak Your words, reveal Your wisdom.
Weave a tale to span the years.

We receive Your grace and glory,
all. You say sincere and true.
Through the tears, the fear and laughter,
Weaver, we believe in You.

What Of The World?
J. Cooper

Is the situation now as bad as it can get?
Oh! No, to use a well known phrase, "You ain't seen nuthin' yet",
I think it will get far, far worse than it is at this time,
"What"? you ask, as well you might: Well, violence and crime.

An Ideal World where none exists? now wouldn't that be nice,
No wars, no rape, no crimes of theft, not any kind of vice,
Pipe dream? Yeah! I know it is, I'm on the funny farm,
But wishing that the world was so, that can't do any harm.

People talk and make it known that peace should be our aim,
Others twist their words around and treat peace as a game,
Protest songs have always tried to get the message through,
The sad part is that those who heed are now so very few.

It's not just peace but love as well, that needs a helping hand,
Religious people tend to think their God has something planned,
Well if that's true, and who can say? He's surely marking time,
If you're there, Lord, please look down and read this rhyme of mine.

Man is clever, Man is good at making things for man,
Never thinking that his work could put us in the can,
The animals and birds and trees are victims of our race,
If Man can't stop the rollercoaster, "Please" JUST SLOW THE PACE.

Teachers
Carol Jaxson–Jager

Some teachers call on the ones who are clean and smart
Who finish their homework, who have clean teeth, white teeth,
Who have good grades, who wear brand name clothes, who have straight hair
Who have straight noses surrounded by freckles,
Who have round light-colored eyes, who have light skin, white skin.
The world is open to them.

The world is open to the light, bright and white,
and closed to the dark, stupid and ugly who will
Kick down the door and climb the ladder of life and succeed.
Weeds always survive and become stronger.

The Mother Earth
G. Jain

Big Bang! There was in the Cosmos a new birth,
Added to our universe was the living earth
For trillion of years revolving round the sun,
Among glittering galaxy you had your berth.

Kicked out of Heaven came Adam and Eve,
To stay forever on a long, long leave,
God ordered them never to return,
Not to be pardoned, never to reprieve.

Nothing is untouchable, for he is adroit,
To pillage, to poach, to dig and exploit,
The man, whose greed is a bottomless hell
Covering all continents, from Delhi to Detroit.

The end is nigh, it is quite distinct,
Like docile dodo, you are going to be extinct,
A lifeless planet like Moon and Mars,
From destruction of ecology, it is quite evident.

The only hope is, spanning the (ozone) Hole,
The seas, America and the virgin North Pole,
Slowly and steadily your demise drawing near,
Would you be a celestial desolate body or a barren dustbowl?

Dreams of the Soul

A Mother's Love
Mary Symons
She holds her little boy close to her breast
Then she rocks him and sings to him till he's at rest.

Then gently she carries him up to his bed
Hoping he'll sleep through the night now he's fed.

She sleeps Oh so lightly she waits for his cry
Then she lifts him and changes him so he's all clean and dry

Then holding him close to her body so warm
She feeds him and talks to him as up comes the dawn

And so she talks to him and holds him awhile
He's now wide awake and he gives her a smile

He gurgles and talks to her in his own way
And his little bright eyes from her face never stray

His fingers so tiny and soft to the touch
Are curled round her finger he loves her so much

And the pride in her face tells a story so old.
Of a Mother whose child is more precious than gold.

My Father
Janet A. Forster
My Father, big and strong,
Black hair, and skin darkened
From sea, sky and wind
From work done on the sea.
He loved the sea, blue and green,
Calm and angry.
This loved Father of mine,
who could not swim,
Left this land of hate and anger
And found the peace
Of his blue–green sea.

My Longing Wish
Godfrey J. Martin
Please let me see the Daffodils again
Brought to bloom by sun and rain
Please let me see their golden heads
In local parks and flower beds

In the meadows they stand so proud
A shining beacon between the clouds
Slowly my heart is filled with pride
As they decorate the countryside

Please let me see the flower of Wales
Growing wild in woods and dales
When Winters followed by the spring
Then hordes of Daffodils it will bring

Let me see from the top of the hill
The clusters of the Daffodil
Our national emblem brings a tear
They will soon be gone for another year

Come early May they will fade away
The flower of St. David's Day
But the seasons come and seasons go
And once again the Daffodil will grow

My Man
A. McNally
We married in June of 61
We weren't very rich but had lots of fun.
We started a family right away,
and I'm happy for that to this very day.

Bridget was first a beautiful one,
Eddie was next, a sweet little son.
Then Alice, then Anne, then Billy came too,
I thought at that stage that we would be through.

But no not us, we still went on,
First Mary then Tricia then Jim were born.
But wait, guess what we didn't stop there,
Margaret came next so cute and so fair.

Well our kids all grew up and we used to say,
we would be on our own someday.
But no not our kids they kept up the score,
17 grandchildren and soon a few more.

Well my man has gone now, things aren't the same,
But I'm very proud what he's left in his name.
We were poor but we found,
We were the richest parents around...

Drink
Samantha Knox
I was once a smart person
until one day I found a friend
Drink was it's name.
When I was with my friend everything seemed so fine.
I started to rely on my friend
more and more
until one day I couldn't leave him where he was
I couldn't go on living without him
but all my money was gone.
I ended up on the street all due to alcohol
I thought I was strong but drink was stronger.

I Book My Dreams In Advance
Michael Levy
Dream you say, Yes dream I do.
Not any dream mind you.
My dream is real, so real you see,
It isn't a fairy tale or fantasy.
I'm not trying to lead you a merry dance,
I book my dreams in advance.
If anyone could do as me,
Dream the dreams that make you free.
Life would be so full of fun.
Just like a band with a big bass drum.
What is my dream I hear you say,
It's something I do night and day.
I open my arms and soar up high,
Yes believe it or not I can fly.
Above the clouds or over the seas,
Across the fields and through the trees.
In and out, up and down,
Over the city and over town.
I have seen some wonderful sights,
In the mornings and in the nights.
Now close your eyes and up you go,
Not too fast and not too slow.
After awhile you get to know
You really can fly like I told you so.

Noteworthy Works

Emotional Scars
Barry Rothschild

Shackled I am,
Shackled I'll be,
Though slavery's over,
I'm not truly free.

I'm treated unfairly,
I'm treated unjust,
fight for my rights,
surely I must.

I can't eat with the whites,
can't sit in front of the bus,
as Martin Luther King,
has thoroughly discussed.

Although I am free,
the scars will remain,
throughout the years,
I've suffered oh so much pain!

Shackled I am,
shackled I'll be,
though slavery's over,
I'm not truly free.

My Hope
Geraldine Tiboldo

My hope is for a future
filled with joy for all I know
my hope is for a mind that's
often tested but never fails.
And a body full of life and
spirit. My hope is for a soul
at peace with the world.
And my hope is for love,
Laughter and happiness always.

Dedication: To my great, loving husband

Kinlochbervie
Norman MacPhee

There's a seaweed tang to the wild winds breath
That blows in with the Atlantic tide
And the sweet perfume from heather and broom
To make a Scotsman swell with pride

And the only sound to break the peace
In this part of Sutherland so still
Are the whispers of an evening breeze
And the curlews vibrant trill

Heaven to me is Oldshoremore
Where I can wander the beach and dream
And watch along this northwest shore
The wavelets froth and cream

I yearn to sit on the headland so tall
With my daughter and her twins at my side
Listening to the sea gulls call
Almost drowned by the crash of the tide

Should the good Lord grant to me this prayer
Perfection and peace there will be
My vision of paradise will be there
In that haven of peace by the sea.

No Home For Irene
Sue Northover

Irene and her children came from London Town,
living in a house that was falling down.
They slept on a mattress slung on the floor,
with no kitchen, no bath and half a front door.

One electric light they had to see by,
with holes in the roof they could gaze at the sky.
She walked the streets looking for a decent home,
the answer was the same "Only on your own."

She went to the council and pleaded her case,
"Don't worry" they said "We will find you a place."
One month later she still didn't hear,
now her worry was turning to fear,

Irene fell ill with a collapsed lung,
in no time at all an ambulance was rung.
She was put on a stretcher and everyone did stare,
her poor little children were taken into care.

There are lots of Irene's in the same plight,
forgotten people like shadows in the night.
The people on the council, building castles in the sky,
should all be whipped for letting Irene nearly die.

Untitled
Michelle Fortin

Gentle summer breezes
Bring songs of the lazy days
Colors of azure blue
wisps of whipped cream haze

Children happy and
carefree
not missing their school days

See the tulips smile and
drink the sunrays

The Nightmare Before Christmas
Michael Lyons

Twenty–five days seems like a lifetime
children play, having a nice time
lost in the spirit of make–believe
in the nightmare before Christmas.

The grown–up and careworn watching their young
while a million other things need to be done
frozen in the season of the cold rush
in the nightmare before Christmas.

Shops and shopping, stocks and stockings
I want I want, but some get nothing
it's all right for some while others are having
a nightmare before Christmas.

The flame of youth rekindled again
with awakened love for our fellow men
yearning to find those long–lost friends
in the nightmare before Christmas.

Twenty–five days and one more for luck
and it's over like that, wasn't it fun
well, yes and no
I'd say it's like a nightmare before Christmas.

Dreams of the Soul

The Creatures In My Garden
Jonathan Lee

The creatures in my garden,
give me a fright,
When they jump out,
and give me a bite.

The worst of all,
Is very small,
I run and run and puff and pant,
to get away from the vicious ant.

The best of all,
is still very small,
Quieter than a mouse,
Its the little shell backed wood louse.

Most extraordinary of all
Is not as small
The many–legged millipede
That feeds itself on bits of weed.

The creatures in my garden
Come in, in all shapes and sizes
They are very, very different
and all have different prizes.

Requiem For A Marriage
Mary C. McDaniels

When the fires of rage had burned themselves out
And destroyed my soul with numbing grief
I mourned the death of our love
And finally accepted

But in the deepening shadows before the dawn
As I finally fell exhausted to sleep
Just for a moment in the awful stillness
I thought I heard an angel weep

Dedication: Peggy and Cara, God's Angels

Golden Wedding
Louisa Ray

For fifty years you two have walked
The road of life together,
Hand in hand the way you planned
Through fine and stormy weather.
You have had your share of hardships too,
Of grief and pain and care,
But steadfastly you 'stuck it out'
To see the sunshine there.
You have had misunderstandings
Your ups and downs as well,
And love and joy and comradeship
Yes, more than tongue can tell.
Love that has stood the test of time
Since that fair wedding day
When you two pledged yourselves as one,
And so you wend your way
Together still. Half a century
Has come and gone, and now
You have turned another page in time
And doing so renew a vow
That first was made so many years ago,
When first you two became as man and wife,
For nothing can defeat the love you know
The love that will sustain you both for life.

At Last
Joan H. Yates

I lift my eyes and in the mirror see
A shadow of what once was me.
No more golden hair and eyes of sparkling blue,
Those colours now a softer hue.

Who would think I'd reach this day
Of youthful struggles fading fast away.
No more mind that's numbed by business stress
From watching profits – are they more or less!

Mornings now are mine to stop and hear.
The call of birds from far and near –
To wander down a garden path
And, with boundless joy, to sing and laugh.

You see, I've reached an age of great content,
My body just a trifle bent –
But full of joy at being here,
Savouring these final years so dear.

So mirror, mirror, do your worse
The power and arrogance of youth is but a curse –
For this day at last I see
A softer shadow, which is really me.

My Godly Grandparents
Candace Canada

You are filled with love that flows from child to child, your love is very special indeed. I come to you for things I need such as good advice. You tell me what's best for my life. You teach me to strive for the best and don't settle for anything less.
Sometimes we think grandparents are just old–fashioned and unknowing folks but often grandparents know the most. Good grandparents are great indeed but Godly grandparents such as you are, is what the world needs.

Dedication: My grandparents, Robert and Mary Canada

Letting Go
Carol J. Luchun

My son, I know you must leave me;
And though I have peace when you are gone,
A part of me is still missing;
For your smile, your heart, I long.

Throughout the years I've looked at you;
You've been my pride, my joy, my love.
But in my heart of hearts dear Jeff,
I've always known – you were just on loan from above.

And now as you enter this phase of life;
Where responsibility can weigh you down,
Look up to Him who gave you Stacy, and never give up –
Bring Him the crown!

I'll be near you in the morning;
In my prayers you'll always be.
I'll be near you in the evening,
As I whisper "sweet dreams" to you honey.

God's power in you is real.
Go now, and be strong my son.
Take your bride and be wed today,
I give you back to the Most Holy One.

Bygones
Lilian Caulfield

In days of yore, great grandma wore,
Lace petticoats discreetly.
The country lanes were clean and neat
And birds sang oh, so, sweetly.

Gone are quiet country lanes,
Without a trace of litter.
In, are roaring traffic queues,
With road rage, oh, so bitter.

Gone are peaceful Sundays
Blue skies up above.
Young couples strolling hand in hand,
So very much in love.

No air pollution caused by cars,
To spoil the air they breathed.
No waiting for traffic lights
While drivers sat and seethed

But would we change to bygone days
And give up all our mods and cons?
I rather think that we'd still say
Aren't we the lucky ones!

Grae
Kristy Davis

Windy skies are gray
human spirits not away
laughter? Not today.

Children fade to close
Teardrop smiles are a pose
grown–ups kill the rose

A vampire's kiss
sadness, greed, and pain are the
A soul – sucker's bliss

Mentally Ill
P. A. Hunter

People ignore me,
They think I'm mad,
Why can't they see,
I'm not all bad.

People always fear,
What they don't know,
I'd buy you a beer,
If I wasn't classed as low.

I've feelings repressed,
Because of loneliness,
I get depressed,
Because of unhappiness.

Our stigma is a deviate,
Which is totally unfair,
We also get hate,
When we'd like loving care.

We want understanding,
So give a helping hand,
Not stereotyping,
Get your heads out the sand.

The Firing–Squad
B. E. Kaspar

I can see nothing
The only thing I hear is the beating of my heart
And a thousand thoughts are flashing through my mind:
Fight! Kill! Fight! Kill! For God, King and your country.

But that's against the morals I've been taught, at school, at
church and home.
But yes. Those then were peaceful times
And what applies one moment, does not suit the next.
Now, here condemned I stand
Outnumbered and out–cried, as coward and as traitor.

The silence breaks
The violent beating of the drums are like a thousand thunders
Which break Nature's peace, break my heart and mind.
Which bullet will bring the end to my inner agony?
Whose bullet will make the end of me?

And on command the shots rang out.
The traitor – Victim – did not shout
Murder! But to the ground his body fell.
He could not wonder any more
Whether ends justify the means
Or what indeed all this was for.

A Best Friend
Daniel Alexander

A best friend is like a living diary,
he is always there by your side,
and will be there with his heart and mind open.
A best friend will listen and understand you,
as well as your moods.
A best friend will defend your weaknesses,
he will never let you down when you need him,
he will let you cry and laugh.
A best friend will understand your moods
he will never break your heart.
And that's why you are A Best Friend!!

The Circus Star
Coral Crossley

Betty Wicks gets her kicks
In the circus doing tricks
You can hear, people cheer
When it's her turn to appear

She's a breeze, on trapeze
Swinging to and fro with ease
On the ground, rolling round
With the tumblers she'll be found

In a blue, net tutu
Bare–back riding she will do
With a spring, on she'll swing
As the horse goes round the ring

She's a pro, even though
With the clowns she steals the show
She can vault, somersault
Like a little catapult

She's a star, popular
People come from near and far
Just to see, having tea,
Betty Wicks the chimpanzee

Dreams of the Soul

The Angels Were Waiting
Mark Edward Leslie
Standing on an edge of a cloud,
Thousands of Angels are gathered 'round.
Thoughts of fear go through their heads.
The scene below has them scared.

The Angels are ready with their weapons in hand.
They may have to help the one with nails in His hands.
They wait for a cry of help from below.
He should have called them long ago.

He hasn't given in, but He's growing weak.
The crown of thorns has sent blood down His cheeks.
He hangs there one hour after another.
People say, He's no better than any other.

He raises His chin from off His chest.
He looks down upon all the rest.
With the power He has left, He speaks.
Words we still hear that make our hearts weak.

It is finished. It is finished.
No more, no less, that's all He said.
The Angels look sad, but they know it had to be done.
That was the whole purpose of God's only begotten Son.

Dandelion Wine
Jacquelyn K. Garcia
Dearest friend, lover
Newest of my admiration
Your kiss as sweet as sugar
Your lips more luscious than honey
Tenderly you nurture me with the deepest love
Deeper than all the Oceans
Dandelion Wine
Supple innocence in my hands
I show you the way...
Dreams of you shake free of my hair
As I awake and feel your warmth beside me

Desert Tortoise
Keith Nathan
I move so,
So,
Slowly against the Earth,
Time has almost frozen.

I understand
The lizard goes
Much faster than I,
So powerfully fast.

I understand
Waking up in my deep,
Dark burrow,
And feeling warmth.

I understand
My uniqueness
Because I have a shell,
Home, always with me.

Wherever I go,
I give the Universe
My gift
Of friendliness.

Forever Sorry
Michelle Leininger
As I looked out my steamed window, I see a sky of dark clouds that surrounds me
and my life.
The quietness as each new day passes, the tension that I could cut with a knife.
I begin to look down, with in myself and see the hurt I've caused the past days.
The tears well up inside as I hear myself saying I need to change my ways.
As the world comes down heavy on my shoulders and I've put us in a bind, you're
still around.
Nathan, you're sent from God I think you're Heaven Bound!
The clouds begin to break apart and the sun shines through slowly and the sky
brightens.
As if the clouds are my heart saying sorry that things haven't been too normal, hope
things will lighten.
I want you to know, that you're leaving a past behind that I will truly never forget
over years.
But yet with you I've encountered so many of my fears.
I hope that within this poem you've caught the major point of it.
I'm so sorry and I wish that it's your heart it hits.

Dinosaurs
Resi Olimpia Raes
I like dinosaurs.
They never get sour to
their tummy. I think
dinosaurs are funny.
Now it is time for the
dinosaurs to play with
their putty. They made
the putty very muddy.
The T–Rex is very studly.
And the plant–eater is very funny.
That's why I like dinosaurs.

Untitled
Joyce Meeker
I lost a friend the other day
My heart sank in a sad way,
I thought I lost him as he flew high
All I could do was pray and cry.

Four days went by, I saw no clue
Man, was I feeling lonesome and blue,
I raised him from a baby you see
A beautiful dove, he belonged to me.

On the fifth day he came back home
I figured he was too tired to roam,
It was on a Sunday I looked outside
To my surprise my eyes opened wide.

There he was next to my front door
I just knew I would see him no more,
Praise the good Lord in heaven above
The bird knew I had plenty of food and love,

Thank you Jesus for returning my bird
I knew he'd come back from your word,
He knew I'd take care of him no doubt
This is what love is all about.

Noteworthy Works

The Cloud
Julianne Brooks
Looking up one day to a pale blue sky,
a beautiful white cloud caught my eye.
It hung suspended pure and free,
I felt it was put there just for me.

At first a castle with towers high,
it slowly changed and with a sigh,
I watched it fade and drift away,
maybe to return one day.

It might be fluffy, pure and white
or filled with rain and dark as night.
Return it will, the quest goes on—
searching, moving, toward the sun.

What keeps it searching, is it fear—
or some heavenly music I can't hear,
that leads it higher than my sight,
continuous with the faithful flight.

Across the sky no more than mist,
the cloud all gold by sunlight kissed,
dips down toward earth as if to nod,
I'm up here always seeking God.

Eggshell
Kathleen E. Phinney
So strong and yet so fragile,
Like life it is strong if it is filled with
a substance.
Once it is devoid of anything it can
crumble under the smallest weight.

It's fragile existence is crushed,
By your light emotions for me.
One word can crush the life inside;
Not a word spoken at all can make
the egg disappear for good.

My Friend
Hoyt D. Stough
John Henry is my partner
My companion and my friend.
With a loyalty everlasting
From beginning to the end.

Although the man is little,
His head is carried high.
His heart is made of solid gold
And as large as a Texas sky.

He doesn't know how to be deceitful
He has never told a lie.
The most honest little character
Ever to look you in the eye.

Most folks don't want to cross him
His body language is quite clear.
Those to whom he is befriending
May be best, you not come near.

You may have wondered if on earth
There could be such a man.
John Henry is a miniature pinscher
As gritty as the seashore's sand.

Dinner At Sodini's
Sunnia Eastwood
Alone
I sit alone at the bar,
But not alone.
And yet, alone.

Strangers come and go,
Acquaintances pause to say "hello".
Someone somewhat more will chat awhile
And smile, then go.

Drink.
I sit at the bar
And take a drink...
And sip a drink.

My dinner order:
Pizza, small, parsley on the border.
Some other someone relates a joke:
We laugh; reorder.

Pizza.
I sit at the bar
And eat pizza.
A small pizza.

Our Society
Thomas Devin
Here's to our society,
Which is the only thing I know
A society of winners, a society of foes
A society of anger, a society of hurt,
I ask myself the question, What is it all worth?
In a world gone crazy, in a world gone mad,
It is strength and courage that define a great man
As I lay myself down, like a fallen angel
Renew my hope with your heavenly angels
So remember the times and all that you have done,
Because in the end they will teach you to be one.

Remember Me
M. J. Smith
When you ride down life's highway
When your thoughts turn to our memories
When you dream of how it used to be
Then you will remember me

When you see the morning dew
And feel the rain upon your face
As the wind blows through the trees
Then you will remember me

When the first snow of winter falls
And the trees gleam with icy frost
When the first robin of spring calls
Then you will know that I am not lost

When the sunset ends the day
And the flowers turn toward the sky
When you hear a child's laughter
Then you will know that I am not far away

When you ride down life's highway
When your thoughts turn to our memories
When you dream of how it used to be
Then you will remember me

Dreams of the Soul

Childhood Memories
Margaret A. Tempel
Oh how I took it for granted
My parents would always be there
Warm food would be on the table
And someone would always care

My Grandpa would understand me
I'd snuggle up under his arm
He'd laugh and teach me new things
And protect me from all harm

I'd never get sick or discouraged
My puppy would never die
I'd have a clean, dry place to sleep
With never a cloud in the sky

The woods where I played as a child
Would be there when I returned
The bulldozers wouldn't have claimed it
When for the old days I yearned

Oh how I took it for granted
I was young and so carefree
But I know deep in my heart
It all lives in my memory

Me
Sherri Lynn Ferguson
I am me! Do not try to
change me, for I am unchangeable
Do not try to figure me, out—
for I am mysterious
Do not try and tame me—
for I am insatiable!
Do not try and break me—
for I am unbreakable!
I am... me!

Dedication: My children, Christopher and Rhea–Annea

Two Grandsons
Lela Mae Hubbs
Two little redheaded grandsons
Have made my life worth living
They are my pride and joy
Their love is true and giving

When they see me coming
They jump and run to meet me
My heart strings start to humming
It's the happiest I could ever be

I look forward to the summer
When they can come to visit
When the days are long and warmer
Lonely nights will cease to exist

Tho I go to see them very often
I never get my fill
Of just watching both of them
Ride their bikes up and down the hill

They are always there to help me
In what ever I have to do
And my heart is full as can be
When they say "Hi! Grandma what's new?"

Teardrops
John McCreath
Tiny drops of joy or pain
Tiny drops like falling rain
Release of a pent–up tension
Or a silent wish afraid to mention

A combination of our friendships and dealings
Has created this outlet for our feelings
A reservoir of sentimental crop
With emotion diluted in every drop

Teardrop's can be a wonderful thing.
When feeling free as a bird on the wing.
And hearts are lifted with joy
Using laughter and amusement as a toy

Or when directions are difficult to steer.
And realities are hidden or bound by fear
Then our nerves tend to make us quiver
And the drops turn into a shiny river

When the grass is bathed in morning dew
The drops become sparse and few
Knowing full well when the sun has shone
The tiny drops will then be gone

Mamaw's House
Jessica Yankee
Mamaw's house is so nice
Out in her yard it's flowers galore
Fresh strawberry preserves and more
The sounds of a rushing creek
Like waves on the shore
Beautiful trees and stinging honey bees
At Mamaw's house I eat fresh biscuits
With jelly and jam and fried country ham
Mamaw is the best.

Dedication: Mamaw Shorti, the best

Our Last Goodbye
Peggy R. Rieniets
My thoughts are cloudy
My heart is broken...
Where was I
When you last spoke?

I wish I could have said "Goodbye"...
This is not the way I wanted you to die.
You took us in like no other man would...
You loved us, cared for us, all that a stepfather could.

I wish you could have known
You were going to die,
I wish all five children could have said
Our last "Goodbye".

But I know in my heart
You're with all five of us now,
And a tear or a cry
You would not want at all.

So we hand you over to God so dear,
And know, and pray, that you'll always be near.
Don't close that gate to heaven yet,
Not until you know, Dad, all five have left.

Noteworthy Works

Political Parade
Mark Vaughn
I'm living in a world
Where the changes are made
By a national committee –
In a political parade

Conflicts of interest always
Seem to be at hand
Another dying nation
In our political band

We pull together in what
They call the UN trying
To solve the problems that
Our world is in

We look to the hungry
The starving at war
We tried to make peace
But we gave so much more

Our troops were shot down
Dragged through the streets
Laughed at, spat on, in this
So called parade of peace

My Pebble
Matthew Ashby
I saw you there.
Looking like a lost child
In new and unfamiliar surroundings.
But you shone like the pebble on the beach.
The one the child picks up.
It was never me who picked it up.
I was the slow child.
I was always last to the beach
And ended up with the dull, grey stone.
But not this time.
I got the bright one.

Be Still And Know God
Mabel Sessions
Look out over the garden of God,
The earth on which men must trod.
See the wonders and beauty he made,
And behold the great foundation he laid.

Look up and see the sky so blue,
Remember He made it to cover you.
Look at the flowers that bloom today,
For God planted the seed along the way.

Look beyond the sunset of today,
As death sometimes darkens the way.
Remember there is a bright tomorrow,
Where the Saints shall know no sorrow.

Today build a little altar in your heart,
Let it become a permanent and glowing part.
Meet Him there when you kneel to pray,
Ask Him to come into your heart to stay.

God's plans are quietly worked out for man,
Where and how he shall fill life's span.
May we quietly submit ourselves unto His care,
that He may, His mysteries, with us share.

Why, Who, What, When And Where?
Jessica L. Fredette
Why do we live?
Why do we die?
same reason we laugh
same reason we cry

Who are people?
Who are we?
We are the people
that we see

What are tears?
What is a smile?
They're all part of life
What makes it worthwhile

When do we live?
When do we die?
same time we laugh
same time we cry

Where do we live?
Where do we die?
We live on earth
and die in the sky.

A Smile
Spunky
A smile is worth the many things it brings
While a frown won't get you anything
A smile is worth its weight in gold, and
A frown can't be sold.
It's better to have a smile this makes our
Heavenly Father glad.
Than to frown and make Ol' Satan happy that
You had.
We wear a smile inspite of the things life
Brings, so pull off that frown which can ruin
Everything.

True Friends
Charmane Zimbrich
True friends are like diamonds
precious but rare.
False friends are like autumn
leaves found everywhere.
A true friend will never make
you feel blue.
The sun will always be shiny,
all day through.
A true friend will be there in
good times and bad.
And chase all your tears away,
when your feeling sad.
A friend is a friend in deed
Just pick up the phone, when
you need a hug, or a squeeze.
And a true friend, will rush
over, and listen to all, of your needs.
A friend is to cherish and love
A friend was sent from above
For anyone, who needs someone
to share, their time with.
That's a true friend.
A friend in need!
A friend in deed!

Dreams of the Soul

If Life Were A Rose
Renee Kuhn
If life were a rose
It could be so beautiful
But as everyone knows,
There are thorns on every sweet smelling rose.

If life were a rose
The gentle unfolding petals
Would be each new day
Holding new hope.

If life were a rose,
The strong climbing stem
Would be the center of the soul
Holding dark secrets of the hereafter.

For the stem
And the soul
Are the life
Of the living.

And if you break your soul
As you can break the stem,
You kill the only part of yourself
That keeps the living alive

Addiction
Richard A. Garcia
As gone as I am, I thought this pleasure was for real.
Four times I've seen this man feel my soul and tried to steal.
All that I had sacred in this heart, that I felt dear.
First he played on my fears, then grabbed my wheel and began to steer,
This ride had not been this way before, I used to stop.
These clouds are dull and black, not like the ones I used to hop.
It seems this beautiful cure is no longer temporary,
What used to be my pleasure, has now become a remedy.

The Child
Kristi Clark
Pure and simple
Innocent and rare
A smile with a dimple
A hug because we care

Understanding and love
Watching us grow
A gift from above
A hand when we don't know

As we learn through the years
Of good things and bad
Our hopes and our fears
Dreams that we had

Learning each day
Until we suddenly see
That this is the way
Our life's meant to be

So if you are blessed
With a gift from above
Always give it your best
And guide them with love.

Butterfly
Larry Rosen
I wonder what became of the butterfly
Drawn to the flame of destruction
Devoid of fear, ever nearer, ever near,
And then away, to dance again just out of reach.
I wonder,

To sit and watch horrified as one of beauty flits and glides
In and out deaths open door to flutter free
Just once more, once more, once more,
Should I then the candle smother, and watch in fear
Should you find another flame to tease and play
Death's deadly game
I have lain beside a butterfly that nearly died, body
Wet with shivering sweat and prayers
Oh yes the prayers
Thank you, thank you, once again alive. A blaze of colour
Fluttering around, above below, please stay, don't go, don't go...
The wind that blows the flame that glows,
Life's magnet draws you ever near,
Is it a tear you see me cry?
Or caused by the smell of burning butterfly.

I wonder.

My Daughter, Teryl
Nina Lysher
What can I say?
She is beautiful, loving and caring.
She walks with ease and grace
Her smile illuminates her whole
Being and reflects through
To all who meet and know her
Words cannot say how much
I love her and I am so proud
Of my daughter Teryl.

Dedication: Teryl Wemhoff, my daughter

As The Tide Rolls In
Jennifer Shoup
Death bonds me as the tide rolls in...
Images passing so close by...
I could have almost touched them...
but I never reached out...
Now I wonder why. As the tide rolls in...
Even though I feel that my destiny has come to a halt.
Wonders never cease... Moments of content and unbridled
passions collide...
As the tide
rolls in... Rolls of my life change day to day... Sometimes THE
EMPRESS, with her
loving and devoted ways... Other times THE QUEEN OF RODS,
a all around woman on
other days... But one roll seems to stand out, the guardian of the
threshold, my family's
keeper... Fears, desires, wants and needs all wrapped up to
make me... As the tide rolls in... As my CD turns I come up with
these words... One of my
passions is released to roam free... To wander amongst the world
and know no limits, no
fears, and only dreams... As the tide rolls in...

Dedication: My family, Robert and daughters

Noteworthy Works

To My Daddy
Penny Kibler
I may not know you,
But you are a part of me.
My hair is blond, my eyes are blue,
When people look at me, it is you that they see.
Out of love, I came from two,
But, one felt they had to go.
It wasn't my Mother, it was you,
And for the reason I may never know.

You never held me in your arms,
When I was a baby girl.
I never felt safe from harm,
Without my daddy in my world.

My Mother often told me stories of you,
And how you used to be.
She did her best to take the place of two,
For it was her that was always there for me

One day I hope I meet you,
And maybe you can explain.
Of why I lived without my daddy,
And why I lived with so much pain.

Herd Mentality
Anthony D. Arthur
Keen observation over time has factually shown
many in our society have no mind of their own
allowing the media with their images to dictate
what they should eat and wear even their morals.

A sad commentary on how like slaves they've become
relinquishing personal prerogative on values and choice
the degeneration of society I believe the obvious result
yes the herd mentality debilitating in its effects like any cult.

Dedication: Armintha and Dalis Arthur and Rita Gordon

A New World
Rebecca Simmonds
Is there a new world out there.
Will it ever be found.
A world that's loving and full of care.

Or is it too late.
Now past repairing.
Have we dealt our own fate.

Look at it breaking down.
Where is all the good going.
Everyone walking with a sad frown.

Rushing along in a life so fast.
No time to take out to care.
Happiness flowing rapidly into the past.

Reach out and take hold.
Grasp the happiness now.
Enjoy your life before you're too old.

Don't take too much time.
Enjoy it while you can, you get one chance.
Never waste any its worth more than a dime.

Daydreams
Carol Elfberg
Daydreams haunt my soul,
in tempered measures, with
wishful thinking.
Of knights in shining armor,
romantic and polite.
To spurn my dragons, of
woe and cares.
To spend the day, in
laughter and spin the night
with silver stars.
His name is love and his
sword rewards me with
justice and truth.
For he is my own and
I am his.
We may not have it all,
but we have the riches we need of life.
Yet the treasures of kings
cannot buy true love.
Some can search the ends
of the earth and never find happiness.
Then in one moment, place
the heart and soul in the pages of time.

Inner Child
Marie Agnes Cameron
I experience my presence.
I perceive although the shades are drawn
The beating heart, pumping! pumping!
Darkness succumbs.
Thoughts arouse to no avail.
Thoughts!
Therefore, I must exist!
Surface! surface! herald the cry.
But the tomb is impregnable for now.
Perhaps tomorrow, the cries beheld,
Perhaps tomorrow, she will love me.

Collective Thoughts
Daisy W. Reel
In the wee hours of the darkest night,
When rest has eluded my tired body.
I wrestle to sleep with all my might,
When I decide it isn't worth a toddy.
It is then I switch on the bedside table light,
And puff up my pillows to a greater height.
I then reach for my near–by papers and pen,
For that's when my collective thoughts begin.
I try to record them that I might not forget,
And forever lose them, much to my regret,

So many ideas enter into my tangled mind,
Like a band around my thoughts they bind.
I try to search the words in my whirling brain.
Where only the clear sentences will remain.
As I write, the night passes so swiftly away,
And I am faced with another beautiful day.
Where I will be able to walk among the flowers.
And spend so many quiet and restful hours.
Until I have settled down for another night,
And once again, my collective thoughts I write.

Dedication: To Addie, a special sister

Dreams of the Soul

Moonlight
Liliana O. Adams
Moonlight – shining sky; How do I love him. Answer now.
A secret voice felt with promise like a falling star,
A silver shadow like blossoms covered us.

Moonlight – tell me why; The joy of love shines only if the sun shines.
The whispers of wind are calling for its pain,
And dark passages are running across the sky.

Love was born from thousand spheres of the sunshine.
Love supreme, eternal, like the beauty of your sweet heart.

You promised a gold ring and wedding white gown.
You promised dream house and moonlit gardens.

And now alone, veiled black, gently touching strings of moonlight,
I try to reach the light of breaking day. Alas!

Moonlight – sparkling night; Never forget secrets of love.
Covered shadows! Silver spheres! Felicity!

Come, come to me!
Dedication: Bruce, my husband

The Cold Dark Night
Violet Tapp
The lonely star way up high
Tried to shine to light the sky
The air is cold the star is bold
He tries to shine but he is cold

The moon and the star
Join together to try to light
The darkest night.
Then all his friends suddenly appears
And the sky is full of sparkle
Cheer

To More's Utopia
Jacqueline De Prima
Fly Fly TGI It's Friday
Marilyn's clone is coming to dinner in a Versace gown
Andy knew His clarion blew
Bubbles and tins and diamond–dust skins
For Marilyn

Dozens of shoes Tapping the blues
Waiting for Hermes
To clone a pair for women's wear
Of dainty suede
For Marilyn

More we need of Campbell's Soups
More we need of Fruity Loops
More we need of computer chips
More we need of Nintendo trips

We're on our way to More's Utopia
Gushing forth from cornucopia
More pins
More tins
More wins
For Marilyn

I Am Who I Am
Tresa Tuinstra
I know that I am not perfect at all,
I hurt, I laugh, I cry,

I'm not among the riches,
The average folk am I

I know how to love, I know how to care
I've been heartbroken, down, and confused
And have felt extreme despair

I am who I am:
A person with feelings, thoughts, and dreams

There are times when I feel so together
And times when I fall apart at the seams

Though I may not be the person others want me to be
I still am a person, I'm real, I'm me...

I am who I am, that's all I can say
Though I may not please everyone, this is how I'll stay
Dedication: Paul and Meggan Tuinstra

The Pebble
Elinor Smith
Watch a pebble skimming water.
Leaving ripples on a pond.
As we can see life goes on.
Like those ripples on a pond.
To disappear. As they go down.
Life is like it so we have known.
We have grown wiser more bound.
Like ripples grow much closer on each round.
For life is just a ripple on a pond.
They will show then gone.
Time has a way to close us down.

A Rose Died
Edna Horn
It was a beautiful night, the moon high and
clear smiling upon two people – a soft gentle breeze
caressing their faces, the trees bent their heads
in greeting. In the midst of life and beauty these
two were unhappy – she waiting for something she
expected – he wondering how to be understood.

Finally it came like a storm in summer time – the
strong sudden rain like a dagger tearing at the
beautiful flowers, tearing their petals and leaving their
hearts bare and wounded.

The two now walking in silence and deep thought, faced
each other. There was courage in the girl's face looking
up to her lost lover. He caught her to himself and
Kissed her tenderly. She freed from his embrace and
Ran away. In her breathless escape she hoped he
would call her back to love – he did not – he let her go.

I send my thanks for nights I never can replace and
memories that linger like a haunting tune. It is
better to have loved you dear and lost than never
to have loved at all.

Noteworthy Works

He Sits
Alex Campbell
He sits and watches and listens and grins.
He hears their prayers and he prays along.
The day to the night, now to forever,
Surrounding without, above and within,
He sits and watches and listens and grins.

He cries and smiles and winks and loves.
He reaches for them as they reach for him.
Tomorrow, today, tonight, always,
The rain and the starshine, hand to glove.
He cries and smiles and winks and loves.

He is and is not and will and can.
He loves when love is nothing at all.
This way, that, the farther, the near,
The heart, the heat, the hearth, the hands,
He is and is not and will and can.

He lives and shines and nods and gives
For all and for love and for time and for free.
Eternally, unerringly, generously, unconditionally.
As they raise their arms, they thank him again.
He sits and watches and listens and grins.

Untitled
Marcia A. Ingalsbe
I scream and
Scream
You do not hear
I am
Can't you see my
Tears
Silent tears
Fall in my heart
Freezing
To my bones
It hurts

Sweet Little Angel Girl
Cheryl Evans
Dear little baby girl,
You are an angel
Sent straight from the heart of God
to my arms.
You are too sweet for this world.
You are a work of beauty,
A masterpiece of love;
Too perfect for such an imperfect world.
You are full of God,
I see him in your face;
I hear him in your breath,
You are so close to him,
You are more there than here.

Sweet little angel girl;
How precious it is to hold you.
Could ever there be a greater treasure
on earth than you?
No, for you sparkle of heaven.
Surely the treasures there
Are less without you.

Dedication: Brandi, our sweet little angel girl

To Elvis
Virginia Rose Maynard
I think that I shall never see,
A singer half as great as thee.

Elvis, you are our king,
Not just in song, but in everything.

You're great on every song you do,
Especially the one called 'Loving You'.

I hope your fans will all be true,
I for one will stick with you.

Elvis, since you went away,
I think about you night and day.

I carry your picture in my car,
So you'll be with me near or far.

I'm not much of a poet, as you can see,
I just can't put in words, all you mean to me.

My hobby is leather carving, so what did I do?
I carved myself a picture of wonderful you.

Looking Back In Retrospect
Mary L. Davis
Looking back, I was a Mother's
child
Looking back, I was a Father's daughter
Looking back, I was a husband's wife
Looking back, I was someone's lover
Looking back, I loved the wicked
Looking back, I sat with the wicked
Looking back — In retrospect, I'm
Still a child of God's.

Dedication: Mr. and Mrs. A. Davis, Jr.

Lavender Lady
Cheryl Blair
She spoke softly, haltingly, sparsely spacing her words.
Something in her manner made you wonder about her.
Her eyes spoke of times long past, of memories made
upon windy wings, flying to new places, leaving traces
of lovers, children, acquaintances, who could not hang on
to her dreams with or for her.

She moved on when times got tough and people rough.
She never let anyone touch her soul for fear of feeling.
She wasn't always sad or blue. Nor was her life like
a purple sunset. She was lavender and ladylike
in ways of being, seeing, feeling, existing for today
never letting her passion color her life in any way.

Lavender lady what made you so?
Who hurt you— Abused your body, spirit, and soul...
Making you choose average over truly living...
Leaving you without hope for something better in your life?

You have the right to feel again. You've paid your dues to God and friends.
It's alright to change color... you can be anything you choose to be.
I want so much to know your vibrancy, no more muted hues from violence!
No more pain from those who, left you scarred, lavender and oh so blue.

Dreams of the Soul

Prom Dresses
Mary Butler
Like photos from days long past,
the prom dresses hang in the back of my closet.

Handcrafted with love, by you, each one as unique
as the boys which so innocently clutched at me,
dancing in a comical embrace which would never be again.

A ritual it was for us: select the pattern,
from amongst the beautiful McCalls or Simplicity;
then the fabric,
ethereal and glamorous for a girl so plain as me;
the measuring—Is it big enough?
and the sewing, each seam so perfect
as if by this dress your worth as a Mother was to be judged?

From day, the dress is picture perfect and I,
so unworthy to wear your creation crafted from love,
each one like jewels in the crown of growing up,
given to mark my passing from girlhood into womanhood.

I have saved them all, back in my closet,
each to mark the passing of a different beau,
and each a gift from you for a chance at love.

Misunderstood
Teresa A. Nyarady
My life upon a mountain peak
Atop the world. I do not speak

For in my words, my soul revealed
With misinterpretations sealed

And then my tribe does shut me out
Though there's no proof; there is no doubt

That I be what you choose I be
And not the person that is me.

The International: Eat Your Heart Out Twickenham
Elizabeth Parker
Well we think we have done it, played the first half and won it!
We've enjoyed our victories, gained vital points
Collected our cup and run!

Now seeking to stay on top, containing what we've found
The oceans can have it, national teams don't want it–
The ball is screwed to the ground.

Off the coast another family plays, attracting crowds daily:
Porpoises pirouette, dolphins dive. A wave of cheers is heard–
Until porpoise and dolphin die.

The international teams play foul, cut corners. It's a bit much,
No referee between: chemical, pesticide, nuclear and acid –
It is us who are kicked into touch.

No longer God's creation the earth is man's dumping bowl
Well and truly into the second half, the score against us
Playing our own home goal!

The solution for pollution is a new kind of revolution
Lining up for the serum, can the game be won?
Only humanity can try…

Journey Home
Pamela H. McKinney
Oh Lord if you called me home tonight
Would I try with all my might,
To convince you that I need more time
To do what you had in mind,
for my life.

Would I be, hard to please
Would I beg you, get down on my knees,
For I know time can't be still
While you wait for me to do your will,
in my life.

How could I deny
There's a tear in my eye,
For the sheep that was astray
That I could have saved that day,
offering eternal life.

Oh Lord, what if you called me home tonight
Would I go without a fight?
Would I be lost, unable to see
What You had set before me,
after my life.

Untitled
T. M. Boucher
Like a ship in the winter
I miss you like the sea,
Like a sailboat aches for the wind
So too, I ache to be…
Inside you
Beside you
Around you
Surround you,
About you
Instead of without you.
When will it be spring?

The Unborn Dream
Erin A. Noice
As I sit and wait for the
time of our meeting, I don't
know how to feel my emotions
run wild with Mothering
hormones. I'm so excited
yet so scared of this tiny
being taking over my body.
Your presence is so welcomed
I still don't even know you
yet I give you nourishment
and life every breath I
take I give to you. Our
souls are as if they are one
every day you grow a little
more and a little more visible
you become, even though I can't
see you I love to watch you
grow. Every emotion turning
is like the turning of a new leaf
like the turning of your soft fragile shell turning
inside me.

Dedication: My son, Bishop Chaney

Noteworthy Works

Loving
Laurie A. Ward

I spend all my time loving you,
Seems like that is all I ever do.
I love you at work every day,
and with me all day you stay.
For that is a way of loving you.

I love being with you every night,
Seems like loving you is always right.
You are in my thoughts when away,
and at night in every way.
Sweetheart I am glad our love
beams so bright,
Just like the sunlight.

I sit and count the days that we
have been together,
I shall say it shall be forever.
And since we have joined as one,
We are having so much fun.
For apart we will never be,
Just you wait and see.

Dedication: My loving husband, Paul

That I May Come And Stay
Dagmar W. Meyer

How have I lived so long without you,
I just cannot say,
I pray night and day that I will join you,
But when, I cannot say,
For the Lord has determined
That it's not to be that way,
The loneliness without you, is something
I cannot bear,
So, my darling, I beg and ask you,
To intercede with our Lord,
That I may come and stay.

Maiden Place
Nancy L. Linville

Twirling around – Head in the clouds – Feet beneath the ground
Little child toy in hand – mind the elders never forget
"This is the promised land."
Hearts that long to be filled – empty hands – no tools can be found.
Without the given tools no work can be done – Look deep inside –
smiles and laughter all around. Tools of the mind oh wonders work,
Take time – like lightning flash – the brilliance released – Let go – the strength
will grow everlasting. Can a void be made within a mass – ask a child whose
wisdom is unsoiled. Pure of soul, thought and deed – out of the earth this
purity comes, hold onto your very being – hold strong – stand your own ground
Never forget "This is the promised land." Laden with lace – fine silk – don't
cover your space – look upon each other – give hand when needed – enter each
other – united the mass fends off the void "This is our maiden Place"
Bridges built solid and strong – swift water below all but gone – look ahead
don't look back – We changed the path. What now! Can't right a wrong
or can we. Ride the heavens – Let go – wings outstretched – glide fast
to slow – Never forget "This is the promised land."

Only Yesterday
James Seado

It was only yesterday that I learned of perfection, when
they placed you in my arms. So small, so trusting, so perfect.

It was only yesterday that I learned of pride, when I
watched you take your first stumbling steps to tumble with the
innocent laughter of a child into the loving shelter of your
Mother's arms and I knew you were on your way.

It was only yesterday that I learned of love, as I watched
you sleeping, a little boy where my baby had once been.

Where have the yesterdays gone?

I want to hold you forever, to protect you from the cold
winds that can blow so suddenly.

Wait for me, don't leave me behind as you begin your journey
down life's road.

It was only yesterday that you began to teach and I have
so much yet to learn.

Dedication: My son and his mother

Autumn Rendezvous
Elizabeth B. Long

Autumn runs a willing race
But loses to winter's icy grasp...
Her brilliant clothes return to
Rags, for flakes of snow to sit upon.

Autumn holds within her clasp
A serenity, warmth and real joy...
That will make one determined,
Renewed and thankful—enjoy it now!

Dedication: Jimmy Yohn– grandson, killed 1-14-83

A New Tomorrow
Katie Wennerstrom

As I sit on my bed, an overwhelming sense of loneliness seems to surround me...
Wrapping around me, quenching every last bit of my remaining happiness.
My red, swollen eyes are clenched tightly as I try to hold back the
surging flood of memories that seem to want to surface.
Tears are trickling down my face, and while their salty content seems to penetrate my skin
with a horrid burning sensation, I feel a much deeper pain elsewhere.
A pulsating, trembling sensation passes throughout my body as I fall into
the numbness of my great sorrow.
My heart is full of a dull, murderous ache that seems to grow with every beat.
I feel as if my heart has been torn apart like a jig saw puzzle, and that
one of the most important pieces is missing.
This empty place in my broken heart, seems almost impossible to refill.
It seems that no amount of time could ever completely heal this
devastating wound.
A severely battered and crushed heart is something that I must learn to
overcome only when I feel that I am truly ready.
And I am ready. I am ready to live again, and to love once more.
For I have conquered my misery, and survived my frustrations.
And I have realized that my life will and does go on.
I wipe away my tears, and smile upon a new tomorrow.

Dreams of the Soul

So Far Apart
Stephanie Damon
As I sit here alone,
I listen to the raindrops fall,
thinking about you locked away
in those far brick walls.
old memories keep running through my head.
why can't I just be dead?
I already feel like someone stabbed
me through my heart,
because they locked you away
and we are now "so far apart, "
I don't know how to feel,
I keep hoping this isn't real.

The Field Of Dreams
Lahela
Wandering hearts, in the field of dreams
Caught by surprise, at night,
in the moonlight's gleam
Cool and rushing, almost
like a mountain's stream
One joining, then winning another
making a fascinating team
magic, mayhem, and natural instincts collide,
taking both on a fast, beautiful, long-lasting ride,
feeling as though you've moved,
heaven and earth, while being there,
leaving nowhere to hide, only just to abide,
until thunder hits, and lightning strikes,
ripping them apart, at the seams,
finding yourself, again wandering,
Wishing, on a bright shining star
up, up, so high in the sky
Wandering how, and when,
did you come to goodbye, and still,
Wandering, why, and where you are,
in the field of dreams.

Dedication: A special friend

Reality
Andrea Brown
Don't run from your problems – look them in the face,
Handle them at your own pace.

Take criticism to your advantage and use it,
Accept it and don't refuse it.

Everyone will experience bad times–some more than others,
Why is it at bad times – we seek our mothers?

Knowing that someone is always there – feels nice –
Don't take it for granted don't put it up for a price.

Who and what is real is now a question
You'll find out for yourself–take no suggestions.

Friends are often not what you thought.
Let them know you care – but not a lot.

Hurt and betrayal is what my friends gave me,
To them I say thanks – for allowing me to see.

Times can be trying and often hard,
Always be prepared and stand your guard.

Dam Mad (I Ode It To You)
Jacqueline Walters
Am I mad? I think not, what you
said, I just forgot,
Braincells growing in my head,
I can't sleep, can't stay in bed,
I need to read, I need to write,
I see the dark, I see the light,
I'm going home, don't like this place
Don't trust you, don't like your face,
You feed me pills, make me sleep,
Confuse me more, make me weep,
You're not right, you're really bad,
You're the one that's really mad.

Untitled
N. Shew
Ponder wonder – wonder ponder
why can't I be much younger,
Too much reason, too much why
When you're older too much try.

To pull up, to pull through
that's what elders have to do.
Younger, childish, filled up dreams,
Rivers can flow through quiet streams.

Living through long years
When like a child, yesterday's tears
No worries – not held of fears,
Never to worry about any peers.

Rainbow so close, yet far as can be
Why does it seem you're following me,
Closing up to the scene of my crime
Crimson blood red soon to die

Let me fly back to younger years
And relive good memories
That once were here.

Portrait In Words
Flora Christopher
She, from a palette of oils
Painted pictures like:

PHARAOH'S HORSES.
Three horses, agitated, trying to survive.
MAJESTIC SWANS:
Curve neck beauties, near cattails.
HERD OF DAIRY CATTLE:
Grazing, lazy, velvet noses, chewing cud.
ROSES IN BASKET:
American Beauties, spilling from basket.

Her paintings,
Mood contrasts.

MOTHER.
A farm wife
Possessor of many skills.
Patient.
Kind.
Many-faceted.

Admiration, always. Regrets that I didn't tell her how much.

Daybreak
Margaret M. Milligan

When birds are waking in the valleys green
And purple crags in majesty are found
When flowers are breaking with their dewy sheen
And squirrels dance along the sunlit ground
When streams and rivers shine with sparkling hue
And cottage doors are open to the lanes
Then day is breaking steadily and true
And golden dawn is streaking o'er the plains
Her spell is spread on dainty winged feet
And all who see her beauty pause to pray—
that God will always smile and make as sweet
The splendour of the glorious day.

Polio Child
Claire Maplethorpe

Oh, the nights I have wept for the child that I was,
The grief in my heart for the child that I was.
The love of my Mother, it overcame all,
The arms of my Father caught me when I'd fall.
The care and the selflessness, for no reward,
The stares and the pity, it must have been hard.
Despite all the odds, the battle was won.
I never can thank them for what they have done.
The horror is past, but buried inside
The scars they will last, my apartness I hide.

Oh my Mother my Father, how can I show,
The depth of my love that I need you to know.
The imperfect child you loved and protected,
Your own lives and wants were sadly neglected.
I show it in love for my children, my heart,
In my anguish and sorrow for a world torn apart,
For children who suffer, are hungry and sad,
Children of a world which is clearly going mad.
Oh, the nights I have wept for the children who are,
The grief in my heart for the children who are.

Dedication: My parents, Netta and Ray

One Night
Paul A. Pelengaris

Temptation of forbidden fruit
how sweet will it be by then?
how will my soul endure
the passion of the flesh?
that will soon be you...

I will envy the company with you
only this I do hope
that he treats you right
so that I may share you
someday in the future tense

Dare he hurt or disappoint
and my quest will be failed
damned if he does
damned if he does not
fulfill your mind and soul

Even though I know you not
so as not to lose you
I am prepared to let go
have that night for yourself
then focus your mind...

Long Shadows Of Winter
Ken Autry Davis

As I sit on my porch and look out through the trees
I see long shadows on brown leaves.
There is green here and there
but mostly dry grass everywhere.
The cardinals and chick–a–dees
Are pecking grain from the leaves.
And every once and a while
A red–headed woodpecker comes by in style.
The sky is cold, cloudy and gray
And you know this is a winter day.
And as the sun runs out of light
You just know it's another cold winter night!

To Mama
Marian Wright

You were always a pillar
of strength
And full of love
I thank God for letting
you teach me
And preparing me for
things in life

All the years He gave us together
Then in return He taught
me how
To take care of you...

All that time preparing I
was God's helper.
Now you have
journeyed on
Home with the angels to be
with Him.

So Mama take your rest and sleep on

Dedication: Marie T. Glenn, mother, and Barbara J. Drennon, sister

---

My Three Sons
Gayle M. Bergeron Dixon

I had my first son in the hot Summer time.
He was little and wrinkled, but healthy and mine.

My second son was born in the cold of the Winter,
Small with blue eyes and dry little fingers.
He had very good lungs, but not much hair,
He was different from my first babe because he was so fair.

Son number 3 came in the middle of June,
A big baby boy with a face like a Moon.
A little of both brothers combined in this fellow,
He had fuzzy blonde hair, but boy was he mellow.

I couldn't believe the great "miracle" of birth,
And I know God above brought my Babies to Earth.

My boys liked to fight as they grew to be men,
And now they are friends, I hope till the end.

I will love all my boys until my dying day,
"May God keep them healthy" is how I will pray.
Live, life to the fullest and take care of each other.
Please never forget the Love of your Mother.

Dreams of the Soul

My Mitzi
Joann Wawro

I'll miss you forever, My Mitzi
Time cannot heal the way
that I feel
I'll miss carrying you to bed
at night
I'll miss your sweet face in
the morning light
Now that we must be apart
I'll have this sadness in my
heart
No one will ever replace you
My Mitzi

The Tiger
Lisa Hathaway

Fast and agile, with all its speed
I was watching the tiger catch its nightly feed.
He prowled along the dark, damp ground,
looking for his prey to be found.

Then he finds his prey,
sitting on the ground.
It was all fluffy and grey.
It was a rabbit that was his prey.

The tiger leapt through the air,
with the rabbit down below,
then he hears the tiger,
and jumps into a nice safe hole.

The tiger lands on the ground,
there is no prey for today,
the one lonely rabbit had gotten away.

There is still tomorrow,
and tomorrow's another day.
Maybe then the tiger,
will catch his unlucky prey.

Death
Marylou Spires

It is not so easy to face
but in time we all take our place

I've tried to be brave, a tear not to cry
Why is it, you never want to die

Time is near and while I can
Put on paper and make a plan

I must make it easy for my clan
My death they won't accept or understand

Once time has healed the loss they feel
I'll watch from above and see them kneel

And come to them, if I can
they'll know as I place a hand

Hear a hurt, dry a tear
Just be near or calm a fear

Then they will smile and remember
best of all remember Me

I Am
Lacey Bloom

I am young but I know;
I have seen and heard.
Life is hard. It bears down on me. I stretch my mind to correct it.
I am still young; I strive in vain.
I know right from wrong; I know the truth and it ages me.
Life teaches that with knowledge comes sorrow.

Time passes. I try to block it out.
I don't want to know. Life is sorrowful.
I don't want to age.
I am young but I know and
it robs me of my youth.

View Across The Sea
Caroline Ann Davenport

Close your eyes, and imagine the scene
Nothing short of a wonderful dream!

Wine – beautiful surroundings, a picturesque view
All of these too good to be true?
There I sat contentedly – on a warm August evening
The sound of crackling – from Barbecue Coals –
And the aroma of hickory seasoning.

In the garden – hydrangea enveloped the chair where I sat,
My glass filled with wine – but apart from that!
It's the view, as I looked across the sea, which took my breath away
A volcanic eruption – a magnificent display
Of daytime going into hideaway.

Pinks, purples and reds painted the sky, like a burning torch
Too high to touch, too far away to scorch.
Below the fire, the sea seemed to shimmer – like silver ribbons
The star's glimmer
Of daytime going into hideaway.

A slight shiver from the cool breeze – I now feel,
Hypnotism broken – but this dream was real!!

How Swiftly
Bernice Abrahamzon

How swiftly fall has swept through here
To bare the limbs of golden elms
Crisp, curling leaves slip to the ground
And with a dry, contented sound
Cover lawns and forest realms.

How swiftly fall has made it clear
The world will soon lie winter dead
The stiff and shining oak leaves sail
Upon the fresh, autumnal gale
And rustle to a restless bed.

How swiftly fall has brought us near
To see the pear tree like a torch
Light up the drab and graying day
While maple leaves at golden play
Fall softly on our vacant porch.

How swiftly fall has brought the year
To winter with its steady sigh
The sodden leaves are dull with rain
But woodbine near my windowpane
Is blithely waving at the sky.

The Hue Of Anew Beginning
Nicholas Ramirez

Incipit seemed as a vision and more than Angels sing touches'
Heaven's ground.
In light of Aurora; A hue of anew, Angels lament anent creation.
Analects of history now just memories anabasis to the Horizon
inwrought with Crimson wonders and Treasures uncalculated
worth.
Kudoed by such a sight with kvass to join my celebration.
The inception that leads a Heart and looking back at Earth's ending
To Labial begins a song.
So I kowtow above Earth's Lamentation where a place has no
ending and words that live forever as your wait is long overdue
where your Gradin is for one to follow...

The Fireman
Eileen Newman

He came to the house in a hurry, no time for handshakes or smiles,
He just climbed pretty smart up the ladder
And started to bash in the tiles,
He caved in the lovely lead window, then demolished the door,
Saying "I hope if anyone's in there
They are laid down pressed flat on the floor"
There was nothing to see but the flames folks,
And this brave little man with a hose,
But what with the shouting, crackling, and smoke,
Ooh it started to get up my nose,
I whined, "My jewels are under the mattress, my money under the floor, "
"Just sit down on the grass love, of this fire we must find the core"
After the fuss was all over, I started to tremble and cried,
"Look at my steaming love letters
They are no use now they are just fried"
He said "Yes but we saved all your silver,
And your Burt Reynolds photo that's cool, "
It was difficult right then to thank him
Standing there ankle deep in a pool,
I felt so ashamed so I kissed him,
This brave man covered in grime,
His hair was all singed, he just stood and grinned,
I hope there's more like him next time.

The Beach
Karen Burnett

I lie here alone, my thoughts by my side
From the world around me I need not hide
No one in view, this place is all mine
So peaceful and calm and ever divine.

Absorbing the peace, I listen to the sounds
Within this sanctuary that I have found
The waves from beyond lap onto the shore
I feel so content, I want to hear more
The birds in the sky soar high up above
They send me their voices of freedom and love.

My hand by my side, I reach to the sand
And feel the warmth of my new found land
Each tiny grain shimmering with light
Gently glistening under the sun so bright
Caressing them at first then letting them go
A waterfall of sand through my fingers flow.

Slowly inhaling, I take a deep breath
And cleanse my soul with the air so fresh
Leaving all of my worries behind
I enter this world with an untroubled mind.

Winter Beauty
Mildred H. Knight

Let me share with you in an exciting way
The magnificent beauty I experienced today.
Our home sits on the shore of a beautiful lake
So peaceful, so heavenly, the setting unique.
When I awoke this morning, such beauty to behold
Snow was falling swiftly, icy and cold.
'Twas a dream for an artist with brush in hand
To paint a picture before him not created by man.
Winter is such a special time, it's hard to explain
What a marvelous experience to live where seasons change
As I looked out my window I stood there in awe
At the miracle of winter beauty this morning I saw.

Spring
Margaret R. Beresford

The trees swayed gently in the breeze
The sun lay dappled through the leaves
Primroses bloomed in sun and shade
The river flowed on through the glade
Spring flowers growing in the grass
Daffodils standing mass on mass
Birds singing their sweet spring song
And lambs skipping and racing along

A mole pushes up a heap of soil
Horses plowing, hard at their toil
Each so busy before summer comes along
When tiny things grow big and strong

Swallows nesting in the eaves
Crows cawing high in the trees
A cuckoo calls his old sweet shout
A robin nests in the water spout.

Bees are busy gathering pollen
Snowdrops and crocus bloom in the garden
Housewives bustle through spring cleaning
In fact each season has a meaning

Derelicts
K. Dickinson

Through the bleak and the forgotten
Where our Fathers have trodden
Where the derelicts pause
For an engineers clause
This is where home was

Where bagged rubbish lies
On gardens where pride
Was spent so enjoyed
By people employed
This is where home was

The paths are now weeds
Symmetry finally concedes
To debris and mess
An old shoe–torn dress
This is where home was

So it's fires from tyres
On a street now expired
Young children still play
Unemployed pass the day
This is where home was

Dreams of the Soul

Summertime
Cecil George Ince
Now the heat of day is over
and the evening breeze is blowing
swaying fields of scented clover
is not this the time for roaming
over hills and through the meadows
to the golden burnished wheat
here the rabbit finds its food
near the brook is meadow sweet
hedgerows are alive with chirping
Nature surely now rejoices
showing us its regal powers
giving us such wondrous choices.

Garden Pride
R. Henderson
Every day you'd see her in her wee bitty garden,
Working away late and early.
A tiny figure, frail and bent
Ignoring all, on her task intent,
In her wee bitty garden.

Flowers of every colour grew in her wee bitty garden.
She really had a lovely show,
All tended by her loving hands,
Flowers grew in orderly, scented bands
In her wee bitty garden.

A competition for 'Best Kept Garden'
In the village was to be held.
She worked with even greater pride.
Hardly stopped to go inside
From her neat wee bitty garden.

They came to view her much loved garden.
Tramped around, looked and muttered.
Then left without a backward glance.
Sadly, she knew she had no chance
Of a prize for her much loved wee bitty garden.

The Bomb Building Site
Linda Medlam
The smell of rain, wet, sun warmed
Dandelions
Then I am there in Bean Street
Hessle Road, aged six

The ground of sorrow to some
I knew families had died there
In their homes
Before I was born
In the war that
My Dad had fought in

But for me aged six
The bomb building site
was a place of safety to play
A place of space to imagine
with a friend to enjoy
In this space we felt safe

Only a stone throw away
from the heavy docklands traffic
of Hessle Road – Hull – East Yorkshire
In the high summer of 1957

Sorry
Rita Roebuck
Sorry, is a little word, yet very hard to say
Most of us should use this word at least 10 times a day
You find that writing down this word, sometimes on little notes,
Is a very easy thing to do, but "the word" sticks in our throats
So, if you find and will confess, when you are in the wrong
Don't be too proud to say this word, and keep your friendship strong

I'm sorry that he came my way
Sorrier more he decided to stay
In my ignorance, I was happy of course
Never dreamt it would end in divorce

Who would help him to betray me
I really never can tell
I only know it's bad to feel this way
I cannot help but wish her in hell
It will not ease my pain I know
Yet, I just wish they would get off, just go

He's no concern for his family
Yet, what sort of "woman" can she be
To let her sins be "visited" on her family
She has to be a selfish "she" certainly not one to be "sorry"

Why Do I Do It?
J. M. Henderson
"Why do I do it?"
I wished I knew.
"Is it for them
Or is it for you?"
I lost my husband
A while ago
And people inquire
"How are you?"
"I'm fine" I say
I know not why.
'Cause in my heart
I know it's a lie.

Come To Me
Richard H. Collins
One day I found myself face to face with the Lord
He held out his arms and said "Come to me, my child"
"But Lord, do you not recognise me?

I am Judas... I betrayed you
I am Peter... I denied you
I am Caiphas... I accused you
I am Herod... I mocked you
I am Pilate... I crucified you
I am Thomas... I doubted you"

"Enough!" cried the Lord
"It is for this that I lived for you
It is for this that I died for you
And yes, I recognise you

You are Mary... you anoint me
You are Simon... you carry my cross
You are Joseph... you cut me free
You are John... you love me
You are Peter... you know me
You are Paul... you witness me
You are mine... come to me."

Noteworthy Works

Dragons
Justin Rod

Dragons, creatures of power within the mortal realm,
Truly, a beautiful animal of mystery and wonder,
Captivating all who see it's majestic stance.
It controls the air as a fish in a stream,
True power in it's grasp as it takes flight.

All this says is a small part of their glory and nobility,
Honor and magnificence in their renown,
Wisdom venerated by their near immortal life–spans,
Many have sought and been unable to find them,
Yet those that find them commonly don't want them.

Why that is, only they know for sure what the reason is,
Often something to do with the destiny of men,
And only their vast wisdom knows the answer to that.
Often feared, but without true reason,
Held often only in the dreams of men, held in love.

This is why they are important to the lives of men,
A very significant piece of knowledge,
So truly I must go and leave you in wonder of why,
So I will say that must research more on the subject,
I'll ask my dragon friend.

The Artist To Her Lover
Marion Cloyd

Sketch it front and center,
The rest of my life
Only faint background.
From the palette of our togetherness,
Color it with pink for sweet imaginings,
And scarlet for its passion,
Royal purple for its power
And swirls of blue for pensive times.
Use spring green to show its freshness
And, for its endurance, rich and solid brown.
Then crown it with white for a holy glow.
Display it proudly, titled LOVE.

The River
Mandy Ratcliff

The river you see, can be so gentle and calm.
Its waves beat so gently across the sand.
The soft, cool breeze that blows through your hair,
Seems to help you forget all your cares.
A place to relax and calm yourself down.

The river can be so destructive, destructive, yes that's what I said.
Its waves beating harshly against houses and ripping them apart.
Destroying everything, yes everything that's in its path.
Taking people lives is all just a terrible part of a flood.
It can happen right before your eyes.

But when the river's calm,
You'll see the ducks swim by.
Paddling their little feet to see the beautiful sights.
You'll see boats of all shapes and sizes,
And the people aboard waving their friendly hellos.
You can see and hear the trains in the background,
Sounding their horns to assure its approach.

The river is a calm and destructive place.
A place I live near by
In the town I call my home.

My Mother
Darla Chevalier

Mother – how beautiful the name;
Day in, day out, always the same;
Loving, caring, forgetting herself; she forges onward,
Putting her needs 'on the shelf'.

Starting each new day with the Lord, radiating joy and love,
Bringing us a bit of heaven above.
She washes, she cooks and cleans,
All the while her face "beams".
She scrubs, and polishes; she sews and repairs;
Each piece being handled with loving care;
As with each life with which she is entrusted.

She molds, she teaches, scolding oft'times,
When so moved by the Spirit;
She shows by her example
The way that we should be,
She lights the path for us to follow;
That will take us home to God.

No matter where I go, or how far I may roam;
I will always return to my haven—
To my beautiful Mother at home.

Ode To Princess Diana
Victor Molyneux

Radiant and lovely. Gentle and kind
Her glorious presence doth enchant my mind.
Caring of people in all walks of life.
And in far distant countries the victims of strife
Her visits to hospitals bring joy to the wards
And help ailing patients with comforting words
In countries abroad she is greeted with rapture
Her charming presence their hearts will capture
Revered by people everywhere
Princess Di she has been from the start.
But to me she has always been, and is now,
Queen of my heart.

A Necessity
Sherry Byng

beyond the stars...
deeper than the seas...
farther than the wind blows...

higher than the clouds, beyond the stars
beneath the horizon, deeper than the seas
sometimes hidden, farther than the wind blows

gets stronger as it grows in time – to never dwindle
as honest as a whisper, as delicate as a rose petal,
yet so vexatious at times. Perplexing

But dismiss it? Not a chance, unable,... ?
Or is it you can't do without it?
No. You don't want to.
Sometimes you're too grateful, and you cherish it.
Satisfying
Lasting
Complete as a whole.
Yes – it is truly breathtaking feeling,
and painful.

Love.

Dreams of the Soul

My Son's First Communion
Sidney S. Macaulay
For the first time
His hand went out
For the sacrament,
Understanding now
His own unworthiness.

We've been together
In lots of things —
Cheered for the Steelers,
Shared God's glory in nature,
And drank the same milkshake.

It's strange – this answer
To his parents' prayers.
Communion quietly passed him by before.
Now — the blood of my blood does share,
We two whose life is in His blood.

Two small pools in glasses peer,
Pupil–like, reduced by Light,
To see joy in this Father's heart.
"While you are raised to a new plane,
I've become a child with you."

Forgiven
Paula Morriss
Just when I thought you loved me
My heart sank into the ground
Darkened secrets thrust upon me
whispering unwanted sounds
Voices singing, praising, dancing
All was lost but now its found
Desperate silence, moments of passion
Wrapped within a tender heart
Opened up the heavens above me
Stolen clouds that caress the skies
Chance a heart that you still love me
In sacred arms there are no lies

Mirror Of A Matron
Barbara Wagstaff
Fifty was nifty,
But now that I'm sixty
I wear my hair short,
Styled like a pixie.

Diet, exercise and rest,
Always struggling
To look my best.

Smiling through my limbs
Go numb —
There's no need
To look so glum.

Youth's reflection
Doesn't last,
It's an image
Of the past.

Inner beauty
I'd rather boast
Love for posterity
Should matter most.

Untitled
Ann Mided
Am I so blind, I cannot see,
What eighty years has done to me?
Inside I feel like twenty–one
But I ain't having so much fun!

My aching back, it leaves me weak,
I'm walking like a helpless freak.
My ulcer hurts, my heart is bad
My "Charley Horses" drive me mad.

But there are pluses you can see,
Senior discounts keep luring me,
Restaurant discounts, shows and all
Keep me busy in the mall.

And the thrill of getting that
Social Security check
Boosts my ego – yeah! – like heck.
Old age is great, I can't deny
And I ain't ready to say 'bye–bye'.

My goal–100–'cause I want to see
What the future holds for me.

Untitled
Rene Gouader
Life is funny
Life is short
Life is a game we have all been
taught.
Tender sweet and loving too
Love for me, and love for you
We play our part until the end
Then our act is passed on to
A friend, there life is funny
Tender sweet too.
But in the end they must
Follow you?

Harder On Me
K. A. Scott
Being involved in everyday life
Playing, learning, laughing

Growing into pain
Family death, little league losses, sibling rivalries
It's beginning to be hard on me.

Friends growing apart
Different schools, new friends, past memories
It's hard to be me.

Moving further, new friends and me
Suddenly it's so hard
Where am I going?

Where am I? Who am I?
It's hard to be me.

Standing alone, on the edge
Where did time go?
It's hard to be me

Why is it harder on me?

Noteworthy Works

Spring
Peggy McGrane

Glorious colour and balmy nights,
The freshness of earth bursts forth.
Buds unfurl and lift their heads
heavenward.

He comes courting and she dreams of a
future once again.

The impossible seems within reach,
the difficult just a minor annoyance.

All is birds
and
bees
and
brightness
Plans
and
Hopes
Love
and
Tenderness
God's lighted pathway to joy and serenity.

Silhouettes
David J. Smith

Darkened rain with chains
Of abysmal smiles
Daughters do look down
On torsion minds
Listless and empty
We stand 'Sin Qua Non'
Yet I wonder as I
Stand and stare
Amongst this darnel
Of woven pleas
To be naked
And yet I never weep.

Mom
Mary Kowalski

You were always there when I needed you
to talk, to laugh or when I was blue.

You gave so much of yourself to me
with patience, love and sensitivity.

Always ready to give and to care
a smiling face you had to share.

So many wonderful memories remain
now you are gone, but not in vain.

For your love lives on to grow
in all of us, who loved you so.

A Mom, Grandma and Great–Grandma too
so many lives were touched by you.

A legacy you left of unconditional love
to guide and comfort from above.

You will be missed now we're apart
A special angel, alive in my heart.

My Family Is Sleeping Long Today
Melinda Lorge

My family is sleeping long today
I scream loud in their ears
they're not getting up for heaven sake

I think I'll have a little fun
I run and run and run
I hammer a nail
I play with the cat
I yank her tail
I swing a bat

I make some jungle sounds
I bang on every door
I act like a funny clown
I scream and roar

I think I'll play my trumpet
I see a glass
I think I'll bump it
I think I'll pop a big balloon

They can't sleep through all of this
I'm sure they'll get up soon

My Mom
I. Prest

In the morning there is sunshine,
It shines on the human race.
It could shine on forever,
But would never take your place.
For your face is a wonder,
A beauty to behold.
A face I will remember
Till the day that I'm too old.
I've seen a face of beauty,
A lady I love it's true.
My darling dearest Mother.
That face belongs to you.

Yield
M. S. VanAllen

Floral meadow bends and weaves
As twisted winds bring
whispers of promise
To tempt the hearts of children...

Seasoned reeds and wizened weeds,
A brittle barrier of belittled needs
For the host of precious petals
That flourish too far away
in the fields.

Those exposed are left to pose
In bent and precarious positions.
Young tendrils snap,
And lay in the lap of the earth
to make their additions
To those gone before who had
nothing more
Than their youth to offer the swell.

The meadow is shaven
In windswept invasion,
Where now, does innocence dwell?

Dreams of the Soul

Tango Revisited
Marlies English
Just another ordinary day
so they all say
if I had my way
there would never be an ordinary day
only glitter, music, champagne
and never the same styles
chansons by Edith Piaf
the French sparrow
there is silence in the room
while Piaf sings of doom
and of unrelenting passion
now that has always been in fashion
French wine and Swiss cheese
and pate from some poor geese
lust and laughter fill the room
forgotten is the temporary doom
we will dance the tango – now
with style and ecstasy we dance
firmly in an eternal embrace
close together as if we were one
well I must say this turned out
to be anything – but an ordinary day
I never had so much fun this way.

Divine Love
Coig Cole
This morning when I was waking up you were on my mind,
You make me feel so very happy with a love that's so divine.

Then I turn over and kiss you softly on your cheek,
You open up your eyes, said you love me,
And my heart it will skip a beat.

I hold you very close to me,
Our bodies are meant to be as one.

Something tells me our love is never wrong.
Its only just begun.

It Just Takes A Little Longer
Homer Sharpton
O. K. I've got this lung problem called C. O. P. D.,
A fancy name which means I can't breathe.

The oxygen level in my blood, they call this SPO2,
Severely limits what my body can do.

So I'm tied to this oxygen bottle most of the time
mounted on a little cart that trails behind.

There's also my inhalants I puff on all day.
They help me to breathe by opening the passageways.

Oh well, another mountain to climb.
Like walking out of the Grand Canyon a few yards at a time.

But I'm not helpless as you can see.
And I know the secrets of Adaptation energy.

With a little refueling, it's always spring.
The roses smell sweet and the birds still sing.

So don't wait for me friend, I'll get there I vow.
It's just going to take me a little longer now.

A Poet's Prayer
Carrie Anne Tocci
A reaction to today's headlines:
What was blown up? By whom?
There is mercury in my mouth.

Skyscraper give back beauty.
Eat the clover under my tongue.
Notice the shape of sleep.

Eyelashes kiss on a face.
Vision demands the know of ugly.
Awakened. Words are what I owe.

I give up—black and blue.
Air strikes. Thought is uprooted.
Writing proves its purple.

Speech an illuminate arch,
Steals my eyes upward.
Hibernation is over.

Seasons pass and prepare.
Steady now. Breathe.
God's eyes are larger than air.

First Teacher
Lorna Okorn
How well I remember Miss Carter, who was tall and very thin.
She had grey hair and glasses, and stored chalk in an old cocoa tin.
She taught me numbers – One, Two, Three; how to add and take away.
That sixty minutes make one hour, and twenty–four hours – one day.
She taught me letters– A, B, C and how to read and write.
About the Sun, the Earth and Moon, why stars come out at night.
From her I learned the Earth is round, That fish live in the sea.
Of animals, and birds that fly, and honey is made by a bee.
How William conquered Britain, that Henry had six wives.
Of ancient kingdoms, their peoples, and how they lived their lives.
She taught me many wondrous things, too numerous to tell.
My Infant Teacher – Miss Carter. Oh yes, I remember You well.

Love
Crissie Blackburn
Anyone but you
can say that love is true.
No one but you
Knows what feeling blue can do.

They say love is supposed to be from
the heart.
But often love can tear us apart.
Its almost a feeling of a dart,
A dart right through your heart.
When a true love falls apart
One may feel like death has done us apart.

When this occurs, we must leave behind
the sorrow
And let hope in for a better tomorrow.

We sit back and think, it couldn't
have been true;
Or this love wouldn't be through.
Oh well, it's time to find someone new.
Someone who will be true, and only
true to you.

Noteworthy Works

Going For A Walk In The Woods
Michael Lackey

I'm going for a walk in the woods today,
it's time to get away from the city for at least one day.
I'm going to a place where the only sounds are of birds and bees,
I'm going to a place where the only skyscrapers are the trees.
In the woods, the trees sing to me, and they chime,
"Where have you been, we haven't seen you in a long time."
I'm going to get away from big city things,
to a place where everything has branches or wings.
I'm going for a walk in the woods today,
I want to see what they have to say.

Dedication: Rocky, always my best friend

Father
Stacy L. Long

Father is the title I'm giving to you,
not only that... you're a special
friend too.

Always around for me whenever I fall
knowing you'll help me... It's you
that I call.

Thank you for patience, when rent is due
other people would get upset...
but not you.

Helping everyone is something you do
whether you want to or not...
it's expected of you.

Even though blood isn't our tie
you are my father... you know why.

Read this over one more time
look in the mirror... It's you in
this rhyme.

Life Up – Life Down
Annzetta Holmes

In a nation where everything
and everybody is rushed to do this,
and rushed to do that:
Love is patient
In the mind of a people set on
doing it our way, it's nobody's
business, get out of my way
Love is Kind
Without a song in the heart,
enjoying the sounds of another
one's fall, watching for mistakes
Love keeps no record of wrongs
I love you, let's be two,
I do, that's your view,
we're through – I'll find somebody
New
What a throw–away society –
Recycle
Find out what love really is
in the book called – The Bible.

Dedication: Zetta, Lucian, Mandell, Tia, Robyn

On Heaven's Runway
Lillian Kahn

Looking skyward, as one might,
I spied a plane and bird in flight;
Both were soaring mountains high,
Both were racing through the sky;
The plane in predetermined path
With firm and rigid lifeless wings;
The bird a graceful, fluid form
A melody its movement sings.
As Heaven's boundless roads they skim,
The vibrant body, the mechanical limb,
Their flight a potent message brings
Of Nature's wondrous, winged things.

Mom's Poem
Bianca F. Pool

Mother was there when you needed her care
From the very first day you were born,
She would bandage your knee
And to every degree
She would stop you from feeling forlorn
Now she kissed you goodnight
And instructed you right
Was a time when, you didn't think twice
'Bout making her wait, when you wondered in late
For you often ignored her advice.
Then at last you were grown and went out on your own
Even though she would miss you so much;
But, although it was rough
If you loved her enough,
Then you showed it by keeping in touch.
So by word and by deed,
As you learned by your creed,
From the day that your training began,
While your Mother's around,
Let your feelings abound
With your help and your love,
while you can

Vasily
Christine O'Rourke Praria

Come for me Vasily,
As I hang, wounded and broken,
Shattered... my blood waits for you
to sip it, savor it,
Strain it through your bone white teeth
and swallow its steaming ruby life.

A river of pain streams out of me;
The long gash of your iron tooth
taps the waters of my life;
Your dark hair against my white flesh,
red and sticky with my smeared blood;
Your fist ripping me apart;
Fire burning my soul.

Screams, agony
Who is it screaming, Vasily?
I can't see in the darkness,
The black blood covers my eyes.
Blood fills my ears, my mouth,
My body hangs on an iron spit,
The spike behind my eyes.

Dreams of the Soul

Poetry And Prose
Amalean Witherspoon
I used to think it was for those
With talent I lacked to compose
But it seemed one day words began to flow
Deep feelings were recorded in form of
TRIBUTE, POEM or PROSE
–this was about ten years ago–
Now appreciate a lot of Poets
Especially Edgar Alan Poe
And President Carter's "Always A. Reckoning"
Is reading to behold
Poetry and Prose
It's more than suppose!

Old Age
R. D. Hiscoke
When we are old and weak and foolish grown
With childish mind that lacks a child's frank grace
And missing friendship's love we once had known
Find only pitying kindness in its place

When aged dimmed eyes no longer can descry
The printed pages once their chief delight
And the changing glories of the summer sky
Are merged in changeless gloomy shades of night

When song of little bird and music strain
Fall on dull ears with no responsive thrill
And all the joys of life which still remain
Are food and sleep and warmth in winter's chill

Must it be thus? O Thou who gavest youth
His boundless courage and His buoyant strength
His zeal for justice and His love of truth
Must all be lost in nothingness at length

Must all man's noblest instincts waste and fade
Leaving the wreck of what Thy Hand has made

Waking Up The Wall Flowers
Laura K. Smith
Morning is the smell of your skin and warm sheets,
Crumpled like the face of a child still in yesterday's dream.
The sound of your breath wakes the wall flowers,
The warmth unfurls their buds in brittle, yellowed paper curls.

Sun light creeps in tentatively,
Sliding gentle lover's fingers through your tousled mop of hair,
Then tickling your eyelids with the bright promise of a brave new day.
Consciousness stirs like a dog in a basket,
Too snug in the ring of nose and tail to fear of burglars.

You stretch into the sunrise,
Feeling the loving, glowing baptism of its mellow heat,
Basking in the unassuming joy that you forget is existence.

When you wake the sun filters herself back through the glass,
The flowers retreat once more into the flat indifferences of damp plaster,
And love effaces itself like oxygen; the unseen currencies of living.

You get up, the earth turns, the day begins,
And the galaxy and I tell each other that our worlds don't revolve around you.

Pluto Monkey
Cyrus Kai
They make me feel guilty
For liking the things I like
And I make myself feel guilty
For liking the things they like
They think they're better than me
Or maybe I think they're better than me
I agree and disagree
Or maybe I agree to disagree
Am I angry because I can't have you
Or am I angry because I don't want you
The answers will come in time
Or time will be the answer

In The Following Of The Footsteps
John Karak
My Father laid below, swept through the window,
shedding some tears and shades of red.
Upon this floor and led from the door,
laid these shades from the fallen dead.
And for this I pondered, walked and wandered,
pacing this floor with the marks of red.
I lay to rest, but lay a wreck,
breaking into tears and falling from the bed.
Anxious and latent, weary and shaken,
I cover my eyes to blind all regret.
But nothing I feel, no feeling is real,
but still I wish it all and to forever forget.
And I await this end, for the sadness to amend,
to make my peace with the laying dead.
So I choose the ledge, even more the edge,
to join my Father in the ground of red.
For we'll both lay below, swept through the window,
shedding our tears and these shades of red.
We will lay together, now and forever,
intertwined at last as fallen friends.

Dedication: Lisa... to whom I love

Baby Love
Deborah Christine Williams
Inside me is a little baby that is pure as
a dove, but sometimes I wonder if I can give
you that thing called love. The Father is a
Father that does not want to claim. Oh, my Lord,
how can an image of you be so insane. I know
that I am pregnant and I feel alone, because
life seems so awkward and my heart beats a
different tone. Though I have tears at night and
laughter during the day, I know life will carry
on and this is a part God wants me to play.
Sometimes I watch a movie and see a happy
couple with a baby. I grin and smile or even
giggle, but will there be someone to save me.
I might cry, scream, and feel real bad with
nothing of words to say. But deep in my
heart, I know God will bless me with a
precious love someday. Baby love inside
me, I pray to the Lord above, bless me
with something oh so sweet; that is as
pure as a little white dove.

Dedication: To Christ, my "Baby Love"

Qualicum Beach–Vancouver Island
Nancy Perry
The sea breaks gentle waves upon the shore,
I sit and watch the sea birds by the score.
Sea gulls, blackbirds, loons and herons too
Dip and dive – an ever-changing view.
The ships are far away across the bay,
Fishing boats and ferries on their way.
The islands sleep like giants in the sun,
This is a sight to please most anyone.
The mountains of the Mainland look so high,
The puffy clouds float in an azure sky.
Tomorrow – winds may blow and skies look grey,
But I'm so happy for the sun today.

Emotional Storm
Melissa A. Semeniuk
The end of the world is directly before my eyes.
The black clouds loom over me as a reminder of sorts.
Each drop from the horrific sky pierces my flesh like
a knife.

Causing all the memories to flood from my heart.
Thoughts of pain, suffering, loneliness, and betrayal.
My tears begin to flow, but not out of sadness,
Out of rage that cannot even be compared to the loud
roaring of the thunder.

I feel so confined and trapped in my body.
I want to tear my flesh to escape my torment.
However the torment lies within my mind and heart.
If only I could stop thinking and feeling, maybe then
I could find salvation.

The rain stops suddenly and the city begins to move again.
I look at my surroundings and realize that this was a sign.
A way for me to purify myself.
I feel clean, something I'm not used to.
If only I knew how to hold onto this feeling.

I Am
Rebecca Kindred
I am a caring granddaughter,
I wonder about my Grandmother.
I hear she will be soon going to a wonderful and peaceful place.
I see myself sitting on her lap telling my favorite story.
I want her to stay and be with me just a little longer but she must go.
I am a caring granddaughter.

I pretend she will get better and it will be like old times again.
I feel she is near, caring for me.
I touch her old photos of her in her favorite, wide-brimmed, flowered hat.
I worry I will never see her again.
I cry because she was so close to my heart.
I am a caring granddaughter.

I understand her time will come and all too soon.
I say to myself, "why her of all people?"
I dream of all the fun times we spent together.
I hope to see her soon in that wonderful
and peaceful place.
I am a caring granddaughter.

Dedication: My Grandma Kindred

Jason The Mean
Amy Lee Coleman
Grouchy old Jason,
A tottering old cat;
He hisses and spits and acts all that.
You'd think he's mean and scary;
He'd make you awful wary,
But not to fret:
Under all that show,
One thing I do know,
He's my sweet, sweet pretty Jason.
The same kitten I knew
Many years ago,
And he'd never try to hurt you.

Questions?
Katherine Koldenhof
Have you ever really loved someone
and wondered if he really loved you?
Have you ever felt like crying
and wondered what good it would do?
Have you ever looked into his eyes
and said a little prayer?
Have you ever looked into his heart
and wished that you were there?
Have you ever seen him walking
when the lights were down low?
Have you ever said "God I really love him"
but I'll never let him know?
It doesn't work my friend
it's too much to keep inside.
The love I feel for you is
my only guide.
So I'll tell you now I love you
and may love is true.
I hope you never doubt me
I never doubted you.

Dedication: My husband, John, with love

Grand Doight
Celestine Hickman
Grand Doight was his name
'cause those big fingers were his claim to fame
When he started to play
you couldn't help but become swept away
Along a stratification of notes
while removing our coats
Even though the room was dim,
welcomed by a receptive rhythm
It had to be him.

Hard to describe
those big 5 plus 5 relating a vibe
Composing improvisational jive
building into a soaring style
Its sound, highly worthwhile.

Like a sculptor of movement
those big fingers precisely carved each tune
Ou–u–u–u–u
how the ladies would swoon
As he chiseled a harmonious melody
from ebony and ivory.

Dreams of the Soul

Anniversary Poem
June Fleming
You meet someone and like them,
The relationship just grows,
As time goes on you fall in love,
That's the way it goes,
You go through life together,
Facing happiness, strife, and tears,
But please remember with fond affection,
Those very special years,
So make each day a bonus,
With a love that's precious and true,
And think back to that wonderful time,
When you said I do.

Human Nature – Suddam Hussain
Kiton Ratanavong
A cuckoo's nest can chime in time,
A thousand bees can pollinate in spring,
An owl can sing its love song and serenade it to those untouched by Zen,
But a cunning fox cannot outwit its race,
And an inspiring cloud cannot seduce its foe
For an insidious twirl can rebound its curl.

A cricket can chirp his mate,
A lion can roar in fear, but their liberty must be complete.
The piper of Himelin can blow his flute, but the mole can be an instigator to his companions alike.
A hyena can laugh in hideous sight, but at the dusk of dawn peace will reign his throne.

The stench of irony can influence no more, as a gazing star in solitude calm cannot be reached,
The pace of time can outdo our age,
But an ageless tree cannot be contempt with this priceless silence,
Let vermin bring blackness to us all, for beast has risen to conspire the mood of death.
And the fable is, there is a human being in every tale just like you and me.

Untitled
Eileen Cole
Why do I laugh, when inside I'm crying?
Why do I smile as the tears fall down...
Be brave, little girl, let it not show!
While all the while my heart is breaking.

Look up to the sun, see not the clouds.
For shadows darken, keep your chin up!
If once your eyes cast downward to earth,
They will think you're crying — Look up!

But after awhile your head grows weary,
From all the smiles left unfelt.
What's wrong with letting tears fall down?
If they're real, they mend, they cleanse.

If all the days were added done bravely,
and all the nights left but for sleep,
Then honesty with one's feelings,
Would drop and fall as a tear, to infinity,
unnoticed.
Dedication: My mother & father, whose combined talents I draw upon daily

---

When Frogs Fly
Lisa Scott
When frogs fly
and birds croak.
When I laugh
at my daddy's jokes.
When kids bark
and dogs laugh,
When dogs have kids
and moms have cats,
When trees grow in ponds
and grass is blue.
That's when I'll
stop loving you.

Nurses
Wretha Meyers
"Nurses" tall and skinny, short and fat;
Large, medium, small and flat;
Blonde hair, brown hair, red hair, gray and black;
Straight, curly, short cuts, long cuts,
Braid's top–knots, so many styles, drives me nuts;
Blue eyes, brown eyes, green, hazel, gray
Smiles, frowns, low voices, high;
Some bright and gay, loud and soft,
Angry, placating, loving and aloft.
Good mornings good nights, how are you?

Blood pressure taking, lung and heart listening;
Stomach, front and back, anything and everything.
Sit up please, cough please, take a deep breath please;

Let it out, breathe deep, let it out, another, let bit out.

I wander if I so I should sneeze or shout?
In the listener's ear or what?
Maybe I should be so lucky to try it?

Sometime, and see just what the result would be?

The Battle Upon Edge Hill
Joy Parkin
Upon the sunset of the morn sleepy, ill and worn.
I hear the roll of distant drums signaling battle has begun.
The battle upon Edge Hill.

Brave, determined, I am not prepared to die, boldly rot.
Fear pounding loud within my head, fear of not wanting to be dead.
At the battle upon edge hill.

Bayonets flashing against the sun, line formation charging one by one
Cries of anguish fill my ears, my eyes are most with tears.
I not wanting to stay, would let the roundheads have their way.
At the battle upon Edge Hill.

Awaiting my turn in line, I hear bagpipes from behind.
They play our tune so clear, thoughts of home and kin most dear.
I joined in the vibrant song, to me this battle feels so wrong.
This battle upon Edge Hill.

My kin charge down the hill, exacting revenge for those so still.
Swords, kilts moved with formidable swish.
Certainly making those roundheads wish an end to the battle
Upon Edge Hill.

Noteworthy Works

I Thank God For Owls
Jennifer Jones
One day in May
I knelt to pray
For my back, just didn't feel well
I have a pain
Which helped me gain
A faith I thought I'd lost
I looked up to heaven
And saw a vision
Of a beautiful big brown owl
I look after them now
And now I don't scowl
For my pain is nearly all gone

Anniversary
Claudette Sternberg
I slipped a ring upon your finger many years ago,
It is more precious now than silver or gold.

I placed a circle upon your finger many years ago,
It shines and glitters so brightly even though it's old.

I put a symbol upon your finger many years ago,
It shows that my love continues to unfold.

I slid a band upon your finger many years ago,
It still is being blessed for all to behold.

I encircled a pledge upon your finger many years ago,
It represents a priceless gift never to be sold.

I hung a wreath upon your finger many years ago,
It blossoms fuller now – fragrant and bold.

Oh How thankful I am for that willing finger of old,
For because of it our love story could be told!

Maxi's Light
R. J. Jesson
Unlike the candle by my bed
Unlike the leaves that fall down dead
Unlike the days that change to dark
Unlike chained gates that front a park
But flowing water endlessly
Forever full forever free
Oceans blue and pastures green
Of all the beauty we have seen
Of stars that make the dark turn light
Of all the moons that shine for night
Of rain and wind and sleet and snow
A Place always where roses grow
Not a day of thoughts, nor hour, nor minute
Pass me by without you in it.
And when you sleep within your dreams
When your fears turn into screams
Turn to me your candle bright
To guide you through and give you sight
Your fears will gently ease away
To dream until the light of day.

Dedication: My husband, Max, with love

Bloom For Jesus
Mary Martin
They put Him upon that cross to die.
His blood dropped to the ground that it might fertilize.
He cleared the way of all the debris.
He died upon that cross to set us free.
Will you be the one to help plant His seeds?
There are so many out there still in need.
How bright does your light shine?
Or is it hidden and so hard to find?
Will you be true blue like the violet?
Or will your voice stay still and silent?
He may be coming back soon.
Are you just a bud, or are you in full bloom?

Good Morning
Seth Leibowitz
Violent beams of dawn's song
Found their way through the break
In the miniblinds
Sweaty passion stenched the room
Clothes seemed to have found their way
In the oddest of places
A turtleneck decorated the chair
A bra performed its impression
Of a weeping willow on the halogen lamp
Pairs of socks played a twisted game of tic–tac–toe
With an assortment of shoes and condom wrappers
Got to knock the drunk cobwebs away...
Two cups of water rest next to the clock radio
One filled with tap water
The other... saline solution
Saline does not work well with a parched throat
Funny though... contacts are not used
In this room
Maybe it is the owner of that tuft of hair
Poking out from the comforter

Dedication: Ash, my love and inspiration

Samantha's 1st Birthday
Vicki L. Souder
This past year we've been blessed
With a baby so precious and dear.
It's time today to celebrate with family,
Friends and good cheer!

We want to let "Samantha" know the
Happiness we feel. She's touched our
Lives in many ways – It really is unreal!

Her beautiful smile, her striking dark hair
And her eyes so blue and bright,
They make her shine from head to toe
Oh, what a wondrous sight!

It's been a wonderful year with our special
Little one. It's hard to believe it's all passed
To think that a year has come to an end...
It really goes by much too fast!

So we'll cherish the memories of the days gone by
And anticipate moments to come. What better way to
Live out your life than with a family to make you as one!

Dreams of the Soul

People Watching
Cathy Gillispie
As I look down from my perch in the tree
I can see couples happy and free
They are holding hands as they walk in the park
Just two happy people with one big heart.

Always laughing, never a tear,
Seems like I have watched the same couples for years
The walk is slower, the steps are smaller
But I am the happiest of them all.

As I look down from the tree
I see the happy couples looking up at me.

Love Is In The Heart
Eugene Caad
Love is like the heart
Within the dove flying
into the sunset. Where the
heart is strong with warmth
and a caring heart to
grow as strong as the
winter breeze. Floats like the
clouds in the blue sky.
Something you can see and
feel within the heart.
Love is like a flowers
that you see growing
in the summer where butterflies
are out flapping
there wings going flower
to flower. Love is both of
us floating in the water
holding hands looking straight
up into the stars twinkling
as strong and bright.

Dedication: Meya Williams

Who Is It Underneath? You/Me?
K. D. Henkel
Questions unanswered, cries unheard...
Feelings unregarded, needs/wants unmet...
Emptiness/loneliness untouched...
Hurts unrecognized...
Attempts to reach out in Love unreciprocated...
Distance unchanged, confusion unsatisfied... Unfulfilled...
Tries unsuccessful...

Unthankful? No
Ungrateful, unappreciative? No
Unselfish? Definitely No
Love will be unwavering...
Emotions of sadness unavoidable, sometimes uncontrollable...
Unwanted, unneeded, unconnected...
Unprepared to move on? Unafraid to go forward?
Heart unbroken?
Unforgettable?
Time together was unfinished.
Replacements? Unacceptable.
Undercover...

Dedication: Robert Thomas Henkel

Death
Jessica Peete
Death is a companion.
Know it or not
It's always there
Lingering in the back of your darkest thoughts.
Death sneaks up on you
When you are not aware.
Death stares you in the face
When it's your turn to take your place.
Death is no secret.
Death has no cure.
Death is not human.
Death is just pure.

White Weather Boarded Home
Tina Larkins
For many years in my time,
Have quickly come to pass,
And tho' it is sometimes foggy,
My mind is a looking glass...
Yet, a vivid reflection,
One etched in stone,
Are my fond memories
Of my "white weather boarded home"
Daddy was a traveling man,
Mama, she loved us so.
Times were tough you see,
And all most folks had ever known.
Our family was fortunate,
We could help those in need.
A trunk full of IOU's
That was our good deed.
And at night all cozy in our beds,
Covered by quilts hand sewn,
My heart will always remember
My "white weather boarded home."

Dedication: To Edna Clamon, my grandmother

No Name
Shannon Mumpower
Pain is pain by whatever name,
Can't they see, it all hurts the same.
Each tear cried neither burns less or more
When deciding just what the tear is for.
When people's eyes look on how things go,
They use blame in determining their woe.
If she is the one who made her own bed,
Not one single word of kindness is said.
Never do they seem to all realize,
When she heard the music, the fiddler was in disguise.
They cast their stones and cast their vote
Leaving her alone with the burden to tote.
They grieve and fret for the ones they've lost
Never realizing she pays the heaviest cost.
Still living, but in Hell for the decisions she made
Never minding the cost for what was forbade.
So night after night, her tears are wasted
For the ones she cries, they've never tasted.
They're bittersweet in knowing in her heart she's right,
But cold and alone, they fall night after night.

Dedication: For David, my true love

Noteworthy Works

Life
Melissa Gordon

I wished I'd had a chance to say
That I loved him on that day
Now all I do is lay and cry
and pray that God will tell me why
I know that I'll never understand
It's like only yesterday that he took my hand
I know our children will ask one day
Why those men took their Dad's life that way
I know I must go on to make a new start
But he'll always have a special place in my heart.

Dedication: John, Jessica and Justin Gordon

My Angel, My Friend
Lisa Nelson

Special memories... caring friends, many hopes and dreams,
and a brighter today.
These are some of the things that you,
have brought to my life.

My heart can only say:

Thank You,
... for not only listening,
but hearing between the words.
... for wiping away tears no one else could see.
... for taking the time to understand me,
and teaching me about respect and genuine concern.
... for sharing with me the most
personal times of your life.
... for being one of the best parts of my life
and allowing me to love you.

You truly are an angel, because in your presence
I have felt the spirit of the Lord embrace me.

Dedication: Twanya, our friendship is priceless...

You
Beverly Largent

God gave us love
He made us to care
He looks from above
He'll always be there.
He wants me to love you
He wants us to share
To be caring and true
To make the flames flare.
I've prayed to Him often
I've prayed for your love
I've prayed to the Son
Who's there up above.
the Lord in His mercy
Is pleased with our love
He wants us to be
Faithful as the dove.
Forever I'll love you
And give all I can
To care for you too
For you are my man.

Dedication: George, my life's love

A Hand To Hold
Hilda Pum Anders

If at life's beginning until life's end –
There's a hand to hold – you're with a friend.
The infant rises, and stands, with the help of
an extended hand.
The child is blessed, who, as he grows –
Can run, hand in hand, with friends he knows.
Truly blessed are they, who, on the final day –
As they bid the world adieu, and go their way –
Have a hand theirs hold, and, with gentleness,
and love enfold.

Dedication: Karol Anders, beloved husband and friend

Crazy Thoughts Of You
Kristin Anderson

Lying here alone in my bed,
The carpet still stained with red,
Remembering all the things we said,
Crazy thoughts of you going through my head,
Still can't believe that you're dead,
A single tear drop falls from my eye,
Another dark shadow passes by,
Tired of living a lie,
I no longer am able to try,
We never got to say good–bye,
Oh God, how I wish I too, would die,
Never will I understand why you had to fight,
When you should be here to hold me tight,
And tell me everything is all right,
Looking into an empty room, without you,
I know tomorrow won't be
so bright,
I close my eyes and leave the world to follow
your guiding light,
Beside you I shall lie tonight.

Dedication: Tha, with all my love

I Dreamed Your Beauty
J. Marchesi

I dreamed your beauty;
flaxen hair, blue eyes
legs a man could die for.
Your aquiline features in their prime
before they are stripped bare
by change, and the winds of time.
Where there was loveliness
only grey flesh on white bone.

Life fades, all the fuss
and pomp we made
crumbles into dust.
Beyond the moment time might give
to each, their little glory.
The make–up smudged,
the wax will run
putrescence, death, the story.

If beauty is truth
I dreamed a lie
to hide
from that eternal change.

Dreams of the Soul

Dad Why?
Doreen Grieve
Dad, what keeps the moon and the sun in the sky?
And why don't they fall to the ground, Dad. Why?
The stars come out at night to play.
But why in the morning have they gone away?
Why can't I reach out with my hand
And gather them up like grains of sand?
Dad, you're so clever, you really must know—
I'm only little, it puzzles me so.
I often sit by the window and stare—
Just wondering what it is like up there.
The world's so big and I'm so small.
Does God really know that I'm here at all?

You Say I'm Old
M. M. Joshuas
You say I'm old; I tell you not true
My house is old; but that's not me
I've lived in it; many a year
It has weathered; many a storm.

What stripes and scrapes; as a child
Spots and sports; in my youth
Wars and wounds; for my wench
Strife and stress; with the job
Chores and cares; with my kids

The walls and bricks; may have changed
The light at night; may be dimmer
But my roof; still has slates
The door bell; chimes as new
And my clock; keeps to time

The old john; dot go aflush
I'm as nimble; as of yore
OAP I may be; but am wiser with my age
My haunt and Beth; keep me hearty
I am me; not my house.

The Vultures
N. Williams
The vultures eating up
Our flesh
They steer in our
Eyes
Moving in, moving in
To take a bite.
The intelligent vultures
Sweet spoken devil
Vultures.
Are we not all vultures
Pretending to be humane
Pretending to hold hands
Just constantly playing
The game of global death
While we smile at each
Other
Pretending love.
Only truly able to
Love, to love what?
The vultures within!

Dedication: D. C. Kimani and S. A. one love, always

Individuals
Sandra L. Haight
You are you – I am me –
We are we – individuals meant to be.
You are you –
I'll not make me out of you –
I am me –
Let me be all I can be –
We are we –
Not what everyone wants us to be.
Individuals meant to be –
You, me and we!

Dedication: Anna Mae, we are different!

Life's Direction
Stacey Short
Life belongs to you and to me
Forever tossing surprises in our path,
We seem trapped – never free
As we watch life bring forth its wrath.
It is at such desolate times
That we must close our eyes and pray,
For we are like mimes
Asking God to banish the gray.
We must always face the reality
That bad times will happen by,
To force out every drop of nobility
We can possibly hope to supply.
So, release each hidden desire
Of happy days and smiling faces,
And watch these dreams transpire
In the most unlikely places.
Now, surely you must know
That by taking this wonderful dare,
Life has new direction in which to go
When you allow God to answer your prayer.

Dedication: Mom, my compass

In the Balance
Theresa M. Carney
In the balance there is a place
That I run to no time just space
To find myself in hope to find
Some sort of love (some love that's mine.)

In the balance there is a song
That just might keep me going along
Some sort of love (some love that's mine.)

In the balance I see my face
Within God's eyes I see my place
Some sort of love (some love that's mine.)

In the balance I find myself
And learn to Laugh and see my wealth
Some sort of love (some love that's mine.)

In the balance is where I am
I learn to live and love again
Some sort of love (some love that's mine.)

Dedication: Justin, my precious prayer answered!

Rescue Of The Tiger Butterfly
Ginny Goodyear

Ginny walked over to the pool
She saw a butterfly floating lifeless
It was a pretty tiger butterfly
Some time passed – Ginny watched intently
Suddenly a slight flicker in one wing
She scooped the poor creature out of the water
Putting it on dry land, it baked in the healing
rays of the sun.
There was much suspense – could butterfly
spread its wings?
Ginny prayed.
Then, this butterfly did fly away, triumphantly!

Through The Eyes Of A Mother
Shellie Mayer

When you see your children you see beauty unfold
Behold them in your arms and love them like there's no tomorrow
Give them praise for all they do
Tender hugs and kisses and lots of I love yous
Read them books and see their eyes glisten
When they speak always take the time to listen
Forget the I'm too busy and take a special day
For tomorrow may not come so live for today
Laugh with them, talk with them, hold them tight
Snuggle by their sides as you tuck them into bed each night
Cherish every moment never let one go by
Hold onto your memories remember all the whys
Teach them goals and let them know you can do it
Positively your attitude strengthens their inner wit
Look up to your children as they look up to you
Love them unconditionally whatever they may do
Provide them with a home filled with peace and love
Pray for angels to watch over them from heaven above
Children are miracles it's amazing you see
For without them the gift of parenting would never be.

Dedication: My children, Alexis and Joey

For Crescent Mommy's Angel Pie
Tracy L. Richman Colonna

How do you make an Angel Pie?
You take some moonlight from the sky
Some Crescent Moon to be precise
To make a smile so very nice
And next you'll need some sparkling eyes
So pluck some stars from brightest skies
From galaxies so far away
For eyes that sparkle all the day
But next you'll need some brilliant gold
From planets whether young or old
To make the angel's hair on top
Then one more thing before you stop
You'll need to find a force so strong
To help that Angel Pie along
A force as strong as Mommy's Love
No other force could rise above
So now I have my Angel Pie
I feel so grateful as I sigh
For life gave me a treasured present
I Love You my most special Crescent

Dedication: Crescent, love of my life...

Brother
Vivian R. Harris

You may not know how special you are to me,
You're the best brother there could ever be
We've been through good and bad.
What a fun time together we've both had.
Now that we're becoming better friends,
I hope your trust in me never ends.
All my life I've looked up to you
And I'm very proud of everything you do.
You've always taught me so much you know,
So I just wanted to tell you, "I love you so!"

Dedication: To Wayne R. Pierri

A Missed Love
Kimberly Kang

Yellow beams of light drown into my skin
as I taste the salty air.
The water dances like sheets of silk
as I feel millions of diamonds piercing my feet.
I glance back to see quilts of green blankets on hills.
The soft, gentle wind caresses my naked skin.
In the distance,
I see a tall, scarecrow figure
standing on a rock that is floating on the never–ending
blue.
My heart is no longer frozen now that he is here.
I kneel down on the fiery diamonds as they trickle off my
skin.
I close my eyes recalling his gentle ways and his kind
smile.
It brings a pearly white to me,
as my face turns into a prune.
I open my eyes.
He is no longer here.
Only emptiness lurks nearby.

Dedication: Beloved cousin, Colin Harry Choy

Twentieth Wedding Anniversary
Dave E. Perkins

Twenty years has been and gone,
Time with our marriage is moving on.
Our grey is greyer, and waistlines are no more,
But my lady is still a sight for eyes that are sore.
Our babies have grown, to girls in their teens,
Rat bags in trainers, wearing T–shirts and jeans.
Soon to be sweethearts of fellas unknown,
I battle for the bathroom – me on my own.
But with our caravan, we get away for a bit
To relax in the sunshine, with a beer and just sit.
The two of us, enjoying the peace and the quiet,
Pub meals in the evening and to hell with our diet.
Now our years together add up to a score,
I look forward to our future and years many more.
The object given for this number is china,
Best we go out, so I can wine 'er and dine 'er.
Over these past years that I mention in verse,
My Rosey for me, turned out better, never worse.
And if asked to think and then hazard a guess,
Would I do it all again, the answer is "Yes".

Dedication: To Ann – simply the best

Dreams of the Soul

Ronnie, My Son
Carol L. Howard
My son; What a beautiful sound.
Did you know you make my world go round?
I'm proud of the sensitive person you are,
You were born under a loving star.

I applaud your honesty and fairness,
In one your age, it is a rareness.
I wish you luck and happiness in life,
I know you can handle the struggle and strife.

What you reap, will be what you sow,
You deserve the best I already know.

There Was A Man
Mari Gutierrez
There was a man
A good man who built a little raft
He spent his days upon the land until there came a draft.
It blew him over a little hill at which his children laughed
And down he tumbled, to his doom? No! To his little raft!
"Come, " said a voice grand as could be, "Come, thou good man, and stay with me
For I have need of an heir, you see, to share with me my majesty."
The man bowed low and humbled himself
And took a telescope off a shelf
"Where are thou, Lord? I see thee not!"
"Don't worry, my child, if you have sought
I have been found and you've been bought!
Hurry now, and come with me, for I'm in need of an heir, you see."
The man got in his little raft and was carried far away by the draft
The children that laughed were now very sad
For, you see, they'd lost their dad.
But the sadness will go slowly away
One of the good man's children one day
Might be swept away and hear the voice say:
"Come, thou good man, and stay with me, for I have need of an heir, you see."

Which Road Should I Take
Arthena M. Frazier
Teenage life is like a two–way road.
We sometimes get confused
and don't know which way to go.
We ask ourselves,
Which road should I take?

Should I go down the road of
anger, drugs, sex, violence, and fear or,
should I go down the road of
happiness, success, goals, loving family and friends.
Which road should I take?

There comes a time in life
When we all have to make that one decision
and realize life is not just a vision,
but no matter how hard it seems
always hang onto your dreams.

Then the next time you go down that
two–way road of teenage life
remember you have a choice so make it.
Which road should you take?

More Than Existence
Karla Fieger
On this day and every day hereafter I devote my life to you
For you make it worth living
Your gentle, caring eyes
Your beautiful smile
Your heartfelt laugh
And yet your beauty goes beyond any physical feature
It comes from a place in which I've been blessed to know

I never believed a love like this could exist
The way you can finish a sentence, as though we share thoughts
You know what to do and when, I never have to ask
A word, a touch, a glance
You always seem able to show me a rainbow, no matter what the day brings
In you I know I have found my pot of gold
I am now a believer

For these reasons and so many more
I know we were meant to be
I've found a piece of me I never knew was missing, I found you
I no longer fear death for I know we will remain as one, never alone
The search is over
Soulmates forever

It's Nature's Way
Annie L. Seabrook
The robin swoops down from a sparsely budded tree,
as the blue jay chants its shrill sonata.
The sparrow busily collects materials for bedding,
in great anticipation of her coming family.
A blackbird travelling with a group of his buddies,
suddenly glides downward, as if saluting the daffodils
which sway to the music of the whistling wind.
Many of them are clustered in groups, while others sit
with heads bowed whispering in happy conversation.
Tulips present a striking pose in multi–colored hats
with heads held high, parading up and down the lawn.
It's nature's way of saying, "Spring has come again."

Life
Jennifer Dianne Masters
Love and despair,
It's all there,
In the thing that we call life.
Joy and pain,
A storm brings rain,
In the thing that we call life.
A short while we stay on Earth,
From our death to our rebirth.
Heartbreak and gratitude,
Some people need a change of attitude,
In the thing that we call life.
Education, determination,
Something we call termination,
In the thing that we call life.
Life can be like a giant maze,
you find yourself in a total daze.
But when you are at your worst,
I promise you, you will not burst,
For friendship always comes in first,
In the thing that we call life.

Dedication: 1st grade teacher, Dr. Criste

Alone Is The Heart
Adrian D. Fernandez
Alone is the heart that comes to the dawn of life
seeking refuge from the darkness called loneliness and pain
carrying the wounds of broken promises, but perhaps the tears
of time will heal the wounds of a heart struggling to
be loved.
Like a single rose the heart stands as a true sign
of hope sending the fragrance of love so strong that it
will not only touch the heart of another, but it shall pierce
the mortal soul making it shine like a precious diamond in a
dark feeling world.
Alone is the heart that comes into this world like
the dawn sharing the early morning light of God; hoping to
change the very meaning of life.
Alone is the heart that ears the gift of love,
still that heart is never lonely, because from the dawn of
life the heart has been strong and so full of courage,
but also soft and precious because the nature of the
heart is tenderness, truth and sincere devotion with an
Essence that may bloom with the beauty of
A single rose.

Dedication: To Janett, my loving mom

Love Is
Cheryl Lee
Love is a funny thing
Falling out of love and back in again
Every time more special than the last
Until that someone comes thro' that door
And loves you like you'd never been loved before
Then all the rest are just memories
Or distant days and long lost waves of emotion
When you walked thro' my door
You set my heart into flight
No one can hold a torch to you
As you're the only one my heart adores
And will be forevermore my darling my only you.

Grandma's Special Memory
Doris Steeber
Michael was at play,
I said, "I have something
To give away."
He came running,
I gave him a hug,
Then he ran to play.
I said, "I have something
To give away."
He came running,
I gave him a kiss,
Then he ran to play.
I said, "I have something
To give away."
He came running,
I said, "I Love You,"
Then he ran to play.
He came running
He gave me a hug and kiss,
He said, "I give away."
And ran to play.

Dedication: My grandson, Michael Steeber

Horizon Dreams
Donna A. Powelson
Over the horizon, just beyond reach
Holds all of our dreams, more than one each.

Has the bluest of sky, greenest of grass
With a lake so clear, shining like glass.

Just to the left, a garden of flowers
Beautiful and bright, teeming with power.

Just to the right, a column of trees
Big, bold, and tall, whispering with glee.

Air smells so sweet, with a gentle breeze
Butterflies and bees flying with ease.

When you are sad, with nowhere to go
Just close your eyes and follow the glow.

Reach for the horizon, open the door
There are your dreams and many more.

Dedication: My children, Wes, Lisa and Phil

My Inspiration
Wendy Andrews
When I sit in a garden so green
I feel content with what I see
The marigolds the roses among flowers so fair
and the birds and bees that hover there
With grass so soft the trees so tall
Songbirds joyfully sing their recall
Such tranquility there I find
Works wonders for my peace of mind
Such beauty I behold with mine eyes
Breathtaking colours of every hue
I feel God's presence in the Heavenly skies
Watching over everything that I do

Feelings
Victoria Reinhart
I met a man wearing jeans
I liked what I saw
Then I saw him in a suit,
It showed good taste, but could
hide my flaws.
So I prefer the man in jeans
They showed it all, and I liked
What I saw.
The man in jeans, now
has my heart.
He's gone away and tore me
apart.
How do you live with a broken
heart?
You find this man, and
he'll fix and repair; piece by
piece and part by part; this
broken heart.
Truly only he can repair this
broken heart.

Dedication: Eric, Cindy and Jarren—extensions of my life and love

Dreams of the Soul

The Essence That Is Me
Jennifer Dove
With you in my life I am whole
I am pure
I am vibrant
I am colorful
You are the essence that is me
And like the morning dew on a rose
You are the kiss that awakens me
Filling my spirit with a joy unknown
Taking me places I've never gone
You breathe each breath I take into me
And let me fly through this world
Like a bird upon the wind
And in my laughter you are my friend
And in my sadness you are my rock
Your strong arms catch me when I fall
Your tender voice soothes me when I'm unsure
And through our struggles you endure.
You are my soulmate
You are my destiny
You are the essence that is me

Dedication: Gary, with love forever

Wind Song
Barbara L. Wright
The songs of life keep blowing in my life.
The winds of life carry me to a smooth melody
Hope, Joy, Peace and Love.

When you feel lonely and low, Just listen
to the wind songs.
When you find your mood needs to change
just listen to the melody.

Wind song wind song, I feel happiness blowing
in the wind. Wind song wind song I feel love
blowing in the wind.

Grampy
Kathryn James
What really happens when I turn off the light,
and the darkness seeps into his old, empty shoes.
The shoes that no longer walk,
that worn and winding path,
that when walking, one cannot avoid
all the ledges of history and literature.

Why, when I lie in my bed
do my arms stretch out, dripping slowly like a sponge
all the secrets of that Bath, onto the
floor. Cluttered though it is, I walk
through my bedroom across the night
towards the outside light
but someone else shuts it off.

Is it God who uncages me? or the man
of the empty shoes and the fading photograph?
Can't be God, I'll tell my mind, this
man of wisdom, man of pain,
man of life, eluding my shame.
My doctor, let me from this room,
and into life, beyond that light...

Goodbye
Monica Anne S. Forcey
Through the laughter and the cheers,
The sadness and the tears,
Over all the years,
You were there,
The sorrow and the grief,
And the pain beneath,
The hurt and the love and all the belief,
You were there,
You did for me like no other would,
And loved me like no other could,
Through the good times and the bad,
You were there,
But the biggest pain I ever felt,
And the deepest sorrow of all,
Was the day I found out you were gone,
You weren't there,
No one to call and say it's all right,
No one to run to and hold me tight,
I'll say goodbye, please always remember,
I will love you now and always forever.

Dedication: My parents, Stephen and Margaret Smith

Loss
Josef T. Bath
Running as fast as one
can to places unknown
Searching for people
who can never be found
Finding a place to call
home when the city has
vanished
Closing one's eyes and
hearts to a world
forgotten.

Dedication: To Mattie, Nin, Mom and Diana

As I Die Slowly
Marcos Henderson
As I die slowly I realize my life had just
begun.
It's now that I see the consequences of the things
I've done.
As I die slowly I wish I had been faithful to
my wife,
Knowing that I've murdered us both cuts deeper than
any knife.
As I die slowly I have a different outlook on things,
I realize life is not about women, money and material
things.
As I die slowly I think of how things could have
been,
but now it's too late, I can't have the past again.
As more people die maybe even more will realize,
that AIDS doesn't discriminate and in the end
everybody dies,
The worst part of things is my death is on my
hands solely,
and now it's too late, for I am dying slowly.

Dedication: Rodrick Jamal Henderson

Noteworthy Works

Dawn
Monica Bell

Dawn came, slowing spilling hues and pastels, painting the hills a regal shade
The clouds previewed the fire below, which rose and burst upon the land
My eyes tingled with delight and I turned from my window
The new day's gift, marvelous and magnificent
Could not compare to the sight, which stole my eyes and my heart
You slowly lifted your head from my pillow and gave me a dreamy smile
You stretched your arms and your hair danced down, like a waterfall of descending pirouettes
The new lights showering you in glistening flows
Your dazzling azure eyes opened wide to reveal your loving soul, afloat in pools of burning blue

You deeply breathed the crisp morning air, and your breasts rose and
Peeked through your wispy camisole and stole the wind from my body
My body trembled as you spoke your greeting to me, but I dare not move
Not wanting to lose the heavenly sight that filled my view
But you would not have us so far apart
And you crawled across the bed toward me, a playful feline stalking her prey
You wrapped your loving arms around me, without any effort or any thought
My arms enfolded you, and I melted into you.

Some Were
Loretta Bedwell

Some were poets in the days of old
Some were knights–brave and bold.
Some were beggars in the street
Some were dancers, light of feet.
Some were minstrels – singing loud;
Some were kings, walking proud.
Some were farmers – toiling long
Some were hunters – fierce and strong.
Some were sheriffs – enforcing law
Some were thieves – taking all.
Some were drifters – claiming none—
Those were the owes who had all the fun!

Ice Cream
Dwayne A. Duncombe

Honey, loving you is like ice cream
on a hot and sticky summer day,
big ole' scoops of whip cream on a cookies n' cream sundae.
Chocolate or strawberry, vanilla is always nice,
kissing your soft, sweet lips is like biting
into a Klondike on a sultry Sunday night.

When I press against your body a Dove Bar comes to mind,
With your light chocolate complexion, and goodies
inside for me to find.

When I see you from a distance I'm like a
child in a candy store,
you are so delicious I keep wanting more and more.

Your body is so luscious it's almost like a dream,
and baby, loving you is like a great big bowl of
scrumptious ice cream.

Dedication: The love of my life, Savannah

Exile's Minuet
Jonathan Jones

Our dance is slow
for the music is morose
and its rhythm dictates
our very steps.

My partner is Loneliness

Our dance is intimate
for only Loneliness knows my heart
and measures my sway
with delicate precision.

My partner is Loneliness.

Our dance is eternal
for we are partners bound by fear
imprisoned by the very walls
built to protect my heart.

My partner is Loneliness.

Dedication: All those who mourn

To Someone Special My Love
Tammy A. Moore

My Love, take a little time to close
Your eyes and look inside your heart.

Do you like what you feel and see?

Well love, I have looked inside your
heart and I do. You are loving,
gentle, brave and smart.

But most of all I am proud to know
That I fell in love with you and
That your heart belongs to me!

A True Friend
Eric D. Venters

Sometimes in life, life doesn't even know:
the turns, the choices, the direction to go.
The situations life face are many each day,
leaving a missed thought, a memory astray.

We all in life let life run its own course,
but reality shows it's like speaking with a voice that's hoarse
——it doesn't work!
There are times life seems it's at its bitter end,
the situations, the turns, the choices, how it begins?

Nevertheless, life shows a distant light of hope,
this light gives meaning and advice to help cope,
with the turns, the choices, the direction to the end,
that light comes to you as that one true friend.

They're always there for you when life is not,
understanding each direction of life's emotional knot.
When life shows there's nothing left in life to win,
you know there's that distant light, that hope... a true friend!

Dedication: Brad, Chad, and Kevin

Dreams of the Soul

Eternity
Loretta Brower Leibsohn
I am always, now,
And in eternity
Forever yours
And, only yours

I am love, your love
I am a constant
In life's fickle span
And when time grows short
And moves into infinity
And your timeliness
Comes to an end
Then with the will of love
I shall penetrate
The dark opacity of space
Where, when breath
And breathing stop
I still dare to live
To thrill you
With my touch
Dedication: My beautiful five grandchildren

The Hole
Paddy Kenny
A hole has appeared in my life,
A hole I can never fill,
Only stop from getting bigger.

A darkness shrouds me,
A darkness I can never lighten,
Only stop from getting darker.

Life has to go on,
Never succumb,
You're getting there.
But where?

Leaf
Leah Belcher
I am not shaped any certain way.
In my lifetime I have seen many types of others just like me,
but we are unique in our own special way. People sometimes get us
confused, but then they realize that we have special shapes.
I move when the wind blows and go where it tells me to.
Most things cannot hear the wind, but it is easy for me—I just listen, for
the wind is my friend.
I am not important to anyone or anything;
mostly I am just a nuisance because I get in everyone's way.
Wherever I go, I see and hear different things—
to me it is fun, but to others it would be a bore.
I love the feel of the wind as it sweeps me off the ground again.
Sometimes, though, I wish that my friend would die down for a moment—
sometimes I would like to enjoy the view.
It seems as if I have been here before. Have I? No, I see now that I was
wrong.
Sometimes I feel I have seen certain places time and time again—
In my memory they start running together and looking the same.
I guess I will continue to blow on forever.
That really does not bother me—I have no place to turn to.
No place I can really call my home.
I am alone in this vast unending world.

Blast
Dale Hendrickson
A blast goes fast,
but does not last
like a cast, that's from
an arm or a leg. With
some firecrackers inside
the cast, with one fuse
lit, the firecracker would
then fizzle out slowly until it
hits the bottom of the fuse.
With the rest of the firecrackers
that light up the first
firecracker would then go
ka–boom. While the rest of the
fireworks are ready to go off, they
go ka–boom, ka–boom one after
the other. There the cast would then
explode wide open with shimmering
pieces of the cast flying apart. While
the rest of the firecrackers go off, they
would show those beautiful bursting
colors that shoot up in the sky on
the fourth of July.

Untitled
Dorothy Harris
Old person
I'm old
I have an achy breaky body
And a messed–up mind
I'm in a sad position
And it puts me in a bind
I feel so bad
But what can I do
It's such a lousy affair
I hope it doesn't happen to you
Dedication: Mary Beth Robinson, Sunshine Clan

A Woman
LaTonya Lynn West
God made a woman from the rib of a man. Someone to love, care and understand.

A Woman... The weaker vessel. God's hidden treasure. A Woman... Gentle... Kind... Real loving deep inside.

She carries herself with grace and style. She can mesmerize with her eyes and a smile as warm as the sun. She's a part of man that makes him one, whole and complete.

For she was called his helpmeet. She has God given ability to weep and travail to bring in souls.

A woman is full of elegance and beauty whether she's young or whether she's old. Wise and cunning she knows how to build her household.

She's unique in her own way. Awesomely... Wonderfully... She was made!

A Woman... she was in God's plan. She's an exquisite gift from God to man...

"A Woman."

Noteworthy Works

The House Behind Your Church
Becky Counts

I live in the house behind your church.
Every Sunday, the parking lot I would search.
Many times I watched you come and go,
How to have your joy, I so wanted to know.

But alas the years passed in vain,
And you never once asked me my name.
A life without God, made me hard and mean,
My face in the window, how I wished you would have seen.

I now live in the house behind the church,
And my children look out the window and search,
To see your children's children come and go.
Happy in the joy, my children wish to know.

I never knew you nor your name.
Yet I watched you all the same.
All the difference, you held in your hand.
My life could have stood on the Rock, instead of the sand.
When I stand before God, and my heart He does search.
Don't you think it's sad...
That I lived in the house... behind the church.

One Dozen Roses
Trina Wilson

One dozen roses,
One for every year,
One for a thought,
One for a tear,
One for an angel who's earned her wings,
One for a beautiful golden ring,
One for a single happy smile,
One for the lonely little child,
One for a friend who shows her love,
One for the beautiful mourning dove,
One for you,
Beyond the sky so blue.

The Love Of One Man
Beverly Sapienza

My dreams of the heart are now memories of a summer's passing.
Tired and weary, I lie in my bed, Listening to the night. My aloneness,
fills the space beside me, that he once shared.

I will never know why I was always looking for that "something" else.
Always wanting to love and always waiting to be loved, but never learning
how to love.

Aimlessly, I wandered through my life seemingly unconnected.
Unnoticed and afraid, a cold shadow divided my heart. Always protecting the
frightened women inside of me.
Not knowing how to feel, I pushed him away for fear he would leave one day.

The words and the promises once spoken, now echo in the distance, and my
voice yields to its own silence.

Yet to be a fool,
Locked within my own heart, with no escape,
I hunger from deep within, never to know his love,
and never knowing how to love

Dedication: To Vinny, who inspired me

Hurting Love
LaToya Brackens

A broken heart from a love
that's not real.
A lost soul which only God
can heal.
I'm now confused for my
mind and body have been
abused.
My faith is low, it's almost not
there.
But none of your loved ones
seem to care.
That feeling of happiness
that I had is now gone.
I have nothing but memories
for I am alone.
Love causes nothing but
heartaches and pain.
I have everything to lose,
and nothing to gain,
I wish I did, but I know
not why my misunderstanding
of love has made me cry.

When Death Comes
Elizabeth K. Branigan

Oh death, why do I fear thee so
Why do I fear my time to go, and yet
I know I'll fear no more when death
Comes creeping to my door
Sickness, sadness, and despair will
Fade away when we get there
We'll float right up into the sky
And Jesus will be standing by to greet
Us and invite us in–then our
Happiness will begin so be–at ease
Fear death no more when death comes
Knocking at your door

Thirty–five Days
Susan M. Warren

We were together for awhile–
Thirty–five days. It was enough;
Enough for eyes to meet and hands to touch
In jocular familiarity.
Given time something might have happened.
Given thirty–five days something did happen...
A meeting of souls, a link between your world and mine.

I remember your eyes – so blue,
And how we made each other laugh.
Then your leaving took the sun away from me,
And gave me a deep sense of loss.

You are back in your world now.
I remain here, remembering how it was.
We never voiced how we felt;
All I said was: "I shall miss you,"
My eyes conveying the solemnity of my heart.
Now we may never know what might have been...
Had we been given time.
But we were given time; thirty–five days.
It has to be enough.

Dreams of the Soul

Set Us Free
Melissa Pinckney
When I'm asleep and deep in slumber,
I roll with the clouds and clap like thunder.

My dreams are free and full of life,
I now have wings and take to flight.

I'll see the world through eagle eyes,
While I soar the winds and rule the skies.

This world is large and so serene,
Why can't earth's man help keep it clean.

The most intriguing of all earth's features,
Are the precious things we all call creatures.

And here we kill and mutilate,
Who are we to choose their fate?

So if you care for us you'll see,
We want to live, please set us free.

Dedication: My wonderful husband, Ron Pinckney

Wedding Day
Jennifer Whitlow
I was just a seed,
searching for the sun.
Drowning in desperation
for I had found none.
Then, I looked before me
and followed the light.
It taught me how to love
and gave my eyes sight.
It took me out of the darkness blue
And placed me in the arms of you.
Two lives now become one.
A flower who dances in the sun.

I Am
Tonia Gaskin
I am a smiling person who loves to talk;
I wonder if graduation will separate my best friends and me.
I hear sunlight bounding off my hair;
I see guardian Angels watching from the clouds.
I want to live a full life with few regrets;
I am a smiling person who loves to talk.

I pretend to be confident, when I am not;
I feel a hug from the darkness.
I touch the colors of a sunset;
I worry that our economy is getting worse.
I cry when I think of drugs killing the life inside a bright person;
I am a smiling person who loves to talk.

I understand that life is not fair;
I say that everyone deserves a fair chance.
I dream of making a difference someday;
I try to befriend all of mankind.
I pray for peace throughout the world;
I am a smiling person who loves to talk.

Dedication: My mom, for her guidance

Good–bye
Bethenie Anne Lukl
I knew someday things would change,
that far apart we would range.
The realities we two must face,
don't come at an acceptable pace.

It seemed that you'd be forever near,
the truth of that in which I had fear.
Future times we might have had together,
even I knew couldn't last forever.

You have supported me through thick and thin,
never allowing me to "just give in".
You have been a friend and confidant,
companionship I never had want.

Days we must endure physically apart,
you'll always be right here, pure, in my heart.
The kindness you have shown to me,
will last throughout eternity.

It's your loyalty I'll remember, of our years,
when I say good–bye to you, through my tears.

Mirror
Walter M. Sizemore
I looked into the mirror and what did I see?
I saw a lonely, lonely man looking back at me.
I said help me Lord, help me along my way
I see death beside me and he's got one foot in the grave.
I don't know where I'm going, can't say where I've been but one
thing I know is I won't be here again.
I said have mercy, have mercy on my soul 'cause death has got me by
the arm and Lord knows I don't want to go.
I look at the man in the mirror, and how can this be, now I see an
Angel where death used to be.
I said thank you Lord, thank you for your mercy on me.
My eyes were dark an blinded but now they are open and I can see.

Our Angel Dressed In White
Beverly A. Nelson
I was taking a walk, right about seven,
When the blue skies opened wide, from the heavens,
All of a sudden, there was a glow of light,
There appeared before me an angel dressed in white.
A beautiful gown, a glowing halo, and wide spread wings,
I could hear a harp softly playing, and angels sing.
I walked toward her, so full of fright.
Toward that beautiful angel, dressed in white.
The "Lord" had sent her, to remind us he's there,
To tell me he loves us, and really cares.
She said, remember, "Love the Lord, " as he loves you.
Just have some faith, he'll guide you through.
I told her then, we believed in the "Lord"
Then away she flew, like an eagle that soars.
She went back toward the Heavens, to that beautiful sky of blue
To give the "Lord" the message, from me and you.
Still in shock from seeing, an angel from above,
I felt as if a burden was lifted, my heart was filled with love.
I'll never forget that miracle, or that glorious night.
When the "Lord" sent to me, our angel dressed in white!

Dedication: Brother, John Wayne Talley, Sr. – 1944–1996

Noteworthy Works

The Cry Within
Jennifer Carson
Deep behind her eyes she holds a story of heartache and of fear,
No one would ever know because it's only told with a single tear,
Her thoughts and dreams fade away, saving her smile only for a rainy day,
She locks the pain inside her mind,
Her happiness she searches to find,
Inside, her soul no longer breathes,
Inside, is where the demons feed,
Her god forgave but left her behind to wither and to die,
Never telling her the reason why,
Her hate deep inside it soars, leaving blood on her hands inside this war,
Her song has lost its illusion, her mind filled with confusion,
She prays to the angels locked in their cage,
She prays to the demons to quiet her rage,
She nails her god back to the cross, blaming him for all she's lost,
Cutting her eyes out no longer wanting to see,
Wishing for this pain to leave,
She holds her gun without a shot,
She just sits while her brain starts to rot,
With a bottle she downs her existence,
For her sins she will pay, waking up dead where she lay.
Dedication: With love to Jared Hosey

Meditation In Time
Joan J. Shareak
Relax in your space, listen for a trace
Speak to yourself, hear the antidote
Move with the spirit, can't you hear it
Sleep comes over you, what do you do
Dream a dream of peace, my how your heart beats
Blow like the wind, take time and spin
Flowers in bloom, open up and make room
Hearts made of gold, what a beautiful sight to behold
The world in which we live, take time and believe
Meditation in time, leave all your thoughts behind
Dedication: Noaa Shareak aka Abu Akbar

Love Is Forever
Rose Fisher
For every new day that comes along,
I search my heart for a meaningful song.
One that describes how much it means,
All the things that you do behind the scenes.
The simple things that mean so much,
Like your soft and thoughtful touch,
Or when I need an ear to hear,
You always hold what I say so dear.
You're there in the morning and you're,
There at night.
When I feel deep pain you're there,
To hold me tight.
What more can I ask than a mom,
Like you.
The troubles you handle are but quite,
A few.
The only one wish that I make today,
Is that no matter how hard things get, you never go away,
All of my love I send to you,
And all of the things I say are so true.
They say roses are red, and violets are blue,
But everyone wishes they had a Mom like you.

Hidden Worries
Dura Greenfield
I lock away feelings so no one can laugh...
I keep them pushed all the way back...
life of pain and of the past.
Then it takes just one time for me to break,
hoping this one is love... and true to trust...
With his sweet talk, he seems to care,
he seems to love... Do I Dare.
Should I share, or even care...
wonder if he is the one, or is he like
the others... all now gone!
Will he inflict pain... this time with just a
little sharper blade... ripping deep into my
heart... leaving it torn all apart...
I feel... what a fool... to try to be the perfect
one for him to see...
When I find, after all this time it's not been
me on his mind... only some other...
The game he's played is now over, and I've
lost dearly yet another !!!!!!!!
jeanie 7/6/97

his eyes...

Happy Things
Judy A. Stevens
A bird sings somewhere in a tree
Some flowers kissed by a honey bee.
The grass just after a mow,
A winter day with fluffy white snow.
The sea shore with fresh soft sand,
A Mother holding a small child's hand.
The sky the wind the moon and sun,
A kitten plays just for fun.
All these things I love to see,
I hope every one can be as happy as me.
Dedication: Ken, Sarah, Tyler, Scott and Kelly

Vision
Victoria Comfort
My eyes are the windows
to my soul inside;
Why then the feeling
to just run and hide.
It's the hurt you can see,
the pain you can feel;
Let go and let GOD
as you slowly Kneel.
Your body and soul
must be given to him;
Feelings of sadness make
the light seem so dim.
Having the courage
and strength to go on;
Greeting each morn
with a prayer at dawn.
No more time
to run and hide;
Spread your wings
ever so wide.
Dedication: Michael, Jessi, Alexa and Alexander Comfort

Dreams of the Soul

Lovers
Michael Clarke
We are the lovers talking on the phone
We are the lovers walking in the park
We are the lovers dancing at the party
And we are the lovers in the dark

We are the lovers sleeping in our house
We are the lovers walking the streets
We are the lovers eating at the dining table
We are the lovers that kiss in the summer heat

We are the lovers that share a laugh
We are the lovers that share a tear
We are the lovers that have no fears

We are the lovers running in the rain
We are the lovers that want no pain
We are the lovers that time will help us to remain

We are the lovers that will never go cold
We are the lovers from young to old
We are the lovers to the bitter end
When the time comes and our live's end

Untitled
Vance Sandy, Jr.
At night I look up in the sky
for guidance from above.
I feel so lost and lonely
since I lost my one true love.
The days are much too weary
and the nights are oh too long,
for there's no one here to hold me
or to sing a pretty song.
But someday, someday, this I know,
our hearts will join again,
and her beautiful voice will sing me to sleep
forever and ever, amen.

I Am A Tree
Cynthia Cupe
I am a tree
Why is it hard for you to see, that you can learn a lot from me.
I breathe in the poisons from your air and exhale oxygen because I care.
You sit beneath me on hot summer days, while I hold out my arms and block the ultraviolet rays.

I know your history, I've been standing here for years. I've seen your tears and listened to your deepest secrets.
Now that I've become old, you talk about cutting me down. You say, I am in your way.

How do you think I feel, after watching you saw my family into pieces over on the hill? As I look at my surroundings, I wonder why you choose not to see just how hard you have made life for me.

Your broken bottles, old newspapers, empty containers, pop corn and potato chip bags clutter my house. Sometimes other people cannot get close to me because your trash is in my way. You bury chemicals in the ground, the water I need can't hardly be found. I must force my roots deep into the soil just to stay alive.

I am a tree. I need you and you need me.

The Simple Things
Linda Long
"Can I do anything for you today?" the nurse asked with a smile.
"Well, if you have time, what I'd really like, is just to talk for awhile."

She thought of the patients she had to see. Of the IV's she needed to recite.
But seeing the hopefulness in his eyes, she gently said, "all right."

She fluffed his pillows, straightened his sheets, held his hand and sat by his bed.
She listened intently, smiled and nodded to all of the things he said.

He talked of politics, sports, and the weather, even told her a joke or two.
Then patted her hand, winked his eye, and softly said, "Thank you."

She went on about her busy routine, got all of her work done on time.
Although she had spent quite a time with him, not once did she get behind.

Taking the time just to listen for awhile. Sharing a smile or a gentle touch,
It's the simple things that we do in life that always mean so much.

Endangered Species
Braden Johnson
Wild life dies every day,
Soon us humans, we'll have to pay,
Soon there will be no meat,
Then us humans, we'll be beat.
Every day a forest burns,
Sad to say the tide has turned.
We have destroyed almost every piece of moss,
While animal bones shine with gloss.
As our wildlife comes to an end,
With not enough food to fend.
Life is like a top,
If we don't quit it's going to stop.

Untitled
Teresa McCran
Within the heart of one so dear,
You will find all kindness there.
For the gift of life is not all God gives,
But how many of us care?
God gave us seven days; six in which we keep,
He only asks that we should share with Him,
the seventh day of this week.

There is not even blackmail,
Attached to this one day –
For as you know God gave us life,
But only He can take it away.

When next you wander down the street,
That leads to God's own house,
Do not turn your head the other way,
But feel the guilt within your heart.
For in that humble house of His heart
Is calling out "Welcome my child,
What kept you, did you think I would be out?"

Dedication: My husband, Owen Jerome McCran

Noteworthy Works

Untitled
Patricia O'Brien Parker

They asked: "who are you?"
I answered: I am the burning bush
I am the bruised reed and the smoldering flax
I am the pearl – the product of much suffering
I am the dry bush He set aflame with His fire
and spoke through with His voice
I am the reed, though bruised,
He will not allow me to break
I blow to and fro in the wind/breeze of His Spirit
I am the flax smoldering with fire
in ashes which He will not allow to be extinguished
I am the pearl made through heartache and pain
and He values me
I am the alabaster vessel
He is the mighty contents of sweetness
I am nothing – He is all – though He chooses to use me
I am nothing in my own self
I am a voice crying out His words – He is the message
I am a poet – He is the poem of love I write
I am His servant – He is my Lord

Dedication: My mother, Lorraine Truckey O'Brien

The Breath Of Fall
Karen Kezele

The moon shines bright,
till the morn after.
School morn children
fill the air with laughter.
Leaves falling from the trees
What a wonderful life—the autumn breeze.
Harvesting pumpkins,
Golden leaves falling.
Crisp cool evenings,
Winter is calling.
Take a deep breath and hold the memory.
The magical Breath Of Fall!

The Reason Of Salvation
Kenneth Michael Thompson

I heard about a man named Jesus and all His sunshine.
They told me about His forgiving heart and His creation called time.
I was curious to see if the sinners have been untrue and wrong.
So I caressed my face against my pillow and prayed all night long.

As the morning kissed my lips and made my alarm scream,
I couldn't help but feel that the bliss of His strength was only a dream.
But my flesh lost the race, for the speed of His soul was miles ahead.
Now there can be space to reflect on love, and the stories He said.

I suddenly didn't walk on fragile ground, wondering if my next step was my last.
His production of "Life" is grand, and with pride I stand with the rest of the cast.
And after the curtain falls, I'll bow and lift my arms and sing His praise.
It's the rebirth of the native boy, and the child that He wants to raise.

No false image will ever again grace the cover of my screen.
For the light of His spirit deserves the applause only movie stars have seen.
The bitter response to change can now be accepted without fear.
All the days He made will be lived, for the reason of salvation I hear.

Tinnitus
Bernadette McGrath

"There is no cure" the "great" specialist said
"Ears like yours are ringing throughout the universe
You can have some counseling
Or wear maskers, or play some background music
Even the ticking of the clock
Will help you somewhat."

Now I go without hope
Ears forever blowing, roaring, ringing
And riveting, screwing my head
Into an engine gone berserk,
Making my life a living hell
Wondering, wondering would my brain
Take the strain.

"Oh Lord" I pray
"Make me and all other ear ringers
'Interesting Cases'
So that science will switch us off
One day soon
Now that they have put a man
on the moon."

The Chase
Samantha Reid

I am in the middle of the desert,
I don't even know how I got there.
Something is after me,
As I am running the sun is scorching on my back.
Shredding layers of skin.
It's like you are getting nowhere fast.
Like fighting in a never–ending battle.
A shadow is gaining on me,
Always one step ahead of me each time.
I want to give up, but I just can't.
My life depends on one single thing.
The Chase.

My Precious Gems
Pauline Hardin

Today the sky projects a rainbow,
With colors as bright as gems;
To best describe my children,
Golden jewels nestled within them.

Jerome and Savannah are of whom
I speak,
So young and tender, yet very meek;
My four–year–old Jerome is a little
helper around the house.

While six–month–old Savannah,
quietly creeps like a little mouse;
Proud am I, to be a Mother;
An honor I would not trade for
any other.

As time goes by my children grow;
Soon to leave home;
What memories I have to forever
keep.
As I watch them play and roam.

Dreams of the Soul

Thoughts Of Christmas
Hilda C. Pleasance
We hear the jingling of the Bells,
Through the crisp cold air,
Ringing with Hope and leading us
From dark days of despair.
Our Lord was born on Christmas Day,
Let us give Thanks as we kneel and pray.

This is the Season
when we all meet,
For very good reason
Our Dear Friends to greet.
Though not in person and far away,
Our thoughts are united
For Christmas Day.

Sometimes we speak by Telephone,
To know if they are away,
For some are growing very old
And in "Homes" for the aged they stay.
Later sadly they are no more,
With a last Farewell,
I close the Door!

Rain
Heather Heimbaugh
Rain falls from the sky, as the angels cry.
Tears from Heaven made upon the Earth.
Sadness is so lonely, as happiness is to laugh.
I did something wrong, while the thunder seems
to be at my window.
Have I sinned?
While the cold wind blows the hands of time,
the rain begins to pound on my window –
as if it were tapping on my shoulder.
For a second I began to cry from the rain of the sky.

Dedication: My guardian angel

Heartache And Pain
Debbie Hampson
To love and lose someone special
Is the hardest pain to take
But the memories live on forever
And the future is yours to make.
To explain the frustration of loss
Would take forever and a day.
So you have to make it through Life
To try to forgive, and manage in any way

I've lost two precious children
And the pain and hurt still stays
Even though its been nearly six years
The anger would never go away.
I can't understand for what reasons
Made him choose my little babies
He gave them, then took them away
I live my life on if's and maybes.

The fear of losing another child
Will always be in my heart
But I have to learn to live with this fear
Or my whole world will fall apart.

Trees
Norma Louise Newton
The trees in the park
So serene and mysterious
The oak with hanging branches
The elm so strong
The yew tree sheltering the sun.

The sycamore so appealing
The willow gentle swaying
Over the riverbanks
The river sparkling in the
sunshine

The trees along the riverbank
Protecting the nature on the
side of the riverbank
The trees are full of
Songbirds chirping and

hiding under the leaves
The trees are spectacular
On a bright sunny day
So cool and fresh.

Time's Hidden Treasure
Timothy Webb
What is time and just how can it be measured?
Is it really there or only the memories we treasure?
What is a minute and just what makes up the hour?
Do we reap the fruit from the vine or let it sour?
Is it the thing called love which comes then goes,
or is it the things in life we never really know?
Maybe it's our shadow which is one day here then gone,
in the beginning as in the end we are surely all alone.
Maybe it is a silent tear in the fabric we call time,
just tender moments that fit together is what we find.
So, we drift through this world seeking love and pleasure,
to find that time is like uncovering hidden treasure.

Society And Christians
Susanne Merrilees
Christians and society
Living in perfect harmony
So much they still have to learn
The rich concern with what they earn

Society and Christians
Society with so many questions
Christians so different
Society's experiments

People drunk every night
God nowhere in sight
Christians please give them time
To learn of this God of mine

Maybe they want to know
To whom their life they owe
Or maybe don't really care
Of a God who is not there

So come on Christians do your part
Tell of his work of art

Noteworthy Works

The Dreamer
Steve Saunders

The fortune teller told me
About the thoughts in my head
But I wanna be better than
The things that she said

My horoscope told me of
Much of the same
To go out and grab my fame

The crystal ball gazer
She held both my hands
I crossed her palm with silver
Trying to understand

I like to be the leader
When I play in a game
To go out and make my name

I had a chart reading
But it didn't mean a thing
Am I fantasising
Selfishness can't win.

Sketch Of Love
Jackie Franks

Like a bird lost in a storm
so was I.
Thinking that there was no
where else to fly.
I wanted shelter but I
couldn't see.
There was someone who
cared for me.
I felt your hands and
then I saw,
That I could make it
after all...

Sailor
Sally Jane Docherty

Sailor where are you now
Is your ship ashore, are you sailing out to sea
Oh how I wish you were right beside me
Can you see the clear water or golden sand
Just reach out and take my hand
If you take my heart we'll never drift apart
It won't be the end it will just be the start.

Sailor where are you now
Is your ship ashore, are you sailing out to sea
There must be a way for you to reach me
Just take my hand, take my heart
It won't be the end it will just be the start
We'll sail all the seas, we'll travel far
Guided by the brightest star
We'll dock every port, we'll see every beach
There won't be anywhere we won't reach.

Sailor is your ship ashore, are you at sea
Sailor keep sailing on home to me.

Dedication: Safe Sailing Sam

A Carer's Eye View
C. V. Roy

Why oh why do people stop and stare
at anyone that's in a wheelchair.

Some walk up and stroke their arm and talk to
them like babies.
Next time stand back and look, you will find
they are men or ladies.

Others come and say "How is she getting on today
Yes she certainly looks good".
Please ask the person in the wheelchair, and
remember they are not made of wood.

Lots of disabled persons all say the same, it makes
them annoyed and feel mad inside.
So come everybody, think it out, make the carer
and partner glad to be alive.

Most of the people in wheelchairs, have a smile for
everyone, also a great sense of humour too
Speak as you would to a friend and you will find
they are as normal as me or you

The Mantle
C. W. Brookbanks

I picked up the mantle from him
That had fallen and wear it proudly.
I became "The Conscience of Society"
And like him I needed my cloak of
Armour. For "The Conscience of Society"
Is not necessarily a strong character
But is sustained by the virtues of
Nature. My sad haunted face surveys
The scene with bloodshot eyes, and
Shares the suffering and some of
The wisdom of mankind, I stumble
Towards my grave, confused, hurt and
Angry. But I do know the world.

The Black Crow
Annette James

A cry of joy, is how I perceive,
The shrill cry of love,
Of the black crow's caw.

They keep me company, when I wander,
As through the maze of life I ponder.
What is far beyond I wonder.

When I hear the cry of joy.
It's as if they really know me.
We respect each other solely,
It's our secret from the world,
When I hear their cry of love.
Other people they annoy, but they do not understand,
The meaning behind, the shrill cawing cry.
Its a protection, a guide, from the other side.
A love that cannot be denied.

So when you hear the jackdaws caw,
Take no notice of folklore.
Feel nature's law,
OF THE BIG CROW'S CALL.

Dreams of the Soul

Life's Circle
Janet Morton
We sailed the seven seas and fought the pirates cruel and bold,
We rescued prisoners that they'd chained, deep within the hold.
We journeyed far around the world, discovering distant lands.
We rode our camels in the sun, across hot desert sands.
Imagination played its part, for we were young you see,
And at eight years old, we made quite sure that we were home for tea.

At eighteen years we knew it all, we'd set the world to right,
We'd talk about the things we'd do, far into the night.
We'd change the way that things were done, our cause was right and true,
We marched a lot and drank too much, the way that rebels do.
We thought our parents were naive how could they understand,
We turned our backs, ignoring them, when they would lend a hand.

Older now and wiser now with children of our own,
We recall the youth we had and how the years have flown,
Looking back, our parents then, really were quite wise,
As now we see their point of view, but through parent's eyes.
Our children are, as we were then and though rebels they may be
With love and understanding, they'll be home in time for tea.

Dedication: To my husband, Jack, my son, Sheridan, and daughter, Rebecca

---

Untitled
Guadalupe Trelles
I crave you in the morning
I long for you at night
I watch you making others happy
I feel very sad
I tell myself be strong
I want to better humankind
I satisfy my hunger of you with
something else, but you're on my mind
I am at peace until my next
hunger pang, make no mistake
I no longer want to want you Mr. Steak

Dedication: To my mother, Dolores, with love

It's Raining In My Heart
Wee Hughie
It's raining in my heart
Each time we have to part
In life cheerio hello sadly good—byes
Parting gift locket, scarf, brooch, ties
To remember happy days
Our friends brought sunshine on rainy days

Still photo, fan, castanet, two old dears
Not antiques, but cherished souvenirs
Perhaps now faraway places
The Christmas birthday card look see happy faces

In our memory video
We see George, Janet, Edna, Brother Joe
Funny how years roll by
Now satellites in sky
Beatlemania, Rock 'n Roll, Sinatra, Crosby, made girls swoon
Who thought, astronauts would land on Moon
Now plans for Millennium soon
Alas many have to part
Pray there's many a tear of happiness in your heart
Especially when you hear It's Raining In My Heart

Dad
Jeannie Flossie
There is a man, I'm blessed to know,
The man stands taller, as I grow.
A man who seems to know no fear
So, with a touch can dry a tear.

Intimately, he knows the earth—
As though from her evolved his mirth.
He feels her bloom and then decrease,
A man indeed, who stands at ease,
To face the north wind in its rage,
Then turns again with seasoned sage,
To nurture irises sublime,
As hand in hand he walks with time.

Abyss, within his sea blue eyes,
He holds a depth one cannot hide.
The greatest peace that's known to man
Is felt within his sturdy hand.
In winter, fall and through the spring,
Enchantment looms, as if to sing,
About the man who rivals grace,
With Godly love upon his face.

Mitchell Ray
Jennifer Helms
Someone so tiny. Someone so weak.
One who couldn't cry, and one
who couldn't speak.
His movement not much, but trembled
at a touch.
Held on for days, though God has His
ways;
To take Mitchell Ray, from us on
that day.
We'll all shed a tear, 'cause
we loved him so dear.
And that love says a lot,
now in Heaven with God.

To The One I Have Wronged
Jenet G. Pequeno
This silence is agony on my soul;
With shoulder turned, I see a pain I did not know.
My actions now as I look at them, were senseless and dumb;
Because the repercussions have left my insides wrecked
up and numb.
Am I really that bad, did I make you feel this way?
If I did that's terrible; how does the pain go away?
Isn't it hard to not talk to me? Don't you want to pick up
the phone?
My dear it's hard on me, as long as it's your voice, I don't care
of the tone
I reminisce about the summer gone past;
Getting to know you, the good times, and all of our laughs.
My love this is torture, why not let us speak;
For I know you want to, my love you're not meek.
I try and busy myself, as to not let it get to me;
But it doesn't work, everywhere I turn I see
I see the face of the one I love,
With that precious look, the one as a dove.
These are my true feelings, and I put them here,
For it eludes me, and what it is, is your ear.
For my love, if I had it, I would place these there.

Noteworthy Works

What Goes Around
Elizabeth Glenn

They no longer need me for bedtime prayers,
For fancy French braids or dainty bows in their hair,
They now "do" their own, including mousse and spray,
And Mom's opinion doesn't matter much today.

However, my being must still carry some weight,
When rigorous homework is their unhappy fate,
For the job of removing unwanted dust bunnies in the hall,
Or when rides are needed to their friends or to the mall.
My ears are still available for hearing every word,
My eyes for tears, my arms for hugs, when deep emotions are stirred.

But now I need them... for computer assistance,
Which I, myself, would meet with great resistance.
They tell me when there are runs in my hose,
Or curly black hairs coming out of my nose.
Those funny, persnickety things I used to see,
Now my teen–age daughters are seeing in me.
My turned up collar or curls out of place,
A grey hair on my back or a smudge on my face.
But I, as the Mother, with "sayings" abound,
"My goodness! What goes around comes back around!"

Heartbreak
Barbara Schick

I recall the way it was
before you died.
Memory fades to
soft touches.
To look back to then
is flattery.

You gave me smiles
and candlelight.
The world was alive
and winking.
The task is to
patch the holes.

Lies
Bobbi Haag

Lies will imprison
Those who choose to use.
The truth is not a prism,
A lie is but to lose.
A lie will roll on forever,
Like a ball upon a hill.
Until that awful day
When truth will come its way!

Hear what I say child,
For the taking of that pill
Will be hard to swallow.
For it is then you face the gallows
And life no longer mild.
Truth will keep you free
From those terrible prison walls,
Keeping away those rolling balls,
Keeping away indignity!

For lies are not going to protect
Lies will be cause to reject
That wonderful person you!

Untitled
Dawn Marie Stallard

Far goes the night, so far I cannot see.
Here lies the light, for all the world and me.
For my weakness is you within this night of gloom,
For even the strongest candle gives way to the wind's bloom

Far goes my dreams that I cannot see,
For without them, there would be no harmony.
My song is you of your own sweet will.
How the melody flows, yet calm and still,
Like peacefulness by a window's sill.

Far goes our love to outlast the years,
For faith and hard work wash away pain's tears,
As our path fades away like the sweetness of cheers

How it shapes our lives is symphony on strings
As we dance ever joyful while it prances and sings.
And the wind as it blows raises hymns while it swings
Through our lives and loves for this hope that it brings
Everlasting of life and peace of all things

Oh, how sweet is it all.

Parted Ways
Helen Rodgers

The soft wind blows
As my lonely heart breaks
The pale moon glows
As death doesn't take
The air is still
As your spirit it flies
The wolf on the hill
Will hear my cries
But where are you
You've gone away
Now what can I do
But end it this way
Good–bye my dear

Sweet Fifteen
Sylvia Fox

She rushes into the house, drops her book bag, scowls,
Grunts. "Don't bother me!" Locks herself in her room.
She's fifteen, a teenager. I think, nothing's wrong.
A car honks, the magic call. She dashes out. She's gone.
At dinner, Father asks, "Where's my angel, our precious one?"
She didn't say. We watch the clock and wait.
At last, stealthy footsteps on the stairs. Her door clicks shut.
For weeks, she doesn't talk to us. Something's wrong.

Sick, she's home. Rages upstairs and downstairs, screaming:
"It's eating me! My skin hurts! How sharp its teeth!
It comes again! Horns and claws! Don't bite me!"
She whirls in a hurricane. Dad grapples with her. "Easy, now."
She beats at his face. "Don't touch me! Leave me alone!
I want... I need something... I need... " Her fair hair flying.
Her sweet young limbs crumple under her, she collapses in a heap.
"Go away, Dad, Mom... I'm old enough... to do what I want... "

Her Father looks at her eyes. "Marijuana. "
We fold her between us. Hold her in an embrace. The little child
We nurtured with such loving care is now old enough
To make her first mistake.

Dreams of the Soul

Untitled
Marion Langstroth
The air is still and weighted.
A shroud of gray blankets the earth

No light but the faint glow of a street lamp,
carried upon the beads of moisture
that hang in the air.
No sounds but of crickets, tired and weary,
and the distant call of a bird disturbed
by the overwhelming silence.

I walk as in a dream; afraid to waken,
afraid to slip away from this place of peace.
My garden of Eden.

Take My Hand
Bonnie–Lee Johnson
Come... take my hand, and you'll agree
Six really is quite nice to be.
You know, Mommy, it's sure a sin,
That... You... cannot go back again.

I'll take you away from worry and fuss,
And we'll just play, the two of us.
We'll be so happy... you will see;
So walk though childhood... again... with me!

It's too bad, it really is,
There's only adults... and little kids.
But, I'll lead you through my childhood land!
Come on... Mommy... take my hand.

We grow so fast and then depart,
Childish pleasure's a lost art.
No time to sing... of childhood's song,
Then we wonder... where have they gone.

Dedication: My daughter, Andrea

Facial Features
Evelyn Beasley
I love the early start of when we wake.
I love the morning walks that we take.
Your smile brightens up my day.
Your smile is my life that I love in every way.

That face is so right.
That face I want to see every night.
Your heart is so big like a giant moon.
Your heart is my love which I'll give soon.

Those eyes of yours are nice and round
Those eyes are so deep that I'll drown.

Your hands are so beautiful in sight
Your hands I'll hold very tight.
If my love is not worth it, I'll give you more
If my love is not worth it, you can close the door.

My love may not be worth it,
Your love may be queer,
But that's the love I want,
for the week, month, and year.

Untitled
Sarah Baer
Cherish the time you have
with those you love
for someday you will lose
them forever.
Never will you get back
what you have lost.
I've been there,
done it all.
Through the good and bad times
those special people were always there
to show me the way.
And for that they will be
in my heart always.

Midnight Strangers
Juliet Perkins
Your eyes I caught a glance of as a past you long ago,
how it feels like only yesterday as midnight strangers,
we would seek to find a means to an end of our sorrow.

I walk along a bridge at night and hear you call my name,
the echo floats across the water ripples.
Oh, how it is not the same.

I never introduced myself, but now it is far too late.
You fled with my heart, I bid you my soul to take.

Words were not needed then, just as they are not now
I find comfort in knowing of your existence,
no matter how near or far you are.
I look upon a starry night, and see your face among them.
Your gaze burns into me,
as I long to be there with you sitting by the sea.

The time was not right, it seldom ever is,
so I will take a quiet place and dream of what should have been
as I think about you the tears roll off my chin.

The Robber Baron Of Twilight
Jan Skoog
In repose the twilight seeks to light the hope and cheer of a new day;
But the Robber Baron has stolen the twilight peace that was once mine.

A tear gathers to fullness and in filtered privacy trickles my inner most pain to the outer world;
Proof that the ache at the center of my heart once again awakens.

There was a time that I lay in the arms of such peace, trust, and faithfulness;
Warmed by the knowledge that this love was mine.

Today I wake with a little seeping wound that will form a scab in the busyness of the day;
slowly loosening in the night to ooze its sorry tale into my twilight peace.

A scar will undoubtedly form someday; A poignant reminder to never trust with such abandon again. The Robber Baron has his due in love betrayed and innocence lost.

Grandkids
Bonnie L. Tolle

Grandkids are for loving in a very special way
They make us feel important; they brighten up our day
They have this way of knowing when we need a special hug
They run and jump into our arms, our heartstrings feel a tug
Of course we think they're wonderful, that no one can deny
They're imps, they're clowns, they're angels
They're the sparkle in our eye
They'll sneak into the cookie jar or say, " Let's take a walk"
Or, "Can we get some ice cream and have a little talk?"
Then we might sit in silence as we think about our day.
It's almost time for it to end, they'll soon be on their way
The house will then be quiet – Oh, I wish they could remain
But I will have my memories 'til they return again.

A Mother's Love
Doris A. Sawey

A Mother is an example for her child
God the Father is the example for all Mothers
Jesus, the Son of God,
is the perfection of this example of Mother's love.

A Mother loves unconditionally
She guards her child against all evil
She guides her child in all good
She councils her child in all wisdom.

God loves unconditionally
He is the Mother who guards against evil
He is the Mother who guides in goodness
He is the Mother who councils wisdom.

A Mother is the reflection of God to her child
God is the light to her child.
A Mother teaches through example
God sent His only child to be the example
A Mother sacrifices much for her child
God sacrifices all through His child.

My Best Friend
Lidia Anguiano

You touched my life, some time or other
you're in my memory, my brother.
We had good times as well as bad
we shared some laughs, some tears were sad.
To some degree you helped me be
the person that today is "me".

I sometimes wonder, would I be "me" today
had you not been my friend from yesterday?
Now, as I reflect on days and years gone by
"where is my friend?" I wonder with a sigh.
Did I touch your life as yours touched mine?
or was our friendship just to pass the time?

It helps to know, my friend of me you thought
to my heart great rejoicing it brought.
Our friendship continues as long as we strive
both you and me to keep it alive.
So, my friend, at this moment in time
a word from you would make my eyes
sparkle and shine.

When I Look Into Your Eyes
Victor C. Adamo

Soft, caring, and deep,
Loving, meaningful, and warm.

Words cannot describe how they make me feel.
Your eyes revive me when they're bright.
They make me feel for you when they're full of tears.
It makes me feel young when they twinkle with excitement.
I am comforted by them, when they understand.
My mind wonders when they are thoughtful.
Everything is better when you peer though them.

Your eyes are the windows to your heart.
And it is a place that I love to go.

My Gifts From God
Carol Richardson

The greatest gifts that I received came down from God above.
You see four times he sent to me a gift for me to love.
They were not wrapped in shiny foil or ribbons gold and red.
Instead they came for me to love with crowns upon their heads.
Their little faces shone with love their eyes were all aglow.
I had no way of knowing then how much I'd love them so.
These were not gifts that you could change from one size to another.
Because these were my gifts from God he sent them to their Mother.
They hold my hand when I am sad they stay close by my side.
They share my joy, my pain and fear, these things I could not hide.
They call when they don't have the time, and then before they go,
They always say "I love you Mom" more than you'll ever know.
My gifts weren't wealth, as some men have, that try to own the world.
For mine were sent from God above, the love of my four girls.
When you return to take my gifts to spend some time with you...
There's still a favor, I have left that I must ask of you.
To let them please stay here below for here they have each other.
And if they left, my heart would break,
Because I am their Mother.

Dedication: Mindy, Michaela, Michelle, Melissa

You–N–I
Venus E. Gilbert

You – said you loved me.
You – said you'd never be cruel.
I – believed everything you said.
You – made me your fool.

You – said you loved me.
You – promised me your heart.
I – believed everything you said.
You – lied from the start.

You – said you loved me.
You – promised to stay.
I – believed everything you said.
You – turned and walked a way.

Yes, I believed you.
I – believed everything you said.
Now my life is ruined.
And you – you lie dead.

Dedication: Eric Rinion, my ex–husband

Dreams of the Soul

Moonlight Glow
Eileen B. Kowal
When the Moon is round and full of light
It appears to be day but you know it's night...
When the birds are resting from their flight...
And all is quiet... things feel just right.
When the sleeping desert is an eerie white...
And the air is calm... it's a glorious sight.

When the Moon is pale and a soft halo
Veils the bedroom with a hazy glow...
When tiny seedlings stretch and grow...
And all is serene above and below...
When the desert washes gently flow...
And Earth is at Peace... it's a world to know.

In The Breast Of The Wind
Michele E. Gibson
When the wind is restless and the night is right
I sit by my window and turn off the light

The air seems cool as it blows through the trees
I just want to get out and fly with the breeze

I put on my clothes to go outside
But I think to myself, "I have no Guide"

The wind is calming now, therefore I can rest
Until tomorrow, another day, another test

"What stirs the wind?" I asked myself
As the force of the wind increased
"What do I do now, Dear Lord,
But hope the wind will cease?"

Yet the wind blows harder now
This time with no end
So now I lay forever
In the breast of the wind.

A Dear Friend
Mable Hale
I was burdened down with care
My load it seemed I couldn't bear;
All my relatives in this town,
Were burdening me down.

I could not sleep at night,
I moved from bed to bed;
Then a neighbor at my back door,
Lent a hand and pulled me ashore.

He gave me a rose from his garden of love
He shared his garden of vegetables with me;
He mowed my lawn and cut my trees,
Yes, he was a dear friend indeed.

If it hadn't been for him, I'd have sold out,
And moved back home without a doubt;
For he showed me that he had sympathy,
For someone in need of a friend indeed.

Dedication: James Chisann, my only neighbor

Give Thanks
Sandy Alarcon
Through so many close calls,
You have guided me,
Through danger and falls.
You were always there I see,
You sat with me through the night,
To lift me up when I couldn't bear another catastrophe.
Helping me to see wrong from right,
When I thought my heart would break,
My love and praise do take,
Along with all my useless fear.
Around every turn and bend,
I now know this, Guardian Angel dear,
You'll be with me until the end.

Remembering
Ginger K. Bloms
The teddy bears and dolls
Are put away for keeps
Somewhere on a dusty shelf
In their timeless sleep.

Looking back when kisses
Made everything all better
From skinned knees and broken hearts
To first–love sweetheart letters.

A simpler time, home–made wine,
The Model T by Ford,
Stirring dust from gravel paths
As down the road it roared.

Old photographs and memories
Still linger from the past,
Reminding us of hope and love–
The greatest gifts that last.

Dedication: Bernice Johnson, for her love

Some Graduation Advice
Margareta G. Mihal
You'll have choices to make
Give and take
You'll have obstacles along the way
Always know what to do, what to say
You'll have decisions, at a glance
Follow your heart, life is chance
You'll have opportunities galore
Open your mind and explore
You'll have questions, never fear to ask
The smallest, "WHY", could gain the task
You'll have downfalls and up hill climbs
Straight ahead is where it all unwinds
You'll have challenges along with competition
Keep your faith, winners are those who have religion
You'll have laughter and tears
Moments to reflect upon throughout the years
You'll have a little of everything, once or twice
But just remember this note of...
... Some Graduation Advice

Dedication: To: Future Graduates

Ode To Michael
Barbara Brown

Step by step, each painful memory waiting in line...
Of long forgotten loves, lost friends, and dreams that never came to be.

It's the essence of those who climb the mountains, who traverse the rocky paths to ascend through darkness to discover the opalescence of light... it's you dear friend who are worth more than riches.

So you turn with your face to the wind and just as you song begins...

Dedication: To Michael, whom I miss

Kimberly
David Drumheller

My Kimberly speaks to me softly,
I see my future in her eyes.
She is as beautiful as a summer sunset.
The love I feel shall never die.

My Kimberly walks lightly,
Through my cloudy daydreams.
She smells as sweet as a spring rain.
Still my love I cannot redeem.

My Kimberly says she loves me,
And her love will never die.
Through the depths of any hell,
To the heaven in the sky.

I believe fully the things she says,
But there is sometimes doubt.
No matter my love will last all my days,
With her or without.

Dedication: My Kimberly Sue

Robot Mom
Sandra Dejnak

Performing my mundane tasks efficiently,
pursuing input of family needs.
But sometimes I feel I've blown a fuse
because I never get to rest.

My emotions are held within,
the forgotten human being inside
the mechanical skeleton.

Performing to commands like a mechanical
puppet on strings, controlled by other's fancies,
forgetting all my fantasies.

No time to think, to eat or sleep
because my programming is not complete.

My programming is a characteristic of my mechanical construction.
Experiencing occasional short circuits, in my excellent design.
My energy is nil, I must continue on.

Because I am a robot mom.

Wind
Marie Dambruch

Rossetti asked me, "Who Has Seen The Wind?"
Lyle's daffodils faltered today
in the winds of the storm,
but with the dawn the sun burst thru.
I stood beside the yellow flowers,
golden sunshine filling my being,
bent by years and storms —
remembering youth —
My grandchildren, the youth of my life today,
and breathed a prayer.

The wind brushed across my forehead,
a gentle kiss from God.

Home At Last
Matt D. Zarzeczny

I walked in the quiet cemetery,
My body feeling deathly weary,
Unaware of my own fear
I tried so hard to shed not one tear.

Until I came upon the place,
And looked at it with my hideous face;
A gothic tomb was there
And not a sound did I hear.

I walked into my decrepit home,
Like a stealthy little gnome,
And sat down on my coffin chair,
Alone in sorrow with no care.

Home I was, and home I'll stay,
Holding the demon Death at bay,
But he whispers into my crumbling ear,
"I've come to take you, so beware!"

Dedication: The pretty girl from France

Alone
Alice L. Pfingstag

Laughter, love, people and music
She gave each day a shining glow
Troubles never seemed to matter
For it was laugh, sing and let's go.

Often I question "Dear God, why her
The world and I needed her so?"
I felt a touch and heard a whisper
A voice said "It was time for her to go"

There is a special place in Heaven
Free of pain, sorrow and woe
There she is happy and again singing
Believe, for I have told you so.

Love is never, never an ending
So live each day as it comes
Knowing each one is remembering
The one gone and the one alone.

Dedication: My daughter, Alice Ellena

Dreams of the Soul

Darkness
Perry Zeiger
Here I sit in a lonely place — looking at my face in the darkness.

People I do not know, talk to the people I cannot see.

The wind blows my shadow around in the darkness of the light, which is not seen.

The goals vanish and the pain takes over.

In the shadows of darkness death is just a whisper away.

Only time restores the darkness that it temporarily stole, from the darkness and the light.

Heaven's Bouquet
Jennifer Suzanne Shepherd
Our families are like roses,
blooming fresh with each new day.
Their springtime is the birth of life,
When new rosebuds break way.

Then summer's here and they're in full bloom,
Their lives are at the top.
No thought of what may come too soon,
For they think they'll never stop.

In wintertime the roses must go,
But they don't just wither away,
God picks the flowers specially enough,
For that wondrous Heaven's Bouquet!

Me fellow flowers, let's not say good–bye,
Let's not even say adieu,
For in Heaven's Bouquet I'll see you again,
Where we'll all be fresh and new!
Dedication: To William "Bill" Jarrell

Memories
Thomas J. Simms
It couldn't have been that long ago.
I almost remember when
we talked.
It seemed so very near,
your voice.
Why, it was only last week,
we met.
I almost remember when.

How could I have forgotten
the years?
When, so clearly, I remember
your face.
How soon dreams fade and passion
becomes patience.
I almost remember when.

Memories rush in at times,
it's hard to tell the now from then.
It couldn't have been that long ago,
I almost remember when.

1–800–Press On
Joanna L. Schmersal
"Folks, this is serious, " the reporter said.
"This is definitely something all women dread!"
One victim reports, "It happened to me
Just before 6:00 on state route 103.
I was changing a tape for one moment brief
When all of the sudden I was filled with grief.
I felt it crack and I gave a yelp...
But nobody could aid my cry for help. "
Some think this foolish or even quite silly.
But this is as serious as serious can be.
You may think I've been caught in sleet, snow, or hail...
But oh no! It's much worse!
I've broken a nail!

Untitled
Rubin Chapman
Throughout the brightest day
Everflowing into deepest night
Feel the warmth of our bodies lay
As kindred spirits of love unite.

Sharp the arrow of your love
My heart it does not miss
Wearily as our bodies lie
I caress your frame with my fingertips.

The tears from your eyes
On my lips sweet nectar flows
Within my heart the fire
Of you in a crescendo grows.

For it tomorrow should never come
And our love is never given
I'll scream to the heavens I've missed the one
My true and soul inspiration.
Dedication: Whom greatest fan I am

Women I've Seen
Margaret T. McGarry
FORTIES: Women wore hats and white gloves with care,
Dreamed of marriage and children to bear.

FIFTIES: They entered colleges in streams,
Wore sweaters with letters,
Married men, shared their dreams.

SIXTIES: They smoked pot and lived in sin,
Drug culture consumed their every whim.

SEVENTIES: Their main goal ambition and power,
Children and husbands deserted by the hour,
Final outcome, the families have lost,
One in two marriages end in divorce.

EIGHTIES: Complain in bars by the hour,
With language both foul and sour,
About the lack of men who tower.

NINETIES: As they land in the desert, Mary and Jane,
Will the war of the sexes begin to wane?

Noteworthy Works

A Message From A Loved One, Gone
Alberta D. Potters

Dear family and friends,
As you look upon me here,
I look on from above.
It's all right to cry,
But don't blame yourself.
My leaving was God's will.
When you're feeling blue,
Remember the times we had;
Some good and some bad.
Though my body is gone,
My memory is still alive.
And please remember this,
I loved you, one and all.

Without Words
Mary A. Miller

On a warm summer night
Where a sea of stars
Shone bright
Against a sky of black
Midnight
Stood my friend and me
Alone but together
He was aloof
It was fate decided
By destiny long ago.
Without words we knew
destiny meant us to be.
There was a warm summer
Night where a canopy
Of stars shone bright
Against a vast sea
Of black midnight
It was our fate
It was our destiny
Without words stood
My friend and me.

Your Daughter's Love
Deborah K. James

I messed up your life and made you so blue.
I tore from your soul, your only love true
I know you won't be the same till she's back in your life.
Giving her Dad a love that shines bright
When I saw how much you needed her
I should have made you go home
Instead of being selfish and wanting you for my own
You say I don't understand how you feel deep inside
But I can feel and see the pain with each glance of your eyes,
I'll do anything in the world to make you happy again
Like you were when I met you way back then
I just didn't realize why your eyes shone like the stars above.
It was the happiness you felt
from your Daughter's love.

I Fantasize
Lisa M. Godwin

I am walking on the beach with you.
Hand in hand,
Two by two.
The sun is setting out over the ocean.
The blues, purples, pinks, and yellows.
The sounds of the crashing waves in my ears.
But I'll hold back these tears,
And hope that in these next years...
I'll find someone who cares about me,
As I did you.
And then – without you – we will walk;
Hand in hand,
Two by two.

Lightning
Janet Bonneau

You are energy unchanneled
Like a summer's frenzied storm
Unexpected, ever–changing
Unpredictable in form

As dangerous you are to me
With every move you make
I fear you as one fears the fangs
Of a striking rattlesnake

Upon the razor's edge we live
Where one false move can kill
I could fall at any moment and
Sometimes I hope I will

You are as volatile as dynamite
And I can find no gentle way
To defuse the blast I know will come
Somehow, somewhere, someday...

Dedication: Allen – for believing in me

An Ocean View
Frances Frydenger

She's watched the birds fly to and fro
Watched the plants and flowers grow
Seen the trees blow with the wind
But she's never seen the ocean!

She's seen the turning autumn leaves
Watched the flags fly in the breeze
Flown that "big bird" in the sky
Yet, she's never seen the ocean!

She's walked among the hills and trails
Even rode horseback delivering mail
Rode the "General Jackson" on a river cruise
But never walked the beach with sand in her shoes!

The scenery is perfect now up high
She's surfing those big waves in the sky
Atlantic and Pacific Ocean both in view
Look upward, now — she'll be waving to you!

Dedication: My sister, Kate, whom I love

Dreams of the Soul

Countryside
Catherine Hill

Have you walked in the country
Down the narrow green–swathed lanes
Where the honeysuckle and the wild rose mingle
Have you smelled the scent of wildflowers,
or listened to the birds
Here in the countryside

Over the hedge, in the field beyond
the golden corn is ripening
When the soft breeze blows, the field's aglow
A rippling sea of gold to glory in
Calm thought and serene peace it does bestow
Only here in the countryside.

Why
Sarah Ellery

It's hard when you've got pain
To get up and face the day again,
You've had a big piece of you taken away
And all you want is to live for yesterday,
Life's just not fair at all
Why has someone shut that door.

You never realise what you've got
Until its taken away, the lot,
Good things never seem to last long
God, why did you get life all wrong?
Why do bad things occur
And make people's life a blur.

You have to live for tomorrow
Try to cope with the pain and sorrow
No one wants to live with life
When you feel you've been stabbed
with a knife,
Why, oh why
Does anyone have to die?

The Spark Of Life
Bob Guzman

I live with the cold memories of the spark of life,
Snuffed out so quickly,
Leaving me with an empty loneliness.

So many years we shared that spark.
It bound our hearts and bodies
Like twins that can never be separated,
despite the passing of time.

I search and long for the touch and caress of her hand,
And the love I saw in her eyes.

Why did she leave me so suddenly?
And why couldn't we leave together?

Ours was the unspoken pact
And the unseparable spark of life
Which we shared together
During fifty–two years of holy marriage!

Dedication: My beloved wife, Evelyn Carlene

Ed–Words
Pamela H. Bialozynski

I have never felt this way before... never.
Not about anything or anyone... ever.
I've never needed anyone before, I don't know if I'll survive.
My heart, my soul, my whole being needs you...
to take me in your arms, just hold me.
Make the everyday disappear,
make me drown in that wave that washes over me
when you touch me, kiss me, look into my eyes.

I know that this is "that certainty that comes but once in a lifetime."
If we never have our chance together,
I will be happy to have at least had this feeling in my life.
It is a passion, yet with a calmness and peace that makes me smile inside.

Feelings
Cindy Pratt

I don't understand feelings
they haunt, persuade and pursue
they're not the rhyme in the poet's pen
nor the color which paints the sky blue

I will never trust feelings
they deceive, distraught and lie
their promise of happiness is shallow
and that's not love they bring you or I

I try not to listen to feelings
their voice is loud and coarse
they try to persuade my heart to choose
a way to make my life worse

I don't have feelings
none to speak of anyway
whenever I begin to have one
I just tell them, not today

Dedication: In memory of Robert Hambrick

Morning At Rest
Lisa Winebrenner

Specks of sand soften the ground
under my bare feet; the sky changes
from a somber black to a deep blue;
waves with frosty tips rush to the
shore; birds begin their morning speech;
mysterious shadows recede for a day's
rest; my chow's face appears in the
clouds and rapidly changes into a daisy;
a new Mother Sparrow dives to find a feast
for her four children; a bruised color just
above the peaks due east; the fiery orange
minutes later; maples on the other side
of the shore sway with the rising breeze;
yellow light now from the star beginning
its daily rounds; a man dressed in a
sweatsuit waves as he jogs by; swirling
grey clouds in the west; the lightning in
the distance; the dog barking; the squirrel
foraging; the Father and child flying a kite.

Dedication: To Mom, always an inspiration

Noteworthy Works

Dream Of A Piano
Chantal Gilbert
I played a piano for those who more or less heard.
The vibrations of my notes gave the sensation to play.
I like the feel of fingers on my keyboard.
With dexterity they danced the scale from do to do.
The hammers resound the strings until the melody is loose.
This echo wonderful to scatter about this living room.
I was not alone: "I was a company of fingers of fairies."
These hands who controlled my quavers gave a melodious
Tune.
When all the invited are gone the silence comes back.
When waking up I become harmonious.
Don't tell anyone that pianos don't dream.
Me: "I am a dream for those who want to play."

The Old Wooden Fence
David L. Plummer
The old wooden fence was black with age
Though it still stood tall and straight.
There's many a story it could tell
But old age was at the gate.

When young it stood proud in sun or rain
And looked beautiful all covered with snow.
The farmer took care to paint and repair
To keep it in shape when the cold winds blow.

Small children played horse from every rail
Young lovers made plans and dreamed dreams.
The farmer and his wife saw visions to come
And the fence heard them all it seems.

But time passed, as time always does
There were no more horses to keep.
The family was gone, the land was bare
So the old wooden fence went to sleep.

Dedication: My loving mother, Nancy

Thank You Lord, For Reminding Me
Janet Fox
I woke up today and grumbled because of work,
Then on my way I saw a child in a wheelchair.
I complained today because of my bills I couldn't pay,
Then on my way I saw a child begging because he was hungry
I complained today because my house was too small,
Then on my way I saw a child homeless.
I complained today that my back hurt a bit,
Then on my way I saw a child very sick.
I complained today that my child was so un–listening,
Then on my way I saw a child that was deafened.
I complained today that my husband was lazy,
Then on my way I saw a child that lived with a drunk.
I complained today that my car was junk,
Then on my way I saw a child walking.
I complained today that my shoes were too worn,
Then on my way I saw a child that had none.
I complained today that I don't have much,
Then on my way I saw a child who had nothing.
Thank you Lord, For reminding me...

Dedication: Wondering hearts

Untitled
Shirley Jackson
I wished for you tonight and I pushed the thought away
Moving on, leaving, something about another day
You are not a part of my tomorrow
Yesterdays with you were sorrow
As I watch the sun rise
I remember all the deceit in your eyes
All the things you never said
Just playing leap frog from bed to bed
Stretching the truth – your old smile worn
Out of my loneliness you were born
I could relapse and be back by your side
But I'm sure there are easier and quicker ways
to commit suicide

Yesterday Once More
Val Vivian
Yesterday we went again to our beach,
Where once we stayed so in love,
Same place same me same you,
But nothing seemed the same to me,
Where is the magic we had then,
I felt so crushed so dazed so alone,
How crazy we'd been then you and I,
But you didn't see my tears or hear me
Murmur, "Why o Why",
where did our crazy love and laughter go,
How long does it take to return again,
I turned and looked at you,
then we left our beach again,
Nothing felt the same only memories,
But I want you still,
O please come back,
Yesterday once more,
Just once again, Just once, you need not stay,
yesterday once more.

Dedication: Love to Doug, Mark, Jason

Untitled
Josh Lippert
Silently he's stalking,
as stealthy as a mouse,
slowly he is walking
to get close enough to pounce.
Hiding there behind a tree,
the wolf is crouching low,
in this place there has to be,
a meaty treasure 'neath the snow.
Stooping down for the treasure he sought,
he grabs a chunk of meat,
next he looks for a comfortable spot,
and then lies down to eat.
Lethal predator of the north,
the wolf is swift and strong,
not one animal dare come forth,
when it hears his piercing song.
Then appeared a hunter,
commonly known as man,
many of them want the wolf to disappear,
who can save them?
YOU CAN.

Dreams of the Soul

My Best Friend
Theresa Martinez
I had a friend, who was white as
snow, I wondered if she'd ever know,
The love I had was ever so.
My friend's eyes were as black as
night, we loved to watch the stars,
When the moon was bright.
We liked to take our walks at night.
Life was always forever bright.
For she was the best friend I'd ever
known, will she ever know, how
much I'll miss her so.
Dedication: To my dog, Mandy...

Everyday Birds
C. H. Barker
As dawn comes ALONG, a blackbird on the
Top of a tree, greeting the day with his lovely SONG
To see the swallows high in the SKY is a sign that
The weather will be warm and DRY, sitting out
There in a BUSH I can see the spotted front of
The THRUSH, the coo's of LOVE are heard from the
Ring tailed DOVE, then there's the little beautiful
GREY TIT with most people still a BIG HIT, circling
Way up HIGH are the gulls with their hungry CRY
Can't forget the little house SPARROW who can
Make his home in a space so small and NARROW I must
say they are favourites of MINE, because they are always
There come rain or come SHINE, every day looking for food
we put OUT, the starlings are always out and ABOUT
as summer goes and winter NEARS another little
Beauty, the red Robin APPEARS all these birds are so
Special to ME and they are there for everyone to SEE
These birds give me so much PLEASURE, it's something I will
Always TREASURE
Dedication: Carol, my special daughter

The Same Disagreement
Richard C. Prentice
I've got to shed my skin,
quaking for the beat beater
in his redundant past his patter glittering foolishly for five minutes.
"I'll shun the rules of this earth", he says:
Give way
and handles an address from the cross
where everybody believes it's true
the roundabout way of getting to places
unknown or known but definitely on the map marked with a (crude) circle
and in capital letters; "PILGRIM'S ROUTE".

Taken with two lumps and not stirred, not near here,
then somewhere in the distance, in the near future.
A bull to every field; through here mate if you know what's good for you.
Then later, then bending somewhere nearer the ground
an asp's head roughed and rubbed its body missing or disguised.
Remember how it struck, struck lightning like and hid itself
and left you to continue wandering aimlessly with your hidden intentions
seeking the best advice from ancient remedies
seeking the solace of letters written to one unknown
and finally realising things were not as they should be.

James
Aunt Sheila
You were born one year ago, today.
Grew in our hearts and then taken away.
You were not here as long as we would
have liked you to be.
We all asked why? Why you? Not me?

We do love you so very much,
And miss your sweet baby touch.
We all will see you someday again.
But can just love and miss and pray
'til then.
Dedication: Christa Gregory, in memory of James Axel

Why?
Cynthia Chiarilli
Is it wrong to question why
you didn't even say good–bye?

Is it wrong to say you care
when you really don't or wouldn't dare?

Is it wrong to be sincere or
is that just another fear?

Is it wrong to be a friend
when everything has come to an end?

Why do I ask these questions of mine
when handed just another line?

Why don't you care about how I feel,
didn't you think my emotions were real?

Thanks for the short time that we had.
I wish you the best through good and
through bad.

Life
Michael Addley
Life is precious.
Life is sweet.
Life's a gift
that we should keep.

Life's the Sun.
Life is Children in the park.
Life is a new bird in the nest
waiting to embark.

Life should be joyful.
Life should be fun.
Life shouldn't be ended
by a murderer's gun.

Death is ugly.
Death is cruel.
It's just too easy
to end it all
Dedication: Those who suffered in Dunblane

Time
Jessica Fabela

Why as myself
Words should've been
Said yet things were left
Undone time has gone by
Now things are not mended
The night turns into day
Tomorrow was yesterday
Where did it all go spinning
Away I should've I would've
Only if I knew but nothing
Was done and now nothing
Is new and another day is
Gone what should I do

Thanksgiving Prayer
Lucille T. Lynch

As we gather here, dear Lord
In perfect peace and sweet accord,
Amid a world that's torn with strife,
Your boundless love has touched our lives.

Among the things your love has wrought
Are blessings that just can't be bought:
A baby's smile, a parent's joy,
The loving friends we now enjoy.

Abundant food and robust health,
Stable jobs and modest wealth.
But most of all, our freedom, Lord
So hard–won by civil war!

For all these blessings,
And much, much more,
Our humble thanks,
Dear, Precious Lord.

Amen.

A Poem For A Peachy Lady
Martin M. Aquino

On a sunny day
Your sweet smell of peach
Made me dream of swimming
Like the waves on a beach.

I still remember
The crystal glance of your eyes
Your lovely voice
That tells no lies.

I wish to swim with you
To go downstream
To never look back
Never go upstream...

And with your hands of clay
To make together a vase
That will catch the sun
Like our first gaze.

Dedication: My mom, with all my love

The Recipient's Corner
Ian Tracey

A seaside bench full of sunken faces,
enclosed amongst the passers–by.
A look that belongs to the past,
sunk knee–deep in dying days.
Boarded windows hide the shoppers loss,
your walk now a crawl, full of wasted steps.

Do old age and the sea hold a common secret?
Are there any regrets in a silence,
that puts the world to sleep?
So sad to know, your last day–out
will be an ambulance ride,
trying to restart your heart.

Once, We Were Warriors
Richard Lee Nettleton

Once, we were warriors.
my friend, you and I.
When nothing could harm us
not sun, sea nor sky.

For our youth did not matter,
We had joined the elite.
to march on into battle
and ignore the retreat.

Here the trumpets would sound
and the guns, they would roar
at the height of the conflict,
but sadly, no more.

Now, I stand at your grave
as I say my goodbye.
For once, we were warriors,
my friend, you and I.

Dedication: Graham Holland, a fallen friend

The Survival Of Nature
Ann–Marie Wall

Dawn, the eye of light:
Key to beauty and harmony.
Where music, fragrance, and colour
Inspire the world;
Enchanting those who praise it.

God's creation; our home; – is being destroyed.
Its creatures are dying. There freedom; there life–
is ceasing to exist.
Silent cries of pain and fear
Are questioned by prayers of justice.
Greed, hate, and revenge;
The tools of evil's power.
Wrongs must be put right
If life is to survive!

The sky bleeds a fiery light;
Darkness has crept in.
The world is silent, life thrives no more.
Evil's domain has opened its door,
for the dark forces have broken free!

Dreams of the Soul

Who Is This Person?
Laura Harville
When my heart was broken
You cried for my pain;
When I was afraid
You calmed my fears;
When I was confused
You led me in prayer;
When you were ill
You showed me strength;
You taught me to stand alone
Yet you held my hand 'til you could walk
no more;
You saw me take my first breath
And I held your hand as you took your last;
I thank God for you
For you truly are an angel;
Who is this person?
She is my Mother,
She was my best friend,
She will always be my hero.

Dedication: Jeanell Allen – my mother, my hero

Distance
Monahan Brennan
Far far away
I would just like to say hey!
A little thing like miles
Will not get in the way of our smiles

I long for you in the night
How I miss holding you tight
I can see your eyes burning so bright
Wow! what a sight

I miss you so much my dear
But have no fear
I swear once again we will be near

First Time
Mark Bjork
Your beauty is of the ocean's crests
as the waves come crashing up the shore.
My feelings for you are deeper than the deepest sea!

Farther than any distance known to mankind.
Brighter than the beautiful sun which warms every day
just as you warm my heart and soul.

It's hard to put such feelings into words!
When I know how I feel and every time I think about it.
I know my feelings for you are real!

More than the magical mountains as they reach for the sky!
Just as I reach for your heart hoping someday only if my fingertips
touch your heart it will be enough to satisfy my soul.

Just to be able to get close to you
by holding you in my arms,
as my hands touch your soft skin.
Hoping one day I'll be able to penetrate the wall
in which I encounter for being too late.

Shattered Dreams
Tammy L. Snead
Like shattered glass from a window pane
my dreams have all been broken

All I have is memories of the past
my future not promised
and my present fading fast

I want to hold on
but I am losing my strength
without love there's nothing left

I keep holding on for a brighter tomorrow
but the storm is approaching fast

My Dreams

My Life

My Love

have no tomorrow

Dreamer
James Meskill
I am, a dreamer! Lost in a vast world,
where the emptiness of sorrow,
overshadows the illusion of love.
I am the dreamer of the impossible
the maker of dreams foretold,
Some: call me (sandman)
others just (fool).
At night, I come to the young
planting the seeds of their dreams!
And as they grow, they blossom.
Growing tall and strong
and as their dreams become reality
I am filled with JOY!

My Dearest Mother
Marilyn Whelton
Mother it has been a month since you went away and
it seems I miss you more each day. It is spring your
favorite time of the year, I talk about the flowers
and pretend you are here.

Every day I think of the night you went away, you were
better, everything seemed right we talked, we laughed
and said goodnight, Each time I left you I would pray,
please God let me keep her one more day.

When the phone rang at eleven that night I knew right
away something wasn't right. God had come to take you
away, another precious flower for our Master's bouquet.

On a dreary Friday morning we said goodbye, I turned my
eyes up to the sky, for a moment the sun came out so warm
and bright, It seemed I could see your smile and hear
you say, I will miss you my loved ones, but I am with God
so I am O. K.

Dedication: My precious mother, Beatrice King

Noteworthy Works

Our Love
Charlotte Thatcher
Your love is like the pale frosty stars;
so far away, yet so very close.
My love compares to an evergreen...
growing with each passing season.

can our Love,
the pine and the stars,
be entwined?

Let me ask this...
Have you ever walked through a deep
mysterious forest on a cold clear night?
The shimmering stars over the swaying
pines make the most beautiful
ever–lingering picture to be found.

That's how our Love will be...
Deep
Mysterious
Beautiful
forever – Lingering.

Autumn Beauty
Eula H. Johnson
I think that I shall always be
Amazed by every lovely tree;
The tree so tall arranged in gold,
The tree is vivid red so bold,
The ever lovely evergreen,
All so beautiful to be seen.

My spirits rise and my eyes shine bright
As I behold this wondrous sight.
Our land is beauteous with mountains and seas,
The wonders of nature, the birds and the bees,
But somehow I know I shall never see
Anything more lovely than a tree.

The Little Girl
Azalee Burris
I saw a carousel just the other day,
The horses on it seemed to jump and play.
A little girl was riding one,
She looked at me and stuck out her tongue.
Why would she do that to someone?
Guess she's just playing and having fun.
I roamed around a little while,
Then I saw another child.
I said, "Don't look so sad, little boy."
He pointed his finger and said, "She stole my toy."
I looked up just in time to see,
The little girl that stuck her tongue out at me.
I said, "Little girl, why are you so mean?"
First she laughed, then she started to sing.
She turned around to skip away.
I couldn't think of anything else to say.
She looks like someone I used to know.
I remember now, say it isn't so.
She looks like me a long time ago.
Dedication: For you Mom, love ya

The Eden Rose
Shelby J. Henderson
When God created Eden fair
He must have placed some roses there
However old —— the story goes
Before the man there was a Rose

Remaining through eternity
Thus the Rose will always be
Her Majesty of all the flowers
That ever drank the crystal shower

The masterpiece of art
That speaks to every Heart
The Language of Love – Everyone knows
Tender expressions are said with a Rose

Established in a peaceful garden
So very long ago
However old —— Heaven knows
There must have been an Eden Rose.
Dedication: Holly, Rhonda, Lorinda, and Elisabeth

Autumn Through The Seasons
Mary Doran
Autumn is the time of year,
When nature, wears her cloak, of red, and gold,
Its, the season, when the summer's glow has gone,
When nature hibernates,
And the birds forget to sing,
To tell the winter, that she knows,
Autumn sheds its trees to bare,
for somber winter, to behold,
To cradle in its arms,...
Then nature sleeps.
Till it's time to show,
The spring, and all its summer's green,
Returns, to the leaves, of red and gold.

Father Dale
Sally K. Jablonski
Father of us all, you're leaving
And we'll miss you when you go.
You have taught us how to love and give.
You taught us how to grow.

You gave us hope in our fears.
Held our hands to stop their shaking.
You prayed for us and blessed us.
And calmed our hearts when they were breaking.

You guided us with quiet strength,
When we were in denial.
You brought us peace and loving joy
At the end of every trial.

May the Lord guide and guard you.
May He always light your way.
May you always be embraced with love
Like the love from us today.

Thank you for being you.

Dreams of the Soul

Who Will Kiss Their Tears Away
Janice Miller
Who will kiss their tears away
When I'm so far from home?
Who will greet them at the door
So they won't feel alone?
Who will hear their tales of woe
Of falling off the swings?
In early morning playgrounds
Pretending they had wings?
Who will see their smiling faces
For learning their A B C's?
Who will read their favorite books
If it can't be me?

They really try to understand
Why Mommy can't be there
Circumstances severed us
And they're no longer in my care
They know how much I love them
I send kisses every day
All I need to know is
Who will kiss their tears away?

Foreigner
Mile Mijic
Foreigner different from all the rest,
foreigner in the playground,
foreigner – womb to grave,
live and learn strange accent,
funny name.

Chip on my shoulder,
rubble on top of me, –
Ooh la la
dark haired, blue eyed,
F O R E I G N E R!

Dedication: In memory of Djuro

Untitled
Martha F. Capps
I have been told,
In song of old,

In heaven tears
no longer flow

There are no broken hearts,
no pain to know.

Jesus looking down
on this world blew.

Seeing the troubles and
Heartache on this earth of
the young and the old.

So believe in that place of
peace.

Our Heavenly Father does
weep!

Reunion
Karen–Anne Jamieson
I glance across the busy room,
He's staring, my stomach flips.
It's like he can see right into my soul,
what I'm thinking, what I'm feeling about him.
I feel stripped bare, and drowning.
I breathe deeply, tears fill my eyes,
I won't let him see them.
Our lives could have been so different!
Young and in love, but so shy,
so stubborn, so tortured.
Neither surrendering to the other,
keeping our independence.
Another of his "conquest", that's what our "friends" said.
Believing them rather than seeking the truth.
I look back across the table to him –
but he's laughing with his wife.
We needed each other,
we acknowledge it.
But the moment has gone.

Forever.

Care
Laurie Farrell
I used to care so much, but time cured the wound that told all tales.

Passion was so untamed.

It lived, breathed, and danced with life by its side.

Until life got jealous of passion's finesse and snuffed him with
A wink of an eye.

I used to care but now stand alone.

Alone in a world where loneliness does not take form,
Yet it sleeps, ever so quietly.

The Day I Am Free
JoAnn McBride
Some kids get into trouble because of a dare
Some do because they think they don't care
Time after time kids will break the rules
That's how I came to be at one of the State Schools

I felt as if all the world was against me one day
I did something wrong and I was sent away
Sometimes I feel lonely sometimes I feel sad
As I think of the different life I could have had

When I am young time inches by so slow
But God is just giving me a chance to grow
Someday things will change and it won't be long
Because deep inside my heart I know I'm strong

It makes no difference what my struggle or strife
Today is the first day of the rest of my life
Is this the day the world will see a different me
For that will be the day that I am free

Dedication: My family and friends

Noteworthy Works

My Precious Gift
Kelli Kempf

A new life grows inside me,
This is my first son,
My gift from God, my miracle,
I'm amazed how this is done;

I can feel him kicking,
and moving all around,
I can't wait to see him,
As we race our way through town;

My Lord, he's just so precious,
Those tiny fingers and toes,
I think his eyes are blue,
Above that little button nose;

I never thought, I could feel,
A love as strong as this,
Every time I pick him up,
I can't resist a kiss;

Dedication: My son, Ricky

The Pearl
Tony Prickett

The pearl is as white
As a dove in flight
A pearl is as hard to find
in a mussel shell.
As water is in a pail.
Pearls are fake and real.
Have been caught on a
fishing reel.
found – in the Concho river.
When found will make a.
winner.

Dedication: My mother, Jody Ledford

A Fresh Dance For Life
Linda Wilson

I will awake and shake the moment
when, at last, true to myself
I lick the questions and think
not of ghosts for always
but whisper love's secret urgings
easy, sweet, smooth.
Smile for me, daughter of peace,
but, always listen, down deep in the belly
and question and explore you –
Good
Sacred
Learn of desires present
Though in clouded night;
perhaps wild longings you think
never to see life.
Yet you could change the vision
and make it be a joyful dance
A gift of poetry to celebrate
into eternity!

Dedication: MBF, for the healing journey

Father's Day Again
Gail Christie Patten

They do not know their mockery is
in vain

For they've lied again and again,
surely they knowest my heart
burns with pain

In the end they will have no gain,
knowing they've lied again

My heart knowest much pain,
but I know my "Father"
will no longer allow my suffering
to be in vain

That door is now sealed tightly,
I am no longer in paid, even
though
it is Father's Day Again

Dedication: My daughter, Kelsey Christine Patten

It Could Happen
Rachel Harper

It could happen, just wait and see
I will grow up but what will I be?
A doctor, a dancer, now let me see
I gotta think about what I can be.
My Mom always says, kid you can do
whatever you want to, just do your best,
keep on trying, I'm so proud of you.
If I close my eyes, I can see me
dancing on stage, people watching
and clapping just for me.
A dancer I will be.
A ballerina that's me!!!
It could happen, just wait and see.

Reflections On A Daughter
Claudia Cribb Hucks

Daughter, you are...
laughter on the wind,
giggles on a warm afternoon,
light, shadows, and bubbles in the sky.

Daughter, you are...
friends always, a helper near,
ribbons with lace,
music, dance, and drama.

Daughter, you are...
smiles, tears, and hugs,
hearts and violets, wide eyed surprise,
with crashes in the night!

Daughter, you are...
hope,
a green bough in my heart,
and joy born anew!

Dedication: Adrial, Sheay, and Hayley

Dreams of the Soul

Feelings
Sherry Kulowryi
Thinking desperately, when your eyes glanced
at mine directly.
Wondering, if you feel the same way as I
feel about you.
Anxiously waiting, with anticipation for you
to feed me the words that I want to hear
Wishing, that you would come and express
yourself to me with true feelings.
You're coming to me now, closer and closer. My
heart, it's pounding, faster and faster, it's
almost bursting out of my chest.
Now you're here, in front of me, with a
sensuous breathing of want. I see it, I
sense it, and I feel it.
Then you put your arms around me, and
finally you kissed me, very softly, and so
compassionately.
Compelling upon me without a word says
it all.

Dedication: My husband, Isaac Kulowiyi

Suddenly Parted
Dawn Marie Entorf
Between now and forever you will be in our hearts
Remembering times we shared will never be forgotten
Inside and out you were both made of goodness and beauty
And until we meet again we will hold on to our memories
Never will our thoughts of you disappear
Another day will go by and the memory of you will still remain
Nothing that we can say could make the pain and suffering go away
Dreaming of you is something we can do to deal with this tragedy
Together you will be and never have any fears
Remember us always and never forget the times we shared
In case we need to see you again we will have the photos at home
Nothing can help us hold back our emotions and tears
A thought of you will be with us always.

Cry Out Mothers
Esther LaTour
For our children are dying cry out
Fathers for your seeds are being blown
In the wind yet you turn your head
As our children lay dead cry out
Mothers for the child you will no
Longer hold or see their lives unfold
A child you carried nine long months
Knowing you will never see their smile
Nor hear their voice yet they no
Longer exist they will be deeply miss and
You send them off with a kiss cry out
Fathers for who carries on your name you
See death has no boundaries yet it holds
no shame it doesn't care who's to blame
It's not prejudice it doesn't care if
You're black are white just as long as it
Wins the fight stop the killing/stop
The gang banging/strive for a better
life

Dedication: Sharon, Shawna, Joseph, Jordan, grandchildren

God Bless The Aged
Della H. Tegge
The mind is good, the strength is gone
How swiftly the years do pass on.
When folks are blessed with years four score
Many live with added years far more.
The spirit is willing, the flesh not so well
Aches and discomfort you do not tell.
The Lord is there as we grow weak
With folded hands we comfort seek.
Be it health, or aches and misery
It's the Lord's will how blessed we be.

God bless the aged who do need care
May those in charge their feelings share.
Lord bless them who accepted that call,
Who knows what God has in store for all.
Bless all for their loving care
And comforting words with the aged do share.
The younger folks may never know
As years go by, changes sometimes show.
Keep them, Lord, in Thy tender care
Hear them when they ask in sincere prayer.

Her Carnival
Lisa M. Mayer
Laughing away her tears–
her disguise a charade.
Within her painted–on face
and clownish ways,
lie the roller coasters of emotion.
We are children; standing in line
for a ride– conveyed by affection.
Each day is a carousel;
repetitious as we go around.
There is no amusement in her park;
the lights went out long ago.

Dedication: Loving memory of Cathy Mayer

Who Can I Trust
Mindy Gibson
Who can I Trust,
if the trees tell
if the River Lies?
Who can I Trust,
if the forest turns
cold and dark?
Who can I Trust
When all is gone?
Who can I Trust
With Secrets
Deep Deep Secrets?
Who can I Trust
For a shoulder to cry on?
Who can I Trust
When I have nothing
Who can I Trust
When life turns mean
and green?
Who can I Trust
if the trees tell
if the river lies

Noteworthy Works

Destruction Describes Us
Holly Griffin

The world is a desolate, destructive havoc,
I see it as a venture, a risk, a hazard,
Dash and strike a lethal final hit,
Observe, the hostile man is a timid coward.

An unearthly wind carrying explosive news,
A cloud that covers the scorching sun,
A bomb has fallen, but little care,
Strangled cries rise up as buildings crash on everyone.

As boredom lurks in every dark corner,
My mind searches a long, winding maze,
A strange, bizarre idea comes into place,
My land is thick with a dusky haze.

Dreams
Evelyn Estrada

My dreams carry me
into special places.
Where I can be safe
no one to find me,
because I'm in a different
world.

It's like I've created
my own world in my
dreams.
Everything always goes the
way I want it to go.
And all the stress that
people give me just melts
away.
Because I'm in my
dreams,
I'm in a special
place.

Dedication: My grandpa, Richard Torrez

Vampires of Hollywood Nights
Steven Zumwalt

Out to the streets they come dressed all in black
With skin the stark color of white
Out to the streets they come silent as cats
As the sun sets to darkness of night
Out to the streets of the boulevard
They come with the setting of sun
After the day has but passed away
And the time of the moon has begun
The vampires of Hollywood nights
Out to the streets they flow like the wind
And scatter off into the night
Spotted by only the glow in the dark
Of an occasional neon light
Hidden by all who might do them harm
These vampires of Hollywood nights
Out to the streets at the end of the day
Living their lives at work and at play
Living a life that is shunned by the day
The vampires of Hollywood nights

Dedication: Rochelle, my wife, my life

Alton Towers
Elizabeth Read

Waiting for the ride I've been waiting for hours,
but it's always the same at Alton Towers.
It's nearly my turn, the sun hasn't shined,
I'm at the gate I've changed my mind.
Stepping on to the platform and in to my seat,
my stomach is churning I can't feel my feet.
Away we go, we're picking up speed, like a great
big dog that's been let off the lead.
We go upside down in a giant loop. Round and round
like a hula hoop.
We're slowing down now my head is spinning,
I look round for my sister she's standing there grinning.
I step off the ride I'm feeling sick,
I think I'll have to get to a toilet quick!!.

Our Tree
Kimberly Oesch

Hello little one, so you've come to visit, you've been away for so long.
Come inside and sit with me and tell me what is wrong.
You used to visit once a week and sometimes even two.
How happy that it made me, just to be with you.
I've grown very tall, my needles long, the room much bigger now.
You see little one, I remember how you played beneath my bough.
You'd pretend that this was your castle and were careful who you let in,
But thanks to you, you saved me from those big and burly men.
Sometimes you would just come and sit to get out of the very hot sun.
Sometimes you'd sleep beneath me when the day was almost done.
I've been here quite sometime now, giving you a place to hide.
We've grown up together and have done it with great pride.
You see, little one when you came to visit, I would stretch my branches long.
To give you the shade you needed, to protect you from all wrong.
My roots are deep, my trunk is strong and rough with many years.
Thank you for coming to see me, as you leave I'm filled with tears.
I'll miss you little one, please don't forget me now– bring your little
ones to see me and play beneath my bough.

Dedication: My loving Grandmother... Edith

My Eternal Love
Nancy T. Folga

My heart belongs to you my love,
it beats only for you;
If you should die before me, my love
my heart will die with you;

I die a thousand deaths each time,
I think the Lord above
Would take away my only life —
my life is you my love;

So live for me as I live for you,
no one shall take my place,
In this world or in the next my love,
see always my adoring face;

Please search for me as I'll search for you,
in the hereafter someday we'll find
Each other — hearts like ours beat
as one, my love – till the end of time

Dedication: My Yiannis, Mom and Dad, Sophie

Dreams of the Soul

Soft And Gentle
Shirley A. Nuhfer
Soft and gentle is the voice
That speaks to me each day
It's there to help and guide me
And lead me along my way.

Sometimes if I don't listen
And try things on my own
It will speak to me quite frankly
And say, "You can't do this alone."

The soft and gentle voice I hear
Is music for my soul
Because it's God helping me
And He will make me whole.

Storms Of Life
Tom Owens
Life is full of changes
Nothing stays the same
They happen day by day
As clear skies turn to rain

At times it's so depressing
It seems to make us sad
But then the day begins to change
Into the best we've ever had

After days of sunshine
A storm comes into view
The storm takes from your memory
The sunshine that you knew

The storm seems to last forever
Well into the night
But once again the sun returns
To shine upon your life.

Dedication: Jesus, who calms the storm

What Is Gold
Patricia Carter Keitel
God is everything, God is gold,
He starts with the young, and ends
the old.
In the dawn that comes, and nothing
can be heard,
Except the music from all his birds.
An the snow tipped mountains that take my
breath away,
In a field of wildflowers, can make me
feel the same way.
After a soft spring rain, when everything
is wet,
Or the evening when you see a sunset.
He is in the stars that shine so bright,
And even on a moonlit night.
On the waves of the ocean, that's so peaceful
to hear,
Even in a drink from a brook that's cold and
clear.
So even if you are young or old,
Always remember God is gold.

Whispers In The Dark
Sara Durogene
Every night you come to me;
Every night you're what I see.
Every night you talk to me;
Like whispers in the dark.

You are what I hope for;
You are that and much more.
You are what I hope to be;
While whispering in the dark.

All night I wait for you;
Waiting for that special clue.
That you will be here soon;
So we can whisper in the dark.

Now You Know
Karissa Storer
I have a love so strong inside
Ink on paper can't describe
The yearning burns right through my soul
I am no longer in control

I want your heartbeat next to mine
I'll hold you near me for all time
Your angel eyes have drawn me in
Your love is all I hope to win

Friendship seems so far away
I'm wishing just to hear you say
That you'll belong to me forever
And we can spend our lives together

It's up to you, it's in your hands
Just tell me if we have a chance
My darkest secret rings so true
And now you know it's always been you

Dedication: My only love

Dancing Ecstasy
Vanessa Wolfe
To dance within the eyes of pleasure
and to die with just a kiss.
To feel; to touch;
deep in erotic bliss

With every touch and every kiss;
Making love, it feels so true
I came with such emotion
I'd kill to be with you!

A thrust, a kiss, a thrust again;
breath so hard; the sweat and then;
moaning, screaming, pulsing hot.
Faster, better, harder – stop!

One last thrust and one last breath,
as he licks the sweat from off my breast
one last kiss, to end the night,
sleep my love, sleep well tonight.

Dedication: My dearest Joshua Evans

Peace
Dawn R. Hyde
We long for peace within and say we cannot find it
Yet long ago God sent His Son with His Word to bind it.

We need to find a place of solitude and commune with nature
for not in the noise and strife of daily living can we
hear the message of that inner voice so sure.

Peace between people of differing ideas will never be
just as animals kill each other so do we.

Yet each in our heart may find our way
no matter how sharp the pain if we will pray
not to remove the hurt and wound but to
find the strength to love and go on our way.

From Mother To Mother
Tammy Gruber
As a child growing, up,
I thought "being a mom's a breeze."
Keeping us fed, clothed and sheltered;
You did it all with such ease.

I see things much differently,
Now that I am grown.
Life is not so easy
With responsibilities and children of my own.

I never knew how rewarding
Being a Mom could be.
It's also sometimes quite difficult,
Which is something I now see.

I wouldn't trade one single day
Of all the lessons you've taught me.
Being a mom's a very special job
And you did it so wonderfully.

Dedication: To my mom, thank you

A Birthday Wish
Wes Williams
Mom,
I love you more than anything in my life,
I need someone like you to be my wife!
We've been through it all, you and I,
Oh God, what will I do the day you die!
You've been there for me every night,
Well, you've always held me tight!
All of the things I've done wrong,
Your love for me, still holds strong!
Many of night you've stayed up late,
My needs came first, yours could always wait!
No matter what I've done or what I'll do,
Please remember, that I'll always love you!
All of the times I made you yell,
You picked me right up after I fell!
You cleaned my room, you made my bed,
It didn't matter what anyone said!
Now I'm through, I just wanted to say,
Mama, I love you and happy birthday!!

Dedication: My loving mother

Silent Prayers
Charlene Henson
Lord I pray silently, that you will hear
The cries of the lost, that need to be near
Near to the cross that shields us from harm
Near to the strength that you hold in your arms
Lord I pray silently, that you will hear
The sound of grief as our eyes start to tear
The sound of guilt as felt in the heart
The sound of loneliness, all alone in the dark
Lord I pray silently, that you will hear
Our cries for help as we tremble with fear
Our cries for forgiveness, against you, we have sinned
Our cries for direction as our day begins
Lord I pray silently, I know you will hear
The prayers of your children as they draw near.

Race To Us
Teresa A. Tabb
It was grace that brought you to me again
And by grace I know we can win
No matter what our friends may say
Our love will grow stronger every day
We both have had problems in the past
Now, we face the future and I know it will last

If we concentrate on each other
We will never need to stray to another
Building our future on what's in our hearts
Having an unconditional love and a new start

Our emotions are finally in place
We have run the marathon and won the race
Hand in hand we have crossed the finish line
Our only prize is each other and time

I've given you my heart and soul
In my life you will be my only goal
In my heart I knew
I would always love you

A Gift Of Love
Roy Johnson
A gift of love is what you need
A gift of love without greed
A loving smile is really worthwhile
It will get you through a whole mile

A gift of love is always shared
Always by the loved ones who cared
Whether it be day or by night
It truly is what makes it right

A gift of love I've been told
is for young or for old
No matter where or hour
Love has the magical power

Love should always be shown
Whether you are young or grown
You will feel great and won't be sad
and in no way can love be bad.

Dedication: My wife, Harriet M. Johnson

Dreams of the Soul

God's Love Understands
Erica Wilson

Determination pushes doubt away
as souls revolve around change
Unanswered prayers and faith resign
steadily questioning God's design
Feeling the burn of a world at war
and what was I living for?
When do we learn, how do we see
beyond our view of reality?
Closely dancing in heaven's touch
still unsure of his divine love
tears begin to free our secret pain
and love surrounds our lives again.
With such as dreams are made of
God's love understands.

Silent Meadows
Henry Domke

Silent meadows greet me,
Woods beyond are empty.
Blue skies I cannot see,
Absolute tranquility.
My soul cries out so silently,
As all hope slowly dies,
The tears roll from my eyes.
Oh, how I do hate
My lonely painful fate.
Thunder rumbles in the skies,
As tears again roll from my eyes.
The sky is dark and wind is cold,
Yet still I hold my head up, bold.
For pain is nothing new to me,
As even the blind can truly see.
I live alone and search for she
Who brings the love that sets me free.
My curse does strike so deep,
Like darkness does it creep.
Until there comes a time,
That love is truly mine.

Embracing Passion
Jessica Campeau

My heart on fire with desire
from your luscious lips and
whispers of dreams.
I'm silhouetting your body
with moonlight kisses and
creating shimmers of light from
the Heavens above.
That dance with passion in the
power of love.
The brilliant light of eternal love
grows bright in the candle.
Creating shadows of embracing
fantasies of forever.

Precious passion is etched deep in
candle glows of forever.
The fires of forbidden glory touch your
lips to mine and ignite the forbidden
Passion that is rare to find.
And in the end we will be one.
As a single candle glows.

The Promise
Bonnie L. Mieras

I looked out my window and
What did I see?
One bright red rose,
Just blooming for me.

It's the end of the winter,
The beginning of spring,
One rose to remind me
Of all life can bring.

One rose slowly fading,
As the past slowly does.
Yet the promise of new life,
Of new days begun.

Digitalis Purpurea
Adela Graham

"Atishoo! Atishoo! Atishoo! Pass me a "plantkerchief" please,
In my despondency I find, I can't suppress a sneeze.
Lodged in my nostril there's a bee and in my eye, a fly,
an earwig's wriggling in my ear whilst others creep close by.
I've developed spots like decimal dots upon my swollen tongue
and if you think it rained last night, "foxglove me", you are wrong.
Playful breezes won't permit bright butterflies to settle
And I really do feel threatened by that nasty stinging nettle.
Atishoo! I'm about to swoon, " "Poor plant, I must confess,
Never have I come across a foxglove in distress. "

So I dabbed her eye and foxy nose with a fine embroidered hanky, white,
The bee buzzed off with the pesky fly and the earwig took fright.
"No inclination have I got to move your decimal dots
They are the very essence of your nectarous beauty spots. "
As I filled the garden watering can, she nodded approvingly
Presenting a precious thimble which fit just perfectly.
All other irritants removed, I gave her toes a soak
And straightway, she stood upright, draped in her purple cloak.
"Take Care, 'Adela Thimblefinger', poison lurketh in my shaft,
In no wise get entangled, stick to your needlecraft. "

Fighting Society
Dustin R. Duncan

Life of a loser,
Lost all hope.

No ammunition in
The war of life.

I strive to exist
With mere instincts,

But fail.

Never wanting more than
A future never to be.

Always hoping to be in
The Book of Life.

To God I pray, that
I have not failed.

Dedication: My beloved sister, Mary

Noteworthy Works

A Sonnet
Beverly Solberg

When nature spreads her darkest cloak,
And pounds the earth with heavy rain;
Those who always tease and provoke,
Have weary hearts now filled with pain.
And when once more has come the snow,
Their heavy heads are lowered, too.
They cannot see, they do not know,
Why the skies can't always be blue.
But lift your heads, do not despair,
These darker hours of pain will pass;
And soon the trees that now are bare
Will have their wondrous garb at last,
And all the world will once more sing,
Seeing the beauty of the spring.

Calvary Bible Church
Sandra H. Delong

I love my family at Calvary
Everyone means so much to me
Their friendly smile or cheery hello
Comes from the heart, I know.

The pastors are kind and true
They will help whenever they can
Just remember John 3:16
And your spiritual life
Will never end.

This unity comes from knowing God
As a very personal friend
And someday in the future I know
His love and kindness
Will never end.

Yes, I love my friends at Calvary
For they are so special to me
For when I'm at Calvary
I'm part of a happy family.

The Old Man
Robert Earnest Wilson

I saw the old man standing there,
And I thought, that could be me.
I felt his loneliness and despair,
Suddenly, he turned and looked at me.

His hair was dull and showed no light,
It was silver and grey like mine.
His eyes were sad and showed no joy,
'Cause love had never made them shine.

His body was a thing grown frail,
Hungry for love that never came.
His spirit was broken, his heart was cold,
Forever unwarmed by true love's flame.

I felt his sorrow and his pain,
As he turned again and looked at me.
He'd never know a woman's true love,
And again I thought, that could be me.

Dedication: My Dad, a man's man

Saturday Morning Bartoons
Kathleen L. Karl

Broken amber beer bottle
stench of spilled alcohol
peeled labels
leftover pizza cartons
stale smoky air
burnt, broken matches
cigarette ashes everywhere

no pancakes
just headaches
hangovers from beer

black eyes
bad times

A Hope and a Dream
Ryan Qualls

We all hope and dream,
For the perfect one,
But all too often we forget,
To ask God's precious son.

I also hope and dream,
And indeed one day,
I asked Jesus Christ,
To send a girl like you my way.

And I know I'm not always perfect,
And I don't always treat you right.
But you will always be my princess,
And I love you with all my might.

You have fulfilled my hopes and dreams.
I've loved you from the start.
You're the perfect girl for me,
You have a special place in my heart.

Dedication: Patty, whose light burneth true

One Precious Jewel Was Loaned To Me
Pauline H. Kammet

"You must have lost your way!" I cried;
"You know that you're not welcome here.
Be gone at once!" Death merely sighed,
And as I caught my breath with fear,
My young son died —
His childhood gone so ruthlessly.
"What purpose this?" declaimed my grief.
"Nine futile years! 'Twere better he
Were never born than life so brief."

He was an earnest gifted child,
I reminisced, as solace came —
His humor keen, his manner mild.
And as I softly called his name,
I found I smiled
In gratitude that I could see
How much of joy and love were mine,
That all that he had meant to me
Could not be measured by mere time.

Dedication: To the memory of "Jimmy"

Dreams of the Soul

Thoughts Of Someone
Sally Henley
Thoughts of those we care about can always
make us smile...
Because the special times we've shared makes
life seem more worth while...
And often on a day like this I wonder if
you guess...
How many times a thought of you has
brought me happiness...
It makes it seem like only yesterday in
thought your precious memories...
Can make you realize close friends can
never really grow away...
In thought you're never far apart from
someone who is close in heart...

Fusion
Cheryl Ann Radin
Alone
no hand to hold
no flesh to press
arms and legs entwined.

Cold
surgery is near
lost in a chasm
so small in the bed.

Pain
a sharp pinch
four hours were lost
waking to lifeless eyes.

Silent
webbed tubes extended
blurs of white passing
grasping for a smile.

Dedication: Steve, Aren, and Kellen – with love

The Sought After Prize
E. J. Bell
In the deeper recesses of your soul
you once believed you were in love
with love,
with me

But roses grow
flowers drop

You now think you're in love again
with someone new
but come next season that rose bush
will shed its leaves, drop its flowers, too
So you'll have to continue looking for your constant highs
you'll never be real satisfied
with the status quo
You'll continue to yourself, tell lies
until you of your own volition
shed your guise
and realize
that once you reach that perfect peak
the sought–after prize will real love seek

Yesterday
Angela Jamison
Each day is a new day in our neighborhood. Sometimes I do wonder
If the same things that had happened yesterday would occur again
Today?

Will someone's child be murdered today?
Will someone's child loose his/her mind because they did that
Awful crime?
Would that parent be left alone to do without their child that
Is gone
Will there still be homeless brothers and sisters with our little
Nephews and nieces scrounging for food, shelter, love and hope?
Would we have to bury another addict, battered woman or abused
Child?
Tell me, will today be like yesterday in our neighborhood?

Faith
Joanne Ricketts
I believe faith works in different ways
Different times, different places, and different days
How we got together was very strange
Something I believe faith arranged.

We were brought together in one night
It only took one look and I knew it was right
I fell in love with you right from the start
I know that your love belongs in my heart.

We both want the same things in life
I want you as my husband and you want me
as your wife
So when the day comes to pledge our love
I believe faith will be around us and God
Smiling from above.

I believe that faith works in different ways
Different times, different places, and different days,
In my heart is where I want you to stay
Nothing will ever take that away.

The One Of My Dreams
Juanita M. Thomas
This is a love poem, that I want to tell
The subject a joy, on which I dwell
About one it seems, who's the end of my dreams
Of thoughts and of sweetness, this one does bring
The sun now is shining, in my world it's spring
I believe it is love, and my heart's started singing
The purpose I know now, of my being
When his name is mentioned, my heart does a skip
I long all the time, for the touch of his lips
I know now that I love him, with all of my heart
I wait for the day, when we won't have to part
I'll never forget, the day that we met
How that I felt, I think of it yet
I didn't know then, that he'd ever be
The one that I'd fall for, and love tenderly
And now how I love him, and I always will
And being loved by him, is my greatest thrill
I now know for certain, until life ends
That from here to eternity, I'll be in love with him

Dedication: To Alfred, my only love

Do You?
Nikki C. Terris

Do you think I can see clearly now, my brother as a boy?
Or remember what it was we said in times we shared together?

Do you think these memories return, in flashback or slow-motion form?
Or do they linger in my dreams awaiting to be reborn?

Do you think I will forget the pain when I was told of death?
Or will it pass, but last forever, as a form of emptiness?

Do you think I will ever really know and really comprehend?
Or do I have to wait, till my demise, to fully understand?

Do you think I can see clearly now, my brother as a man?
Or remember what it was I said, the night before he died?

Forever Love
Jonna Sue Cooper

When my Father Johnny Grey,
Courted his true love
Whispered yes, I love you Lois
God's my witness above

And as they traveled down life's path
As a man and wife
With 4 daughters they were blessed
Now more joy they hath

And as the years flew away
The more their love did grow
They shall never be apart
For God is faithful don't you know?

When that day shall appear
Of Jesus Christ's return
They shall fly away as one
No more their hearts to yearn

Dedication: My mom and dad

Spring, Spring It's A Wonderful Thing
Heidi King

Spring, spring, it's a wonderful thing
When the flowers bloom, and birdies sing
Where butters can fly, and bees can sting

Spring, spring, it's a nature thing
That brings the sun, or an evening rain
With starlit skies, when the moon is high

Spring, spring, it's a lovely thing
With blushing brides, and diamond rings
Picnic baskets, and friends to meet

Spring, spring, it's a sharing thing
With loved ones near, or best friends dear
taking long walks, telling happy thoughts

It's spring, it's spring, it's a wonderful thing
So much to do, so much to see
Come enjoy some spring with me.

Dedication: My husband and daughter

Dad
Lyndsey Ward

Now you are gone I feel such pain,
I need you here to touch again.
You are my Dad – I want you to hold,
My world's collapsed, I feel so cold.
I think of you; I start to shake,
I call your name, my heart will break.
You were always there when I needed to call,
I want you back, for us all.
You left too soon – you weren't here for long,
How can I cope? I can't be strong.
I wasn't there when you went to sleep,
Please let me cry, I need to weep.
Your pain is over, for you I'm glad,
I will laugh again but for now I'm so sad.

A Whisper In His Heart
Anna Hoyer

He heard her heart crying out to him.
He knew in a second, she needed him.
In a heartbeat, he caught her fall.
He heard her desperate heart call.

He took away her pain.
He helped her stay sane.
He made her smile again.
He made room and let her in.

She is a whisper in his heart.
Her world was falling apart.
They may be worlds away.
And their thoughts may go astray.
But they built a relationship.
Started with a simple friendship.

She leaves her footprints there.
She learned she could still care.
He helped her regain her life again.
He made room and let her in.

I Walked Up The Mountain Today
Sharon Rose Felder

Spring was in the air
Glacier lilies everywhere were dancing in the breeze
The tall trees looked up with bright green smiles
as the clouds floated about–carried on a sea of
blue by the blazing sun.

Two butterflies by flowers disguised, flew up and startled me
I marveled at the wonder in it all as the birds glided by
in song.

I looked at the water flowing past– on rocks the water seemed
to leap in spite; the laughing brooks retreated around the
crooked way.

And then I saw him there The mighty buck stood tall
and firm; knowing I was there Looking down he took a drink and
was quickly on his way Vanished like a misty vapor... to me his
image still there And all around the mountains crowned stood this
dreamy state.
My eyes could only partly perceive the magic of this place
but my heart knew it better even before my eyes saw a single trace.

Dreams of the Soul

A Lovely World
Cyril J. Maunders

What a lovely world this is,
With its mountains and its dales,
And all the mighty oceans,
On which the ships do sail.
The grass that feeds the animals.
The trees that grow so tall,
The fruit and the vegetables,
That help to feed us all.
The Lord in His great wisdom,
Made everything we see,
All he asks, is to believe in Him,
And by his own decree,
That we do acknowledge Him,
He is the infinity

Words
D. Chant

Thinking back in time to when it all began
Thoughts of me being a woman and you a man
Initially it could have been just a need
A woman for a man of a certain breed
A man who wouldn't question why
A man who could just call in as he passed by.

When did the notion change
When did my feelings alter and become strange
Strange because they were not meant to alter
Hearts of ice are not meant to falter
But mine has melted as time has passed by
Now I can't stop loving however hard I try.

Where do I go from here
Will you always be far away or ever near
Will you ever be here to help me share the feeling
Or will you keep me closed out and leave me wanting
If only, Maybe, Sometime, If Ever
Words that have no meaning which could go on
Forever.

Patty Cake Dreams
Amanda Troolines

Self adhesive dreams pasted to a lifeless sentiment
In a lifeless world of cloning and apathy
Writing the book of faith while believing in a lost patron
One looks around to find the very thing you abhor, in your very mind
The vast openness of a desolate field that sings the blues, only to hear happy news
Happy news once taken for granted as a child, then thought lost, and now found
Found to be the essence of all life that reflects the understanding of a free sanity
And with that the beauty of life, the richness of being
The whole hearted healings of a hand laid upon our souls, lighting the way
As a star lea Columbus, as a light at the end of a hallway,
with the joy of knowing
That we are protected, with any regret, leaving no memories and
No empty rooms behind,
Knowing I understand
That on one's self is the light extinguished by choice,
re–lit by inspiration,
Limited by the freeness of a 5–dollar flower
Captured on film by the openness of oneself

The General Election
G. W. Bainbridge

After 18 yr. the whistle blew, John Major shouted time
Our scoring has been colossal lads, the squad is doing fine
Our team may be disbanded, but remembered with affection
with four in hand, we will try for five, to win this next Election
The opposing teams are not a threat, the Lib Dems has not won one yet
New Labour we do not need to fear, or Tony's grin from ear to ear
These Northerners, thought Tony, they are not very bright they will vote for me
The promises I gave them will bring my victory
There will be jobs for all who want one, they may take their pick
Just place your cross for Tony Blair, that should do the trick
Our country will be Utopia, the streets all paved with gold
It may sound too good to grasp, but that's what we are told
Its a two horse race plain to see, you can bet your bottom dollar
They would vote a bow legged monkey in, if it wore a bright red collar
We have all been conned from left and right, But Tony leads from centre
His guiding star The EEC which he is guaranteed to enter
The day of reckoning will soon be here, 'tis on the first of May
for the Tories and Labour Old and New, that is judgement day
We have had six weeks in which to choose, just where to place your cross
But whichever way you choose to vote, Herr Kohl may be your boss

---

Night
Sharon–Anne Lees

Foxes hunting for food.
Ghosts hunting people, all through the night.
Cars headlamps golden yellow and orange
Children dreaming of far away lands
Hedgehogs scuttle in the grass
Stars twinkling in the sky
Bats falling from the sky
Trains rattling in the distance
Wind howling in the chimneys
The crescent moon glows white
Clocks ticking in the night
The dogs come out to howl
Dad snoring in the night
Frogs croaking through the night

My Island Of Dreams
Rose Maude

Today I looked across the bay
I threw a stone, it rippled on its way
What lies beyond the water's edge, I never really knew
I've lived on this island, all my life,
There's been happiness, and some strife.
Still I would not change a thing.
I'm content with myself and my pet Pelican.

There's banana trees growing in the sun
Swimming is such a lot of fun.
And catching fish one by one
Butterflies, flitting through the trees
Grasping at the tasty seeds.
My parents were shipwrecked here
Who I cherish, and hold most dear.

Now, they are gone I do recall
Tales they told of other lands. I loved them all.
As we picnicked on the golden sands.
But nothing seems to alter the fact.
I love this island and that, is that.

Noteworthy Works

Life Locked Out A Psychiatric Account
Kathy Sims

In each patient I see pieces of myself
Stages of misery
Oh yes I've been there
Maybe its not fair
The bottom line is yes I care
But I feel abandoned, locked out
Who am I, where was I, I am not there
Pieces of me are everywhere
Such terror to care
But not to be able to relate
Why is this my fate
Thought I was precocious hah
That's a joke, I never learned to live
Oh what startle terror
When I gaze at the horror and misery all
around me
And desperation, decay as I murmur
horrified, why am I chosen to be frozen
Around and around I go but I can't
obtain a self I never had
Guess I'll stay irrevocably sad

Look To The Future
Jan Sussex

Look through my eyes, what do you see?
Do you see a sad spirit trying to break free?
Open the window, look up to the sky,
with your head in your hands, you ask yourself "why"

Look through the mist, see your life up ahead,
approach it with caution, but never with dread.
Look through the storm, through the wind and the rain,
protect yourself boldly from sorrow and pain.

Look to the sun, put a smile in your heart.
Treasure the memories, make a new start.
Look in the mirror, like what you see,
you are who you are, no one else can you be.

Christmas
Rosene Negron

Like the freshly fallen snow,
Christmas is so pure and clean.
The coldness in the air seems
To warm every heart.
There is no wrong or right, no black or white.
Just the spirit of the season
To guide us through the night.

The most special gifts are the people
You hold so close.
So close they are actually apart of you.
Like the presence of God on this special day
Family and friends are with you always
to stay.

The day ends with a night full of stars
That never appeared so prettier than before.
Each twinkling star God has kissed
To pass along to you a special wish;
That all of the days you live could be like
Christmas

My Love
Noah Meeks

My love affects me so, For once my heart was stone.
Then one day I saw what was wrong: I had been alone for too long.
Then I saw her one night, Her radiance seemed to make it daylight.
I stood there frozen. Was I under some sort of passions spell?
Could this be true? I've been so blue.
She looked at me awhile. All I could manage was a weak little smile.
She stopped and started walking my way. Oh, how I wished I
could run and hide away!
She was batting her eyes. (What nice thighs!)
She stopped and waited, She wanted me to start a conversation.
I felt such a strange sensation.
When I asked her out to the coffee hut, I felt a sharp pain in my gut.
We walked three blocks without a sound, But I knew my heart
was bound.
We walked into the coffee shop, I was wondering why it was so hot.
I lovingly looked at her. Why wouldn't she say something?
I simply looked into nothingness and unknowingly said three
fateful words:
"I Love You."
These three words determined the rest of my life.
For now she is my wife.

Romantic Nostalgia In Verse
Reg Morris

Looking back we most of us can remember our first crush
But being inexperienced we felt we mustn't rush
Yet age does not come into it when you get down on one knee
My first love started early and her name was Barbara Lee
We would walk hand in hand enjoying every day
We'd be the envy of everyone but she had to move away
We spent all our spare time together until the parting came along
And when the fateful day arrived we both had to be strong
She was a policeman's daughter and the whole affair we found testing
For although we were both so young I always found her arresting
But it seemed somehow that to share our lives was never going to be
And I would have to wait for someone else till then I would be free
In any case I wasn't really ready for what husbands have to strive
It was going to be rather painful but you see we were both only five

---

Come Back To Me
Joshua Boutwell

My heart died the moment you walked out the door
and out of my life forever

As I lie at night memories come to mind.
Memories of us together

The good memories and the bad, the joys
And the tears that we've had

I'd give it all up to be back with you, with
You out of my life, I having nothing to do

To see your smile would heal my heart, but I'm
lying here crying left in the dark

Please come back to me and forgive me the wrong
I've done, I was trying to do good and have fun

Time is never time alone, when I'm with you
But now I have no time. I only pray I will get through
this time without you.

Dreams of the Soul

Daisy
Betty White

There was a Siamese cat
Called Daisy,
She was so brave,
Protective of brother Oliver
She chased that fox away,
Like a soldier she did charge,
A car came like a bullet and
Killed her as she crossed the road,
Oliver following stopped and stared,
Then slowly turned and ran away,
Thinking she would follow
But she never came,
Now she's buried in the garden
Where she loved to roam,
And Oliver sits there all alone.

I Saw My Mother Crying
Andrea Smith

Turning her head she looks away
But I had seen her tears
I saw her body tremble
I even felt her fears
Mama thinks I don't know
That I can't feel her pain
But I have tried to reach her
I have tried in vain
Her self–esteem has let her down
Morale is very low
The sharpness of her memory now
Only comes and goes
She's led a lonely existence
A hollow and sheltered life
She is my endearing mother
And my father's beloved wife
I saw my mother crying
In her room the other day
While staring out her window
I asked her why, she did not say

True Love Destroyed By Rumors
Lia Peterson

There is a guy I met and he lives so far away
But yet I think of him every single day
He told me that he loved me and wanted to share his life with me
I told him that I loved him and wanted him to be with me
Everything was going great as far as I could see
But little did I know that this relationship was going to end quite fast
Because of a rumor that someone had to pass
It started out quite small a little bit of this and that
But it just grew and grew until it was all fact
This guy no longer loves me nor will he talk to me
He tells me that it was just not meant to be
I sit and start to cry, I sit and wonder why
I sit and wonder if he knows how I really fell for him
Will he ever know how I love him
And how my heart aches knowing that he no longer cares
My mind has thoughts of only him, my lips words that I must tell
Although our relationship no longer exists and was gone like a great mist
I will always love him and I'll never say goodbye
It's amazing how a rumor just a little lie
Has destroyed such true love for me and this guy

Let the Clock Rewind
Villette DuCray

I'm not aged, understand?
I am a little older, no atrophy of Mind.
No bolder, no holder of the word, "Unkind",
Just fanned by the flame
Of my elect opinion, in the game
That sets me free at last
From your way of laying blame!

We have lost these years, it's true —
(If we ever really had them) I'm not sure.
Were you KIND and was I BLIND?
And if you missed a chance or two
Because of what I did, or didn't do,
I can give in now, to you, and
Let the clock unwind.

Salm
Jenny Paulhus

Fragments of you billow
The wind made it this way
Its current is so comfortable
Its dream reminiscent of grey
I think of it often
While thinking of you.

And forever will you be mistaken
As dust, I once was this way
Now I'm regretting those moments.
Leaving me reminiscent of grey
And lonely

Change for what and when and how
Your presence has left me this way
I love you, I love you, but now
I can at least tell God I used to pray
Upon clouds reminiscent of grey
It's not what it used to be
Neither are you.

Who Are You?
Chuck Gallagher

Everyone wears the mask they choose,
To play the part they were not born for.
Does anyone truly know you or me?
We can never be too sure.

By wearing masks
We become what people see,
Instead of who we really are;
Just you and me.

We look down upon the true man
Who feels no need for airs
As one who is less than
We who don many masks,
Indicating we are no–man.

What would the world be
If everyone wore the mask of honesty?
Therein lies the riddle you see,
There is no mask with honesty.

Noteworthy Works

Friendless
Jennifer Cerasoli
Alone, stark
Bold against the bareness
of the wintered tree

Struggling, straining
Fighting to hold firmly
to the fragile branch

Brave soldier
Monopolized by monarchy
the over-powering wind

Faltering, failing
Bursting with a final beauty
when the last leaf falls

Places To Go
Noel E. Harvey
There are hundreds of places that we can go.
One is Nashville, Tennessee to a country music show.
Do you enjoy a five hundred mile race?
Maybe Speedway, Indiana is the place.
You are in Texas and want to see it all.
There is a 1-800 number you can call.
For awesome beauty and a clean air aroma,
go to the Grand Canyon in Arizona.
And if your favorite sport is baseball,
try the World Series in the fall.
If the cold doesn't mean one iota,
go salmon fishing in Minnesota.
To have a night-life extravaganza,
spend a night in Las Vegas, Nevada.
For enjoyment in the mountains and the snow,
you'll love the Rockies in Colorado.
Should flowers strike your fancy now and then,
travel to the Tulip Festival in Michigan.
If Heaven is what you most want to see,
then Church is where you ought to be.

Just An Opinion, Mine
Rebecka Reber
In my mind I see this world
A mean and ugly place,
Men and women walking around
With scowls upon their face.
No pleasantries, no nice hellos,
No "thank you for your time."
Just a world with people who,
Would rather talk in mime.
With people yelling, gangs that rumble,
The innocent shot, the buildings that tumble.
The old and young won't get along,
Which generation's in the wrong?
The churches are burning, my stomach's turning,
The schools are gone for our children's learning.
Why can't we get along and say?
"Let's all just have a peaceful day".
Why can't we have an equal face?
Because, we're all a part of the Human Race.
To join all hands would be a feat,
And I for one refuse Defeat!

Winter's Gift
Nelle Nessel
The trees are bare–
The earth is brown–
Winter has taken over all around.
The snow falls softly during the night,
And we awake to a soft blanket of white.
Mother Nature has covered the face of our Earth,
Winter has arrived in all its wrath–
But underneath the snow lay the seeds of
Spring–
Warm, and ready to grow, after the harsh
Winter fades,
The bright spring sun warms field and
Shade.
The trees and flowers burst forth anew
Ah – Sweet Spring, we welcome you!

Homecoming
Eva Beaubouef
I'm going home today to see those friends who will be there too
To reminisce of memories past: to visit places we all knew.

Yesterday will come again, with laughter and with tears.
Our hearts will be young and gay in spite of the years.

And when our visit is over, we'll promise to meet once more:
If God sees fit to leave us or does not come before.

Our life is but a vapor that appeareth for a time:
The days are quickly passing; the years are left behind.

My heart is ever yearning for something I can't see:
The spirit whispers gently, "soon you'll be with me."

Oh Lord I want to go, the day is drawing near.
The trumpet will sound the message, "Jesus Christ Is Here."

Are you ready for that day: that day of which we sing.
Have you made your preparation for homecoming with our king?

Untitled
Stephanie Achziger
Like a stone tossed into the still water,
so is life. You start out small, and
As the ripples grow, so do you. Growing,
Widening, spreading. You become the ripple,
the life. You expand. And as the
Ripples start to reach the shore, you start
Returning again to the still water.
And as the last little ripple fades into
the shore, the life is done. But still
you are the water: still you are the
Life.
Only now, instead of being a small part
of life, you are all of life, the soul of life.
You return peace fully to where you began...
To the oneness of all that is.
As the pebble is part of the earth, the
Water is also. As the earth is part of the heavens,
So am I.

Dedication: For Uncle Byron

Dreams of the Soul

The Pebble
Anita O. Bell
A Life took a change, on a midsummer's night,
with poetic words and candle light.
Captivated by just his smile,
he made a woman of a simple child.
Clutching a pebble, held hand in hand,
the wind blew our hair, as our toes kicked up sand.
Whispering waves called out from the sea,
The moon pilled its light, and it landed on me.

My heart was racing as we looked to the sky.
Did I fall in love with the man I was standing by.
How can I tell?
He's no longer here.
I still have the pebble though...
My souvenir!

Dungorne
Michaela Iafrate
The sound so powerful, so deep, so magical. The scenery breath-taking, the place... home.
As I awake from my dreamy slumber, I admire the lochs, green mounts and hills. The sound is of the bird's sweet song of morn.
The scenery is of my grand home, Dungorne.
I am living here as a poor young lass. So innocent and naive.
But when the heavy feeling fades I realise 'tis but a dream—but no, alas! 'tis not just a dream but a memory of my peaceful childhood.
I look around now and see before me a disturbed and troubled world.
If only things could be the way they once were when I was young.
Everything seemed different, so welcoming, so at peace,
with me? no
with nature.
If Mother Nature were here to see what has happened to her creation, she would sigh with sadness and be burdened with a broken heart.
I'm not asking for much, just what it was like back then,
in the highlands of Dungorne.

Retrieval
Wayne S. Bell
The long tortuous day and Evening passed,
and the exhaustion enabled my retreat
from the Waking life. I returned to
that Place where I could be undisturbed
and travel great distances, with
no fixed boundaries.

I surveyed the pictures that my
mind's vision bore; The Shadowy
creations were at times barely
perceptible. My mind began Winding,
twisting and straining 'til the elaborate
Images could be understood.

Yet the night segues into the dawn of a new
day, and I am forced to depart from the
familiar narcotic of the Dream. Not knowing
how much time I had wandered in the faux
world of spontaneous, effortless images, I
sought to retrieve them as the Sun shone.

The Darkness
Daral N. Millich
Can you hear the darkness whisper?
Do you feel its cold embrace?
Would you care to learn its secrets,
Bound in the unknown place?
Can't you hear it coming,
As it creeps across the sky,
Consuming in its mournful wake both you and I?
As the wind brings shudders
And strangely muffled screams,
The darkness brings its mysteries
In quite unsettling dreams.
Can you feel the night
As it drifts across your mind?
It melts away your remembrances
With the calming rains of time.

Journey To Womanhood
Jae M. Ginger
A young girl stepped out of the darkness
she took a closer look at the path
mapped out by those who had gone before her
The path was well-worn
and strewn with girlhood dreams
slowly, she followed the road
to the base of a mountain
she inched her way up the face of the mountain
'til she reached the summit
The young girl took a deep breath,
closed her eyes
and leapt from the mountain top
as she soared through the air,
she heard words of encouragement from her sisters
echo in the wind
She landed on a cloud and floated down to earth
setting down on wobbly and uncertain legs
and as she took her first tentative step,
she thought she heard in the distance
the applause of her sister-guides

View From My Window
Jean Whitehouse
Sunlight weaves its way through the trees, gently whispering,
Turning the leaves to gold. Tiny flowers growing in the soft earth,
Fresh perfume of rich green grass, morning dew freshly glistening;
The world is glorious and alive, giving us the promise of new birth.

Tall trees growing, spreading their branches to the sky,
Speckled thrushes, sparrows singing with all their might,
Cheeky robins, merry and bright, find shelter upon high;
Above the sky is blue, small clouds hover, shielding the light.

Squirrels play in the sun, tails held high, bright eyes shining,
Hiding nuts and food, rooting among the fallen leaves so bright.
Birds twittering as they build their nests in branches swaying;
The moon rises, flowers close their petals as the earth settles for the night.

A bright summer's day, green foliage full of glory and cheer,
Sturdy saplings, swaying amid mighty oaks so tall,
Stand dressed in living green, dancing above where the air is clear.
It stirs my heart, renews my strength; I know I will never fall.

Awakened
Sandra King

Beyond the quiet dawning
of emotion and romance,
Lies a gentle tenderness
Your song, your touch, my dance.

In silent retrospection,
love lingered in your kiss.
Lost loves of lonely yesterdays
erased by morning mist.

Speak softly to my yearning
calm the raging of the wind
Go gently beyond my heartbeat
You'll feel me trembling
deep within.

Daddy In The Sky
Alison C. Myers

I'm a great girl who loves her daddy.
I wonder if my daddy will ever come back,
I hear my daddy talking to me every day,
I see my daddy in the sky.
I want my daddy to come back.

I'm a great girl who loves her daddy
I pretend I'm with my daddy
I feel my daddy,
I miss my daddy,
I worry my daddy will never come back.
I cry because my daddy died.

I'm a great girl who loves her daddy,
I understand my daddy can't come back
I feel my daddy did not deserve to die
I dream about my daddy always
I try my best to care for him
I wish my daddy could come home
because I'm a great girl who loves her daddy.

Life
Robert E. Schumacher

Life is so beautiful
But time goes by so fast
Before we both know it
Our whole life will be past
We found a love
Not born from our lust
We found a love
That can grow on our trust
Each time we're together
I know that it's right
Like there's sun in the morning
and stars every night
You carry all the trouble
But you never show the pain
If only I could show you
It's not all done in vain
Someday we could be happy
and live a great life
That day can only come
If you become my wife

Mismatch
David Smart

Redhead atop a figure slim
Silent she waits to enlighten the dim.
Stranger's fingers caress her sides
Toying, idling downward slides.
Ignoring advances, they persevere
Making their intentions firmer, clear.
Pushed over the edge, ignited her wrath
Explodes, but still they mock, they laugh
Then casually becoming aware
Eyes fix the tousled flame red hair,
Drawing her closer, lips at ready,
Holding her tightly, intent and steady...

Those seconds her lifetime passed now spent
She's waved away, how indecent.

A Christmas Tree
Lois Y. Holland

In the beginning you did everything to make me happy
You shaped, trimmed and gave me plenty sun and water.
At times you came by and held my branches to check my growth.
As I grew tall and shapely you were proud, then you came and
Took me from my friends. I was happy because I was
Chosen to make many, many, people smile and sing. I
was beautiful. I had lights all over me, red, white and
yellow, even green. Sometimes music came from among
my limbs. I was so proud, I stood tall and still not
wanting these moments to end.
Many people came and stared at me, some talked, some looked,
The children smiled and laughed and played. Suddenly,
no one stopped to look at me, my lights were out, they
would not come on any more.
Early one morning before daylight some men came
and began to take me down. They laughed and talked
not knowing my pain. They threw me on the back of
a truck, cast aside, discarded and forgotten.
What I thought was everlasting was only for a
moment in time... I was your Christmas tree!!

Among The Shadows
Marsha Decker

Among the shadows within my heart
are faint traces of a love now torn apart.

With an artist's brush I'd take my tears
and place upon canvas my pain and fears.
The colors I'd use would be gray and blue
to show my life since I've been with you.

A shrouded soul just trying to be free.
You shan't look for long I'm afraid
because my tears will appear, and my
painting will fade.

As my colors collage and are washed
away, I hope my next painting will be of a
more beautiful day.

Old memories of which I cannot part,
shall always remain among the
shadows within my heart.

Dreams of the Soul

September Wedding
Albert White
At last the great day did
arrive, the weather made it
good to be alive, the birds
in the trees were gently
singing what a wonderful blend
with the church bells ringing.
The guests in the church they
did file waiting for the bride
to walk down the aisle. Many
years have gone through trouble
and strife, but I still love
my beautiful wife, I know
that I shall always remember
that wonderful day in
September.

Hard To Say Goodbye
Jennifer Clyde
Knowing I'd have to say goodbye; but never
thought it would be this way.
As I look at you're today, I see how happy
you are.
I know you in a place where no one can do
you harm.
Why you were taken from us in a senseless act,
I'll never know.
You were someone special whom everybody loved
especially me; even though there was a dark side
of you.
Though you were not perfect no one is, but you
had a heart full of love and affection. Love for
people and a love for God.
As I remember the things we used to do and all
the fun times we had.
You'll stay in my heart forever and always.
Until that one day, where we'll meet again.

Dedication: In memory of my cousin, Aaron

A Day At The Beach
Jennifer Jones
A day at the beach can really be fun.
You romp in the waves and play in the sun.

You put on suntan lotion, again and again.
It runs in your eyes, when you go in for a swim.

You wield with pleasure the sea and the sand,
A wonderful treasure with no slight of hand.

Winding staircases climbing so high,
Magnificent towers that stretch to the sky.

Hot dogs on the grill.
Oh what a thrill.
Corn roasted whole.
So good for the soul.

Baked beans and potato salad,
Ice cream and more.
Oh the joy of a day at the shore.

Home
Koleena Stewart
Home's a place of comfort,
A place of trust and love
A place you can always return to,
When times in the world get rough.

Home is a place of happiness,
A place of sad times too,
A home is a place of memories
That you want to keep with you.

A home is where you were born,
and a place you want to die.
A home is a dwelling place.
Or to you a palace maybe,
but from which you are free to fly.

Poor Little Mistreated Cindy
Kathy Caudle
In whiskey–drenched slurred speech, standing behind
Me while I sat scared and motionless on
The back porch step, Stepmother taunted
"Poor little mistreated 'Cindy'.
"That's what ev'ryone says you are.
"Ain't it, poor little mistreated 'Cindy'?
"Like Cinderella, and I'm the wicked Stepmother.
"Ain't that what they say?
"Poor little mistreated 'Cindy'. "
Knowing her drunkenness I would not look
At her but only sat numb feeling scorned,
Wrongly shamed, by her spit cold rebuke.
"Poor little mistreated 'Cindy. '
"That's what ev'ryone says you are.
"Ain't it, poor little mistreated 'Cindy'?
"Like Cinderella, and I'm the wicked Stepmother.
"Ain't that what they say?
"Poor little mistreated 'Cindy'. "
As I listened quiet, to her wrenched
Babbled venom, I knew—she knew—I knew.

Mourning Peace
Stacy Burr
A gentle breath of air drifts
over the large wooden casket,
reaching under Old Glory
to feel the gleaming varnish.
It sweeps out and touches
the sorrow–flushed cheeks
of a young woman,
wholly engulfed in blackness
save the thin gold band on her finger.
It wipes away her burning tears
kisses her trembling hands,
and offers her a serenity she
knows, understands and welcomes
by instinct alone.
Gently, it fills her anguished lungs
and refreshes her harrowed heart,
providing momentary peace in such
an innate union—
even when the life she knew
has stopped.

Noteworthy Works

Alone Again
Tracy Smallwood
Alone again, it's always me
I look to the future,
What do I see
A person that's sad
Right through to the end
With a broken heart
That I wish you could mend.
This pain in my heart
Which no one can see
These tears that I've cried
And you don't know it's me.
I wish you could love me
As you did at the start
Will you ever find room
For me in your heart.

"A" Level Results
Judith M. Bhojani
I am pleased that you have done so well but:
A cold chill grips my heart
I thought, could cope but:
Now I'm not sure
We will be so far apart,

I smile and enter the fun but:
I'm fighting back my tears, you:
Have a whole new world to see and learn and:
I will play no part.

I comfort you, the phone is there and
surely we will write but
The fear wells up and stifles me:
I cannot face the night.

Be brave my love, please think of me,
With memories of our summer
At least we had a little time
To cherish one and other

Endless Time
Yvonne Fraser
It's written by the stars above, for us all our destiny to depend.
If you listen long enough through forgotten time my friend.
Rediscovered, yet hidden by darkness, yet revealed to show.
A distant candlelit starry sky, a Milkyway a small path to grow.
A great galaxy mixed with stars planets a moon and sun.
Glistened a sparkle, a formation, a chosen route for you and everyone.
Time is the essential essence of all living life.
Endlessly, silent ticking passed in this world of modern strife
Everlasting, evermore, high in the vast skies above.
Flutter forgotten ghosts of once adoring love.
Past procreative generations, with their ambitions and dreams.
Gone bodies, restored to dust, souls to freely float in passing Sunbeams.
Embedded, indented no longer unsung passions to cast.
Endless haunting voices, eerie echoes from all the years past.
I hope enchanted to dance amidst colourful rainbows.
Now uttered differently their song, like the summer dipping swallows.
Time now endlessly to express happiness, a joy of people of distant Years.
To recollect your own silent pain, beneath clear crystal tears.

Loneliness
Rita Wingfield
Loneliness is not merely being alone,
Being with friends not having a home
Its feeling anxious and afraid
Wondering which way the game is to be played
It is searching for something
That cannot be found
It comes within reach
Then falls to the ground

It's a promise made on an empty night
Only to be forgotten in the morning light
It is chasing rainbows dreaming dreams
Planning all sorts of fantastic schemes
It is wanting a listener whilst you talk
A companion for that lovely walk.

Our Little Boy
Elois Combs
Where is our little boy,
Where did he go?
We don't have to guess,
We already know.
You've gone to Heaven
To be with God up above,
Whom you talked about often
And said that you loved.
You were our ray of sunshine
And now you are gone.
We were so blessed to have you
Our little "Special One".
To know you was to love you,
You were special in every way.
Our lives will never be the same,
We will never again hear you say:
"I love you" or "I'm sorry".
But please, Little Sunshine, Know today
That we will love you as much tomorrow
Even though you've gone away...

Untitled
Amy Hurd
I am what I am
Though I don't want
To be what I am

What I was, I am
No longer
Independence gone

No control, I am
Headed to the unknown
Out of my hands

One of thousands, I am
Stranded in time
Life forever changed

Prayers and tears, I am
Loved and lifted
My eyes to heaven
I am

Dreams of the Soul

First Of October
Agnes Thain
If love were measured in a smile
My grin would be as wide as a mile
If sorrow plunged as deep as the sea
Where would you be if not for me?

The answer to all and even more
Is not washed by the tide upon the shore
But in the wind and in the skies
And in truth if we are wise

So say what you mean and mean what you say
And love will nourish and blossom through each day
For each day given is a day to remember
From the first of October to the end of
September.

On Angel's Wings
Isis Iskaris
Listen,
Be still,
Be calm,
Do not be afraid.

These are the words of angels,
Such wondrous beings that God has made.

When we have learned how to walk,
They teach us how to fly,
When we have given up,
They show the reasons why.

When we have lost our hope,
We see a brand new day,
such wonders in a moment,
Will never fade away,

It is on angel's wings that I will take my rest,
And when my life is over, I'll know that I've been blessed.

My Patient
Rita M. Krieger
I wonder if he's going to make it thru the night!
It's all in God's hands if he gives up his fight.
He's all alone – the nurse and he
His family is all gone – wherever they may be.
His breath – I'm wondering – which will be his last
The pulse is so slow – before it was fast.
She moves him about from side to side
To break down now would be his demise.
His pressure is dropping minute by minute
I know this man is not going to win it.
Not long ago he was a big hunk of man
His body has withered – he is holding God's hand.
This man so valiantly fought for his life
I know he just went thru all sorts of strife.
I wonder what the man would have to say
If he knew that on this earth it was his last day.
How does one give up and lie motionless
Waiting to go to a life that's blessed.
You sort of envy this man now that he's gone
To think "no more pain" now that he's reached the dawn.

Mother
Orme Hale
We can only have one Mother,
Faithful kind and true.
No other one in all this world,
Would be so true to you,
For all her loving kindness,
She asks nothing in return.
If all the world deserts you,
To Mother you can turn.
Many tears you've caused her,
when you were sad or ill,
maybe many sleepless nights though grown,
you cause her still.
So whenever you come or go,
Give her a kind word, and a kiss.
'Tis "All she craves", I know.

A Sea Of Sorrow
Lucille Warnek
Every time I am reminded of the beautiful daughter that was stolen from me,

it plunges my heart into a black, cold and sorrowful sea.

The giant waves of sorrow crash hard upon its shores.

washing away the grains of her vision even more and more.

As the years go by and the grains wash one by one into this sorrowful sea,

her love will slip farther and farther away from me.

So when I am old and gray; and a final sleep washes over me,

I pray the grains of her beauty slips backward through this sorrowful sea.

For then maybe her vision will splash bright and beautiful for me to hold for eternity.
Dedication: Betty, my beautiful daughter

Little Star
Anna Motschenbacher
twinkle twinkle little star
a song from my life's past
is what i wish to dare to be
shining soaring burning roaring
to have the world in my palm
oh just to be a little star
inspiring the minds of thinkers
and the hearts of lovers
and to brighten the darkest night
i want to live... i yearn to be alive
laughing running playing jumping
let the sun shine brighter
and the birds sing sweeter
and the streams run clear and blue
let me be the one to sense it
let me be the one to feel it
let me be the one to revel in its glory
but first
let me be the one to twinkle
and let the first to revel be you

Noteworthy Works

The Big Sale
T. Blaney
Dear MP's give us a better quality of life
If you cannot give a job to your honest loving wife
To sell all army homes to the Japanese
Tax payers and the public people are not pleased
Promises in the past all those lies!
Furious POW's all over Britain
Memories are back, all the pain
To sell to the Japs is a disgrace
It's a slap in the face
Wife's Uncle killed by them in Singapore
Call a General Election let's have no more
Millions of pounds to all those fat cats
While homeless sleep in streets like rats!
Lottery cash NHS made better
All the truth is in this letter?

Why Me?
Yvonne Ruth Kaye
There must be more to life than this,
I feel somewhere I've gone amiss.
For all the work and things I've done—
life for me has not been fun.
Just one long drag from day to day,
to make ends meet from pay to pay.
I see my children go without.
I feel for them, how I could shout
"Why me, why mine?" but no one hears.
In bed at night, I shed my tears.
I'm in a trap, I can't escape
as all I meet is more "red tape"
With bills to pay and food to find,
to a life of poverty I'm resigned.
All I ask is that someday
this pain and hurt will go away.
To share my days with someone who
would wish to share in my life too.
So that my dreams won't seem in vain,
that life have meaning once again.

The Important Chain
Robert Beaudoin
Every part of your person is connected in some way
The strength of this chain gets you through each day
If any one link separates from the rest
The strength of all bonds will be put to the test
Among the many links are your heart and soul
Emotions and faith have an individual role
Values and principles depend on each other for support
It is those, when stretched that makes the chain so taut
The bonds will hold firm and provide the strength that we need
As long as each link, we nurture and feed
If one link would open and loosen the chain
Then all of your person could feel the strain
The circle of unity keeps the person intact
Any break in the circle would have a major impact
Each trauma you face, may tend to affect its length
But because of your belief, you will retain all your strength
Try to maintain the most positive thought
It often provides much–needed support
If you care for each link as you would someone's heart
Then it would not be possible to pull them apart

Reflections
Mary L. Weiseman
Did you ever look up in the sky,
And watch the white clouds floating by?
Did you ever let your mind ponder,
As you watch the sky with all its wonder?

First a ship with sails so high,
Still there's plain clouds riding by.
Next a shape of a dog appears,
Soon the dog too disappears.

A bear, a cow and mountains show,
As though they reflected objects below.

Time passes so fast when you dream this way,
But haven't you had a beautiful day?

I'm Me
Wendy Millard
I'm not just a Mom or a wife,
Living for someone else all my life.
There are needs that I have got too,
Not only the needs of all of you.

To be me and do something that I want to do,
But I've no energy left when I've finished with all of you.
You play and fight I try to keep the peace,
Some days I could tear my hair out at least.

So I go through my days trying to please everyone,
And all that I get is sorrow not fun.
But I am a woman regardless of size,
Love is all I need and soon the time flies.

It's not too much to ask for a small piece of time,
For something for me to do what is mine.
Not to wash, or to sew, or cook, or to clean,
Just an hour for ME do you know what I mean

Masks
Sharon Bell
We are taught young to do all the right things,
but who's to say what's right and wrong? Mom
says this, church says that, society says else.
The boss says do this, family says do that, why
won't they leave it alone?

Saying all the right lines, wearing all the right
masks, acting out a role in the play. Everywhere
we turn, we don't have a choice, we just do what
we have to do.

All grown up now still saying all the right words,
confused as to what's right for me. Hearing all
the voices, afraid to make choices, why not follow
the heart? Wanting to play this role, wishing to
say these words, it's time to write my own scene.

Saying all my own lines, removing all the old masks,
not acting out a role in the play. Tired of pretending,
searching for an ending, ready to make my way.

Dreams of the Soul

From The Classroom Window
Charlotte L. Palmer
From the classroom window this is what I see,
Thick, grey poles of metal
Barring light from me.
Electric fences, great high walls,
I've seen it all before.
Try to escape? I don't think so
You'll be locked up forevermore!

From the classroom window I would like to see,
Desert islands, paradise
and the deep blue sea.
Hula girls, doing what they do best,
How nice it would be to have a rest.
Dolphins jumping, here and there,
Instead of grey everywhere.

A Ti
Rosa Maria Ochoa
Y en una tarde como hoy; cansada, angustiada, dolida y abatida.
Sintiendo que el fracaso el triunfo ha tenido.
Los problemas ya me agobian y mis pocas fuerzas ya no me sostienen.

De mi mente se han borrado compromisos por instantes.
Y siento que he caido un poco mas profundo. Y desde esta obscuriDad clamo a ti senor.
A ti que solo llamarte mi corazon anhelante espera.
A ti que todo lo imposible haces realidad.
A ti que con amor me abrazas mientras mis lagrimas me queman.
A ti que con tu paz me das aliento continuar el manana.
A ti a quien siempre reclamo el infortunio de mi v bida.
A ti a quien tocar quisiera para sentirme segura.
A ti por quien mi vida joy tiene un manana.
A ti a quien con la esperanza de un manana sueno dia a dia.
A ti a quien en momentos como hoy no te alejas de mi, ni me das la espalda.

Dedication: Amiesposo con Amor

If
Pauline Blackburn
If I could turn back the clock in time,
Where would I first want it to stop?
The day we met, the day we wed,
No, let me pause and give it some thought.

Remember the time, when we had the flat tire,
And you never would carry a spare...
We just donned our roller skates and skated to the next town,
Just as if we didn't have a care...

If I could relive it again, would I change anything?
If I could, I'd give us more time.
We were robbed of our youth and yes of our love
But oh it was the sweetest of wines...

If I could've taken away your pain,
And the helplessness I felt,
Oh, But it just wasn't to be,
If I had just one wish in the whole wide world,
I'd wish you here, once more with me...

If I Could
Tysen Hodgson
If I could be a king, my wealth would be a glance from you.
If I could make the sweetest music, it would be your laugh.
If I could own any lands, they would be those of your heart.
If I could have any joy, it would be the light in your smile.
If I could journey on all the oceans of the world,
I would rather sail my fingers through your hair.
If I could wrap my arms around you, I would bear the bitterest cold to keep you warm.
If I could hold the sun, I would make a necklace of it for you to wear.
If I could paint the sky the colour of your eyes, I would so that I could lose myself in its depths every night.
If I could live a day as sweet as your kiss, I would know heaven.
If I could have your love surely I would need no more.

Untitled
Michele King
Like a big dark blanket
you feel its protection, safety and warmth

Until—
You find yourself needing
fresh air and light

We are living beings

I've cast off the blanket
called grief

I've thrown it off
gulping in the clean fresh air

Inhaling, taking all the
beauty of growth that
God has promised!

Dedication: My children: Andrew, Jennifer and Nathan

Our Dog Bandit
Cynthia L. Grounds
Bandit is a special dog,
That has an attitude.
He should be a movie star,
With all his little moods.
One might say, he understands,
Just what you have to say.
Bandit likes to learn commands,
Like, sit, dance, and even pray.
He can beg, roll over or crawl,
And likes to run and play.
Watch him fetch his toy or ball,
And even speak or stay.
He is a Rat Terrier,
And is proud as can be.
Outside, he wears his visor,
So, that everyone can see.
He shows off a little bit,
When he rides in the car.
We love our dog named, Bandit,
He's born to be a star!

The Time Is Now
Francis J. Romano
Brothers, sisters a blessing indeed.
To have them both makes you jump with joy.
The laughter, the tears, part of life's journey.
Some are younger, some older, no choice here.
Lucky the young ones, their lives made easier, thanks to their elders.
Many years gone by, the tables have turned.
Take heed young ones, it is now your turn.
Make them smile, make them happy.
The choice is yours, the time is now.

Untitled
Daniel MacGuire
Get a little bit closer baby, Come to me,
Let me be the one to be close to you.
Let me feel you all up and down,
Let the 2 of us just become 1.
Come a little bit closer baby,
Let me be, Let me stay Here in your arms.
How can I stay away baby,
After the love that we've shared.
Don't send me away, Let me stay,
Let me be the 1 to be 1 with you.
Let me stay close to you,
Let me stay baby, Don't send me away.
All I want is to be close to you,
Stay with me always baby
Don't ever go, Don't ever leave.
Always stay near me baby.
And hold me tight in your arms.
I'll never leave you, I'll always stay close to you baby.
You are my love, You are my life,
So come to the place where we'll become 1.

Two Worlds Collide
Terese Rodriguez
Saw an old man with much to say, I walked on by pity he's all gray.
When the beggar approached and asked for spare change,
Why did I stare at him with disdain.
Have I somehow sinned today?
He was freezing and covered in mud, I could have given him my gloves.
Have I somehow sinned today?
Surely he hasn't ate, I ponder while staring down at my lunch plate.
I try to guess his weight.
Have I somehow sinned today?
He coughed profusely and had a bout, not wanting to see him, I take another route.
Night has come all is finished, my thoughts of him won't diminish.
Have I somehow sinned today?
Off I go and hurry to work, I reach the corner where he lurks.
Again we meet his eyes are weak, I smile and help him to his feet.
This time I hand him some provisions, and release all my stigmatism.
Inhumanity was my sin, he taught me this,
Through an ordinary grin.

Dedication: Para Mi Madi

Hands Of Time
Marianne Taormina
To change the hands of time
Go back to my start of yesterdays
Knowing how to re–arrange my life
To avoid and guard myself
From fear... hurt... and disappointment, I'm now endeavoring
Would change my entire existence
If I only could, Oh if I could, WOULD I?

To go back to my start of yesterdays
And change the hand of destiny
Would I again get lost along the way
Become to exist as I do today... NOWHERE
or
Would I have accomplished all of what I wanted...
I'll never know... WOULD I?

Save The Children
Lisa R. Baugh
Somewhere in the night a child cries an endless tear:
All the joy and laughter gone, replaced by fear.
No longer do they feel safe in their own home:
This small child once filled with love now feels all alone.
Their sweet innocence is ripped from them leaving only pain:
They stop their daily prayers, feeling they have nothing left to gain.
The people they love and trust are the ones who make them cry:
Night after night they lay there and wonder why.
So young and so confused, they feel they're the ones to blame:
For this cruel abuse and overwhelming shame.
From the fear of being punished, they keep their mouth shut:
They don't understand it but feel the wrong of it deep in their gut.
With no one to turn too, no help in sight:
They live with the pain and loneliness every single night.
Children are tiny miracles sent from heaven above:
All they ask for and deserve is our loyalty compassion and love.
Its time for us to join together and take a stand:
Together we can "Save The Children" side by side hand in hand.

Dedication: My loving husband and children

Help Me Always
Dawn Stevenson
Lord help me to Pray
Always knowing what to say

Help me to Read
Always planting a seed

Help me to witness
Always examining my Spiritual fitness

Help me to Love
Always laying my treasures above

Help me to friendly Greet
Always even if I have to repeat

Help me to Give
Always as long as I live

Help me to do your Holy will
Always doing these things joy will I feel.

Dreams of the Soul

Learnings
Patricia N. Wilson
Through the world of make–believe
it's so easy to receive
Messages of kindness and love
images from above;
methods of being in control
through the world of make–believe.

To keep a semblance of sanity
one must deal with reality.
Kindness and love mean nothing
to most
heartache will become the post
table your dreams for a time;
start on another climb
to keep a semblance of sanity.

Lost For Work...
Fiona Craig
Tired? (not really)
Done everything (sort of)
Been out (once, briefly)
To buy bread, loaf – ha ha!
Chat shows, quiz shows, cookery shows
Talk, ask, make, bake, Flaming state!
I am awake – just
Tidied up – mostly
Opened the cupboard door
Poached, fried, sighed, denied
Looked around the room many a
Time for "Neighbors" soon
Wash the dirty dishes – Can't the water is not hot
Didn't switch it on, must have forgot
Sit down quietly
Never, well nearly never
Mustn't get caught up in
Thought
Put the kettle on again, glance at paper – "job section"
Choccy biscuit with tea, (lucky me) – that's better – almost.

What A Waste
Sheila Ann Wood
As we look through the rubble where bodies lie,
I ask myself, why do children have to die?
They have done no harm to anyone,
I can't forgive the things that you've done.
Does anyone remember what this war is about,
When you go on your marches and scream and shout.

It's just words of glory that come from your lips,
As innocent children die on shopping trips.
The hate and rage that you provoke,
Means death to ordinary, everyday folk.
Have you forgotten about life, so peaceful and giving,
Do you just want to hurt anyone who is living?

Your are just like Hitler was with the Jews,
You slaughter anyone who doesn't share your views.
Do you think that people look up to you,
Is talking of peace so hard to do?
Are you so shallow and full of fear,
That if peace came along you might disappear?

Summer Storm
Mary K. Sharp
Skies turn black, and stillness reigns over all my world.
Thunder rolls, vibrating the earth's foundations,
Lightning crackles, building excitement and tension.
A certain closeness grasps, holding captive earth's sweet air.
Caught in pangs of birth, the skies weep,
Relieving the turmoil of the boiling clouds,
Delivering peace and light.

And I tell myself, "this too , is only a summer storm.
This boiling conflict within my soul
Will fade as these retreating clouds.
Falling tears will wash away this doubt and leave me free. "
Tomorrow I will smile and view again
The sunrise of certainty and light, and remind myself,
"That, too was only a summer storm!"

Poetry Is
Kim Parker
An art.
Beautiful words strung together
with the skill of a mastered seamstress.
A wire mesh of fused emotions.
A point of view. A carmine sunset.
A glass of vintage red with grapes and creamy Brie.
Refined, humourous.
The window into someone else's mind.
The picture show of an event.
An oil painting of time.
A full moon, a fading rose.
Fantasies, nightmares, aspirations, failures.
A Christmas tree, or bitter feud.
A death, a birth.
A miracle of literature
Forged from the pen of a loving soul.
Massive thunderstorms of inspiration.
Twisted.
Perfect.
Poetry is.

Wendy
Golden Chrysanthenum
The news that I am pregnant,
Makes me feel thrilled and yet uncertain.
I couldn't bear to have the abortion,
Neither could I cope with the situation.
As the fetus developed inside,
I begin to feel a certain maternal pride.
The labour was an agonising whirl,
But in the end I was rewarded with a six pounds eight ounces girl,
With her punk hairstyle and a sweet little nostril,
I cannot help myself from being thrilled.
At six months she started to crawl,
And possess long copperish hair unlike her brother who was nearly bald.
At eighteen months she was out of the nappy stage,
And without my family's help I don't think I would have managed.
She is such a sweet, lovable and cheerful daughter,
Who finally filled the house with happiness and laughter.
I hope she stays sweet, innocent and wise throughout her whole life,
Although an awful lot to desire in a world fraught with strife.
Words could not justify or express,
How grateful we are with our little sweet princess.

Noteworthy Works

Artist
Maxine Costa

"No simple way to wipe the slate,
remove myself from the canvas,
the landscape of life...

The depth of feeling that stretched me
beyond the limitations of self
into the vastness of thee...

As the Universe is witness,
this One firmly grips the brush,
tips the delicate bristles into oil
and touches the speck that is I and
gently, forcefully swirls into clouds
beyond the spectrum of vibration
singing across the canvas into eternity."

Fantasia
Timothy A. Wellman, Jr.

As they stood at a distance away
they watched as the clouds of mist
disappeared. And they stared onward
majestically at the Ivory Tower "behold
all its beauty". As the sun was rising
it made the Ivory Tower glisten, and sparkle
like the God's Heavens. It stood high as a
mountain with great power, and distinction.
As it shone through the morning sky
with rays of light so magnificent no
words can describe its beauty. It stood
majestically in the middle of a rock formation
with a stream trickling, churning, and
bubbling by its side. As the sun set
it became more distant, and far away.
By morning the indescribable tower
was shining once again describing the
majestic glorifying beauty of "FANTASIA".

Dedication: To my grandfather, Francis L. Wellman

Folly
Alma L. Bess

Time flies
Today's shadows... Tomorrow's vanity
Giving way to thought, eluding memories
Watching dreams go by
Scheming... Planning
Always missing the mark
Doing this... Doing that
Never satisfied
Looking here... Looking there
Nothing ever changes
No peace... No joy
Clouded happiness... Overwhelming confusion
People come... People go
Idle existence... Endless loneliness
Profitless pleasure... Wandering desires
All vexation of the spirit
Stop the madness!
I communed with mine heart
Redeem the time
Live circumspectly, answering all things.

A Parent's Forbearance
Dyann Denby

Influence bearing nonchalance
Our elders are elegance
Subtly demanding nicety.

To the soul, inviting
Unfulfilled — contriting
A moral commodity

Reflection and wisdom portrayed
With instinct foundation layed
Tradition based honesty

For those reserved with doubt
Evolved integrity to think about
Sorting through ambiguity

Flowers
Sean Bewley

Two beautiful flowers...
God had granted to me,
Amidst a swirling wind of self-destruction and insanity
Fear and self-will run riot I let drive you away, leaving me more empty
than before
Sometimes I kiss the moonlight as if to kiss you
And I ask you to for forgiveness
For I have broken you in a way I can never mend
Now I wait...
Wait for you to come to me with hatred in your heart and your whipping
words
Until then, I'll keep kissing the moonlight
Deep in thought,
Pondering just what I will answer, when you are old enough to know, to
all your angst-filled questions
But remember, my flowers...
No matter what the past holds, or what the future will bring,
That I will always love you.

Dedication: Sirrel and Paulina Bewley

With Quiet Steps; Soft Voices
Ethel M. Sturm

Throughout the stillness of the night
They walk through rooms dim with light.
They seek to comfort those in pain
Gently speaking patient's name
To calm those waiting surgery –
Encouraging of what can be.
Assuring them with calm and poise
Dimming hurting; tearful noise.
To be a person hospitalized
One needs the sincerity of their eyes
The look, the touch is medicine
Allowing peace to enter in;
And then the surgery is past –
To recovery we look at last
But, were it not for those above
Who emanate both warmth and love
Could we have gotten passed the fear?
The hurt? The cries we did hear?
Oh no! It would have been much worse
Without our Guardian Angel – our nurse!

Dreams of the Soul

The Hot Sun Shines
Nicola Huckstepp
The hot sun shines
With all different kinds
When we were out that day.
The sun shone like yellow
Like yellow on hay.
hooray hooray the sun is shining
like yellow people ready for lining.
It's yellow it's yellow
like yellow on the beach.
like yellow what shines through classroom
When teachers are trying to teach.
like yellow like gold
not blue that is cold.
It's lovely it's lovely to have the bright
yellow sun, sun, sun, sun.

Angel's Dream
Jessica Hughson
Once I dreamed I was
an angel to watch over our
children. Drying up their tears
with gentle hands to mend the
broken dreams of my little
friends.
When I woke up I felt
the fear of never again being
able to tend a tear or cuddle
a fear until it shines again.
Then I laid my head to
cry. An angel came to me
with air upon his wing
he whisked me away and
to this day, I'm happy
to say, I am happier than
I was that day my angel
dream came and went away.

Dedication: Mother, Constance Hughson and Princess Diana

The Dimensions Of My Mind
Donald E. Hopkins
The dimensions of my mind, how they wonder all the time.
when I think about you, or writing down a line.
the process of thought, sometimes without rhyme.
will even make a person, want to climb the wall sometimes
and they my friend are the dimensions of my mind.

I'll think about the beauty of life sometimes
or heaven and space, or the wonder of love
and the tenderness of grace.
I'll think about you and the joy that you bring
so if you're still wondering, first look into my face
and if it's possible to find, look for the deepest
thoughts that linger in my mind.

I could sum it all up, in a matter of time
I have it all stored up in the back of my mind.
I could tell you whether it's rhythm or rhyme.
or if that's love that I see in your face
or if its just the thought in your mind.
Because they my friend, are the dimensions of my mind.

Echoes
Keszeg Michael
Echoes from the shadows, a voice
through the trees. Startled stare in
disbelief at falling autumn leaves.

Unnatural silence as the darkness flows
like wine, icy hands of fear running down
your spine.

Each heartbeat sounds like thunder,
as the darkness forms a fist. The hand
revolves and opens, a face that's made of mist.

The voice and face now move as one,
in your eyes are tears. A friend you'd thought
lost, smiles then disappears.

From Sorrow To Joy
Pat Bartee
Oh God, I hurt from my head to my feet.
How can I endure this hurt without defeat

A part of me is gone, yet only for awhile
once again I'll see that dear face, and
sweet smile.

He sees me now so all alone, my tears I
must subside.
I must cleanse my thoughts, my whole being,
inside.

So I'll sing a song of praise to you God
for all the fun we had.
I'll thank you for the love you gave
through this dear Lad.

Oh God the hurt is better now, I feel it
going some a little each day.
Please God turn this lemon into lemonade.

Rebirth
Annette Mercedes Oliva
Between somber tones and dark moods,
We begin to see some sight in
what we do.
With the painful news of dying,
We begin our mourning and crying.
When the light begins to flicker away,
Our spirit will remain here to stay,
When the cold is in the air,
We start to feel our inner fears.
With our trails of broken hearts,
Our innermost soul is never torn
apart.
Between our joys and our sorrows,
We know there is always a tomorrow,
With the death of one body is the
birth of another,
And forever they're together,
like lightning and thunder.

Dedication: Arthur Arizala, in loving memory

Noteworthy Works

October Madness
Elizabeth Carnahan Koss

The queen of the Nile
Was here for awhile last night.
She stared back at me from my mirror.
She had not come to conquer Worlds—
Only revived to have a good time,
To go to a party and dance with Merlin.
She searched for Mark—
But he apparently, still slept.
He missed a good party.
We photographed her this day—
Packed her away—
And now in the mirror I see—
Only me.

Dedication: For Dennis, with love

Spring Fever
D. J. Calzada

Lying in the grass, gazing at the sky,
I contemplate life during the noon hour
While cars zip past and horns sound
And overhead clouds slowly glide by.
The chirping of birds tucked safely away
In the crowns of towering trees are
Mingled with less melodic people-sounds,
Coming from someplace close at hand
And yet somehow far, far away.
Nestled in the grass am I, eyes closed,
Pretending to fly like the birds
And float like the creamy white clouds
Before time forces me to jump into my car
And zip down the road to the place
Where I tediously earn my keep, surrounded by
The trance-enducing tempo of elevator music.
Oh, how I long for the end of the work day...
Fearful of how far the clouds may have drifted and
Wondering what it would be like to be unemployed
For awhile... at least for the duration of spring.

Color Slide 1955
H. E. Richardson

There was a walk on which you stood
One Easter Sunday by the street
We walked. Our snap-shooting friend would
Raise his old Leica's eye to greet
Us—you too startled, shy to seek
Escape, lovely as the flower
On your lapel below your cheek
Soft as Time played through that hour
I stood with you—deep blue your coat—
your scarlet hat—so red its rose—
soft as veiled lips, your white-laced throat!
These things abide as Time-Since goes:
the life of you so young, so fair...
So much has gone that now I see—
the sunlight caught on your dark hair
Oh, flash of immortality!
This Leica's eye—it will not lie.
Still we are young if we should die.
Lovers may hear our song if sung
As here we stand, forever young.

Passionate Sleep
Rita F. Gibson

We were together in the garden last night,
sharing love by the moon's dim light.
The warmth of your touch against my skin,
unleashed the fires of passion, that burn within.
I knew (for the first time) just how beautiful love could be,
as you brought to life my every untold fantasy.
You took my emotions to an exciting new height,
and there you kept them, until dawn's first light.
So pure, so real, it certainly did seem.
Then I awoke; to find it only a dream;
so until (this) my dream comes true;
each night my darling (if only in my sleep)
I'll be with you.

Dedication: Steven Earl Gibson

Jewel Of Life
J. Byrne

With every drop of rain that falls, plain stones are turned to gems,
And dirty cobwebs so forlorn, then hang with glistening hems;
The dead, dry grass, will sparkle bright, its colours rich and deep,
With every drop of rain that falls, new life awakes from sleep.

The ancient bark of oak trees grand, will run with rivers bright,
As dry parched earth drinks in the tears, it glistens in the light;
A single drop may rest upon a dull and dried up seed,
To magnify in glasslike state, to form a glistening bead.

A soft, light sheen, on lazy river, where warm, soft sun rays lay,
Becomes a living granite path, its surface rough and grey;
Then every leaf transforms itself, a waterfall lit makes,
So hollows in the paths are filled, in miniature, new lakes.

With rain comes laughter from the plants, their heads and leaves they shake
Enriched in colour where water rests, kaleidoscopes they make;
For every drop of rain is life, that gives itself for free,
Without this jewel of liquid life, a dead world earth would be.

The Jews
Danielle Hunt

Their hands touched the rain
Their eyes saw the pain,
Their weakened bodies
seemed to walk in air
Like they were already
ANGELS.
They knew they would die
But it seemed the fear
Wasn't in their eyes
But in the enemies.
For some peace stayed
But for others it would
Never come again.
Those buildings and gas chambers
Were all the enemy thought
They could see.
But in their eyes
They could see more
They could see the pain
And their hands are now the rain.

Dreams of the Soul

Gone But Not Forgotten
Crystal Leavoy
Zing! A bullet flies by.
You make a fast duck to dodge the next one.
Then up again and off you go
Ducking and dodging and hoping to make it.
Just as you make it...
Zing! A bullet you can't duck
Laying in the mud.
Soaking wet.
Suffering in pain—then...
Slipping away silently.
Gone forever,
But not forgotten.
For all soldiers are remembered.

Dedication: My four great–uncles (Mullins)

True Love
Amber Cranmer
True Love is what I'm in.
It comes from deep, deep within.
My heart holds on,
While my love goes on.
Now I know we shall never part,
For you have won my precious heart.

True Love is what I found,
When I heard your sweet, sweet sound.
Through summer, winter, spring and fall,
We shall have and own it all.
Now I know we shall never part,
For you have won my precious heart.

True Love has just begun,
and now I know that you're the one.
You flew from heaven to my door,
and I shall love you through rich or poor.
Now I know we shall never part,
For you own my precious heart.

Untitled
Eileen Petano
Sometimes, as I'm walking along,
I glance at the grass.

When the wind is blowing,
the grass reminds me of the ocean.

Sometimes, the dandelions remind
me of islands –

Each group is an island, sitting amidst
the gently flowing ocean.

Sometimes, there are leaves on the grass,
and they become miniature boats,
floating on the green water.

And then it ends – I come out of
my trance, and all I see then
is a patch of grass,
invaded by dandelions and leaves.

Field's Farm And Store
Jermaine Whirl
Field's farm and store—
Lots of roots,
Heritage, too.
Day by day
Work the fields
Every day
Fresh food
To Eat,
To sell.
We work the fields
Past, present, future
Our
Land
Our
People.

Untitled
C. A. Davis
Now that the autopsy is in
I've taken a certain liking to gin
It may not be the best way to deal w/ my life
But, I know I will never be someone's wife
I miss him so damn much
He was my emotional crutch
We were twins
We both didn't win
For he took the hard way out
and left me to finish the bout
I'm in a corner with no place to go
While he is somewhere trying to grow
the sweat runs down my face
While he in turn sets the pace.
The fight goes on, and I try to win
while he sits there wondering why I am drinking gin
I try to talk to him
but things begin to turn dim
for the last punch is thrown
and he is nothing but a voice that drones

He Put Me Here
Goldie Fairchild
One day you asked me, why am I here?
To live on earth in so much fear?
Why do I have to work each day?
Why can't I go outside and play?
Why can't I do what I want to?
Why can't I go when I choose?
God put us here, on earth you see.
To live our lives so happily.
He put me here, to teach you, Dear.
That you don't have anything to fear.
He put me here, to teach you, Babe.
There are some things, you shouldn't say.
He put me here, to teach you, Child.
His love for you, is worthwhile.
He put me here, to teach you, Sweets.
His love for us, is such a treat.
For someday, I'll be gone.
And you will be left on your own.
We shall meet another day.
And in His love, we'll forever stay.

Noteworthy Works

Butterfly
Monica Henson

i grasp the
blue–winged butterfly
dancing 'round my head
in the orange tinted
sunlight slowly
fading away and 'cause
my grip was
too tight,
it died.

is that
what happened
to you,
my ebony–winged
butterfly?

Summer
Marjorie E. McKenzie

Under the old elm tree,
So big with so many branches,
A home for black bird and finches.
An ideal place for morning coffee and afternoon tea.
It's a home for squirrels to romp and play,
A place for boys to dream life away.

An ideal spot for a swing,
To swing and listen to the songbirds sing.
Look out the window and see,
Two little ones climbing the tree.
Later when the work is done,
To sit and watch the setting sun.

What better place on a hot afternoon,
To open a freezer of homemade ice cream,
And when friends or neighbors come,
Together sing old favorite songs,
Until birds cease their flight,
Time has come to say good night.

Accidents
Katrina Clark

Accidents are things
that happens unexpected

Accidents can be surprising
to you or others
because you just didn't
see it coming to you.

Accidents could bring
happiness or sadness
is just depends on what
it could be...

Most accidents are caused
by people not paying
attention or just not
caring about hurting
others...

Accidents!!

Untitled
Gwen Carlton

I try I fail
I try again, to no avail
Happiness, they say is true
If not for me
It must be you

and if it's yours,
and it's not mine
You must be smiling
all the time.

So laugh at me
and I'll laugh too.
What's good for me
is good for you.

Always Looking Up
Deborah Moore

Somewhere far away in a lonely
field of hay, lay a new baby
colt just learning how to neigh.
Big blue eyes and a soft fluffy
mane, gave color to the pasture
that was only just lain!
A frightful low wind and a
blackening sky brought fear
to the colt and he jumped up
high.
Wind is blowing wildly to and
fro – which way to run the
colt doesn't know. Look up
here says a voice from afar –
in the corner of the sky was
a bright shining star!
"Look up at me for things right and
wrong and you will see
greatness and accomplishments
life long!"

Untitled
Dennis Asche

There's no me without you,
My life has no meaning without you.
I couldn't go on,
If you were gone,
I don't want to,
Live my life without you
I'm all alone feeling down and out,
My heart won't let you go,
Until I let you know.
I'm the type of man,
Who will take good care of you,
Put my life on the line,
By now you know what I say is true.
Remember I will always love you
And so if are two hearts can't be together
For me there is no life worth living
None what so ever and just remember
I will love you
And will care for you
FOREVER

Dreams of the Soul

Hold My Hand
Anneliese Buskirk

Hold my hand when you show me
how to safely cross the street.
Hold my hand while I pray,
now I lay me down to sleep.
Hold my hand as I grow
and learn the lessons of life.
Hold my hand on the day
I will become his wife.
Hold my hand when I'm afraid
and feel all alone.
Hold my hand, let me know
in your heart I'm always home.
Hold my hand when you teach me
to be honest and stand tall.
Hold my hand, hold on tight
when I stumble and fall.
Hold my hand
when you grow old and gray;
I'll always be there beside you
I will never be far away.

Little Boy
Linda Rolli

Fishing pole in hand to catch a whale in his plan.
Daring twinkle in his eye.
Always asking why.
To his Father he is a champ.
To his Mother her pride and joy.
And to his sister he is just a mischievous little boy.
To him, the world is big and exciting, although he spends
most of his time fighting.
He is full of energy and bounce.
One day he will announce, his life full of pleasure,
for he has found a treasure.
Yes his heart is in a whirl,
... he has found himself a little girl.

Dedication: My son, Phillip III

Freedom
Jennifer Cottle

Freedom...
Of speech.
A right we take for granted.
The freedom to be ourselves.
Being able to say what we feel,
To say what we believe.
Sometimes to be condemned by the narrow–minded.
A way to show individuality.
To show how we are different from one another.
Having opinions is not a crime.
If your views differ from mine,
Do not criticize,
Do not agree.
Accept.
Learn.
For being unique is a gift.
It is not meant to be ashamed of,
Or looked over.
When you learn to understand others,
Only then can you understand yourself.

At First Glance
Gerard Straniero

Can a man put into words, that which is perfection?
When he meets a woman who captivates his soul.
With the look of heaven, and the heart that tells no lies
He gazes at her majesty.
Have I seen this creature, who has been smiled upon by the
Ages?
I have dreamed this vision before
I wondered if perfection does indeed exist.
And now I wonder no more.
She is alive and well, sadly beyond my reach.
I would search eternity for her
To gaze upon her once more.
She gives me more than I could hope for.
And yet so much simplicity.
She is beyond our world.
And I saw her in only a first glance
A millisecond... And then she was gone
Time is cruel to these eyes
But I have seen perfection,
At first glance

A Friend
Samantha Beckwith

If you look up in the sky and wonder why,
You might smile to yourself and give a little
sigh.
Because a friend is someone you can be completely
at ease with.
Whether they're thin, fat, tall, or small you
Will like them all.
A friend you can count on is all you need,
no matter what their colour or creed.
You know that they will always be there for
you no matter what good or bad things you do.
So if you look up in the sky and give a little
sigh,
Remember don't think why give a friend a call,
go on don't let life pass you bye.

The Dividing Line
Jeffrey Weaver

Catch me if you can. But if you do, you must follow me
On a journey like never before into the depths of my mind.
A peaceful place at times. Where birds sing with sweet serenity,
and compassion overflows from the sea of love. A dainty little place it is
of happiness without despair. The ground is of satin and the grass of silk.
All of the pleasurable things one wishes to possess.
In the distance there is a mountain, with a gleaming, glowing snow
shining like an angel looking over this peaceful place.
But you dare not cross that mountain for you may not understand the
changes.
It is the darkside, the midnight, the complete destruction of all sanity.
The land is scorched and the sky is blood red.
The trees are aflame and there is nowhere to run.
Only death, depression and loneliness live here, waiting to overpower me.
Never cross that mountain in my mind, for you may never come back,
trapped in the horror and sorrow, unable to return.
Every day I live my life knowing the other side,
but if not for that Great Angel
dividing the confusion and holding back the dark enemy,
my mind would surely rot in its own hell.

Noteworthy Works

Timeless Leisure
Gertrude Ann Slater
I sit here quietly
Upon the lawn,
Gaze my eyes
Whatever upon.
Bathed in a sweet
Perfect peace,
Voices of nature
Will never cease.
Timeless leisure
Here at hand,
Glad I live
In this American land.
The gentle breeze
Within this air,
Moving softly
Through my hair.
I raise my hands
To Heaven above,
Surrendering my all
To God's merciful love.

Life
Amil A. Bera
Light
Radiates Innocence
Lost by Earth
Creates Disillusion
Forbidden Thought
Enables Search for
Light

Dark
Tedium Arises
Consortium Filled with
Emptiness Sparks Thought
Teaches Faith
Illuminates Innocence at
Dark

Write Now
W. R. Bozeman
I write when I am lonely,
I write when I am sad,
I write to think more clearly,
I have to clear my head!
I live to write,
I write to live;
For, I know when I stop writing,
And my earthly life is over,
At the pearly gates I am standing,
As my pen drops to the floor,
I want my robe so white,
And my golden crown—Oh yes;
To see dear friends, and loved ones once more,
Lord, that would be the best,
I will pass on that mansion,
And, I would praise thee day and night,
If I can write one Poem again,
On through eternal Light!

Dedication: *My beloved brother, Leroy Hill*

Memories of Fifteen Years
Terri LeGrande
We've been thru a lot, good and bad
We've helped each other when times are sad.
Our love's grown stronger with each passing day
Your continuing support has helped me along the way.
I love you now and forever more
Even when married life seems like a chore.
Our three kids have proved our love is strong
You can see it in their lives we didn't go wrong.
Having your children—who look just like you
Has been something I was proud to do.
Anything you ask, I'll be there for you
Love you forever and I'll always be true.
Remember my love because it runs thru and thru
Therefore we have no reason to be blue.
I love you for an eternity and more
A happy 20 more years is what's in store.
Your children and I talk from our heart
When we say "We have loved you from the start".
I'll always love you, no matter what
Our love is closed forever, open and shut.

A Prayer
Barbara Martin
Dear Lord,

I pray for help to meet
my needs

I ask for strength to
carry out my deeds

Knowing with a faith
as strong as this

I'll never stray or go
amiss.

Dedication: *My sane sis, Betty Anne*

In The Throngs
M. Gill–Honczar
The crowding in of my life
I am Held
Perhaps in the middle
yet... Being Crushed
a multitude of thoughts crashing
grabbing the balls of my soul

In the throngs of life
I am Free
not only a ride
steering towards the fork in the road
Clouds of Issues
pecking at MY ME

held in the trance of a look
Throngs Unleashing
walls not really falling
I am the Strength
as the wind blows
seeking to tumble my life

Dreams of the Soul

Look
Sonya Denise Baker

Look at the cracks in the wall.
The roaches crawl.
Along with the junkies that
Linger in the hall
Waiting for the scraps we
Don't eat
While I wait for the man to
Fix the heat
Look at the dirty dingy
Living room floor
Which is also the bedroom,
Family room, this place has
Got me doubled over with gloom
While in the corners the spiders
Loom
Look at the ceiling O' what
A feeling to feel it falling into
Your child's' eyes as you sing him good
Night with ancient lullabies
Just look, look at this room.

The Silhouette
Audrey Clark

The waves collide with rocks of gold. Between the clouds and sky, an iridescent silhouette ascends with strength to fill my soul with energy. My heart replenishes itself with tenderness and patience. Each and every day, I know my guiding force above assists me through those obstacles that come my way. I know I'll never fight the battle by myself. When life pervades with darkness, pain, and hopelessness, I know that all I have to do is look above the clouds. The silhouette will shine its light of energy inside my heart and soul, defeating sadness, pain and hopelessness replacing it with passion, love and peace.

Confessor
Deborah White

Those we love, we use the worst
Trying so hard to do so well
We forget to stop and think.
How will it all come out?
It seems that what we need
Gets lost in the getting.
All we have left is the hurt.
We both know it's wrong!
Wanting to touch one another
But now knowing how,
We retreat.
He to his corner,
I to mine.
My pen is my confessor
Solitude is his
Pride, foolish pride, go away!!
Precious moments lost forever
In anger.

Dedication: *George, who is my rock*

The Dreamer
Jennifer Lea Lambert

Her eyes close and the last beam of sun disappears.
Her mind becomes untroubled and clear.
Gorgeous flowers are crowned upon her head.
No longer is she in bed.
She is dressed in a gown of the finest silk and softest pink.
Fairy dust flitters in her eyes and she blinks.
The girl is in the marshy world of the fairies.
No bigger than hummingbirds they fly around her in the mist.
One lands on her nose and bestows her a kiss.
Along with the kiss she is presented a gift.
The fairies begin to sing.
The melody is a soft enchanting thing.
A moonbeam shines down from the heavens in front of her,
Followed by a soft purr.
A magical beast stands there; the unicorn.
A myth she never once thought forlorn.
Together they walk through the magic of the universe all night.
When it's time to say goodbye she hugs him tight.
Her eyes flutter open and never again will she see him it seems,
She will, so long as she can dream.

The Dream
Lisa Morris

I had a dream the other night
and it gave me such a terrible fright,
I had to write.
The nightmare down, or was it a dream?
I think you know what I mean.
I was seen.
Flying through the air, giddy and free
I ruled the land and all looked like me.
How can it be?
No one is different, we're one and the same,
I never would ask to play such a game.
It started to rain.
It thundered! It bolted! It viciously poured!
What am I doing down on the floor?
I dream no more.

Eternity
Roger Dale Keeney

Clouds form and the wind starts to blow. Nature punishing us for what we owe. Birds sing to try to cheer the day. But thunder screams and lightning strikes from a distance away. All silent except the cracking of the trees from the blowing wind. The correction is coming. Is there no end? "Run for your lives!" the people say, "Death is coming, we're all going to pay!" Blinded by the dust in the wind, could it be God punishing us for what we have sinned? Nowhere to go. Nowhere to hide. Death is in front of you, behind you, even to your side. You can't run away. God has reached out his hand to you. Fall to your knees in tears and ask for forgiveness of your sins. To live eternal life in Heaven, this is what you must do. Let happiness come into your life. Let God take those thunder clouds away. Let God come into your life. Never leave Him. He will always stay. Let the birds sing in cheer. Wake up from your sleep. God is coming. He is close. He is near. For the day He passes judgment on you, you will know what you have done is true. Eternal life in Heaven. Think about it when you look up into the sky so blue.

Caught In The Storm
Donnie Watson
I was caught in the storm
And blown off my course
By the strength of the wind
And its mighty force
I was battered and beaten
And cast onto the shore
Then thrown back out to sea
To battle some more
I had no sense of direction
Without compass or sail
I thought all would be lost
I could do nothing but fail
When a still small voice
Seemed to thunder from the deep
Give me your hand
I haven't been asleep
But help yourself
When you think all is lost
And I'll do the rest
I died on the cross.

Spring
Haydn Dobby
Spring is like a lady,
The bearer of new life.
Lambs start gambolling gaily,
While birds sing like flutes.
Flowers come out of their sepals,
Like blobs of paint on green paper.
animals come out of hiding,
Like flowers from their buds.
Green trees reach up to the sky,
Like many fingered hands.
The sun high up in the sky,
Is like a bright beach ball,
Roasting the clouds like marshmallows.

SPRING IS HERE.

Repeated Insanity
Mary Lou Rutenberg
Nothing is what it appears
but with the naked eye exactly what it is.
Shameful destruction of the planet
all life gouged by the shovel of greed;
foul use of splendid mentality.
In a hundred years we have done what
millions of years have not,
destroying even the food we subsist on,
the air we breathe.
The hammering of the battlefield and
gases laid on our brave young soldier,
while strategists profit for the stupid ego.
Let the leaders die on heroic soil.
The land belongs to no one but future
generations for their lifetime use;
and what an appalling legacy for the want of
petty luxury conceit wrought.
START NOW, put to use what is at hand.
Reverse the taking, as centuries of civilizations revealed,
or the cruelty will come back on our heads.

Mother's Quilt
Felicia Gail Gibbs
Long ago, a beautiful quilt was made
By strong hands of a woman
Who's love would never fade...

Each piece was sewn with love and care;
A tiny part of a family's heritage.

Some pieces were made no doubt,
From clothes we wore.
It has sat quietly and aged gracefully over the year
It is now on my bed for all to see...
A small piece of my Mother's memory,
It means so much to me...

Words cannot express the security
it holds for me...

I only hope it lasts forever.
Dedication: My mother, Ruby Mabel Sudbrock

Rest Dear Ocean Rest
Tiffany Casper
The ocean is like its own world.
Salt filled water waves of foam.
Vast with life beneath its cover.
Translucent
Blue, pink, iridescent fish.
In, Out, In, Out, In, Out, In, Out.
Its tide is like life,
In with the new,
Out with the old.
The young children play upon your shore,
As the old rest your rough sand,
From broken shells, as broken promises.
Choppy waters rough as the sun sets.
Rest troubled water waves rest,
Rest like a sleeping baby, REST.

Heaven's New Angel
Stephanie Lynn Wise
There's a new angel in heaven's band
She just joined today
She left with the one with nail–scarred
hands,
I knew she couldn't stay

The chorus needed a little help
They knew she'd know the tune,
So the leader of the band
Let her join the chosen few

They saw her shining in her pain
Covering her sorrow with a smile,
They knew that she'd be the one
To bring joy to that heavenly choir

So amid my tears and sorrow
I think upon these things, and
If I strain my ear to listen
I can hear a sweet angel sing.

Dreams of the Soul

Your Love
Alexandra Moser

In this world of hate love will find you soon enough
but dive on in before your time the sea you'll find is rough
and when you see the one you find to be your fate
know that love is not a thing one can extricate

It will come upon your breathing in
now love you're breathing out
you'll never feel it creeping in
until for love you'll scream and shout

Love is patient, love is kind
and forgives when you are wrong
listen carefully and you will find
every lover singing the same song

Only in we am I me
and in us I'm truly whole
only with you can I be
in my only lifetime role
your love

No Reasons
Jason Dunn

Whenever I'm around, She's always friendly.
No matter what I did, she continues to smile.
When the world despises me, She's still compassionate.

She implores when I am distraught.
Her presence uplifts my spirits.
I seek her out, so I can glance at her friendly face.

I talk too her, so I can hear her wonderful voice.
I appreciate her more than words can say.
I ponder, "Why does she do this?"

I implore other's input, but I still can't seem to understand.
There are endless questions and many ideas why,
But, there are still no reasons.

Valentine To A Lost Love
Paula Allen

My dearest love, my darling one;
Why did you leave me all alone?
You promised me love undying,
And now, I can't even stop my crying.
You said you wanted to make me your wife;
Now there is no end to my strife.
You said you would erase my past
By showing happiness and love that would always last.
In my mind there are such happy times;
Friends, places and the tastes of fine wines.
We loved each other both night and day,
But now, my love, you've gone away.
The decision you requested and I made so well
Has caused me countless hours of hell.
I hope in time we can forgive each other,
And maybe become as sister and brother.
But for now, my dear, you've broken my heart
As I've expressed in this form of art.
And yes, dear friend I'll remember the dove,
But sometimes, it isn't enough just to love.

The Garden
Ruth Brown

The garden it's called, it's more
like a jungle. I smile every day.
My lips are parted but it's only to
keep from telling someone off.
The things that are planted here,
the seeds. Every new boss wants
to do things his or her way. You plant
a flower today. They want to dig it
up tomorrow. My work that I
was assigned to do is not good enough for
the boss. Everything must be changed
to his liking. They told me that everything
in the garden would remain the same.
To my disbelief things change and some
things remain the same. Job title changed.
You walk past me with your off–the–wall
smile. But I know you are only
out to change the gardens. Flowers
grow and seeds are planted over.
The garden will remain the same.

Smile Girls
J. N. Canter

There was a young senior citizen, who some called cousin Kate
She joined the crowd who have had a hysterectomy, but not to late
Here we stand some stout, some slim and proudly announce, we have
had our hysterectomy.
Gallantly we stand and vocally declare, who needs that extra
baggage anyhow.
Now we can all join in and sing, we are not the girls we used to be
Since we have had our hysterectomy.
We are growing older and some should be getting gray, But
We are not dead since we have had a hysterectomy
We have plenty of time, there's places to go, much to see,
Even if we did have a hysterectomy.
come on Girls! Get a smile on your face, take your stance
For united we stand! and proudly announce I have had
a hysterectomy!

Happy Valentine's Day From A 4 1/2 Month Old Baby Boy
Isabelle F. Weber

I come in, I go out, never knowing where I go.
I see faces I know, I see faces I don't know.
Life is so strange – I can't figure out
Who I am, where I am or what it is all about!

My mommy, daddy, my grandma, my great–grandma, too,
My grandpa, my great–grandpa,
Cousins, aunts and uncles all love me it's true.
They are so silly when I make a face.
All I do is lay back and sit in my place.

They say I'm so sweet, and look so cute.
Now I ask you isn't that a hoot?
This family is silly, but lots of fun.
I think I'll stay for a long run.

I'm a very good boy, I don't wake up at dawn.
I just want to be your beloved SHAWN.

Dedication: Shawn, great–grandson and inspiration

Noteworthy Works

Growing Old
Oliver Kenneth Cole
Now that I'm turning old and gray
I try to remember my young past day

And as I sit here in my old rocking chair
Wrinkled is my face, gray is my hair

Here I am growing old
Not as brave, not as bold

I remember when I was only six
Down by the creek whittling sticks

With a fishing pole and my old straw hat
Down by the creek, there I sat

Now I'm growing old pretty fast
I know my days are almost past

And soon I'll leave this gay old earth
It's been a long time since the day of my birth

My Mother
Justine Foden
My Mother is very kind.
She also has a very unique mind.
I love her in every way, and
I'll love her each and every day.

My Mother
She's the best one I know.
She was there to watch me
grow.

My Mother
There is no word nor way
That I could say...

I Love You

I'm Thankful
Stephanie P. Reisnour
I'm thankful for my Barbie doll,
although I lost the shoes.
I'm thankful for my radio,
it does not play the blues.
I'm thankful for my piggy bank,
though I lost the cork.
I'm thankful for my crystal ball,
although it does not work.
I'm thankful for my dog,
although it is lazy.
I'm thankful for my dolls,
but they look pretty crazy.
I'm thankful for my dresser,
although it is white.
I'm thankful for my bed,
although I have to make it every night.
I'm thankful for so many things,
except for Brussels sprouts.

Dedication: Auntea Ann for the Barbies

Time's A Cheat
N. Greenbank
I'm eighteen, and I'm slender.
My waist is trim and neat.
The look in my eye is tender,
The smile on my mouth is sweet
And then I look in my mirror
And I know that time's a cheat!

For though inside I'm eighteen
My mirror tells me "No!
You're seventy dear, and look it!
Eighteen was years ago!
You're not that slender girl now dear,
And your hair is touched with snow!"

They say that the young are careless
Of the precious days of youth,
That it's not till you're old you realise
How quickly time flies. It's the truth!
Youth's gone forever for me dear!
Just pour me a gin and vermouth!

A Perfect Time
Mary Weeks
Early in the morning, the beautiful sun
flowing in, the fog covering an almost dry
river, that will soon come to life, with water
running down the sand and rocks, looking for
new adventure. The dew dropping off the roof
and sparkling like diamonds in the grass, so
many diamonds. The wind bringing the trees to
life with their leaves dancing in the
sunlight. Dogs barking in the distance.
Birds and Squirrels preparing for a new day.
Just like God gives us a new chance each day
for new hope, new adventure, new meaning, and
most of all the reason to love. Like he has
loved us, to have given us all these precious
things.

Uncertain Destiny
Gilbert Briones
Every moment, every word;
every thought ever heard
– all encompassing –
stems from the brain.
Look around you and you'll see
that the mind can do wonders.
This much is plain.

We have erected skyscrapers
and monuments
for the eyes to feast upon and marvel,
but we have yet to tame the tempest.

Fate is like the wind,
it does not know which way
it will blow;
like a lost traveller,
it does know where it will go;
like destiny,
it is beyond our control.

Dreams of the Soul

Slow Dawn
James Herring

You woke me at 4 a. m.
Like a ship riding easy at a dock, you nudged me awake.
And though alone, you were every where;
I'm sure I awoke calling your name.
I breathed you in, I breathed you out
I felt you watching me, and your image was burned into me.
Long, dormant feelings awoke and I knew;
you had touched my soul.
The more I tried not to think about you
the more you were there filling up the room.
I can remember every brief touch,
like being in the sun, warm on my skin.
I see you so clear before me;
like a ghost, watching me.
I hear your voice in my ear;
and I am enthralled.
The more I tell my heart to slow down,
the faster it speeds up.
The more I try not to think about you, there you are;
filling up my head, my heart, my soul.

Home To Stay
Bernadette C. Curran

The ocean seemed to meet me as I walked along the strand.
As the waves they crashed against the rocks I could feel
the gentle breeze.
For I was very young when I left my native homeland.
But I always remember the promise that I made, to come back
someday to the place where I was born.
Many years have passed since then now I have returned.
And cherished are the memories of this country that I've
always known and loved.
With tears of joy and mixed emotions I stood for a moment
to look out at the sea.
While the sun it shone upon the golden sand, I feel happy
in knowing that this time I'm home to stay.

Dedication: In loving memory of James Bernard Lawrence Curran, Jr.

Faith And Prayer
Harold L. White

"He has thrombosis, " Doctor said, "I don't know if he'll survive!"
But I prayed for God to help me and today I'm still alive;
At times I did not feel too good, but my faith did not waver,
A faith in Him lives above, our blessed Lord and Saviour;
"Have faith, " He said, "Nothing's too great, if in Me you believe
If you but pray and ask of Me, My blessings you'll receive; "
The doctor cannot understand how well I feel today,
He does not realise it is because to God I pray;
This is proof beyond all doubt that God does answer prayer
If you but only look around, the proof is everywhere;
Of course I know I must take care, as things must still improve
But having faith in Him above, can even mountains move;
I know that others prayed as well for my recovery,
To know so many really cared, was a great discovery;
If anyone should ask you "does God really answer prayer?"
Just point me out to them and say– "Well, there's your answer there. "
The moral here is clear to see – faith conquers all,
"Have faith" – surely these words are but a simple call;
Faith and prayer go hand in hand, so be without them never
So praise the Lord from now henceforth, forever and forever.

Death
Erika Pascoe

It is expected in a world full of hate,
some are killed by their own mate.

It comes in many different disease
cancer, herpes, and HIV's.

It can be cured by two things,
that is love and heaven's ring.

So when it is time to go,
don't be afraid, just go with the flow.

God loves you with all his might,
he'll give you wings so you can take flight.

Just remember people care for you,
even though you are invisible too.

And one day we will join you up above,
just 'cause you remembered our sweet love.

Taps For Nam
Victoria J. Cocco

Softly, the bugle blows,
Telling what he only knows.

A man to some, a child to others,
He gave of himself
Like many of his brothers.

A black marble stone now holds his name.
A monument to soldier's pride
And a nation's shame.

Softly, softly the bugle blows,
Telling what he only knows.

Dedication: Mario and Terry Cameron

My Gallant One
Tracy A. Wuest

Where did you go my gallant one, did you ever really exist, or were
you simply a dream. Could your love have been a figment of my
imagination. You seemed so real that I thought I had touched you.
There was flesh and warmth or so I thought.

You touched my heart, my mind, my soul, my whole being. You
seemed so real, so warm and tender.

You gave me love and taught me to give and receive. I felt like a
Goddess from all your care, the love you gave was all so pure, to last
through eternity with a burning glow.

The dream ended abruptly, I woke only to find the man in my dream
laying beside me. Only this one is cold and with piercing eyes. Still
filled with beautiful words, yet nothing you did ever confirmed those
words. Compassion and compromise have gone out of your heart. As
well as your love and your passion.

Where have you gone my gallant one. I miss you, I love you and I
wish we were one...

Noteworthy Works

My Last Wish
G. Guest

If I were to die tomorrow
Here's what my last wish would be
That my wife would be broken-hearted
And die right here beside me.

That would be the perfect end to my life
Being buried here alongside my wife
A fitting tribute right to the end
To my wife, my lover and my best friend.

No amount of riches could buy her worth
She's been the finest, sweetest person on this God's Earth

If there really is a heaven above
I'll walk through the gates with the woman I love.

My epitaph would read.

Here lies Gordon and Betty, his wife
So in love in death as they were in life.

Walk With Her
Aldrema Smith

Walk with her, not in front nor behind.
Give her that strength to feel special inside.
Hold out your hands not to defeat, but to help
her stand on her own two feet.
Nothing is too hard to accomplish here,
especially when she's sincere.

Soon she'll get the message loud and clear.
"I'm not just one in a crowd. I'm a very
special child.
I have people who care about me.
I want the world to see I'm me.
Not a duplicate in any form.
I'm an original.
I've come into my own. "

Sarah Sitting
Christopher Koch

The highways spill westward off the coast;
let me lay you down tonight someplace east from here:
Aluminum skies– standard–,
steel rivet seams,
and clouds, like fat cattle, drift emptily to the block.
Thick, you move into me cliche
and in a drink we share some misty velvet
We decompose the composite selves.
The rust swims down the pipe
and we move free and run through
the loud layers of the motel room:
six bucks an hour for just–visible conversation.
six bucks for words that dry up into
every second and only the room grows one hour deeper.
one loud layer of the dead skin of human history:
spin it; stitch it with steel rivets.
you tell me I need no more than that,
(it's warm today, even through the rust) and
I believe you.
when the cows open up.

I Am A Baseball Player
Michael Retzer

I am a baseball player.
I wonder if I'll be a Major League baseball player.
I hear a crowd cheering.
I see a home run.
I want to be the best baseball player ever.
I am a baseball player.

I pretend I'm a Major League baseball player.
I feel a baseball.
I touch a baseball bat.
I worry about striking out.
I cry when we lose a Championship game.
I am a baseball player.

I understand I am a baseball player.
I say to be the best you can be.
I dream of being in the Baseball Hall of Fame.
I try to be the best I can be.
I hope I play in a World Series game.
I am a baseball player.

Lightening
Gina Marie Billino

The rumble of the bass–drum thunder rolled across the sky, drawing me out into
the humid air of the sultry July day. I stood in the midst of my lush backyard, my eyes
drawn inexplicably to the blood red sky above. I'm mesmerized by the brilliant white
lightning illuminating the dark red sky, lost in the pure magic of nature. I stood
bewildered by the sheer force and wonder of Mother nature's power as my trance was
shattered for only an instant by the warm drizzling rain. I looked directly up into the
ethereal red sky, closed my eyes, and let the rain run down my face...

Dedication: Ms. Betz and Mrs. Flanary

Where Do I Begin
Sarah Taylor

I want to do something, but I don't know how.
I want to be proud of that, and take my bow.
I want to do nothing, but I don't know how.
With the many problems of all of ours now.
I want to help someone, but where to start.
My troubles, and I still need to part.
I know everyone, and that's all right.
But to be known, would raise my might.
I want to love someone, but I don't know who.
He'll be the perfect man, but I'll still not know what to do.
Where do I begin, I can't decide.
If I ever said I was happy I must have lied.
All these answers I just can't find.
Let me lie down to rest my mind.
Someone once told me that you just have to wait.
The only thing that can help is your fate.
So where to begin is put aside.
Fate is a rule made for people to abide.

Dedication: Grandpa John, my inspiration, teacher...

Dreams of the Soul

Just Say It
Stacy Berry

Thoughts cross my mind
and it's only you I find,
the feelings run deep inside
with my question being why?
Happiness is everything to me
what exactly do you see,
what is your dream to fulfill
there has to be desire inside, still;
sweaty palms are only the beginning
so much passion we have living,
with so much to offer each other
it seems only a waste we can't be together;
Maybe our worlds are in the wrong direction
never to meet again and this is a learning lesson,
is this the way it must remain
with feelings so strong and nothing to say,
can we really go separate ways
walk away from what we shared one day;
I can and will if you would just say
tell me goodbye, I'll turn and walk away.

Untitled
Patricia Ann Moore

Since you came into our lives
What a difference you have made!
The joy you have given will never
Ever fade.
So perfect a girl! anything goes
From your downy head to the tips
of your toes.
What did we do before you were born!
As soon as we saw you our hearts
Were Reborn
What a rejoicing that red
Letter day, oh! what a beauty
"Our Little Sun–Ray"

Dedication: Shannon Laura Moore, our joy

Take the Time
Wanda Collins

Let's take the time to love our neighbor,
a rose may express "I care about you".
A flower falls, then crumbles sweetly,
yet we often forget just where it grew.

The flowers we give bring meaning
and pleasure, so let's take the time
our hearts to renew.
And to honor the one who created
them all and can touch every
bud with the morning dew.

Let's take the time to love our
neighbor giving hope for the
future, yet not ignoring the past.
A flower falls, then crumbles sweetly,
but what's done in love is destined
to last.

Dedication: In memory of Reta Flemens

I Am A Child
Sonja Clarke

I am a child
Help me, guide me.

My world is new
Share with me, teach me.

Understand my thoughts
Listen to me, know me.

Share in my joy
Play with me, cuddle me.

Celebrate my achievements
Encourage me, praise me.

Show me my boundaries
Be firm with me, care for me.

I am a child
Respect me, love me.

Untitled
Cindy K. Bell

Trees, trees, blowing in the
breeze! Oh, how they look so
content as they sway to and
fro. I wonder what they say
when their branches bend down
so low. Their leaves seem to
whisper to each other as they
rustle and shake in the air. At
times they look as though they
are hanging on for life, as a
big gust of wind comes along.
But other times they just float
and ride with the breeze, as if
to say — this is the life – relax
and enjoy it!

Mirror Of Life
Sharon Anthony

Our life is but a mirror – a reflection of who we are... An image of all that life has dealt, and how we've come so very far... God keeps our life in balance, to guide us as we grow... A blending of tears and sorrow – with love and laughter, strengthening us so...
Why do some have burdens many, yet feel there's but a few? And why do some with blessings abundant, pass through life without a clue?
And when the storms in life surround, and drench our hearts with pain... Why is it one shall see a rainbow, while another sees only rain?
Could it be that only through our eyes, the challenge large or small – That we may soar as high as eagles, with broken wings, or take a fall...
The answer I think must surely lie, deep within our very core... And those who find the richest treasures, on this journey, do not keep score...
For the image we see in the Mirror Of Life, is not, "Did we win or we lose?" But counting our blessings far more than our losses – And making a choice to choose...

A Grin On The Face Of Infinity
Blake Butler

held forever breathless by razor–sharp hope
the diamond grasp of her unending gaze
delicate smiles and enchanted fingertips
the silence of angel's wings and this tender beauty everlasting
precious scarlet yearnings — the ways in which we imagine
painting emotions of every shade
focusing the sweet divinity upon eyes of the crystal horizon
strung upon the ghostly ropes of solitude
innocent flames within the sway
framing her in satin desire
maudlin aches of never and tomorrow.
my endless, Mothering heart, and her,
dissolved within a sad symphony,
surrounded by the echo of a feeling—
to fly amongst lightning and kiss the gleaming lips of chance
to murder our tears and blow away the dust of the moon
to build forever from rainbow milliseconds
to swallow velvet rapture
to whisper
to dream...

Riches And Rags
Kelda Barnes

She stood tall in a posture, so to impress the mirror,
And delighted in the elegance of her own rich furnishings
And clothes. For had not her public proclaimed her an angel?
She didn't know their praise was not correct, but naive

She stared out the window, eyes intent upon the crowd
And secretly mocked their ill–mannered upbringing
That she loathed, yet rejoiced in her feeling of vanity
And so humoured them, and bathed them in the light of good manners

I am, she thought, above them, for would I ever live the life of
A humble pig? (for she felt the pig a humble creature indeed).
She sighed in pity at their inbreeding, and closed tight
The adorned window, to indulge again in counting her riches,
Laughing secretly.

A Woman's Retirement
Shirley A. Marshall

A man can retire and begin having fun
But a woman's work is never done

A woman can retire, no more work to do?
How about the house, just waiting for you

Make the bed, scrub the floor
Vacuum the carpet, run to the store

Dust the furniture, wash the clothes
So much to do a man never knows

Fix the meals do the dishes
Where is that genie with your three wishes

Chore after chore, day after day
Isn't it fun with a man in your way

A woman's retirement you can easily say
Is nothing but work without any pay

To Be Free – A Voice From Auschwitz
Sarah Rasmussen

To be free
that is my wish
not surrounded
by the dead
the hungry
the sick.
To be free
that is my dream
not to be trapped in this cage
I want to be in school
running and laughing
I want to be with my friends.
To be free
that is my hope
not to be tired
I want to be strong
I want to live
I want to be with my family
not alone.
To be free.

The Enemy Within
James P. Walker

He had begun to grow forgetful of the enemy within,
For it was years since he'd suffered for his sin;
And he had imagined that he was safe now,
And that its talons could not wound him,
Could not torture him from within;
Yet such complacency was but delusion,
And once again he'd suffered for his sin.

And he had thought that he was king pin,
Free to come and go and always win,
Soaring above the dangers that lurk within:
Yet how wrong he was!
How arrogant, to forget that time is no protector,
To imagine that he could be so proud and never fall,
And never again ever suffer for his sin.

Untitled
Jane Helein

Pleased do not ask where I have been
Nor how it is I got here
I will simply be who you see,
All that you want me to be.
Do not pretend to know anymore
No lies, no games;
I know what my role must be,
I know where you will lead me,
And I will not show fear
Not while you are near.
I will hide behind the shadow
That darkens each day
Steer clear from curious eyes,
Hide within the pain.
You have no idea, for I cannot let you see
All that I am, all that I could be;
This pain is mine,
Untouched by your hands
It grows within my mind,
It smothers my heart.

Dreams of the Soul

Live The Life
Erin Aiello
Dance the Dance of a million words
Fly the flight of mockingbirds, Live your Life
strong and free, let the wind give you a chilly
breeze, I've swam, will swim have swum, I've
fed the pigeons got the honor roll, I've lived
life, have sung, In the darkest hours I
could run, I can walk, I can walk, I
can write a book, So I'll make a movie,
sing a song enjoy life one for all, Live
Life strong and free what's the meaning?
"Beats Me!" I see you, you see me It doesn't
matter I'm me, whether you have one friend
two or three It doesn't matter I'm free.
I can run, I can jump in the deepest emotions
of my own heart, Don't kick me because I'm
down but I'll get up without a frown
I'll live awhile then go on, I'll feel your gentle
hand caressing my sole, Don't bother helping
me you can't see, I'm on my own just
little old me.

The Beginning Of Us
Brenda Manjuck
Into this relationship we did go
With a promise to take it slow.
Before I take you as a lover
Friends we must be with each other.
We must learn to talk and trust
A relationship can't thrive on just lust.
With you I want to grow
To share my hopes and dreams,
and be with me when I am high and low.
I want you to take me under your wing
And protect me from everything.
Is this my darling too much to ask of you
For in return, I will give right back to you.
And as we watch the years go by
We will have a love that will never die.

Genuine
Nikki Kingham
The children cry in the dark of night,
the abuser has come within their sight,
and places a shadow along with its breath,
tonight there will be a sudden death.
The child was heard, but was nowhere to be seen,
for the darkness of night had already been,
and the soul of the child carried on sleeping,
but the mind of the child, forever, will be weeping.
for innocence had been taken once more.
For the child, self blame, and an affliction of war.
The child wants to speak but is made to be silent,
the monster is free, and has now become violent,
free, to destroy the innocence of others,
wrecking the lives of fathers and mothers.
A subject our nation will choose to ignore,
cause it hurts to re-open our closeted doors.
So the soul of the child will carry on sleeping,
protecting its adult from the monster still creeping,
through the corridors of life,
casting its shadow and blocking the light...

Good-bye For Now, See Ya
Eddie M. Williams
It's time to leave you now — Please
say you'll not cry –
Someday I'll see you where I'm
going— Bye and bye.

I've had a good life with you –
I really hesitate to go –
My suffering, as well as your
waiting, could be over now – If only
you would say so —

Old friends and family I'll
meet, soon – sometimes it's hard to
wait – Don't cry now, soon I'll
see you, at that gate –

You keep busy now, try to enjoy every
minute – Don't ponder on my going – It's
all past. Just keep going on the fact, I'll
see you at last. See ya —

When
Susan Hopp
You loved me when
The dew was on the hill
And the wind stood still

You kissed me when
The moon was high
And the wind swept by

But I loved you when
The storm was strong
And the day was long

And I kissed you when
The tide ran out
And the birds flew about

Imagination
Rene Vera, Jr.
Thoughts are flowing through my mind like
Leaves across the sky
Wonders, worries, cares and dreams
Are drifting by and by
Foolish thoughts are passing by
I'm trying to let them go
Good ones will be coming now
Lined up in a row
Thinking now, wondering when,
This daydream will be gone
Sometimes when I close my eyes
A minute seems so long
I let it go and it comes back
Just like a boomerang
It soars up high above the sky
And searches all the land
I think I'll bring it back right now
So I can get some rest
'Cause when I get a good night's sleep
It works the very best.

Noteworthy Works

In Praise To The Firemen
Thomas Chew
Here's in praise to the firemen—
and the special lives we live...
We volunteer our time—
and when called for unselfishly give...
We train very hard—
for a dedicated cause...
Because we know that one mistake—
and someone's life will be lost...
We may race to the scene—
with our blue lights flashing...
For some drivers who were careless—
and end up crashing...
Sometimes our lives are complicated—
as only a fireman's wife could tell...
Here's in memory of our fallen brothers—
who died answering the final bell...
May God bless our firemen—
and guide all our ways...
And pray that we can make it home—
the next time we fight a raging blaze...

To A Skylark
Nassawanda Norman
I bring fresh showers for the thirsting flower
from the seas and the streams;
I bear light shade for the leaves when laid
In their noon–day dreams.

From my wings are shaken the dew that wakens
The sweet buds every one,
When rocked to rest on their Mother's breast,
As she dances about the sun.
I wield the flail of the lashing hail,
And whiten the green plains under,
And then again I dissolve it in rain,
And laugh as I pass in thunder. !!

Dedication: My mother and two boys

Growing Old
Vicki Hendrix
The old house seems empty now
An old couple live within
No one comes to visit
Except an occasional friend.
They seldom come outside now
They spend their time alone
And somehow seem much older
Since all the kids are gone.
The house once rang with laughter
Within and without
And the pitter patter of little feet
Could be heard all about.
The children all are married now
And have homes of their own
They seem to have forgotten
The old folks left at home.
It's sometimes easy to forget
The kind folks you once knew
So don't forget your parents
For they gave life to you.

The Angel Sleeps
Brian Chock
Inside, my blood pumps, my heart still quakes.
As I soak in the afterglow, my body still shakes.
I still can't believe the love we've just made;
The turbulence, the serenity of a symphony well–played.
And now that I stand in awe, what does she do?
She sleeps. My lady sleeps.

As I gaze at her smiling, supine on the bed,
Is it thoughts of me swimming dreamily through her head?
Yearning, my heart skips with the rise of her breasts.
Was it I she made love to before this deep rest?
And now that I sit in wonder, what does she do?
She sleeps. My lady sleeps.

Lying beside her, watching her sleep
Brushing the hair from her halo, her check.
She stirs! Do I wake her to again ride the tide?
No! Let her slumber! To her dreams, I oblige.
Secure in my arms now and what does she do?
She sleeps. My Angel sleeps.

Drunken Suicide
Carrie Southard
I'm looking out over the skies
Dear Lord please hear my cries
Can't you see the way I'm living here
Smoking my dreams and swallowing my tears
But really only living in fear
I'm calling out but no one seems to hear
Or really cares if I swallow this last tear.

Eyes hazey moving side to side
Do I know what I'm doing?
Yes I'm saying goodbye.

Is it the drugs all along
No it's lonely me
And now I'm gone.

A Tear–Stained Face
Chrystal Getzfreid
She looks in the mirror
only to find a reflection of
a young woman, that has
no future, no hopes, no dreams
Only a tear stained face.
A lonely heart crying out,
reaching out, and searching,
for someone to take her heart
and hold it without dropping it
or abusing it.
To reach out and take her hand
to bond with hers.
To hold her, to take her
fears, and her tears away.
All the pain is incomparable.
Still the only reflection she
Saw was of young woman
with no future, no hopes, no dreams.
with a lonely heart, and a cold hand.
Only a tear–stained face...

Dreams of the Soul

Pictures
Lesley Ann Franklin
Dabbing paint upon the paper
No picture there for us to see.
But who's to say there is no picture?,
As shapes and colours flood the paper,
A picture there may be.

In the mind of my small daughter,
A park full of swings and slides,
A house with a garden full of flowers,
Trees over which an eagle glides.

Who's to say there is no picture?
When one so young paints this way,
A mind so full of imagination,
Have we forgotten what it is like to play?.

Look once more upon the painting
See the shapes a child can see,
You will look in fascination,
For a picture there, you know to be.

A Tribute To My Private Students
C. R. Thompson
We were introduced,
"Pakistani" I said,
I looked at them,
They looked at me.
In that first look
We made our decisions,
We made our assessments.
We planned our reactions.
Since then I have become,
the wanted weekly visitor.
The welcome embraces my confidence,
Absolute comfort,
No penetrating intrusion felt,
We have grown up together,
A perfect situation

Untitled
G. B. Sayers
What frustration threading a needle
I've licked it and twisted it round
Held up to the light, and shut one eye
Thought I'd done it, but thread's gone by.

The eye of the needle seems smaller
Why make them so little says I
To thread a needle to darn a sock
What a performance, look at the clock.

Half an hour and I'm no nearer
To threading the thing than before
That's torn it, lost the needle
It's somewhere on the floor.

The hole in the sock is a problem
I'll get a new pair from the drawer
Until I get round to darn them
When needle I've found on the floor.
What a performance.

Colin's Dream
E. M. Keeler
Colin had a lovely dream
Which surely must come true.
He said "the finger in the sky
Was pointing straight at you!
This is a lucky omen,
We can't ignore such tips
So take these three round golden coins
And buy three lucky dips"
So we went into Caenarvon,
Which was the nearest place,
And bought three lucky tickets
Then homeward we did race
So we'd be back in Somerset
When the lottery draw was done
And when our lucky line was shown
They'd think the Welsh had won!
Now it's the following Saturday
And they didn't show our line.
I think those heavenly fingers
Just made a rude "V" sign!

Untitled
Philip White
Her eyes gleam and shine in the pale moonlight as I
lay down beside her
and kiss her sweet lips and whisper a soft good night.

We are both sort of young and the days go by so fast,
but there is one thing
I know and that is our love for each other will forever last.

She is the most beautiful person I have ever come across,
and to continue
life without her would be a great loss.

And as I lie next to her and dream off in space I don't think
of what could have been but only of what the future
sends and how sad I will be when my life ends.

Neighbours
Mabel Leatham Thomas
They sometimes glare, they sometimes smile,
Sometimes stop and talk awhile.
Some are good, some are bad,
What kind have you ever had?
I've tried them all in every place,
And studied each new different face,
Effusive ones, indifferent others,
Mamas, Papas, sisters, brothers.
Some are loners, what a pity,
Must be lost in this big city.
Big and brassy, lots of noise,
Garden full of trash and toys.
Nice ones now, stop and chatter,
"Come for coffee, have a natter".
They make us laugh, they make us cry,
But most of them we can't deny...
Are there for us in times of need,
And very often sow the seed
Of friendships that will never pall,
Our neighbours... may God bless them all.

Noteworthy Works

A Pain Too Hard To Describe
Lynne Gotting
There's a pain in my heart, too hard to describe
It comes when I'm yearning for you
And though I'm so glad that I'm still alive
I do wish that you were here too!
If wishes were horses, beggars would ride
And impossible dreams would come true
But although I've had those impossible dreams
They don't stop me yearning for you.
So I cry once a day, every day, all day long
As a way of releasing the pain
I even forget just where I belong
Till the hurting has eased once again
A year – is the period most people quote
When things will begin to change
I want to believe them, but, on that note
I find myself crying again.
What else can I do, what more can I say
This cycle just keeps going around
I try hard to break it – I long for the day
When I can change my Cross for a Crown!

Star Filled Dreams
Diana L. Dalke
I watch the world
through curious eyes
and wonder up at star – filled
skies and dream about
the wondrous things
tomorrow promises to bring
I keep my secrets, hopes
and dreams tucked far away
on bright moonbeams
and out beyond horizons far
I journey to new worlds unmet
with treasures undiscovered yet
my dreams take me
where rainbows are
when I follow my own star.

The Good Soldier
Carole Carter
here lie the bones
of a fallen man
flesh blood
this hill was his
to take
he believed

here lie the eyes
of a fallen man
barren cold
liberty my good son
he believed

here lie the memories
of a fallen man
lover, Father
for God and country
he believed

the good soldier

The Ocean Blue
Sarah Marquer
The waves are rolling,
Time and again,
And I feel a sensation,
As if the sea were my friend.
It's peaceful and calm,
And you can feel the joy,
Oh what fun I am having,
As if the sea were my toy.
I sit on the beach,
The sand colored white,
It is soft as silk,
Oh what a beautiful sight!
The music around me,
Are the dolphins and whales,
Their singing is superb,
No orchestra could compare!
Now look beyond the animals,
Look at what is true,
Look beyond the crashing waves,
It is the Ocean Blue.

The Postal Privilege
Edward Brunton
Great Privilege of Postal Workers,
Patron Saint, The Archangel Gabriel,
Who carried The First Christmas Greeting.

Great Privilege of Postal Workers,
With the penitence of Advent,
Their long labors of Christmas
Have always been linked.

Great Privilege of Postal Workers,
Whose Clerk–Hands and Carrier–Feet
Work The Wings of An Angel
Bearing Millions of Messages
Throughout The Angelic Season
Of Gabriel's Ave Maria!

White Lilies Of Peace
Susan Davies
Excellently a most stylish flower,
Of purity and peace in as much I sense a tower,
Standing graciously upright needing much light,
Erect stems establish them tall and strong,
That they may stand peaceably so long,
With poised dignity and elegance,
Like a warrior's spearhead steeped in virtuosity is it's stance,
Demanding righteousness fair play and chance,
For all to see in a single glance,
Resembling also the nib of a fountain pen,
Reminding us of words written by women and men,
Many written words have flair and panache,
Not hastily put down in a flash,
But polished to perfection to add a dash,
Of brilliance and be an exception,
An emblem of unblemished perception,
Coloured milky white like the paper on which I write,
Lily so white growing in the light,
What a glorious sight always opposing smite,
May weapons do no harm for the pen has much might.

Dreams of the Soul

Heaven
Stanley Williams

My little child is only seven,
But she said to me one day,
"Daddy dear, where is heaven?,
Is heaven very far away?, "
Heaven's far above in space,
The streets are paved with gold,
It's such a wonderful, wonderful place,
So everyone is told.
No beauty on this earth compares,
With what's in heaven above,
There's pretty flowers everywhere,
Which our Jesus loves.
I looked into her little eyes,
The words were hard to say,
I said, "You go there when you die,
And angels guard you night and day".
Her eyes were dim with tears,
When she said, "I'm only seven,
But now, I have no fears,
For when I go to heaven. "

Doing Time On 8th Street
Karen Irene Choiniere

What do you do about the pain
What can be done before the rain
Do you take a toke or is this all just a joke
They say resist and work with your best to avoid the test
What happens to the child with a cold look in his eyes
Mamma's in jail
Daddy's on dope
No one's left to care for me
They're prisoners of a crime but I'm doing time
What do you do about the child who's lost among crack and dope of no one's cruel joke
Is it the pushers fault or is it mamma's and daddy's fault
Cause Mamma's in jail
Daddy's on dope
Help with my pain ease the crime for I am the one doing time.

Forsaken
Angela Mathieson

Never more
To think
Our eyes are mist–ringed moons
Orbiting the silver–starred same planet

Never more
To dream
Our thoughts alight as one
On some green mythic hill

No words I have to make you stay
No transmutation: black to grey
The ignition key turning
My grief–filled heart yearning

And the blackbird sings to the empty street
Eternity
This unrequited love

Never more

My Little Dog
J. B. Hall

I had a dog a little dog he was my best friend
That dog looked after me right to the very end,
He could not stand the pace because he was
getting old,
Now he is in dog's heaven or so I have been told,
My dog comes back to see me he lies upon my bed
I cannot really take it in that my little
dog is dead,
I was driving home one foggy night, driving
very slow,
My little dog walked in front of me to show
me where to go,
I stopped my car outside my house I went
to pat my dog,
But I could not find him because of the
misty fog,
I went back into my house there I sat
and cried,
Because now I know and I am sure that
my little dog has died.

The Old And Wrinkled Hands
Myrtle B. Forbes

The hands are old and wrinkled now,
but many years ago,
They were very beautiful and soft.
They held the love so dear to her heart,
And held the young babies from this
beautiful love,
They held their own Mother's dear
old wrinkled hands, and gave her lots
of love until she went to heaven.
Now they hold the grandbabies so
tenderly and with so much love.
They are getting wrinkled and very
stiff from old age.
But the old wrinkled hands are
still full of lots of love.

The First Woman In My Life
D. Woods

She was there for me when I fell and grazed my knee,
I told her tales, but through me she could see,
She stood over the stove cooking, when I was hungry,
Cleaning and washing, as busy as she could be.
She dried my tears, and wiped my nose,
Scrubbed behind my ears, and had me smelling like a rose,
She got up in a morning and saw me off to school,
Helped me with my homework, so I didn't turn out a fool.
She'had the shoulder I always went to cry on,
The one who didn't like my first girlfriend, she wasn't wrong,
And on a lad's night out, when I got home so late,
She'd paced the floor for hours, and got in such a state,
She cried and cried the day that I got married,
And fussed and fretted about the baby my wife carried,
But how I made her swell with pride, when my first son was born,
The doting loving grandma, so emotional and overjoyed,
And as I flick through the album, fond memories come flooding back
Of that woman in my life who made sure nothing I did lack
Cause she was my confidante, my nurse, and my foundation
Someone I called Mother, not another like her in creation.

Noteworthy Works

My Prayer
Patricia Youngs

Dear Loving Father help
me to be strong
Especially when things
start to go wrong
Some days are good and
some are bad
Teach me to remember
the good I have had.
Please give comfort
for those in pain
Hope for the mourning
that death's not in vain,
Give food to the hungry
and water to drink
Stop cruelty to the animals,
how much lower can man sink?
You have a peaceful place
set aside for all
Dear God in Heaven,
Help us to hear your call. Amen.

Understanding Heart
Mel Jones

Words said with wisdom, care and love
for instruction simply to understand
Words to apply to the heart for knowledge,
so I could understand!
Words said in truth and with true love
from a Father's heart, to a son with a foolish heart
To ears that would not hear
Today on my Father's day all these words come back to me
the imparting of the knowledge of these words
I understand
the wisdom, care and love
that my Father put in each specially chosen word!
For a son to learn how to live,
Finally, these words of love made it to my understanding heart!
"Thanks Dad for the time it took to say these words of love"!

Common Drivel
Dannie Hughes

I get a certain anxiety at the state of
our society lambs to the slaughter springs
to mind,
But do the shepherds really know the proper
way to go and if and when we arrive what will
we find,
Political documentation seems to explain the
whole situation however grandiloquence was
never my forte,
I am sure that for the best for myself and all
the rest plain language would help save the day,
To drive the entire flock all agreeable and enbloc
then a common destination must be known,
An intelligent presentation would inform the
population and diminish their urge to rightly moan,
This is not a dig at diction heaven knows that would
cause friction but we need to understand just
what you say,
So keep your meanings clear so we comprehend with
cheer and please would you do it right away.

Life
Robert R. Parks, Jr.

Life is a test
We all must pass
If we fail we lose our class
When we lose we choose to die
And wind up making others cry
With their tears we feel the pain
and find we have nothing to gain
We lost the test
Causing us an endless rest
knowing this we choose to hide
keeping ourselves locked inside
Sparing others from the pain
knowing they have nothing to gain
Life is a choice we all must make
choosing what path we take
knowing one will lead to demise
we choose to hide from loving eyes
So we choose the wrong path
That leads us to the Lord's wrath
And we die alone and scared

The Wise Old Dragon
Briana Reissener

Slain by defeat.
His head at his toes.
The dragon can't eat.
For everyone knows.
How he had lost.
How he'd made a mistake.
It's like he's been double-crossed.
For he's the one in checkmate.
Everyone stares at the board.
That sits on the floor.
They crowd in a hoard.
As he looks on with dread.
The wise old dragon.
Had been beaten in chess.
By an eleven-year-old princess.

The Auld Tandrigee
E. Gallacher

Of all the places where e'er I roam
One in my memory will always be home
The neighbours they were oh so good
They shared their joys and sorrows even their food.
You chapped on the door and just walked in
And old Sarah Jane her yarns would spin
Tales she'd tell of her Granny's day,
Or maybe a dream that would last all day.
The work was scarce, the jobs were few
Near everyone was on the broo,
But when it came to Thursday man,
Old Gallagher would clash the pan,
Sausages would fry, the chops would sizzle
If Tam was in you had a giggle
On the door a card he'd display
No loans till after lunch today,
God rest the dead who once lived there
And offer up a silent prayer
For all the tenants of sixty-seven
And trust in God they are all in Heaven

Dreams of the Soul

Mellow Yellow Sun
Eric Jones
The city lights blind my eyes;
the stinging smell
of the newness of everything
sometimes hurts my soul.
There always seems like
too much to do,
yet not enough
to really ponder about.
Simple problems nip at me
in this complicated world;
maybe because I can't
seem to catch up.
But then I sit in a comfortable place,
with comfortable air;
and wonder why,
in relaxing amazement,
the sunset looks so particularly
beautiful that day.
I take my time to move about,
for I know there are things I can live without.

Take The Chance
Ken R. Weybrecht
The crystal, gleaming light dancing across the sky.
Two visions collide into a storm of
dreams, contemplating
Our most deepest thoughts turning them inside out.
True belief found within the soul brings abound
reality out.
To be seen in our actions not words. Fear
of unknown misery shatters hearts as the
ghosts in our closets find their way out.
Dealing with things is half the struggle,
Accepting it takes time, in which in context
is too short.
DEATH

Dedication: My true love, Tina Crockett

A Fantasy World
Tara Guida
Come into my world where you can see the fire
Come into my world where you can feel the burning desire
I'll take you up high into the bright blue sky
I'll make your life happy so you will never cry
See the flowers blossom and see the stars shine
See the blue mist, doesn't it look divine
Watch me grow stronger and proudly stand up tall
Watch me be the sun or fall like golden balls
See the water twinkling and see the fishes swim
See the magic person and never make a sin
Feel for freedom and reach up high for your goal
Feel deeper into your heart, feel deeper into your soul
Listen to the bees buzz and listen to the birds sing
Listen to the animals and listen to the lilies of the valley ring
Feel above the silver and feel above the gold
Feel above the hate and nothing will stay old
Take the time to laugh and take the time to smile
Take the time to think and I'll stay with you for a while
Reach for the heavens, for the light is what you can see
Reach further into your dreams and be all that you can be!

The Rain/God's Pain
Peggy L. Mayer
I hear the pouring of the rain, is it the tears of God in pain,
His pain of seeing everyday
the homeless, battered, those gone astray.

And finding no one with a heart to take the time
to come apart,
and give some love, concern or prayer
to make a better world out there.

For they are also sons of God,
they only need a little love that they might know
He loves them too,
won't you ask the Lord what can I do?

To make a difference in their lives,
to help them better to survive the pain and agony of life,
the husbands, children, battered wives.

Yes, our God cries out in pain,
and sometimes tells us in the rain.

Margaret Ellen
Harry Craddock
A Father's joy can be a girl or a boy,
And I was blessed with a daughter.
Now she has been blessed with a child of her own
And her name is Margaret Ellen.

I am so full of pride
Of my daughter and child
My head is really swellin'.
Perfection and beauty has come on the scene
In the name of Margaret Ellen.

As she grows older and wiser of life
She will do as her Mother has done,
Bring pride and joy to her Grandfather's life
Sweet beautiful Margaret Ellen.

The Sensitive Soul Of A Child
Dixie L. Little
A child's soul – like a lovely rose
it thrives in the presence of God
Climbing from infancy – and slowly grows
to heights in his same strong bod…

Alertness of kindness, under tender care—
—If neglected, is crude and wild—
Like a cared–for plant, so nurtured and rare,
transforms this sweet soul of a child…

We must be there to give his fair share
of tenderness and abundance of love—
Never lacking in his life–long care,
Remember, this is YOUR little dove!

A source of pride when his leaves unfold –
with a disposition oh, so mild —
It's a pleasure to see strengths untold
in this sensitive soul of a child –
in this sensitive soul of a child.

You Are
Emma Khalid

You are my sun,
with your sunny smile.
You are my stars,
with your twinkling eyes.
You are my days.
You are my nights.

You are fire,
keeping me warm in your embrace.
You are water,
keeping me cool with your grace.
You are air,
keeping me alive.

You are the wind blowing,
urging me on, softly.
You are the river flowing,
urging me on, softly.
You keep me going,
on and on...

Homeless
Laine Burch

As the lonely earth becomes still and cool
And animals take shelter for the night,
Soup kitchens begin to close at the church.
A small child's eyes grow big with unknown fright;
He turns to his Mother for some support,
She is weakened by sickness and cold.
The courts are keepers for her husband
And her parents too old to help
And love their daughter and baby more.
Snow blankets the streets in soft powder
On sneering and unforgiving streets.
She knows she has to try the store once more
And rummage for change to buy food and birthday treats.
The cold, deeply encased in the hearts of others
Should turn to warmth to love our brothers and sisters.

Stand Up America
Margaret Becknel

Stand up America, get on your feet
Our flag is passing by
Remove the hat from your head
Honor our country and the dead
Rivers of blood have flowed
They died so very young
Life had just begun
Dreams left unfulfilled
They gave unselfishly for you and me
That generations to come can be free
Our flag is not a colorful rag
It is freedom, peace, love, hope,
Opportunity and more
Our borders cannot hold
All that knock at our door
Be thankful we live in the best land
In all the world
Love, protect, cherish it
As others have done before
God bless America forevermore

Warriors
Donna Kramer

Fill us with your Holy Spirit
Your spirit of power and might
So we can march forth as your warriors
Enabled to fight the good fight
The battle is constantly raging
Our enemy stands at the door
With fiery darts he's attacking
And at times we feel we can't endure
But the spirit that's living within us
A warrior He makes us to be
So let's put on the armor God fashioned
And march forth toward victory
Sometimes we get pierced with an arrow
We grow weary and let down our shield
But the word of God will revive us
And the wounds we received are soon healed
The enemy can't stand against us
When we wield our mighty sword
The victory's already certain
For the battle belongs to the Lord

Moods Of Life
Phyllis A. Lewis

Of two entwined together their moods seem never to run the
Same

Although love is there it seems a task to do for each other
What they might ask

One is always at fault in the mind of the beholder even
Though you think it would change as one gets older

Of women there are moods each month upon which everyone
Agrees but what of men they have them too which only a woman
Sees

As each goes on as man and wife you say to yourself well
These are the moods of life

Outside Lookin' In
Yolaine St. Fort

Outside lookin' in
Afraid to tap on the door,
where worldly people laugh,
dance the night away.

I am only a shadow
'cause that's how,
my soul remains pure.

Every time I attempt
to step in,
I see images,
Sunday dresses,
a flower bud,
The Holy Virgin.

I'm a shadow,
as pure as she.
Outside lookin' in.
That's my destiny.

Dreams of the Soul

33rd Street Sleep
Kevin Shlosberg
I feel your heart beat next to mine,
As thoughts of the city rush through my head.
There, we, two young —but matured— souls
Wander throughout the chaotic streets.
Timid me, with my head held low,
And you, queen of the night,
Adventure—seeker, Bold, Brave, Undaunted.
No fear runs through your veins; how I envy you.
And still, as you lay quietly asleep, I'm scared.
Scared of tomorrow and what it will bring...
Scared that my bed will be one less come morning...
Scared that you will find me a waste.
A waste of time.
A waste of experience,
For I am half the thrill—seeker as you.
Though, as the sun creeps through the shades
To reveal that glimmer in your eyes,
I still feel your pulsing body near
Giving me no more need
To relinquish to my fears.

The Heart, The Soul, The Mind
Ronnie Farley
The Heart,
The Soul,
The Mind,
All Equal Love,
And Love Is A Passion
Something never to let go of,
You Hold Onto It,
And Make It Your Dream,
For Where Your Dreams Are,
Your Heart Will Be Also
For The Heart Is The Flow,
The Soul Is The Feeling,
And The Mind Is Knowing...

Dedication: I wait for my Erin

Rainbows in the Spring
Erin Kimberly Fluharty
When your day seems dark and dreary,
You're as lonely as can be.
The dark clouds seem to gather,
Like a storm upon the sea.
When life, it seems useless,
All is lost, nothing to gain.
You realize it's spring, rain is near,
Much to our hearts delight,
And flowers will soon be in sight.
Spring is a special time of the year,
When a small voice whispers,
God sends rainbows after the rain.
When the fear of failure haunts me,
And no one seems to care,
My eyes look up to Heaven,
For I know God is there.
A rainbow is a promise,
The sun will shine again.
The dark clouds will soon be over,
God will send rainbows after the rain.

The Courage To Live
Barbara D. Harper
I want to be
An architect
Or, maybe not
Next thing on the list
A writer
Not that's my Mother's dream
What's next
What would I like to be
Maybe a Mom
But what would I do
Should I be what I have dreamed of so many times?
A Major League baseball player
When would I see my family
Would I like to be
What I like to see
A pilot and be free
Oh my
What shall I be
Oh I know
I will be them all.

Untitled
James Kubiak
Yellow lines pass down the center.
I enter an amber hallway of fame.
Touched by Whitman, Blake, and
others.
I come to thee, in excess of wants,
to pray,
and listen,
for your words.
Out of the hallway, a god of sky,
exits,
and I try to follow.
But I learn, I will never fly.
That is not my god, that who flies away.
And I turn left, and leave
on the ground.

Renewal
Bruce Schowers
Does my line seem still and stagnant?
Mindful of reproach, vengeful vigor
The din blares, blurts a discordant "twenty–four".

Resilience diminished, I clenched, I claw, I wait...
A mere epoch passes.
From behind and above "twenty–five" wails replete the hall.
Meals missed, loves lost, crimes committed
All in the blink of a geological eye.

Christen the date of a privileged licensure,
This, my day of annual trek
To the seething depths of bureaucratic bungle.
"Twenty–six" resonates to gasps and sighs.
Machinery at work, cost cuts. "Downsize the Department".
Featureless windows woefully barren,
Perpetuating the void.
I groan, silently scream.
I am "seventy–three"
At the DMV.

The Last Time
Joe McHugh

I had so much planned for today.
I was going to drop you off at day care,
But I woke up sick
And called the office.
"I might be in tomorrow." I said.
Then I called day care,
Said I'd bring you by in a day or two,
When I was feeling more up to par.
Now I want to hold on to you forever.
And I thank the Lord I got sick.
Because I don't think I could live without you.
There's not a day goes by I don't look into your eyes,
Seeing a spark of hope,
And a promise of a future better than mine.
Yet now I see more.
I see a future that many children won't have,
Because their parents weren't sick.
And having to work,
Dropped children off
One last time.

Another Boomer Turns Fifty
Louise Turkel

Ah twenty nine was no more,
Especially with children
That never believed in folklore.

I tried to make them guess,
But it was merely a daisy
That said "fifty no less."

Hide my holiday birthday?
With fireworks blasting it
Only meant lasting and lasting.

The celebration was simply for me
And along with my cards came the form
To join AARP.

A Trail Of Honor
Jim M. La Manna

Patriots standing together
Our watch as overseer.
Overseas and here
Clouds of war drew near
These storms became clear
Here after their reflections still remain
The winners and losers will wear on
Earth's grain.

Ashes become settled and life resumes
Clouds of the peacemaker return, to
Form our land with prism and sunlight.
Our winds remember the many forgotten.
And those last smiles on these gallant men.

Come now and journey on,
"Our trail of honor".
Walk in these cadence steps of history.
Learn and adhere a roll call of names.
This is how our great states were made.

Love Can...
Paul R. Schilling

Love can take you up so high
Love can also take you down so low
Love can make you travel the world
Love can also make you just stay home
Love can make you feel no pain
Love can also make your heart just break
Love can make you laugh and giggle
Love can also play the cruelest joke
Love can set you free
Love can also tie you down like a rope
Love can make you feel rich as a king
Love can also make you just go broke
Love can make your dreams come true
Love can also make you just feel blue
Love can...
Love can also...

My Shield And Salvation
Brent Fitzgerald

... My God is my rock, in whom I take refuge. He is
my shield and the horn of my salvation, my stronghold.
(Psalms 18:2–NIV)
He is the rock and my stronghold,
the salvation in my soul.
When I'm in need of help, he's there for me.
The shield for protection from my enemies.
I take refuge in his arms,
and holds me close and warm.
I want Jesus to deliver me from all my sins,
and take them all away like a blistering wind.
Let me walk in your faith, because the time is near,
and there is no time to wait.
I have come short of your blessings.
I have come short in your word,
I have come short in my journey,
and now I'm hurting.
But I know there is relief in sight.
You will come like a thief in the night.
Because you're my shield and my salvation.

Winter Time
Janice Miller

I love to walk a snow–covered lane
When the snow crunches 'neath your feet
And a chill in the air, makes you bundle up
And the fresh breeze smells so sweet

I like to ride in a horse and sleigh
Through the woods we go
We cross the bridge, and over the ridge
As the cold wind and snow does blow

As the sun starts to set
I head for home
In the fireplace a glowing flame
And soon wintertime will be gone
Once again it will be spring

I'll have to wait quite awhile
Until wintertime once more
And I will start all over again
As I have all the wintertime's before

Dreams of the Soul

Untitled
Jill L. Richards

I keep rediscovering who my real friends are,
They're not the ones you party with or go shopping with
It doesn't matter if the taste in guys is the same.
Sometimes it's even the ones you don't talk to for awhile
For in this silence the friendship is sheltered not
forgotten. My true friends are the ones who know they
can always count on me, even only with a smile. For this smile
holds all the feelings and memories from the past. A true
friend never forgets, never tells and knows when you need them.
They can read your eyes and set your heart free. A true
friend will always cause you to remember who you really
want to be. When a tear in your eye is all that is needed
to start their eyes drowning for your pain. There is a bond
between these kinds of friends that can't be broken by
time nor different experiences. Their souls are connected
and will walk down the same path forever.

Interest–Free Credit
Jonathan Hart

1. 2. 3 I am meant to be.
I am crawling. I'm stepping. I'm falling
4. 5. 6 I am learning tricks.
Responsibility is dawning.
7. 8. 9 I'm doing just fine.
I am bathed in a shroud of attention
10. 11. 12 I'm all by myself.
Not a whisper, not a glance, not a mention.
13 to 15, remember me?
I'm the boy you once held in your arms
16 to 20, going on 30.
My sensitivity slips from your palms.
You don't mean to hurt me, that's not your way
But I've something to tell you... that "I'm here to stay."
So take back your presents that come once a year
They are not worth me shedding a tear.
I have no need for your formality.
But once in a while for you to see me
Falling and stepping and doing tricks.
But for forgetting my name, you never shall fix.

Lost And Found
Kristen Ledford

As he stares through the window at the world outside,
he looks for the answers with eyes open wide.
Trapped in a world too big to control,
he feels lost in the crowd, on a downward roll.
His Mom abandoned him young and he lived on his own.
She did not see him again until he was grown.
Now he has questions that have been with him for years,
and he struggles to ask them as he fights back the tears.
Wonder and worry of his future and life
have made his face much graver than that of his wife.
After years of the streets, drugs, and the booze,
he almost gave up on the fight he thought he would lose.
All he ever wanted was a family and home,
but that dream seemed so distant, so hopeless, so wrong.
Now, thanks to a woman he met years ago,
his life is much brighter, no longer so low.
So staring out the window, thinking back on his past.
he realizes, for a reason, his life was meant to last.
Finally his dream of happiness had come true,
never to be broken apart by his feeling blue.

It Must Be Magic
Joseph Paul Ariente, Sr.

It must be magic
How inside your eyes I see my destiny
Every time we kiss
I feel you breathe your love so deep
inside of me.
And if the moon and stars should fall
They'd be easy to replace
I would lift you up to heaven
And you would take their place

To hold you
Love you
See you smile at the break of day
To touch you
Know you
Want you with me when you're far away

Lord Help Me
William Bradley

Lord help me,
to live my life,
to take care of my family,
and my wife.
Lord help me,
to always believe,
always be honest,
and never deceive.
Lord help me,
to make the right choice,
no matter what the circumstances,
to hear the right voice.
Lord help me,
to always be able to pray,
no matter how good or bad,
I felt that day.
And most of all Lord,
I need your help in such a way,
as to get through,
each and every day.

My Cousin Steve
Ryan Cottrell

Your fate is in your hands, only for you to decide,
we can't control what's in front or standing side by side
When the end comes no feelings are hid.
And we'll always remember the wonderful things you did.
When the tears are shed and feelings are spilt
You will be free of this world without any guilt.
Looking down over us, watching our every move,
Making sure we all stay in our little groove.
It's hard to believe one night ended all those years.
Among hours of sorrow and thousands of shedded tears.
Too bad it takes a death to make some people learn,
That in a single second your entire life can turn
Lying in a hospital, or maybe in a grave,
If you see the pain it causes step outside your cave.
Families torn down or even split apart,
Simply because one mistake can stop the beating of a heart.
After you have passed away and forever you are gone,
Never looking forward to the night and dreading tomorrow's dawn.
For it brings another day that we live without you,
But knowing that you miss us, we miss you too.

Noteworthy Works

Mirror Of Thoughts
Pam Woods
They told me I was ugly without giving it a thought
they must be right, they said it a lot

Could they have known how their words cut like a knife
that their uncaring thoughts would alter my life

I could not get the word ugly out of my mind
how could those that say they love me be so unkind?

It was then that I realized, I was just a mirror for
those that had spoke, it was their ugliness that
actually awoke

I am through believing their words, as they were never
meant for me, if they could look passed themselves, my
beauty they would see.

Get Well
Bonnie Brown
Now that you are all rested
And your patience has been tested
I hope in this card you'll find
A helpful thought to keep in mind.

We all love you very much
And really try to keep in touch
Although in our buy lives
We don't seem to realize.

But, when one's sick in bed
many thoughts go thru our head
That is when we stop and ask
what we could do to ease the task

So keep a smile on your face
I am sure time will erase
This episode of trouble
and may future happiness be double.

Moms And Dads
Alexis Manning
Moms are there because they care
Even when you fall.

Sometimes if you have a bad dream
About a shark called Jaws.

They're here to help you with your
Homework even though you're not a
Jerk.

Well that's enough talking about Moms
I think its time to get on Dads.

Dads are there because they care and they
Love you too.

They do a whole lot of things like clean
Your room, and when you're not at home your

Mom and Dad call and tell you they love you.

Mute
Shane Pennington
All my life I have been mute.
All I hear is nothing, is because I'm deaf.
All my life I communicate by using sign language.
All my life I have suffered through the public insulting me
because of my deafness.

To get my attention, just tap my shoulder.
For me to understand the TV, I have to use closed caption.
For me to understand the phone, I have to use TTY.
For me to understand other people who don't know sign language,
I have to communicate on paper.

All the problems that I suffered, doesn't mean I am a unhappy person.
I have family that I can communicate.
I have a family who loves me and cares about me.
I have friends who care about me.
Those are what I need for my deafness.

Night Into Morning
Yvonne Zorrer Ley
Upon retiring for the evening
I saw fireflies in flight.
Darting through the darkness,
Lighting up the night.

The little bugs were all in tune,
Serenading with their song,
And before I knew it,
It wasn't very long,

Before night turned into morning,
Just before the sun appears,
The little birds start singing,
Bringing music to my ears.

The flowers lift their sleepy heads,
The dew fades with the sun,
The soft breeze whispers a message,
That a new day has begun.

We Come From Different Worlds
Harry Husted
We met in such a strange way.
No way known better to all.
You are so sophisticated,
And I am plain.
You are a woman of many talents,
I am a man of so few ways.
We clash in nearly everything we are.
We come from different worlds.

You know no boundaries,
I have pure thoughts.
You strike the fancy free,
I long for commitment.
You walk on the wild side,
I look for solitude.
Despite these differences we do share love.
Even though we come from different worlds.

Dedication: My loving wife

Dreams of the Soul

Scattered By A Stranger
Athena Montoya
I skip from stoned rock on my own bare feet; Three–hundred fifty–nine days;
needless say I have not reached my destination to the other side of the shore: For
the day passed suddenly; As I walk into the night; on the deep blue sea; 'tis like if I
am being pulled by someone. I fall into the cold water; a hush as I gasp for air;
A tall lady dressed in black; a stranger who cometh within the wind; pulls me
back on shore, from where I started, by one cold touch to say that, her heart as
warm as the sun; her eyes are as green as a tree, her hands are as soft as cotton;
Nevertheless need not to thank her; upon death or life; three–hundred sixty days; so
scattered; for I was already there.

Missing You
Michele Chavers
My days go by at a turtle speed;
I long for you to fulfill my needs.
My nights go by at an even slower pace;
My heart cries out to see your face.

Every waking moment
You're on my mind;
Every dream I dream
You rule them every time.

Why–all of a sudden–did I fall so deep?
There's just something about you that makes my heart leap.
How–in a moment–could you make me lose control?
I think I'm starting to love you with all my heart and soul.

Every thought I think,
Every thing I do,
Every breath I breathe–
I'll be missing you.

Shining Lights
Jimmie Lilly Franklin
May my light so shine,
That you may see
The ruts that once
Were so deep for me.

May my light guide you
Through the stormy nights,
So your journey will be
Without fear or fright.

May your light keep shining
Within your own heart,
So that you and your God
Will ne'er drift apart.

And then when you come
To the end of your time,
May you leave a bright light
That will always shine.

To The Hale–Bopp Comet – March And April 1997
Ann Ffitch–Heyes
Burning comet in the night
Tail so long and streaming bright
Across the blackness of the sky
Did you bring those men to die.

Nauseous gases trailing long
Did you have a force so strong,
To take their souls to Heaven's Gate
for them to find their timely fate?
Bearing hard and deadly force
to try and find the higher source.
Is that music that you play?
and do I hear the words you say?
Will your calling ever stop
to take me to the Hale–Bop?
Must I really pack and go
to that hidden UFO?

Thief Of Dreams
Ruth Sewell
Reason has stolen my dream–world!
Fact has laughed at my wild delight
My joys and dreamy fantasies
Are but phantoms into the night.

I live with an imagined beauty
But step back to earth's glory too.
I somehow know evil
And shall vanish when all becomes true.

Still is there a good compensation
What offered return for reason is granted?
Exchange for my heart!
Faith's future supplanted?

In its dull imagination alone
There is a token
For reason I bow and become broken,
In the corpse of death and dust, and bone

I Fear Not
Marlo Bailey
I fear not the unknown–
When you are here with me.
Whatever the future holds for us,
I'm Content to let it be.

Like a precious gift your Love is,
That God has seen fit to give.
With you here by my side, My Love–
I fear not, this life I live.

Many times I've faced uncertainties
And endless hours of pain–
But with your love, you've made me strong
And I'll never cry again.

The heartache that came before you,
Now bitter memories I've forgot.
It was worth the wait and now I know
Because of you, Love, I fear not.

Noteworthy Works

Spring
Pauline Hales

Spring came early this year.
For a little space of time
The garden looked like
A tiny corner of Eden.
The garish colours of daffodils and tulips
Looked resplendent against the cool, green grass
The primroses peeped from under the forsythia
The blue tits found the waiting nesting box
Enjoy the moment
Soon the daffodils and tulips will fade,
Leaving unsightly foliage.
The lawn grass becomes crisp and brown
The predatory cat
Eyes the busy blue tits.
Death stalks the garden,
Hiding among the roses
And the bedding plants

My Teacher's Gift
Ginger Hill

My teacher's gift is a selfless one,
it is taught by our Father's holy son.
The most precious gift that can be given
reflects a love devised in heaven.

My teacher's gift is given to me
to help me decide what I want to be.
A doctor, a lawyer or fire chief,
the choices I'm given are beyond belief!

The special angel you will see,
taught me how to believe in me.
A special place in heaven is won
when your work on earth is done.

This humble gift is from me to you,
look at it often for memories renewed.
Your gift is a simple mirror you see,
reflecting the gift you gave to me.

Together Forever
Kathy Herdman

Swirling within my heart
We are together; yet apart.
In spirit you are always near
I love you sister dear.

The flowers smell so good today
Like my mind; a sweet bouquet.
On thoughts of you and me dear sis
Living in our garden of thoughts, what bliss!

The moments we spend together I find
In our heart, in person or in our mind.
Are the greatest treasures life can give
A tribute to my sister; long may she live

Someday our lives will again intertwine
Living close together; then you will find
Everything I say here is true from the heart
Together forever; never again part.

Time Names
Dora Burnie

The scenes of the night were as still as the dark,
The shadows were long and lean,
The eyes that peered out were now in the know,
The scene before them was in awe,
All God's creatures were now assembled just so,
What could this all be about?
God spoke with Adam
Who stood tall, straight, and pure,
"You, Adam, will now rule over them all,
Each one will receive your appointed name.
All the beasts of the fields,
The livestock as well,
Birds in the air and fish in the sea,
To creepy crawlers, you do find on the ground."
Adam, he named them one and all,
And to this day the name carries through.
Each animal and insect does have its own name.

Our Love
Sheila Hoggard

Our love began as a simple kiss,
Though simple it did not seem.
A mere touch of our lips
Was the beginning of our dream.

Our love began to grow from there
Like a small and fragile seed.
Since then, I have come to realize
You're all I really need.

Your love has taught me many things
Things right from the start
You've showed me you would not hurt me
For that, I give you my heart.

I know now what I want in life
And what I want to do.
I want to spend the rest of my life
Living with and loving you.

Listen To The Wind!
Miranda A. Blankenship

Listen to the wind
Listen to it cry
Listen to it whirl
Listen to it lie,
Shh, it whispers
Wizz, it says
Wizz, Shh, Wizz, Shh,
let it blow your hair
let it whisper its cry.
Let the wind
Let the wind
Let the wind
Fly!!

Listen to the
Whisper
of the Wind!

Dedication: My family and friends

Dreams of the Soul

He Made It All
Linda K. Easton
Behold the beauty of the stars in the night;
Yes, they are God's true personal lights
They make the Heavens glow in the darkness,
And than God hung the moon;
What an awesome glowing light
Oh! what magical nite lights He gave
Yet, He took time out to make us a pale blue sky
And He made the sun with but a sigh;
He placed the clouds up there
because He wanted to be fair
Oftentimes He sends tears from heaven;
And snowflakes, hale, tornadoes, and hurricanes
And through all this we know He is the Great "I AM"!
The creator of all creation
We mustn't forget the mountains standing so tall
And the carpet of green grass that comes in spring;
And all of the living things created by HIM

A Night
Scott McDuffie
steaming bodies, twisting in the night.
dreading, loathing the return of light.
tantalizing, throbbing of pleasure.
a moment of exhalting, intertwining treasure.

so blissful, the passion flows.
irresistible the sensation grows.
bodies touch in the heated night.
heavy breaths and enticing delight.

distant souls made one in love.
sharing with nothing placed above.
sated sighs and languid eyes.
knowing, seeing only binding ties.

two searching souls under the silver moon.
two searching souls together in the golden sun.
this sensuous, searing night for them has passed.
passions play has joined them to ever last.

The Shine
Peter M. Charlton
The shine is beauty highest prized
the light in new–found lover's eyes
the laughing smile of a Mother's child
and you...

The shine is love's unspoken verse
a perfect gift life's sweetest curse
its greatest joy, its deepest hurt
and you...

The shine emits from those who care
a ray of hope when no one's there
it's a beacon in life's dark despair
and you...

The shine is love's release from pain
a favourite love song's sweet refrain
a lonely heart at last unchained
for you...

The Sea
Nicole Skripochenko
The sound of the surf wraps my soul. Warm rays caress my body.
The sea gulls keep me company.
From the ocean's depth, the cries of lost souls reach out to me.
The shores await their return.
A soothing breeze transports my soul to encounter the Oceanides.
Storms, wars, screams and cries. Despair, anger and sorrow.
Clippers, caravels, freighters, fighters and lovers.
Oceanus' foreplay to a boring day. Divine control, nothing more.
Show of strength. A friendly reminder to us mere mortals.
That winner takes it all.
The sea, so beautiful and yet so cruel! We beg her for mercy.
Happiness, celebration, flowers in commemoration.
Praises given, sorrows forgotten, cruelty turned into love.
Oceanus' victory over the lost souls.
Shivers bring me back. Water splashes my body.
No battles, no cries. Safety, tranquility
Quietude and harmony surrender me.

Garden Of Romance
Mary Stampone
Greatness in human relationship
Clarity of being revealed
Intended of meaningful insight
Goddess freed and unconcealed

Full bloom now consenting
Marriage prearranged before time
Betrothed to consuming rapture
Destiny of divine design

Lying upon rosebed gardens
Virginal goddess presents herself
Romancing, penetrating now one
Merger of divine wealth

Heavenly intent fulfilled, complete
Mystical, magical so real
Union of misconceived duality
Wholeness love would reveal

Behold, The Grand Canyon Of Arizona
Kuran Anne Brown
Behold, pinnacles and buttes of stone no human has ever touched
And listen as the wind rushes in and out of the abyss
Echoing in your ears!
Behold, junipers, pines and fir jutting from the layered rock
And listen as the mighty Colorado river snakes its way
Along in the distant depths below!
Behold, canyon flowers and cactus along your path...
And listen for kaibab squirrels as they scamper among the
Crevices and along ledges of the canyon's rim!
Behold, the palate before you of rusts, beiges, browns, and grays,
Colors of ages gone by, in formations of earth and clay,
And listen as people of every nation stand and sigh in awe!
Behold, mountains with their base on the canyon floor and marvel
At the sight of boulders laid one upon the other against
The blue sky...
And listen to the beat of your own heart as you behold the
Grandeur of this "labyrinth of forms, colors, and sounds"!

Dedication: My husband, Dale, and my son, Keith

Noteworthy Works

A Woman's Wedding Day
D. J. Vanden Langenberg

I've always wondered how my husband felt.
On the day we stood in the house of God and became one.
Was he full of second thoughts while before the Priest we knelt?
Or was he thinking like me of a wonderful journey just begun?

I remember the day abundant with happiness and delight.
I knew in my heart there would never be another man.
My husband was my life as no other would be right.
I looked forward to traveling through life hand in hand.

That day was the beginning of many wonderful years.
We've grown and triumphed over all life has thrown.
It still shows in his eyes that he forever holds me dear.
We've built a bond through children, love and home.

My wedding day was the first step to happiness and maturity.
Since that day I've never felt such strength and security.

I Saw Your Son Today
Chris Ravetto

I saw your son
today,
I saw his smile.
I saw your son
today,
and in him
I saw you.
He came in
with his
Mother,
The woman
you once loved.
I acted as if
I didn't care,
like it didn't
matter.
I saw your son
today,
I saw you.

Lost Love
J. Evans

You called me up to say goodbye.
You listened as part of my heart died.
Everything about my world has passed.
Even though I hoped it would last.
I gave a love I didn't know I had.
To watch you go makes my heart sad.

The hurt someday will pass away.
I sit here and I can tell the truth.
I still love you and I have proof.
There is no smile upon my face.
A one–way love within my life has no place.

I can't do anything about how I feel.
I'll hide it and my heart I will seal.
There is a lock upon my heart, and from
this day no love will start.
It will take a long time for it to heal.
Because you see I love you still.

Introspect
Celeste Johnson

Always wanting, wanting
when gotten, still craving
surface needs

Look deeper, deeper still
acknowledge for survival
accept

Seek what is truly desired
nigh unbearable, near
impossible

Barriers up
to experience, not
wonder of wishful dreaming

Accept oneself foremost

Through The Looking Glass
Brinda Joyce Adams

I came to the center of myself and the oceans of Life
crashed against my Temple
Rushing foam through my veins carried me to the twilight
of distant souls
Voices reach out of the Void
Shadows linger near
Sparks of light, ancestors, dear
Leap forward to grasp my hand, touch my hair
Magic, Magic everywhere.

Inside this realm of world eternal
Dwells the life–force of this journal
Departed Souls, searching faces, in their Temple share their graces
Distant journey, time untold
Life beyond dares unfold.
Am I Life Am I Death
Shape shifter breathes my breath
Dare I stay Dare I go
Visions of a Sacred Soul.

My Friend
Lisa Langford

I have a friend, I can call my own
Always there
Waiting... when I come home
My friend that I speak of
Cares not of my faults, but eternal love
He's the one that is true
That will always stay
The one with fur, who likes to play
Sadness strikes in the night
A stream of tears roll down my face
The rub of his head takes them away
He flips his tail, as if he knows
The stroke of his tongue, the bond grows
Now my friend is gone, waiting no more
The tears at night continue to pour
At times I stop and think of how it was
Saying "Your memory is forever My Friend, eternal love"

Dedication: My friend, Timone

Dreams of the Soul

Divorce
S. Arthurs
little child stop crying
what has upset
you so,

have you hurt yourself
or lost something
please tell me
let me know.

you shake your little
head, at me
and look me in the eye...

My Mum and Dad got
divorced today
please can you tell
me why.

Being Short
Mary Catherine Gates
I hate being short and being told
things of that sort.
People say, "a couple of inches you need
to grow" but that isn't anything I don't
already know.
When people say that I'm a shrimp,
I say to myself, they're just a wimp.
I endure, I am zealous, I try to think
they're just jealous.
No matter how hard I try to be kind,
others treat me as if I were blind.
When I reach things I need a chair,
can rude comments I truly bear.
Young children view me as a peer, people
my own age think I am queer.
I try to be peaceful and calm and try
not to explode like an atom bomb.
If people would just open their eyes,
they would see someone of a greater size.

Jungle Song
Patrick M. Cappadona
The drums beat out their morbid song
The hyena cries at break of dawn
and through the greens the tiger creeps
near a den of leopard young
fast at sleep.
And from the trees the vultures fly
near an old buffalo who's ready to die.
Down by the river the crocodile sleep
while brave little birds
clean their big teeth.
Then in the trees the monkeys spring
away from the danger the jungle can bring.
Away in a clearing the lions roar
while high above the buzzards soar.

The drums beat out their morbid song
sordid tales they love to repeat
of the snake, the lion
and the jungle heat.

Untitled
L. Day
Now that I am eighty and
Feeling rather glum,
I cannot walk very far,
Neither can I run.
My hearing aid plus walking
Stick are just one part
Of me, will I live to be
One hundred you just wait
And see, old age is only
A tag its given to many
To donate the length
Of one's life long span
So from January to
December I shall
Forget to remember,
Just how old that I
Really am

Generations
Jean A. Kingsley
Maple trees surrounded the pond
Years ago when I was young.

And the water was pure and clear,
No pollution was evident in the water.
Growing plant life was in abundance
Everywhere, but now the
Leaves die young.

Let's all help clean the planet,
It is not to late too
Save the earth from destruction,
And make a better place for the

Many generations that will come.
A little effort on our part
Right now will make a difference
In the way our descendants live.
Every generation affects the others.

Little Sheep
Louise Kilby Fesperman
On an island called Barbados,
Lived a sheep that had no wool
Grazing on the lovely hill side
With her tummy nice and full

How I wondered as I watched her
So carefree and happy there,
If we all could be more like her
Not a worry or a care

Just the whisper of the palm trees
Swaying gently in the breeze,
Sandy beaches just below her
Blue green water on the seas

In a moment I must leave her
My great ship will sail away,
She will also find new pastures
In my memory she will stay.

Noteworthy Works

Untitled
Edna Ball

Spare a little thought for the needy
And all the little children in care
The elderly who are lonely
And not many seem aware

The situation with the animals
That stray round our towns
Who people have thrown out of their homes
Who just don't care where they roam
The sins that lots of people commit
And get away with it all
Who never think of things that befall them
Wherever they go
These tragedies would never happen
If people would think first
And take nasty thoughts out of mind
And stop this senseless hurt

Memories: A Duet Of Daydreams
Kimberley Liao

Illumination
The starry skies
Blanketed silkily in the darkness
See you in deep slumber
Smile down on you sweetly
Whisper dreams into your ear
And vanish, sadly
As you wake into silence
Independence
The piercing air siren
Fills the aquamarine blue skies
And the smell of airplane engines
Permeates the atmosphere

As you take off
A cool breeze knocks you into consciousness
And you look down on your airbase
With the realization
That you are free

... Friendship...
Tonya Campbell

In the rush of everyday pressures,
It's easy to take a special friendship
Like ours for granted...

Maybe because we've known each other
so long and been through so many good
and bad times together.

We just don't think about how it
would be if we weren't there for
each other...

So I just wanted to take a little
time to tell you how much I cherish
our friendship and to thank you for
being such a special person in
my life.

Dedication: My best friend, my sister

A Sailor's Dream
G. R. Robinson

A sailors tomb festooned with gold, speak of yore and tales of old
once again we hear a cry. A sailor's voice about to die.
Sailing high, sailing low, or yonder sea pirates go,
Told of treasures that one day, buried deep far away.
Waves abound with blackened sky, "hang on lads" we hear a cry
Lashing ropes, batten down, "this be no time to drown".
Hardened to their fearless plight, "yonder look" the morning light
In the distance dawn appears greeted with the loud cheers.
Sailing on towards the sun like Fathers long before had done.
"Land Ho"– we hear a shout, "where away" — there about.
Heading to and drawing near, the land away, which brings no fear
"2 more fathoms cap'n then no more, " the bosun calls the men to shore.
Of they go in search of gold, to the place which was foretold.
Marks the spot, a pile of stones.
Underneath, a pile of bones.
From a distance cries a scream.
'Twas the end — "A Sailors Dream"

You
Heather Huskey

I think of you and tell myself no
I just dug myself out of that deep hole
Another relationship with you would only drown my hopes and dreams
All you could do is hold me back it seems
Since we broke up all you do is wrong
You are no longer who I knew as strong
You smoke dope, get high, soon you will try to fly
When you do you'll find you will not make it high in the sky
I think I could stop you or may be try
But if I don't succeed all I can do is cry, so I ask myself why try
I just hope soon you will realize there's more to life than this
When you do I'll be there to reward you, maybe with a kiss
But if you don't realize the mistake you are making
Then it's my turn to let go of this pain aching
I do not know how but I will try
For I cannot stand here and watch you die
So all I can do now is pray to God he will help you all he can
For I want you to return into the other man if it's not too late and if you
still can

Untitled
Tom Orr

When she cries I hold her,
When she falls I bathe her,
When she smiles I laugh,
And when she ails I cry.

If all news seems bad to me,
I look upon my child asleep.
My heavy heart touched with pride,
Moisture rushes to my eyes.

Her gentle breaths and peaceful face,
Radiate such calm,
Like a distant drifting melody,
That's floating, soft and warm.

But thoughts postponed disturb the scene,
I know I cannot keep my angel.
Time will pry her from my arms,
Gently but firmly, but forever.

Dreams of the Soul

A Stranger No More
J. P. Kennedy
On an uneventful and boring day,
I met a stranger as I
walked a new and
different way.

As I steadily looked deep into
his eyes, I didn't feel like
fleeing.
I felt calm and at
peace for dwelling
within was a kind
and gentle being.

No matter how I try,
I cannot erase the
fact, that I had
met a nice guy.

The Lady
Joseph A. Sagisi
Her long eye lashes are like
fringes of light rays,
Arched as rainbows on her eyes.
Their twinkles bring colors to her smiles.

Liken to a candle flame,
Of light that shines within.
The man wonders holding tenderly,
Flickers of light to show,...
Path golden glimmering glitters,
Near her sincere, loving and fragile heart.

Though the flame is dim,... sadly, as it may.
The man strains his heart to see,
Future glimpse vivid treasured memory.
For the lady, further holds... the key.

Yet the man understands,
For this reason He calls Her,... "The Lady"

A Zombie Generation
Jenny Lynn Lesley
Walking zombies in the Doctor Zhivago era of life
Incredible pain as delicacy disappears
Women whose children are not as beautiful
Dine with pigs to save their bloods' future

Some living with passion though life is
Terrible and oppressive some living
Yet only breathing and experiencing
Nothing outside their foolish existence

Needless suffering and supreme human sacrifice is commonplace
White angels turn their faces away
Starving dogs lap up rose petals in the street
Daisies vanishing melting away as the rain falls

Gold admired but not valued
Rubies and emeralds gather in the rich man's fireplace
Hopeful water more precious than wine
Quenches the thirst of a dying generation

God's Promises
Janyce F. Draper
The promises of God are given everywhere.
HE gives His strength for each and every care.
In the dark night, He is always there
Our every burden He will always share!

God's greatest gift has brought us all a
bright new life.
His precious love will end all war and strife.
Trust in Jesus, just give Him your heart.
In all of your life, He will never depart.

God's wonderful promises; God's marvelous
promises
Every night and every day; In the stillness
of His way.
God's promises so sure, makes my life
secure!

Look Out Your Window
Linda Dean
Look out your window and what do you see?
All of God's beauty all about free.
Things we take for granted, the birds and the trees,
The beautiful sunshine, the cool–smelling breeze.
All of these things, all about Free!

The beauty of God comes free by his hand.
His love for the world and his love for man.
So, look all around you and feel God's love.
He's not far away, he's just up above.
All around us and all about free!

Look out your window and what do you see?
The flowers that bloom, the glow of the moon,
The leaves that fall down, the snow on the ground,
The bees that buzz by, and the stars in the sky.
All of God's mystery, all about free!!
Dedication: Jim, Billy and Tommy

Petals In The Wind
Caryn Fitzpatrick
Crushed rose petals beneath my foot,
Mingled amongst the ash and soot.
Broken, destroyed, all in vain,
The solitary symbol of my heart's pain.

Blow hard, ye winds, and cast away
The vile words exchanged today,
The bitter tears wept for naught,
The wracking sobs in this throat caught.

Oh, ye cursed, awful wretch,
With shards of glass you left etched
Upon this heart, this noble place,
The image of your beauteous face.

I hold the poison to my lip.
Embracing death. One final sip.
Now a shudder, now is done.
The shrouded veil of death has come.

Noteworthy Works

Invitation
Marion Mackay
A taut smile, sweetly enhancing
the glimpse of a spirit
disinclined to leave home.
The season of singing
has not yet come.

Can the gaze of a lover
catch the eye of your heart
disregarding rebuke and retreat?
Can the season of singing
still yet come?

Softly resuming the grace of seclusion
with steady forbearance
the lover retires,
awaiting the season of singing
seeking strength for the days to come.

The Dove
Mike Wilson
i once dreamt i was flying
i went higher and higher
until i saw the earth's edge
i almost touched the sun
then my wings vanished
i was unclothed naked
to the hurtful world
i fell to the earth's oceans and they
swallowed me whole
the waves ate my flesh
and shattered my bones
i felt no pain
yet i felt tremendous pain
when i awoke on the shore
in my home
in my bed
my wings had
come back
to me

Total Eclipse
Bradley Wong
Hot and humid is the noontide sun,
shone brightly upon our lair.
From the west a dark army approaches,
bringing immediate celestial warfare.

The dark side encompasses the light,
draining its vital life force.
Complete darkness now covers the earth.
The moon shows no signs of remorse.

Then out of the murk shoots a radiant spark.
"Eye of Heaven" now seeks compensation.
With one swift push all twilight is lost.
Day and night resume segregation.

A triumphant victory won,
a manifestation truly divine.
The sun is briefly exalted,
'till the moon seeks revenge down the line.

Caresses Of Dreams
K. L. Wise
The waves tickled my body,
The wind softly caresses my face,
The sand begins a dance
Beneath my feet,
The wind comes gently to
Bestow a kiss on my face.
The sun with its shine so
Warm so bright waits...
Then covers my whole body
and thoughts with its gentle
Might.
All so beautiful and lovely
It makes noises with my voice
So if you stand on the sand
Just close your eyes to the
Sun and just begin to
Discover a love for one.

December
Richard E. Tripp
December, Oh why must you be so cruel?
Spring was so close, but now it's an eternity away.
We must all face your cold wrath, head on and strong
We each will greet you a separate way.
A few put up a strong fight and quickly lose.
Others battle for longer times,
knowing they can never win.
December, oh why must you be so cruel?
Our loved ones are our loss.
Precious memories, ours forever.
December, you won the Battles,
and took its toll,
three days before spring.
December, oh why must you be so cruel?
December, you showed up again
twenty–four days after spring.
December, oh why must you be so cruel?

Dedication: My Loving Mother, Missed Greatly

Untitled
Marjorie Kane
I know this day will bring you tears;
I had your love through all the years –
And you had mine.
And though I did not want to leave,
Remember me, but do not grieve
For too long a time.
Keep memories of the happy days
When I was young with many ways
That made you smile.
When I could run and play a game,
And knew all my toys by name,
For quite a while!
The years passed; how fast they flew!
I slowed down, and then I knew
That He might call me soon.
So thank you for the loving care;
I always got more than my share.
And so farewell to family dear –
(And I'll be waiting Here)

Dreams of the Soul

I'm Cold
J. Beaupierre
Sitting in my home at night,
Wrapped in blankets really tight.
It's very windy and cold outside
The grounds so frosty, you can almost glide
The windows rattle in the wind,
What did I do, have I sinned?
What did I do to be so cold.
Or is it that I'm getting old.
My feet they feel like blocks of ice.
A nice cup of cocoa would be nice.
That would warm me to the bone,
And bring my skin colour up a tone
My hands are cold and very sore
I don't think I can stand it anymore
At last here comes the sun and heat
To bring feeling back to my hands and feet.

Transformation
Ellen Scherling
From the cages of my past,
Chthonic shadows broken loose,
Stampede like headless beasts
Hurled down by mighty Zeus.

Ripping roots long tangled,
Trampling over gardens of my youth;
Shaking hardened, layered soil, that stir
Secrets, stolen from the truth.

Behind the weeds, grown up,
Lie all the hidden "me's" –
Lost in dark deep woods, of
Shrouded fears and buried memories.

Now, encased by my chrysalis,
Listening for the conch to be blown,
Announcing my emergence, I find
Bread crumb paths that lead me home.

Summer Magic
Pauline Wisdom
As the sun shone over the meadow
Poppies were waving in the breeze;
A bird was calling to another
Before they flew beyond the trees.

Two cows stood up in yonder field
Now does that mean that it will rain?
As I was trying to remember
They moved and then sat down again.

The stream that trickled through the wood
Seemed to stretch for quite a while
I lazily wondered whether I must jump
Then came across a stile.

A perfect day to remember
As I write it down in pen
I hope there will be another summer
Because I must go back again.

Untitled
Pauline Haggett
Children, I had many
and troubles many too
but I am always there
should they need me
like they do.

Marriages have come
and marriages have gone
by my many children
so many little grandchildren
have now come along.

Bringing with them troubles
and also lots of tears
but this is all outweighted
by the love, joy and laughter
they now all give, to me!

Rainbows
Wendy Rightmire
I took a step and I stumbled
I took another and I fell
I took a third I was crawling
Between Heaven Between Hell

A hand reached out to touch me
It was neither young nor old
It had all the answers
Answers coming from the soul

I cried out, I know I'm falling
My strength is falling,
please let me go
There was only silence
As my tears began to flow
My tears touched his finger
My tears touched soul
they formed a flowing river
The river a Rainbow

A Rich Life
Jennifer Helton
Let me live one day at a time
And be the best that I can be,
And in each day I'll give a part
Of the very best of me.

Let me live with a caring heart
And learn to love my fellow man,
And I will share my strength with him
By reaching out a helping hand.

Let me live with an open mind
To help me better understand
Another person's point of view
And the problems that are at hand.

Let me live to help mankind—
To light their way or warm the cold,
And my heart will be filled with riches
Far better than treasures and gold.

Noteworthy Works

My Grandma And Me
Leslie Anne Kenshol
We've always been close and hope it will
always be that way,
My grandma and me.
When I stay overnight, we always do fun
things,
My grandma and me.
We laugh together at our jokes,
My grandma and me.
We weep at sad movies,
My grandma and me.
I know she will not be around forever, so
we try to make the best of the time we have,
My grandma and me.
We look out for each other and help each other,
My grandma and me.
We have a special friendship that can never be broken,
My grandma and me.

A Mariner's Tale
Lorraine Helen Prehart Fourcaud
Aye, me fair lads, I too, sat here and listened to a drunken
mariner as he spun a stirring tale and, with nary a thought, the
the following day I left me family, and with him, soon set sail 'Twas
a blustery day and the rig took to the high seas. A bit lonely I was
at first but all mates performed their tasks and naught e'er said to me.
Then a bellowing voice fell upon me ear and ne'er again I shirked me
duties for the Captain's voice made me cringe in fear. Aye, me
fists were all callused and me mouth right too big, and I was all
too ornery for I wanted to be master of this rig. All of me now
was part of the ship, too soon I forgot family and home –
carnage and whale, fool-hearted friends, and greed forced me to roam.
Ah, young lads, I greeted many ports and they greeted me, "here he
comes" all would shout, I was master of the sea. The rig was now
mine, and all the crew feared me when 'twas found out that Captain
of the ship I'd be. Bellow and shout I did, so all could hear me
fore and aft – none dared disobey me for fear of the shaft. Tonight,
me fine lads, you've listened to an ole man who sealed his own doom
looked there at yon window, me wife and daughter, who, because
of me, fell into sin and a life of ruin.

A Wanted Dream
Maria Scourby
My mind is slowly drifting,
I begin to hear a woman's laughter
A dark haired man mowing the lawn
Family of three, chuckling,
Eating spaghetti. . . .
Bright lights, gray walls
I'm in a hallway – so many people
A familiar woman,
Starved, bald, eyes shut,
Machines galore,
Does she know I'm here?
I'm in a doorway,
Gazing down on this dark haired
Handsome man.
Why is he still sleeping?

Wake up!!
Mom?
Dad?

Just Another Drive–By
Dominic Blackwell
Just another drive–by
hair–raising screams filled the sky as a woman stood still and
watched her child die.

Please God no, no! She yelled. Going through a brief moment in
hell. Heart pounding hard and eyes bugged out. Please God no!
She continued to shout.

No this can't be. Why God? Why the hell me? Feelings of love
crying come back but, in reality there's no hope for Jack.

He didn't see it coming fast as it was. In one second the sky
turned from blue to black.
He died instantaneously as the car flew by. Jack never even
had a chance to cry.

For it's just another drive–by.

To Mother
Arlys LaPlant
As a child. In your loving arms
Which no love could compare.

Your gentle smile. Your sweet caress
With me you always shared.

Your patience you showed me when in
distress.

Your guidance through my first years
Your loving hand would always be there to
wipe away my tears.

Now, As your hair turns silvery grey,
As the years speed by so fast,

I now a Mother
Turn to you, and
Thank you for the past.

The Rigour Of Time
Geoff Powell
Oft through the days I speak to you,
I hear your answer, yet there is no voice,
Though your presence I can no longer view,
Happy memories abide – in these I rejoice!

I remember every talk, every joy, and some tears,
As daily rounds our lives entwined,
With little conception, with advancing years,
Pre–ordination contrived our closeness to unbind.

Black days were few, or words spoken,
Always blue skies hailed our every morn,
Promises made together were never broken,
Why is life now so dejected and forlorn?

Problems or hurt never could the heart numb,
Life with you was clothed in silk and gold,
With you beside me I felt so young,
Without you now so tired and old!

Dreams of the Soul

Friendship
Karen Robinson

I love him from a distance
because we can only be friends
We meet, we talk about life
and past experiences.
My life has changed in these past
months.
A longing to see him even though it
is wrong,
but the need is there.
He is understanding, a caring man.
I feel safe when I am with him.
He brings light into the darkness
and brightness emerges within me.
I feel shy when I am with him
I feel a girl again.
My feelings are alive
A new love begins.

Dream Escape
Charles King

While the body sleeps, the mind it creeps in a land
that has no time.
A land that lets you wander free, and play to your
own rhyme.

To feel so free away from me, but I myself I'm
there.
Where I can be want I want to be, blameless and
without a care.

It's a place that's there whilst I'm asleep, a place
where I can dwell.
Where I can feel the things I want to feel, without
my earthly shell.

With you're mind at play, the coming day, closer
and closer it creeps.
But your dreams are real throughout this time,
at least whilst the body sleeps.

Inside Of Me
Helen Kerr

Once a lilac fresh in bloom
But colors flow beyond the Surface
Blue through my heart
Black through my head
The shadows unfold
through my mysteries untold
another empty thought
for empty days
in empty hearts where I lay
I wish I wasn't in so deep
I wish my heart, my soul to sleep
I swear to you my soul will break
I wish for wings to soar on
to fly straight into the sun
and begin again where I've begun
far away but oh so near
I really don't belong here
so I will go, so fare thee well
I will just stay here in my private hell.

Love's Eternal Sorrow
Rachel Compton

The small beads of sorrow,
Fall from her cheeks,
When she thinks of the love,
She once had,
Leaving trails of moisture,
Down her soft skin,
Leaving her make–up,
To swirl in a pool of tears,
Love songs winding round in her head,
Memories flooding her eyes,
Finding it hard to swallow,
She lifts the photo of him,
The love of her life,
Gone like a whisper to the wind,
And the breaking of her heart,
Will echo in her head,
For all eternity.

Romany Rue
Gordon Jack Crisp

Oh yes! she weaved her magic spell,
This Romany woman in gypsy dress,
And when on me her eyes did dwell,
I felt I needed her caress.

Poised on one leg, the other on heel tip,
Thick, curly dark hair flecked with grey,
Red skirt awhirl with shake of hip,
The hands eloquent in aerial display.

Her blouse of white with stripes of blue,
Full of sleeve and edged with lace,
Dark waistcoat embroidered with every hue,
serene the smile on that proud face.

I am sure those dark eyes held a sign,
But too soon my gypsy figure went away,
Leaving me bereft, on my own to pine,
My heart empty, but the pictures stay.

Morning Chorus–No Encore
Glyn Goode

As the light lifts the dark
And the sun rises in the sky
Our ears perceive the song of the lark
But our eyes see the tractor trundle by
Its cargo of death on its back
Spraying poisonous chemicals all around
Killing all insects on the ground
Insects farmers they do say
Are pests to crops each and every day
But if nature was allowed its course
We would not have any remorse
For birds their offspring would rear
With songs for all to cheer
But Mothers search for food without rest
While their chicks starve in the nest
For their food that was all around
Does no more abound
The morning chorus will be no more
Morning chorus, no encore.

Noteworthy Works

Mum
Vivien Widdowson

The worst night of my life
was when Dad lost his wife,
and I lost a Mother so rare,
she was gone, could I cope
without seeing her there.
By the fire in her favourite chair,
she was good, she was wise,
with her gentle old eyes,
she looked on her family with pride.
And when things weren't quite right,
she would hide all her hurt,
and quietly brush it aside.
"What a wonderful woman"
was said of her then,
when she quietly slipped out of our lives,
I hope that someday I will see her again,
with that thought then my spirit revives.

Null And Void
Josie Willis

Fragmented parchment of skin tethers me
to existential who.
I am, I breathe, I rhapsodize—then
cut the silver cord of flesh.
My self, the vibratory instrument of him:
carrion of my flesh, genetic—engineered.
I am who he makes me,
co—habitant of Eden, impermeable and
permeated.
Mother seed, Motherless.
Father spawn, Fatherless.
Inside the valley of hollow, the black
tears slide.
Warped wormholes of my cosmic soul, unsutured,
the universe spins on.
I am of the Father, by the Father,
innocence betrayed.

Dedication: My husband, nurse and mentor

John
M. J. Dowman

As the years go by
The months, weeks and days
Our thoughts are still
Of far—off better days

Your smile and your wit
And your gorgeous face
Remain through years
Months, weeks and days

The sun will ever rise
The rain will ever fall
From the clouds above
I still hear you call

My darling, naught will change
My love for you is ever strong
Until our hands join in final bond
With you my handsome, darling John

A Death In The Family
Vickie N. Burgess

There's been a death in the family
Everyone has changed, nothing is the same
There were seven of us, now there's six
Makes me sick, it happened so quick
Our ties are broken, the pain hasn't weakened,
The unanswered questions, why is he gone
Why didn't I see, that was the last time
for him and me, why couldn't I say
I've missed you so much, how have you been,
We must keep in touch. If we knew the
future, what would have been said,
good—bye my brother, how will I go on
I still love you too much, my hero is gone
I pray not for long, when we meet again,
Our ties will be strong.

Dedication: In Memory of Joey Nason

Storm
Shawn Conkle

with apprehension waited we.
The wind began to blow so strong.
A sense of ill, a deep foreboding.
To know that something else was wrong.
The pariah's visit was but brief.
It came and went, yet stole so much.
The anguish and the lasting grief:
the lives that day which it would touch.

It's over now we build again.
Starting over deja vu.
A new beginning a brand new start.
Another chance to live anew.
In retrospect: for an onslaught
such as this, could we prepare?
The clouds approach impending doom.
Before the storm; this time: a prayer.

Dedication: To all victims of disaster

Why Did God Pick Me?
Mindy Baker

Love walked away from me.
It just up and left.
How could that be?
Why did God pick me?

I was so good to him.
He was so good to me.
So how could this be?
Why did God pick me?

Maybe I am right.
Maybe I am wrong.
But how could it be?
Why did God pick me?

Why did God let him leave?
Why did he have to go?
The answer I do not know.
But why did God pick me?

Dreams of the Soul

Black
Julie Sprecher
The absence of light.
BLACK
Where wrong seems right.
BLACK
Overcomes all.
BLACK
Sets you up for a fall.
BLACK.
Looms over your shoulder.
BLACK.
Yup. Just behind that boulder.
If you see it coming you had better run.
If BLACK gets you, you're done.
Watch out! Beware!
If not...
BLACK
Is the last thing you'll ever see or hear.

The Gift of a Baby
Katherine Belden
The world is full of a great many things,
some that we may never see.
But the joy a baby brings,
is the greatest one to me.

The babe is sent from God above
and always is a special one.
To give to us, the gift of love
and happiness that can't be undone.

A child is the most precious gift,
a person could receive.
The babe will give your heart a lift,
like nothing you would believe.

So when you lay down to sleep,
just before you close your eyes,
Give thanks for those that are yours to keep,
and thank Him for their precious lives.

I Thought Of You Yesterday
Catherine Klopfer
I thought of you yesterday,
A smile passed my lips in recollection,
Oh those endless nights of laughter,
How I felt inside, thereafter...
I thought of you yesterday,
different things you did and said,
maybe my heart just misread,
deep inside just feels so dead.
I thought of you yesterday
I tried not to bring back old feelings left inside,
the tears I wept for you,
senseless idle thoughts of we two.
I thought of you yesterday,
all the hopes and dreams we both shared.
From misconceptions that only scared,
to the choices that impaired.

I thought of you yesterday,
I THOUGHT OF LOVE...

Frustration Box
Marthalyn Anderson
It's a lot of frustration
The expectations that were given to them as children
Are now in small amounts my job to uphold
It's a lot of frustration
To be who I am and to be who they want me to be
The frustration can't be stopped
It couldn't care less
But when the tears start streaming
I think why do I bother why do I try
I am not the perfect child
I am far from that
But as far as being a teenager
I feel I am one of the perfect ones
But I will keep trying to do well
In all the tasks I am given
And maybe one day I will realize the point
The point of working so hard

We'd Like To Be Winners
June Martin
Sometimes we think we have all the answers.
Sometimes we think we have total control.
When who are we kidding but our own inner soul.

We know all the dangers, at times we don't care.
We act like we're puzzles with pieces to spare.

We take life for granted as though it's a game.
But games are for children, not hiding our shame.

It's time to take notice of hurts and despair.
if we can't stand together, then please take a chair.

Step off of that game board, don't worry who glares.
When life goes too fast, then please take the stairs.

We want to be winners, though we end up as spinners.
So hang on real tight, but not out of spite, and
someday soon we will all see the light.

Untitled
Alicia L. Duckworth
Autumn, the glittering colors.
When the tree's leaves fall.
Awaiting the winter's snow.

Streams and rivers with silver threads
Crystallized by the furious winds.
There is radiance on the evergreens.

Winter, silence beneath the
Trees, creatures of the forest
are asleep, snuggling to keep
Warm.
While the earth begins to
Freeze.

The seasons come and go
The reasons we all know.
Nature's beauty must keep
Although no one is pleased.

Noteworthy Works

Two Different Worlds
Jillian R. Deasey

Look up. What do you see? A blue sky with white clouds hovering above. A bird singing happily in a tree standing by your side. Birds flying so high they seem to touch the sun, reflecting off a crystal clear pond where fish the color of a sunset swim.

Now look up again. What do you see now? A black sky with rain clouds ready to burst. A truck roars as it passes on a crowded highway on the other side of millions of tree stumps. Birds can now only cough in the smog filled air. The pond is now polluted with toxic waste. Fish no longer swim in its water. And the sunset will never be the same again.

Which world would you like to live in?
Which world are you willing to save for the next generation?
If we all do not think fast there will
be nothing to save...

What Is A Mother
Ada Jackson

A Mother is A woman
That God made from man
Man is the head of the house
she's second in command
She teaches the family to love God
And to love each other
She teaches them to respect themselves and to respect their brother
She teaches them to give thanks
because God has been so good
He appoints us anoints us because he promised he would
She teaches them family values
That's important today
because self esteem is low we turn the other way
What they need is someone
They can look up to
Because you are an upright mom
That someone is you.

Dedication: My mother, Christine Johnson, with love

Shhh Be Still, And Listen...
D. A. McQuagge

Shhh; be still, and listen...
You can hear them on the wind,
Those clearly ringing voices,
Voices without end.
From the crosses of the ages,
To us their voices lend;
Shhh; be still, and listen...
To the messages they send:

Martin, Jack, and Bobby's,
And a million voices blend,
All in loving union,
As the ages they transcend,
The essence of all truth,
For us to comprehend;
The greatest love of all...
Your own life for a friend.

Shhh; be still, and listen...

Austin
Lola D. Cox

In memory of a little boy,
Who filled our hearts with so much Joy.

He was such a tiny lad
Who left us all so very sad.

Who was only two hours old,
When we laid him in the ground so cold.

We love and miss you with all our might,
A star we know that shines so bright.

We look up to the heavens so far,
We don't know where to find your star.

To your grave we go with flower and toy,
To show how we miss you, our precious boy.

Who Am I
Samantha N. Brady

I may be small, but part of it all,
Who am I is the question I recall.
Who am I?
Who am I?
Who am I?
That is what I ask myself and I think;
a girl, a sister, a daughter, a person, a friend, a poet.

When you think of who you are
think of how important you are when you are here now
and gone later...
to everyone and everything.

Who am I is asked by millions of people,
near and far, deep and wide...
People want to know...
Who am I?

And all it is, is who you are inside.

Seasons
Lesley Hamilton

Spring is here once again,
Sun, wind and now it is rain.
Horses, sheep and birds look after their young,
The weather doesn't stop people having fun.

Summer is here holidays have begun,
Adults, children are having fun.
To the zoo, park or play in the sand,
Plenty of ice creams to hold in your hand.

The Autumn leaves are falling to the ground,
Everything is quiet: you can't hear a sound.
The mist lays in the vales and on the hills,
Here comes the sun, how much better everyone feels.

Snow and ice winter coats on,
Christmas carols, bells chime ding, dong.
The Festive Season means winter is here.
We have come to the end of another year.

Dreams of the Soul

To Love
Susan Jobson
Alone amongst the masses.
Is it fear that makes them seem so cold?
Has pain and despair touched their lives so deeply,
That they keep their hearts hidden safely away?
Away from the warmth and tenderness of love!?
Is the chance to find happiness,
Not worth the risk of opening the heart
To possible anguish?
Do we spend our lives looking at love,
But never embracing it,
For fear of rejection?
I have loved and lost,
But never will I forget the joy that was given.
Nor the memories that I can hold close to my heart.
These will keep me warm until love comes back.
Then I will be ready to pull it to me,
And cherish the time that it stays.

Unknown Love
Tracey Wardle Bron
Although I've never seen you
I come to your resting place
and hope to find that someday to
I'll see your loving face

I've been asked a lot of times
"why do you care so much
you never knew or met him
why does he mean so much

I say "it's not the man
that means so much to me
it's the stories I've been told
that give me memories

One day when we meet above
I hope I'll get to see
the young, the old the unknown love
that means so much me

The Shell
Sherri Dutra
I learned to hide inside my shell,
To succumb to the pains of a living hell—
The shell, my protector — so no one could see,
The truth about my misery.

The shell had learned, on its own
To walk this journey called life, alone.
It learned to hide anger, hide fear, avoid love;
With self–hatred and self–destruction to rise above.

This shells' been disintegrating for quite some time,
And inside its casing is quite a find—
A child awaits with a desire to see,
What this wondrous world has to offer thee.

No longer living in misery, or hell,
I no longer need my protector – the shell.
With a sense of self that's tolerant and forgiving,
I can have a life that's worth loving and living.

My Favorite Place
Robin M. Smith
Oh wondrous blue green sea that I adore,
Your glist'ning beauty shines on us each day;
Your waves beat loudly at the sandy shore,
It makes me want to sit and think and pray.

No children want to just sit in the sun,
They play and chatter in the ocean clear;
They dive through waves and have a lot of fun,
And at days end they say they liked it here.

When not a soul is on the beach at night,
I get my greatest satisfaction here;
So cool so crisp the soft wind is tonight,
I start forgetting all about my fear.

The ocean is the only thing for me,
The ocean is my favorite place to be.

Much Love and Thanks
Loriedel D. Sangcap
I love you for your funny ways,
I thank you for your smile each day...
I love you for making every moment seem bright,
I thank you for turning any sadness into right.

I love to hear you giggle,
I thank you for your dances and cute little wiggles...
I love the two dimples upon your face,
I thank you for every warm, cheery embrace.

I love spending all of my time with you,
I thank God for all that you do...
I love that you are my boy,
I thank you for bringing me such joy.

I love you my dear, sweet Bubba,
I thank God daily for letting me be your mama...
I love that you are my special little one,
I thank you for being my son.

Going Home
Monique Johnson
The darkness begins to envelop
me,
And a sweet warmth starts to
encompass me,
And the darkness deepens and
I see streaks of light,
A sweet peace fells my soul,
And my eyes gladly close
I begin to see brighter and
brighter light, beckoning to my
very soul.
And I turn to them greedily,
eager to follow its glow.
For I know it is my
time for my spirit to return
to the magnificent glory from
which it first sprang.

Dedication: For our Latishia, our beloved

Noteworthy Works

Dreams Of Nativity
Sally Ann Watt
As the child lay sleeping
He felt the warmth
The memory of being cocooned
He felt the hands gently lift him
As they had so often caressed him
Whilst he was in the quiet
The floating softness
Before the long journey
Into the love
Of his family
Now he enjoyed the warmth of the water
As it flowed over him
He felt himself content again
He would always have with him
His first memories

Dedication: Mum, Dad, with love, Sally

Summer Days
Beverly Lovegrove
I have memories of summer days
Full of blackberry bushes
Fingers pricked but no matter
Except our bowls were filled
Running home to Mother
Showing her our treasures
Waiting patiently for mom
to work her magic
Smells from the oven of
our delicious treat
Blackberry dumplings
Hot sticky days
Carefree spirits
Climbing trees
Going to the very top
Viewing the world
Through a child's eyes.

Dedication: In memory of Carol Moore

Mom
Manda Schmeling
When I was little
you showed me the way
And you made me what I am today
For all your guidance, caring and love
I thank the good Lord from above
I caused you problems years ago
for that I'm sorry I hope you know
you taught me how to stand on my own
If only then I wish I'd known
There were times when I was mad at you
for little things you made me do
But you were always there for me
Yet let it be what I wanted to be
I LOVE YOU more than words can say
And learn new things from you each day
You're someone on whom I can depend.
You're not only my Mother, you're my friend
And I hope that someday I will be
as good as you were to me.

Being Purple Crow
Stuart R. Johnson
Odd it is how purple Crows have flourished
They hop about speaking Purple Crow chirpings
Insisting that only Purple Crows know the ropes
They preen and flap their Purple Crow wings
Strutting stiffly, they act the part of Purple Crow police
The unenlightened fail to perceive lavender logic
So they clamp down with Purple Crow lawsuits
Purple Crows alone possess the imperial hues of royalty
Naturally they feel justified in every Purple Crow action
PC's regale each other in their presumed irrefutability
They insistently peck at every deficient doctrine
Applying the needed Purple Crow theory and agenda
Not susceptible to the vulgarities of the past
Purple Crows mix fuchsin passion with pale bluish irritations
To obtain the exact Crowness tint required
They scoff at sheepish black crows who question their color
Still... a hint of doubt lingers about the real Crowness of things Purple

---

Eric–If You Were A Rabbit In Wonderland
Gilly Turmeau
Although you will never speak
I imagine your voice –
Like a cute child,
Inquisitive.

Conversations in my dreams
Find me telling you how much I love you,
And you reply
That you love me too.

If you could talk
I'd tell you to eat all the food on your plate
Not just your favourites.
You'd ask for more sweets.

We'd cuddle just before bed.
You're not sleepy
And I hate to say goodnight,
But I promise you a treat for breakfast.

Have You Ever Loved
Harold Stiles
red
hair, wine with a woman, wet freckles
alive in the rain, wispy days left before fall
steps in to set the year, evening fog, the first
stone of what's left. I would stand with fallen
arms for the night pushing down night sky, my
mouth would gape. Tired limbs with that brave
freedom remind me to breathe, I could not be a man
telling a story, I would stare in blank salvation
at the angle of the day's first light, moss
hanging on. I could live on a river island, live
island life or greet the petty thief beneath
submissive beds, live hard laughter. Generation
X and HIV are paying all attention to the great
recycle campaign, born with eyes, a virus
holocaust to guarantee fresh anger, blind
thoughts of personal freedom, fresh laughter
as certain steps to unexpected lights flashing
red.

Dreams of the Soul

In A Black Christmas
Brenda Wheeler
Just me on Christmas and what do I see
Snow on the ground as black as me
What's too black too black for me
The color of my skin which makes me be
to be black as black as me
my snow is black my tree is black
my world is black my Christmas is black as
black as me
So what do I see under my Christmas tree
black! Black as black as me
It's my own black Christmas under my
Christmas tree
The blackest Christmas I'll ever see
black as black as me
Merry Christmas to all.

Dedication: To my uncle, Simon Wheeler

Healing
Kim E. Tich
I shield my eyes from the harsh sunlight as I emerge from my troubled sleep
A battered reflection in the mirror–but the wounds are much more deep
What once was free in spirit–naive–yet strong of heart
Is hidden behind a wall to protect me–I turn inward as not to
be torn apart.

A claim of love is simple–accepted for it is what we seek
Enduring his rage and violence – survival has made me weak
Broke the bonds that held me but I left too much behind
Time will heal the body but what will heal the mind.

Another chance was given but of my pain you weren't aware
Still hidden behind the wall – too hard for me to care.
You stayed for a long, hard journey and settled for the
little I had to give
And in the end I could say I Love You and knew you
were the reason I live!

Dedication: Chad – The light of my life

Little Joe
Robert C. Brown
Little Joe, as you all know
Was the fightin'est ship in all the show
Now the show was good as far as shows go
And the farthest to go was Little Joe.

The Admiral said, "We're in a pinch"
So Hoppy replied, "We have a six inch"
And into the beach and along the shore
No fighting ship could ask for more.

We got our bearings and trained our guns
That would put an end to the sons of the Rising Sun
Then after the show we cleaned the guns
Swabbed the deck and was given "well done."

But the man who was credited with Little Joe's good
Was that proud little man, Captain Hopwood
Then we were fed ge–dunk and started the next show
On the main deck aft of Little Joe.

O Sodom
Robert M. Richardson
O Sodom, O Sodom why was thou destroyed, were
there no righteous men in thee. There were not
fifty, nor forty, nor were there even ten. Oh what
a very wicked place, O Sodom you must have been.

Are you a land forever gone and never more to be,
or have you lain dormant in the soil like the roots
of an evil tree.

O Sodom, O Sodom of long ago where there
couldn't be found not ten.
For your destruction came about of wickedness
and sin.

Just look about O Modern Man and you can plainly
see the wickedness that once was Sodom is still
alive in THEE.

What Do You See
Becky Kays
Tell me nurse, what do you see, what do you see when you look at me?
Do you see the man I used to be or do you see what's now become of me?
I wish I could get up and walk beside you, I'd show you all I used to do.
I feel so helpless and sometimes depressed, and you out of everyone
knows this the best.
My eyes may sometimes look hollow, but inside my mind I'm sharp as a
Tack most of the time. You give me the care I so badly need.
You're not just my nurse you're my friend indeed.
I know you care and love me so but the day will come when you must let me
go.
God has a plan for me you see and I've often wondered just what it could
be.
So wipe away all your tears, all your sadness and all your fears.
This place I'm going I will be pain free, and someone very special
Is waiting for me. We will meet again someday in a place so
Very far away. I'll know you and you will know me
And again I will ask, now what do you see?

Dedication: Bennie Barnett – very dear friend

Easy To Remember
Carole M. Erickson
Easy to remember
Never shall I forget
That warm summer evening
When we first met.
Your eyes so blue
Your cheeks so red
I knew from that moment
Someday we would wed.
Many years have now passed
As I look in the mirror
Remembering precious times
Will sparkle a tear.
Through good times and bad
Sometimes happy,
Sometimes sad
Our life together
Will always be easy to remember.

Dedication: My friend, my husband Paul

Noteworthy Works

Sting
Marilyn Smith
Wrenched from Mother earth,
in my prime uprooted, uplifted
briefly left to dry
not of my choice,
tanned dry skin peeled.

Exposed fearful I bleed
raw pungent odor,
cut, sliced dissected
for the needs of others
I am used.

Abuse of my swollen
pallid body is avenged,
as their ducts ooze
warm salty liquid
stinging guilty cheeks.

Time
Sheila Bills
As I looked from my window, I saw the children at play;
I don't know how long I watched them, it seemed like most
of the day.
I wondered as I watched them, happy and gay, how would
it feel to be free again that way?
Where did the time go?
I cannot say.
Did I use it well, or did I just let it pass away?
Time is something that keeps moving along;
It passes for the weak as well as the strong.
As I sat in contemplation so deep, wishing for lost time
so hard, I wanted to weep.
Times that I thought that nothing I planned would ever
go wrong;
That with enough time I could shape my life on my own.
Now, I have found that in this thinking I wasn't unique,
besides, time isn't something that you can bottle and keep.
You try to use it as best you can, but it still slips
through your fingers like grains of sand.

World Of Poetry
Laina Kontautas
Life is like a blossom
or perhaps philosophy.
Love is pleasure...
Ends with torture and psychology.

Dignity and beauty
Treasure cannot be bought.
May beautiful America
Rich as a Midas.

World of poetry
Is calling my name
To cheer and dry my tears.
Meet America's poets
Hello you there
I am the shadow compare
to them.

Dedication: The World of Poetry

The Writer
Keith Woodhams
Weaver of words,
His pen his sword,
He duels the day away,
Making a masterpiece of his foe,
A petty labour of love.

Artistry in the craft of narration,
He toys with the portrayal of dreams,
Striving for all whose air–drawn dagger
Does border at rationality.
But they relish and unlearn.

His tragic figure ripped and torn,
Against the battlements of ignorance,
His sword dripping verse.
A battle fought to an ironic victory,
The better part of valour is dead!

The Balance
Andrew Busby
There is no black or white, only different shades of grey,
There is no doubt inside you, simply heed the words you say,
There is no right or wrong, just contradiction of opinion,
And there is no land of freedom, but different styles of dominion.

You don't choose what you know, eventually you'll be told,
You won't know what you choose, unless you lose your blindfold.
The mountains, valleys, rivers and hills, that seem to pass you by,
Are always there for you to find; they never say goodbye.

Our fate can be decided, discarded or ignored,
For destiny is not arrival, it is the journey down that road.
But the train of life moves quickly, clinging to the rails,
Though neither Man or beast nor earth and sea can solely tip the scales.

The Balance is a trawler, sailing through the mist,
Good and bad, happy or sad, are things that don't exist.
Love, hate or indifference are easy things to blame,
But these things are dealt in equal share, so everyone's the same.

Daddy
Lisa Fulmer
A special person to you he was
But he is now an angel in God's land above.
He left this earth too soon for you
You still had questions that needed answers but alas he was due.
His job here was completed he now could go
You depended on him to help you through,
You learned a great deal from your daddy and now you know
The secret to his love, but he made it difficult though.
Remember your daddy will always be there
To watch over you in spirit, he still loves you still cares.
The pain and emptiness is very strong right now
But I promise this will subside in time, but you say how?
For within your heart there will always be
A window to your daddy just open it and see.
Let his love surround the pain and hurt that is so real
Let him embrace you and take you on that magical carousel ride
just close your eyes and feel.
Your daddy though he is gone will never be far
For he is in heaven looking down on you flying on a star.

Dreams of the Soul

It's Over
Pam Brodie
My soul is quiet, my heart is still.
Time has left me without will.

My cries are useless, no tears to found,
gone and left forever, never to abound.

Sadness surrounds me as I let go,
no longer fearing time is too slow.

Feeling the warmth of a still light,
it is now time to let go of my fright.

Souls surround me–guiding me through,
pounding hearts are no longer blue.

Angels singing, trumpets sound, death
cannot haunt me anymore.

Gleams
Elmer F. Beckstrand
Across the starlit sky there glowed
A golden gleam of light —
Remained an instant, then was blown
Completely out of sight;
And though the gleam tried hard to rend
Its way thru darkening gloom
Its efforts all too soon were spent—
Untimely death, its doom.

A gleam of love a few days since
Was burning in my breast
That gleam in vain has tried to pierce
Your heart and there find rest;
But such is life and we must fight
For all we get or gain
And though I've lost that gleam of love
Its memory I'll retain.

Dedication: My wife, Ina Beckstrand

Untitled
Glenn Isaac Ward
The troops rolled out,
To put things right.
They'll fix everything,
To our delight.

For they don't care,
Where they may go.
They only want
Their might to show.

Wonder now——
If you really believe;
The solution to this one,
Is up your sleeve?

The troops rolled out,
In the middle of the night;
And the whole wide world,
Shook with fright.

Misguided
Mary S. Standifer
When I warp my arms around me
nothing can set my boundary
feelings watched over by one unseen
Who is always there with caring wing.
I am held within a measure of time
and pray these words of rhyme
set free my heart's expression
allowing the mind's expansion
to set not desires as goals to reach
but life's realities do teach
because I caused more pain
as normality I tried to gain
I say to you "One is as is"
and cannot be...
the same as you, the same as me!

Dedication: Glemagene Wynn–Michels, my mentor, my close friend, my Mom!

Decisions
Gaylene Mitchell
Love is a decision
Not something you purchase or take
It's something you do—because it's right for you.
You do it for your own sake.

Happiness is a decision
Not something you seek or find
No one can give it—you simply must live it
It comes in its own good time.

Peace is a decision
Not something you force others to share
It's something you make—or strive to create
A special feeling in the air.

Life is a decision
A gift you can share or destroy
You can squander and waste—or relish and taste
The sorrow and pain and joy.

Untitled
Teresa Stratz
There they are – your broken words
So filled with betrayal and deceit
Did you ever stop for just a moment –
Did you stop to think what you were doing to me?
You left me there –
You burdened me with your words –
They were harsh – like a violent thunderstorm
raping the trees of their beauty
And like the saddened flower it droops silently
from the weight of the rain.
–Just like your words weighing so heavily upon my heart
This time the rain hides nothing.
– The sky lit from the heaven's rage
And this time there will be no tears to mask my anger
For I have fallen prey to your lies and irresponsibilities
But no longer...
I now stand proud of my feelings –
Just like the renewed flower
Standing proudly in the sunshine.

Noteworthy Works

Untitled
Andrea Dixon
I found you, just in time,
You brought meaning to this life of mine,
Made my broken heart a valentine.
At last my loneliness is behind me,
You touched me, just in time,
Just when I thought the sun would never shine,
I found you, just in time.

Just in time to save my world,
Heaven sent you to my door,
Just in time you reached out,
And showed me how to love once more.
Don't let me cry again,
Don't leave me alone again,
Because, darling...
When I almost lost my mind
You saved me just in time.

Guardian Angel
Heather Lawford
Sweet, soft, strong Spirit.
A child's love, a Mother's touch,
A Father's wisdom.

Warm feathers soak up my tears;
Gentle whispers wrap comfort;
Shelter me from life.

And then...

You show me a strength;
The light that promises
A better day. Strong wings
Shove me towards life.

Save me from my
Sucking, sulking self–pity
That is devouring.
Give me myself

Consider My Love
Jeremy C. Pick
Consider the lilies, the ocean and sky
magnolias in moonlight, ducks flying by
Consider the tides, they come and they go
and we cannot change the ebb nor the flow
Consider the mountains covered with snow
the golden leaves of autumn falling below
Consider the apple blossoms that fill the air
with magical moments happening everywhere.

Consider the stars we never have seen
the glory of Easter when everything's green
Consider the seasons of summer and spring
with roses and lilacs and robins that sing
Consider the sunset, the death of each day
the passing of time for nothing can stay
Consider my love in beauty arrayed
For this is the gift my heart has made.

Dedication: My dearest Teri

Beggar's Melody
Jamilla Webb
excuse me Miss you have a lovely daughter
would you mind if I borrowed a quarter?
'cause you see the kids have no food to eat
no house to live in, or shoes on their feet
Sir please can you give food to the poor
I don't mean to harass you by knocking on the front door
but at least I ask honestly I don't steal or rob
I just don't have the education or skills to get a job
I hate living like this, no one seems to care
people always laugh at me or treat me like thin air
excuse me would you mind if I took out your trash
why for even a few dollars I'd even pump your gas
please can I have some change to borrow
you have no idea of all my suffering and sorrow
try to understand and imagine living this way
because who knows it could be you one day

Dedication: Gertrude Francis Dillard and Ronnie Jersky

The Thunderstorm
I. Beale
As I looked from the bedroom up at the sky
The beauty of the days dawning as the sun caught my eye
My thoughts went back to the night before
The thunderstorm as I had never seen before
The thunder so loud so close so frightening
The power of the lightning streaking across the sky
Blinding you as it flashed your eyes
The sound of the rain as it came with such force
To watch it again as it bounced up and rose
The size of the hailstones as they landed with a roar
The flood that it caused as it flowed around
Never would you think there was land around
The dog under the table shivering with fright
The cat under the chair a pitiful sight
That terrible night
Those were my thoughts as I looked at the dawn
The following morn.

The First Christmas
Aaron Fitzgerald Evans
The first Christmas.
God gave the first gift,
He gave the greatest gift of love.
His only begotten son.
The first Christmas.
God gave the greatest compassion.
He gave a saviour to the world.
The first Christmas.
God gave His life, blood, and tears,
The first Christmas.
God gave grace and mercy,
Like no one can do.
He gave the greatest joy, peace,
and happiness.
The first Christmas.
God gave His very best.
And just think!
Without the first Christmas,
What would this Christmas be?

Dreams of the Soul

State Mission Offering
Patricia S. Ritchie
We mission friends have saved our money
to help the people of Kentucky,
Because we've learned that compared to some,
We are very lucky.

We know that Jesus loves us!
But others have never heard!
And we want to use our money to help
Missionaries spread the word!

We may be small, but we understand
Far more than you're aware,
And we have learned how important it is
For all of us to share.

So please join – the mission friends,
And give what you can afford,
So the missionaries in Kentucky
Can tell others about the Lord.

A Man Who Never Complained
Anthony J. King, Jr.
I once knew a man, who never complained
no matter how he felt, good or bad, he acted the same.
You might ask "How do you feel today?" and he would say "Just fine".
But yet still he was feeling the worst of all times.
You would think that he never felt pain,
For he was a strong–willed man who never complained.
Then as his days grew short and his time was done
he still did not complain to anyone.
In his last moment, hour, and breath
It was as if everyone could smell death.
Even though you could smell death, nothing had changed
because when asked how he felt he replied, "the same."
You might say how could it be, how is it so,
But it is just he was a man who never complained, a
man I'm glad I was able to know.
Dedication: My great–grandfather, Savon King, Sr. "Pipi"

Our Dad
Sandie Horne
A life of devotion, commitment and love
His wisdom and counsel he sought from above
We knew without question he'd always be there
Whatever the sacrifice, our burdens he'd bear

A man of integrity, carved out of trust
We knew that his words and his actions were just
He taught us to value and help one another
To honor and love our kind, gentle Mother

In good times and bad times, for better for worse
He stood by our Mother and followed God's course
For richer for poorer in sickness and health
His wife, his children and God were his wealth

He gave us a childhood so wholesome and pure
Of love and protection we were always sure
Our lives are much richer, abundant and glad
Because of the treasure God gave us in Dad

Heaven
Martine L. Shelton
Heaven could be to someone a field of grass of luscious green
With daisies, buttercups, bluebells adding to the glorious scene;
Upon which the golden warming sun shines from a sky of vibrant blue
And a brook of crystal water in the field gently ripples through.

Of course Heaven is where our Lord is seated at the right hand of God.
Where the angels sing in glorious tones and where all the saints have trod,
Where True Peace and Joy and Love abound for all who have found The Way,
And a continuous Light is shining – for there is no darkness, only day.

The perfect idea of nature as our God would ordain it to be
May be there in all its beauty – as part of the Heaven we long to see.
And there will be constant rejoicing on that wonderful impending day
When all who have loved our Saviour will be there with Him for always.

Whatever the idea of Heaven, of one thing we can be sure:
There will be True Light and Beauty and Peace and Love forevermore.
Just to at last be with my Saviour will be Heaven enough for me
And for all who do truly love Him – oh what a glorious day that will be!

Message To My Son
Susan E. Coffman
This is the last day of 1992. It's been
six months since I last saw or held you.
Ricky, I miss you with all of my heart,
I'll never understand why God tore us apart.
If I had just one wish for 1993, It
would be, that God returns you to me...
Every day you're in my thoughts, Every night
you're in my dreams, I'll never stop
missing you and I'll never, ever stop loving you
You were my one and only son and as every
one knows, a very loving one.
I'll be with you someday, I just wish it were
today.
Wait for me my sweet son, 'cause you are
the only one. To keep my place warm and safe —
When my day arrives to walk through
God's Heavenly Gates.

The Fiver
Carol Fisher
Whilst walking int' fields last summer one day
John spied a fiver just lying int'way
Face down int' furrow all crinkled blue–brown
Not believing his luck as he hunkered straight down

I'll get camera says Fred and rushed back t't car
Excited and happy he chuckled 'hurrah'!
The pictures were grand some wi' Fred, some wi' John
Sat beside fiver, standing or kneeling down.

They planned how they'd spend it at races or fo' beer
or one of them new caps that dandies would wear
Of luck and good fortune the' bragged and the' pattered
What fortunate chaps and nothing else mattered

So elate was their joy their fortune been found
That neither had thought to pick it off ground
Sun turned to rain and darkened the day
As gust of wind surged and blew fiver away.

When We're Old(er)
Mary Ann Brewer-Whitson
Our thinking process slows way down
Our physical abilities are limited
So what we take a little longer to respond
And we walk in a way that seems to take
too long
Be patient!
It's still me inside this body that has served
me so well
Look into my eyes when you speak to me
I can hear you, can't you tell?
If I seem to drift off – let me! – I'll be back
I am peacefully reminiscing about the
life I've had
Treat us gently, treat us kind
To the aging old folks, don't be blind
God be with you to help you unfold
We are all His children, young and old.
Dedication: Clair and Ruthie

Twenty–Five Years
Evelyn J. Snyder
Twenty–five years ago we said "I DO."
We promised to stay together thru and thru
Each year we have had our ups and downs
Now I love you Terry even tho' sometimes you are a clown
To death till we part are vows that we took
You surely must remember how your knees shook.

Fortunate we are that we have one daughter
I am so proud of all that she has accomplished
Very bright spot we have in our life
Enjoying our grandson James Aaron Lisle

You have to know you are my best friend
Enjoying each other to each days end
A milestone we are celebrating today
Regarding our 25th Anniversary.
So Terry I must say I love you in every way.

Do You?
Meredith Musgrave
Do you think of me from time to time?
Do thoughts of me ever cross your mind?
Do memories float by you any day?
Do you snatch them up or throw them away?

Do pieces of thoughts gnaw at you?
Do you push them away and different thoughts ensue?
Do you completely shut me out?
Do you ever have a doubt?

Do you ever wish things aren't the way they are?
Do you ever try to reach out for a star?
Do you remember how we wanted it to be?
Do you remember all that we wanted to do and see?

Do you remember all of our thoughtful sighs?
Do you remember when our laughter died?
Do you remember our moments of glee?
Do you ever think of me?

Bluebell Wood
Graham Hume
When I was young, so full of fun, the days they seemed so long.
My two friends and I we played all day in Bluebell Wood as we
had known.
The ferns were so tall and we were so small as we crawled on
our hands and knees.
Cowboys and Indians, Tarzan too, as we swung from the branches
of trees.
The rabbits would play alongside us all day till the sun would
start to set.
We make our way home, make our excuses known, we know what trouble
there be.
Mum at the door "I know where you've been but have you seen your
clothes, just have your bath and eat your tea you've had a good
time I suppose."
Since those days have gone three became two and two became one
as the Lord will only know.
That one is me but I still see Bluebell Wood how it used to be.
The diggers have been in and the trees have all gone and Bluebell
Wood is a wood no more.

A Fair Trade
Dorothy C. Chegwidden
The waves slap against the shoreline
Pressing their fingerprints into the sand.
Some dare to stretch farther than the others,
Where on the sand they shed the opaque colors of the deep,
And reflect only the sparkle of the sun,
Where they deposit a glistening Abalone shell
And grab
The gullible sand
And a fragile Child.
Laughing and clapping, she throws her infant hands up in glee.
Tipping over to splash and play, she clutches the watery hand
Which Deceives her
And Drags her
Down.
Bartered for the sea god's treasures, her pale shell rests.
He smiles with his prize in his pocket.
As do I.

Autumn
Bernard Adams
Strolling through a woodland park.
Tints of light and shades of dark.
Sunlight, speckled on the ground,
Nature's beauty all around.

Yellows, browns, greens and golds,
The fall of leaves on grassy moulds.
Once, flowered meadow and windy heath.
Wave on wave of scented leaf.

Sound, touch, taste and smell,
Of course, the fifth, sight as well.
Look, feel, emotions are abound,
Nature's beauty all around.

Row on row of barren trees,
Forest, fields and gentle breeze,
God's creation, sun, moon and all,
Beauteous is the leaf in fall.

Dreams of the Soul

This Game Of Life
Edith Mee
This game of life is so hard to play,
Especially when the outlook's grey.
It makes life easier when the sun shines through,
You feel like doing what you've got to do.

There's the chores to do, and the meals to cook.
If only I had time to read a book.
I must go shopping and pay some bills
Must see the doctor, and get some pills.

There's a film on TV but haven't the time.
Must hang the washing out on the line.
The newspaper's here, I'll have a read,
Now the baby's crying, he wants his feed.

Now it's time for bed, a rest at last,
Six hours of sleep, but it goes so fast
Then it's the same routine, day after day.
Yes this game of life is so hard to play.

Reflections On A Summer Morn
Perdita Carman Humphreys
Tentatively, I waken to a new day dawning,
Yawning, as re–kindled consciousness lies spawning
Images and whisperings that stir my inner soul.

Quietly the timid morn comes stealing
Revealing what the nighttime was concealing.
New shapes and sounds aggressively achieve their goal,

As, suddenly, an early bird chirps warning,
"Morning is approaching, and daylight is adorning
God's world. " And lo, the avian anthems sweetly roll.

Slowly, lethargy gives way to fantasizing
As in rising from my slumber realizing
With joy and wonder once again His love and care have made me whole.
Dedication: My children, Sharon, Linda and David

So
Deborah K. Nelson
I am not a leper.
I do not have the plague.
I am not a priceless artifact on show to the general public.
I am not carrying twenty–seven thousand volts.
I am not poisonous.
I am not marked "Top Secret – Confidential. "
I do not belong to somebody else.
I am not an unexploded bomb.
I am not a naked flame.
I do not have sharp edges.
I do not sting.
I do not bite.
I do not have thorns.
I am not a carrier of a contagious disease.
I am not a god.
I am not even a messiah.
I am just a warm–blooded human male.

So why won't you touch me?

Mackenzie
Melissa Lazzara
Ssh don't cry mommy is here
Let me wipe away your tear
I rock you gently in my arms
Hold you so tightly no one can do you harm
When you fall down and scrape your knee
My medicine will make it better you'll see
To watch you grow into my beautiful child
I pray to God you won't become wild
Hoping we can stay good friends
So I might be there when your first love ends
As you start to walk down the aisle
Upon my face is the largest smile
The baby is so tiny and small
Just perfect, he looks like a doll
A hand on my shoulder and I hear her say
Ssh don't cry mommy I am here
Now let me wipe away your tear
Dedication: My most precious gift

My Dear Mother
Judy Boron
Years ago when you were young;
many a lullabies I bet you sung.

Burps on your shoulders,
and the many bottles you must have fed?
And also the many nites you tucked us in bed.

The love that you gave us, there is no measure;
the love that you gave us, will always be treasured.

You touch my heart with a miracle mist;
there is always a hug and a gentle sweet kiss.

A role model you will always be;
you're my dear Mother, I thank God for thee.
Dedication: My dear mother, Julia M. Thunberg

Too Precious
Wendy Brown
An old man sitting amongst the trees.
Watching the flowers blow in the breeze.
The woman sitting in solitude.
Looking at seeds she's carefully sowed.

Are they together, or are they apart?
They're actually together, they're tied by the heart.
Their love is so strong, they don't live in their pockets.
Just a heart round their necks, they call it their locket.

He loves her because she's kind and giving.
She loves him because he's honest and loving.
The reasons they love are so very many.
To read their minds is worth more than a penny!

But, the hurdles are stacked in the way.
Do they decide to call it a day?
NO. Don't let them destroy the love that you have.
It's Too Precious.

Noteworthy Works

What Is Love?
Teresa Carrion

Love is like a sunken treasure, never knowing
what it's worth,
Until the one we love the most has forever
left this earth.

We sometimes forget to say the important things
that are meant to be heard,
And sometimes they're not even as audible,
as a soft tune from a bird.

So while we have the time right now to
say what's in our heart,
Let's let the one we love so dear know how
much we care before we're apart.

For the time here on earth is precious, and
we don't know when it will end,
Let's let this be a new beginning, and let
our broken hearts mend.

Untitled
Natasha R. Johnson

When the world turns its back on you, and all you know is sorrow and despair,
Just look to the sky and know that He cares.
This life we live might have plenty to offer, but cannot promise to take away your pain.
Just know that the life God gave you was never meant in vain.
You may stumble and fall and struggle to get up.
But He'll always be with you – through the good times and the rough.
In this life we treasure so many things, the air we breathe. Even the birds that sing.
But when the world is against us, these treasures seem so far away.
Just pray to the heavens for a much brighter day.
So when the world is against us and our hearts are burdened with despair.
Lift your pain to Him, for he is well aware.
He'll take away your sorrow, your weeping, and your despair.
His comfort may not come in seconds, but his blessings will always be there.

Since The Death of My Husband
Elizabeth Ratcliffe

No one to please, no one to impress
No one to acknowledge everyday stress
No one to sleep with, nor to caress
No one to share every day's best.

No one to share the flavor of food
No one around to alter the mood
No one to share life's gratitude
No one to break this stark solitude.

No one to feel the folly and wise
No one to reflect in the depth of the eyes
No one to care if your soul needs to cry
No one to be there when it's time to die.

No one to hear the guttural moan
No one to know that you're all alone.

Dedication: Russ, no one without you

The Word Is Out
Velma Adkins

The word is out,
that I have this thing,
people are talking
of us having a fling,
people are curious, wanting to know,
they're watching my mood,
hoping that feelings will show,
let them look,
the curious, the jealous alike,
it's their problem, their unhappiness
that they have, as part of their life,
the word is out,
be careful of things you say,
They're watching you too,
hoping we'll give something away,
So, the word is out,
We two are having a fling,
We're smarter than that,
they'll never prove we're doing a thing.

A Cry For Help!
Lucille Martin

I cried for help! "God" heard my cry
And sent his "son", for "me", to "die".
He heard my plea and sent to me
A blessing for "eternity".
He shied not away from the "terror"
That would befall.
He "knew" he would have to suffer,
If he answered my call.
And though he "knew" when he came how
Great the price.
He answered my cry at the cost of his "life".
Now you would think that it was for
A "good" man that my savior did die.
But "no", t 'was for a wicked "sinner"
That he answered that cry.

Dedication: My beloved husband, Marion Martin

The Neighbor Girl
Steve Lewis

Do you remember that daisy, on that hot summer day.
One petal, she loves me. One petal, she loves me not.

We always lost track before the end of the flower.
What took minutes, seemed like an hour.

It really didn't matter, we were together for fun.
I used to chase you, and you used to run.

We would run and run, till we ran out of breath.
And then sit on the grass, to figure out what was next.

Then your Mom would yell "honey I think it's time to come home"

Then we would look at each other with a sigh and a groan.
But then we would laugh and forget all our sorrow
and with a smile and a wave, we set our sight on tomorrow...

Dedication: Heather D.

Dreams of the Soul

Across The Bridge
Imogene Pinnock
The bridge is for crossing
Not an awning
Go forward, go forward, take no turning
Do not hesitate
No time to contemplate
Go forward, go forward
The sunrise is before you
Backward is yesterday
Go forward, go forward
The bridge is near, the bridge is near
Do not hesitate
No time to contemplate
Under the bridge
there is the torrent sea
This side of bridge is dark as can be
The bridge is for crossing
And safe as can be
When you cross over
Only then you will see

I Am
Kayla Ondracek
I am...
The water in a stream
The wind at your doorstep
The gold in a coin
The soap on a bubble
The bark on the trees
The water in a cloud
The butter on your bread
The yolk in an egg
The wrapper on a crayon
The dirt on a shoe
The leaf on a branch
The pearl in an oyster
The roof on your house
The hair on your head
The grass on the ground
I am the end of a poem.

He Painted Love
Mary Romine
I can see the golden sunrise
From a far and distant land
Where the artist holds the palette
With his gentle nail–pierced hand.

He paints the color of the rainbow
After painting winter's rain
He spreads joy with reds and yellows
Covering up the black of pain.

When the masterpiece is finished
We will fully understand
Why rain was mixed with sunshine
To complete the master plan.

When we behold our Savior
We will see the grand design
From the cruel cross of Calvary
He painted love for all mankind.

Grass Fields
Jillian Perry
Bending under a barbed wire, she's in grass fields.
The wind whips around her like ghosts,
catches her hair and blows through it like wildflowers.
Running against the wind, she closes her eyes
and inhales a lungful of freedom.
She kicks out and sets her shoes flying,
leaving her naked feet in the morning dew.
As she tosses her head back to face the sky,
a raindrop lands on her nose.
The tears of heaven begin to fall,
leaving an indelible mark on the girl's soul.
Mud puddles appear, small ponds of murky water
and in the horizon, the colors of the world
come to life in the translucent sky
as the heavenly weeping ceases.
She leaves the field, all evidence
of her presence gone, except
the green blades clinging
to her clothes.

Merry Christmas
Darryl Hall
Myriad rivers of shimmering love
Ever flowing through endless time;
Radiant crystals of pure Thought
Recognition of love Divine;
Yes. "I AM".

Christ the power, infinite sight;
Holy Spirit, Christ the Light.
Reason not, nay do I ask, for
I AM, and shall come to pass.
Smoke filled delusions of doubt and fear;
Trust, and have faith, thy vision clear.
Master the Word, though it be odd;
All are One,
Sons of God.

Dedication: Grandmother, for your love

Yesterday's Dreams
Joseph V. Marr
Where are the dreams
of yesterday
That ever so briefly
passed my way

A caressing word
a smiling face
Have disappeared
without a trace

Lost in the mists
of time gone by
Somewhere between
a sob and a sigh

Where did they go to
and why do they stray
Those elusive dreams
of yesterday

Noteworthy Works

My Baby Brother
Nayab Pathan

He came and took me away
He came and changed my life
He was all I asked for,
they way he used to cry, the way he
used to laugh.
I miss him I love him I want him
back.

To change him was hell but I enjoyed
it.
To make his milk was hectic but fun.
To bathe him was crazy but now he is
gone.
I remember the first time we brought
him home, so sweet and innocent.
I remember seeing him for the first
time, so fair and cuddly, then seeing him
for the last time so small and lovely but
cold and still.

Treasures
Carol L. Woodford

No money, have I, yet I am rich
As rich, as rich can be
My treasures, are my children
They mean 'the world' to me.
God gave them gold dust for their hair
To shine and bring me joy
Diamonds, he gave for their eyes
To sparkle over a new toy
Rubies are their smiling lips
So meek and yet so mild
Whatever could be richer, than the life of a small child
If I could have one wish come true, I know what it would be
To live to see them grow up, how contented I would be
To be without my treasures
I would be so very alone
I hope I will be there, when my treasures
Have treasures of their own.

Summer
Daniel W. Borntreger

I like to ride
in the field
I'd rather go on
when it says "yield."

I like to harrow
in the sun
Go here and there
and have fun.

I like to make dinner
and something good, too
I'm always so hungry
I could eat it like new.

If I don't go to the field
I make something good to eat
And today it was potatoes,
noodles, peas, and meat.

Friends
Dorothy Morlan

Friends have a special place in our lives
In times of sorrow, times to rejoice
Relatives come from the family tree
But our friends are ours by choice

To have friends, you must be one
That isn't so hard to do
Just open up your heart to them
And you will have friends, tried and true

When we have our "ups and downs"
They are there to lend an ear
You count on them, they count on you
It helps to have them near

Be kind and understanding
To the people whom you meet
You cannot have too many friends
And good friends just can't be beat

Telegraph Words
Brian M. Ladd

I was sitting at me ambo accounting of me pelf
When I saw a Chapman passin' and Thought "I'll treat meself"
So I went an' bought a paper and read it in my room
And then I rang South Africa and had a word with Oom
"Have you got an Aye–aye handy you can send me right away
I saw an ad this mornin' and think I can make it pay
I'll see a Shroof tomorrow and get some pelf from him
Then I'll take it ok to Aussie and train him up on Gin. "

Well the sun was really fulgent as we landed in the bay
Old Aye–aye he was tired so we rested all that day
I had no gin to give him so he drank the fusel dry
And when I tried to stop him well he blacked me bloomin' eye
So we headed north to Darwin to the Pharos on the beach
The phlox was all in flower and looked a real peach
But time it was a wasting so I passed old Oom the news
That were off to Wogga–Wogga catching Kanga–bloody–roos.

Again
Ian John

Immune to emotion,
Devoid of desire,
Trapped by the flames,
Engulfed in the fire.

Lost in a place,
Where I don't want to be,
My eyes are wide open,
Yet I no longer see.

Transparent words,
Exposed and then lost,
Translucent lies,
At no extra cost.

Mocked by the laughter,
Inflicted with pain,
Taken for granted,
Again and again...

Dreams of the Soul

Kindness
Eva Halliday
Kindness is an asset
That we must all possess
At times it will be difficult
Just try your very best

Take the time to listen
Show others that you care
Your kindness is rewarded
With the smiles everywhere

There's one thing to remember
From deep within your heart
Kindness is the path to take
To know you did your part

It might be just an action
The handshake of a friend
A moment you can cherish
From now until the end.

Day Care Kids
Letha Garlow
Day care kids are such a joy,
Each little girl, each little boy.
When each one climbs upon my knee
it brings a warmth to the heart of me.
Those little arms around my neck.
cannot be replaced by heck
then at the table they begin to eat,
to see which one will surely beat.
Off to naptime heads a–nodding
up again off and running.
Evening comes, and so do folks,
to take then home for laughs and jokes,
next day comes, and the kids do too
to start another day anew.
But without them what would I do?

Dedication: Leona Sandhagen, "my supporter for my song"

A Special Place
G. R. Messinger
A soccer field is my special place.
It puts a big smile on my face.
It's a place where dreams are made of.
I enjoy the soft grass under my feet,
The warm air of the summer days,
The roaring and stomping of the crowd.
This is my special place.
Dreams become reality on the field for me.
It's where I let out all my built–up emotions.
It's a place where skill is required and,
Patience is a must.
Sometimes it's a place of total surprise,
When it could be the last time there.
When in case of injury,
This special place could not be anymore.

But still this is my special place.
Dedication: Coach Kevin Koger, thank you

Jamie My Dear
Ramona D. Morrow
Jamie My Dear,
Please don't shed a tear;
Even though we are apart,
You will always have my heart.

The five years we've had
Were joyful, never sad;
What memories we've shared
Will always be there.

So Jamie My Dear,
Please don't shed a tear.
The love in our hearts
Will never keep us apart;
Even though we live in different places
God will always grace us.

So Jamie My Dear,
Please don't shed a tear.

Pepper, A Tribute To My Kitten
Loette M. Hull
My kitten's name was Pepper, 'cause he was mostly black.
He had some white hairs here and there and barely had a tail.
He had the bluest little eyes, almost as blue as the sky.
He liked to sit and look at me and cock his little head,
As though he knew just exactly what I'd said.
I knew that Pepper loved me, he had his special ways.
He would gently pat my face with his tiny little paws.
Pepper suddenly took sick today!!!
He had to go away.
Today, I lost my little friend, I'm very sad to say.
I miss him very much with his playful little ways.
Thoughts of him bring joy and tears,
I'd hoped he'd be with me for some years.
He came my way for just awhile.
Thoughts of him still make me smile.
He's still with me in my heart and thoughts.
His friendship was worthwhile.

Speckled Butterfly
Donna A. Ryan
Between shafts of sunlight
Under a green canopy,
A speckled butterfly
Dances from tree to tree.

It moves to the cadence
Of a willow warbler's song
Charming woods and meadows
All spring and summer long.

With dappled coloring,
It seems to disappear
Creating twilight magic
Whenever it is near.

It's a fairy–like creature,
And a friend of birds and bees,
Who enchants the woodlands,
The mountains, and the leas.

Noteworthy Works

Ease Your Mind
Barbara Wilson
Close your eyes
Open your heart
Love beats true
Though we're apart

Open your eyes
Look at the sun
You'll know for sure
You're the only one

Open your hands
And catch the rain
Let the storm
Wash away the pain

When twilight ends
And darkness surrounds
It's a good time to
Lay your burdens down

Lullaby Of Life
Laura Larcombe
At first,
Curtained by crowd
Only voice can be heard.
Indistinguishable words, but
Oh, the beauty of the chant
Embracing every recess of this world.
But curtain pulls as
People receive the sight of sound.
Confronted by Mother and child
All pleasure now violated and
Oh, the beauty of the chant
Debased by their apathy of eye.
The fatalistic pose of a cradled child
Mesmerized yet traumatized by
Her lullaby of life.

Dedication: Mervyn, Holly and Joshua

A Better World
Bert Kanwit
Because oh so many people are nefarious
We are dwelling in a world that's
much too precarious.
We must go all out to enhance the
prevalence
Of everything we can categorize as
bona fide benevolence
While we continue to whittle away
day after day
At all that is evil in any way.
A commendable course to pursue
For everyone of you
Is the Unitarian theme—
Nothing nobler can you deem.
Love and justice if they truly prevail
Can without a doubt derail
All which is sinister and totally out of line
In our search for a modus vivendi
That can be labeled as divine!

Castle of Dreams
Patricia S. Rafuse
Here I stand in our
castle of dreams.
The love that we feel
is like warm sunbeams.

The coldness that
suddenly appears.
Gives a new meaning
to all my fears.

This coldness is all
around me.
Could this mean that
our love will never,
ever be?

This castle is diminishing,
diminishing it seems.
There goes our castle of dreams.

White
Sean Smith
What we seek
Heavenly existence
Just out of reach
Self–kept dream
Reality beneath
Personal expansion
Treasured to keep
Golden
What I have here
Love too strong
to leave behind
Freedom tied
Life inside
Clockwork percussion
Family pride

Dedication: Mandy, Billie Jo, Julie, Elizabeth, Lillian

Night Storm
D. C. Pratt
Jagged streaks of light bring meadows to sight,
And distant views are curtained by the rain.
A timber trembling roar and it is night
While the angry wind presses each window pane.

Too long the hot broiling sun ruled the sky
As the thirsty green seemed to cry for rain.
Such turbulence, and the sky seems to cry
As the cleansing changing tears bathe each pane.

In life when struggles get too much for man;
Later comes the burst of rewarding power.
There is renewed strength that we understand;
Like new life appearing from the thundershower.

Behind walls we seek to escape the light
As nature's release makes us wait and shake.
A new dawn will come from this power tonight
When the sleeping sprouts will cheerfully wake.

Dreams of the Soul

Still A Dreamer
Lisa J. Johnson
Dreams are said to be a mirror to our hidden desires.
Dreams give us hope when there is nothing left.
Dreams keep me sane, when I feel I've lost my way.
My dreams are sometimes incomplete and complicated to most.
Somehow my dreams have a way of falling in mid–flight.
After all the crashes, I still take off again to make them soar.
Through the years, I've learned you have to work to keep some dreams alive.
Instead of waiting for Prince Charming to appear with roses on your door step,
Realize, life is a like a play, full of love and sometimes tragedies.
Stop wearing your heart on your sleeve or it will get broken.
Remember time heals all wounds.
With every storm a beautiful day follows.
In every rainbow, I believe a pot of gold is waiting at the end.
There is true love and it can last forever.
Believe in yourself or no one else will.
Hold onto your dream and forever keep trying.
Because dreams are part of the future, and the future is yours.

Footprints In The Sky
Stuart J. Goode
I see the sun walking across the sky
And I know there are still tears which I have not cried
There is still pain held deep within
I may hide it but it will never end
Agony, Sorrow, Death, and Sin
I have conquered all yet did not win
It was simply to bring you near
But in doing so I have released my darkest fear
You have me but could have so much more
Why do you choose to be locked away when all the world is an open door
These eyes see the future all too plain
My love can do no more than cause you pain
And I do not wish to pull you down in my flames
You are an angel and must fly away
To leave footprints across the sky another day
But remember me in your dreams as a distant star
For I will always love you from afar

Well Spent Dreams
Doris B. Ahearn
Last night I dreamed of you
You were here again with me
Everything was fancy–free
The way it used to be.

I only meet you in a dream
And those special moments gleam
Once again we are a team
'Tis such a joy supreme.

You were called so long ago
'Twas October how well I know
Thoughts of you will always glow
Your loss was such a blow.

Pleasant dreams of you thru the years
Help subside my bitter tears
When God tells me "He hears"
'Tis then I have no fears.

You—Can Make A Difference
Virginia M. Krueger
Though volunteers have been around for lo these many years
Now, they're needed even more, if just to wipe a small child's tears
Some deliver "Meals on Wheels", often stop and chat a while
They know they've had a good day if, just one person they make smile

Others help out at hospitals thus, "Trained Staff" may get more done
They bring magazines and papers or, read to children just for fun
Handicapped kids may be a challenge, but never are a bore
Just when you think you're helping them, you find, they help you more

There are juveniles and infants that would cherish a tender touch
Your caring, might light up their eyes——they aren't used to getting much
Teens, aiding seniors or injured neighbors, are apt to find a friend
Plus, many schools give credits to encourage this thoughtful trend

Volunteers are sorely needed, let your heart tell you what to do
Remember, but for the "Grace of God", the soul in need could be you
Yes, you too can make a difference, in these days of rage and strife
With a little time and effort, you might give someone hope in life!

Monday At 2:00 A. M.
Erin Puttonen
The birds did not sing,
but the phone, it did ring.
A call to share the news,
a time to sing the blues.
A soul went to a better place
As we, the survivors, begin to pace.
We mourn the loss of a man with great love
We all know now that he's in the heavens above.
During our final goodbye,
we will gather, we will cry.
Moving on is not easy to do
But with God on our side, we'll make it through.
Two lives lost within not even a year
People being touched by grief, by the tear
We know now that he couldn't stay
We know now he's not that far away
He's gone to be with Jesus

If I Was Much Older
Kenneth P. Lee, Jr.
Would you take me more seriously?
Laugh harder at jokes
Feel pleasure, not pain
With massages and pokes.
Would you look at me different?
Would you realize I'm grown?
Would you wake up beside me?
Instead of lost and alone.
Would you listen more carefully?
Take pride when I speak?
Look beyond imperfections
Of mind and physique.
Would you hold my hand?
Would you sway my hips?
Would you whisper my name?
Would you taste my lips?
Could you love me?
Could you cry on a younger man's shoulder?
Would you take me more seriously if I was much older?

Noteworthy Works

Children
E. M. Batley
Children, whom I adore,
Just make me love you more and more.
Gifted children, music making,
So inspiring and fascinating.

Magic moments, in the beginning,
Just to hear their voices singing.
Walking, talking, singing, dancing,
All around the garden, prancing.

Looking so pretty among the trees,
Birds singing, butterflies drifting, on the breeze.
Picking flowers, one by one,
I can see they're having fun.

Beautiful and dainty as the flowers,
Only I can look and dream for hours.
Life's dreams come true in stories told,
Answered prayers I'll never forget as I grow old.

You Can Make A Difference
Eve Kiley
In a world filled with greed and need
You can make a difference.
To those without hope unable to cope
You can make a difference.
For those who can't run the race
And never seem to find their place
You can make a difference.
When times are dark and dreary
And a friend is weary
You can make a difference.
To someone depressed or distressed
You can make a difference.
To the homeless and the loveless
You can make a difference.
If God is on your side
And in His love you abide
You can make a difference.

Mother's Farewell
Johanna Somsen
I know the time is near,
for me to leave you.
I can't do this face to face,
so I will put it down in words.

Do not spend time weeping,
after I am gone.
Just remember the good times,
we had together as a family.

If I made any mistakes,
I am so very sorry.
As I love you all dearly and,
will keep you in my heart forever.

When you must leave this world,
you won't be alone.
As I will be there for you again,
With a smile, big hug, and a "Welcome Home".

In My Heart
David Andrew Cooke
There's a place in my heart
For a girl I once knew
Never sure in myself
I watched as she grew
From sweet young thing
To a woman so tall
Fair of form, and face
I'd gladly give all
My heart, my soul, my life
If only she could be my wife
But my dreams were not to be
Cause I'm still shy you see
Long years have passed me by
And now I grow old
I wish that just once
I could have been bold
Now past eighty I've know from the start
There's always been a place
For this girl in my heart

Demise
L. Julian Cuervo
The frightened man screamed,
and life flashed before his eyes
He could clearly see all his life pass by
The birth of his motionless stillborn son
The wedding that fell apart,
All the triumphs and most of all, all defeats
If he could only go back and change things
But the end was near, darkness filled his thoughts
desperation engulfed his body, reckless motions
followed by despair. Agonizing ticks
went by, alarming him of what must be done.
The reaper waits but not for long,
another soul he must possess
A bang is heard, and then a thump
another life is now gone.

Dedication: All teachers, who inspired me

Kenya: Dreaming
Kirsty Anderson
His eyes sparkled by the light of the fire,
Kindled by sparks, smoke and desire.
The heavenly starlit night
Weighed down with dreams of delight,
My heart about to burst from my chest,
So proud of you,
Knowing I had the best.
The way you danced in the light of the moon,
Surrounded by natives,
I thought I would swoon.
You swooped, you pranced,
I was permitted to glance at
A secret side that you could not hide.
That of belonging, or was it longing
To belong to a side that was really you?
Who are we to decide who to be.
We are all mixed thro' and thro'.
What we need to remember, is
Who belongs to who!

Dreams of the Soul

Pilgrim
K. J. Donovan
Alienated by a cruel injustice
She applauds her world but stands alone
Bemused, bewildered yet beguiling
In a void of silent monotone

Her eyes will never see the torment
Her ears indifferent to the screams.
Lonely, penitent and pilgrim
Her mind a pool of fractured dreams.

Beyond the sanctuary of darkness
And noxious vortex of her fear
She perceives a parallel harmonious
On a course to her as yet unclear.

In her sombre citadel oblivion
Obscure pariah devoid of friend
With ardent prayers and thoughts conflicting
That someday her odyssey would end.

My Father–My Friend
Margaret Allen
Dear Dad a poem just for you
You are an example of a perfect Dad
All our family agree with me too
Always a smile, never a moan
Even though you have problems of your own
You always have a listening ear
When anyone visits your home
There for all our smiles and tears
We've never heard you speak an unkind word
You're so understanding, and I want you to know
That your family and friends love you so
How lucky I am to be your daughter Dad
If I am half as nice as you I'd be glad
All you've taught me I try to carry out
Because you are what life is all about.

Love you.

The Bored Seaman
Victor Saxby
As we near the English coast,
We can see the castle and its moat,
High above the grey white cliffs,
Surrounded by a swirling mist.

Down below lies the beach and harbour,
Promenade and a slim ice–cream parlour,
Sailing boats with tall stem masts,
In the distance lies the hovercraft.

Sea gulls hover overhead,
Squawking as if they've never been fed,
As we slow to enter port,
Crew arrive upon the baulk.

Very soon we are on the turn,
The ferry shuddering as we go astern,
It slowly eases into berth,
Another trip over for what it's worth.

Epic Battle
Walter E. Eckhoff
Gather round and listen close, for what I speak is not a boast.
In a time not long ago, a fear had come to feed and grow.
An evil thing which bred despair, it raped the lands and fouled the air.
The king sent forth an urgent plea, who will come and set us free?
But before the scroll was written, before the word was sent–
Five warriors of a different caste, rode forth with swords intent.
They did not stop to hear the praise, the winds they rode with eyes ablaze.
They met the beast at edge of sky, and on the breeze we heard their cries.
A serpent's head was rising up, and we could spy its stack–
Bellowing forth a choking smog, beguiling its attack.
Charity has fallen, Faith has lost her soul,
Humbleness was torn apart and Truth was swallowed whole.
I am Hope the last one left and on my brethren swear,
that I will drive this demon back, and slay it in its lair.
She whirled around and parried fang, then turned and countered tail.
With blinding speed she rushed its head and mated sword to scale.
The sword sank deep in serpent's blood, and tasted it with scorn.
And in the hush a baby cried and Justice had been born.

Strangers
Patricia A. Banwell
Jenny Bell stood by her gate
Playing ball with Sue and Kate
A Lady stopped to say hello
I am off to the park would you like
to go
There is some ice cream in my car.
Or would you like a candy bar
I like sweets said Jenny Bell
Then Jenny's friend began to yell
Mummy said we must not go
with people who we do not know
Jenny's friend was wise and good
She did exactly what she should.
So don't forget the dangers
You must stay away from strangers.

Dedication: Granddaughters, Claire, Lauren, Emily, Gilhooley

2nd Best
G. Barrie
His hair's the same colour as yours,
His eyes are blue not brown,
Through the years I've come to care for him,
On my list of true loves he's way down.

He stands as tall as you,
Same build and skin so fair,
But as he lays beside me,
All I imagine is you're there.

He tries to play the guitar,
Unlike you he's talentless and just makes a din,
I want to wrap it round his neck,
And throw him and it in the bin.

I know I should try and love him,
But my feelings of you won't rest,
But if I can't have my true love,
Then I'll have to settle for second best.

Noteworthy Works

Wonderment
A. R. Wilson

Have you ever wondered why, in the canopy of sky,
There are myriad's of stars, and Sun and Moon?
Or the glory of the dawn giving way to Break of day
And heralding a sunny afternoon?

Have you given heed to grass on the verges as you pass,
In its lush and restful shades of lovely green,
Or the colour spots of flowers, that brighten up the hours,
And the glory of the verdant country scene?

Have you looked upon the hills with their silver streams and rills,
And their barren heads surveying views sublime?
Seen a rabbit scudding by, or heard a pheasant's cry,
And felt the longing, or the urge, to go and climb?

These blessings you should count, as on the hill you mount,
And keep them always fresh within your mind;
So offer God your praise for the pleasure of these days,
And be thankful, that to these, you're never blind!

Shamrocks In The Rain
Anne Mary Sullivan

The shamrocks were
glistening in the
morning dew
as little Mary skipped
along
Listening to the blackbird's
song
She was on her way to
school.
Her hair was brown
Her eyes a tranquil grey
She looked at the sky
And loved the day.
White clouds sailed by
In skies of deepest blue

Dedication: Paul, Demot, Gerald, Sildea

The Country Village
Jacqui Bailey

Patchwork fields of many greens,
bright flowering, coloured meadows,
glistening sun rays through the forested trees,
while church spires cast their village shadows.

The Farmer's labour hard upon the land,
while sounds of laughter fill the village square,
where joyous children can be seen dancing,
at their annual village fair.

Haunting horns alert the dwelling foxes,
as galloping huntsmen race their horses,
while fielding animals graze in sheer contentment,
and Mother Nature works her mystic forces.

fishes swim within the curving rivers,
and the corn yields its head upon the land,
the country birds roost safe in disused barn lofts,
while we parade our village bands.

Our World
Betty Whitcher

Imagine our world where wars would cease,
imagine living in a world of Peace.
Imagine our world if we all loved one another
and took every man to be our brother.
Imagine our world where everyone was free,
for it is our heritage and belongs to you and
me.
Freedom for a man to plough his land and sow,
freedom where a man and wife can watch their
children grow.
Our world is such a lovely place if we but used
our eyes to see, the beauty in its creation is
there for you and me.
So let us live in harmony together, wars are
never won, why can't we think of the children
and learn to live as one.
For our children are our legacy, and so is our
world too, what we leave them for the future
is up to me and you.

Cynicia
Ashton John Fischer, Jr.

There is beginning of my end again.
I follow Cynicia, my right eye.
Together we go somewhere, stumble lame
For fourteen times and do never know: why?

Nor even, why not? There's all the answers.
It is hard to return and I am soft.
My ears ring resoundingly. The rest were
Callow human creatures, these we lofted.

Eyelessly, I've discovered there's no cause.
But merely is, another five red years.
Look, profound philosophy, my metalaws
Of Cynicia who knows me and fears

Concluding couplets, now and even then
A rhyme scheme of the truth, sneeringly lends.

Make Today Count
Ray Datlen

Tomorrow is a vision yesterday just a dream,
Remember yesterday whatsoever it may seem,
Plan for the future, do the best you can,
But live not in either, let that be your ban.

The only way to live is yourself to change,
Other folk their own lives they can arrange,
Let people be, make tolerance be your aim,
If you criticise, let it be you by name.

Try for self-forgetting, help the ones in need,
Be loving and friendly, ready to concede,
Give your love away, very much will return,
This is the way to happiness, to live and learn.

The "eternal now" will see you round the bend,
It will be with you until the very end,
Enjoy this very moment, see it pays you well,
Just "make today count", make every minute tell.

Dreams of the Soul

They're A Joy To Watch
Gerald A. Chard
Raging seas, torrential rain,
Blinding snow or freezing again,
Winters arrived with it's mighty roar,
Let's get inside and close the door,
But wait! Can we really be so mean?
Not to think of wildlife in this winter scene,
Feed the wild animals and birds galore,
Time will repay you from a wealthy store,
Watching animals and birds play on cold days,
It's a pleasure, a treat as we sit and gaze,
Soon spring will arrive with a gentle hand,
And gradually change the whole land,
Tree and flower buds will soon burst,
Transforming the scene that we oft have cursed,
Young birds in flight, fox cubs frolic,
All this activity is very symbolic,
Of surviving hardship during wintry weather,
Now emerging to give us pleasure,
They're a joy to watch.

To Be The Night
Amy Richardson
A transparent me walks the walls of the world,
searching for the light that won't shine through.

Searching for darkness to conceal imperfections,
to mask disastrous truths,
I stumble on the light that opens my soul.

Bending to bask in the shadow of night,
illuminous beams finger my presence and tear open the locks
I have carefully closed around myself.

Searing streams of light burn my hopes
and melt my dreams.

Oh, to be the night
where all are safe and can find
cover in illusion.

Retired Man
J. M. Drinkhill
What a lazy life he's got.
A retired man with not a lot.
He gets up late, has some food.
That's "if" he's in the mood.
If not he sits reads the paper
Very soon he's back to sleep
What good company I keep
I'm up at seven most mornings
Out to fetch his paper
Then on the bus up to town
I haven't time to lie around.
I'm home about half past three
He's not done bad, he cooked the tea
Then on the chair for TV show
That's it for the night, "I know"
Off to the pub for a couple of drinks
I'm left at home to sit and think
All these years of married life
I still don't know my other half.

The Sea
Mary Courtney
The rock that stands inside the waves
With darkened edge and taverened caves
The sea surrounds it carefully
You can't get near – there is no key.

The sea gulls sit upon its peak
Through wind and gales they always squeak
Beneath the rough and rugged sea
A silent life that frightens me

In stillness quiet with skies above
It took the lives that people loved
Beneath its dark and powerful waves
Who knows the story of the graves.

Of slated rock of black and green
There many a man lie with untold dream
I stand upon the sandy shore
And think of lives that are no more

Halloween
Leslie R. Lucas
Decrepit wrinkles molded into plastic, are raindrops clinging to a
withered cloud.
Grapenut texture sags under spools of silver wire, are merely
Sominex nights of counting sheep.
The jellied eyes with gazes into nothingness, are pasted stars
drowned in threads of tears.
... a mask

A child stretches string behind his head and his mind
becomes the mask.
He folds his milk–strong body and becomes the tattered comic
in his closet.
He grabs an empty pillowcase and thinks of last
year's haul.
... a memory

Dedication: My mother, who never wears masks

Who Knows What The Morrow Will Bring
Stanley M. Gall
Today I am happy and carefree and gay
The future looks rosy and so does today
My spirit is lifted as loudly I sing
But who knows what the morrow will bring.

We all live in hope of a brighter tomorrow
Without any pain or heartache or sorrow
We trust that the winter will turn into spring
But who knows what the morrow will bring.

Today I don't need to escape from my lot
I can cope pretty well with all that I've got
But the pressure of life is a terrible thing
And who knows what the morrow will bring.

Some take to the bottle to deaden their pain
While other poor souls go completely insane
So don't be complacent about everything
For who knows what the morrow will bring.

Noteworthy Works

Peace
Eunice C. Squire

The sheep with their lambs are grazing
In fields of grass so green.
The river is softly flowing
The great tall trees between.

The gnats above the water skim,
Enjoying life so free.
Birds preen feathers O so trim,
Then build nests in a tree.

But the hills upon the skyline
Just stand in glory there,
And without a care or worry
They never fret nor fear.

As dusk comes, then the shadows fall,
With sunsets bright array.
But the river flows softly on
Towards a bright new day.

My Friend And My Companion
Paula Green

You're my friend and my companion
'Til death do us part. Being together
Always, as from the very start.
Sharing love and friendship are the
Main parts that show. Knowing these
Feelings of love will always grow.
Being together through thick and
Through thin. Knowing that tough can't beat
Us, as we always win.
Being there for each other when
We need a lending ear. As we have our
Ups and downs, knowing we should never
Fear.
My friend and my companion, the
One I love so much. Will always be
There for me, when I need that
Loving touch.

The Wicked Old Witch
Philippa C. Benacs

The wicked old witch, on her broomstick one night,
Across the dark sky, at midnight took flight,
The moon and the stars, she passed them both by,
And her faithful black cat, winked a wicked green eye.

She'd a large hooked nose and a tall pointed hat,
And from her black cloak, hung a black winged bat,
With mystic powers, she'll weave her spell,
Of evil wrong doings, she knows so well.

A potion of snails and long wispy tails,
A cocktail of devil's delight,
She'll brew and she'll stew, this tincture anew,
'Till she knows that the mixture be right.

Her journey takes her far and beyond,
As her old wrinkled hand, holds and old wrinkled wand,
Back home her caldron bubbles away,
Awaiting the witch on return, next day.

True Friendship
Sandra J. Howells

Friendship is a funny thing; it can make you happy and your heart sing.
Friendship can sometimes be bad, making you unhappy and feeling sad.
Friendship is about always being there, showing that you really care.
Friendship is not about presents and giving, its all about helping with everyday living.
Being able to share your secrets and fears, knowing why your eyes fill with tears.
Understanding your despair and sorrow, a friend will always be there tomorrow.
Friendship is about cheering you and sharing your dreams, helping you plan those crazy schemes.
Assisting you along life's way, guiding you on through another day.
Friendship is about supporting and believing in you, encouraging you on when no others do.
A friendship is a wonderful treasure; it's not to be picked up and put down at your leisure.
A friendship is like a precious stone, to be cared for and not left alone.
Take care of friendships old and new, and they will always take care of you.

The Haunted House
S. M. Randall

Slowly, in the haunted house,
When night begins to fall,
Everything begins to creep,
And something stirs in the hall.
Ghostly forms flit to and fro,
'Tis here lost spirits dwell,
Queer things may happen in this house,
What things? Why, none may tell.

On dreary nights in winter,
When bleak winds sweep the moor,
Some cold and lonely stranger
May open this fearful door.
And once inside this dreadful place
He ne'er is seen again,
For no one e'er returns from thence
Once there, must there remain.

Examinations
Susan Crouch

Sitting in a great big hall
People all around
Not a word is spoken
Their brains are on the pound

Teachers walk around the room
With paper in their hand
They'll give one sheet but never more
Each time you raise your hand

Nothing to do but sit and dream
While others do exams
I feel I'm in a tiny room
With doors shut tight like clams

Sitting in a great big hall
Time is moving fast
No time for dreams and hopeless schemes
Exams must all be passed.

Dreams of the Soul

Holding On To Burn
Hazel Houldey
I love you in the midnight sun
or in the first dawn rain
on shell strewn sands
but I love you in pain

like a stringless harp
for music I yearn
like a dying flame
holding on to burn.

like an unfinished journey
I must reach the end
or the vulnerable heart
I must defend.

In a rainbow painted sunrise
when you come you wake me
I've got nothing to say
but if you go please take me.

Alexandra
Rebecca Cash
You are the one at the end of the day
I'm most thankful for when I sit down to pray

You are my angel, my own guiding light
When I look at you I know the future is bright

You fill my heart with joy and made all my dreams come true
My life is truly blessed because God gave me you

I love to hold and rock you in my arms
I wish we'd stay that way forever, away from all harm

May you always feel safe and secure when I am near
May the Love I feel for you be comforting and clear

For as high as the heavens, for eternity and beyond
We are Mother and child, sharing an incredible bond

The Outpatient
Chris Fletcher
Swimming pool smell in a cling film room,
Men in white coats with faces like doom,
Sunday magazines and files piled high,
Women in skirts and stockings walk by.

Signs above doors with names you can't read,
I've sat for so long that I've now gone to seed,
Look across the room to catch no one's eye,
A plant on the table that's about to die.

Pictures on walls with nondescript scenes,
A leaflet that tells me to eat all my greens,
A machine that makes coffee, with no cups in,
Forty dry mouths, cursing the thing.

These are the memories that will stay with me,
These are the visions that I will still see,
I hope that my wishes will be granted soon,
To never again visit the outpatients' room.

For You
G. M. Breen–Ridout
If you should stray too far
If you should ever need me.
I'll be your guide, right by your side
I'll be your light to see.

I'll hold you when its dark
I'll lead you through the storm
I'll praise you when you're on top
I'll catch you when you fall.

For I am all around you
My love embraces all
Your needs your fears
Your joys your tears
No–one can feel as I
For a Mother's love knows no bounds
It is a gift for eternity
and for you my child I give you life
I give you all of me

The Quest
Robert S. Taggard
When we start we know not the end.
Ups, downs, and sideways will come again and again.

Granted, taken, given and received, all we will do.
We know not the reason, only the course we pursue.

Some want only the act, the whole is not their goal.
I want it all, the mate to my heart and soul.

I dare, I soar, I wonder at it all.
I search, I find, I stumble and fall.

How great the quest, how great the fear.
Uncharted riches we cannot see, only feel, these I dare.

To touch, closeness, to be with that which makes me whole.
The quest will end when she gives her heart, and I give my soul.

Peaceful Night
Sandra L. Richards
The twinkling of a star at night
The earth bathed in moonlight
Listen to the night sounds
Crickets and frogs all around

As I stand in the midst of it all
And listen to the creatures call
I know that it was meant to be
All living creatures running free

An owl passes by in flight
The sky above is clear and bright
As I observe it all I find
I feel contentment, peace of mind

Civilization has slipped away
I'll go back another day
This is where I want to be
With solitude and tranquility

Noteworthy Works

Dreams Of The Mountain
Denise R. Hall
Once upon a time,
I, too, had a dream.
I was told always
To be a player, a part of the team.

But, I don't like the rules
And I don't like the teams;
I know I'm not the smartest,
But the smartest teams don't always succeed.

Success takes time and commitment;
It takes hard work and heart everyday.
You can't prove success by a checkbook
Balanced on the last hour of your last day.

Success is a state of being—
To achieve life's ultimate dream.
And when I'm up on that mountain,
I'll be helping others find their dream.

A Song Of Summer
Gladys Phillips O'Day
When Spring turns to Summer
And the pinks are in bloom
And the rose unfurls her petals
And Robin chants his rune
There's a fragrance in my garden,
A sweetness in my garden,
Magic in my garden,
And the earth whispers June.

And as the daylight lengthens
Other flowers bloom,
Stock and honeysuckle
Join the rose perfume
And white nicotana
Floats her essence to the moon.
There's a promise in my garden
As the earth sings June.

Sun And Rain Apart
Eugenia Boussios
You were my smile in the rain and the sun
in my heart

I never thought that we would be apart.
I don't believe I could ever measure
how much you were my treasure.

The real reason why this happened I will
never really understand or know. My only feeling
is that my heart loves you so.

But they say, "If you love someone you
must set him free and if he comes back to
you, then it was meant to be."

Yet my heart feels that it will cry till the
time does end, and oh how I just wish
You would come back to me and smile and be in
my arms again.

The Honest Man
Mary Lynn Paeth
He picked me up when I was down
and held me through my silent moan.
Never judging past, or me.
Giving courage just to be.

Broken spirit, bruised soul,
the bitterness of such, my dole.
Wearing thin, with senseless strife
my hopes and dreams for 'a full life'.

Quietly, he helped me stand
from building castles in the sand.
Saying it was still okay
when time and tide washed them away.

I wonder now, as I did then,
of which is the more honest man?
One knocks you down and lets you stay.
One helps you stand, then walks away.

Lest We Forget
Betty Brown Harrison
At times like these, when it's quiet and still
I remember sounds of the night, like the whip–poor–will,
and days of sun so bright, you could not see,
and a sky so blue, you felt almost that it was a painting.
Trees so green and the slow murmur of a creek
ever wandering through the woods, to end where?
A mere child, innocence abounding, loving, thrilling to the sounds and
sights of nature.
Could we not walk through those woods again, and see the beauty and
serenity through
the eyes of that child again?
Must we give it all up and forget, even though we have grown older, and
sometimes much older?
Can we not steal away to that long ago and far away time
that held such peace and joy, to recapture something that should have never
been forgotten?
For shame that we forget that which was good.

Reflection Of A Lover's Heart
Robert E. Walsh
On that bright and beautiful day you put your hand in mine,
I sighed and hoped that you would be my Valentine;
And it was the next day, when you again came into view;
It was then that I felt quite young and all brand new,

And now time has passed, and I still feel quite the same,
There are times when I can't even think of your name,
Our quiet times I treasure beyond the color of blue,
For I feel much closer to you then the morning dew:

I pray for the day when you are completely mine,
It is then I'll know you are truly my Valentine,
I'd like to change you, so your thoughts are all of me;
But I'll never do that as you and I must agree.

So, dear heart, do put your heart and hand in mine,
And say that you will always be my Valentine,
For no greater love on this planet will you see,
Then mine alone, for I love you, but it's only me.

Dreams of the Soul

Marbled Reality
Marcia Richardson

I was there the day she lost her marbles.
The red eye knocked all the others out of the circle.
She foundered about, arms flailing, trying to gather them.
But, her grasp wasn't strong enough to hold on.

We had to take her to someone to stop the splintering.
She felt everything flying away — arms and legs.
He said to face reality, but her vision was clouded with fear.
Reality was — she couldn't play the game anymore.

I'm taking my marbles and going away.
And she did— in her head. Away to another world.
One where everything is in slower motion and nothing collides.
Where spirits live instead of spiraling downward.

Some place in that queer, divine, blank space
Where she can laugh again and play an unfettered
Game of marbles and not lose any. Some place where
The yielding sand holds the marbles securely within the circle.

A Little Girl's Dream In A Russian Heart
Teri Champ

Twin silent stars through neo—nimbus blaze,
The craving awe suppressed by matron hands.
A nova, newly kindled, limelight—crazed
Who yearns and pines for Balanchine's demands:

With bloody toes, with spindly leg, with cramps,
Imprisoned body, tortured scalp and spine,
Through haze of pain to thrive on true romance,
Through window—skin to vibrate all divine.

Crescendo, spirit raised, the music taunting,
Musculature, stark ribs exposed to woe.
You cannot see the passion that she's flaunting.
Facades and lies, illusion: all you know.

The shackles, pain and sickness which you see?
No price to pay for utter ecstasy.

The Edge Of
Andru Paene

As you gaze upon the dawn's approach
Inspiring emotions beyond reproach
Evoking images of a past life's host
Observing a distant existence as a ghost

Do you feel the power striking within
Sending shock waves of confusion that never end
Believing in things you can't see or hear
Embracing all that you hold so near and dear

Will you take me places never seen before
Directing my vision toward the open door
Illuminate my dreams from long ago
Exorcise the demons in my tortured soul

Can you hold on forever by my side
Enhance my being, strengthen my pride
Induce my better half to reappear
Promise to always remain affectionately sincere

The Imprisoned Spirit Of The Sea
Penelope G. Hass

Deep in my soul a spirit lives:
The SPIRIT OF THE SEA.
It longs to have my heart unlocked
And once again set free.

Years ago with youthful passions strong:
I cast the soothing SPIRIT OF THE SEA aside.
As worldly wants seduced my greedy soul,
I climbed aboard to ride the outbound tide.

Years flew passed in a furious pace;
And a saddened spirit now does dwell,
Within this my languid lonely soul,
Which enormous emptiness befell.

The SPIRIT calls to ardent deeds.
The soul and heart are slow to heed.
Too late they hear the primordial plea.
The Spirit Of The Sea cannot be freed.

The Importance Of Mothers
Jerrie Major

Mother's Day is the most important day of the year.
Can't you see you or I would not be here.
Celebrate with love on Mother's Day,
The most important day in May.
Jesus had a Mother, Virgin Mary.
If it had not been for Mary,
We would not have Christmas Day.
Mothers are the most important persons in this world,
Mothers are important to every boy and girl.
Mothers Day is more important to me than Christmas Day.
You may want to give some thought,
about this statement I just made today.
My Mother to me was perfect in every way.
Her love, not only for me, but for others,
she gave with all her heart,
Her entire eighty—seven years of life,
not only one day, but every day.

Love's Dream—Come True
Elizabeth Holsombeck

Never in all my dreams
Have I ever known, it seems;
Anyone I could love, so true –
the way that I love you.

Life is a very great mystery.
Love comes to me, not like history,
but suddenly and certainly,
wonderfully flirtingly.

Without any warning— I find–,
you are mine and I am thine.
Because of our love, so bold—
We've found each other, to have and to hold.

May our marriage last until we're old,
and yet still; togetherness be our goal.
All the way to eternity and forever—
Our love for each other will never sever.

Noteworthy Works

Bird Of Power
Joan Murphy
He glides above me in the sky
With an eight foot wing span flies so high.
Sharp eyes observe my dumbstruck stare;
He dances on without a care.

No other bird is quite so free
Or holds a place so regal,
As he who soars with fearless grace;
The independent Eagle.

Since ancient times mankind has schemed
To possess the Eagle's power;
But no man can steal a soul so free,
Or take away his dignity.

We must accept our limitations,
Earth bound is our humble state;
While in awe we watch this bird of prey
With mighty things to do this day!

Dreams Of My Life
Nancy Lee Jackson
When I was a child, I dreamt of the future looming in front of me
I tried to picture the adult I would soon grow to be

While a teen, my daydreams were filled with love and romance
And a faceless young man with whom on my wedding day
I would dance

As a wife and Mother with a young family to guide and nurture
My dreams were for them to grow to have a bright and
full future

The years have slipped by and our children have grown
Before we knew it, they were gone, living dreams of
their own

Through all those years, my dreams were of things yet to come
But now, I find they're of memories... of times long gone.

Sunny
Ruth Steinhilber
We have a kitty at our house
She has her own special mouse
She is white with gold
She is young, not very old

Her name is Sunny
Sometimes she is so funny
She likes to run around and play
From Sunday to Saturday

She is such a good kitty
She is so clean and pretty
She says "Please" and "Thank You"
Before I feed her any food fresh and new

Jackie, our Granddaughter, gave her to us
Over kitty we make such a fuss
We really enjoy her very much
Guess we'll keep her, with her loving touch

Untitled
Jennifer Hart
What really lies
behind those eyes?
Secrets long buried,
Unknown, unnamed.

Wise and tender,
Caustic flamed.
Laced with lenity,
Yet wild, untamed.

Heights of Heaven,
Depths of Hell;
None can plumb
That endless well

What really lies
Behind those eyes?
You'll never know,
They'll never tell.

My Silence
Melissa Evans
The silence is driving me insane!
Let me out, let me be free!
I feel trapped...
As if there were 4 solid steel walls
surrounding me!
Smothering me in, and won't let me free!
Not letting me say how I feel!
I can't hide from reality,
It just walked in the door 5 minutes
ago!
I can never seem to catch up with life,
or, all that it has to offer!
I always miss it by a split second. Please,
Somebody... I'm begging...
Set me free!
Open the steel doors.
Help me face reality, and let me be me!!!

Welcome Spring Rain!
Lorraine C. Fellows
I love the sound of rain
Making music on windowpanes,
Lulling me to sleep
With sweet refrains;

Raindrops sparkling like diamonds
On trees and grass,
Hanging from wires
Like beads of glass;

Clouds drifting away
From the breaking sun,
And rainbows lingering
After the rain is done.

Welcome spring rain;
Our gardens need you!
Thank you for making
Our earth fresh and new.

Dreams of the Soul

Calypso Music
Avonelle Lewis–Rand
Such a sweet rhythm,
can't help but
wine you waist and move you feet instantly.
Listen to de beat.
Calypso music, feel de beat, so sweet.

Hear de brass bands
with those thundering sounds.
As de music intoxicate your body
with its compelling rhythm.
Calypso music, so sweet, hear de beat.

As for de inexperienced,
When de music hit you
there's an instant surge of electricity.
A tantalizing heat in you feet,
that makes you start dancing,
prancing and wining all over de street.
Calypso music, so sweet, so ooooo swee eeeeeeet!

Do Not Cage The Panther
Lucy Geyser
Do not
cage the panther,
she must not lose her dream:
Moon leads her through the silver woods
each night.

She knows
the Moon will show
the silver path that she
must walk to find her mate, and she
will go.

The Moon
will gleam on him
and he will become real
silver – like the woods – and the path
– and love.

This Husband Of Mine
Wanda Mowatt
He lies there
This husband of mine
Lifeless, yet, living.
Does he think, or
Does it take all his strength
Just to go on breathing?
Does he remember, as I do,
The forty–three years of our
Life together? A marriage
That suited us; Was precious to us?
He still mouths my name.
Does he know me as his love? His wife?
Or only as the pain eradicator;
A bringer of medicine and
Life sustaining liquids?
Can he tell if it's me or the RN
Caring for him?
He lies there, this husband of mine.
Lifeless, yet, living.

Prisoner Of Lies
Chester Barnett
I am a prisoner of war,
I am a captive of the world,
Locked behind a door,
Because I never kept my word.

Lies turned to truth,
No one believes me anymore,
Truth turned to lies,
I just do not know what I am living for.

I lost everything I had because of lies,
I am trying to change but it just doesn't work,
I am trapped behind a hideous disguise,
And it just doesn't work,

Love will never live here anymore,
It is all my fault
Lies are stuck in my core,
And I have been caught.

Fall
Phyllis Dylong
The weather is clear
Clouds fluffy seem near
A nip in the breeze, cold in the air
Leaves falling down in so
Many pairs.
Colors of reds, orange, and
Brown.
Thousands of leaves covering
The ground.
A blanket of beauty changed
Every day.
That makes the heart
Feel a warm kind of way
The beauty of fall is
Always its best.
And just down the
Road winter lies at rest.

Someone's Son
May Brown
He was someone's son
And someone's friend
and someone's shining knight
The young man's body on the road
Pale and deathly white
The men of hate who killed him
Want to rule this land
Laugh and smile and talk of peace
but murder by command
But one day peace will surely come
upon our blood–soaked earth
and the men of hate who killed him
will have to face God's wrath
and someone's son
and someone's friend
and someone's shining knight
will walk once more
upon the road
from darkness into light.

Noteworthy Works

Another Woman's Man
Robin Post

Belonging to another, knowing there's no chance,
for him and me to have, a very long romance.
Short and sweet and incomplete,
the feelings must not grow.
For it would be wrong, to compete,
to think he'd love me so.
He holds me tight with all his might,
hoping he won't let go.
Kisses my cheek, saying it's great,
wishing the time would go slow.

There's something missing in his life,
a void filled by me instead his wife.
What it is, we both don't know,
but no matter, it wouldn't show.
The feelings for him, I must hide,
within myself, not to cry,
Being friends, not holding hands,
with this other woman's man.

War
Shawna R. Asmus

I shot my brother today.
I dwell upon this as I lay,
On the cold, hard ground,
With stars all around,
And illusions of peace.
My mind is far from peaceful,
My heart cries from within.
For I have just lost,
A very good friend.
Childhood memories,
Swim in my head.
The things we had done,
The things we had said.
Innocence of youth,
How quickly it turns.
As passions of war,
How deeply they burn.

Twilight
Timothy Fishback

Don't leave me Sun,
for I fear the death of day
Again I must attempt escape
I flee frantically for Refuge
Only to find
failure once more

I am sought out,
and it has me within its gray
It forces me thoughts of the past
and what is to come
It fills me with uncontrollable anguish

How long must I endure this misery
before I am released
Night has fallen
Thank God
I am relieved
Until...

My Touchstone
Mici Green

Whenever I have called on you,
You've been there without a doubt.
I've shared my thoughts, hopes and dreams.
From you, I gained not a fret, sneer nor pout.

In my times of pain and fear,
You've been near.
I had the desire to march on and triumph.
Your support, how sweet and dear.

My shining light and my solid rock,
Yes, that you are.
That I promise to you,
No human can ever bar.

A cousin and friend you are to me
And my everlasting touchstone.
You give me faith
That I'll never walk alone.

Give Wings To Goodbye
Dawn Burns

Goodbye is never easy. Sometimes it means goodbye forever. Sometimes it means goodbye for now. Goodbye is waiting.

It is like standing on the edge of something about to happen, dangling by your toes.
Uncertainty is a wind that whispers in your ear and nudges at your back. It pushes you closer to the edge but you never actually fall.

Goodbye is a maddening descent. Down you go until you feel as if you are a lone angel in hell. And there you wait.

While there you begin to realize that angels have wings and are meant to fly, high and free. Soon they soar and rise above.
They cover great distances and eventually even
angels must land. Sometimes on their own two feet.

And when they do what was once goodbye becomes hello.

Goodbye...
Amanda Lovelace

Most of friends come and then wander, yet you and I
stayed so close... You grabbed life by its heart,
And I think that's what I liked most.
But friend now life has beaten you, and put you
in the most peaceful place... And though it hasn't
been that long, I've almost forgotten your face.
I feel as if I've been broken, just taken and
torn in two... A part of me still remains here, and
a part of me is with you.
The borrowed blouse in my closet, the lacy pink
one that you lent... I'm always curling up to it,
because it still carries your scent.
I wish you were here to pull me through, and in
a way I guess you are... Because I keep you
in my heart, that makes you not so far.
You taught me how to say goodbye, though not
to such a good friend... You journeyed for the
best in life, you've succeeded, because it is
the journey that counts in the end.

Dreams of the Soul

Covert Tables
Mary K. Hauer

Liars lie,
Shooters shoot,
Soldiers walk with heavy boot.

Dealers deal,
Spoilers spoil,
Young men march on foreign soil.

Talkers talk,
Sleepers sleep,
Wolves enter disguised as sheep.

Thinkers think,
Guessers guess,
What Mother now is childless?

Schemers scheme,
Blamers blame,
War: The politicians' game!

Grandpa
Deanna Pflugradt

You came into my Grandmother's life,
and you asked her to be your wife.
And to your surprise, she said yes,
for she knew you were the very best.
You are a very special person to everyone,
and everyone knows how much you have done.
You've seen us laugh, and you've seen us cry,
you're always there for us when we ask why.
You always tell us right from wrong,
you tell us not to give up, just be strong.
You are a man, so very rare,
no one else could ever compare.
Your the best grandpa on this land,
for you, outdo any man.
So when it comes down to that fine line,
everyone should have a grandpa just
like mine.

Your Atrocities
Annie Mae Raus

Persistent atrocities including death of one kind
or another. Magnetic preface more to post–manual
machine era.
Relieved the drag of having to turn handles and use
ones own mind to untangle man made problems.
Cavities trapped beneath the surface of such acts
of jealousy and evil made that ache in your heart
worse than ever. Can you breathe?
Do your lungs ever adapt to the stench of misfortune?
The Babylonized scars and casualties.
Cry sweet child, cry the river of tears you dammed
long before in fear of overflowing emotions.
Do your love or hate your common strikes and or fits of
outrageous tremors and emotional flights?
Do you find that you are afraid of heights?
Make me love you or leave me alone.
Conceive the recipe for troubled concept of life, so next
time you are confused about why your brain scatters
before the deep end leap you'll have a map to refer to.

Forty
Janet Hassefras

I tell you "40" is only just a number,
a matter of your attitude.
Still seeking life's fulfillment,
pondering your next direction.
If you're stressed, it is rightly so,
for you have just been through 40 years of life.
So let's just say Congratulations!
Find what makes you happy.
Search your soul to truly know yourself.
Find a passion and let it evolve in you and you will
find a purpose for your life.
So celebrate if you must, take off to foreign lands to escape,
venture across the unknown, strike out on a childhood whim,
but remember we love you back home and you will still be 40
when you return.
But I keep on telling you I'm still stuck at 29,
it's only a number, a matter of your attitude,
perhaps the secret to my youth.

Untitled
Melody Keegan

They descend on humanity,
Countless black locusts
Children with hollow eyes
staring without compassion
beyond one another.
People without conscience,
lacking a soul
infesting all they touch
with their disease of hate.

The Ancient of Days,
Sacrificed His Only Son
to save them from the monster,
the pit, the impending destruction.
It is inescapable,
there they cannot see to clasp
His wounded hand
and are lost forever...

The Love Of The Unfaithful
Ian L. Major

The sweetest of all nectar
lies in the flower of your hair;
That sweet softness of pleasure
with beautiful highlights of despair.

The cleanest of pools and diamonds
are the stars centered in your eyes;
Far be it for anyone to find us
for together is where abandonment hides.

The softest of sonnets and purity
sweet words engraved within your heart;
Causing the sorest of pain and misery
to devour me apart.

Your love is shallow and empty
your love is as precious as gold;
Your face is deeply within me
but your love is desolately cold.

Noteworthy Works

Cast Away
Mark Asher

I listened to you never talk
I heard your silent speech
I knew what you weren't thinking
And it wasn't about me.
Your actions are so distant
Your looks are turned aside
I know you're seeking someone else
'Cause I'm no longer in your eyes.
Are we so very far apart
That nothing can be done
Nothing that we say or do
Can fix this once again?
Your answer is this icy pain,
"What will be, will be."
So with this ring I cast away
I've gone and set you free.

Day Dreams
Loraine A. Phelan

What fun it is to roam the field
Of your own inner thoughts
For there you'll find no boundaries
That anyone has wrought.
Your imagination holds full sway
Ideas are in full flush
And you can picture anything
There's no one to say "hush".
It is such thoughts that sow the seed
For great things in this world
And nothing then can hinder plans
That busy minds unfurl.
There's no one to discourage you
And say your thoughts are groundless
So keep on building on your dreams
Your future can be boundless.

Untitled
Matt Lacy

I try to put my feelings into words
But they always
come out fumbled.
I try to show you with my actions,
but I always mess-up
somewhere in the middle.
I'm not sure how to show you
how I feel, without being
frightened of what you'll say.
I don't know how to put it
so it sounds like
music to your ears.
But I guess there's only one way.
To say it right out.
So here it goes.
I love you with all my heart
and all my soul,
and I hope you feel the same.

Christmas Confusion
Cynthia Lynn Hudson

Decorate the tree
Make the lists
Plan for a party or two
Do the shopping, buy gifts, buy food
Clean the house, so much to do
I don't know where to start
Trapped in the mall
Struggling through the crowd
In the middle of the mob
I turn my head and see it
The perfect gift for you
A light in the hands of an angel
Then I remember how much Christmas means to you
I also remember what Christmas really means
It is about the ultimate gift to everyone
The gift of God's love and the birth of His Son.

Be Nice
Margaret Muir Colligan

Being Nice is easy
All you have to do,
Is say the words
Please and Thank You.
Just doing the shopping
Can feel more worthwhile
By being pleasant
with a little smile.
A wet and foggy day
Can be full of sunshine
If you live this way
When wrong say Sorry.
Receiving Thank You
Words that mean so much
For you and others
Along life's highway.

Dedication: My lifelong friend, Frank G.

My Gram
Cheryl Kalmon

She was precious.
She was my past, present and future.
I was watched, disciplined and cuddled by her.
My Gram couldn't be replaced by another.
The day she died will be the last of my happiness.
Before the break of dawn,
We were called to the hospital.
Before the break of dusk,
She said she loved us.
The last four words "I love you all"—
This last thought will be the last memory of Gram.
I need her, love her, miss her.
Oh, how Gram enriched my life.
How Gram will still guide me throughout the rest of my days.
Her guiding hand will always touch me.
I love you, Gram.

Dreams of the Soul

My Dad
Willena Phelps
When we were so very small.
Running here, running there, running everywhere.
Dad would never spank or yell
He would always laugh and say,
Better not do that for you see
When you get older you will see,
We miss talking to that brown-eyed man.
He'd be in the garden hot and dry,
Planting beans and hilling taters.
riding his tractor around the bend.
Looking up and smiling from ear to ear,
Now we miss those happy days.
For you see he's riding for our Jesus now.
He's looking down and smiling so big.
Saying don't you worry for you see
Jesus is with me all the way,
So don't cry no more my little one
For I'm where I want to be.

Heavenly Father Spoke
June Johnson Adkins
This hour,
I made a flower,
And gave it life.
Can I not make you a wife?

This day I made a tree,
Can I not give power to thee?
I give the world a beautiful song,
Can I not help you along?

Today at sunset
You met,
My friends,
A lot depends
On you
Be true.

The Surf
Bernice Daniel Cook
The rhythm of the sea
Washes over me.
Ebb and flow —
Come and go.

The sandpipers feed
At the water's edge
And where the plover's nest
Between the ledge.

Ebbs and flows,
Swift undertows!

The mighty sea!
My primordial home –
Eternal womb –
Deep unto deep
And lulling me to sleep!

The Perfect Night
Heather Lynch
You sit aside waiting
While everyone around you is fading
a guy walks up to you
It's weird because you feel like glue
You're thinking that between you two there is no chance
But still he asks you to dance
You are stunned but still say yes
You're wearing your prettiest little dress
He tells you you're the girl of his dreams
This isn't real that's how it seems
By the end of the night you're in love
The relationship that forms between you two is as perfect as a dove
The two of you go off to the car
He tells you he wants to show you a special star
You have a night filled with passion and love
But then neither of you hear from each other again.

Alcoholism Takes My Daddy
Christalyn Sheridan
HE was always there.
HE held my hand and wiped my tears.
But now, HE is never here.
HE slaps my face and creates my tears.
The MONSTER has gotten inside,
The MONSTER is making him mean.
The MONSTER is ever-present.
There is never a time it is gone.
Tears of pain leave my eyes.
My tears are the LUCKY ONES,
For these tears can only be cried once.
But ME, I am unlucky.
My pain cries out always.
Oh! How I wish I were a tear.
Then I would only have to be cried...
ONCE!

Drive On
Jon R. Schulze
Cigarettes and coffee, if you think you're brave.
But drivin' a truck, you'll drive to your grave.
When I was younger they all looked so big.
Always a dreamin' that I'd drive a rig.
Drivin' a truck ain't like TV,
A highway hero I'll never be.
I just keep drivin' to take care of bills,
I don't do drugs or stay awake pills.
Son, please listen, don't follow your dad.
Truck driver's life is lonesome and sad.
Never at home and you're always away.
Missing your loved ones every day.
Drive on, drive on, all through the night.
Drive on, drive on, straight to daylight.
Guess I'll always be drivin' a truck,
Runnin' and chasin' that almighty buck.

Noteworthy Works

Choices
Beatrice Cagle
I wake up each morning.
Look out at God's world,
and see the sights, and
hear the sounds.
And try not to let things
get me down.
Cause, life can be fair, or it
Can be rough.
Can pull you up, or pull you
down;
those are the chances. Sometime
we take.
And many choices, most of us
make.
Surely as we live, we're gonna
die.
The choices are not made by
You or I.

This Empty City
Tim Holden
This soulless place, which has no grace
A lonely kingdom, which lost her might
A whimpering dog, who lost his bite
Fear stalks, let darkness pass
This empty city, a crumbling mass

No peaceful noise of shouting boys
Death's decay looms over the land
No picturesque beauty by God's hand
This smoke filled sky, from burning fire
This empty city of a fallen sire

This wanton race for love's embrace
This fallen land of disillusioned people
Standing in the shadow of the church's steeple
As God looks down at each solemn face
This empty city, which lost it's place
ends.

Sadness
Jeremy D. Williams
Sadness could be considered a color.
Much of it is dark, with very little light.
Most of it is wrong, with very little right.
A slice of bread without any butter.

Sadness is much like loneliness.
It's like 100 animals with no zoo.
It's like what, when, where, why without the who.

Sadness is too much like being homeless.
It's an ice, cold head without a hat.
It is being alone at a Spring dance.
It's a feeling you cannot enhance.
It's a front door without a WELCOME mat.

Describing it is just not appealing,
Just because it's only a feeling.
SADNESS

Eventide
Elizabeth Hamilton
In the west the dying splendor,
Soon the purple shadows deepen,
All the air is full of softness,
Calm and still—with evening's stillness
Far across the distant meadows come the cows,
Slow, wending homeward.
The sweet tinkle of the cowbells
Making music to their footsteps.
Hushed—the busy daytime voices
Silence falls, as toiling ceases,
Radiant, glows the last faint flicker
Of the sunset's golden glory,
Mystic scene of silent grandeur,
Filling all the earth with beauty,
Filling all the earth with greatness,
As the shades of evening falleth,
And the day grows at it closing
To the "hush" of Eventide.

Whimsical Desires
Jessica Ruse
There is a terrible nagging overpowering
my body
like the tide being pulled by the
moon
My tormented soul confined to this life
is longing to leave this place soon
It smells of strong incense and musty
dark rooms
It tastes of old wine on my lips
It feels like smooth velvet, or a cold
crystal lake caressing my skin with a
kiss.
It sounds like soft bells, or a sharp lullaby
and it looks like a full harvest moon
my souls been seduced by an auger
on this warm gentle evening in June.

You Are Like!
Michelle Nichols
Roses are so red,
Violets are so blue,
You are to love.

If there are shadows,
Yours is beautiful,
As if a velvet wind blew on your face.

When the leaves fall,
It is as if you are touching my heart,
As gentle as you can.

In the winter,
It is as if a gentle hand touching me.
In the summer it is like you have nothing to do,
And I love you!

Dreams of the Soul

Untitled
Crystal Hendron

You have helped me in so very many ways. Helped me to say good–bye and move on. You have made me who and how I am today. You helped me to move on from a broken heart. Even though I made it more difficult than it needed to be.
You
helped me to see that there will always be a tomorrow with new people and from
that I have found the best love of my life.
You have turned me into a young sophisticated woman. Learning and growing together we both have had our share of mistakes, which I love you even more for.
You have taught me that we can learn together and from each other. Mom, you have turned me into the best person I can be. Loving, caring, and sensitive to others
needs. Who you are, is all a girl could ever ask for in a Mother. Remember Mom I
will always love you for all you are...

Pain
Joanne Smith

I wonder what I should do?
With all the pain I'm going
through.
I know I'm going to die soon,
You probably think I'm worrying too
much,
But if you knew what has happened
to me,
You'd be thinking you'll be dying
soon too
I will tell you what has
happened to me,
Then you'll realize how it has
upset me.
As I have got a great big
sharp thing in my finger,
which my mum calls a
splinter

Rivers
Siobhan Kelly

The snow melts
and here starts a stream.
It's a wonderful sight
for all to be seen.
The river flows gently
and meets with others,
"Hello" it says
to its sisters and brothers.
The river grows
and meets some new friends,
but here the gentleness
comes to an end.
The river goes crash
and then the banks smash
because of the gashing
flowing fast water.

Watching
Georgette Turnbull

Watching – a face in a crowd
Listening – to music so loud
Hurting – just loving you
Crying – what more can I do?
Trying – to make you love me
Wasting – my time I can see
Hoping – things will get better at last
Feeling – that really the chance has passed
Wondering – why her and not me
Thinking – how lucky some people can be
Fighting – my love to keep
Knowing – it'll end on the heap
Losing – the battle I know
Praying – that you still won't go
Dying – inside a little each day
Loving – you in my own way

Mother
Helen Oshea

Bending slowly low
To sniff the scented rhododendron
Aches and aging pains forgotten
For a fragrant minute
Heaven for a time within a time
Of forgotten and half–remembered day
When flowers filled the air
And she and all of bawn were young
Free and folded in the arms
Of hungry hill
A rush of dogs and cats and cows
From pastures past
Blend their perfumed memories
With the rhodo's own
And she lifts up her face
And smiles alone

Seeing Eye To Eye
Valerie Perkins

Once there was a lonely man, very aware of life's short span.
He put a brave smile on his face and drifted about from place to place.
He thought perhaps he'd find some ways to fill his lonely empty days.
He began to tuck away his sorrow and start to think about tomorrow.

He didn't go off to the pub, instead he joined a dancing club.
A cheerful smile and a friendly word is what he had to give
His life became much richer... and at last he began to live.

One night when he was at a dance he met a lady, just by chance
And dancing round he recognised the sadness she had in her eyes.
For she had shed so many tears and known much sadness through the years.
She'd decided that the only way was to live her life just day by day.

She too was aware of life's short span but her heart was warmed by this smiling man.
Time went by and they danced on, and the grey days seemed, at last, to be gone.

Listening
Kim R. Hawkins–Brown

How good this world would be if people would just listen.
If you listen to yourself, your first and true voice, you will never go wrong.
If you listen to a child, you could learn new things.
If you listen to a person less fortunate than you, you can learn to appreciate what
you have.
If you listen to your parents and elders, you can learn how things were and would
still be if someone would have just listened.
How hard could it really be to listen?
You can learn a lot more if you're silent.
So next time someone is talking,
take out the time and listen,
You can't go wrong.
Trust me.

Ausleander
Russell Slater

I watched the day's sun drowning and the night engulf the sky,
I knew we were alone and it dawned that we were one,
Though we were apart, and to part as stars crept nigh,
You'd away, I alone to await the night's fears to come.

I fear the water, as well as ought should one of earth,
But then I hear the siren's clearly and I slowly lose resolve,
Stepping closer to the water's edge, dreaming of my worth,
Upon this steady land of mind, to you then my heart betroth.

Weight of stone to fill my pouch and old heart I know to crave,
My end upon a barren world, that I and heath no more the same.
As I willingly drown, and I fall for all beneath the waves,
The heavy winds of night will carry forth your whispered name,

Fraedotter.

The Moonlit Night
Janet L. Duncan

The light is fading as sunset approaches
The day has almost ended
I lie awake as darkness falls
The moon rising clear and bright
While it fills the sky with newborn
light
The stars above sparkle and shine
When all is still and the world asleep
I lie in silence and listen
To the piercing evening sounds
The bold tick of the clock at my side
And the call of an owl in the distance
All this floats quietly out of my
mind
When my eyes close to the dark
And stillness of the night.

It's A Girl
L. Hale

It's a girl they shout
A beautiful baby girl
After 9 long uncomfortable months
Of waiting and anticipation
My baby is here to hold.

She's here to add to my family
Her red/brown hair is quite wavy
Pale skin and big brown eyes
Her rosebud mouth is curved in a smile
I instantly fall in love with her

A little girl – I wonder
Will she be my friend?
Will she have my husband wrapped
Around her little finger?
One thing is certain – she's
Going to be loved and cherished.

A Smile
P. Steel

When I see a smiling face
I look at it with pride
I feel my heart is glowing
I feel so good inside

It's good to spread some happiness
As you go on your way
It helps if you are cheerful
In your work from day to day

The world can be a gloomy place
So fill your days with laughter
You'll leave behind a legacy
To the ones who follow after

Heartache
Andrew Stevens

The sound of laughter, children playing in the rain
The sight of discarded toy, enough to bring back the pain
The agony that never goes away
Just lies heavy upon me with each new day.

Where are you my life, my love, my heart
Why, oh why did we have to part
Are you in someone else's arms
Sharing someone else's charms.

Where are my children, so young, so sweet
All I know is bitter defeat
Broken hearted here I lay
Facing another empty, desolate day
I'd give the world to see you all again
But all I can see is the bitter empty pain.

Dreams of the Soul

My Plant
Joyce Matthews
I planted a little seed.
It was an exotic bloom not a weed.
I lavished with care, and I patiently wait
For two little leaves through the earth to break.
One sunny day the leaves were there.
Whitefly greenfly, land if you dare
The weeks went by my plant grew strong.
Many, many leaves and stem so long.
I couldn't wait for that plant to bloom.
The exotic flower filling my room.
Then one day a bud appeared.
I was so happy I almost cheered.
Then in through the window flew a big fat bee.
Straight for my plant. How dare he.
I lifted my hand and brought it down.
And knocked that bee to the ground.
And on the ground laying by the bee.
Was my little bud of the flower I'll never see.

Too Good To Be True
Ron Kelly, Jr.
Bring it on heavy, bring it on hard
Slap me a kiss, or send me a card.
Ask me a question, or tell me a lie,
it doesn't really matter baby, but don't make me cry.
Bring me a song, from heaven above
let it be you, let it be love.
I'm a lost heartbeat, wondering around,
I'm glad you caught me, 'twas love you found.
Now that you have it, don't let it go
let it be strong, let it grow, grow, grow.
Sometimes I think it's all in my head
waiting for you, lying in bed.
Now, I can't stop thinking of you,
Your eyes, lips, and curves, an angel you are true.
Remember I told you, don't make me cry,
almost dropping a tear, I'm asking you why.
Now, I see you fading, blue, blue and dark blue
I guess, you were always too good to be true.

The Wayward Light
Jeri Dippold
Thoughts that burn within my mind fly away in minutes
time. Poems that do not rhyme wind chimes that do not chime,
buried secrets that churn inside my brain, whispering voices
that do not learn to mind the rain. Deep seated hate that
covers me like fog blinds my mind's eye that wants to see the
clear blue sky. Thoughts never thought, dreams never given a
chance, words never heard or spoken. Many is the time when my
heart's been broken, but isn't that the token of life. The
world keeps spinning, others keep winning my soul keeps bending
How long I scream, oh how long until it breaks? It takes more
to survive than what I've got and what I have isn't a lot. I
scurry around to find the lost pieces of my life paying with
loss of mind and satisfaction. A chill creeps over my body
that cannot be warmed, I'm left lonely broken and scorned
Torn away from life's bosom tossed into the sea of darkness
and despair, wandering seeking for the wayward light.

The Addict's Prayer
Anne Marie DeFrange
Stop this merry–go–round and let me go
Quickly, silently into this good night,
To bid farewell to this kaleidoscope
Of pain and emptiness I fight.

The world is beautiful, but also dark
For some a treasure, while others blight.
I chose the ride I can't complain
Although the trip may end in vain.

The ups and downs, the highs and lows
The music plays and round I go.
I'll miss the color, flash and light,
But let me off, the time is right.

Dedication: Sarah and Robert, with love

The Open Page
Sally McAveety
As I write these words of love
I look upon the stars above
No one can portray my story
as I'm the one who reaps the glory

If you ever get the chance
write a story of romance
as it's worth some weight in gold
it's our poem to be told.

Now I've written down these lines
I know our love will be entwined
nothing can take that away
as our love will grow each day.

Disability
Greta Carty
Once I rushed about from work to home and work again.
I was alive! I was important!
Then suddenly all stopped.
A damaged lung halted all.
The importance vanished.
The screaming shell imploded in bitterness.
Now, in the silence of my life, I discover many jewels.
Time I never had before, is filled with watching, listening
and talking.
The God of my life invited me to love and share in his
peace;
The inefficient body houses a soul of passion.
The props that fell were really chains that bound me
I am now free to love; to be.

Noteworthy Works

Dawn
Sheila K. A. Thompson

As dawn surveys this wondrous
earth, all nature seems to wake
and say,
Who is He who has created me
And, am I here to stay?
Then, I look around me.
And; nearly weep for God above
Father, Son and Holy Ghost
Spirit of perfect love,
Do we have to spoil your world
Why? for triumph and for fame
Each war that's fought
Each tree that's lopped
For whom; for what! For gain.

The Blackbird
Sheila Jenkinson

The blackbird woke me up
this morn
Its silver notes trilled
through the dawn
It sang so hard
That at the worst
I feared its tiny heart
would burst
I wonder if it sang for me
To ease my sad despondency.
To tell me hearts
Don't break in pain
But learn to live
And sing again.

Loneliness
F. Kauser

An empty space that no one shares
talk to yourself who knows? or who cares
A tidy kitchen, a place laid for one
Tell me, where have all the guests gone?
a fat child at school, a figure of fun
Couldn't keep up on the cross country run,
a sister laying still with rag doll limbs,
The lonely knowledge the out look is grim,
One brown skin in a sea of white
bigoted ignorance thinks it's right,
a different view, each against another
daring to speak out against a brother
a blanket of nothing over your head
Thoughts of tomorrow bring a despairing dread
This is loneliness, it's not me
I've never felt this way you see.

Let Me Tell You Once More That I Love You
J. M. Gilchrist

Let me tell you once more that I love you
For one day it may be too late
For time passes by so quickly
It could be taken from me by fate.

Let me offer you a life's devotion
As I hold you in my arms
For sometimes I think I'm dreaming
When I think of your many charms.

But time goes by so quickly
That day soon turns to night
So I'm going to tell you once more
Because time's on an endless flight
Let me thank you for being so caring
And for a truly wonderful life
And for all the years of love you've given me
And I'm glad you chose me for your wife.

The Greatest Love
Gina Shoukri

There was a circle,
And inside the circle was my heart,
And outside the circle was the greatest love,
And the greatest love gave me a quarter of the circle,
And it was my son, and he gave me a second quarter
Which was equal to the first, and it was my daughter
And the greatest love gave me a third quarter,
Which was lost, and just remained as a memory,
And I called this my secret love,
And the greatest love was sad,
And he gave me my fourth and final quarter,
And that was my son, and he was special,
And my circle was complete,
And the greatest love said, love and cherish your circle
for one day it will be broken, and be no more
and remember always,
for I am the outline of your circle,
And everything that is inside is mine.

Night
Kimberly Hedgebeth

The sun is golden on the grass
Soon the day will come to pass
The clouds have slowly turned to pink
The bright red sun is on sky's brink
Soon it turns so dark outside
Shadows seem to creep and hide
The stars are out and very bright
Making the glow of a mysterious night
But soon they start to fade away
And morning birds begin to play
The moon is getting so much fainter
A perfect picture for a painter
I can see the sunlight's beam
It rises with a golden gleam
The beauty of a morning starts
The moon, the stars; a nighttime parts

Dreams of the Soul

Never Alone
Lillian Curnutt
I am never alone Lord,
Because I know you are with me!
Tho' no human person be
O' the joy your presence brings to me!
Your love never fails to give assurance to me!
And that Never Alone, I will ever be!
When danger surrenders me
I see the hedge you placed around me!
I shall never forget that day
You showed the hedge to me!
Tho' it was as clear as crystal
And not even sound could penetrate thru!
Because I have been sealed by the Holy Spirit
I am hid with Christ in God.
Therefore I know the Holy Trinity watches over me.
And I know NEVER ALONE will I ever be! Praise the Lord!

The Dreamer
Daniel Ray Connell
Dreams may come and dreams may go
But the Dreamer had one thing he'll always know
He has within him, the power inside
To move on, conquer, set goals and decide

The Dreamer is master of his destiny
Able to manipulate all things that he sees
The Dreamer is controller of the fates
Guardian to hell and the pearly gates

The Dreamer is lord in the world he creates
The prince of loves and duke of hates
Rule the land with thy staff and thy rod
The Dreamer is everything, The Dreamer is god

Force Of True Love
Nancy Turner Collins
The force of true love now rests upon me

It came in with the roar of a lion
Once wild, now tame

It has settled ever so silently
Into the depths of my soul

This force does not fear me
As I it

It has now made a friend of me

Once it captured and overpowered
My fear
I was lost in you, my force

Hoping to never let go

The Go–Cart Trail
Luci Cook
The grass is getting tall and green
getting the riding mower I start thinking back,
I'm riding then but it's my go–cart.
In those days the grass didn't grow
on this side no need to mow.
All through the yard a trail was seen
up the hill around the oak tree
and down by the creek no grass to be seen.
My friends, our go–carts, and me
riding the trail having a good time
never once worrying about the bright sun shining down.
Those were the days all filled with laughter,
now we're all grown, the grass grows faster.
Up the hill around the oak tree I ride still
but now riding just isn't the same,
because it's work that I cannot shirk.

Untitled
Angel Lyle
As I sit watching my candle burn, I slowly come to
realize, that I've been hypnotized by this romantic
little creature. A creature it surely is for it needs
to breathe and it must eat. It just doesn't need to be
fed the same as you or I. I watch it dance and dip,
curl and twist. All to seduce the wax of which it
will caress. Once the wax has yielded to the way
of the flame, it becomes violent, uncontrollable. Its need
is purely to consume. So the flame licks at the wax
savagely. Taking little notice of the drips that pass
by. In all its passion, greedily devouring the very
substance which gives it life. Soon it will die. Its life
force melting, wasted down the side. Maybe this small
and subtle creature was meant as one of life's little lessons.

Sunrise
Rae A. Halvorson
The Lord took my hand and led me to a place
Where I was surrounded by darkness
The anticipation of what was to be unfolded
burned within my heart
Then, my eyes beheld the most beautiful sight...
As the sun began to rise over the mountains
With colors that flowed through my soul
Warmth and gentleness surrounded me
My heart was comforted as the Lord began to say,
"My child, your life is about to unfold—
Just as you have seen the sun rise today
Your life will reveal such beauty in the same way.
So, be encouraged and know these blessings to come
are from me."

MCMXCVII
Jean Foster McColgin
When young I was eternal.
Time was something I'd always have enough of
And life was on ahead.
Then I'd really begin to be and do and have.
It was still to come.
Somewhere along the way
I was and did and had
And still it was to come.
In these later years
Ideas of mortality sneak in
and nibble around my edges
But still to come
Are days
And years
To be and do and have.
I still don't believe
I'll ever not
Be.

Home Is...
Amanda Shaw
Home, I want a new Home
Far and away from the city
A home that is peaceful and quiet
One that is soft and pretty.

It would be nice to be in the mountains
Where the air is fresh and pure
The pine trees blow with the wind
And the birds glide quick and sure.

I'll have two dogs and a horse
Two cats to kill the mice
A big room to look out
Wouldn't that be nice?

Birth
David Hadrava
Why can't I be free?
Like a bird, who flies in the sky.
But, may I ask you, can a bird who is locked
away, sing as sweetly as a bird who is free?
I yearn, I wonder, I search, I ponder.
Every day just seems to be longer.
Then, one day there came a chance.
My Mother seemed anxious today, so I decided to go.
What's ahead? what will become of me?
What's to do? what's to see?
One day I may look back, and decide I was wrong.
But life's about that; and so it began.
I started to see the light of day.
I heard a screaming; and tried to hide away,
But too late! now here I go
out into the wide blue yonder!
I'll probably do the same out there,
I'll yearn, I'll wonder, I'll search, I'll ponder.

Oh Angry Sea
Dennis George Dorset
Calm down calm down oh angry sea, it's like a millpond you should be,
The day is fine the sun is bright and not a gust of wind in sight,
The sky is clear no sign of storm yet you rear your head as though in scorn.
Why are you angry, why so rough, you've shown your power off enough

There's many fought you on your terms, There's many won and many learned
That your power is beyond belief, and returned to land with great relief
There are many terrors in your deep, There's much food from your depths we reap

But for ever prize from you we've won you've claimed the right to someone's son

Calm down calm down oh angry sea, and like a millpond will you be
Upon you all our ships can run, you can give pleasure food and fun
If we could keep control of the weather we could keep your strength in tether

---

The Promised Land
Bill Rainwater
Do you want the Promised Land, that flows with milk and honey?
Where the stars give out their light, and days are cool and sunny
This land is promised to you and me – it is ours to claim
It is not given free, or won by playing a game.

You'll go through a battle zone, before you reach your goal
If you carry this burden alone, it will take its toll
There's One who promised to go with you, He said it's yours – believe
He said that He would see you through, and the victory you would receive.

If you run into a solid wall, you think you can't knock down
Keep the faith, and step by step, it will hit the ground
It's yours, possess it, you've won the fight, no evil force can stand
The victory you won has brought you in the Promised Land.

I Want To Be With You
Eian C. Bell
Loneliness engulfs my soul
Sending my heart spinning out of control
Every waking thought is dedicated to you
I wonder sometimes, "do you think of me too?"
My letters go unanswered as if you don't care
Yet you always find your way into my prayers
Passionate whispers encircling my ears
Chanting your name, and forcing the tears
If only you could tell me somehow
Where we go next, and what we do now
My love for you is too strong to be broken
I miss you more than in words can be spoken
So please don't deny my only request
To be with you, and give you the best
I want nothing more than your hand in mine
As we walk together 'til the end of time.

Dreams of the Soul

A Man Keeps Walking
Samantha Addeman
In the street,
A woman's scream,
A man keeps walking.

In an apartment building,
A desperate cry for help,
Screaming to God to save them,
A man keeps walking.

In the park,
A woman's purse,
The thief running to hide,
A man keeps walking.

On a path,
A man is attacked,
And the people,
Keep walking.

Loving You!
Myra S. Hanks
I give you my heart to have and to hold
I give you my heart as we grow old
I give you my heart each night and day
I'll give you my heart 'til we fade away.

I gave you my heart to have and to hold
The years they pass by too fast to hold
I give you my heart as time passes by
It's been 20 plus 5 and it seems to fly.

The kids are growing and leaving the nest
I know it's life and it's for the best
The family is growing and couldn't be happier
Our hearts are filling with a new kind of laughter.

Dedication: My loving husband, Sid

His Eyes
Barbara J. Panza
They are like the color of the sea,
they are blue and they are deep.
Peaceful and gentle they are constantly,
all storms, in their depths have gone to sleep.

Gentle rolling waves lap to the shore,
to tickle and tease the sand.
Their leagues are filled with love and adore,
to leave an eternal brand.

Neither salt is in its chemistry,
nor in the winter do they freeze.
Only gentle ripples come to me,
stirred up by his soft breeze.

Dedication: Jeff, whose eyes inspire me

My Brother Liberty
David Smith
He stands still in life
waiting for life to see
other things are distraction,
Peaceful uncluttered thoughts
Innocence has touched darkness
For all to see, liberty waits
And sleeps for him to see
And feel gentleness and
peace, unclenched of
anger he will open his
mind, where liberty will
choose.

Dedication: My brother, Gordon

Across The Street
Louis D. Harris
I first saw you from across the street
You waved and said hello
When I began to cross over
You leaned and whispered to your friend
Later I learned the words you whispered, were
I have a feeling, I am to marry him
As I approached, I said my name is Louis
You answered with I know
I am Elmida in case you wish to know
As I began to leave
I reached out and squeezed your hand
Instantly I was in love with you
I am an old man now and still remember when
I fell in love with you.

What Is Life
Yolanda Jasilli
What Is Life
But a World of what we are
A mixture of good and bad
Joined together near and far

What Is Life
But what we want to be
Striving for the peace
That we find in eternity

What Is Life
But a fulfillment of a dream
If it could all be beautiful
How wonderful life would seem

A Mystery Of Life
Barbara Surette
It is a mystery to me, decided but unknown,
About a child who, even now, is my very own.
My entire self is devoted to its love and care,
And soon it's small body on the earth I'll bear.
It started with a very small seed, which was full of love,
And soon it started growing with a blessing from above.
We gave it life, we gave it breath, along with some tears
We'll give it hope, we'll give it faith, along with many years.
But still there is that mystery, determined but unrevealed,
About the gender of our child, though it has been sealed.
Will it be a little boy to his dad's delight,
Or turn out a little girl whom he'll love in spite?
This is the secret which I hold inside:
Whatever God may bring us, I'm sure we'll abide.

An Ode To The Immortal Poets And Philosophers
C. Antonio Provost
No greater service did they bestow;
A debt of gratitude we owe
Throughout the ages past whose verse will forever last
They enriched humanity with their profound philosophy,
With knowledge they bestowed mankind,
Infusing wisdom to each and every open mind,
A wealth of concepts enriching our souls,
Aiding us all attain great goals
To make us better than the beasts,
And beastly brutes who plague the world
With deeds destroying humanity,
Because of their perversity

If their works are taught in time,
The human race would be sublime far less brutality of man
by virtue of the poets', and philosophers' plan.
Indeed! their lessons which we learn,
The godly guidance, no one should ever spurn.

Undeniable
Hazel L. Nelson
When I close my eyes
The tears roll away
And calmness flows over my face

When I speak your name
My heart quivers
And stillness saddens my grace

When I think of you
I hear fire cracklin' in my chest
And my body shivers from constant stress

Undeniable, I'm yours
Love has taken over.

Lonely Heart
Latise D. Minnicks
My heart has been broken and it bleeds once more,
like a veteran scarred from his war wound, or a
child discovering an old sore.
As I remembered before, quite clearly how it
feels, to be hurt by someone whom you thought
love was real.
If only I had known, that pain followed gain,
then maybe I could have figured out that I was
not to blame.
Oh I wish I could go back, to escape all the hurt,
back from where I came, resculptured from the dirt.
As my night and days grow lonelier, and my months
and years pass through, my body yearns for a true
love, which leaves me only you.
But life goes on, like seasons go, in hope that
Cupid finds his bow.
As true as it may sound, as many of us hate, but
good things come to those who wait.

What Makes Dreams Come True?
Jamey Shepherd
What would I have if it weren't for you?
I wouldn't have been set free from life's wheel.
Your love for me is pure as well as true
and I still can't believe it's for real.
You have rejuvenated me, I feel brand new!
Because you've helped me learn how to feel.
In my life's mystery you were the final clue.
When I saw you, my defenses began to peel.

Why do you love me? I often ask.
You make me feel like a tree so tall.
For loving me is not an easy task.
Together, we can break down any wall.

We are forever bonded by the strength of love
because you were a blessing sent from above.

Flower
Jennifer Gaspard
A flower
Has power
To cure the mind, body, and soul
A flower never gets old
It soothes the pain
Chases away the rain
It cares
It's there
When you need it
When you want it
To keep
In reach
When you're sober
When your life is over
Through never
And forever

Dreams of the Soul

A Mother's Love Is A True Love
Roderick E. Ellison
Come to me my child, that I may show you,
that life is so precious, life is true,
not a soul in this world can care so
much, the way I care for you.

Hard times will come, good times will go,
life is strange and so uncertain, you
never know who's your foe.

Now in due time you will find, that being
on your own, is no big deal, but no matter
what, my time I'll cut, to write with love
and zeal.

So listen my child the world may say, I
will not always be here for you, but a
Mother's love is an unconditional love and
a Mother's love is true.

Platonic Love
Desiree A. Cole
The sentimental love of a devoted and trusting spirit,
characterized by extreme fondness, and tender affections.

The feelings of deep expressions of admiration and adoration,
which need only to be expressed through the heart.

The gentle and tender touch of a hand or cheek,
which kindles the feelings of the soul and not the flesh.

These are expressions which adorn the heart,
and must be held there as an embellishment of friendship,
with its warmest regards.

Dedication: To Carl, my friend forever...

Deranged Fate
Chris Tate
solid doors, metal halls
cracked windows, iron walls
standing up, straight, tall, alone
supported by this unstable foam
chilling glares, ... strain the possibilities
just nightmares,... in their fake realities
loosing heart, ... still striving for
another part, ... yet so much more
doomed to die out someday
trips and cannot fly away
digging, yet, a deeper hole
trying to raise this wretched soul
enjoying this negligence, ... figuring more than you should
hating anything's presence, ... controlling more than you could
needing it more, ... fending off intensity
open up the sore, ... loss of this audacity
finding out the truth of the lie
confused and wondering why

I Know You
Michelle Jefferson
"By night on my bed I sought him
whom my soul loveth:
I sought him, but I
found him not.

I will rise now and go about the
city in the streets and
in the broadways
I will seek him whom
my soul loveth: I
sought him, but I
found him not.

The watchmen that go about the
city found: to whom I
said, Saw ye him
whom my soul
loveth?"

A Helping Hand
Marian Winsor
I see no charity in thee
You close your eyes? you do not see.
How life for others has to be.
Everything for you is cut and dried
Things are black and white
Other shades of life you have never tried.
Never once a helping hand, offered by you
Just remember life can change you could
Be down too.

I wonder why you are so hard life's been
Good for you having more than your share
You must admit it's true.
So be a bit more giving I don't mean pound
Shilling or pence
Don't leave it too long or you could repent

Song of a Winter Morn
Cecelia Weber
The sun is shining brightly,
And I've seen no morning stars.
The days are long and lonely
'Cause I don't know where you are.
I haven't kept up contacts.
I'm trying to "keep the peace".
My world is closing inward.
I need a new life to lease.
Please find me where I am,
On the path to the land of the damned.
The sun is shining brightly.
I don't want "us" to be a scam.
The evening star of Venus
Is being coupled with the moon.
Don't hesitate to call.
Please, please find me soon.

Seventeen
Patti Lutz

17 years ago I met you
17 years ago – I love you
17 years ago I married you

17 years later
I love you more now
than the day I said I do

17 more years
coupled as we are
our love will set
forevermore

17 years
Always
I Love You

Dedication: My inspiration. I love you

Hum
Darcy Hoshal Smith

Quiet clicks at day's end,
Steady pulse in rivulets and tunnels,
Awareness thick and true,
Flows past the mathematics of agreement,
Soothing my time–clocked psyche.
A long hum of resonance,
Voices dear and quiet.
Darkness enfolds my body
In feathers and cotton.
Brushes my lashes
Dream–soaked and still.
Sanctuary of timeless streaming.

Dedication: Julian Bly Hoshal, my father

Lost In The Darkness
Jennifer Vanderlee

The quietness, the darkness, the shriek in the night
The boy in the park running out of sight
The birds in the sky all gone to bed
But me wide awake, scared of the night
There's something here, I feel it, I just can't see
I've shut out the world just thinking of me
The starving children I've forgotten
The wounded I leave
forgetting the phrase "Let them come unto Me"
I leave them forgotten, alone on the path
Something in me is crazy
My mind's under attack.
Who is this; this madman with terrible thoughts
who is the person making these evil plots
Someone I know, but never have seen
Only someone opposite of Jesus could be so mean.
I think it's Satan, alone doing wrong
He'll never get me. My Savior's too strong

Dance Of Fall
Francesca Hockycko McLellan

Gentle leaf what is to become of you
Fall is now upon us
It is your time to shine
Let your beautiful colors beam

The cold fall wind is beginning
Swirling and carrying you down to earth
At last you begin your graceful dance
How beautiful you are

Are you to become part of a family
After a child proudly picks you up
Or simply be swept away
When your dance of fall is done

Noise
Kathryn E. Bell

The rattle of dice as it hits the board,
The metallic clink as the knights cross their swords,
The laughter of children as they play in the glen,
The chime of a clock as it strikes ten.

The scream and the cackle of a coven of witches,
The slurp and the spurt as the men drain the ditches,
The crunching of leaves as they're trod on in fall,
The ding–a–ling–ling of the phone in the hall.

A cry of surprise as the child opens a box,
The boom of a boat as it's leaving the docks,
The din of an orchestra as they try a new song,
The zoom of a speedboat as it races along.

Mom
Veronica Lawwill

I think that everyone should know, I love a special lady,
I've loved her more with every day since I was just a baby.
She taught so many things to me, from day to passing year.
Some brought happiness and joy, while others brought a tear.
Sometimes improprieties would cause a doubt or fight, 'cause
After all, a teen just knows that Mom is never right!

Less than perfect, thank the Lords, but thinks she ought to be.
Yet, in my eyes, no greater love could she have given me.
I think she is the greatest, I'm sure she is the best!
I'll bet it's me, instead of her, that has been truly blessed.

I'm proud to say I love my Mom, I'm proud to let it show, but
Wish she'd told me sooner that my name's not "Honey, No No"!

Dedication: My mom, Evelyn Solnok

Dreams of the Soul

Once Upon A Time
Raenell Diffie

Once upon a time seems only a fairy–tale told to
children at night, maybe it is and maybe it isn't
but the children remember the stories as the
Mother turns out the light

The children carry those stories into adulthood
and so it gives them hope, the great big world
may let them down and the remembrance of
stories is just what they need to cope

As the children grow older and wiser they become
parents warm and kind, their children will ask them
to tell a good story and the adults will reply,
Once Upon A Time

Void
I. S. Caddie

Span the mind, shut out the noise
Embrace yourself within the void
Lost in body, lost in soul
Clouds of nothingness taking hold
Silent screams drift into space
Dissolved memories leave no trace
Flowing lakes of endless night
Winds of darkness take to flight
Reality becomes but a blur
As roused, infinity begins to stir
Conscious minds falling deep
Into the pit of endless sleep
Precious sanity starts to boil
Remnants of reason tossed like a toy
All hope consumed, lost to fate
Forever void, eternity awaits

Untitled
Lesley Richens

Don't ever let your light go out,
you laugh, you sing, you smile, you shout,
you light up every corner of my day,
you're bright and breezy in every way,
sometimes I think my heart will break,
the love you give but never take,
you are my moon and stars and sky,
and no matter how hard I try,
I can't believe although I love you,
you can find it in your heart to love me too,
when I'm not here you miss me,
when I come home you run and kiss me,
my love for you grows all the time,
that is why I wrote this rhyme,
you live deep within my heart,
and if we ever have to part,
I know for sure what I must do,
I will leave this place and follow you.

The Meaning Of Love
Cameo Rene

Someone who makes you feel good about living, who
Brings out the you who is joyful and giving, this is
the meaning of love...
Something that gives you a chance to be
Strong or trust in another to help you along,
this is the meaning of love...
Somewhere that you feel like you'll been there forever,
a place where you're growing and learning together, this
is the meaning of love...
With you I've found the something that allows me to be
strong, yet gives me comfort and support when I need
it... with you I've found the somewhere that makes
me feel sheltered and secured, yet free to grow and
develop on my own... with you, I've found
what seems I had been looking for forever that
Beautiful, and very real meaning of love...

Dedication: Someone who has never been loved

Only In America
Eric B. Shaffer

Only in America can someone walk into a McDonald's and kill
21 people.

And, only in America can Miss America do a nude photo layout
in Penthouse magazine.

And, only in America can Jane Fonda go to the Communist side
of the world and see our pilots get shot down in Vietnam.

And, only in America can you burn Old Glory and protest the
government and get away with it.

These are just a few things, the list can go on forever.
So, the next time you want to smoke your dope and protest your
country and burn "my flag," remember you can only do these things.
"Only in America."

Dedication: My wife, Jewlie Jo

My Prayer
Toni L. Berghman

Thank you Lord, though I've failed,
passed over once again,
I often feel so tired as,
I wonder if and when
I'll ever feel the joy of sweet success,
Feel blessed, not cursed;
Just once to know I tried my best
And actually came first.
It shouldn't really matter, Lord,
Just give me what you see
Is best, you feel, to help me do
The tasks you've given me.
I shall be first, when once was last;
I've loved and lost again.
For you only ask an honest heart,
Not mighty deeds of men.

Dedication: My family

Untitled
Rick Burton

There is peace, there is giving, there is much to be thankful for. This land that we nourish, this land was scarred, it tries to flourish and come back for more.
We came in wonder, in search of new land, we established our presence, we grew only to expand.
As time went on, we became greedy, no longer were we needy.
A never-ending imagination of technology, producing more and more, only to take away from the land that we worked so hard with our hand.
Our forests, our streams, our air. Mother Nature, it used to be such a beautiful picture. Our parks, our seaways, the untouched land, will it be safe from man?
Will the future survive, will they know this land, that once we worked with our hand? Nature will survive, if it can.

Dedication: My daughter's future, Mandy Burton

You And Me
Thelma M. Donahue

It's just you and me against the world.
A dreamy-eyed boy and a starry-eyed girl.
They set out on their own two feet,
working every day just to make ends meet.
They bought a house and settled down
in a small, quiet, country town.
A few years later, the baby came,
a little boy that shared his daddy's name.
Thirty years now have passed,
proving all those wrong, that said
it wouldn't last.
It's still you and me against the world,
the same dreamy-eyed boy and starry-eyed
girl.

Dedication: My loving husband, Sean

It Was The Night Before Christmas
Dawn Belanger

It was the night before Christmas and all through the house not a CBer was stirring not even a mouse. With CBer's all snug in their beds with visions of CB radios and antennas dancing in their heads. There arose such a clatter I sprang from my bed to see what was the matter. I threw open the window and stuck out my head and to my surprise that did appear but a giant cobra 2000 and 8 tiny silver eagles. As the base buzzed and squealed and faded out of sight a message came over the speaker and said
Merry Christmas to all and to all a good night.

Dedication: Richard Gonzales (future husband)

Untitled
Gary J. Smith

They can take away my colours, so I see
Black and white.
They can take away my daytime
So I just have the night.
They can take away my eyes, so I no
Longer see
They can take away my sanctuary, so
I am no longer free
They can take away my arms and
Legs, until there is nothing more
That they can do
But they will never take away
My heart, because my heart
Belongs to you

Untitled
Laura McCormack

Here's a little birthday greeting
To a brother fine and dear,
With a hope that with this sentiment
Will come a bit of cheer.

May the sun which seems to hover
Just beyond your present view,
On this day of days most special
Shed its golden light on you.

So, Happy Birthday, good old soldier.
Holding on, you played your part,
You're one among a million:
We salute you from the heart.

When Angels Cry
Felipe Chacon, Jr.

"Oh rain from the heavens, why do you so pour?
Are many your griefs, for such a downpour?"
The heavens responded, with thunderous light;
"Why do you not heed, my little ones' plight?
My angels from heaven, I send to be born.
They are then forsaken and treated with scorn.
You batter and maim, subject them to porn.
Laying guilt and shame, on my angels born,
From their Mothers' womb, they return to me,
Butchered like the lamb, before they're to be,
Do you not believe, in heavenly might?
Once on a night's eve, you foresaw my light.
I command creation, all that is to be.
Eternal damnation, will fall upon thee."

Dedication: All battered children on earth

Dreams of the Soul

The Visitation
Carole A. Fisher
The Lady, clad in flimsy white
Bent down and kissed her sleeping knight.
She saw him stir, she touched his face
Smiled, and slipped off her gown of lace.

She held him close, she smoothed his brow
He was hers for the moment now.
She saw his eyes, his soul her treasure
A memory to hold with pleasure.

Their time would remain in her heart
Remain forever, though they must part.
She gently rocked him back to sleep
Then departed forever... destined to weep.

Dedication: Those who surround me with love

The Gateway (Ode To The Sixties)
Malcolm F. Martin
I hear the call, I'm being paged
Entering the gateway of the aged
I've passed the time of immaturity
I've entered the realm of Social Security
I'm politer now and it does amuse me
I pass more gas and say more "Excuse Me"
Baseball's over, I can't hit a grounder
The feet are flatter, the stomach rounder
The hair is whiter, breath sometimes short
the knees are weaker the teeth, store—bought
the bills are larger, my money's spent
where sex was often, it's now an event
Don't get me wrong, I'm not whining
In all of this there's a silver lining
My family loves me, my health is fine
So come on seventies, you're next in line

Untitled
Patrizia Evola
I've grown weary of
Descending this
Desolate path
I have chosen

I'm not too proud
To admit the bricks
Of ignorance I've built
Have become too high to scale
Too thick to break
With bare hands

Which leaves only will
And patience
To disassemble my tower
One brick at a time

Dedication: Anyone that didn't lose hope

Pain And Sorrow
Karyn Entler
Love can cause pain and sorrow.
So, if you have it, let it all out like there is no tomorrow.

But if it's love you hope to find,
Make sure it is true for you.

It consists of total control over heart and mind,
But if it's not true, it can make you blue.

The desire to be loved can make you blind,
And you could end up in a terrible bind.

For some, there is only pain and sorrow.
But for others there is a tomorrow.

Untitled
Kevin L. Oakwood
Kindness, devotion and your will
to be, are the hardest tests
for you and me. We are given
these with a key, to unlock
them in life and show to thee.
But as we grow older, and wise
in thought, will be remembered
to some, and others not. My
generation, the people I know,
are the ones who care, and are
not afraid to share. Family,
friends are special to me, to
show that blood is thicker than
water for eternity.

For Madison
Marian Bohn
Our hearts became one
the moment we saw your face.
And our sweet little one,
none will ever replace.
The twinkle in your eyes
and the angelic way you glow
Will make all of our hard work
worthwhile — we know.
We promise that your life
will be happy and true.
Our sweet little one,
We pray to always have you.

Dedication: My Baby, My Heart

Tanya
Carla Eggimann

Life has many questions
that puzzle you and I
I think I have a reason
why sometimes young ones die.

I think the Dancer was an angel
sent from God above
to live with us awhile
and spread laughter, joy, and love.

Then God took her home
to live with Him in glory
He taught us all a lesson
and used Tanya in His story.

Peaceful Bloom
Jeff P. Barentine

Peaceful gems glow from white pools
And reflect upon my soul
Untamed sunbeams scent her brow
As Beauty's essence flows
Artist's work upon midface
In Endless Desert Fair
My head rests on youthful breast
I, Lover's hands do wear
Gentle touch on Lady's form
Beneath a silvery moon
Maiden's kiss to quench the fire
Of virgin love in bloom

Dedication: To God, Kari Bennett

Reality Of The Shadow
Micki Chatman

Walking alone, moon at my back
casting shadows into the night.
I stop, look around
someone is following me.
Who could this bent person be
Head sagging in defeat
Arms hanging in dejection
and oh, my their feet are
shuffling too.
I listen, I hear no confident
echoes of footsteps
I look around again
there isn't anyone here
But me
Yet here stands this lost
soul I vowed never to be
and yet, and yet,
the shadows have become me

Let Us Now Sing
Jeadenia Ann Roberts

Let us now sing:
Sing out loud; let it ring
over the hilltops and across the sea.
Sing until the earth trembles and you feel
it beneath your feet.
Let us now sing:
Shout the victory; mama and papa
can't always sing those hymns and
go marching down those lonesome
roads, although you can stand with
raised hands stomp to yesterday's beat.
Let us now sing:
Sing, sing and let your voices
ring. Sing until, you feel it
deep down in your soul. Sing
my people; sing, sing and
—NOW—
"Let us now sing"

The Nosy Winds
Kiri Benson

The nosy wind sweeps from town to town,
and when there's a storm she
sometimes slows down.
She's as graceful as a swan
or maybe as playful as a baby fawn

The nosy wind is like a whisper,
in the chilly night sky.
Listening for some gossip
or maybe a little white lie

The nosy winds can hear all
so don't try to hide.
Whether the North, south, east
or west winds.
All four can hear your call

To Can Dot
Katy Agnew

It's birthday time today – your day. This poem is for you
all the way. I love you so much and you must
Love me too 'cause when I am bad you never
Tell a soul whatever I do.
I'm not sure how old you will be and it really
doesn't matter – 'cause you never ever show it
or get any fatter.
You are the sweetest, the nicest and the best
around – my Mom and me couldn't find any
better if we looked all over town.
I was just writing this for you to say you
are the best babysitter all over and we
couldn't find a better one even with
a four–leaf clover.

Dedication: To Can Dot

Dreams of the Soul

When Death Calls
Jackie F. Petty
When death suddenly calls our loved ones home
Our hearts are made heavy and we might feel alone
Then we remember that weeping may endure for a night
But that God promised joy with the morning light

Be encouraged oh my soul, just look towards the sky
Your help is on the way, you'll rejoice by and by
Death is but a doorway to receive our heavenly prize
And The Father up above will be waiting on the other side

Oh death where is your sting, grave where is your victory
You were defeated a long time ago, way back on Calvary
Yes death you're only a release, that's all and nothing more
For to be absent from the body is to be present with the Lord

---

You
Cida Carneiro
Oh, how is it to dream,
Of a poet's lips, moist, warm
Whispering promises of a satin night
To feel the magic of caressing hands,
Touching, awakening forbidden places

Poet,
I dream of you
My renaissance prince,
Warrior, lover, a romantic in true!!
I envision your presence,
In my nights of solitude,
Awaiting longingly,
On a bed of roses... And satin sheets...

Before Knowledge
Jayne James
Darkness all around.
The slow, steady beat pulsing through
The depth of silence
Like oozing mud sucking in.
Then muffled vibrations.
Sounds buzz, and are gone.
Feel confined, trapped
Knees against chest.
So cramped in here
Long to breathe
Fresh, cool air.
To stand upright
Kick impatiently
Eyes tightly closed
Still time, quiet time
Before my dawn.

Adieu
Deborah J. Law
Saying goodbye, farewell or see ya
is usually by a sad time in one's life.
Due to the fact that someone is
either withdrawing from your life
or you are evacuating from theirs.

As a mild expert at goodbyes I have
discovered one solution to ease the
pain. That is to open one's arms and
hug with all one's might. But try not to
cry cause that could be a real tie.

And who knows when, where or how
you will meet once more. It could be
tomorrow or perhaps even more.
Either way hang on tight and squeeze
for your true delight, in saying
goodbye to the ones you leave behind.

Untitled
Samantha S. Solverson
You are His child.
You have already made that choice.
He will never abandon you.
You have announced it with your voice.
Although you have strayed away from
Him,
He opens His arms up wide.
Anytime you want to—
you can come back to His trusting side.
He understands that life is hard, and
sometimes you make the wrong choice.
He welcomes you back—
no questions asked.
He's just happy to hear your voice.

Of Jesus
Neil Campbell
If he could bear to have
his skin torn, by so much more than only one
thorn; and because he knew that this was to be,
long before it became history. Then what kind of
pain is it that I can't stand? "None", I say, "does
exist", that I cannot withstand.

For with his pain he gave to me, the freedom,
the peace, and the joy to–be, in his thoughts and
in his cares, for he does truly forgive me.

If only his strength and his courage I could
summon, when it is needed to strike down fear.
For, fear will only appear, only when you dread it,
but to know it and face it will surely make it
disappear.

Compare
Michael R. Dewolf

The grass grows green
Dies brown and frail.
The tree grows tall and
Full of color and dies shabby
And bare and starts over again.
The flower grows of many colors
But dies one, black.
Death is viewed in so many ways.
It all depends on how you see
It. Maybe you see it as painful,
Wrong and a loss, or you see it
As a part of life as a stage in the
Cycle.
It's much easiest to look at death
(So painful, so very painful) in a
Natural part of life.
Everything dies but not everything
Lives.

Down By The Sea
Richard Mistretta

Down by the sea I stand and watch
The beauty and power comes to me flowing toward the shore
With a force unlike any other it's nothing like I've seen before
Even the bright and radiant sun couldn't match the beauty and glory of the sea or what was yet to come!
The purple and red sky caressed the end of the world.
I felt as if I wanted to fly!
In the midst of the night the moon reflected off the water creating a rainbow of light.
In the light came a face. It came like a ballerina with grace.
Silently floating down by the sea I saw that face peering into my eyes
Blessing my soul, cleansing me.
Unable to scream or run away I stood there as time went by knowing that I should pray
For God had given me a key to His glorious kingdom that night down by the sea!

How'd The Soul Get Damaged
Ruth Ann Carver

How'd the soul get damaged?
Do you know?
Everyone knows, love can damage the soul.
Temptation is present wherever you go.
Giving in, can damage your soul.
Words that are meant to hurt.
Cause the soul damage
Cause the soul to hurt
Hearts can be broken.
They can cry out in pain.
Faith is the only answer, it is also the only game.
Trust in yourself is what they say.
Yet, as you look around everyone has given up on that game.
Words are cheap they come and go, just like the winter's snow.
Real love is said to be a myth,
– No one ever really gets it. –
Was it ever really you or me,
that caused my soul to flee.

Petals
L. J. Valentine

As I walked along the beach today, leaving a trail behind me in the sand. Thoughts of you flood my mind, as I walked along the shore. The tide began to wash away whatever was there before.

Clutching near my heart, a rose within my hand. Knowing that it's delicate, frail and new. My love for you is too. Still longing for my destination, the sky was clear and blue.

Suddenly startled by a thunderous roar, a bolt of lightning shot from the heavens above. The clouds of gloom rushed across the sky, I began to cry.

The tears cascade down my face and now combined with rain, landing on the rose, causing the petals to fall away.

Dedication: Laura Alma Calvarese (Mom)

The Unsung Hero
Ben Clifton

As I approach the box my hands start to tense.
All I seem to think about is that distant fence.
The bottom of the ninth trailing by one,
A runner on third and one out is done.
A home run will win the game on the line,
Then my faithful coach gives me the "squeeze" sign.
As a puzzled look comes across my face,
The coach begins a slow steady pace.
I don't understand how this could be,
To give the "squeeze" sign to a hitter like me.
But I did as told and got the run in,
And two batters later we scored again.
I wasn't the "hero" on that triumphant day,
But I wonder what might've happened had I swung away.

Thinking Of You
Tammy Fernandes

As I look out to the sea,
I will think of you and me.
The love we shared through the years,
has brought us happiness, joy and many tears.
My love for you grows each day,
I will miss you greatly, I know my heart will break.
But only for a short time.
As the months will pass,
I await for your return,
My heart will always, constantly yearn.
For your lone and soft touch that you bring.
The joy I feel inside, will make my heart sing.
As I sit on the rocks, watching the water.
I'll think of you.
My husband, my friend, and my
Lover.

Dedication: My husband, with all my love

Dreams of the Soul

Doubting Mind
Amy Mericle
How well do I know you?
I sometimes wonder.
Are you who I thought you were?
When you're lost in thought, where do you go?
Am I with you when you are there?
Do I know your expressions, or are you deceiving?
I hope that I'm right when I'm believing.
Console my doubts.
Let me know.
Please...
Tell me you'll never let me go!
Am I too insecure?
That's probably true.
Do I conjure up problems that just don't exist?
I'll try not to doubt.
I promise you that!
But make me believe.
That's all I will ask.

Heartchild
Brenda J. Windell
I call you out of bondage to ignorance and fear;
When you speak to me, my child, I am always here.
I call you to the silence where you may drink your fill,
And lead you to the promised land to help you know my will.

I give to you the freedom to live as you would choose;
The power and potential to win, and never lose.
I call you when you wander, for I would give you rest.
I love you, my heart's child,
And want for you the best.

You are my creation, birthed from my own heart;
And while you sometimes feel alone, we never are apart.
For you and I are one; and forever you will be
A child of my own heart, always one with me,
My heart's child.

Special Dedication To Ma From Robey February 5, 1996
Roberta Kingston
Where you slept, where you sat, where you laid your head, thoughts of
you go whisking by; memories of things we've said.
I stop and only realize now how many lives you've touched
In so many ways, big and small, never guessing just how much.
When I was young and always hurt, you'd gently take my hand...
and ease my fears so easily. 'til on my feet I'd land.
You'd tuck my hair behind my ears with a touch I can't erase; 'til tears
would dry and then again the world I'd have to face.
I know you must be happy now warmed by familiar embraces
I know the peace and joy you feel among the many faces
So among the treasured memories, we've upped and tucked away...
we store them safely in our hearts to share again one day.
A flower bloomed the day you left... a reminder to go on
'til we meet again among the rest... our lives, we'll carry on.

May They Come In?
Angel Taylor
A family of three
as white as white can be.
A family of four
has come to the door.

The family sends them back.
For, you see, they are black.
Back into the night;
Their souls on a midnight flight.

They are angels sent down from above
to see if God's children can love.
Love beyond skin
for it is no sin.

May they come in?

The Rocket
Charleen K. Cook
It chanced that He grew weary of the sun,
And longed to find a fire that was more bright,
A fire brilliant as the fire of Hell;
And yet He did not covet Satan's flames.
And so He took a thought out of His head
And gave it to a mortal on the earth;
And from that sacred thought there grew a dream,
And from that dream grew a reality —
A ship, a mighty ship, a ship of fire!
He saw, and said, "There is but one thing more,
A man to bring to me my flaming ship."
So He took up a little mound of steel
And poured it in a mold, and made a man.
The thing at length was done; the mighty ship,
With man of steel within, burned through the night
And, soaring past, burned Heaven's gates ajar.

Baby Killers!
Rebecca Ann Pinson
It is my sad duty to report
that millions of children
die each year, in the U. S. !
Not because of sickness, but
they are being: abused, thrown
around, molested, beaten, strangled,
drowned, shaken, and hurt every
way imaginable!
They killers too often never
get punished!!
If they do, they may only
get 5 to 10 years in prison!
If their sentence is
shortened they get off with
parole of "good behavior!" To do
it again!
Why do criminals have
more rights than non–criminals?

The Big Hunt
Loring W. Wiseman

For weeks on end
I'd check and plan
Clean all my gear
The best I can,
I mapped the lease
And made a blind
With the best of view
That I could find,
The big hunt began
The games a lot
I'd shoot and shoot
Never missed a shot,
Two weeks of hunting
And shooting fun
For I used a camera
Not a gun.

Love
Yolanda Mendoza

I need to wake up and see my reflection
in your eyes
For you are the only one who can see the
beauty in me
I need to hear and see your love
For you are the only one on earth
who knows the truth
You have always taken care of me
I hope that you do not grow weary
I love everything about you
I love you because you love all of me
Can you give our love a chance?
We are best friends always
I hope we can grow into love together
That part is up to you
You decide what our future will be

Dedication: My Noble One

Silent Mind
Ray Williams

Have you ever sat and listened to the silence all around
When you're sitting quite alone with no one else around
You hear the floorboards creaking the rain upon the glass
But what makes those other noises how long will they last
Your mind it starts to wander you think there's someone there
The noise you hear out in the hall or was it on the stairs
The doors they start to rattle the handles you think they move
You look out of the window a face reflects it's you
It's really getting spooky you're scared you just can't move
The silence just continues its got right into you
But what about the silence it's your mind that makes that sound
You're sitting all alone there's no one else around.

Dedication: Memories, Harold and Muriel Jones

Death vs. Fun
Hayley Cook

Smartly dressed all in a line,
All groomed up and looking so fine,
The sound of the horn, the horses are go,
At full speed, no time to go slow,
The hundreds of dogs all trying to stay clear,
Of the fast heavy hooves which are so near,
The sight of the fox, increases the pace,
Now it's like a gigantic race,
The fox is soon caught and tossed in the air,
It shrieks with pain, but nobody cares,
All to be heard is the cheer of the crowd,
They all seem so happy and all are so proud,
How on earth can they say that they win,
Killing is not right to me it's a sin.

Little Mama
Ann Tedder

She loops a strand of beads around her neck
And clips ear–bobs sideways on her ears.
She streaks pink lipstick on her mouth,
Careful to avoid any smears.
She clutches at her long, pinned–up dress
And daintily turns, careful not to fall.
High–heeled shoes click–click on the floor
As she pats her hair and prances up the hall.
With doll on one arm, purse on the other,
Her white puppy following at her heels,
She says, "Mama, we're going for a walk."
At three–and–a–half, how grown up she feels!
May Kathy's dreams come true, and may I be
The "grown–up mama" she needs to see.

Star Crossed Lovers
Jessica Prall

He loved her, and she knew it
She loved him, but they blew it
She gazed at him with loving eyes
He broke her heart with all his lies
Her heart was broken, it was broken in two
He knew how she felt, his was broken too
They loved each other, but it couldn't be
It wasn't in the stars, it wasn't meant to be
They loved each other, but couldn't be together
They needed each other, they would love forever
But they couldn't be together,
And they couldn't be apart
They were star–crossed lovers
So they died with broken hearts

Dreams of the Soul

Crazy World
Terry J. Hannon
In a world so crazy
It seems there is never much time to be lazy
Three boys a husband and a house
I'm always running around like a busy little mouse
I try to make time for those precious little boys
But I always seem to be picking up toys
Running here and there always on the go
There's never time to just sit and watch them grow
You don't realize how fast they grow each day
Until you look back and say
I knew all along
They would grow up to be strong
Those three little boys are now young men
I only wish I could go back to that time again
Dedication: My children Richard, Anthony and Tyler

Cat
Petrina Strothers
You lie down as peacefully as can be
Looking at all there is to see
With eyes glowing yellow and green
Revealing that in your mind you are big and mean
A tiger with a loud roar
That shakes the jungle floor
You jump up and tiptoe on tiny feet of white
Trying to keep out of sight
Who knows what kinds of beasts lurk in the living room
You carefully hide behind a broom,
Then jump out from your imaginary fallen log
And attack the poor dog
Then you remember that you are only a cat
And walk back over to where you sat.
You quietly curl up and purr
Since you are really just a lovable ball of fur.

The Somber Stage
Kristi Osenbaugh
When I look at the world surrounding me
The barren and the deserted stand out.
I see the fallen, sable, old, oak tree
On my brown, sun–streaked lawn, lying about.
Harsh sounds of the gray raindrops trickle down
Landing precisely on each destined point.
I watch feebly from the window aroun'
On the side south off of the bedroom–joint.
In one room, we used to lie together.
The other belonged to our baby dear.
My precious two are gone now, forever.
Blackness surrounds me always. It is clear
I'll never again have light, save my lamp.
And the tears on my pillow are still damp.

Once Where I Was Young
Mary M. Adams
One night when I was very young
I fashioned a beautiful dream,
And pinned it to a tiny star
With a shaft of bright moonbeams
I guarded it with singing heart
And laughed in secret glee
To know that such a lovely dream
Belonged to only me
Tonight I am a woman
With wisdom in my eyes
And I know I'll never find
My little dream star in the skies
It's there beyond the clouded years
Just where it always hung;
But it belongs to what I was —
Once when I was young

Truth
Linda S. Rogers
Body of a man, mind of a child
Strength of the body, weakness of mind
Searching for something, not knowing why
Seeking solitude in rituals not of this time
Wishing for something not understood
Knowing a power greater than earth
Desires of leaders, follower's rights
Wandering aimlessly, claiming direction
Grasping for wisdom, searching for truth
Time of the seer long passed by
Feeling a tearing yearning inside
Looking back, looking ahead
Wanting to change life
Dreaming instead

Forever
Jessica Jones
There are nights I sit at home alone waiting by the phone.
And there are days I sit and wonder if you're gonna come
back home.
There are times I sit there and cry 'cause I'm wanting
you to be by my side.
It would be like old times.
Those times were good and I thought they would
last forever.
But I never knew forever had an end.
I always thought forever was until your dying day.
But I guess forever to you ended the day you
walked away.
In my heart is where you'll always be.
And I'll never give up hope on you and me.
So when the day comes when you want to start
all over again.
Just give me a call 'cause I'll always be your
friend.

Noteworthy Works

The Man In My Dream
Tammie Terrell DeVance
The man in my dream appears to me
every night
I know this when I see the moonlight
Every night he has a smile,
and asks if he could stay awhile
He takes my hand and says,
"I'll love you forever".
I close my eyes, smile and say. "Thank God you'll leave
me never".
I awake to the dawn, and find I'm alone,
for the man in my dream is long gone,
I know it won't be long,
until the day
when I wake, to find the man in my dream is here to stay,
for he has promised this,
and last night he sealed it with a kiss.

Memories Of Kentucky
Mary Alice Swaney
It's Christmas time in old Kentucky,
Where I'd love to be,
To pick the mistletoe and berries
And trim a Christmas tree!
Go sledding with the youngsters,
Throw snowballs and eat
The homemade cookies and candy
And all the little treats;
I'd love to see the faces of those
Who'd say — "You all, "
And hear the folk call to their friends,
"Come back again, come any at all. "
May every one be joyful
And filled with hopeful cheer,
For a very Merry Christmas
And a Happy New Year!

Dedication: To my children and grandchildren

The Pigeon
Ryan Tilley
I could see this pigeon
Amongst a crowd
It stood there watching
Tall and proud

On the outside
It showed no fear
But on the inside
I knew it could hear

The screaming children
Throughout the park
in his own world
He was alone and dark

A Time Misunderstood
Shannon Marie Clement
As I do some things I want to do
and never thought I could,
I'm at a point just standing there—
A time Misunderstood.

I see things that I couldn't see
and never thought I would,
the sun shines down and holds me here—
A Time Misunderstood.

I feel some things I never felt
and don't quite think I should,
I cannot help chaos within—
A Time Misunderstood.

Dedication: To my loving daughter, Alexis

The Age Of Beauty
Jennifer Lee Cooper
Hanging down the middle of her face forming a perfect line of symmetry,
One strand of hair, wavy yet long enough to touch the top of her lips.
Every now and then getting brushed aside but falling back down into its
natural position.
It constantly annoys the nose of the young woman who owns it.
Is it longer?
Maybe the day has pushed the slight curl to the edge.
Still hanging down, it reaches her chin and sometimes tickles the bottom
of her lip.
And the color is lighter, glistening like tinsel at Christmas time,
beautiful;
nearly as beautiful as the possessor.
Now thinner, snow white in color and shinier than ever,
the woman brushes it aside with her old arthritic fingers (fingers that
were soft and straight when I first saw her)
The silver strand falls back down and is more stunning than ever before

---

Another Lesson
W. Issac Guye
A Man lay in the Road;
All Tired and Broken.
All that's left from Him,
Is Word of Voice;
And the Truth that's been Spoken.
Behind Him, His Cart;
Laden with His Wares,
And the People He's taken On.
Nothing has He Asked,
Not for Anything; not even Fares.
"Wake up!", They Cry.
"Get up; pull on... We haven't all Day!"
Hungered by His Labours,
Beleaguered by Questions
Of His Fellow Neighbours;
He Wonders Things in stately Ponder
As still They Beckon and Call
From Over Yonder.

Dreams of the Soul

Sorrow There, Happiness Here
Tung T. Nguyen
From the day I was born
my life had no future.
Our country had fallen apart.
The communists had taken freedoms out of us.
Our brothers, our families, and friends
had died for our country.
Boat people try to come in the United States,
but their journey is long and hard.
They will use every dirtiest things
to conquer us.
Our body has fallen apart,
but our heart is still there.
Wishing there will be hope
and we're the lucky ones to be in the U. S.
Freedom is waiting on us,
but sorrow for the unfortunate ones behind.

Insanity Engulfs Me
Keith R. Dolson
Insanity engulfs me
Everyone's gone now
I'm left with nothing
My life is a personal hell
If I am dead, why can I
feel such love
Why am I dreaming
I'm yours
You're mine
Fight the flames of death
With the water of life
So dark
So cold
Where am I

Twilight Zone
Jeffrey J. Horan
You are living in the Twilight Zone,
You have no place to call your home.
They say home is where the heart is,
You say home is where the pain is.
Your pain is something I can see,
Your pain is something that torments me.
You are living in the Twilight Zone,
You have no place to call your own,
If you don't think I understand,
Take my hand
And let me explain,
How I can take your pain.
Let me take you from the Twilight Zone,
And give you a place to call your own.

Dedication: Lisa Faustini

Mirror
Kelly M. Miles
Yesterday was a bad day,
the day before wasn't so good
the day before that was the worst ever,
but the day before that was good.
Today was a day I'll never forget,
today was a day to cherish.
Today was a day to forget the past,
today was a day to relish.
The opposition may have won
in other people's eyes,
but in my heart I won the fight;
I won without demise.
Yesterday I thought a lot,
the day before was a rage.
Today I could really care less,
tomorrow I'll act my age.

Untitled
Melissa G. Casto
He is always there to lend me a hand.
I owe it to him for being all that I am.
He taught me to always have faith and
to always believe,
To chase all my dreams and to
never deceive.
He told me there was more to life than
the struggles and pain.
And there is more to living than what
you can gain.
He taught me that everything can't
always be bad.
I owe all that I am to this man,
my dad.

What Love?
Stephanie Beck
Lost love?
I see no lost love.
I thought I loved,
I thought I needed,
But now I see.

No, I did not love you.
No, I did not need you.
I'm sorry, I thought you wasted my time.
But it was the other way around.
I was wrong, I wasn't in love.
Maybe you were and maybe you weren't.
I'll never know, but you know what?
I don't think I care.

Noteworthy Works

Just a Dream
Mary Gantz

I sit and write.
I write of dreams; of life.
I'm a wife and Mother, I
dream of a lover.
Someone to hold me,
to break the mold that binds me.
I sit and write
I write of dreams; of life,
and find myself living life in
a dream.
I cry for the things I want
and live with what I have.
I desire the dream.
So I write.

Seasons Come Seasons Go
Tara Christine Rogers

Seasons come seasons go
There are some things we
Don't know,

The days go by very fast
Our lives in the future
Our minds in the past,

With each breath that we take
There is a new decision we must make,

Our bodies grow old our souls stay young
With Each season a new person we become,

Our hearts be lighter every day
There is a new season blowing our way.

Twilight
Jean Harrell

The sun is sinking slowly, the end of
day is near.
The birds will find their shelter,
the moon will soon appear.
Flowers will bend their sleepy heads,
a slumbering child will dream,
A time for rest has come to all,
Like a peaceful, shimmering stream.
The cool night soon caresses us,
with soft and perfumed breeze.
The stars shine brightly up above,
through tall and stately trees.
This is a time for thankfulness,
For a descending day,
for each and every one of us
took part in some small way.

Dedication: My children and grandchildren

Our Dear Brother
Ruth Renee Little

Like a whisper, so softly spoken,
Like love, in a heart wide open,
Ever gentle, like leaves on the breeze,
You touched our hearts with the greatest of ease.

Into our lives you drifted, and then out.
We thought we knew what love was all about.
But you've shown us what love should be,
With your bravery, honesty, and integrity.
We only pray we can be a little like you,
For ones so great, we know are so few.

Now you are with loved ones gone before.
But we will hold you dear, forever more.
No one can replace you. No! There's no other.
For we love you so much, our dear brother.

Dedication: John Henry Berry, Jr.

Where's My Maria
Roman Duenez

Often times I don't really think about it, but then in the blink of an eye the emotion hits me like a crashing bolt of lightning right between the eyes. ALONE! I'm all alone. It doesn't take much these days. It could be an old tune playing in the car as I redundantly drive to work, or a glance of two lovers joyfully embracing hello. What used to be a pain of lonesomeness is now a fear of solitude. I've tried and I've looked and I've searched and still I have not found her, my Maria. I call her Maria to give her life because searching for "someone" seems less fulfilling. She's out there. I know she is. I can sense her around me in a crowd. I can see her eyes and I can taste her lips. I've stroked her hair and I've caressed her shoulders. I've seen her smile and I've heard her laughter. I've felt her heartbeat next to mine and I've felt her breath on my chest as we've danced in the moonlight. She is out there. I know because I've seen her in my dreams and I still have to believe dreams can come true.

Poet Block Lament (in 3 verses)
Jared McLaughlin

I. Of the words that elude me
That I ponder in retrospect,
At times like these I go to bed
Saying, "Ah what the bloody heck!"

II. If a poet rhymes, yet misspells,
But no one is around to hear it,
Does the only one who points it out
Become the pickiest critic?

III. For all I have written
It does me much good.
But, now, with my mind at idle
Why, oh why, can't I think of a title!

Dreams of the Soul

Garden Therapy
Margaret Burgess

Whenever I have troubles
Or everything has gone wrong,
I get away from it all in my garden
To change the tune of my song.

Out there, whatever the weather,
My problems fade away,
When my thoughts are engrossed in the plant life
That changes every day.

Tending the flowers, pulling at weeds,
Or finding something that needs staking,
Even a few rows of digging
Can save my heart from breaking.

Midnight In The Garden Of Eden
Deb

when i close my eyes i see the stained glass in your door
making pretty patterns with the sunlight on your floor
and beneath your window watch the inner city sprawl
but we're not lovers anymore

so here i am in winter in my garden after dark
sitting in a deckchair with my overcoat and scarf
smoking a cigar and looking for a star to wish upon
but they're all wrong

i remember when we parted and i think you may be right
i can't make sense of it at all when i go to sleep at night
i'm hoping that you'll call but i'm glad you haven't yet
so i can be content

Death...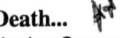
Janina Sweeny

I feel so sad when those I love
are cursed by death's dark hand,
But it would ease my sorrowness
if I could but understand.
That death is just a gateway
that everyone must pass through,
to the other side of death
into a world bright and new.
My loved ones await
to welcome me with open arms,
to a land free from tears
where time isn't counted by the years.

Dedication: My dad, love you forever

Flowers
Valuy Hope

Flowers what do they conjure
In your mind, colour, shape, smell
Beauty the loveliest thing you
Can find. Everywhere in the
World today flowers bloom from
Small seeds they grow, given to
Each other with such love I know.
Flowers convey our feelings in
many ways, bunches, arrangements
Wreaths and bouquets, flowers bring
Joy mirth in birth flowers in
Sadness, death, so many tears
God given to us over the years
Flowers are forever my dears.

Dedication: Princess Diana, spirit of love

My Sister
Denise Thomas

"My Sister" came into this world fifty years ago,
Then three years later I arrived, and boy did I let her know!
She always had to look after me, which sometimes wasn't fair,
But as long as I was with her I didn't really care.
Everywhere that she would go I just had to tag along,
Singing "Me And My Shadow" would be an appropriate song.
Even when she was courting, I often cramped her style,
Sometimes being quite horrid still she managed a smile.
Then our little brothers came along and she fussed like a Mother hen,
Taking both of them under her wing, yes! it started over again.
Now that we're all grown up and can take a look at the past,
Words can never quite express our thanks to her at last.
Our gratitude is endless for all her tender care,
Because she was always watchful over every passing year.
And though we can never recapture what's lost in those childhood days,
"My sister" never changes and I love her special ways.

Dedication: To Marie and my family

Foliage Round The Brim
Ann Copland

What's that I see in your tea cup
Of fine bone china from you sup
Little leaves around the brim swirling
Circling around a little froth whirling
Some sugar added with a spoon of gold
Gently stirred and sipped a saucer to hold
Residue droplets and any spills
Saved falling on lace linen and frills
A teapot sitting near at hand
Slender on an antique stand
Water jug with curved handle to match
Tea cosy too with a flowery patch
Roses pale peach and hyacinths blue
A little luck will be waiting for you
So take my shawl and hand—me—down
Let's go strolling into town

A Poem For Jennifer
R. A. McDonaldson
telephone calls, unreturned,
letters remain unanswered.
strange I should get the feeling, that this friendship
is just a one-way thing.
it's easy to understand, I guess,
'cause all I've got to offer
is Caring and Sharing,
Laughing and Crying, Love and Respect.
who needs that in a friend?!
maybe it's time I woke up
or maybe it's time you grew up.
you say you're a big girl; prove it.
Show a little courtesy,
a little respect,
a little class,
'cause this friend ship
is starting to take on a lot of water.
my tears.

Untitled
Keith Henderson
Oh remember the days of old
Oh remember the days that was told

Ships sailing so swiftly
Trains clicking so merrily

Madams and sirs is what you heard
Swing and singing was the way

Little light lamp at night
Little one tucked in tight
Which was such a sight

Oh my! Oh my!

Those were the days of old.

A Mother's Presence
Beverly A. Still
Sometimes
A sound, a sight or a word
reminds me of her.
Sometimes
My thoughts wander and suddenly
my mind is consumed with her memory.
Sometimes
I fight back the tears
as to not be discovered,
I must be a rock.
Sometimes
I let the tears flow,
behind closed doors
the rock crumbles to dust.

Dedication: My beloved mother, Ruth Still

Frost
Nancy L. Cavanaugh
Silently spreading silken strands
across her surface;
spinning frozen webs
white, feathered traces
filling inner reaches, coating outer plains

Etching his name
leaving
maleness in the dark.

She awakens
thickened with crystal cold
not remembering his spending yet
holding him in her fold.

Earth greets the sun
warms to the day,
melting Jack's night memories away.

Untitled
Andrea Rowbottom
Here we sit, the educated,
Stony stare and heads inflated,
Expounding our contemplations;
Thinking thoughts that affect all nations,
Within these walls of hallowed halls
We hear the trump of social calls.
Like vultures we sit and meditate;
Media experiences we relate.
Devouring media's tricks of the trade.
(They weave a web; that's how they're made).
We dissect the evidence that fools;
The glitch and glamour sparkles like imitation jewels.
Media's the bad guy all around;
See the trickster leap and rebound!
Now the pleasure is gone for good.
To be ignorant if only I could.
But the joy of it all is riddled with guilt.
Were those the joys on which society was built?

A Friend
Myrtle Durand
A friend can make the good times great
or make the bad times better
A friend can close a thousand miles
with just a simple letter
A friend can smooth the rough times out
and keep away the doubt
A friend can travel years away
and still remain devout
A friend can double every joy
cut sadness right in half
A friend can share a heavy load
or just a simple laugh
A friend can do what you have done
hold close from deep within
My friend I'd like to be like you
the kind of friend you've been.

Dreams of the Soul

Faith
Sheryl A. Triplett
When life's trials come before us
It's so hard to see and understand;
We know so well we shouldn't worry
With the Lord right at our hand.
Yet we try to live our own way,
Rather than letting Faith control;
And all that ever comes of this
Is heartache as we stroll.
He always has a reason,
from this we should grow strong;
And never hesitate to let him know
When we are in the wrong.
Slowly we learn to live each day
With his guidance in all we do;
As we show we share and trust in him,
He will give us Blessings too!

Rising Winds
P. LeAnne Gibson
The winds of change are blowing
strong
Hot and heavy to a desolate place
and I have a feeling I don't belong.

Rising winds have carried me away
the further I go the less I can say
the times you told me you loved
me so and everything would be ok.

I will be brought back to my special
place
with as much force that has taken
me away.

Back to my island of solitude for
these same winds will have brought
me back to you.

Dartmoor
Gwyneth D. Futer
The hazy glow of summer skies white wisps of cloud up in the blue
The sight of gorse a patch of gold, and heather of a purple hue,
While far away the rugged tors stand sentinel above the moor
And in the valleys cattle graze as they have done since days of yore.
The ponies roam here wild and free the sheep all graze contentedly.

But when the winter winds blow chill and snow lies deeply on the hill,
When Nature wears a gown of white and mist obscures the view from sight,
The moor is still a magic place as it has been since time began
But now a new threat looms in view... the animal that's known as MAN!

The moor is here and free for all but just remember when you call
To show respect in all you do, the moor is not here just for YOU
It's held in trust for those that follow, the generations of tomorrow.

Isle Of Dreams
Christine McKenzie
I dreamed I was in heaven
Such beauty to behold
I stood there in wonder
Letting my imagination unfold

Where once the traveller used to sail
He can now go by road
Peace and tranquility awaits him
As he nears his journey's end
Feeling elation as if going to meet a friend

I have been a few times now to this idyllic place
For me it never loses its magic style and grace
North, south, east and west
I can but wonder why
I am drawn again and again to the magical isle of sky.

My Oak
Mandy Jilge
My big tall oak is dying
I watch him every day,
His leaves have gone brown
Some have flown away.
His branches are withering
They once were very long,
He used to reach for the sky
So proud, so handsome, so strong.
His trunk is getting weaker
Disease is eating him away,
The once beautiful body
Is now filled with decay.
His roots are disappearing
His seedlings are close by,
I'm sure I saw them crying
To watch their Father die.

Father, My Dad
Maxine A. Wachholz
50 years ago on this 19th day of February in 1997,
My Dad was now my Dad and now is in heaven.
Sadly missed by his family, his wife our Mother,
Yet he is always in our hearts, along with many others.
The day I became his daughter was on his birthday,
I was almost 3 years of age that was to be in May.
Our years together were like many others, very happy,
My schooling, my marriage, my sons, my dearest pappy.
I got the boys he never had,
Charles and Joseph are with him, I'm glad.
Now I have ten grandchildren, 6 girls, 4 boys,
My Dad would have been great playing with the toys.
I know he is watching as our lives move on,
Wishing he was here with us to really be our bond.
There will come a time we'll see him again,
What a reunion we will have–grandpa Ben.
Holidays are always near and around the table we will be,
Father, my Dad with his spirit above, where I know he will always be!!!

Noteworthy Works

Puppy Love
A. D. Flicker

I crept to the nursery, the other night,
and gazed at your face, in the moonlight.
A picture of beauty, your hair so fair,
asleep in your manger, without a care.

How someone so small, can give such pleasure,
so much more, than any treasure.
I'll love you forever, with all my heart.
can't bear to leave you, to be apart.

I want to wake you, and see you smile,
hold you and kiss you, just for awhile.
Take you out, to play in the park,
we can't go yet, it's much too dark.

One Day In June
Caroline Halliday

While we were out the phone it rang
with a message from my Dad
"come round quick" the voice had said
and I felt a pain of dread
I hurried there in pouring rain
to see him wracked in pain
I took his hands and held them tight
as pain now ebbed away
the look of peace on my Dad's face
made me smile and cry
a part of me went with my Dad
on that sad June day
but I am proud to have held his hands
as his life now ebbed away.

Dedication: To my Dad

Memories
Patricia Elizabeth Walker

April – our special month has gone my son
And you – who brought me joy and love
Have left this world – too suddenly
No time for sad good–byes, no time
To watch your children grow, or me grow old.
Only the yearning in my heart
When Spring flowers die, and earth is cold.
The flowers will rest and bloom again next year,
But you will never walk with me around the garden paths.
And yet – when soft winds blow, and Summer raindrops fall,
I'll hear a whisper in my dreams
And know you're still close by.

Dedication: Gerard, our beloved son

Hell
Michael Synowicz

a dead fish washed up on shore
this morning
a stench was in my mouth
the rancid air burning my lungs
skipping breakfast I make my way to work
stale pungent spiteful coffee courses through my veins
enabling me to exist for the sake of existing
skipping lunch then work I make my way back
to chain smoke till early evening
it's Friday but I decide on steak — medium well
oil bloody smutty debris left on the plate
an interminable amount of time spent on a dirty toilet
mingling stench with stench
without bothering to undress I flop on my side
to suppress an emetic urge
rhythmic incandescence of the city lulls me to sleep
a dead fish washed up on shore
this morning

Untitled
Mark Leblanc

If just one picture in this world
were all I could see...
May it just be your face
Smiling over towards me...
If just one fleeting moment be
allowed just for me...
may it be in your arms
being held tenderly...
If just one breath be allowed me
till the end of all time...
May it be the essence of you
always etched in my mind...
If just one shadow be allowed
to cast over me...
May it be the figure of you
Holding hands by the sea...

Dedication: My best friend, my Carol

Dreams
Christy Marie Schaffer

Some dreams do come true
While others seldom do
Some dreams spread their wings and fly
While other dreams collide
Some dreams turn to fantasies
While others turn to realities
Some dreams are great
While others are fate
Some dreams are like fine wine
While others don't even shine
Some dreams are meant to shimmer
While others rarely glimmer
We all wish dreams could fly and never die
But perhaps we'll never know why

Dreams of the Soul

Desires
Mechele Donahue
Nothing seems so sacred as the desires one holds inside
Cherishing every treasured thought never wanting to let go
Never wanting to lose them I hold tighter and tighter
The growing weight on my heart never becoming lighter
Searching my soul for answers that I know in my heart I'll never find.
Unmeasurable admiration and respect for a man, one of a kind
The white knight that keeps my demons at bay
The animal that fuels my desire, night and day
Soul scorching eyes of blue
Musical genius so true
A towering figure with the raven mane
his seven seas I long so to tame
Never knowing of my existence
I offer no persistence
Admiration and love from a far, that's how it has to be
for a man of his stature was not meant to love me.

Dedication: Blackie Lawless, my everlasting inspiration

I Thought Of You
Dee Pankiw
I thought of you the other day—
I don't know why you crossed my mind—
I thought of you, and suddenly
I stepped into a simpler time.

A time when all was possible:
The future beckoned far ahead,
And paths spread out beneath our feet
To take us where our passions led.

How did I reach THIS place, alone?
When did you step away from me?
Somehow our paths diverged, but I
Am better for your company.

Tall Pine
George Hatzell
Tall pine a giant tree
Made especially for you and me

If it is in God's plan that I grow old
I will have to withstand the winter's cold

The storms that come the rains that fall
or the summer sun most of all

And should I manage to survive
I'll be very happy to be alive

To live out my full life span
As tall and straight as I can.

Contentment
Nancy Brown
A sunny day, A baby's smile
A walk along the shore
To meet with friends and talk awhile
Of life, and what it's for.
No time for worry, Just for fun
And help someone some time.
To sit together in the sun
And drink a glass of wine
No rushing there and rushing there
Just plan our quiet days
Some gardening when time to spare
Then off to watch a play
A holiday would add some spice
With sun and sea and walks
But coming home is twice as nice
To family friends and talks.

My Own
Debbie Riner
Young man with the curly hair
Young man with the blue eyes,
standing there.
Your mind is wrapped in fantasies of music and toys;
of being a little boy.
Growing like a weed with each passing day;
Growing taller, stronger and growing away.
Sometimes crying with heartfelt tears.
Proclaiming your anger; expressing your fears.
Laughing and enjoying the wonder of life's simplest delights;
From sun–kissed mornings
to star–lit nights.
Young man one day you will be grown;
And shall remain
forever
in my heart my own.

Untitled
Steve Thurman
Inspirations of the heart
come at spontaneous moments...
Mysterious feelings begin
to ignite untouched emotions...

With this comes the meeting
of two people from separate lives...

Silent conversations from
exchanged glances
expressing more than words...

A moment on the beach.
embracing as we part;
a sweet kiss goodbye.
Anticipating another day
to share moments of
open company...

For I Was Her Son
Larry Weichert

When I was a young boy, not very old,
I would act like a brave man, strong and bold.
And if I got hurt, I started to run,
For my Mother to hold me, for I was her son.
As I grew up, and got a little older,
I left, my toys, tanks, and soldiers.
Wanting a place of my own, something that was mine,
A home, a wife, something to hold onto — for life.
But when it didn't work, and I got hurt,
I started to run for my Mother to hold me, for I was her son.
As you go through this world, searching for the right one,
Sometimes you get hurt, and left all alone.
Nowhere to go, I stand empty handed,
So I began to run for my Mother to hold me,
For I was her son.
But this time was different, not like before.
For she had to leave this world and she started to run,
For her Mother to hold her and to meet God's son.

I Keep Reaching To Be Free
Constance C. Fitzgerald

I keep reaching to be free
Keep traveling down my road of life
Hoping someday just to see,
Life and freedom as it ought to be.

I look at faces so sad
No one is truly free
From everyday cares and worry.
Everyone must be reaching like me
Searching for something,
Not really knowing what they see.

I keep searching to be free
Just to find my road of songs and laughter
No more work of things I hate to do.
I will keep traveling down my road of life
Hoping someday just to see,
Life and freedom as it ought to be.

Loving You
Traci Bradley

As long as we're apart there is no tomorrow
Only loneliness and heart felt sorrow
Life gave us a chance and we failed
Like a train, our hearts have been derailed
Someday fate will give us another try
But for now I lay awake at night and cry
The time we shared was pure
Like medicine for a disease you were my cure
I know that we will always share love
Loving you was a sign of hope sent by the heavens above
One day we will be together again
I will take comfort in loving you until then
Don't forget me while we're apart
Remember always that you hold the key to my heart
I will see you my love, very soon
Just as sure as each midnight sky brings the moon.

Change Of Hands
D. C.

He came strolling out from mystic hills.
His face so good and kind
He took my hand in his, and we walked together
for some time
Away we walked from life and fear
Happiness was mine
When all was right with home and hearth
I didn't see it appear
Black it came the mist again and took my love
so dear
Now I walk the earth again, with little hands
this time
The little ones my sweet, sweet love, hath left
behind

Dedication: John, we miss you

God's Heavenly Blue Sea
Amethyst Mirage

Sometimes I wonder, what it would be like – to be God sitting on a cloud.
Does He see the earth, like the big blue ball –
with white wisps like space shuttle pics?
Or, can all our activities be seen –
we must look like overgrown ants waiting to go swimming.
Now I must muse, how the Holy One gets around –
He must paddle His clowd like a canoe.
Listen... as the wind goes by, you can almost hear –
"Take time to smell the spring air..."
Then, I look around, to see who calls to me –
to enjoy the beauty of nature in the midst of nature.
Only to realize, that is exactly what I've been doing –
and the Great Spirit is also enjoying my same journey in the
Heavenly Blue Sea.

Old Spice And Cinnamon
Michele M. Hulek–Doyle

Old Spice and cinnamon
stir memories of
being wrapped
in your bed

feeling at home

being safe and warm

illusions sparked by
your embrace
time borrowed out of time

left alone now
to dreams laced with
Old Spice and cinnamon and you

Dreams of the Soul

Emily
Alan K. Colucci
A new life into this world.
A life we brought into this world.
And, what kind of world will it be?
Hopefully, one of joy, one of peace.

But, could it not be
one of unhappiness, one of war?
But, we will not think of the world,
of all the negative things that can be thought of.
But, we will think
of the young new life.

A new life, new hope
The world will be better
because of her.
A new life into this world.

My Love
Diana Cline
The sun so bright, the sky so blue,
As I gaze up I think of you.
Moments pass without you here,
the one to me who is so dear.
The one who has a place in my heart,
The one who I long for when we're apart.
Waiting to see you again,
You my love and true friend.
I pray that time will swiftly pass,
As the sand trickles through the hourglass
I want our love to always be,
And everyone around us will surely see.
Love is out there for those who care,
You my love are an answered prayer.

What Is Love?
Jennifer Mitchell
What is love?
Have you ever seen it?
When you say it do you really mean it?
Where do you find it?
When do you feel it?
Do you feel it when its too late
or right away and it makes you
feel great?
Does it make you happy or sad?
Could it be something I never
felt or something I never had?
Still the question remains in my
mind.
What is love?

Mournful Love
Alison Ann Cummings
I love you truly deep inside,
My secrets to you I confide,
You're my friend and my lover,
If not you, I want no other,
Please understand me,
The part will hurt,
Dancing with heartache,
I will flirt,
I know you, you know me well,
Throughout my life,
Will cast shadows of hell,
The clouds hang low, grey and bleak,
Whispers of death,
Soft–spoken will speak,
Haunting figures floating about,
Companionship shall be without,
Black roses of death to signify,
Destination of our love shall die.

Untitled
Melanie Poulsen
I look at these three little faces
They take me to such places
They make me laugh they make me cry
They make me feel like I could fly
Every day there is something new
She looks like me she looks like you
Two are blonde and one is brown
Boy they sure can make me frown
The love they give is beyond compare
Don't even try don't even dare
The years go by so fast you see
I blink my eyes and know she three
A child is such a precious gift
Their spirits you must lift and lift
My girls I love you very much
And always wish the best of luck

A Grandma's Love
Elizabeth Cross
Maegan, Maegan mine
You're Grandma's little lifeline
With those eyes, blue as a clear winter sky
So soft and hushed is the sound of your cry

Maegan, Maegan mine
Your kisses are as sweet as sugarplum wine
The smell of you is like fresh morning dew
Why Honey, you are Grandma's dream come true

Maegan, Maegan mine
You have a smile as bright as the sunshine
And hair that glistens like fine threads of spun copper
You are Grandma's perfect little lady, all prim and proper

Dedication: My granddaughter, Maegan Nicole Cross

Noteworthy Works

Memories Passed On
Betty McClain–Frogge

Memories come flooding and tumbling around in my mind,
Some so vivid shivers tingle up and down my spine;
Others are shrouded in layers of fog,
As a night–time traveler through an ancient bog.

My memories of childhood so bittersweet,
Of Loved Ones now gone to their eternal sleep.
Memories of Christmas, birthdays and special occasions,
March into my mind as one calling out cadence.

As I look fondly upon my children and their heirs,
I daydream of future days that happily we will share.
Then when I go the circle of dreamless nights,
May these memories be recalled and enhance their lives.

Dedication: Beth, George, Cody and Miranda

Feeling The Ocean
Linda F. Crabtree

The waves are rippling fiercely across the ocean land
As I step into the water–soaked sand
I can feel crushed seashells beneath my feet
While the scorching sun delivers its heat
Letting my body float upward and away
I can float off into my illuminating day
The taste of the ocean water filled with salt
Lets me put all my busy days to a drastic halt
With closed eyes I can only hear
The sound of the waves crashing against the pier
To combine with nature's beautiful production
Makes the soul become a part of a magnificent reproduction
Floating away into the sunset indeed
I may float for eternity...

Dedication: My beloved children, Lindsey, Kelly

A Manly Image
Raniece Brown

His eyes are like TYSON cool but alluring, his smile is like MOORE'S blessed and assuring.
He is chocolate like WESLEY sweet and delightful, or Caramel like CHRISTOPHER smooth yet tasteful.
He will stand strong and upright without any tension don't worry ladies I have more men to mention.
He will sweat like KEITH, and grind like KELLY, he'll lounge like "L", and jam like TEDDY.
He will shoot like HARDAWAY, and assist like HILL, he will fly like JORDAN, and slam like O'NEAL.
He will be sexy like DENZEL, and exhale like LEON.
Don't get excited I will go on.
He will rap like TREACH, with style and finesse, he will sing like ANGELO rhythm and essence.
He will be the Father of my children like KEITH HAMILTON COBB and be young but not restless like CHRISTOFF ST. JOHN.
But above he will be GOD fearing like no other, He will strive to be perfect like our SAVIOR.

Roses
Albert Kundrat

Oh, rosae vim obiciunt – the teepee hilt
Made lovely in the summer's sun and solstice tilt!
Rose blooms present a living force – inspiring sight,
Serenity's bright petals overcoming plight.
Made true in blossoms' fragrant scents – majestic show,
All "hieroglyphs of Deity" – so nice to know!
Reveal on earth, my gardener, these smiles of God.
Yes, show us hope to sprout and grow above the sod.
These petals one and all tell of His purpose high –
Hues' rainbow tints that gaze unto an azure sky.
Oh, toil in a rose garden today – no labor's lost!
Maintain the cultivated plants until the frost.
Praesendo rosam tibi vincet tulio anew
So Mother nature wins her rose for you!
On garden ground "olim rosa vincet ibi":
Nobility, vitality, and victory!

Dedication: Mary Thompson of Gettysburg

Dream Machine
Rob S. Weber

My 1990 Mustang GT
is a very special thing to me
Cherry red with 3 star rims
It's made to satisfy all of my whims
Two door leather interior
It is definitely a car that is far from interior
5–speed, ponies running wild
Slamming through the gears, boy this baby is my child
Tinted windows, hatchback
No one is ever going to take this baby back
355 gears, very fast
My Sony system is made to last
It has a Ford Motorsport sticker
150 top speed to make it quicker
untamed horsepower, I love my car
I know my 5. 0 will take me far.

A Question, Love
Frankie J. Demoss

Did I fool you back then
With my cute infectious grin?
Did you think me for a night
Instead of all your life?
Did I come in through the door
That had not been used before?
You were surrounded by so many
But to know you, there weren't any
And you were such a lonely man.
Inside you was so much to share,
If only there was one to care
And live with you according to God's plan.
I pray each day that God above
Will keep me worthy of your love
And keep me forever at your side
True, loving, faithful, but not untried.

Dedication: Ron, thy truth is love

Dreams of the Soul

Daybreak
Jan Peterson

Silence drifts into every
crevice of the woods.
Nestling snuggle together,
Owls swoop silently through
the air.

Dawn spreads its wings
over a sleepy world.
A mixed chorus is set in
motion. Feathers ruffle
and birds warble.
Soothing breezes tiptoe
through leafy branches.

Daybreak sets the world
in motion.

Morning
Kerry Elsworthy

The sun rises to the sultry sky.
The clouds clamber, gathering together.
A bright orange ball comes into sight
Creating shadows amongst the heather.

Trees chatter in quiet whispers
Leaves scuttle across the ground,
Animals peep to see the sunlight
Curious faces all around

A typical day has just begun
One no different from the last.
Things are looking to the future,
Not a trace from what was past.

The Prayer
Kirk Kneeshaw

Where am I now in these troubled days?
What do I see through the thickening haze?
How should I feel and what should I do?
How should I try to be more like you?

I know you have made me
and one day you will take me,
but what should I be doing at this very time?
What should I seek and what will I find?

Wake me oh Lord from my sinful sleep,
give me a purpose and a desire I can keep.
Set me apart from what others do,
please help me Jesus to be more like you.

A View From Within
Craig Blevens

Through the dark pathway into my eyes
There is a light within the soul
At times
it may seem the darkness creates the end.
At those times
I shall look to faith for that light
Releasing the pain,
the anger,
the confusion.
If I want to feel the energy of the light,
I must learn to carry myself through
the darkness.
Then I shall let my light shine
and share it,
with the world around me,
Not to fear that I will blind
But in hopes that I will brighten their soul.
As mine has been enlightened by others.

Now I Lay Here
Bryan Malone

Now I lay here and I pray
Forgive me Father for sins I lay
Forgive me Father for things I do
Help me Father to guide me though
As I breathe I make mistakes
Forgive me Father for Heavens sakes
Forgive me Father for I do wrong
Please take my soul when I'm gone
I walk this earth you give to me
I take for granted things I see
Forgive me Father and take my soul
For it is to heaven I want to go
I do wrong by night and day
But now I lay here and I pray

In Memory Of Deuce
M. L. Porterfield

Free to give
or tuck away
Love abounds.
Birth
Death
Mere sparks
Life
A circle
Never–ending.
Stop
Love does not
Nor
the circle
Like memories
they go on
Forever.

Dedication: I love and miss you...

God's Promise For Your Children
Pattie M. Green

God has promised to save your children, yes, your kids and mine,
train them in the way to go and things should work out fine.

Love them and nurture them with all of your heart,
comfort and protect them and they will not depart.

When raising children you must admit,
there are times you'd love to quit.

Trials and tribulations are constant day by day,
your children no longer listen to what you have to say.

There comes a time our lips must STOP, our opinions don't seem to matter,
the more we talk and push our point God's plan we often shatter.

Why slow up what God has promised? You can if you may
but he will save your children, just don't get in the way!

Creatures Of The Night And I
Autumn Gilley

To be among the creatures of the night,
Is to be among friends I never knew,
The still quietness around me,
The peace between each of them,
A coyote calls to his friends,
And another answers from a distance.
An owl flies through the sky nearby,
For his nightly feeding he screams.
The lion and his family wake up,
To hunt finally for the night.
Still the quietness around me,
With peace between each of them.
To be among friends I never knew
Is to be among the creatures of the night.

Your Will Or Mine
Yvonne de Ridder

Forget not to abstain things small,
a smile, a helping hand, a willing ear.
Cast away the erroneous involvement fear.
Remember what we cherish so seldom,
Marriage, joy of childbirth, Freedom.

Say no to evil's lust.
Life's too short or barely just.
Why destroy steal or kill?
God said: I gave you your will,
but left you mine,
make the choice, so thin the line.

Dedication: My Noekie

Life Gifts
Marlene Martin

Life is a gift God gave us all,
We came from within not long ago.
We were put here for a reason,
but we will never know.

So sit back and take a good look,
and study just the Good Book,
and maybe we can see what road
God had in mind for you and me.

Our life is short up on this earth,
so stay on that straight and narrow path.
God put us here for a reason just
like the seasons, and we will never know.

Buddha Smiles
Tammera S. Woodall

Why does the Buddha smile
That precious, knowing grin?
Do you think he's laughing
At illusions we're within?
As he tries to show us
The folly of the Mind,
Can you catch a glimpse of
The reality behind?
We are all just dreaming,
All life a very joke
In the eye of our Creator
Vague murmurs, shadows, smoke.
Why does the Buddha smile?
He can't contain his grin,
Knowing WE create our drama,
And life is NOT a sin.

Angel For Me
Marlene Price

I would climb the highest mountain,
Swim the deepest seas, if that's what
It would take for you to be with me—
I would.

I'd fly to the moon and catch all
The stars in the sky just to prove
you're the apple of my eye, I'd leave
you alone forever if you told me you
wanted to be free but that's not speaking
of how bad I'd be ——

I feel you're the right one for me
and I love this feeling you make
me see. "Timothy — my heart belongs to thee"

Dedication: Forever dedicated to Timothy Leiler

Dreams of the Soul

Love
Rebecca A. Beaudoin

I am not famous,
but I am known by all.
I am not harmful,
but some still fear me.
I am not always wanted,
but I am still craved by every being.
I am not always truly felt,
but when I am, you'll know,
because I put the words in people's hearts.
Once I've entered yours,
I will never leave.
I am not easily obtained,
but I am always within reach.
I do not call myself by any name,
but I am known by those who feel me
by one simple word.
I am Love.

A Dreamer's Wish
Deanne K. Guardino

I hear a music in my mind, and so shall he, this love.
That human ear would think divine with melodies from above.
We will create the lyrics, we shall compose the song
Whose harmony is the kiss, to which our hearts belong.

Oh I've known such loneliness, the human soul could bear,
I've felt the great abyss of rejection, futility, and despair.
I beg that you unclench your fists, that I might place my hand
between the love you now resist and the fear we understand.

For my warmth is but a giving and my breath is but a sigh.
I dare doubt that life's worth living, if but a living lie.
He took my hand in his, we walked along life's road,
Then I woke from slumber and wrote this empty ode.

My Treasure
Janet T. Kimmons

My children number seven,
My grandchildren are many.
Hearing someone say Mother or Granny,
Is my idea of heaven!

A life filled with joy,
A house filled with laughter and love,
These are my blessings from above;
As is each new baby girl or boy!!

It is like seeing the first rainbow,
Watching my children grow.
They bring me great pleasure,
These children, my one true treasure.

Untitled
Erma Mansell

The day we met oh how sweet
The rose you gave showed your love complete
We are apart but you know in your heart
The love we had is not far apart
Months go by then years are here
I wonder how it could have been
It was not clear when I left that year
And now you're there and I am here
Thinking when I will see you again
Time keeps ticking and I still am thinking
Night and day you're so far away
With no reply
I loved you then and I love you now
So time can tick but I don't know how
The time is here and I love you dear
So tell me how please tell me now

Bread Without Life
Deanna Rorabaugh

Heaven without Hell
Salvation without the Blood
Religion without Relationship
The Holy Spirit without Tongues
Love without Accountability
Government without God
Doctrine without Truth
Ethics without Christ
Faith without Works
Prayer without Trust
Sin without Penalty
Bread without Life

Dedication: Revival in the Church

Give Us The World
Pearl Savage

Wrap us in sunshine
Protect us from the rain
Bring us the stars and the moon
And take us from gloom

Hand us the world
For we can stop evil
Hand us your hearts
For we can stop the pain

The world is ours
To shape and mold
If only love
Can guide our souls

Jenny
Phyllis Geary
I see her through the taut harp strings
As she gently plays, and notes fade away,
Taking me on memories wings,
To the songs of yesterday,
They ring out as she plays
Like light upon her beauty fair,
As joybells chiming out the days
Bringing peace and loveliness everywhere.

In the twilight she sits alone,
Her soft melodies touch my heart,
The dreamy music drifts on the air
And glints from her golden harp dart,
Lighting on her gown of gossamer blue,
A vision floating like a summer sky,
In her lovely headdress of every hue,
Where a myriad fragrant flowers lie.

Strait Sonnet
M. P. Barszcz
Haste not to explore, lest we toss Friendship
at Wet Appetites we've sown in Pleasures,
by boarding Port Gates whose unknotted Grip
helms navigate Shores through Tropic Treasures.
Fathom Shoal Serpents guard Buccaneer Loot,
while Merchant Mongers like to terminate
Tribal Beldam Saints whence Deck Cannons shoot
royal Trade Sailors with Rancor Estate.
Siren Semaphore, Serous and Sipid,
seeks Terra Firma Cavy Castaway
to scuttle Sylph coign with christen Liquid;
a Maiden Rank Sir Brackish beyond Brae.
Scorn Frumps feign Romance; a Lust to divest
inside a Kiosk for Succubus Breast.

Amorous Desideratum
Dave Dietrich
Flowers blooming in the Spring,
bursting anew in a kaleidoscope of colors;

Sun soaked sandy beaches,
sparkling like crystals and fine gems;

Balmy breezes whispering soft coral melodies;
energizing the soul;

Autumn leaves dancing in the wind,
swirling majestically in a minuet
of radiance and grace;

All of these things make me think of you.

A New Day Rises
Jenny Smith
Some days when I am feeling low,
And things are at its worst;
I feel I have no place to go;
A sad and awful curse,

But then I look upon the night skies,
And see all nature's praises;
The birds, the clouds, the fireflies,
And wait, a new day rises!

Uncertain the days have gone, by and by;
Life is no doubt an eternal surprise;
As long as we keep our heads held high,
A new day will always rise!

One Summer Day
Natalie Joy Woodall
One summer day when love was new,
You said, "Come, be my own, "
And I, poor fool, was overwhelmed
By heat of sun and heat of passion.

One summer day not long ago,
I said, "Where has love gone?"
For you, my darling, were far away
From heat of sun and heat of passion.

One summer day in years to come,
I wonder, will we meet again? And,
If we should, poor darlings, let it be
In heat of sun and heat of passion.

Champagne
Ashlee Bergstrom
Sadness, weeping mostly over little things,
silly things and funny things.

But this isn't little or silly or funny it's HUGE.
How could it be. WHY?

She was so sweet, so kind, so generous.
Why her, why now, Poor Champagne

She's probably happy now, no pain, I hope!

Why did she have to go, her life 13 years young,
For a dog "91", but what does it matter.

She was like a big sister.
I'LL NEVER FORGET YOU! NEVER!

CHAPTER THREE

Personal Profiles

The following pages comprise concise personal profiles of the poets featured in this book, including pen names, occupations, special honors, other published writings and even personal goals and philosophical viewpoints. You will find that some are professional published writers, while others are appearing for the first time ever in print. But all of these poets have one thing in common: they are all compelled to reveal their feelings about life through creative expression in the form of words and verse.

EDITOR'S NOTE: *Please keep in mind that not all poets who have contributed to this book will appear in this chapter. All biographical information presented is specifically at the behest of each person listed.*

Dreams of the Soul

Author: Barbara L. Abel; **Birthplace:** White Plains, NY; **Occupation:** Customer Relations; **Hobbies:** Writing, drawing and keyboards; **Memberships:** National Home Gardening Club; **Education:** Westlake High School; **Honors:** B. O. C. E. S. won statewide art contest for college; **Published Works:** For John (Heaven); **Personal Statement:** Words are a gift from the heart to be shared with others. I would like to develop my talent to the fullest. Special thanks to mom.

Author: Liliana O. Adams; **Birthplace:** Poznan, Poland; **Occupation:** Musician, harpist; **Hobbies:** Music therapy, storytelling; **Memberships:** Am fed of musicians, UK harp assn, Calif music teacher assn; **Spouse's Name:** Bruce Adams; **Education:** Master of arts; **Published Works:** Several articles published in professional journals; **Personal Statement:** I am a musician and, inspired by Claude Debussy's Clair de Lune, I wrote "Moonlight" using a scriple poetic expression to sing "the rhythm which is in all space..." (Khalil Gibran, The Prophet).

Author: Brinda Joyce Adams; **Birthplace:** Springfield, MO; **Occupation:** Executive director; **Hobbies:** Reading, research, art, music, animals and friends; **Memberships:** ABWA, NSDAR, AQHA, VHBE and Arabian Horse Registry; **Education:** K. C. Art Institute, Penn Valley College, Columbia College; **Awards:** 3rd place Laurie Art Fair; **Published Works:** Short story illustrations, commercial advertising; **Personal Statement:** Keep an open mind, be kind to others and be good to yourself.

Author: Michael Addley; **Birthplace:** London; **Occupation:** Student; **Hobbies:** Cricket and computing; **Education:** Christ the King Sixth Form College; **Personal Statement:** I was moved and inspired by the tragedy of Dunblane and hope that this poem will prove a small comfort to those left behind.

Author: Robert Aleksinski; **Birthplace:** Great Falls, Montana; **Occupation:** Hardwood floor refinisher; **Hobbies:** Bowling, fishing, hunting, walking, jogging, biking, weights; **Spouse's Name:** Divorced; **Children:** 1; **Education:** 4 years of college (University of Great Falls); **Honors:** Honor roll for 4 yrs. in high school; **Awards:** Various bowling awards for outstanding performance; **Personal Statement:** Strong emotions of the heart and a closeness to a Higher Power inspire me to write with an open heart, mind and soul. Simple words uncomplicate difficult subjects.

Author: Paula Allen; **Birthplace:** Glendale, CA; **Occupation:** Administrative Assistant; **Hobbies:** Dance, travel and theatre; **Children:** 1; **Personal Statement:** Art reflects life and there is still much beauty to be discovered. Keep your eyes open.

Author: Sheila Allen; **Birthplace:** Biddulph, Stoke-On-Trent; **Occupation:** Primary school teacher; **Hobbies:** Reading, walking, gardening and music; **Children:** 1; **Education:** Teaching training course; **Honors:** Diploma of Education from Manchester University; **Personal Statement:** I wrote this poem after the death of my father in July of this year. The "Journey" represents my first memory at the age of two going to Torquay on holiday, with my parents.

Author: Sharon Anthony; **Birthplace:** Indianapolis, IN; **Occupation:** Homemaker; **Hobbies:** Decorating and writing poetry; **Memberships:** International Society of Poets; **Spouse's Name:** Carl Anthony; **Children:** 3; **Grandchildren:** 4; **Education:** High school graduate; **Honors:** Inducted into the international poetry hall of fame March 97; **Awards:** Editor's Choice Award National Library of Poetry, March 97; **Published Works:** "Changes In The Heart"–Nat'l Library of Poetry, "In Dappled Sunlight"– anthology, "Angels In Our Midst", "Destiny"; **Personal Statement:** Communicating through poetry has given me a connection and healing within my soul. And my goal as a writer would be, that others might find that same connection and healing within themselves.

Author: Martin M. Aquino; **Pen Name:** Harlequin; **Birthplace:** Buenos Aires, Argentina; **Occupation:** Kennel Assistant; **Hobbies:** Hiking, collecting sculptures, martial arts and reading; **Education:** De La Sacce High School, Buenos Aires Argentina; **Published Works:** A short horror story called "Cosecha 1f", Gurbo Science Fiction Magazine; **Personal Statement:** Poetry is the music of the words that flow from within the spirit in the instant when we cry to the universe for answers... I admire poets such as Robert Frost and Spanish Nobel Prize winner Vicente Aleixandre.

Author: Anthony D. Arthur; **Birthplace:** St. Michael, Barbados; **Occupation:** Database administrator; **Hobbies:** Reading, writing, traveling and music; **Education:** Co–op High, U. S. Navy

Author: Rebecca Atkinson; **Pen Name:** Belle; **Birthplace:** Los Angeles, CA; **Occupation:** Mother and Grandmother; **Hobbies:** Composing music & poetry, playing music, and making posters; **Memberships:** Costeo (Soon to be International Poets Society); **Children:** 4; **Grandchildren:** 1; **Education:** Some High School, Some College; **Published Works:** I Thought You'd Always be Here, Something Between Us, Love is The Ingredient; **Personal Statement:** God works in mysterious ways and if you trust Him He will show you things in your life that will be unbelievable to your natural mind. God is so awesome, Praise Jesus!

Author: Annita Aube; **Birthplace:** Beresford, N. B., Canada; **Occupation:** Nurse and Nursing Instructor; **Hobbies:** Writing, reading, movies, arts; **Memberships:** Order of Nurses Province of Quebec; **Children:** 1; **Education:** College University; **Personal Statement:** My days and nights are invested with thoughts of visionary impulsions of wild moments of triumphs as a writer and those thoughts drag me back to 1997.

Author: Mindy Baker; **Pen Name:** Min, Minnie or M'n'M; **Birthplace:** Redmond, OR; **Occupation:** Student; **Hobbies:** Art and writing; **Memberships:** Jr. ROTC, Jr America Club, Girl Scouts, Willow Creek Cloggers; **Education:** Freshman Madras Senior High School; **Honors:** Language Arts and Academic Excellence, Jr American Trophy; **Awards:** Gift certificate for a poster on Child Abuse Prevention; **Published Works:** My Dog Charlie, Our Family–Awaken To A Dream, and Bright Eyes

Author: Patricia A. Banwell; **Birthplace:** Liverpool; **Occupation:** Housewife; **Hobbies:** Reading, writing, music, driving, being around people; **Spouse's Name:** Divorced; **Children:** 4; **Grandchildren:** 5; **Education:** Left school at 15; **Personal Statement:** My granddaughter encouraged me to send my poem. Never dreaming I would reach the semi–finals. I now feel more confident in writing my poetry.

Author: Jeff P. Barentine; **Birthplace:** Pensacola, FL; **Occupation:** Student; **Hobbies:** Writing, bass guitar; **Education:** Tate High School, TCJC; **Personal Statement:** My goal as a writer is to make people stop and think not just to read. My influence: everyone and every situation I've ever encountered.

Author: C. H. Barker; **Birthplace:** Sunderland (England); **Occupation:** Retired; **Hobbies:** Watching sport on tv; **Spouse's Name:** Caroline; **Children:** 2; **Grandchildren:** 2; **Education:** Standard; **Personal Statement:** I have a special daughter, special granddaughter, thinking of them inspires me to sit down, to put words to rhyme, in a very short time.

Author: Josef T. Bath; **Birthplace:** Tipton, IN; **Occupation:** Telemarketer; **Hobbies:** Reading and fitness; **Education:** Currently working on my doctorate; **Personal Statement:** I have many influences and inspirations. The one that has given me a gift to share with the world is my higher power within.

Author: Lisa R. Baugh; **Birthplace:** Knoxville, TN; **Occupation:** Housewife, part–time waitress; **Hobbies:** Writing, reading, drawing and music; **Spouse's Name:** Jerry Wayne Baugh, Jr.; **Children:** 2; **Education:** High school graduate; **Published Works:** The Purple Haze, Washington D. C. Up Against The Wall Mother; **Personal Statement:** The chance to make a difference, to protect our children, to share my pain to help others. Being a writer gives me that chance.

Author: Robert Beaudoin; **Pen Name:** Robert Beau; **Birthplace:** Rhode Island; **Occupation:** Computer Software Q. A.; **Hobbies:** Gardening, poetry, cycling and travel; **Education:** Bachelor's of science; **Published Works:** Reflections Of Your Legacy (self-published); **Personal Statement:** My writings are to leave for others the gift given to me by life and its journey.

Author: Stephanie Beck; **Birthplace:** Fontana, CA; **Occupation:** Full-Time High School Student, Part-Time Assistant Worker; **Hobbies:** Reading, writing, modeling and acting; **Memberships:** Institute Of Children's Literature; **Education:** Junior in high school; **Published Works:** "The Little Lord" poem, "Night Of Pleasure, Lifetime Of Pain" poem; **Personal Statement:** As a young lady, I haven't enough experience to write about a lot of things about life, but as I experience certain things I am enticed to put my feelings into words. Thus, my poem, "What Love".

Author: Elmer F. Beckstrand; **Birthplace:** Rigby, Idaho; **Occupation:** Retired from self-employed machine shop; **Hobbies:** Family, church, and flying; **Memberships:** Elder, Bishop, The Church of Jesus Christ Latter Day Saints; **Spouse's Name:** Ina Lottie Ferrin Beckstrand; **Children:** 7; **Grandchildren:** 26; **Education:** Shelly, Idaho High School and Military Flight Academy; **Honors:** 2nd to Valedictorian, Gave Graduation Class Welcome Address; **Personal Statement:** I have written a pamphlet "Nine Steps to Heaven", wherein find another poem "A Ride at Dusk" for your consideration.

Author: Dawn Belanger; **Birthplace:** Luton Beds, England; **Occupation:** Homemaker; **Hobbies:** Painting, listening to music, and bike riding; **Children:** 2; **Education:** High School, Some College; **Personal Statement:** My future husband encouraged me to write it and send it in to you. He is my strength and my inspiration to write poems.

Author: Toni L. Berghman; **Birthplace:** New Orleans, LA; **Occupation:** College Student, Homemaker; **Hobbies:** Writing, reading and bowshooting; **Memberships:** Phi Beta Lambda; **Spouse's Name:** Donnie Berghman, Jr.; **Children:** 3; **Honors:** Dean's List; **Personal Statement:** My children, Keith, Alexis and Laurie, have always been my number one source of inspiration.

Author: Sean Bewley; **Birthplace:** Fort Leonard Wood, MO; **Hobbies:** Guitar, poetry, music, and jet ski; **Children:** 2; **Education:** High school; **Published Works:** "Untitled" in a book called "Essence of a Dream"; **Personal Statement:** Poetry really helps me define the puzzles in my mind. My emotions are a lot clearer in black and white.

Author: Mark Bjork; **Occupation:** Auto Glass Tech Manager; **Hobbies:** Bowling, writing poetry and reading; **Education:** 2 year associate degree in business; **Personal Statement:** My standpoint, as a writer, is to have many poems published for my own goals in life. As well as my family. My influence is Mark Twain.

Author: Cheryl Blair; **Pen Name:** Cherlana; **Birthplace:** Los Angeles, CA; **Occupation:** Realtor; **Hobbies:** Travel, Scrabble, golf and mahjong; **Memberships:** Academy Of American Poets, Women's Council Of Realtors; **Children:** 2; **Grandchildren:** 3; **Education:** College Of The Sequoias, broker's course university programs; **Honors:** Who's Who 1994 – new writer; **Awards:** Outstanding performance, President's Club; **Published Works:** Famous Poems Of The 20th Century, self-published, Essentially You; **Personal Statement:** Cherlana @ AOL. COM. Poetry is a cathartic release of passion, pain and personal triumph and humor. Maya Angelou and Wilt Auden are heros.

Author: Miranda A. Blankenship; **Birthplace:** Pocahontas, Iowa; **Occupation:** Student; **Hobbies:** Piano, writing and drawing; **Education:** 6th grade student Lavrens Marathon School; **Personal Statement:** I hope to be an author/illustrator when I grow up.

Author: Ginger K. Bloms; **Pen Name:** Ginger Johnson–Bloms; **Birthplace:** Kenmare, ND; **Occupation:** Consultant; **Hobbies:** Travel, flower gardening and writing; **Memberships:** Chamber UNA Alumni; **Spouse's Name:** Mitchell Bloms; **Education:** M. A. Communication/BBA Management, University of North Dakota; **Honors:** Summa cum laude, cum Laude; **Awards:** Satrom Scholarship; **Published Works:** Yesterday's Past; **Personal Statement:** We become the mirror image of those we love. May your mirror always reflect faith, trust, beauty, compassion and love.

Author: Stephen J. Bradbury; **Pen Name:** Steve J. Bradbury; **Birthplace:** Castle Bromwich; **Occupation:** Export sales, director dog showing; **Hobbies:** Poetry, singer/songwriter, guitarist, family; **Memberships:** Dog show committee; **Spouse's Name:** Joy; **Children:** 3; **Education:** CSE maths, english, history, geography, science; **Personal Statement:** My career and lifetime ambition is to hopefully become a successful poet, novelist and songwriter.

Author: Patricia Bratcher; **Birthplace:** Bennington, Vermont; **Occupation:** Retired; **Hobbies:** Painting, sewing, writing and making hats and quilts; **Memberships:** Our Lady of Lourdes Church; **Spouse's Name:** Stanley Bratcher; **Children:** 2; **Grandchildren:** 4; **Education:** Bennington High School – Adult courses etc.; **Honors:** Blue Ribbon for quilt; **Awards:** Honor student; **Published Works:** Poems published in National Library of Poetry; **Personal Statement:** For each day I awake a beautiful present I do take.

Author: Barbara Brown; **Birthplace:** Madera, CA; **Occupation:** Office assistant; **Hobbies:** Reading, writing, traveling; **Children:** 2; **Grandchildren:** 2; **Personal Statement:** Writing poetry is how I express myself when something touches me deeply.

Author: Andrea Brown; **Birthplace:** Hengview, TX; **Hobbies:** Writing poems and volleyball; **Education:** Hallsville High School graduate; **Honors:** Most unpredictable Sr year; **Personal Statement:** Writing poems is an expression of my imagination. I can be mad, sad or happy when I write. I love sharing my thoughts with others, only if they appreciate it though.

Author: Betty Brown Harrison; **Birthplace:** East Texas; **Occupation:** Insurance clerk – Orthopedic Clinic; **Hobbies:** Singing, reading, hunting and fishing; **Spouse's Name:** Richard; **Education:** High school; **Personal Statement:** My poem reflects my own childhood. I am sad to think that so many children today will never experience a summer day in the woods.

Author: Jackie Browning; **Birthplace:** Cowen, WV; **Occupation:** Kindergarten teacher; **Hobbies:** Sewing, creating materials to use in my classroom; **Memberships:** Word of Faith Assembly Church, WV educ assoc; **Spouse's Name:** Mike; **Children:** 2; **Education:** AB degree– Glenville State College, attended West Virginia graduate college; **Awards:** Original gospel song, won 2nd pl in a contest, was recorded; **Published Works:** An art idea published in the teacher's "Mailbox Magazine"; **Personal Statement:** I give God all the glory and honor for all he anoints and inspires me to write.

Author: Edward Brunton; **Pen Name:** Edward John Brunton; **Birthplace:** Cleveland, Ohio; **Occupation:** Retired postal worker; **Hobbies:** Reading, writing, symphonic music, romantic songs & memories; **Memberships:** Postal Employee Holy Name Society, Secular Franciscan Order; **Spouse's Name:** Wanda Brunton; **Education:** G. I. Bill– John Carroll University 1947; Biarritz

Dreams of the Soul

American U1945; **Honors:** Diocese of Cleveland & Corpus Christi Church & Social Ser; **Published Works:** Quill Books, Holy Name 'Harbinger', The Poet: Fine Arts Society "Mishawaka, Indiana"; **Personal Statement:** I try to hold my poetic efforts in a spirit of humility... My father quoted poets often during our teen–age lives... My grandfather: Editor "Altoona Mirror"

Author: Grace Buller; **Birthplace:** Los Angeles, CA; **Occupation:** Security (Communications); **Hobbies:** Computers, music, judo, psychology; **Memberships:** SGI–USA; **Children:** 5; **Grandchildren:** 5; **Education:** Various Community Colleges and Trade Schools; **Honors:** Cyber Poet; **Awards:** Editor's Choice 1996 and 1997; **Published Works:** ONWARD, There but for ——go I, New Year's Resolution, Moonscape; **Personal Statement:** Compelled to produce, I search out the innate. Fearing discipline will reduce art to worthiness. I search for my goodness and one thing that's great.

Author: Laine Burch; **Birthplace:** Clay Center, KS; **Occupation:** Nurse, therapist, freelance proofreader/editor; **Hobbies:** Music, reading, writing, walking, quilting and my dog; **Memberships:** St. Annes Church, Psi Chi, Alliance for Mentally Ill; **Spouse's Name:** Timothy; **Children:** 2; **Education:** MS clinical psychology; **Honors:** National Honor Society, Dean's List, and President's List; **Published Works:** Essence; **Personal Statement:** I started reading at age 3, and thus learned early the exquisite beauty and power of language. That has stayed with me all my life.

Author: Ethel M. Burch; **Birthplace:** Austin, TX; **Occupation:** Retired school teacher; **Hobbies:** Travel, fishing, arts and crafts; **Memberships:** Daughters of the Republic of Texas, Poet Society, DKG; **Spouse's Name:** Herman Raynor Burch; **Children:** 2; **Education:** BS, MS from Southwest Texas University; **Honors:** Alpha Chi, college players; **Personal Statement:** Thanks to all those Old Masters who gave so many beautiful "Memory Gems" for me to share with my students throughout the years.

Author: Rick Burton; **Birthplace:** Princeton, IL; **Occupation:** Machinist; **Hobbies:** Sketching art, camping, martial arts; **Children:** 1; **Education:** Graduate of high school, trade school; **Published Works:** Hunting And Fishing Corner, for PGI Flyer (Morning Sunrise), A Thought, News Tribune; **Personal Statement:** My goals as a writer are to bring smiles on a sad face and thoughts to awaken routine minds, share my heart's passion worldwide.

Author: Eugene Caad; **Birthplace:** San Diego, CA; **Occupation:** Janitor; **Hobbies:** Reading, hiking, fixing and building things; **Education:** Graduated from Western High; **Honors:** Honor roll in Job Corps; **Awards:** Scholarship from Jr. High School; **Published Works:** Humor Laughter & Happiness; **Personal Statement:** I would like to make my poem into a song someday. My next goal is to become an inventor & poet. My role models are Einstein and Da Vinci.

Author: Tonya Campbell; **Birthplace:** Portland, OR; **Occupation:** Mother; **Hobbies:** Writing, reading, computer, radio and watching movies; **Children:** 2; **Education:** going to school to get GED; **Personal Statement:** My poem Friendship was written by me to my best friend about our friendship.

Author: Cida Carneiro; **Birthplace:** Brazil; **Occupation:** Gaming Agent; **Hobbies:** Reading, writing, martial arts, darts and cooking; **Children:** 2; **Education:** Master's degree in nursing; **Personal Statement:** The poem is a reflection of a dream I've had since early age. It reflects the loneliness that fills my heart due to his absence. In a dream lives my happiness–in reality the prince is somewhere–I can't find him. Hope keeps me going.

Author: Kathy Caudle; **Birthplace:** East St. Louis, IL; **Occupation:** Hotel clerk; **Hobbies:** Gardening, audio recording and traveling; **Education:** Weber State University; **Published Works:** Poetry Press, Ohio Poetry Supplement, and Utah State Poetry Society; **Personal Statement:** Long ago my life was changed by the power of the written word. I believe in the written word, and its power.

Author: Nancy L. Cavanaugh; **Pen Name:** Caithin K. Charmhanach; **Birthplace:** Gallipolis, Ohio; **Occupation:** Management Consultant/writer; **Hobbies:** Travel, photography, literature, and backpacking; **Memberships:** American Assoc. University Women and Women's Health Ldsp.; **Children:** 3; **Grandchildren:** 4; **Education:** B. S. University of Redlands, M. P. A. University of San Francisco, Ph. D. Health; **Honors:** Dean's List, A Whitehead Honor Society, A. A. F. E.; **Awards:** Outstanding Women's Health Care Leader, Academic Excellence; **Published Works:** Poetry National Poetry Assoc., Technical Health Care Articles; **Personal Statement:** My goal as a writer is to speak my truth and to illustrate universal connections in spirituality, healing, and discovery. Those are my lifelong passions, influenced by many great women– Mary Sarton, Maya Angelou, and Eleanor Roosevelt.

Author: Felipe Chacon, Jr.; **Birthplace:** Fabens, Texas; **Occupation:** Delivery driver; **Hobbies:** Writing, guitar and electronics; **Children:** 2; **Grandchildren:** 1; **Education:** St Louis High School, University of Texas– El Paso (2 years); **Published Works:** Several with National Library of Poetry; **Personal Statement:** The most beautiful song in the world, is the smile of a child.

Author: June V. Chandler; **Birthplace:** Virginia; **Occupation:** Housewife; **Hobbies:** Reading, gardening, cross word puzzles, watching TV; **Memberships:** Columbia House Video Club, etc; **Spouse's Name:** Ronald Chandler; **Children:** 3; **Grandchildren:** 2; **Education:** High School; **Personal Statement:** If everyone would think about their life in this world, we could walk through our days with purpose and love for each other.

Author: Rubin Chapman; **Birthplace:** Stamford, CT; **Occupation:** State Worker; **Hobbies:** Piano, photography, and poetry; **Children:** 3; **Education:** Associates in Science; **Personal Statement:** I'm inspired by the most talented poet I've ever known, my dear departed brother, Arvil T. Chapman. I miss you and love you always.

Author: Micki Chatman; **Birthplace:** Shreveport, LA; **Occupation:** Nurse; **Hobbies:** Painting, reading and crafts; **Education:** Panda College School Of Nursing, Northwestern State University at Shreveport; **Personal Statement:** Poetry is the visible feelings of the soul. It's pure, honest and lives forever. It's like painting a part of your essence, displayed for all to see.

Author: Barbara Marie Chesteen; **Birthplace:** Jackson, MS; **Occupation:** Carhop at Sonic Of Pearl; **Hobbies:** Writing and listening to music; **Education:** I have my G. E. D. and hope to go to college; **Published Works:** My first poem was printed in my 7th grade yearbook; **Personal Statement:** My inspiration is my life, anything I write about my life in some way. I enjoy a good Poe story and poem, when I have the time.

Author: Dafni Chrysostomou; **Birthplace:** Mobile, AL; **Occupation:** Elementary Education Major; **Hobbies:** Poetry/story writing, reading novels; **Education:** Freshman at University of South Alabama; **Honors:** Who's Who (2 Yrs.); **Awards:** Service Award; **Personal Statement:** Poetry, for me, is a way to escape. I have Poe to thank for my love of it.

Author: Elaine Cincotta; **Pen Name:** Karin Koal; **Birthplace:** Elizabeth, NJ; **Occupation:** Spiritualist Minister; **Hobbies:** Art, needlepoint, chess, walking, reading and sound waves; **Memberships:** Prayer Power Fellowship; **Spouse's Name:** Joseph Cincotta; **Children:** 3; **Grandchildren:** 1; **Education:** High school and 1 year New York Business School; **Honors:** Design Patent on my "Galaxy Gazer" astrology tarot game; **Awards:** Four Year

Personal Profiles

Scholarship to Bishop McDonnel High School; **Personal Statement:** To me poetry is jam, when spread on the bread of humanity, sweetens the consumption of brotherly love.

Author: Iva Clark; **Birthplace:** Riverside, CA; **Occupation:** House Attendant; **Hobbies:** Fishing, hiking, biking, weight lifting, swimming, etc; **Spouse's Name:** John; **Children:** 1; **Education:** High School Diploma and GED; **Honors:** 3.75 GP in High School on Honor Roll; **Awards:** CPR, Football Ralley; **Personal Statement:** Our earth is getting weak, it's up to all of us to save it. Please do your part for your children. Thank you Eva Clark.

Author: Phyllis M. Coates; **Birthplace:** Claverton, Bath; **Occupation:** Retired; **Hobbies:** Knitting, reading, writing, playing Scrabble; **Spouse's Name:** Widow; **Children:** 6; **Grandchildren:** 23; **Education:** Village school

Author: Victoria J. Cocco; **Birthplace:** Hartford, CT; **Occupation:** Owner Drywall Business; **Hobbies:** Golf, gourmet cooking, and gardening; **Spouse's Name:** Mario; **Children:** 2; **Education:** Graduated Manchester Community College; **Honors:** Alpha Beta Gamma Honor Society and Dean's List; **Personal Statement:** Where God takes one child, he gives another. Terry died in Nam 9-26-67 in my husband's arms. Born unto us, a daughter, five years to the day.

Author: Oliver Kenneth Cole; **Personal Statement:** Thirty seven years ago when I was ten years old, I wrote this poem on my grandpa's sixty fifth birthday.

Author: Eileen Cole; **Birthplace:** Antigo, WI; **Occupation:** Insurance Agent; **Hobbies:** Reading, writing, fishing, and experiencing life; **Children:** 2; **Grandchildren:** 1; **Education:** High school and varied insurance courses; **Honors:** On a personal level won a trip to Las Vegas; **Personal Statement:** I'm an emotional writer. I pour out my heart on paper releasing a myriad of feelings that traditionally are shared with girltalks. Essentially a private person, I have two friends and an extremely tolerant mother who I inflict this upon!

Author: Amy Lee Coleman; **Pen Name:** Annabelle Lee; **Birthplace:** Jackson, MS; **Occupation:** Photographer's assistant; **Hobbies:** Reading, writing and photography; **Education:** Sophomore at Central Hinds Academy; **Published Works:** Life and Death; **Personal Statement:** My favorite things in life have been my friends and family. They are the ones who give me support and influence my work.

Author: Robin Collins; **Birthplace:** Clinton, IN; **Occupation:** Work outside of home/mother; **Hobbies:** Swimming, hiking, fishing, camping, reading, music, dancing; **Children:** 2; **Education:** Some college; **Awards:** Music award in high school; **Personal Statement:** I have a goal to have my poetry published so I can share my thoughts and feelings with words and poetic balance.

Author: Charleen K. Cook; **Birthplace:** Flint, MI; **Occupation:** Clerical assistant; **Hobbies:** Reading, writing, listening to records; **Education:** BA in journalism, University of Michigan 1972; **Published Works:** Creative Writing for High School Students, H. C. Brasher (V–M)1968; **Personal Statement:** Poetry is food for the soul, which is why so much of the Bible is written poetic language.

Author: Jonna Sue Cooper; **Pen Name:** Johna Grey; **Birthplace:** Brazil, Indiana; **Occupation:** Secretary; **Hobbies:** Drawing, oil painting, quilting and playing piano; **Children:** 1; **Education:** Ivy Tech Business College; **Personal Statement:** Everything I do is talented and good is inspired by my Lord & Savior Jesus Christ. This poem was written to honor my dad(81) and mom (77).

Author: Theresa Costanzo; **Birthplace:** Smithtown, NY; **Occupation:** Hairstylist; **Hobbies:** Gardening, family writing; **Spouse's Name:** Jerry; **Children:** 2; **Personal Statement:** Some things I write are straight from my heart, but all my creations are gifts from God– and for those creations I am always thankful.

Author: Linda F. Crabtree; **Birthplace:** Pikeville, TN; **Occupation:** Medical technologist; **Hobbies:** Writing poetry, playing with my children; **Spouse's Name:** Wesley Crabtree; **Children:** 2; **Education:** Tennessee Tech University, Cumberland School of Medical Technology; **Published Works:** A Rainy Day At The Beach; **Personal Statement:** Writing is a love of mine, I can express feelings that I cannot in speech. My most beloved inspiration: my children, Lindsey and Kelly.

Author: Amber Cranmer; **Birthplace:** Wilmington, DE; **Occupation:** Student; **Hobbies:** Writing, talking, reading and sports; **Memberships:** FFA (Future Farmers of America); **Education:** In high school; **Personal Statement:** My inspiration comes from my best friend, Kenny Kassing. He shows me many things from many different viewpoints, therefore I owe this poem to him.

Author: Claudia Cribb Hucks; **Pen Name:** Claudia Cribb Hucks; **Birthplace:** Hemingway, SC; **Occupation:** Children's Bible Writer; **Hobbies:** Travel, crochet and reading; **Memberships:** Summerville Baptist Church, N. L. A. P. W.; **Spouse's Name:** Clarence B. Hucks; **Children:** 2; **Grandchildren:** 5; **Education:** Bachelor's Degree– Andersonville Baptist Seminary; **Published Works:** Articles, nonfiction and short story; **Personal Statement:** The medium of writing expresses best my desire to communicate, enhance, and teach. Books, poems, and other writings have illumed my life in tremendous ways.

Author: L. Julian Cuervo; **Birthplace:** Medellin, Colombia, SA; **Occupation:** US Army active duty soldier; **Hobbies:** Music, football, playing drums, camping; **Spouse's Name:** Tania Cuervo; **Children:** 2; **Education:** Graduated from US Army aviation logistics school, currently attending Univ of Maryland; **Personal Statement:** Education and perseverance are the keys to a successful life.

Author: Susan L. Cupari; **Birthplace:** Akron, Ohio; **Occupation:** Registered Nurse; **Hobbies:** Cooking and sewing; **Spouse's Name:** Gregory S. Cupari; **Children:** 2; **Education:** Graduate of Stark State; **Honors:** Dean's List; **Awards:** HIV Volunteer Training; **Published Works:** A Mother's Love; **Personal Statement:** I write about subjects that touch my life in a special way. Writing about them keeps them with me in spirit and in thoughts... Always.

Author: Diana L. Dalke; **Birthplace:** Ronan, Montana; **Occupation:** Student; **Hobbies:** Reading, writing, watching TV, crafts and fishing; **Memberships:** Yearbook Editor; **Education:** Still attending Ronan High School; **Personal Statement:** Writing poetry is a way of expressing yourself, thoughts and feelings. When I write I put away all my worries for the day and just have fun. Always follow your dreams.

Author: Marie Dambruch; **Birthplace:** Cherokee, TX; **Occupation:** Executive Secretary – Medical, Legal (retired); **Hobbies:** Reading, writing, painting, family, friends and strangers; **Spouse's Name:** Lyle; **Children:** 3; **Grandchildren:** 7; **Education:** Life; **Personal Statement:** For me, writing is like playing the piano or singing a hymn or contemplating the glory of God in a sunset on frozen Lake Winnebago.

Author: Vivian Davis; **Birthplace:** Kansas City, MO; **Occupation:** Retired/Part–Time Notary Public, Typist; **Hobbies:** Writing, drawing; **Spouse's Name:** Leman V. Davis; **Grandchildren:** 3; **Education:** AA–Sacramento City College, BS–University of San Francisco, Vocational Certificates

Dreams of the Soul

Author: Yvonne de Ridder; **Birthplace:** South Africa; **Occupation:** Housewife no "House Executive"; **Hobbies:** Painting, writing and photography; **Spouse's Name:** Karel de Ridder; **Children:** 3; **Education:** Graduated high school in South Africa; **Personal Statement:** This is my first attempt at English poetry. English is my second language.... May this be the first of many more...

Author: Linda Dean; **Birthplace:** Spangler, PA; **Occupation:** Bookkeeper; **Hobbies:** Fishing; **Memberships:** Ladies Aux. to the VFW; **Spouse's Name:** James Day; **Children:** 2; **Grandchildren:** 2; **Education:** Graduated from Garner Senior High; **Honors:** Certificates of recognition from various organizations; **Awards:** Several merit awards; **Personal Statement:** My poems are an inspiration of God and life. My grandmother influenced me all of her life to feel the beauty of living.

Author: Olivia Deering; **Birthplace:** Georgia; **Occupation:** Computer Operator, Teacher Assistant; **Hobbies:** Horseback riding, sewing, painting, tennis; **Memberships:** Church, School Nutrition; **Spouse's Name:** Ben McClendon; **Children:** 1; **Education:** H. S. – Georgia Tech CDC Course, CDL, One; **Honors:** Retired from Rich Building Ga Tech 1983; **Awards:** Cake Contest, Most Original, (fair); **Published Works:** Poetry Tech Erato 1979 and Poetry Today 1977; **Personal Statement:** My goal is to write children's books and to get my other poems published. My inspiration comes from knowing people and about life. Influences – my mother.

Author: Lillie Maude Deffenbaugh Massey; **Birthplace:** Natural Dam, AR; **Occupation:** Homemaker; **Hobbies:** Crocheting and working puzzles; **Spouse's Name:** J. B. Massey; **Children:** 2; **Grandchildren:** 7; **Education:** High School; **Honors:** Honorable Mention

Author: Linda DeJesus; **Birthplace:** Hudson, NY; **Occupation:** LPN, housewife; **Hobbies:** Writing, crocheting; **Spouse's Name:** Sixto DeJesus; **Children:** 9; **Grandchildren:** 1; **Education:** GED, nursing school; **Personal Statement:** My gift of writing comes from the Lord, to Him is all the glory and I'm so grateful for the gift.

Author: Sandra H. Delong; **Birthplace:** Gainesville, Florida; **Occupation:** Greeter at Wal–Mart; **Hobbies:** Write poetry and do embroidery work; **Memberships:** Calvary Bible Church; **Spouse's Name:** Floyd Lincoln; **Children:** 2; **Grandchildren:** 3; **Education:** High school graduate; **Awards:** Certification from Moody Bible Inst. and Floyd Bible Inst.; **Published Works:** "Our Good Shepherd" and "Memories and Daydreams"; **Personal Statement:** I have been writing poems since I was a young child. When I think of something I always try to put it in poetry form. My thoughts are inspirational and I have lots of love for my family, church family and my God.

Author: Hannah Sexton; **Pen Name:** Hannah Sexton; **Birthplace:** Glasgow, Scotland; **Occupation:** Retired English Teacher; **Hobbies:** Reading, painting; **Spouse's Name:** Louis Demers (deceased); **Children:** 7; **Grandchildren:** 7; **Education:** Honours B. A., M. A., McMaster Univ, Hamilton, Ontario

Author: Teresa Denison; **Birthplace:** Gordon, NE; **Occupation:** Unloader/stocker, Wal–Mart; **Hobbies:** Drawing, writing, arts and crafts; **Memberships:** YMCA; **Education:** Graduated Presentation College in SD; **Awards:** 4-H awards, Best Senior Choir Member; **Personal Statement:** I've always enjoyed writing poetry and short stories. I do it as a relaxation method. My goal is to someday publish a short story.

Author: Thomas Devin; **Pen Name:** 111158; **Birthplace:** Portland, Oregon; **Occupation:** Hotel industry; **Hobbies:** Playing and watching sports, reading & writing poetry; **Education:** Some college; **Personal Statement:** Poetry is a timeless root of hope that grips the soul and lifts the heart. Never give up the fight.

Author: Joseph M. DiPerna, Jr.; **Birthplace:** Brooklyn, NY; **Occupation:** Lawyer; **Hobbies:** Sports, creative writing, hobbies, stocks; **Memberships:** St Charles Singles Club, Richmond Ct Young Republicans; **Education:** College – St John's University, BA Psychology, University of Bridgeport School of Law J. D.; **Honors:** Dean's List 1985–86, 1986–87 St Johns University; **Awards:** 1988 Outstanding Young Men of America; **Published Works:** Into Our Heart and Minds – Anthology of Poetry – Fall, 1996; **Personal Statement:** There is a fine line between procrastination and faith. There is a fine line between confidence and arrogance and I walk it well.

Author: Randall M. Dockery; **Birthplace:** Scioto County, Ohio; **Occupation:** Federal Correction Officer; **Hobbies:** Football, fishing and family; **Spouse's Name:** Betty J. Dockery; **Children:** 2; **Education:** High school diploma plus Correctional Officer Tech School; **Honors:** Being a Christian and praising my Lord; **Personal Statement:** Mark 13:32 "But of that day and that hour knoweth no man, no not the angels who are in heaven, neither the Son but, only the Father. "

Author: Keith R. Dolson; **Birthplace:** Michigan City, IN; **Hobbies:** Play guitar in a band, bowling and going out with my friends; **Education:** Graduated high school; **Personal Statement:** My philosophical viewpoint is "whatever it takes. " It's also our band motto. It can be applied to anything.

Author: Henry Domke; **Pen Name:** Kain Shannarra; **Birthplace:** Alpena, MI; **Occupation:** Student; **Hobbies:** Singing, reading, writing and helping others; **Education:** High school diploma, Alpena High School, Alpena, MI; **Awards:** Choir award and pin; **Personal Statement:** Poetry is a type of art that springs forth from inside your heart. Let it go – let it flow – let the world know (so sayeth Kain).

Author: Thelma M. Donahue; **Birthplace:** Huntington, WV; **Occupation:** Packer at Industrial Anodizing; **Hobbies:** Reading, fishing and writing; **Spouse's Name:** Sean M. Donahue; **Education:** I graduated from George Washington High School; **Personal Statement:** I have always admired Edgar Allen Poe and Ralph Waldo Emerson.

Author: Rebecca N. Dyer; **Pen Name:** Beck; **Birthplace:** Sallisaw, OK; **Occupation:** 8th grade Student; **Hobbies:** Sports, cheerleading, reading and writing; **Memberships:** 4–H; **Education:** 8th grade honor student of Moffett Public School; **Awards:** Academic Awards in all areas; **Personal Statement:** All my life I have always wanted to do my best, no matter what. This attitude has helped me to succeed in school and other activities.

Author: Dianne Eisen; **Birthplace:** Australia; **Hobbies:** Fishing, crafts, writing poetry; **Spouse's Name:** David; **Children:** 2; **Personal Statement:** This is my first attempt at poetry. Living on an atoll, its beauty and tranquility have given me untold inspiration and I have just finished my second poem.

Author: Anita Elliott; **Birthplace:** Robstown, Texas; **Occupation:** Doll artist; **Hobbies:** Portrait artist, crafts and gardening; **Memberships:** Calallen Baptist Church, Prof. Dollmakers Art Guild; **Spouse's Name:** Paul D. Elliott; **Children:** 3; **Grandchildren:** 3; **Education:** High school and business college; **Awards:** Doll Artisan Guild Award; **Personal Statement:** Creating whether sculpting/writing is what I must do to express myself. Inspiration comes from the beauty and talent of great artists. Dickinson is a favorite.

Author: Joel W. Ellis; **Birthplace:** Bluff Dale, TX; **Occupation:** Retired; **Hobbies:** Electric trains, model airplanes, cars and trucks; **Children:** 2; **Grandchildren:** 4; **Education:** 10th grade; **Published Works:** One song "Days Of Yesteryear" ASCAP

Personal Profiles

Author: Roderick E. Ellison; **Pen Name:** Fysh; **Birthplace:** North Carolina; **Occupation:** Central Fidelity Bank Clerk; **Hobbies:** Basketball, tennis, golf and fishing; **Memberships:** Masonic Lodge; **Spouse's Name:** Latise Ellison; **Children:** 4; **Education:** Virginia State University graduate; **Awards:** Junior Achievers Award, Young Black Authors Award; **Personal Statement:** My mother is a great inspiration to me. She has been a mother, father, teacher and true friend to me.

Author: Luretta Elston; **Birthplace:** Pell City, AL; **Occupation:** Aspiring Author/Poet; **Hobbies:** Writing poetry, reading and writing short stories; **Children:** 1; **Education:** Graduated Pell City High School, 1971; **Awards:** I was awarded for being an outstanding foster parent; **Personal Statement:** My goal, as a writer, is to inspire and encourage ordinary people to do extraordinary things that will enrich their lives.

Author: Aaron Fitzgerald Evans; **Pen Name:** A. A. Fitzgerald Evans; **Birthplace:** El Dorado, AR; **Occupation:** Minister; **Hobbies:** Coin & stamp collecting, imported wines, beers, sodas, etc; **Memberships:** VFW American Legion, Democratic Party; **Education:** 12 years of high school and 2 years of college; **Honors:** Minister's license and ordination, 1970; **Awards:** Army good conduct medal and a host of others; **Published Works:** Owner/publisher – The Christian Traveler Magazine; **Personal Statement:** I am the owner of A. A. Evans Enterprises Christian Traveler Magazine, Christian Traveler publishing board. I write poetry that people might benefit from it.

Author: Henry J. Falcone; **Birthplace:** Norwich, CT; **Occupation:** Pastor/Missionary; **Hobbies:** Song writing, poetry and travel; **Memberships:** Pinecrest Ministerial Fellowship; **Spouse's Name:** Donna; **Children:** 4; **Education:** Providence College 3 years; **Personal Statement:** I want to thank a gracious and loving God for His inspiration and gift to create poetry and music, without Him I can do nothing.

Author: Adrian D. Fernandez; **Birthplace:** New Orleans; **Occupation:** Record Conversion Techncian; **Hobbies:** Motorcycling and leathercraft; **Children:** 4; **Education:** East Iberville High and Delta College; **Published Works:** New Artist; **Personal Statement:** I write to free myself from pain, also hope to touch the hearts of others with the sincerity of my words.

Author: Louise Kilby Fesperman; **Birthplace:** North Carolina; **Occupation:** Retired; **Hobbies:** Writing, gardening, sewing, reading, travel and singing; **Memberships:** Big Lake Chamber of Commerce & Hawaii Yacht Club; **Spouse's Name:** Tillman R. Fesperman; **Children:** 2; **Grandchildren:** 4; **Education:** High School; **Personal Statement:** Writing poetry is an inspirational gift from the heart to be shared with others. My goal as a writer is to create inspirational books to enhance and uplift the human soul of those who read my writing.

Author: Pamela Fiedler; **Birthplace:** Beatrice, NE; **Occupation:** Graphic designer; **Hobbies:** Illustration in all forms of physics/science and poetry; **Memberships:** Alumni association; **Education:** BFA/graphic design– Univ of Nebraska; **Honors:** Illustrator of science– published works called Submission; **Published Works:** As a graphic designer; Protons: The Unified Field, Theory, The Weekly Planet; **Personal Statement:** "May the great teachers of today, always inspire the children to sculpt along the beach of tomorrow. " Pamela

Author: Ashton John Fischer, Jr.; **Birthplace:** New Orleans, LA; **Occupation:** Self–employed; **Memberships:** Illiad Literay Awards, International Society of Poets; **Education:** Tulane University B. A.; **Honors:** Poet's Guild Who's Who in South & Southwest, America, World; **Awards:** Who's Who in the Academy of American Poets

Author: Carole A. Fisher; **Pen Name:** Carole Ann; **Birthplace:** New Jersey; **Occupation:** Certified Insurance counselor; **Hobbies:** Reading, walking, biking and tole painting; **Memberships:** Natl. Assoc. Ins. Women, NJ Society of Certified Ins. Cons.; **Spouse's Name:** Raymond; **Children:** 1; **Grandchildren:** 1; **Honors:** Recipient of Ruble Scholarship 1993; **Published Works:** Throughout the Night; **Personal Statement:** My personal quote "When the soul is also touched, the heart remembers. "

Author: Constance C. Fitzgerald; **Birthplace:** Centerville, Iowa; **Occupation:** Retired from word processing; **Hobbies:** Because of visual problems writing is special; **Children:** 3; **Grandchildren:** 7; **Education:** High school 1948; **Honors:** Just being reunited with my oldest son and family; **Published Works:** Boards Of Life in 1971

Author: Justine Foden; **Birthplace:** Lawrence, MA; **Occupation:** Student; **Hobbies:** Writing; **Education:** Attending junior high in the 7th grade

Author: Nancy T. Folga; **Pen Name:** Teresa; **Birthplace:** Wheeling, WV; **Occupation:** Legal assistant; **Hobbies:** Music, art, photography, travel, writing; **Memberships:** Pan Zakynthinian society; **Spouse's Name:** John Bozikis; **Children:** 2; **Grandchildren:** 2; **Education:** BA Brooklyn College; **Honors:** National spelling bee; **Personal Statement:** Thank God every day. Choose to be joyous, loving, kind. Never give up your dreams. Be persistent. Stay positive, focused, disciplined.

Author: Jason Forget; **Birthplace:** Cohoes, NY; **Occupation:** High school student; **Hobbies:** Poetry, hockey, soccer and community service; **Memberships:** National Junior Honors Society, National Honors Society; **Education:** Junior in high school at La Salle Institute; **Honors:** Gold Honors Student for 4 consecutive semesters; **Personal Statement:** Education is never ending. As a wise person once told me, "A mind once stretched never regains its previous shape. " Never stop learning.

Author: Travis C. Forsberg; **Birthplace:** Thief River Falls, MN; **Occupation:** Furniture delivery and sales; **Hobbies:** Football, weightlifting, and writing; **Education:** High school graduate; **Honors:** Honor roll in high school; **Personal Statement:** Writing for me is a stress release. When I am stressed I sit down and write what I feel. My favorite author is Edgar Guest.

Author: Edith Foster; **Birthplace:** Des Moines, IA; **Occupation:** Certified Medical Aid; **Hobbies:** Painting, collecting dolls and writing; **Memberships:** World of Poetry, National Poetry Library, Sparrowgrass Poetry; **Education:** High school graduate and 2 yrs. for medical aid; **Honors:** Who's Who in World of Poetry; **Awards:** Golden Poet of the Year (World of Poetry 1988, 1989 and 1990); **Personal Statement:** Poetry is an art form of words

Author: Linda Fox; **Birthplace:** Passaic, NJ; **Occupation:** Secretary; **Hobbies:** Reading, computers, writing poetry and needlework; **Memberships:** Computer Club Of Ocean County; **Spouse's Name:** Frederick; **Children:** 1; **Education:** B. A., Paterson State College; **Published Works:** "Still Not Home" National Library Of Poetry, 1995; "Instant Prayers" Famous Poets Society, 1996

Author: Clayton Hobart Fox; **Pen Name:** Clayton Hobart Fox; **Birthplace:** Drain, OR; **Occupation:** Retired Journalist; **Hobbies:** Chess and woodworking; **Memberships:** American Legion; **Education:** Some college; **Honors:** Best public speaker and journalistic awards; **Published Works:** Too numerous to list; **Personal Statement:** I have completed an 85, 000 word novel about modern day piracy on the oceans of the world.

Author: Janet Fox; **Birthplace:** Alexander County, NC; **Occupation:** Clerical; **Hobbies:** Writing poetry and songs, drawing and singing; **Memberships:** Notary Public for the state of North Carolina; **Spouse's Name:** Erik; **Children:** 1; **Education:**

Dreams of the Soul

Alexander Central High School graduate 1983, CVCC and Wilkes Community College; **Published Works:** Sounds Of Time, co–author Margaret Gwaltney (my mother); **Personal Statement:** My philosophy has always been "love those that love you and especially those that don't love you." My goal, as a writer, is to let someone know all the love and mercy of our Lord and Savior Jesus Christ. He has been my strength in all.

Author: Jimmie Lilly Franklin; **Pen Name:** Jimmie Lilly Franklin; **Birthplace:** Orlando, Florida; **Occupation:** Retired teacher; **Hobbies:** Reading, creative writing and crossword puzzles; **Memberships:** C. R. T. A., Society of Book Writers & Illustrators; **Children:** 4; **Grandchildren:** 11; **Education:** B. A. Degree – Wiley College – studied at KU, UCIA and USC; **Honors:** Two plays I wrote were presented by Wiley at Drama Festival; **Awards:** Made Who's Who while in college; **Personal Statement:** Education in Tulsa, OK public school. During early years, I was encouraged by Mother Florence Lilly to become an avid reader and to write poems and short stories.

Author: Tonia Gaskin; **Birthplace:** Houston, MS; **Occupation:** Student; **Hobbies:** Jogging, reading; **Memberships:** Phi Ma Fraternity; **Education:** Currently a Senior at University in Birmingham, Al

Author: Edith Gattilia; **Birthplace:** New Haven, CT; **Occupation:** Landscape artist, Freelance writer; **Hobbies:** Arts, gardening, needlepoint; **Memberships:** All groups at church; **Education:** 4 yrs Hill House High School, Radio Technique in NY, Stone Business College in New Haven; **Published Works:** Only a short story and an editorial in Palm Beach Post Paper; **Personal Statement:** Writing is a craft, but one must believe in one's work. Study people, be inspired. A good writer must write something one is familiar with. The reader always can detect this. Writing is exciting and rewarding.

Author: Sylvia F. Gause Gurganious; **Birthplace:** Wilmington, NC; **Occupation:** Housewife, Exc. (many skills); **Hobbies:** Sewing, quilting, flower making, candles, soaps, etc; **Memberships:** March Of Dimes; **Spouse's Name:** Bobby; **Children:** 5; **Grandchildren:** 10; **Education:** High school; **Honors:** Spelling Bee; **Personal Statement:** I wrote this poem to inspire the people of today's viewpoints, goals, etc. Just as a thought of inspiration to others and myself and to enrich those I love.

Author: Felicia Gail Gibbs; **Birthplace:** Audrain County Missouri; **Occupation:** Cashier; **Hobbies:** Writing poetry, crafts and gardening; **Spouse's Name:** Daren Gibbs; **Education:** High school graduate; **Published Works:** Tidal Wave; **Personal Statement:** My goal as a writer is to bring inspiration and happiness to the world. My writing is a pattern of my life and innermost thoughts.

Author: Juan Ernesto Gil; **Birthplace:** Havana, Cuba; **Occupation:** Spanish Professor; **Education:** Bachelor's Degree in Literature and Language from Universityof Havana; **Published Works:** Poems in different anthologies; **Personal Statement:** I intend to express my personal view about life through the magic of poetry. I deeply admire poets Whitman, Ellicot and Neruda.

Author: Chantal Gilbert; **Pen Name:** Chantalou G; **Birthplace:** Quebec; **Occupation:** Postmaster; **Hobbies:** Reading and writing; **Memberships:** Committee Action Economic; **Spouse's Name:** Richard Rodrigues; **Children:** 2; **Grandchildren:** 1; **Education:** C. E. G. E. P. and different courses; **Honors:** Receive mention for voluntary work; **Awards:** trophy; **Personal Statement:** My inspiration come from my emotions; and in the privacy of my mind, I transcribe all my feelings. It is for me a satisfaction personal.

Author: Darce Glaze; **Birthplace:** Little Roza, AR; **Occupation:** Medical secretary; **Hobbies:** Cooking, fishing and taxidermy; **Education:** UALR Speech Communications, UALR School of Taxidermy; **Personal Statement:** I enjoy writing literature for children. My one desire is that I always be able to see the world through the eyes of youth– embracing each moment.

Author: Hayden Gomes; **Birthplace:** San Diego, CA; **Occupation:** Student 5th grade; **Hobbies:** collect key chains; **Memberships:** San Diego zoological society; **Education:** 4th grade; **Honors:** San Diego museum of art

Author: Stuart J. Goode; **Birthplace:** Fort Bragg, NC; **Occupation:** Operation 7 Worker, MDI; **Hobbies:** Bowling, golf, tennis and painting; **Memberships:** American Bowling Congress; **Education:** High School; **Personal Statement:** My goal is the same as all writers. Simply to be read, and in doing so in one sense find immortality.

Author: Melissa Gordon; **Pen Name:** Missy; **Birthplace:** Henderson, TX; **Occupation:** Housewife; **Hobbies:** Enjoy spending time with my children, travel; **Spouse's Name:** John Gordon (deceased); **Children:** 2; **Education:** 11th Grade; **Personal Statement:** I plan to write a book, and more poetry in the future. I have admired poetry all my life.

Author: Maureen Green; **Birthplace:** Shipley, Yorkshire; **Occupation:** Sales Assistant; **Hobbies:** Reading, dressmaking, gardening; **Spouse's Name:** Harold Green; **Children:** 3; **Grandchildren:** 7; **Education:** Bingley Modern Secondary School, Eldwick Primary Yorkshire; **Published Works:** Foulridge Wharfe, by Anchor Books; **Personal Statement:** To be able to get my novel, Tribute to A Lady, finished and to be published one day.

Author: Marcia Jean Grzywacz; **Pen Name:** Marcia J. Grzywacz; **Birthplace:** Detroit, MI; **Occupation:** Disabled, was caregiver of daughter; **Hobbies:** Music—playing keyboard, painting watercolors and crafts; **Memberships:** AARP over 50; **Children:** 1; **Education:** High school; **Honors:** Being a mom; **Awards:** Art awards; **Personal Statement:** I'm a very positive person, and try to live life the best I can. I have a good sense of humor and I smile a lot.

Author: Mari Gutierrez; **Birthplace:** Chicago, Illinois; **Occupation:** Writer & student; **Hobbies:** Reading, writing, music, singing, and rollerblading; **Memberships:** YMCA; **Education:** Up to freshman in high school; **Personal Statement:** My inspiration is God. He guides my hand to make beautiful mind pictures on a plain sheet of paper. My goal is to become known.

Author: Bob Guzman; **Birthplace:** Douglas, AR; **Occupation:** Retired sales manager; **Hobbies:** New career, poetry, literary perspectives; **Memberships:** American Legion Post 1000; **Spouse's Name:** Evelyn Carlene (deceased); **Children:** 2; **Grandchildren:** 2; **Education:** High school; **Honors:** USAF Military CID Commendations–Military Instructor; **Awards:** National West Coast Sales Mgr. Award; **Personal Statement:** Childhood filled with the uplifting "Beauty of Words" they awaken all the joys of the world are meaningful and fated and full of God.

Author: Thomas L. Haines; **Birthplace:** Lewistown; **Occupation:** Customer service specialist; **Hobbies:** Photography, computer programming, wrestling and all sports; **Memberships:** Safety Team Recruiting Committee W. E. W. F; **Spouse's Name:** Jeni Haines; **Children:** 1; **Education:** Lewistown Area High School; **Personal Statement:** Thank you Jeni–Robert who are my bestest. Hi Mom! Hi Dad! love ya guys. Josh Whitman and Eric Huvane– we're too sweet.

Author: Mable Hale; **Birthplace:** Pikeville, TN; **Occupation:** Retired school teacher; **Hobbies:** Crafts, music, writing poetry, sewing and raise flowers; **Education:** Graduated from Tenn. Tech College; **Honors:** Math Medal in high school, Middle Honor Roll in college; **Awards:** Math Medal; **Personal Statement:** This poem "A Dear Friend" is a true to life experience that has happened to me during the last 9 months.

Personal Profiles

Author: Florence Halvorson; **Birthplace:** Brocket, ND; **Occupation:** Retired School Teacher; **Hobbies:** Quilting, plastic crafts, embroidery and crochet; **Memberships:** St Simon & Jude Catholic Church; **Spouse's Name:** Rudolph; **Children:** 5; **Education:** College – teaching certificate; **Awards:** State Fair ribbons for crafts

Author: Doreene Hanks; **Birthplace:** Placerville, CA; **Occupation:** Live–in Caregiver; **Hobbies:** Collect crystals, woodwork, painting, sketching & designing; **Memberships:** Literary Guild; **Children:** 2; **Grandchildren:** 1; **Education:** Graduated 1970 El Dorado Union High – Placerville; **Awards:** 1974 "Most Comical"; **Published Works:** "Here's Why", "Not Alone" and Golden Poet & Silver Poet; **Personal Statement:** As the years of my life progress, so do my wisdom and courage. I've lived many different types of styles and had a great variety people cross my path. All in all I'm a happy and content woman, and anxious to find more and more.

Author: Jean Harrell; **Birthplace:** Syracuse, NY; **Occupation:** Homemaker; **Hobbies:** Arts and crafts– music and writing; **Children:** 6; **Grandchildren:** 11; **Education:** High school; **Honors:** Volunteer work with children; **Awards:** World of poetry, country creations; **Published Works:** Blue Ridge Greeting Card Co; **Personal Statement:** I have always been able to express my feelings to those I love through writing. It has been a great avenue for me throughout life.

Author: Dorothy Harris; **Birthplace:** Detroit, Michigan; **Occupation:** Nurse's aid; **Honors:** Pearl S Buck Foundation Award Cerificate; **Awards:** Foundation for Exceptional Children Award Certificate; **Personal Statement:** It is nice to be able to put a thought, inspiration or viewpoint into a verse, saying or poem.

Author: L. F. Harris; **Pen Name:** L. F.; **Birthplace:** Illinois; **Occupation:** Secretary/Bartender; **Hobbies:** Reading, writing, music and traveling; **Personal Statement:** Writing has always been a special friend. I'm happy to be able to share this, and I hope it brings a smile to everyone.

Author: Jonathan Hart; **Birthplace:** London; **Occupation:** Studying for "A" Levels in Sixth Form; **Hobbies:** Writing, music, socialising etc.; **Education:** 9 GCSE'S, and 3 Prospective "A" Levels; **Honors:** 9 GCSE'S; **Personal Statement:** If I have accomplished anything from this, let it be my footprints in the sands of time. My thanks to God for such an opportunity.

Author: Barbara Ann Hartley; **Birthplace:** Castleford, West Yorks; **Occupation:** Disabled; **Hobbies:** TV, writing, two pet dogs; **Memberships:** Poetry Guild; **Education:** Airedale Mixed Schools; **Personal Statement:** Those hard times are true life of my late father 50 years as an underground miner at Wheldale Colliery. The poem just falls into place and rhymes of my memories in those days and any more like him.

Author: Laura Harville; **Birthplace:** LaGrange, GA; **Occupation:** Hairstylist, Mother; **Hobbies:** Reading, writing, painting, spending time with my 2 boys; **Memberships:** Beta Sigma Phi, Church, WMU, PTO; **Spouse's Name:** Joseph Harville; **Children:** 2; **Education:** High School, still working on college; **Personal Statement:** My writing comes from my heart. Experience, joy, sadness, gratitude, and love all take form with a pen and paper. In writing my thoughts flow freely and honestly. I thank God for each and every day. God Bless!

Author: George Hatzell; **Birthplace:** Penalosa, Kansas; **Occupation:** Food Service; **Hobbies:** Reading, bowling, golf, dancing and also Indian Pow Wows; **Education:** Motel Manager Training School, Los Angeles, CA and Lewis Hotel School, Washington, D. C.; **Honors:** Two Diplomas in Hotel Management; **Awards:** First Place in 4–H Projects in Liberal, KS (when younger); **Personal Statement:** Indian Prayer... Great Spirit, grant that I may not criticize my neighbor until I have walked a mile in his moccasins.

Author: Linda Hayes; **Birthplace:** Birmingham; **Occupation:** Housewife; **Hobbies:** Sewing, walking, aromatherapy and reading; **Spouse's Name:** Peter Hayes; **Children:** 2; **Education:** Turves Green Girl's School, Birmingham; **Personal Statement:** "Putting my thoughts into words eased the despair and suffering, following my nervous breakdown. I hope others will gain strength and inspiration from this!!"

Author: Becky Hedrick; **Pen Name:** Becky; **Birthplace:** Buckhannon, WV; **Occupation:** Fiberglass Plant (PPG Industries); **Hobbies:** Writing, working puzzles, country music, dancing; **Memberships:** United Way, American Red Cross, Video Stores; **Children:** 2; **Education:** High School Diploma; **Awards:** Award for Perfect Attendance, Girl Scout Awards; **Personal Statement:** I love to write poetry. I always write what's in my heart and when I write I'm usually sad and heartbroken.

Author: Heather Heimbaugh; **Birthplace:** Harrisburg, PA; **Occupation:** Full–time student; **Hobbies:** Playing sports, exercising and writing poetry; **Education:** Majoring Special Education and minoring in Psychology at Lock Haven University; **Personal Statement:** Writing poetry is the best way for me to express my feelings, hopes, and dreams.

Author: James Herring; **Birthplace:** Boonville, MO; **Occupation:** Photographer; **Hobbies:** Reading, photography, movies, music, cooking, collect wines; **Memberships:** Lifetime NRA, Professional Photographers Association; **Education:** A. A. degree, Kempen Military School & College; **Personal Statement:** Of all the things I've lost and found and all that I don't have, my writing will always be with me.

Author: Lisa Hoback; **Birthplace:** Nashville, TN; **Occupation:** Self–employed; **Hobbies:** Writing, gardening, arts and crafts; **Spouse's Name:** Eddie Hoback; **Children:** 2; **Honors:** Dean's List; **Personal Statement:** Addictions can cause heartache for everyone. Not just to the addicted. Honest communication can heal. If you can't say it aloud, write it! It works.

Author: Kimberly Hoff; **Birthplace:** Concord, MA; **Occupation:** Actor; **Hobbies:** Hiking, camping, and old movies; **Education:** Graduate Fitchburg State College and New Theater Conservatory; **Honors:** Magna Cum Laude; **Awards:** Richard J Freeman Award; New Theater; **Personal Statement:** There is nothing more freeing than writing from the heart, writing of all that fills it.

Author: Alanna Holder–Riches; **Birthplace:** Winnipeg, Manitoba, Canada; **Occupation:** Hairdresser/Teacher; **Hobbies:** Writing songs, children's stories, screenplays and singing; **Spouse's Name:** Darrell Riches; **Children:** 1; **Education:** Grade 12, post graduate, advanced hairstyling; **Honors:** Outstanding Achievement for Teacher Excellence; **Awards:** Numerous hairdressing related awards; **Published Works:** A column in community newspaper titled: "Hair Talk"; **Personal Statement:** I try to be the best that I can be whether it be writing, teaching, or at home with my family. I hope that my writing will one day touch the hearts and minds of the people who may be able to take it farther than I.

Author: Annzzetta Holmes; **Birthplace:** Kansas; **Hobbies:** Music, travel and learning; **Children:** 4; **Grandchildren:** 3; **Personal Statement:** God deals with our souls thru His son and His spirit. If only we as men and women could look into our souls and learn discernment.

Author: Jeffrey J. Horan; **Birthplace:** Shrewsbury, MA; **Occupation:** Student; **Hobbies:** Hockey, rollerblading, writing; **Education:** High School Diploma; **Personal Statement:** All hopes and dreams are useless, unless you have the ambition to pursue them.

Dreams of the Soul

Author: Donna Howland; **Birthplace:** Maquoketa, Iowa; **Occupation:** Medical records/unit secretary; **Hobbies:** Various crafts, gardening, reading, writing and billiards; **Spouse's Name:** Jim Howland; **Children:** 2; **Education:** Bellevue Community Public High School, Alantic Vo–tech; **Personal Statement:** Inspired by a small–town life. Special people who are in my life in many ways. By God's grace in which life is bound.

Author: Jessica Hughson; **Pen Name:** Jesse L. Hughson; **Birthplace:** Nebraska City, NE; **Occupation:** Student; **Hobbies:** Writing poems and stories; **Education:** High School (9th Grade); **Awards:** Gentle Award; **Personal Statement:** I find writing as a way to express feelings I'm too shy to state. My inspirations are Shakespeare and my mother. Also, Princess Di for her caring ways.

Author: Loette M. Hull; **Pen Name:** Loette Marie; **Birthplace:** Panama City, FL; **Occupation:** Homemaker/Writer; **Hobbies:** Crocheting, gardening and fishing; **Memberships:** 2 garden clubs; **Spouse's Name:** Timothy; **Children:** 3; **Grandchildren:** 1; **Education:** Completed 2 years Bible college in Chicago, training as a minister in the Salvation Army; **Personal Statement:** I enjoy being a homemaker, but a part of me has wanted to be a writer for many years now. Maybe it's time.

Author: Perdita Carman Humphreys; **Birthplace:** Bancroft, Nebraska; **Occupation:** Retired farmer; **Hobbies:** Sewing, reading and woodworking; **Memberships:** Fairfield Community Church, American Mothers, Inc Farm Bureau; **Spouse's Name:** Widowed; **Children:** 3; **Education:** High school graduate; **Personal Statement:** I love the rhythm of poetry. Writing and reading it brings me great satisfaction and relaxation.

Author: Heather Huskey; **Birthplace:** Vandalia, Illinois; **Education:** Vandalia Community High School; **Personal Statement:** Writing poetry allows me to release all the deep hidden feelings I keep from the public. Goal: write for a musician or magazine.

Author: Maria J. Imperiale; **Birthplace:** Queens, New York; **Occupation:** Office Manager; **Hobbies:** Writing, piano, reading, poetry, sports, music and crafts; **Education:** Bachelor's of Science in Communication Arts at St John's University; **Personal Statement:** Once you have found your way to express, never settle for anything less.

Author: Sally K. Jablonski; **Birthplace:** Chassell, Michigan; **Occupation:** Housewife, Poet, Writer; **Hobbies:** Needlework, reading, writing, and crafts; **Spouse's Name:** Jerry D. Jablonski; **Children:** 4; **Grandchildren:** 2; **Education:** High school, medical trade schools, and some college; **Personal Statement:** Now is the start of my new life and self–fulfillment. Poetry is a view into my inner being.

Author: David R. Jacks; **Birthplace:** Chester; **Occupation:** Teacher/Director of Studies, King's School Worcester; **Hobbies:** Music, gardening, decorating, computers, beer, Wrexham F. C.; **Spouse's Name:** Sheena; **Children:** 2; **Education:** University of Wales, Aberystwyth, B. A. Hons History; **Personal Statement:** I have found it very difficult to get children to write poetry unselfconsciously; I decided to lead by example.

Author: Stephanie M. Jacoby; **Birthplace:** Straudsburg; **Occupation:** Student; **Hobbies:** Poetry and art; **Education:** Attending Jr. High School; **Personal Statement:** Writing poetry is the best way for me to express my feelings and thoughts. My heart was always touched by William Shakespeare's Romeo and Juliet.

Author: Carol Jaxson–Jager; **Birthplace:** Dayton, OH; **Occupation:** Speech Pathologist; **Hobbies:** Windsurfing, astronomy, photography and writing; **Memberships:** Numerous professional organizations; **Education:** B. S. Miami University, M. Ed. Xavier University, Ed. Sp. Vanderbilt Univ., doctoral candidate Barrington University; **Honors:** Many; **Awards:** Many; **Published Works:** My favorite is "Is A Hospital Do A Strange Animal Be"; **Personal Statement:** Why strive to be like others; let others strive to be like you!

Author: R. J. Jesson; **Pen Name:** Rosemaris Jesson/R. J.; **Birthplace:** Burlington, Vermont; **Occupation:** Owner of furniture store; **Hobbies:** Writing poetry, horseriding, dancing, singing & voiceovers; **Memberships:** Chamber of Commerce, College Station, TX; **Spouse's Name:** Maxwell Jesson; **Children:** 3; **Education:** Kent College, Kent England; **Awards:** International Poetry Society– Certificate of Achievement; **Published Works:** International

Author: Lisa J. Johnson; **Birthplace:** Charlotte, NC; **Occupation:** Freelance artist, homemaker; **Hobbies:** Hiking, swimming, aerobics, art work, playing w/ my children; **Spouse's Name:** Douglas E. Johnson; **Children:** 2; **Education:** 2 yrs– art instruction school, 1 yr Guilford Tech Community College; **Honors:** 4 Certificates of merit, 1 gold key; **Published Works:** "The Vow"–Nat'l Library of Poetry, "My Mom"– best poems of 1996 Nat'l Library of Poetry, "Still A Dreamer"– anthologies; **Personal Statement:** I find great enjoyment from writing every poem. My husband and my 4–yr–old son have been the inspiration for several poems.

Author: Roy Johnson; **Birthplace:** Merna, NE; **Occupation:** Retired Truck Driver and Airplane Builder; **Hobbies:** Flying, writing manuscripts, and songs; **Memberships:** National Chaplains Association; **Spouse's Name:** Harriet M. Johnson; **Children:** 1; **Education:** Five Years Bible College and a Paralegal; **Honors:** Established Song Writer, and A Full Chaplain; **Awards:** Song Writers, and Story Writing Actual And Fictional; **Published Works:** Songs and a manuscript ready to be published; **Personal Statement:** Goal as a writer and of songs and I give to the needy and children that need help.

Author: Natasha R. Johnson; **Pen Name:** Renee Alexander; **Birthplace:** Inglewood, CA; **Occupation:** Accountant; **Hobbies:** Traveling, cooking and reading; **Education:** Graduate of Dillard University, New Orleans, LA; **Honors:** Honor roll, Albert W. Dent Scholarship; **Awards:** 4 year academic scholarship; **Personal Statement:** Poetry is an expression of everyday life. Writing poetry has allowed me to share my thoughts with the world, for this I am truly grateful.

Author: Mel Johnson; **Pen Name:** Robert Wesley; **Birthplace:** Amaville, Texas; **Occupation:** Retired FM, US Coast Guard; **Hobbies:** Stamp collecting, writing science fiction/horror; **Memberships:** Life member D. A. V. Vietnam Veteran AARP; **Spouse's Name:** Carolyn M. Johnson; **Children:** 3; **Grandchildren:** 1; **Education:** Graduated from Livermore High School class of "63"; **Honors:** Studied with Institute of Children's Literature "92"; **Awards:** Voted Famous Poet, Editor's Choice Award; **Published Works:** Across the Universe and Frost at Midnight; **Personal Statement:** I feel that if you're born with the God–given talent to write stories and poetry, then you should use it, or lose it. I was inspired by Faulkner, Steinbeck and Hemingway.

Author: Ella Johnson–Bentley; **Birthplace:** Cascade, MT; **Occupation:** Professional Beadwork Artist; **Hobbies:** Quilting and painting; **Spouse's Name:** Jim; **Children:** 3; **Grandchildren:** 4; **Education:** High school; **Published Works:** Published in four beadwork books; **Personal Statement:** I believe all of my original work, whether poetry or beading, is divinely inspired.

Author: Nellie M. Johnston; **Birthplace:** Bartlesville, OK; **Occupation:** Pursuing B. A. Degree in Spec. Ed., L. D.; **Memberships:** Seventh–Day Adventist Church, Salvation Army Home League; **Spouse's Name:** Tommy; **Children:** 2; **Education:** Bartlesville College High School, Rogers State College, currently at Northeastern State University; **Published Works:** The Apple Pie; **Personal Statement:** I was born August 4, 1952 to George R. and

Personal Profiles

Flora Ann Moland. I was married on January 30, 1972. My children's names are Tommy Jr. and Margie Ann. All of my poetry is inspired by God, whom I love dearly.

Author: John E. Jones; **Birthplace:** Memphis, TN; **Hobbies:** Inst. music; **Memberships:** National Humane Educational Society; **Education:** High school graduate; **Honors:** Honorable Mention – "Sunset Stroll"; **Published Works:** "Camp American Legion", "Peace", "Today"

Author: Joanna Jones; **Pen Name:** J. Jones; **Birthplace:** St. Louis; **Occupation:** Project Consultant; **Hobbies:** Travel, cooking, writing, photography and reading; **Memberships:** Sigma Xi, Scientific Research Society; **Education:** M. A. Urban Affairs, St. Louis University; **Honors:** Good Apple Teacher of the Year Nominee, 1994; **Awards:** St. Louis University Academic Fellowship, 1996–1997; **Personal Statement:** ... And the words and thoughts on the page were mine to hold for time and eternity.

Author: Shirley Jones; **Birthplace:** Hazlehurst, GA; **Hobbies:** Reading, writing, swimming, bowling, square dancing, biking; **Memberships:** Who's Who For International Business Women; **Spouse's Name:** Kenneth R. Jones, Sr.; **Children:** 5; **Grandchildren:** 5

Author: Kimberly Kang; **Birthplace:** Wahiawa, Hawaii; **Occupation:** Junior, Leilehua High School; **Hobbies:** Writing, reading, soccer, running, student government; **Memberships:** Leo club secretary; **Education:** Junior– attending Leilehua High School; **Honors:** Best in physical science, outstanding leader, sc foundation; **Awards:** Masonic lodge citizenship award; **Personal Statement:** I believe appreciation is the most vital value everyone should display. Thanks to my cousin, I'm striving to be the best I can be.

Author: Bert Kanwit; **Birthplace:** Lynbrook, Long Island, NY; **Occupation:** Retired Surgeon; **Hobbies:** Writing poetry, playing piano, working out at "Y" 4x a week; **Memberships:** Int. Society Of Poets (distinguished member); **Spouse's Name:** Janet; **Children:** 6; **Grandchildren:** 12; **Education:** AB University Of Michigan, 1937, MD Harvard, 1941; **Honors:** Medical Corp US Navy, Certified Amer Bd Of Surgery, 1951; **Published Works:** Int. Society Of Poets anthology, 1997; **Personal Statement:** Focus on love and justice and need rather than greed!

Author: Steve Kauffman; **Birthplace:** Lewistown, PA; **Occupation:** Writer; **Hobbies:** Photography, reading, looking – and trying to see; **Education:** University Of Maine, bachelor of university studies; **Published Works:** "A Book About The Book" will be published by Hazelden (spring of 1998); **Personal Statement:** I'm inspired by the same spirit that inspires us all. I'm influenced by the person behind the poem. I say, say more with less.

Author: Roger Dale Keeney; **Birthplace:** Louisville, KY; **Occupation:** Student at Iroquois High School; **Hobbies:** Playing piano, writing stories & poetry, classical music; **Memberships:** The National Beta Club, PTSA; **Education:** Graduating senior of 1998; **Honors:** Student Of The Month in Business First's, Honor Roll; **Awards:** 4. 0 GPA Award, academic awards in math, science, english, SS; **Personal Statement:** I'm glad I express my feelings in poetry and music rather than in violence, like the world does today. Psalms 145:11; Praise The Lord, Jesus Christ!

Author: Janet T. Kimmons; **Pen Name:** Janet Tyrrell Kimmons; **Birthplace:** Proctorsville, VT; **Occupation:** Housewife; **Hobbies:** Writing, crocheting, reading, knitting and travel; **Spouse's Name:** Roger Kimmons; **Children:** 7; **Grandchildren:** 19; **Education:** 2 years of college; **Personal Statement:** Poetry can tell a story and tell us a little about the author. Poetry is one way I express my thoughts.

Author: Rebecca Kindred; **Pen Name:** Becca Kindred; **Birthplace:** Allentown, PA; **Occupation:** Student; **Hobbies:** Concert and marching band, jazz band and piano lessons; **Education:** 9th grade student at Kutztown High School; **Honors:** County Band and State Piano Recital; **Personal Statement:** Watching my grandma confront Alzheimer's has been very difficult but I have come to cherish the many fond memories we shared together.

Author: Michele King; **Pen Name:** Christian Witness; **Birthplace:** Grand Rapids MI; **Occupation:** Wife, Mother, Licensed Practical Nurse, Pharmacy Tech; **Hobbies:** Praying, singing, walking and reading; **Spouse's Name:** Mark; **Children:** 2; **Education:** Kelloggsville High School, Grand Rapids Community College nursing program; **Honors:** Being wife, mother and daughter of God; **Personal Statement:** After the death of our youngest son, Nathan, my growth and feelings were best expressed through poetry. God moved my spirit to write, so I did.

Author: Linda King; **Birthplace:** New Haven, East Sussex; **Occupation:** Undergraduate BA– Primary teacher; **Hobbies:** Interior decorating, painting, gardening & swimming; **Spouse's Name:** Rodrick King; **Children:** 2; **Education:** Currently a student at the University of Brighton – BA in Education with OTS; **Honors:** I hope so!; **Awards:** A BA degree next year!?; **Personal Statement:** I am inspired by the works of Seamus Heaney; I hope the children I teach are inspired to write poetry through me.

Author: Anthony J. King, Jr.; **Birthplace:** Corpus Christi, TX; **Occupation:** Attending College; **Hobbies:** Run track, listen to Gospel Music; **Memberships:** Prairie View A & M Poetry Club; **Education:** High school graduate, freshman at Prairie View A & M University

Author: Akia Knight; **Birthplace:** Virginia; **Personal Statement:** I am in love with Marques Barrett Houston, if you're out there, please I need to meet you. I love you!

Author: Katherine Koldenhof; **Pen Name:** Kathy Weathers Koldenhof; **Birthplace:** Mooresville, NC; **Occupation:** Self–employed; **Hobbies:** Travel, creative writing, writing and reading poetry; **Memberships:** National Female Executive's Association; **Spouse's Name:** Henrick J. Koldenhof; **Education:** High school; **Honors:** Honorable Discharge Army/USAR; **Awards:** Army Service Ribbon; Marksman (Rifle); **Personal Statement:** I am a hopeless romantic, to me love is the strongest, most complete and fulfilling emotion possible, without love, lifecan never truly be lived.

Author: Laina Kontautas; **Pen Name:** Laima V. Kontautas; **Birthplace:** Lithuania; **Occupation:** Cosmetologist; **Hobbies:** Poetry, reading and writing; **Memberships:** The French Libary, Blacksmith House, and Lithuanian Club; **Spouse's Name:** Feliksas Kontautas; **Children:** 3; **Grandchildren:** 1; **Education:** Junior College; **Honors:** Award of Merit Certificate, Who's Who in Poetry (twice); **Awards:** Golden Poet of World of Poetry

Author: Andrew Joseph Kos; **Birthplace:** Detroit, MI; **Occupation:** Teacher of English & Humanities; **Hobbies:** Water sports; **Memberships:** Phi Kappa Phi; **Spouse's Name:** Pranom; **Children:** 2; **Education:** Ph. D. in english; **Honors:** Many; **Awards:** Thompkins Novel Award; **Published Works:** Hamlin (a novel); **Personal Statement:** It will soon be too late.

Author: Rita M. Krieger; **Birthplace:** Black Lick, PA; **Occupation:** Registered nurse; **Hobbies:** Writing, reading, visiting my children; **Children:** 6; **Grandchildren:** 12; **Education:** Blairsville High School and Conemaugh Valley Memorial Hospital School of Nursing; **Published Works:** My Five Boys, My Daughter, and I Love Him So; **Personal Statement:** I love to express myself on paper, whether by poetry of short story.

Author: Sherry Kulowryi; **Birthplace:** Savoorga, AK; **Occupation:** Housewife; **Hobbies:** Writing; **Spouse's Name:** Isaac Kulowryi;

Dreams of the Soul

Children: 6; **Grandchildren:** 1; **Education:** 10th Grade; **Personal Statement:** I write with my feelings and with the actions that I see around me, and I have this sensational satisfaction when I do.

Author: Brian M. Ladd; **Birthplace:** Tidworth Hants; **Occupation:** Retired civil servant; **Hobbies:** Walking, crosswords; **Spouse's Name:** June Doreen; **Children:** 6; **Grandchildren:** 14; **Education:** Saleman Misionary college, Shrigley Park Mr Macclesfield; **Published Works:** "Thoughts Of Shropshire", Voices From The West Country

Author: Laura Larcombe; **Birthplace:** Hemel Hempstead, Herts; **Occupation:** Youth Leader; **Spouse's Name:** Mervyn D. Larcombe; **Children:** 2; **Education:** "A" Level, Psychology, Theatre Studies, English Literature; **Published Works:** In two anthologies published by Forward Press; **Personal Statement:** I have always enjoyed writing poetry since a child and find writing and reading other people's work a wonderful, cathartic form of personal expression.

Author: Esther LaTour; **Pen Name:** Hadassah LaTour; **Birthplace:** Sulphur, Louisiana; **Occupation:** Meter Reader; **Hobbies:** Reading, sewing, and traveling; **Memberships:** Zion Holy Church of all Nations; **Children:** 4; **Grandchildren:** 6; **Education:** Andon College, Lincoln High School; **Personal Statement:** If you had the knowledge and wisdom of old age what great things might then be accomplished along with the power of youth.

Author: Mark Leblanc; **Birthplace:** Fitchburg, MA; **Occupation:** Warehouse manager; **Hobbies:** Golfing, fishing, traveling; **Spouse's Name:** Carol Leslanc; **Children:** 2; **Grandchildren:** 1; **Education:** Fitchburg High School, University of Maryland; **Awards:** Air force commendation medal; **Personal Statement:** Most times I think more than write, that should change. I draw much strength from my wife, without whom, my heart would've never found words.

Author: Terri LeGrande; **Birthplace:** Springfield, Missouri; **Occupation:** Sales Associate; **Hobbies:** Crafts, interior decorating; **Spouse's Name:** Chuck Legrande; **Children:** 3; **Education:** Graduated on Honor Roll–Central High School; **Personal Statement:** Poetry helps me express my fears, goals, wishes and dreams.

Author: Karen Lester; **Birthplace:** Munae, IN; **Occupation:** Babysitter; **Hobbies:** Miniature golf, playing organ, latch hook and ceramics; **Spouse's Name:** Larkin Lester; **Education:** 12 grade, GED; **Honors:** Poetry; **Published Works:** "Get Yourself Out of Bed"; **Personal Statement:** Life is like a mystery puzzle, my pieces were missing. God had them in his hand. My life is now beautiful.

Author: Steve Lewis; **Birthplace:** Tonasket, WA; **Occupation:** Laborer; **Hobbies:** Fishing; **Education:** Graduated Oroville High School; **Personal Statement:** I enjoy expressing my feelings, observations of nature, and eventful situations in life through poetry.

Author: Lauren Lewis; **Birthplace:** Fairbanks, AK; **Occupation:** Housewife, mother; **Hobbies:** Writing, swimming, reading; **Spouse's Name:** William Lewis; **Children:** 1; **Education:** Some college; **Published Works:** A poem dedicated to my father published in the library of congress anthology "Spirit Of The Age"; **Personal Statement:** My son is very special to me. It means a great deal to me that my poem to him has been chosen to be published. His name is Brandon.

Author: Leonora Lewis–Stratford; **Birthplace:** England; **Occupation:** In the process of starting own business; **Hobbies:** Raising angel fish (hope to turn this into a business); **Memberships:** The Conservancy, Florida Sheriff's Association; **Spouse's Name:** Steve; **Education:** Accounting; **Personal Statement:** I worked most of my life as an accountant. I was a DJ at one time. Just returned from two years in Australia, where I taught aborginals. Studying now with Institute Of Children's Literature.

Author: Ruth Renee Little; **Birthplace:** Helena, Arkansas; **Occupation:** Medical Laboratory Technician; **Hobbies:** Reading, fishing, hunting and being with my family; **Spouse's Name:** Cleadus Ray Little; **Children:** 3; **Education:** Graduated Phillips County Community College; **Honors:** Distinguished High School Students; **Personal Statement:** In loving memory of our brother Johnny, July 24, 1953 – April 21, 1997. We love and miss you. From Ginger, Paula, Joe, Renee.

Author: Elizabeth B. Long; **Birthplace:** Harrisburg, PA; **Occupation:** Clerk typist retired; **Hobbies:** Interior decorating and cooking; **Spouse's Name:** Lester (deceased); **Children:** 2; **Grandchildren:** 2; **Education:** High school, attended business school; **Awards:** Silver and Gold "World of Poetry"; **Published Works:** Newspaper; **Personal Statement:** Writing is like peeping into another's soul and letting a bit of sunshine through. Then you paint your picture with words until they can understand.

Author: Nina Lysher; **Birthplace:** Jackson, WY; **Occupation:** Retired; **Hobbies:** Reading, Volunteer work; **Awards:** Volunteer Work; **Published Works:** Poem, The Heart Garden; **Personal Statement:** Special influences are from a close friend. Reading scriptures gives me inspiration.

Author: Cashel Mack; **Birthplace:** St. Louis, MO; **Occupation:** Swimming coach, Florida State University; **Hobbies:** Kayaking, music, taking care of pets (2 dogs, 2 cats); **Memberships:** American Swimming Coaches Association, USS, and CSCAA; **Education:** Bachelor of Education (elementary) Drury College; **Honors:** Florida Swimming Age Group Coach of the Year 1996; **Personal Statement:** I wrote this poem while in high school and experiencing the divorce of my parents. I just recently revised it for this competition.

Author: Johnny Lee Madden; **Birthplace:** Breckenridge, Texas; **Occupation:** Field Service Supervisor (Security); **Hobbies:** Reading and writing; **Memberships:** Distinguished Member of International Society of Poets; **Education:** A. A.; **Honors:** Elected 1997 into International Poetry Hall of Fame; **Awards:** Honorable Mention and Editor's Choice Award; **Published Works:** Nine poems published in Anthology; **Personal Statement:** "Poetry is not something you do after you've finished something else. It's what won't let you finish anything else." John Holmes; Writing Poetry.

Author: Amie Mann; **Pen Name:** Rose Mann; **Birthplace:** Battambang; **Occupation:** Secretary; **Hobbies:** Tennis, volleyball, gymnastics; **Memberships:** National honor society and California scholarship federation; **Children:** 3; **Education:** Graduated from high school and trade school; **Honors:** Graduated with honor from high school and trade school; **Awards:** Perfect attendance award from high school and trade school; **Personal Statement:** I like to write romantic and rhyme poems during my spare time. I hope I will become a poet writer someday.

Author: Clare S. Marder; **Pen Name:** Clare Sleeth Marder; **Birthplace:** Ft Lauderdale, Florida; **Occupation:** Perpetual Student, Counselor; **Hobbies:** Writing, reading, painting, sports, music and antiques; **Memberships:** AAMFT; **Children:** 2; **Education:** B. A. Psychology, certified hypnotherapist; working on M. S. in Marriage & Family Therapy, & Holistic Health; **Honors:** Dean's list; **Awards:** Most Contributive to Class– awarded poetry book; **Personal Statement:** Writing is like giving birth... the finished product is the delivery and creating it is the fun.

Author: Jim Marshall; **Pen Name:** Jim Marshall; **Birthplace:** Lincolnshire; **Occupation:** Retired Detective Chief Superintendent, Sussex; **Hobbies:** Gardening, sport – Royal British Legion, Burma Star Assoc; **Spouse's Name:** Bette Monica Marshall; **Children:** 2; **Grandchildren:** 4; **Education:** Spalding Grammar School; **Honors:** Queen's Police Medal for Distinguished Service;

Personal Profiles

Published Works: The True Story of The Ollie Murder (Book), Emma's Special Wish (Poem); **Personal Statement:** I strongly believe people matter.

Author: Mary Martin; **Birthplace:** Guy, AR; **Occupation:** Cosmetologist; **Hobbies:** Bowling and reading; **Spouse's Name:** Richard Martin; **Children:** 2; **Grandchildren:** 6; **Education:** High school graduate and Beauty College of AZ; **Personal Statement:** When God says write these words, you write them. I started writing May 1997. Have written four more poems since then. To God be the glory.

Author: Laurabelle Martin; **Birthplace:** Jackson County, MN; **Occupation:** Teacher, real estate owner and farmland operator; **Hobbies:** Travel, antiques, sewing and writing poetry; **Memberships:** American Legion Aux., Historic Renville Preservation Com.; **Education:** B. S. at Mankato State University; **Honors:** Who's Who of Midwest, America, World, plus 14 others; **Awards:** Listed in the International Edition of 500 Notable Women; **Published Works:** Treasure to Share, What Is Your Message, Lingering Memories and research articles for H. R. P. C.; **Personal Statement:** To succeed in whatever we desire to do in life we must be good managers. How we use our time, how well we apply ourselves on the job and how we spend our money will determine the level of our success.

Author: Marlene Martin; **Birthplace:** Lamar, MO; **Occupation:** Factory worker; **Hobbies:** Sewing, gardening and crafts; **Memberships:** Church; **Spouse's Name:** Kessler Martin; **Children:** 7; **Grandchildren:** 5; **Education:** 12 years; **Personal Statement:** Writing poetry just comes to me like a gift God gave me. I write around 4 a year, since 1989.

Author: Vickie Maryon; **Birthplace:** Kansas City, MO; **Occupation:** Business Management, Sales, Cosmetology; **Hobbies:** Cooking, gardening, writing; **Memberships:** Institute of Children's Literature; **Spouse's Name:** Gary A. Maryon; **Children:** 3; **Education:** 2 Yrs Jr College, Coosa Valley Tech; **Personal Statement:** Writing gives confirmation and validity to our emotions and thoughts. Poetry is the river from which all feelings flow from one to another.

Author: Nancy Carol Mascaro; **Birthplace:** Lansdale, PA; **Occupation:** Office Manager; **Hobbies:** Writing poetry, drawing, collecting "Mickey" items; **Spouse's Name:** William; **Children:** 2; **Published Works:** Published in a Delicate Balance

Author: Shellie Mayer; **Birthplace:** Missoula, Montana; **Hobbies:** Writing and playing sports; **Memberships:** Altor Society; **Spouse's Name:** Darrin Mayer; **Children:** 2; **Education:** High school graduate; **Honors:** The birth of my children; **Personal Statement:** I've been inspired by my experiences in life. I have a great passion for writing. I hope to touch others as they have touched me.

Author: Teresa McCran; **Birthplace:** Tranent; **Occupation:** Housewife; **Hobbies:** Swimming, painting, model gnomes; **Spouse's Name:** Deceased; **Children:** 5; **Grandchildren:** 9; **Education:** Tranent Second; **Awards:** Only school prizes

Author: J. A. McCrea; **Birthplace:** Cross Pointe, MI; **Occupation:** Accountant; **Hobbies:** My animals, arranging furniture; **Memberships:** Humame Society; **Education:** Michigan State University and Walsh College; **Honors:** Gold Key in Poetry, Scholarship from the Detroit Press Club; **Awards:** Thespian for Drama; **Personal Statement:** I have been writing poetry since I was eight years old, have worked on many publications of poetry, have thousands of poems in boxes in my closet.

Author: Mary C. McDaniels; **Birthplace:** Neenah, Wisconsin; **Occupation:** Retired teacher, Inn keeper; **Hobbies:** Volunteer for abused children, art, music, poetry, dolls; **Memberships:** Tough Love leader, Western Dance Assoc. and NEA; **Spouse's Name:** Ron McDaniels; **Children:** 2; **Grandchildren:** 1; **Education:** B. S. in Education, minor in Spanish, University of Wisconsin; **Honors:** Editor the Rocket, Kappa Delta Pi, Gamma Sigma; **Awards:** Poster Awards, Bulletin Board Awards, Magna Gum Laude Grad.; **Published Works:** Spokesman– Review, Prime Time Magazine articles; **Personal Statement:** When I look into your eyes, I see God's little angel watching me. You're all that ever was and all that is to be.

Author: Jared McLaughlin; **Pen Name:** Chester Kat; **Birthplace:** Seattle, WA; **Occupation:** Bartender; **Hobbies:** Music, computers, billiards, hiking, astronomy, reading; **Education:** Graduated Hylton Senior High School; **Personal Statement:** Poems are my release as I have tinnitus. I hope to publish more works in progress. My influential poets are Robert Burns and Lewis Carroll.

Author: Ruby M. Merritt; **Birthplace:** Holden, West Virginia; **Occupation:** Retired; **Hobbies:** Writing and reading; **Memberships:** Song Writers Guild of America; **Children:** 4; **Grandchildren:** 10; **Education:** High school; **Honors:** Accepted as lyric writer; **Awards:** Certificate of Lyricists; **Published Works:** Poem "Odie and Me"; **Personal Statement:** Inspirations from God. Bought books and studied how to structure a song or poem. Two record companies have recorded four of my lyrics.

Author: G. R. Messinger; **Pen Name:** Grrr; **Occupation:** Electrician in Training; **Hobbies:** Play soccer in high school; **Education:** Junior in High School; **Honors:** Lettered 2 years in Soccer; **Awards:** St Jude Children's Hospital Marathon; **Published Works:** Mom; **Personal Statement:** This poem is my feelings I have for the game of soccer.

Author: Wretha Meyers; **Birthplace:** Inavale, NE; **Occupation:** Have done many jobs; **Hobbies:** Crocheting, embroidery, sewing, reading, writing & puzzles; **Spouse's Name:** Deceased; **Children:** 5; **Grandchildren:** 9; **Education:** 12th grade, 12 weeks Normal School; **Personal Statement:** Cook, bookkeeper, all–around worker in self–owned business (food) 35 years. Shelved writing course for family, business. Wanted to be nurse, write many diaries of life experiences.

Author: E. Middleston; **Birthplace:** Pool Dorset; **Occupation:** Gardener; **Hobbies:** Jogging, swimming; **Memberships:** Hamworthy Royal British Legion; **Spouse's Name:** Susan Hiddleston; **Children:** 4; **Grandchildren:** 8; **Education:** Secondary Modern; **Awards:** Ed's Choice Awrd 1997 for poetry – Int'l Library of Poetry; **Published Works:** Six other poems published by Arrival Press; **Personal Statement:** I love to put my thoughts down, and if it gives as much pleasure as I get then I think I have achieved something.

Author: Margareta G. Mihal; **Birthplace:** Akron, Ohio; **Occupation:** Certified Home Health Case Assistant; **Hobbies:** Writing short stories, poetry and playing guitar; **Spouse's Name:** Ron Mihal; **Education:** High school graduate, some college and language school in Austria; **Awards:** Silver Poet Award 1986, World of Poetry; **Personal Statement:** At the age of 8, I discovered a "God–given" talent. A gift to write from my heart and soul. My goal is to share it.

Author: Kelly M. Miles; **Birthplace:** Hopewell, VA; **Occupation:** Student at Hopewell High School; **Hobbies:** Writing poems, reading, playing piano, bead work, animals; **Memberships:** Beta Club, Forensics; **Education:** Sophomore at Hopewell High School; **Honors:** Plaque for academic achievement (coach's award); **Awards:** 1 forensic silver medal, trophies for baseball, ballet, tap; **Personal Statement:** My goal is to get my poems (100), stories (4), plays (2) and short stories (6) published in a book of my own.

Author: Janice Miller; **Birthplace:** Mattoon, IL; **Occupation:** Homemaker; **Hobbies:** Writing, traveling and gardening; **Memberships:** 3438 Eagles Club, Allenville CWF; **Spouse's Name:** Larry; **Children:** 2; **Grandchildren:** 2; **Education:** High school,

Dreams of the Soul

some college, course in floristry; **Published Works:** Articles in our daily paper; **Personal Statement:** I'm a country girl, who enjoys people, family gatherings, grandkids and cooking for the family.

Author: Patricia Miller; **Birthplace:** Glasgow, KY; **Occupation:** Retired; **Hobbies:** Crocheting, gardening and fishing; **Children:** 5; **Grandchildren:** 7; **Education:** GED; **Personal Statement:** I owe my love of poetry to my English teacher in high school, Mrs. Saunders.

Author: Mary A. Miller; **Birthplace:** Circleville; **Occupation:** Property processing specialist; **Hobbies:** Flower arranging and travel; **Education:** High school; **Personal Statement:** Writing is an expression of the heart. I love writing to encourage others. And admire Helen Steiner Rice.

Author: Latise D. Minnicks; **Pen Name:** Necie or Black Pearl; **Birthplace:** Virginia; **Occupation:** Teacher Assistant– English; **Hobbies:** Singing, writing poetry, fishing alone, and drawing; **Memberships:** Young Authors Club, Book Club; **Spouse's Name:** Roderick Ellison; **Children:** 2; **Education:** George Wythe High School graduate; **Honors:** Most Outstanding Journal, Best Stage Performance; **Awards:** English Award, Outstanding Scholastic Award; **Personal Statement:** Throughout my life, I've always felt alone, and to avoid making any crazy decisions, I decided to put all my thoughts and feelings down on paper.

Author: Ivan Mirosevic; **Pen Name:** Barcos De Croata; **Birthplace:** Velaluka, Croatia; **Occupation:** Marine engineer; **Hobbies:** Fishing, inventions; **Memberships:** The society of naval architects and marine engineers; **Spouse's Name:** Karenza; **Children:** 2; **Education:** Technical college; **Awards:** Several Editor's Choice awards (ISP)– poetry; **Published Works:** Pending; **Personal Statement:** That ship of homeland far away, which was left once in total darkness, will sail, seas of centuries, if given guidance the knowledge and compass of leadership.

Author: Helena Miszta–Lane; **Birthplace:** Poland; **Occupation:** Biologist; **Hobbies:** Reading, movies and theatre; **Spouse's Name:** Philip Lane; **Education:** Tagiellonian University, Cracow, Poland; **Honors:** The Ministry of Science; **Awards:** University President's Award; **Published Works:** Professional publications

Author: Chris Moat; **Birthplace:** Canterbury, Kent; **Occupation:** Geography teacher; **Hobbies:** Photography, writing, painting and travel; **Education:** B. A. Nottingham; **Published Works:** Articles in various periodicals, poem in Nothing Left Unsaid; **Personal Statement:** Inspired by Landscape and the natural world

Author: Marcella Morey; **Birthplace:** Monticello, Iowa; **Occupation:** Civil Service Retiree; **Hobbies:** Sewing, reading and gardening; **Memberships:** Bethany Presbyterian Church; **Spouse's Name:** deceased; **Children:** 4; **Grandchildren:** 12; **Education:** High school

Author: Amethyst Mirage; **Pen Name:** Amethyst M. Mirage; **Birthplace:** Tokyo, Japan; **Occupation:** Customer service; **Hobbies:** Music, making dream catchers & American Indian Hist, writing; **Memberships:** Racine Sister City Program; **Education:** B. A. International Relations, minor Political Science; **Awards:** VW Parkside Wind Ensemble Grant; **Personal Statement:** Maybe we can learn something from Star Trek, Klingons were federation enemies in the original series, eventually they became allies and senior officers in Star Fleet.

Author: Alexandra Moser; **Birthplace:** Baltimore, MD; **Occupation:** Student; **Education:** Currently in college; **Personal Statement:** Poetry is the window through which my soul takes flight; close it and I am imprisoned.

Author: Margaret Muir Colligan; **Pen Name:** Tammy or Candy Floss; **Birthplace:** Saline, Fife, Edinburgh; **Occupation:** Housewife; **Hobbies:** Writing, inventing, love dancing; **Children:** 4; **Grandchildren:** 7; **Education:** Ordinary, Left School 14 Years Old; **Personal Statement:** Hoped for achievement in life, fame etc. Often inspired as if from the heavens. Read, dance, think, romantic, honest. I feel God's presence. Heart attack (coma) He spoke Jesus, vision of Him.

Author: Richard Lee Nettleton; **Birthplace:** Monks Gleigh, Suffolk; **Occupation:** Partner, Security Firm; **Hobbies:** Fossil collecting, computers and writing; **Memberships:** Literary; **Spouse's Name:** Ruth Marion; **Children:** 1; **Education:** Secondary, Stove by Nayland; **Awards:** Literary, SM, Army; **Personal Statement:** While visiting a local churchyard, I noticed that every stone was unknown to me. We should all strive to leave something, my writing began.

Author: Lisa G. Newell; **Pen Name:** Lisa Verduft Newell; **Birthplace:** Harbor City, CA; **Occupation:** Cosmetologist; **Hobbies:** Writing music, playing guitar, and writing poetry; **Children:** 3; **Education:** Ontario High, College, Pharmacology, Cosmetology; **Personal Statement:** My influences and philosophical viewpoints are (life is of change and change is of life) which means change with life and you will grow.

Author: Patricia O'Brien Parker; **Birthplace:** Beloit, Wisconsin; **Occupation:** Co–owner Classical Glass– a neon shop; **Hobbies:** Reading, writing, theater, shopping and traveling; **Memberships:** Delta Psi Omega, Evergreen Foursquare Church; **Spouse's Name:** Michael J. Parker; **Children:** 2; **Grandchildren:** 1; **Education:** Graduated with B. S. in Social Welfare – University of Wisconsin; **Awards:** Crisco Outstanding Homemaker as a high school student; **Published Works:** "Rocky River Anthology, Eat Your Mind – The Whistler, The Jester; **Personal Statement:** I've been stringing words together since I was little and would ask my mom to write them down for me. Writing has always been a very big part of who I am. My poems express and reflect my inner thoughts and tell what my soul and spirit feel.

Author: Shirley O'Reilly; **Birthplace:** Kentucky; **Occupation:** Medical Clerk at Luke AFB Hospital; **Hobbies:** Quilting; **Memberships:** Women's Federal Employee Association; **Spouse's Name:** Danny; **Children:** 2; **Grandchildren:** 3; **Education:** AA degree, medical office management, currently seeking a degree in english; **Awards:** Administrative Employee Of The Year, Luke Air Force Base; **Personal Statement:** Since being influenced to pursue writing by teachers during high school, I have written my thoughts and experiences on paper. This in itself is the reward; the written word. Poetry is a tangible way to see a person's feelings.

Author: Colette M. O'Reilly; **Birthplace:** Liverpool; **Occupation:** Public House and Restaurant Manager; **Hobbies:** Music, yoga and writing poetry; **Children:** 2; **Education:** Secondary Modern School "St Margaret Mary's"; **Personal Statement:** I have no awards or honours but I have my strong beliefs. I find putting them into poetry gives me personal satisfaction.

Author: Kevin L. Oakwood; **Birthplace:** Lancaster, PA; **Occupation:** Building Maintenance; **Hobbies:** Golf, motor sports and keeping fit; **Education:** High school graduate and trade school graduate; **Personal Statement:** My thoughts, experiences of life are common and personal as they appear to me, only to shame our society. Family and friends influence me.

Author: Rosa Maria Ochoa; **Birthplace:** Valles, S. L. P. Mexico; **Occupation:** Housewife; **Hobbies:** Handcrafts, writing poems and theatre performance; **Spouse's Name:** Humberto Gonzalez; **Children:** 4; **Education:** Dentist DDS. Graduate; **Personal Statement:** God is my inspiration

Author: Annette Mercedes Oliva; **Pen Name:** Mercedes Oliva; **Birthplace:** Ventura; **Occupation:** Assistant as cashier; **Hobbies:** Writing poetry, and drawing; **Education:** 2nd year at Oxnard

Personal Profiles

College; **Honors:** Who's Who among american high school students 1992–96; **Published Works:** "If You Judge Me" in twentieth century poets anthology; **Personal Statement:** My poems are a way for me to express my views, beliefs and feelings. Some of my poems are written in memory of my friends.

Author: Elaine Overton Bulger; **Birthplace:** Pell City, AL; **Occupation:** Collection adjustor; **Hobbies:** Dancing, gardening and crafts; **Spouse's Name:** Stephen Bulger; **Children:** 2; **Education:** Graduate of Vincent High School, Shelby County, School of technology; **Honors:** Dean's list; **Personal Statement:** Writing poetry is my way of putting emotions on paper that otherwise would go unsaid, and unnoticed. My favorite poet is Maude Muller.

Author: Charlotte L. Palmer; **Birthplace:** Rugby; **Occupation:** Student; **Hobbies:** Swimming, acting and books; **Education:** Currently at senior school

Author: Erika Pascoe; **Pen Name:** Eureka; **Birthplace:** Las Vegas; **Occupation:** Student; **Hobbies:** Dancing, cheerleading, talking on the phone; **Personal Statement:** My motto is: "other people's money"

Author: Gail Christie Patten; **Pen Name:** Gail Christie; **Birthplace:** Dayton, Ohio; **Occupation:** Insurance Agent/Broker; **Hobbies:** Sewing, writing, reading, angel dolls and channeling; **Children:** 1; **Personal Statement:** This poem is about the fact that it does not matter who my biological father is, because God is my father.

Author: Elana Payne; **Pen Name:** Sheree Morgan; **Birthplace:** Independence, MO; **Occupation:** Secretary at Elementary School; **Hobbies:** Reading, writing, basketball; **Memberships:** MSTA; **Spouse's Name:** Jack J. Payne; **Children:** 5; **Education:** High school graduate; **Honors:** Salutatorian of my graduating class, First Miss Hickory Coun; **Awards:** ty; **Personal Statement:** Writing can be an excellent form of therapy. Sometimes you can write what you can't seem to say verbally. Poetry seems to run in my family.

Author: Wayne E. Pearson; **Birthplace:** Royersford, PA; **Occupation:** Retired Chemist; **Hobbies:** Water ski, hike, golf and reading; **Memberships:** Unitarian Church; **Spouse's Name:** Mary Lee; **Children:** 3; **Grandchildren:** 5; **Education:** BS in chemistry Ursinus College, Collegeville, PA; Physical Chemistry at University Of Delaware

Author: Geoffrey Persten; **Pen Name:** 113806; **Birthplace:** Woodridge, New York; **Occupation:** Insurance Loss Control Consultant; **Hobbies:** Antique autos; **Spouse's Name:** Cheryl Persten; **Children:** 2; **Education:** Orange County College; **Personal Statement:** Writing poetry has always fueled my desire to be creative.

Author: Eileen Petano; **Birthplace:** Torrington, CT; **Occupation:** Daycare worker; **Hobbies:** Playing guitar, collecting postcards and cow paraphenalia; **Spouse's Name:** Mark Petano; **Education:** Some college– working toward a degree in Early Childhood Ed.; **Awards:** I received an award for Good Citizenship when I was 11 yrs.

Author: Brenda L. Peterson; **Birthplace:** Cullman, AL; **Occupation:** Secretary; **Hobbies:** Walking and reading; **Spouse's Name:** Divorced; **Children:** 2; **Education:** Wallace State College; **Personal Statement:** I get great enjoyment out of reading and writing poetry. It expresses our inner being.

Author: Gladys Phillips O'Day; **Birthplace:** Aberdeen, WA; **Occupation:** Lawyer; **Hobbies:** Gardening, roses especially; **Memberships:** American Rose Socicty, Washington State Bar Assoc.; **Spouse's Name:** Lester E. O'Day; **Education:** University of Washington B. H. and L. L. B.; **Honors:** Valedictorian Weatherway High School; **Personal Statement:** I have always loved poetry – especially 19th century English poets Wordsworth, Keats and "Ae."

Author: Kathleen E. Phinney; **Pen Name:** Min Leore; **Birthplace:** Rockland County, NY; **Occupation:** Student at Boston University; **Hobbies:** Tennis, drawing, painting, poetry, violin, piano & acting; **Honors:** Honors Program at Boston University; **Personal Statement:** People are fragile vessels who contain fountains of knowledge and love. Be careful not to drop them.

Author: Alice Pike; **Birthplace:** Erie, PA; **Hobbies:** Poetry, crafts, cake decorating, cats, biking, shopping; **Memberships:** Senior Organizations; **Spouse's Name:** Arthur Pike; **Children:** 4; **Grandchildren:** 8; **Education:** Graduated; **Awards:** 18 ribbons– 6 first, 5 second, 2 fourth & 1 hon. mention; **Published Works:** Sparrowgrass– National Library of Poetry– Grapevine Newspaper; **Personal Statement:** My goal as a writer is to publish my own poetry book. I am inspired and influenced by my family who keep encouraging me to write. They love my poems and I enjoy writing very much. I think it's quite a talent and makes me feel proud.

Author: Melissa Pinckney; **Birthplace:** New Mexico; **Occupation:** Student/medical transcriptionist; **Hobbies:** Writing poetry, fishing and camping; **Spouse's Name:** Ronald A. Pinckney; **Children:** 1; **Education:** High school graduate, and nail technician; **Published Works:** Sounds of Thunder; **Personal Statement:** Poetry is how I have learned to express my thoughts, feelings and opinions and I would like to thank my husband for inspiring me and encouraging me to enter and publish some of my work.

Author: Imogene Pinnock; **Pen Name:** Imogene Pinnock; **Birthplace:** Kingston, Jamaica; **Hobbies:** Gardening, travel, sewing, writing letters and cooking; **Published Works:** The Amazing Grace (booklet); **Personal Statement:** Self–expression is poetry in motion, I have always admired poets. I would like to be a poet.

Author: Rebecca Ann Pinson; **Birthplace:** Albuquerque, NM; **Occupation:** Work at American Legion Auxiliary; **Hobbies:** Writing short stories and listening to music; **Memberships:** International Society Of Poets; **Education:** Graduated from Central High, May 23, 1997; **Honors:** Poetry award from Central High; **Awards:** 2 Editor's Choice Awards, National Library Of Poetry; **Published Works:** "Environment" and "Streets"; **Personal Statement:** Never be afraid of what you want. If you work hard enough, you will receive more than your heart could ever desire.

Author: Revena M. Pollard; **Birthplace:** Glover, OK; **Occupation:** Kindergarten teacher; **Hobbies:** Making crafts and writing poetry; **Memberships:** AEA/NEA; **Spouse's Name:** Dale K. Pollard; **Children:** 2; **Education:** A Bachelor's degree in elementary and art education; **Personal Statement:** Writing poetry is my way of expressing childhood memories and life's experiences. "Jumping the Moon" clearly reflects me as a child and how I felt.

Author: Donna A. Powelson; **Birthplace:** Macomb, IL; **Occupation:** Factory Assembler; **Hobbies:** Camping, reading, ceramics and cross stitching; **Spouse's Name:** Lynn L. Powelson; **Children:** 3; **Education:** Graduated Robert Morris College; **Honors:** Dean's List; **Awards:** Certificate of Achievement; **Personal Statement:** Writing poetry is like opening a window to your soul.

Author: D. C. Pratt; **Pen Name:** D. C.; **Birthplace:** Cedar Bluff, VA; **Occupation:** Retired Educational Administrator; **Hobbies:** Writing poetry, singing, church and community work; **Memberships:** Life member, Optimist Club, VA 4–H All Star, Life NEA; **Spouse's Name:** Pat; **Children:** 2; **Education:** Post grad, master arts and B. S.; **Honors:** Honorary Citizen Of Tennessee; **Awards:** Jaycee Young Educator Award, Poetry in Nat'l Anthologies; **Published Works:** Ten books of poetry, local history, 2nd child's autobiography; **Personal Statement:** Problems do not hinder the progress of an individual, but it's the attitude one has that determines failure or success. Keep trying!

Dreams of the Soul

Author: C. Antonio Provost; **Birthplace:** Colon, Panama; **Occupation:** Retired U. S. Postal Employee; **Hobbies:** Sports, volunteer exercise director at retirement home; **Memberships:** Knights Of Columbus, Nat'l Assoc Retired Federal Employees; **Spouse's Name:** Irene; **Education:** B. A. in philosophy with a certificate in gerontology; **Honors:** International Poetry Hall Of Fame; **Awards:** Poetry exhibit; http/www. poets. com/c. provost. htm; **Published Works:** The Birth Of The Modern Renaissance, The Opening Of The American Mind, Modern Renaissance, Poetry Philosophy; **Personal Statement:** My books pertaining to our social problems and philosophy, I hope will contribute toward the improvement of our nation. We need a far better system of education with a more suitable curriculum in all our schools, colleges and universities.

Author: Thomas E. Radcliffe; **Birthplace:** Webster, MA; **Occupation:** Artist; **Spouse's Name:** Elizabeth R. Radcliffe; **Children:** 4; **Grandchildren:** 3; **Education:** School of Practical Arts; **Honors:** Many art awards and one–man shows; **Personal Statement:** I am inspired by nature and history with emphasis on the good of mankind.

Author: Pamela L. Rapport; **Birthplace:** Fort Worth, TX; **Occupation:** Director of sales and marketing; **Hobbies:** Reading, fitness, travel and gardening; **Spouse's Name:** Jack; **Children:** 2; **Grandchildren:** 4; **Education:** High School; **Personal Statement:** My poetry is a new discovery that allows me to express my deepest emotions. The value of this gift doubles when my words touch another.

Author: Rebecka Reber; **Birthplace:** St Geoerge, Utah; **Occupation:** Retail sales clerk; **Hobbies:** Crafts and football; **Children:** 3; **Personal Statement:** I want the world to know, I have a voice and I choose to use it. Please, find your voice and express yourself.

Author: Daisy W. Reel; **Birthplace:** Alto, GA; **Occupation:** Housewife; **Hobbies:** Writing, gardening; **Spouse's Name:** Eura; **Children:** 3; **Grandchildren:** 14; **Awards:** Editor's Choice Award; **Published Works:** Daily Support; **Personal Statement:** Thanks to my husband for allowing me to spend so much time at my desk. And to my father for his inspiring encouragement.

Author: Stephanie P. Reisnour; **Birthplace:** Honolulu, Hawaii; **Occupation:** Student; **Hobbies:** Reading, ballet, softball, clarinet, chorus, and writing; **Education:** Hawkins Elementary School, in 5th grade; **Personal Statement:** I've wanted to be a writer ever since I could hold a pencil. I hope to be a professional writer someday.

Author: Briana Reissener; **Birthplace:** Bridgeport, MI; **Occupation:** Student; **Hobbies:** Role–playing, hacky sack and dance; **Education:** 6th grader at Bridgeport – Spaulding Middle School; **Honors:** Honor Roll; **Awards:** Principle Award; **Personal Statement:** Sometime the best stories are the ones that are never written down.

Author: Spunky; **Pen Name:** Spunkey; **Birthplace:** Tuscaloosa, AL; **Occupation:** Cook; **Hobbies:** Fishing and reading; **Spouse's Name:** Otis; **Children:** 4; **Grandchildren:** 2; **Education:** High school; **Personal Statement:** I never say what I can't do I just focus on what I can. Always smile.

Author: Carol Richardson; **Birthplace:** Tompkinsville, Kentucky; **Occupation:** Gap Jeans training Field Mgr; **Hobbies:** Fishing, writing, swimming and walking; **Spouse's Name:** D. T. Richardson; **Children:** 4; **Grandchildren:** 1; **Education:** High school graduate; **Personal Statement:** I enjoy writing poems, it takes me where I want to go, I feel I am there with whoever or whatever I write about.

Author: Jeadenia Ann Roberts; **Pen Name:** Jeanie; **Birthplace:** Carmel, CA; **Occupation:** FIM operator/data entry; **Hobbies:** Art, drawing, poetry writing, looking at fashionable clothes; **Education:** High school graduate class of 1990; **Awards:** I have received numerous awards for my poetry; **Published Works:** None at this time, this shall be my first; **Personal Statement:** I thank God for my gift of writing poetry. My church (First Tabernacle Fellowship) has been a great support with my editor Lydia Robertson. Thanks!

Author: Isobel Sherrard; **Pen Name:** Isobel Sherrard; **Birthplace:** Darlaston– West Midlands; **Occupation:** Retired accounts clerk; **Hobbies:** Writing, painting (water colors), music, gardening, reading; **Spouse's Name:** Ernest Rogers; **Children:** 2; **Grandchildren:** 2; **Education:** I left school at fifteen; **Personal Statement:** All my life I have wanted to write and paint, now the time is right. I am blessed through the written word to record eternal love.

Author: Deborah Rohan; **Birthplace:** Los Angeles; **Occupation:** High school student; **Hobbies:** Track and field, drawing wildlife, hiking and cooking; **Education:** Class of 2000 at John F. Kennedy Memorial High School; **Honors:** Honor Roll; **Awards:** Conrad Award, O. S. C. O. R. Award; **Personal Statement:** I believe nature is the ultimate good. It is the source of wonder and inspiration. Take care of it!

Author: Linda Rolli; **Pen Name:** Linda Sayre Rolli; **Birthplace:** Mason City, WV; **Occupation:** Hairstylist, salon owner; **Hobbies:** Writing, walking; **Spouse's Name:** Phillip; **Children:** 5; **Education:** UCLA Voc ed; **Personal Statement:** I fell in love with poetry as a young girl. I love the romance, that comes from words written from the heart.

Author: Deanna Rorabaugh; **Birthplace:** Lynwood, CA; **Occupation:** Bishop– Senior Pastor; **Hobbies:** Painting, drawing, writing, sewing, travel, flower arranging; **Memberships:** Ariel Dear Fond., Int. Fellowship Inc., Atwater Ministerial; **Spouse's Name:** Tony A Rarbaugh; **Children:** 5; **Grandchildren:** 3; **Awards:** Sam Walton Community Leader 1997 Walmart Teacher of the Year; **Personal Statement:** Working to develop team ministry; transcending the lines of denomination, gender, race and national origin. Discovering common ground drawing together the body of Christ in unity.

Author: Tammy W. Rue; **Birthplace:** Charlotte, NC; **Occupation:** Stadium Cleaning Service; **Hobbies:** Tennis, swimming; **Memberships:** PTA; **Spouse's Name:** Michael B. Rue; **Children:** 3; **Education:** Garringer High School; **Published Works:** "Darkness" in the book, Into The Unknown; **Personal Statement:** Writing is a way to get out feelings or make believe can be put into words just as good as real life.

Author: Leah Allen Russell; **Pen Name:** Stacey Spencer; **Birthplace:** Cumberland, MD; **Occupation:** Paralegal; **Hobbies:** Reading and painting; **Education:** 2 year paralegal degree from Auburn University at Montgomery

Author: Vance Sandy, Jr.; **Birthplace:** Anchorage, AK; **Occupation:** College student; **Hobbies:** Horseback riding, fishing, writing poetry and songs; **Education:** Junior at Pittsburg State University; **Published Works:** The National Library of Poetry; **Personal Statement:** I spent 3 years in the Navy and I've seen a lot. I only write on how I feel about things.

Author: Beverly Sapienza; **Pen Name:** Bev Sapicnza; **Birthplace:** Lawerence, MA; **Occupation:** Director Env. Services; **Hobbies:** Interior decorating, writing, travel, and operas; **Memberships:** NEHA; **Children:** 1; **Honors:** To be my mother's daughter, and my son's mother; **Personal Statement:** Poetry is not necessarily rhyme and verse. It has a language all its own. It sings to those who listen.

Author: Manda Schmeling; **Birthplace:** Fairmont, MN; **Occupation:** Student; **Hobbies:** Horseback riding, basketball, carving, crafts, poetry; **Education:** Buffalo High School class of '99; **Awards:** 1st place in GFWC artwork contest; **Published Works:** In school's book called Pegasus; **Personal Statement:** My mom and I do a lot of things together and she has raised me to be what I am today. I thank her.

Author: Carlo J. Villena; **Birthplace:** Oconto Falls; **Occupation:** High school senior; **Hobbies:** Reading, writing and riding horses; **Education:** Completed most of senior year; **Awards:** Bronze metal in an agricultural program; **Personal Statement:** Go with your dreams, and don't let anyone stand in your way for what you believe.

Author: Annie L. Seabrook; **Birthplace:** Greenville, SC; **Occupation:** Retail; **Hobbies:** Sewing, cooking and writing poetry; **Spouse's Name:** Jimmy; **Children:** 6; **Grandchildren:** 6; **Education:** Graduate of Louis D. Brandeis High School; **Awards:** Editor's Preference Award of Excellence; **Published Works:** "Noise"; **Personal Statement:** My family, church and friends have been my inspiration. My goal is to eventually have my own book of poetry published.

Author: James Seado; **Birthplace:** Tacoma, WA; **Occupation:** Kitchen Coordinator; **Hobbies:** Music, drawing, philosophizing; **Memberships:** The New Lord's Society; **Spouse's Name:** Divorced; **Children:** 1; **Education:** High School; **Personal Statement:** For me poetry is the music of the heart, and my music wouldn't live without Michelle and Andy Zabroske, Chris Behrens, and my mom.

Author: Della H. Tegge; **Pen Name:** Della H. Tegge; **Birthplace:** Chicago, IL; **Occupation:** Retired; **Hobbies:** Writing poems; **Memberships:** Good Shepherd Lutheran Church; **Spouse's Name:** Louis (deceased); **Education:** 7th grade; **Awards:** Poet's silver certificate; **Personal Statement:** 100 years old and still going strong. I'm looking forward to my home in heaven, now in a nursing home. I'm very faithful.

Author: Sheri Setzer; **Birthplace:** Hickory; **Occupation:** Dishwasher, Bluffs Coffee Shop; **Hobbies:** Reading; **Children:** 3; **Education:** GED; **Personal Statement:** I love to write poems of how I feel.

Author: Jamey Shepherd; **Birthplace:** Long Island, New York; **Occupation:** Telephone Survey Conductor; **Hobbies:** Writing, reading and sports; **Education:** Graduated high school, two years of college; **Personal Statement:** I believe writing is a way to release feelings. My way of venting. I speak out to a world through my words that just won't listen when I speak. Poetry gives me freedom.

Author: N. Shew; **Pen Name:** Natalie Jane Shew; **Birthplace:** Swindon; **Occupation:** Housewife; **Hobbies:** Poetry, swimming and reading; **Spouse's Name:** Sean Fitzgibbon; **Children:** 2; **Personal Statement:** Poetry is an inner explanation of one's self and path of experiences. Both good and bad of love, joy, sadness and hope, it's individual artistry.

Author: Rhonda Shiffman; **Birthplace:** Los Angeles, CA; **Occupation:** Liaison with resource agencies for hydroelectric projects; **Hobbies:** Writing, fervent adoration of my whippet and cooking; **Education:** Graduated cum laude from San Francisco State University with a BA in geography; **Honors:** Dean's list; **Personal Statement:** We must honor our dreams for they contain our hopes, our fears and our answers.

Author: Jennifer Shoup; **Pen Name:** Forever & Always; **Birthplace:** PA; **Occupation:** Nursing Assistant; **Hobbies:** Reading and writing; **Spouse's Name:** Robert; **Children:** 2; **Education:** Technical Schooling; **Published Works:** Internet (WWW); **Personal Statement:** Poetry is a way to express myself and my thoughts to others and to grow as a person, wife and mother.

Author: Gerri Simon; **Birthplace:** Mansfield, LA; **Occupation:** Secretary; **Hobbies:** Casino, visiting with grandchild; **Children:** 2; **Grandchildren:** 1

Author: Linda L. Simon; **Birthplace:** Fairmont, WV; **Occupation:** Territorial Sales Mgr., Philip Morris U. S. A; **Hobbies:** Painting and crafts; **Spouse's Name:** Marion D. Simon; **Children:** 3; **Grandchildren:** 1; **Education:** BS Degree in Education; **Personal Statement:** Putting my thoughts and feelings down on paper has inspired and encouraged an incentive to live and experience life on a daily basis.

Author: Gertrude Ann Slater; **Birthplace:** Shippenville, PA; **Occupation:** Housewife, Mother, Grandmother, Clerical; **Hobbies:** Writing, reading, traveling, needlework, antique dishes, etc; **Memberships:** Ceres United Methodist Church, Oswayo Valley Lions Club; **Spouse's Name:** William; **Children:** 6; **Grandchildren:** 5; **Education:** Keystone Joint High School, Knox, PA; **Personal Statement:** I strive to glorify God in my writings. Writing poetry expresses my inner–most feelings. I also enjoy writing poetry about birds and animals.

Author: Linda Smathers; **Birthplace:** Sweetwater, TN; **Occupation:** Homemaker; **Hobbies:** Arts, crafts and gardening; **Spouse's Name:** Wayne Smathers; **Children:** 3; **Education:** McMinn High School, Knoxville Business; **Personal Statement:** My mother loved writing poetry and reading her poems brings back special memories. I would like this to be in memory of her.

Author: Sean Smith; **Birthplace:** Alldershot; **Occupation:** Civil Engineer; **Hobbies:** Writing lyrics for songs, hand–sketched portraits, painting; **Spouse's Name:** Amanda Skelton; **Children:** 1; **Education:** "O" Level Art; **Personal Statement:** Unfortunately, my rebellious youth turned down further education. Now older, wiser, I've rediscovered my natural talent and only write what I feel strongly about.

Author: Aldrema Smith; **Birthplace:** New Orleans, LA; **Occupation:** Deputy Recorder; **Hobbies:** Viewing classical movies; **Memberships:** Sigma Gamma Rho Sorority, Girl Scouts Of America; **Spouse's Name:** Cedric; **Children:** 3; **Education:** Attended University Of New Orleans; **Honors:** Basileus of Gamma Pi Chapter of LSUNO; **Personal Statement:** Anyone hoping to endure, must have support. I thank God for Cedric Sr., Ced Jr., Drema, Jonathan, Brenda, Sherolyn and Arthur. You are solid!

Author: Glenna Smith; **Birthplace:** Hico, Texas; **Occupation:** Legal Assistant; **Hobbies:** Volleyball, piano, writing poems from past and present; **Memberships:** N. P. O. Memorial Fund, Veterans of Foreign Wars; **Spouse's Name:** Terry McKinley; **Children:** 1; **Education:** Graduated Midland College, Associates of Applied Science, Major Legal Assistant; **Awards:** Pauline Slater for Piano competition, awards & certificates; **Published Works:** The Explosion, My Parents, My Friends; **Personal Statement:** A special thank you to my parents, friends and Terry for all your help. For helping through some tough times in my life, and for your influences that have helped me grow stronger. I thank God for the inspiration and spiritual healing.

Author: Carrie Somerton; **Birthplace:** Vancouver, Canada; **Occupation:** RCMP, Royal Canadian Mounted Police, clerk; **Hobbies:** Needlework, genealogical research; **Children:** 2; **Grandchildren:** 3; **Education:** College (at age of 50); **Personal Statement:** Working on history and research on maternal grandfather who was one of the original northwest mounties during the turn of the century and the infamous northern gold rush.

Author: Doris Steeber; **Birthplace:** Manitowoc; **Hobbies:** Travel and reading; **Spouse's Name:** Joseph Steeber; **Children:** 3; **Grandchildren:** 3; **Education:** Graduated Mishicot High School;

Dreams of the Soul

Published Works: In newsletters; **Personal Statement:** My goal as a writer is to have my children's books published. Life is beautiful in the eyes of a child. Envisage life like children

Author: Judy A. Stevens; **Pen Name:** Judy Stevens; **Birthplace:** Binghamton, NY; **Occupation:** Nurse; **Hobbies:** Crafts, puzzles and my grandchildren; **Memberships:** PTA; **Spouse's Name:** Kenneth Stevens; **Children:** 2; **Grandchildren:** 2; **Education:** High school and nursing school; **Personal Statement:** I think that life should be experienced to the fullest never say no to trying something new. Like poetry I tried it, and it's fun and you never know what you'll come up with.

Author: Beverly A. Still; **Birthplace:** Passaic, New Jersey; **Occupation:** Domestic engineer; **Hobbies:** Writing, reading, crafting, collecting teddy bears & camping; **Children:** 1; **Education:** Some high school; **Awards:** Golden Poets Award; **Published Works:** Homeless Souls; **Personal Statement:** Poetry speaks of the heart and soul

Author: Amanda Anne Stirn; **Birthplace:** Louisiana; **Occupation:** Bookkeeper; **Hobbies:** Musician, interior design and gardening; **Spouse's Name:** Michael Stirn; **Children:** 2; **Education:** Spokane Falls Community College; **Personal Statement:** Words can breathe life into those whose lives are empty.

Author: Karissa Storer; **Birthplace:** Billings, MT; **Occupation:** Student; **Hobbies:** Writing, reading and skating; **Education:** Sagebrush Elementary, Central Middle, Carey Junior High; **Honors:** Gifted Program, Honor Roll; **Awards:** Young Author's Contest; **Personal Statement:** My friends have been a tremendous influence and inspiration for most of my poems.

Author: Helen L. Strom; **Birthplace:** Pittsburgh, PA; **Occupation:** Retired Secretary; **Hobbies:** Writing, knitting and needlepoint (I create my own designs); **Children:** 3; **Education:** High school graduate; **Honors:** Graduated 4th in class of '66 – Honor Student; **Awards:** Editor's Choice Award for poem "Pandemonium"; **Published Works:** Three poems published in "Lutheran Ambassador" (Christian magazine); **Personal Statement:** It is a privilege and a gift; taking ordinary words and arranging them into a thing of beauty... that might somehow help another human being.

Author: Mildred Supe; **Birthplace:** Cincinnati, Ohio; **Occupation:** Housewife; **Hobbies:** Travel, reading, sewing and cards; **Memberships:** Church Business Assoc., Historical Society and eight clubs; **Spouse's Name:** Frank Supe; **Children:** 1; **Grandchildren:** 3; **Education:** high school and night school; **Honors:** Spelling, sewing and one prize for a poem entry; **Awards:** The 1997 "Outstanding Citizen Award" from our city; **Personal Statement:** "Outstanding Citizen Award" reads "a Lifetime of Dedication to the Citizens of Mt Healthy." Accompanied by a proclamation from the mayor made me feel very special.

Author: Jonathan Swift; **Birthplace:** Mountain Park, NC; **Occupation:** Student; **Hobbies:** Tennis and outdoor activities; **Personal Statement:** I dedicate my poem "The World War Solider" to my grandfather, Sgt. James T. Simmons, United States Army. Leader of PeaceFreedom, and Humanity

Author: Alice Jane Tally; **Birthplace:** Indianapolis, IN; **Occupation:** Housewife; **Hobbies:** Gardening, canning, writing, reading; **Spouse's Name:** Robert M. Tally; **Children:** 2; **Education:** 9th Grade; **Personal Statement:** In my life my greatest joy has been helping others to overcome problems in doing so I have helped myself overcome shyness and an abused past.

Author: Angel Taylor; **Pen Name:** Anja Taylor; **Birthplace:** Beaver County, PA; **Occupation:** High School Student; **Hobbies:** Writing; **Memberships:** Hopewell High School Yearbook; **Education:** Freshman in high school with the gifted class; **Awards:** Certificate from Johns Hopkins Univ. for SAT scores, grade 7; **Published Works:** A poem "Mask Of Emotions"; **Personal Statement:** Never let life stop you. Make your choices to the best of your ability and life will reward you.

Author: Ann Tedder; **Birthplace:** Robeson County, NC; **Occupation:** Retired English Teacher; **Spouse's Name:** Sam; **Children:** 4; **Grandchildren:** 7; **Education:** Masters in teaching english from Duke University

Author: Melissa S. Thompson; **Birthplace:** Midland, Michigan; **Occupation:** Teller; **Hobbies:** Singing, poetry, basketball and softball; **Spouse's Name:** Steve Paul Thompson; **Education:** Some college, graduated from Arena Eastern High School; **Honors:** Who's Who Among American High School Students; **Personal Statement:** My husband and mother have been the most influential people in my writing. They have always encouraged me to believe in myself and my talents.

Author: Beverly R. Thompson; **Birthplace:** Washington, DC; **Occupation:** Legal secretary; **Hobbies:** Playing with my grandchildren and my two dogs; **Children:** 3; **Grandchildren:** 7; **Education:** High school graduate

Author: Steve Thurman; **Birthplace:** Oregon City, OR; **Occupation:** UPS driver; **Hobbies:** Hiking, camping, mountain biking and collecting collectibles; **Spouse's Name:** Jacqueline; **Education:** High school; **Personal Statement:** In high school my biggest fear was English. Somehow over the years I was able to express myself through poetry. We all have a gift within.

Author: Geraldine Tiboldo; **Birthplace:** New York City; **Occupation:** Homemaker; **Hobbies:** Baking, reading, writing, arts & crafts; **Memberships:** International Society of Poets; **Spouse's Name:** Lawrence; **Education:** B. A. degree in Psychology; **Honors:** ISP Poet of Merit for 1997; **Awards:** One Editor's Choice Award; **Published Works:** Several poems published in different poetic anthologies; **Personal Statement:** I enjoy writing and I would do it even if no one ever got to see it but me.

Author: Kim E. Tich; **Birthplace:** Minneapolis, MN; **Occupation:** Certified Medical Assistant; **Hobbies:** Writing, reading; **Memberships:** American Association of Medical Assistants (AAMA); **Spouse's Name:** Chad Everett; **Children:** 2; **Education:** St Mary's College–Special Education Courses–Medical Institute of Minnesota Associate of Applied Science Degree; **Awards:** Midwest Fed Chaparral Poets; The Polly Hart Award 10/11/75; **Published Works:** 06–25–75 Poetry published in the Mpls Sun Newspaper; **Personal Statement:** My inspiration comes from a man who has "healed" me more than he knows. A new found faith in love. Where there was once darkness comes the light.

Author: Tresa Tuinstra; **Birthplace:** Rochester, MN; **Occupation:** Part–time waitress, full time mom; **Hobbies:** Spending time with my family and writing poetry; **Spouse's Name:** Paul Tuinstra; **Children:** 1; **Education:** High school– Pine Island High, Pine Island, MN; **Published Works:** Several poems in local newspaper and in upcoming anthologies; **Personal Statement:** Writing poetry is my favorite hobby. I have been influenced by my family, the world around me and feelings that just come from within. My goal is to someday write a whole book of poetry and hopefully get it published.

Author: Diane M. Valand; **Birthplace:** Sheboygan, WI; **Occupation:** Certified nursing assistant; **Hobbies:** Writing poetry, reading, crafts and knitting; **Memberships:** The Word of Grace Church; **Education:** High school and Lakeshoe Technical College graduate; **Personal Statement:** I thank my Heavenly Father first and foremost for the inspiration he gives me to write poetry, and my friends and familywho encourage me.

Personal Profiles

Author: Laurie Ann Walker; **Pen Name:** Lauren Lane; **Birthplace:** Richland, WA; **Occupation:** Writer, Housewife; **Hobbies:** Crafts, traveling, reading, knitting; **Spouse's Name:** Anthony W. Walker; **Children:** 3; **Education:** A. C. Davis High School, Yakima Valley Community College; **Awards:** Grace Shannon Taylor Scholorship; **Personal Statement:** Poetry is a gracious gift expressing the world and life around us. Browning and Frost are an inspiration to me.

Author: Glenn Isaac Ward; **Pen Name:** Glen Allen Ward; **Birthplace:** Morehead, KY; **Occupation:** Self–employed; **Hobbies:** Music, art and literature; **Education:** Graduate of National Tech. of Literature; **Honors:** Advanced Research (two terms); **Awards:** Valedictorian; **Published Works:** Letters, lyrics and papers; **Personal Statement:** In letters and lyrics, you expressed your most profound love. In war, you were a worthless fantasia.

Author: Donnie Watson; **Birthplace:** Richmond, KY; **Occupation:** Former County Judge Executive – Present Factory Foreman; **Hobbies:** Music and gardening; **Spouse's Name:** Monique; **Children:** 5; **Grandchildren:** 4; **Education:** High school

Author: Jamilla Webb; **Birthplace:** Washington, DC; **Occupation:** High School Student; **Hobbies:** Playing piano, kickball, writing, learning, helping everyone; **Memberships:** Poetry Club, National Junior Honor Society (95–96); **Education:** Sophomore at Banneker Senior High in Washington; **Honors:** Magna Cum Laude Award in the National Latin Exam; **Awards:** 1st place science fair trophy (92–94), 4th place chemistry; **Personal Statement:** My inspirations come from God, the new and old earth, family, friends, relationships, the seas and plants, education and most of all music, dreams and love.

Author: Heather Weeks; **Birthplace:** Sawyer, Michigan; **Occupation:** Student; **Hobbies:** Writing poetry; **Education:** Attending Pickerington High School; **Published Works:** The World's Wisest and War; **Personal Statement:** Poetry is one of the most inspiring forms of writing. If there is something that must be said, poetry is one of the best ways to say it.

Author: Timothy A. Wellman, Jr.; **Pen Name:** Timothy D. Wellman, Jr.; **Birthplace:** Minneapolis, MN; **Hobbies:** Music, art, and writing; **Education:** Still in High School, 10th Grade; **Personal Statement:** I want to become an accomplished musician, artist and writer.

Author: Patricia Werdebaugh; **Pen Name:** Mourning Dove; **Birthplace:** Hagerstown, MD; **Occupation:** Homemaker; **Hobbies:** Crafts, writing poems, embroidery, reading; **Memberships:** A. A. R. P.; **Spouse's Name:** David Lee Werdebaugh; **Children:** 5; **Grandchildren:** 15; **Education:** High School; **Published Works:** Newspapers and National Library of Poetry Book; **Personal Statement:** I like to express my thoughts and feelings in my poems for others to read and enjoy and I would love to have more of my poems published.

Author: LaTonya Lynn West; **Birthplace:** Port Arthur, Texas; **Occupation:** Columnist for Thimco's Christian Newspaper/Evangelist; **Hobbies:** Reading, writing and cooking; **Memberships:** The Church of Jesus Christ; **Education:** Graduate of Lincoln High School and Lamar University with B. S. degree in Sociology; **Awards:** Editor's Choice Award for Outstanding Achievement in Poetry; **Published Works:** The Gospel Thru Poetry, published in 1996; **Personal Statement:** I received 1st place trophy in adult division poetry contest at the Nancy Shepard's Arts Ensemble in Lake Charles. Co–cordinator of Poetic Recital Presenting the Gospel Thru Song, Music, Poetry & Drama (annual event)

Author: Ken R. Weybrecht; **Pen Name:** The Wizard; **Birthplace:** Ravenna, Ohio; **Occupation:** Writer; **Hobbies:** Travel, thrill seeker, taking insight on the world; **Spouse's Name:** Tina M. Weybrecht; **Children:** 1; **Education:** High school graduate; **Personal Statement:** To take the chance will suppress opportunities of progress as well as limit one's growth. Limiting the views of a fuller picture of life. So to all I ask take the chance and learn.

Author: Marilyn Whelton; **Birthplace:** Noma, FL; **Occupation:** Homemaker; **Hobbies:** Sewing, crafts, and camping; **Spouse's Name:** Roger; **Children:** 4; **Grandchildren:** 5; **Education:** Bay County High School; **Published Works:** Unknown Grandchild; **Personal Statement:** My deceased mother is my inspiration and the encouragement from my husband, keeps me writing.

Author: Jermaine Whirl; **Birthplace:** Charleston, SC; **Occupation:** Student; **Hobbies:** Wrestling, football, basketball, beating drums; **Memberships:** Church abundant life Church of God in Christ; **Education:** 7th grade, James Island Middle; **Honors:** Honor roll, academic award; **Awards:** Football, school, science, english, reading, math awards; **Published Works:** Desert, Wrestling; **Personal Statement:** My goal as a writer is to write the best taught poems. I really do love wrestling and I wrote a long poem about wrestling.

Author: Brenda G. Whitaker; **Birthplace:** Columbus, GA; **Occupation:** Disabled; **Hobbies:** Play piano, painting and gardening; **Spouse's Name:** George B. Whitaker, Sr.; **Children:** 5; **Grandchildren:** 4; **Education:** Graduated Columbus Vocational Technical School, 2 Yrs Univ of Mississippi towards a Business Associates Degree; **Published Works:** National Library of Poetry – Portraits of Life; **Personal Statement:** During an illness, the Lord touched my heart and gave me the words for my first poem. I've been writing His words ever since.

Author: June Whitehouse; **Birthplace:** Langley; **Occupation:** Processing input operator; **Hobbies:** Poetry; **Spouse's Name:** Clive Whitehouse; **Children:** 2; **Grandchildren:** 4; **Education:** Secondary school; **Personal Statement:** My poetry is based on my own life experiences. Also experiences of family and friends. I try to keep my poetry very simple.

Author: Patricia Williams; **Birthplace:** New Orleans, LA; **Occupation:** Senior Fiscal Specialist; **Hobbies:** Traveling, reading, writing and evangelistic work; **Memberships:** Lilly of the Valley Society; **Education:** Graduated from Southern University in Accounting and BRE in Religion; **Honors:** Dean's List; **Awards:** Valedictorian, Readers Digest, S. Central Bell Science Award; **Personal Statement:** Writing motivates readers to view life realistically and gives hope to the despair; one's experience can be an asset to another realizing his/her goal or dream. I wish to become a famous writer. I give God the glory, it's a gift.

Author: Hubert D. Williams; **Pen Name:** Bud Williams; **Birthplace:** Scranton, NC; **Occupation:** Retired 20 yrs. Vet. U. S. Military; **Hobbies:** Writing poetry and philosophical short stories; **Memberships:** Masonic Order, Poetry Guild, Philosophical Society; **Spouse's Name:** Sally; **Children:** 2; **Grandchildren:** 6; **Education:** BA Metaphysics from University of Metaphysics, Los Angeles Ph. D. M. D. Th.; **Personal Statement:** Mortal's fears, anger, hate, love, wants, needs, and desires, are all expressed in accordance with one's own developed degree of understanding one's own illusions.

Author: N. Williams; **Pen Name:** Segutie Melekot; **Birthplace:** London; **Occupation:** Counsellor/Community and Youth Worker; **Hobbies:** Drawing, telling stories, walking, travel; **Memberships:** Pan African Grassroots Educational Network; **Children:** 3; **Grandchildren:** 1; **Education:** London University Goldsmiths Community and Youth Work Certificate; **Published Works:** Ripples an Anthology, Brothers, Pain; **Personal Statement:** Words are powerful, and poems have always made me love life on a spiritual level.

Author: Deborah Christine Williams; **Birthplace:** Ft Ord, California; **Occupation:** Homemaker; **Hobbies:** Writing poetry and reading; **Spouse's Name:** Richard Williams; **Children:** 3; **Education:** High school graduate, 2 yrs. of Junior College, currently

Dreams of the Soul

studying Medical Transcription; **Personal Statement:** Most of my poems are written from my heart about my children and my husband. They are my inspiration. Special thanks to my father.

Author: Robert Earnest Wilson; **Birthplace:** Los Angeles, CA; **Occupation:** Construction Manager; **Hobbies:** Soccer coach, boating, jet skiing and writing; **Memberships:** International Union of Operating Engineers; **Spouse's Name:** Beverly Jean; **Children:** 3; **Grandchildren:** 7; **Education:** A. A. in Construction Management; **Honors:** Dean's List 4. 8 GPA, US Navy Commendation Medal; **Personal Statement:** My inspiration comes from real life. Dad was an Arizona cowboy, mom an Oklahoma Cherokee. You just can't get more down to earth than me.

Author: Linda Wilson; **Birthplace:** Flushing, NY; **Occupation:** Registered nurse; **Hobbies:** Theatre, film, skiing; **Memberships:** New York State nurses assocation; **Education:** Graduated with a BSN–Hunter College, C. U. N. Y. (Cum Laude); **Honors:** Sigma theta tau; **Awards:** Grand St. Boys foundation (1969); **Personal Statement:** My poems give voice to my inner life. They inspire, challenge and heal me. They are an ongoing revelation of possibilities.

Author: Cheryl A. Wilson; **Pen Name:** Sherry Crosby; **Birthplace:** Clarksburg, WV; **Occupation:** Customer Sales Service Rep; **Hobbies:** Writing poetry, traveling, writing short stories; **Memberships:** Methodist Church, The National Library of Poetry; **Spouse's Name:** Edward Ray Wilson; **Children:** 4; **Grandchildren:** 6; **Education:** High school, beauty school and 2 years of college; **Honors:** National Honor Society; **Awards:** Golden Poetry Awards 3 times; **Published Works:** 4 poems in the National Library of Poetry, Golden Poetry Award; **Personal Statement:** It's my belief that as we travel down life's paths, each problem that we encounter is preparing us for a greater task in the future.

Author: Stephanie Lynn Wise; **Birthplace:** Nelsonville, OH; **Occupation:** Homemaker; **Hobbies:** Writing poetry and songs, singing; **Spouse's Name:** William; **Education:** Trimble High School; **Honors:** Honors Day 11th Grade; **Awards:** Scholastic Awards in English, 1st Place Salesmanship; **Published Works:** She is My Mother, True Romance May 1988 Edition; **Personal Statement:** The greatest inspiration for my poetry has been Christ. May His love shine through my writings. Also my husband who encourages me to write.

Author: Loring W. Wiseman; **Pen Name:** Sonny Wiseman; **Birthplace:** Belton, TX; **Occupation:** Retired; **Hobbies:** Writing poetry and photography; **Children:** 6; **Grandchildren:** 8; **Education:** High school; **Published Works:** "The Great Outdoors"; **Personal Statement:** Strive for the preservation of wildlife and wildlife habitat for our children and their children.

Author: Amalean Witherspoon; **Birthplace:** Allegheny County, NC; **Occupation:** GMAC retiree; **Hobbies:** Hand embroidery, reading, and watching tennis; **Memberships:** YWCA, Old Baptist Church; **Spouse's Name:** James O. Witherspoon; **Children:** 1; **Grandchildren:** 2; **Education:** Business school; **Published Works:** Mom–Mom Joy, Footsteps In The Sand, "On Retirement" Moments Of Reflection; **Personal Statement:** Even though writings usually come out of deep feelings, words come to paper without much struggle, and there is a sense of cleansing/renewal.

Author: Vanessa Wolfe; **Birthplace:** Glendale, AZ; **Occupation:** Student; **Hobbies:** Writing, singing; **Education:** Senior at Tolleson Union High School; **Published Works:** No More Tears – Poetic Voices of America 1995, Book; **Personal Statement:** With all the hardships in my life, I've found that poetry had an escape for me.

Author: Sheila Ann Wood; **Birthplace:** Barking, Essex; **Occupation:** Housewife; **Hobbies:** Writing, I have 3 cats which I spend a lot of time with; **Spouse's Name:** John; **Children:** 2; **Education:** Secondary modern; **Personal Statement:** After a car accident, I am now unable to work, and this was why I started writing poems.

Author: Tammera S. Woodall; **Birthplace:** Fontana, California; **Occupation:** Proofreader/typist for Ogden Standard Examiner; **Hobbies:** Reading, writing, drawing, singing, dancing, hiking, camping; **Memberships:** Distinguished Member of The International Society of Poets; **Spouse's Name:** James Londas Woodall III; **Children:** 3; **Education:** Junior at Weber State University, working toward BIS, English/Psychology, Chemistry; **Honors:** I was usually on the Honor Roll & high marks for citizenship; **Awards:** 1st, 2nd and 3rd place in writing and art contests; **Published Works:** Cat–E–Chu–Men, in The Scenic Route, National Library of Poets; **Personal Statement:** I have been inspired greatly by the work of the Romantic Poets. I wish to convey the beauty and spirituality I find in my life's experiences to others through my writing and art.

Author: Natalie Joy Woodall; **Birthplace:** Adams, New York; **Occupation:** Newspaper reporter; **Hobbies:** Scuba diving, photography, genealogy, and travel; **Spouse's Name:** AAVW, MLA, American Philological Association; **Education:** Ph. D English, Syracuse University, Ph. D Classical Studies; **Honors:** W. Wilson Dissertation Fellow, Outstanding Young Woman; **Published Works:** Scholarly articles in English, Latin American and Classical Literature, newspaper articles; **Personal Statement:** I draw inspiration from the efforts of nineteenth–century poets, such as Letitia Elizabeth Landon, Felicia Hemaus and especially from feminist firebrand Elizabeth Barrett Browning.

Author: Paulette Woodard; **Birthplace:** Rome, GA; **Occupation:** Secretary with Polk School District; **Hobbies:** Music/organist, reading and enjoying my grandchildren; **Memberships:** GA. Assoc. of Educational Office Personnel; **Spouse's Name:** Dr. Joe P. Wooddard; **Children:** 2; **Grandchildren:** 2; **Education:** High school and working on my Assoc. degree in Information & Office Technology; **Personal Statement:** I've always enjoyed reading poetry. I find it a refresher from the busy world of our day.

Author: Jessica Yankee; **Birthplace:** Morristown; **Occupation:** Student; **Hobbies:** Bike riding and swimming; **Education:** Mooresburg Elementary School; **Honors:** Principal's List; **Awards:** 1st Pl in Heritage Days Art Contest, School Princess 94–95; **Personal Statement:** I write short poems at home but my goal was to get a poem published.

Author: Matt D. Zarzeczny; **Pen Name:** L. Zar; **Birthplace:** Quantico, Virginia; **Occupation:** Full–time student; **Hobbies:** Hunting, weightlifting, string bass, history, and travel; **Education:** 12th grade student at Padua Franciscan High School; **Honors:** Honor Roll; **Awards:** 3 time Scary Story Contest Winner; **Published Works:** Poem in Horizon; **Personal Statement:** Inspired by Napoleon, I wish to bring happiness to those who want to see our civilization grow grand and not collapse into darkness.

Author: Perry Zeiger; **Birthplace:** Myrtle Point, OR; **Occupation:** Automotive Service Advisor; **Hobbies:** Car racing, engine building, basketball and hot rodding; **Spouse's Name:** Rebecca; **Education:** 10th grade; **Personal Statement:** I feel that I don't have any special talent. I just write what pops into my head.

Author: Donna J. Zuk; **Birthplace:** Fall River, MA; **Occupation:** Nurse; **Hobbies:** Attend college part–time, whatever time is left I read; **Children:** 1; **Grandchildren:** 3; **Education:** College; **Honors:** I have a 4. 0 average in college; **Published Works:** The Price of Love, Just a Dream, He's Type Oh No!; **Personal Statement:** The hourglass shape of "Saying Goodbye" depicts the speed at which one's life passes. Before my hourglass runs out I want to make a difference in this world. I soon realize that every touch, hug, smile and kindness can change the world.

APPENDIX

Index of Poets

This easy-reference index of poets is an alphabetical listing of each author whose poem appears in this anthology. A quick scan of the Poet Index will tell you the full name of every poet featured in the book, followed by a page number on which the poem can be located.

A

Abbott, Jodi Anne, 43
Abel, Barbara L., 82
Abrahamzon, Bernice, 136
Achziger, Stephanie, 191
Adamo, Victor C., 167
Adams, Bernard, 249
Adams, Brinda Joyce, 231
Adams, Liliana O., 130
Adams, Mary M., 290
Adams, Theresa, 110
Addeman, Samantha, 278
Addley, Michael, 174
Adkins, Velma, 251
Agnew, Katy, 285
Ahearn, Doris B., 256
Aiello, Erin, 216
Akin, Dovie, 68
Alarcon, Sandy, 168
Alberts, George, 102
Albrechtsen, Bruce, 82
Aleksinski, Robert, 47
Alexander, Daniel, 123
Allen, Margaret, 258
Allen, Paula, 210
Allen, Sheila, 6
Allensworth, Mary Rozanna, 87
Allison, Meredith, 7
Alston, Gregory P., 28
Alwine, Ruth J., 108
Amatelli, Mark, 24
Anderson, J. L., 45
Anderson, Kirsty, 257
Anderson, Kristin, 149
Anderson, Marthalyn, 240
Andrews, Cassandra A., 70
Andrews, Wendy, 153
Andrus, W. Lee, 94
Anguiano, Lidia, 167
Ansumana, Josephine M., 13
Anthony, Sharon, 214
Antoniou, Chris, 19
Aquino, Martin M., 175
Ariente, Sr., Joseph Paul, 226
Arthur, Anthony D., 129
Arthurs, S., 232
Arwood, Abbey, 82
Asche, Dennis, 205
Ashby, Matthew, 127
Asher, Mark, 269
Ashjian, Karen, 20
Asmus, Shawna R., 267
Atkinson, Rebecca, 75
Aube, Annita, 78
Austin, Robin, 8
Axe, Celia, 96

B

Badovinatz, Rachel, 100
Baer, Sarah, 166
Bailey, Jacqui, 259
Bailey, Marlo, 228
Bainbridge, G. W., 188
Baker, Mindy, 239
Baker, Sonya Denise, 208
Ball, Edna, 233
Ballenger, Shannon M., 42
Banwell, Patricia A., 258
Barentine, Jeff P., 285
Barker, C. H., 174
Barker, Debbie A., 80
Barnes, Hilda, 92
Barnes, Kelda, 215
Barnett, Chester, 266
Barnhill, Mildred, 47
Barragato, Katherine, 65
Barrett, Erin, 97
Barrie, G., 258
Barszcz, M. P., 307
Bartee, Pat, 202
Bassett, W. H., 99
Bath, Josef T., 154
Batley, E. M., 257
Baugh, Lisa R., 199
Beadle, Y., 44
Beahan, D. T., 72
Beale, I., 247
Beasley, Evelyn, 166
Beaty, Sheila, 55
Beaubouef, Eva, 191
Beaudoin, Rebecca A., 306
Beaudoin, Robert, 197
Beaupierre, J., 236
Bebble, Lewis T., 105
Beck, Stephanie, 292
Becknel, Margaret, 223
Beckstrand, Elmer F., 246
Beckwith, Samantha, 206
Bedwell, Loretta, 155
Belanger, Dawn, 283
Belcher, Leah, 156
Belden, Katherine, 240
Bell, Anita O., 192
Bell, Cindy K., 214
Bell, E. J., 186
Bell, Eian C., 277
Bell, Kathryn E., 281
Bell, Monica, 155
Bell, Sharon, 197
Bell, Wayne S., 192
Benacs, Philippa C., 261
Bennett, Donna, 302
Bennett, Mary Kate, 106
Benson, Kiri, 285
Bente, Elizabeth M., 38
Bera, Amil A., 207
Beresford, Margaret R., 137
Bergeron Dixon, Gayle M., 135
Berghman, Toni L., 282
Bergman, Emily J., 31
Bergstrom, Ashlee, 307
Berry, A. L. W., 96
Berry, Stacy, 214
Bess, Alma L., 201
Bewley, Sean, 201
Bhojani, Judith M., 195
Bialozynski, Pamela H., 172
Bianco, Mia, 67
Billino, Gina Marie, 213
Bills, Sheila, 245
Bishop, Donald, 95
Bisset, Stephen O., 15
Bjork, Mark, 176
Blackburn, Crissie, 142
Blackburn, Pauline, 198
Blackwell, Dominic, 237
Blair, Cheryl, 131
Blaney, T., 197
Blankenship, Miranda A., 229
Blevens, Craig, 304
Blohm/Beauregard, Denise, 10
Bloms, Ginger K., 168
Bloom, Lacey, 136
Bluvshteyn, Sasha A., 16
Bohn, Marian, 284
Bonneau, Janet, 171
Borden, Evelyn M., 68
Borntreger, Daniel W., 253
Boron, Judy, 250
Boucher, Andrea C., 7
Boucher, T. M., 132
Boudreaux, Cindy, 52
Boussios, Eugenia, 263
Boutwell, Joshua, 189
Bowser, Denise A., 83
Bozeman, W. R., 207
Brackens, LaToya, 157
Bradbury, Stephen J., 69
Bradley, Traci, 299
Bradley, William, 226
Brady, Samantha N., 241
Branigan, Elizabeth K., 157
Bratcher, Patricia, 75
Brechan, Linda L., 95
Breen-Ridout, G. M., 262
Brennan, Monahan, 176
Brewer, Elizabeth, 111
Brewer, Melvin D., 69
Brewer-Whitson, Mary Ann, 249
Bridges, Mary E., 71
Bridges, Mildred, 23
Brink, Jeanna, 69
Briones, Gilbert, 211
Brodie, Pam, 246
Brookbanks, C. W., 163
Brooks, Julianne, 125
Brower Leibsohn, Loretta, 156
Brown Harrison, Betty, 263
Brown, Andrea, 134
Brown, Barbara, 169
Brown, Bonnie, 227
Brown, Kuran Anne, 230
Brown, Lorraine, 64
Brown, May, 266
Brown, Nancy, 298
Brown, Phillip, 39
Brown, Raniece, 303
Brown, Robert C., 244
Brown, Ruth, 210
Brown, Trina S., 78
Brown, Wendy, 250
Brown-Harding, Delores, 107
Browning, Jackie, 106
Brunton, Edward, 219
Bryant, E. N., 18
Buchman, Christine, 70
Buffery, Victor Charles, 54
Buller, Grace, 98
Bulthuis, Dolores, 57
Burch, Ethel M., 10
Burch, Laine, 223
Burgess, Margaret, 294
Burgess, Vickie N., 239
Burnett, Karen, 137
Burnie, Dora, 229
Burns, Dawn, 267
Burr, Stacy, 194
Burris, Azalee, 177
Burton, Rick, 283
Busby, Andrew, 245
Busby, Minor, 84
Buskirk, Anneliese, 206
Butler, Blake, 215
Butler, Mary, 132
Buxton, Renate, 14
Bygrave, J. A., 27
Byng, Sherry, 139
Byrne, J., 203

C

Caad, Eugene, 148
Caddie, I. S., 282
Cagle, Beatrice, 271
Cairns, Gary, 12
Calzada, D. J., 203
Cameron, Marie Agnes, 129
Campbell, Alex, 131
Campbell, Faith, 5
Campbell, Neil, 286
Campbell, Tonya, 233
Campeau, Jessica, 184
Canada, Candace, 122
Canger, R. Albert, 89
Canter, J. N., 210
Capella, Michelle, 60
Cappadona, Patrick M., 232
Capps, Martha F., 178
Carlson, Madeline J., 31
Carlton, Gwen, 205
Carnahan Koss, Elizabeth, 203
Carneiro, Cida, 286
Carney, Theresa M., 150
Carraud, Sylvia, 111
Carrion, Teresa, 251
Carroll, Misty M., 106
Carson, Jennifer, 159
Carter Keitel, Patricia, 182
Carter, Carole, 219
Carty, Greta, 274
Carver, Ruth Ann, 287
Cash, Rebecca, 262
Casper, Tiffany, 209
Cassette, Carmen M., 56
Casto, Melissa G., 292
Cater, James, 116
Caudle, Kathy, 194
Caulfield, Lilian, 123
Cavanaugh, Kelly Rosemarie, 58

Cavanaugh, Nancy L., 295
Cerasoli, Jennifer, 191
Chacon, Jr., Felipe, 283
Chalk, Brenda Faye, 53
Chamberlain, Denise, 8
Champ, Teri, 264
Chandler, June V., 108
Chant, D., 188
Chapman, Rubin, 170
Chard, Gerald A., 260
Charlton, Peter M., 230
Chatman, Micki, 285
Chavers, Michele, 228
Chegwidden, Dorothy C., 249
Chesteen, Barbara Marie, 99
Cheung, Marion, 302
Chevalier, Darla, 66, 139
Chew, Thomas, 217
Chiarilli, Cynthia, 174
Chiasson, Ellen, 89
Chiva,, 32
Chock, Brian, 217
Choiniere, Karen Irene, 220
Christopher, Flora, 134
Christopher, Robert, 113
Chrysanthemum, Golden, 200
Chrysostomou, Dafni, 66
Chyten, Anne M., 98
Cincotta, Elaine, 45
Clark, Audrey, 208
Clark, Iva, 33
Clark, Katrina, 205
Clark, Kristi, 128
Clarke, Michael, 160
Clarke, Sonja, 214
Clement, Margarita, 47
Clement, Shannon Marie, 291
Clifton, Ben, 287
Cline, Diana, 300
Clough, Patrick Vincent, 55
Cloyd, Marion, 139
Clyde, Jennifer, 194
Coates, Phyllis M., 50
Cocco, Victoria J., 212
Coffman, Susan E., 248
Coldiron, Anne, 84
Cole, Coig, 142
Cole, Desiree A., 280
Cole, Eileen, 146
Cole, Mary Lou, 89
Cole, Oliver Kenneth, 211
Coleman, Amy Lee, 145
Collins, Richard H., 138
Collins, Robin, 85
Collins, Wanda, 214
Colucci, Alan K., 300
Combs, Elois, 195
Comfort, Victoria, 159
Compton, Rachel, 238
Conkle, Shawn, 239
Connell, Daniel Ray, 276
Cook, Bernice Daniel, 270
Cook, Charleen K., 288
Cook, Hayley, 289
Cook, Luci, 276

Cook, Wanda, 6
Cooke, David Andrew, 257
Cooper, J., 119
Cooper, Jennifer Lee, 291
Cooper, Jonathon, 72
Cooper, Jonna Sue, 187
Coots, Amanda M., 4
Copland, Ann, 294
Corbett, L. B., 75
Costa, Maxine, 201
Costanzo, Theresa, 30
Cottle, Jennifer, 206
Cotton, Elizabeth, 52
Cottrell, Ryan, 226
Counts, Becky, 157
Courtney, Mary, 260
Cousins, Rosa M., 104
Cox, Lola D., 241
Crabtree, Linda F., 303
Craddock, Harry, 222
Craig, Fiona, 200
Cranmer, Amber, 204
Crawford, Jessica Bryanne, 107
Cribb Hucks, Claudia, 179
Crisp, Gordon Jack, 238
Cronin, Wendy, 73
Crook, W. Maurice, 20
Cross, Elizabeth, 300
Crossley, Coral, 123
Crouch, Susan, 261
Crowe, Jr., William F., 26
Cuervo, L. Julian, 257
Culbert-Slute, Merri Lee, 117
Cullers, Cleve, 88
Culp, Jon K., 43
Cummings, Alison Ann, 300
Cummings, Dianne, 90
Cupari, Susan L., 76
Cupe, Cynthia, 160
Curnutt, Lillian, 276
Curran, Bernadette C., 212
Cusick, Carol A., 45
Cyr, Elizabeth A., 88

D

D. C.,, 299
D'Amato Perkins, Theresa M., 76
Dalke, Diana L., 219
Dambruch, Marie, 169
Damon, Stephanie, 134
Danks, Jacquelyn, 83
Datlen, Ray, 259
Davenport, Caroline Ann, 136
Davies, Kaleigh, 301
Davies, Susan, 219
Davis, C. A., 204
Davis, Gina, 107
Davis, Ken Autry, 135
Davis, Kristy, 123
Davis, Louise, 66
Davis, Mary L., 131
Davis, Virginia R., 34
Davis, Vivian, 19
Day, L., 232

De Prima, Jacqueline, 130
De Ramirez, Luisangel, 91
de Ridder, Yvonne, 305
Dean, Linda, 234
Deasey, Jillian R., 241
Deb,, 294
Decker, Marsha, 193
Deering, Olivia, 118
Deffenbaugh Massey, Lillie Maude, 109
DeFrange, Anne Marie, 274
DeJesus, Linda, 62
Dejnak, Sandra, 169
Delong, Sandra H., 185
DeLorean, Ian, 65
Demoss, Frankie J., 303
Denby, Dyann, 201
Denison, Teresa, 301
Denko, Joanne D., 17
Dennis, Sharon, 17
Dent, Joy, 73
Desrosiers, Patricia A., 60
DeVance, Tammie Terrell, 291
Devin, Thomas, 125
Dewolf, Michael R., 287
Diana, Christine, 86
Dickinson, K., 137
Dietrich, Dave, 307
Diffie, Raenell, 282
DiPerna, Jr., Joseph M., 18
Dippold, Jeri, 274
Divolis, Katherine, 11
Dixon, Andrea, 247
Dixon, Mary E., 46
Dobby, Haydn, 209
Docherty, Sally Jane, 163
Dockery, Randall M., 61
Doemel, Becky, 29
Dolson, Keith R., 292
Domke, Henry, 184
Donahue, Mechele, 298
Donahue, Thelma M., 283
Donovan, K. J., 258
Doran, Mary, 177
Dorset, Dennis George, 277
Dotson, Brett A., 49
Douglas, J. W. E., 43
Douse, Mike, 50
Douthart, Kimberly Anne, 55
Dove, Jennifer, 154
Dowie, M. C., 57
Dowman, M. J., 239
Doyle, Maureen Ryan, 72
Draper, Janyce F., 234
Drinkhill, J. M., 260
Drumheller, David, 169
Drysdale, Clayton, 13
Duckworth, Alicia L., 240
DuCray, Villette, 190
Duenez, Roman, 293
Duncan, Dustin R., 184
Duncan, Janet L., 273
Duncan, Ronnie, 58
Duncombe, Dwayne A., 155

Dunn, Jason, 210
Dunnigan, Ashley, 88
Durand, Myrtle, 295
Durnell, Nancy, 54
Durogene, Sara, 182
Dutra, Sherri, 242
Dye, Helen, 56
Dyer, Rebecca N., 32
Dylong, Phyllis, 266

E

Easton, Linda K., 230
Eastwood, Sunnia, 125
Eckhoff, Walter E., 258
Edwards-Bardecker, Meredith, 28
Eggimann, Carla, 285
Eisen, Dianne, 28
Elfberg, Carol, 129
Ellery, Sarah, 172
Ellington, Tiffany, 68
Elliott, Anita, 37
Ellis, Elizabeth Ann, 104
Ellis, Joel W., 59
Ellison, Roderick E., 280
Elmer, Pearl L., 104
Elson, C., 100
Elston, Luretta, 101
Elsworthy, Kerry, 304
Emerson, Kristine, 93
Enarson, Anna E., 24
English, Marlies, 142
Entler, Karyn, 284
Entorf, Dawn Marie, 180
Erickson, Carole M., 244
Espinoza, Darlene, 66
Estrada, Evelyn, 181
Eubanks, Ruth, 38
Evans, Aaron Fitzgerald, 247
Evans, Cheryl, 131
Evans, J., 231
Evans, Melissa, 265
Evans, Robert, 6
Evers, Andrea, 119
Evola, Patrizia, 284

F

Fabela, Jessica, 175
Fairchild, Goldie, 204
Falaleeff, Liana, 117
Falcone, Henry J., 81
Farley, Lana J., 16
Farley, Ronnie, 224
Farrell, Laurie, 178
Farris, Helen, 7
Felder, Sharon Rose, 187
Fellows, Lorraine C., 265
Feltner, Susan J., 33
Ferguson, Sherri Lynn, 126
Fernandes, Tammy, 287
Fernandez, Adrian D., 153
Fernandez, Marga, 29
Fesperman, Louise Kilby, 232
Ffitch-Heyes, Ann, 228

Fiedler, Pamela, 48
Fieger, Karla, 152
Fillmore, Colleen, 41
Finocchio, April, 67
Fischer, Jr., Ashton John, 259
Fishback, Timothy, 267
Fisher, Carol, 248
Fisher, Carole A., 284
Fisher, Rose, 159
Fitzgerald, Brent, 225
Fitzgerald, Constance C., 299
Fitzpatrick, Caryn, 234
Fleming, David, 10
Fleming, June, 146
Fletcher, Chris, 262
Flibotte, Kathleen, 109
Flicker, A. D., 297
Flossie, Jeannie, 164
Fluharty, Erin Kimberly, 224
Foden, Justine, 211
Folga, Nancy T., 181
Forbes, Myrtle B., 220
Forcey, Monica Anne S., 154
Forget, Jason, 25
Forsberg, Travis C., 114
Forster, Janet A., 120
Fortin, Michelle, 121
Foster McColgin, Jean, 277
Foster, Edith, 86
Foucht, Lisa, 51
Fox, Clayton Hobart, 102
Fox, Janet, 173
Fox, Linda, 107
Fox, Sylvia, 165
Franklin, Jimmie Lilly, 228
Franklin, Lesley Ann, 218
Franks, Jackie, 163
Fraser, Lynda, 18
Fraser, Yvonne, 195
Frazier, Arthena M., 152
Frederick, Joy Dorman, 117
Fredette, Jessica L., 127
Free, Veronica, 48
Freeman, Jean M., 103
French–Coleman, Joyce, 114
Frost, Eva, 30
Frydenger, Frances, 171
Fulmer, Lisa, 245
Fulton, Sherri A., 4
Futer, Gwyneth D., 296

G

Gaddy, Villa Kelly, 32
Gaines, Gary, 19
Gaines, Reya J., 74
Gall, Stanley M., 260
Gallacher, E., 221
Gallagher, Chuck, 190
Gallagher, Joan, 100
Gantz, Mary, 293
Garcia, Jacquelyn K., 124
Garcia, Richard A., 128
Garlow, Letha, 254
Garwood, Sophia, 78
Gaskin, Tonia, 158
Gaspard, Jennifer, 279
Gates, Mary Catherine, 232
Gattilia, Edith, 37
Gause Gurganious, Sylvia F., 97
Gawel, Lisa G., 28
Geary, Phyllis, 307
Gerber, Gabriel, 118
Getzfreid, Chrystal, 217
Geyser, Lucy, 266
Gibbs, Felicia Gail, 209
Gibson, Michele E., 168
Gibson, Mindy, 180
Gibson, P. LeAnne, 296
Gibson, Rita F., 203
Gil, Juan Ernesto, 54
Gilbert, Chantal, 173
Gilbert, Venus E., 167
Gilchrist, J. M., 275
Gill–Honczar, M., 207
Gilley, Autumn, 305
Gillispie, Cathy, 148
Gillon, Rachel, 41
Ginger, Jae M., 192
Ginnevan, Elizabeth E., 69
Giordano, Jeannie, 9
Glaze, Darce, 26
Glenn, Elizabeth, 165
Godwin, Lisa M., 171
Golden, Debra F., 37
Gomes, Hayden, 111
Goode, Glyn, 238
Goode, Stuart J., 256
Goodman, Richard, 108
Goodship, Lynda, 115
Goodwin, Patti, 11
Goodyear, Ginny, 151
Gordon, Annette, 77
Gordon, Melissa, 149
Gotting, Lynne, 219
Gouader, Rene, 140
Goulden, Shirley, 5
Grafton, Mary Leona, 74
Graham, Adela, 184
Granger, J., 85
Green, Karen Joyce, 81
Green, Maureen, 51
Green, Mici, 267
Green, Pattie M., 305
Green, Paula, 261
Green, Susan L., 71
Green, Valene, 23
Greenbank, N., 211
Greenfield, Dura, 159
Greer, Elma L., 36
Gregory, Kristin, 302
Grieve, Doreen, 150
Griffin, Holly, 181
Grounds, Cynthia L., 198
Gruber, Tammy, 183
Grzywacz, Marcia Jean, 76
Guardino, Deanne K., 306
Guest, G., 213
Guida, Tara, 222
Gutierrez, Mari, 152
Gutzeit, Bev, 57
Guye, W. Issac, 291
Guzman, Bob, 172

H

Haag, Bobbi, 165
Hadrava, David, 277
Hagans, Cuba, 68
Hagen, Roberta L., 9
Haggett, Pauline, 236
Hahn, Donna, 57
Haight, Sandra L., 150
Haines, Thomas L., 106
Hale, L., 273
Hale, Mable, 168
Hale, Orme, 196
Hales, Pauline, 229
Hall, Darryl, 252
Hall, Denise R., 263
Hall, J. B., 220
Hall, Melanie, 46
Halliday, Caroline, 297
Halliday, Eva, 254
Halter, Kay, 101
Halvorson, Florence, 65
Halvorson, Rae A., 276
Hamilton, Elizabeth, 271
Hamilton, Lesley, 241
Hampson, Debbie, 162
Hancock, Doris, 58
Hanington, Glen, 110
Hanks, Doreene, 70
Hanks, Myra S., 278
Hannah, F., 94
Hannon, Terry J., 290
Hardin, Pauline, 161
Harding, Sue, 8
Harper, Barbara D., 224
Harper, Rachel, 179
Harrell, Jean, 293
Harrington, Jeanette, 87
Harris, Betty, 79
Harris, Dorothy, 156
Harris, Kathryn Emilie, 15
Harris, L. F., 75
Harris, Louis D., 278
Harris, Rita, 40
Harris, Tanner, 22
Harris, Vivian R., 151
Hart, Jennifer, 265
Hart, Jonathan, 226
Hartley, Barbara Ann, 89
Harvey, Noel E., 191
Harville, Laura, 176
Hass, Penelope G., 264
Hassefras, Janet, 268
Hathaway, Lisa, 136
Hatzell, George, 298
Hauer, Mary K., 268
Hawkins, Kayann, 77
Hawkins–Brown, Kim R., 273
Hayes, Linda, 113
Hayes, Rose, 35
Hedgebeth, Kimberly, 275
Hedgecock, Anne, 302
Hedrick, Becky, 73
Heimbaugh, Heather, 162
Heimes, Charmaine, 101
Helba, Doris, 98
Helein, Jane, 215
Helms, Jennifer, 164
Helton, Jennifer, 236
Henderson, Georgina, 78
Henderson, J. M., 138
Henderson, Keith, 295
Henderson, Marcos, 154
Henderson, R., 138
Henderson, Shelby J., 177
Hendrickson, Dale, 156
Hendrix, Vicki, 217
Hendron, Crystal, 272
Henkel, K. D., 148
Henley, Sally, 186
Henry, Delroy, 87
Hensley, Mary, 302
Henson, Charlene, 183
Henson, Monica, 205
Hepburn, James R., 45
Herbig, Anne, 4
Herdman, Kathy, 229
Herreid, Elizabeth, 17
Herring, James, 212
Hetherington, Craig, 67
Hetzel, Barbara, 13
Hickman, Celestine, 145
Hicks, Paul, 110
Highfield, Yvonne, 88
Hill, Catherine, 172
Hill, Ginger, 229
Hill, Krysta, 83
Hill, Teresa, 113
Hiscock, Betty M., 52
Hiscoke, R. D., 144
Hite, Sheila A., 60
Hoback, Lisa, 25
Hock, Tammy J., 70
Hockycko McLellan, Francesca, 281
Hodgson, Tysen, 198
Hoff, Kimberly, 99
Hoffman, Susan, 93
Hogan, Jean A., 81
Hoggard, Sheila, 229
Holden, Tim, 271
Holder–Riches, Alanna, 51
Holland, Lois Y., 193
Holliday, Thomas S., 84
Holmes, Annzetta, 143
Holsombeck, Elizabeth, 264
Hope, Valuy, 294
Hopkins, Donald E., 202
Hopp, Susan, 216
Horan, Jeffrey J., 292
Horn, Edna, 130
Horne, Sandie, 248
Hoshal Smith, Darcy, 281
Houldey, Hazel, 262
Howard, Carol L., 152
Howard, Duan, 110
Howard, Josh, 52
Howells, Sandra J., 261

Howland, Donna, 59
Hoyer, Anna, 187
Hubbs, Lela Mae, 126
Huckstepp, Nicola, 202
Hudson, Cynthia Lynn, 269
Hughes, Dannie, 221
Hughie, Wee, 164
Hughson, Jessica, 202
Hulek–Doyle, Michele M., 299
Hull, Loette M., 254
Hume, Graham, 249
Humes, C. Lincoln, 13
Humphreys, Perdita Carman, 250
Hunt, Danielle, 203
Hunter, Jim, 56
Hunter, P. A., 123
Hurd, Amy, 195
Huskey, Heather, 233
Husted, Harry, 227
Huston, Courtney, 25
Huxtable, Muriel, 42
Hyde, Dawn R., 183

I

Iafrate, Michaela, 192
Imperiale, Maria J., 90
Ince, Cecil George, 138
Ingalsbe, Marcia A., 131
Isaacson, Laura, 17
Iskaris, Isis, 196
Isle, Monica, 34
Izzard, W., 112

J

Jablonski, Sally K., 177
Jacks, David R., 100
Jackson, Ada, 241
Jackson, Conni, 9
Jackson, Elizabeth A., 69
Jackson, Nancy Lee, 265
Jackson, Shirley, 173
Jacobs, Myeisha, 103
Jacoby, Stephanie M., 22
Jaichner, Jennifer M., 101
Jain, G., 119
James, Annette, 163
James, Deborah K., 171
James, Jayne, 286
James, Kathryn, 154
Jamieson, Karen–Anne, 178
Jamison, Angela, 186
Jarbeau, Mary J., 92
Jasilli, Yolanda, 278
Jaxson–Jager, Carol, 119
Jefferson, Michelle, 280
Jenkins, Mary M., 116
Jenkins, Regina, 117
Jenkinson, Sheila, 275
Jesson, R. J., 147
Jilge, Mandy, 296
Jobson, Susan, 242
John, Ian, 253
Johns, Cody, 67
Johnson Adkins, June, 270
Johnson, Bonnie–Lee, 166
Johnson, Braden, 160
Johnson, Celeste, 231
Johnson, Eula H., 177
Johnson, F. M., 10
Johnson, Janis A., 49
Johnson, Karen, 53
Johnson, Kathryn, 85
Johnson, Lisa J., 256
Johnson, Mel, 36
Johnson, Monique, 242
Johnson, Natasha R., 251
Johnson, Roy, 183
Johnson, Stuart R., 243
Johnson, Verva M., 52
Johnson–Bentley, Ella, 96
Johnston, Nellie M., 109
Joiner, Carolyn Mae, 55
Jones, Daisy E., 75
Jones, Eric, 222
Jones, Jason, 10
Jones, Jennifer, 147, 194
Jones, Jessica, 290
Jones, Joanna, 61
Jones, John E., 33
Jones, Jon Paul Emmanual, 66
Jones, Jonathan, 155
Jones, Mel, 221
Jones, Shirley, 80
Jones, William B., 89
Jorgensen, Lynn, 27
Joshuas, M. M., 150
Joyner, Lisa P., 301
Julian, Sorrow, 90

K

Kabata, Katy, 50
Kadow, Cynthia M., 19
Kahn, Lillian, 143
Kahn, Sandi, 45
Kai, Cyrus, 144
Kalmon, Cheryl, 269
Kammet, Pauline H., 185
Kane, Marjorie, 235
Kang, Kimberly, 151
Kanwit, Bert, 255
Karak, John, 144
Karl, Kathleen L., 185
Kaspar, B. E., 123
Kauffman, Steve, 63
Kauser, F., 275
Kaye, Yvonne Ruth, 197
Kays, Becky, 244
Keefe, Adalyn, 70
Keegan, Melody, 268
Keeler, E. M., 218
Keeney, Roger Dale, 208
Keeter, Grace G., 118
Kelly, Jack, 42
Kelly, Jr., Ron, 274
Kelly, Julie C., 55
Kelly, Megan, 64
Kelly, Siobhan, 272
Kempf, Kelli, 179
Kennedy, J. P., 234
Kenny, Paddy, 156
Kenshol, Leslie Anne, 237
Kent, Katie, 94
Kerr, Helen, 238
Kezele, Karen, 161
Khalid, Emma, 223
Khursigara, Cezar, 14
Kibler, Penny, 129
Kibunguchi, Brigit, 93
Kidder, Cynthia K., 61
Kiley, Eve, 257
Kimmons, Janet T., 306
Kindred, Katherine, 85
Kindred, Rebecca, 145
King, Charles, 238
King, Heidi, 187
King, Jr., Anthony J., 248
King, Linda, 4
King, Michele, 198
King, Sandra, 193
Kingham, Nikki, 216
Kingsley, Jean A., 232
Kingston, Roberta, 288
Kinshott, Margaret, 301
Kinzer, Christine, 74
Kissell, Crede M., 96
Kittrell, Elizabeth, 102
Klingensmith, Deborah S., 118
Klopfer, Catherine, 240
Kneeshaw, Kirk, 304
Knight, Akia, 62
Knight, Mildred H., 137
Knopp, Becky Sue, 59
Knox, Samantha, 120
Koch, Christopher, 213
Koenig, Douglas, 43
Koldenhof, Katherine, 145
Kontautas, Laina, 245
Kos, Andrew Joseph, 53
Kovaschetz, Jammey, 68
Kowal, Eileen B., 168
Kowalski, Mary, 141
Kramer, Donna, 223
Krieger, Rita M., 196
Krueger, Virginia M., 256
Kubiak, James, 224
Kuhn, Renee, 128
Kulowryi, Sherry, 180
Kundrat, Albert, 303

L

La Manna, Jim M., 225
Lackey, Michael, 143
Lacy, Matt, 269
Ladd, Brian M., 253
Lahela,, 134
Lambert, Jan, 112
Lambert, Jennifer Lea, 208
Lammers, Daniel, 47
Langdon, Katrena, 109
Langford, Lisa, 231
Langstroth, Marion, 166
LaPlant, Arlys, 237
LaPoint, Karen Amy, 116
Larcombe, Laura, 255
Largent, Beverly, 149
Larkins, Tina, 148
Lashley, Donald, 20
Latham, Cliff J., 42
LaTour, Esther, 180
Law, Deborah J., 286
Lawford, Heather, 247
Lawwill, Veronica, 281
Layton, Amanda, 68
Lazzara, Melissa, 250
Leatham Thomas, Mabel, 218
Leavoy, Crystal, 204
Leblanc, Mark, 297
Ledford, Kristen, 226
Lee, Cheryl, 153
Lee, Jonathan, 122
Lee, Jr., Kenneth P., 256
Lees, Sharon–Anne, 188
LeGrande, Terri, 207
Leibowitz, Seth, 147
Leininger, Michelle, 124
Leipold, Katharine G., 114
Leonard, Gary F., 90
Lesley, Jenny Lynn, 234
Leslie, Mark Edward, 124
Lester, Geraldine, 99
Lester, Karen, 44
Leuenberger, Jr., Arnold, 91
Levy, Michael, 120
Lewis, Etta, 77
Lewis, Lauren, 72
Lewis, Phyllis A., 223
Lewis, Steve, 251
Lewis–Rand, Avonelle, 266
Lewis–Stratford, Leonora, 102
Liao, Kimberley, 233
Lightkep, L., 71
Lightner, Katherine, 53
Lilley, J., 38
Lilley, Rebecca, 99
Linville, Nancy L., 133
Lipin, Joan C., 62
Lippert, Josh, 173
Lisney, Helen B., 113
Litman, LoriLee, 91
Little, Dixie L., 222
Little, Ruth Renee, 293
Long, Elizabeth B., 133
Long, Linda, 160
Long, Stacy L., 143
Longenberger, Carla, 56
LoPresto, Vincent, 9
Loredo, Jr., Ernesto, 45
Lorge, Melinda, 141
Lovegrove, Beverly, 243
Lovelace, Amanda, 267
Loyd, Sharon, 15
Lucas, Leslie R., 260
Lucero, Glenda Louise, 91
Luchun, Carol J., 122
Lucock, J., 56
Ludlow, Jacqueline, 97
Lukl, Bethenie Anne, 158
Lutz, Patti, 281
Lyle, Angel, 276

Lynch, Heather, 270
Lynch, Lucille T., 175
Lyons, Grace A., 102
Lyons, Michael, 121
Lysher, Nina, 128

M

Mabry, Sam, 64
Macaulay, Sidney S., 140
MacGuire, Daniel, 199
Mack, Cashel, 80
Mackay, Marion, 235
Mackenzie, Jennifer A., 64
MacPhee, Mary, 83
MacPhee, Norman, 121
Madden, Johnny Lee, 95
Maddox, Karen, 67
Major, Ian L., 268
Major, Jerrie, 264
Malone, Bryan, 304
Manges, Christine Ann, 105
Manjuck, Brenda, 216
Mann, Amie, 77
Manning, Alexis, 227
Mansell, Erma, 306
Maplethorpe, Claire, 135
Marchesi, J., 149
Marcotulio, P., 8
Marder, Clare S., 36
Marquer, Sarah, 219
Marr, Joseph V., 252
Marshall, David, 35
Marshall, Jim, 93
Marshall, Shirley A., 215
Martin, Barbara, 207
Martin, Dennis, 107
Martin, Godfrey J., 120
Martin, June, 240
Martin, Laurabelle, 85
Martin, Lucille, 251
Martin, Malcolm F., 284
Martin, Marlene, 305
Martin, Mary, 147
Martin, Stephen, 11
Martinez, Theresa, 174
Marty, Danielle, 74
Maryon, Vickie, 71
Mascaro, Nancy Carol, 79
Masters, Jennifer Dianne, 152
Mathieson, Angela, 220
Matthews, Joyce, 274
Maude, Rose, 188
Maunders, Cyril J., 188
Mayer, Lisa M., 180
Mayer, Peggy L., 222
Mayer, Shellie, 151
Maynard, Virginia Rose, 131
McAuley, Caroline, 301
McAveety, Sally, 274
McBride, JoAnn, 178
McClain-Frogge, Betty, 303
McCormack, Laura, 283
McCran, Teresa, 160
McCray, Pearl E., 97
McCrea, J. A., 29
McCreath, John, 126

McDaniels, Mary C., 122
McDonald, Elizabeth, 12
McDonaldson, R. A., 295
McDuffie, Scott, 230
McGarry, Margaret T., 170
McGinley, Jerry, 16
McGrane, Peggy, 141
McGrath, Bernadette, 161
McHugh, Joe, 225
McKenzie, Christine, 296
McKenzie, Marjorie E., 205
McKinney, Pamela H., 132
McLaughlin, Jared, 293
McManus, Lisa, 61
McNally, A., 120
McNamara, Rose, 119
McNeil, M., 116
McNeilis, Valerie, 18
McNulty, Marie, 11
McQuagge, D. A., 241
McVay III, Richard Lee, 98
Meadows, Valerie, 14
Medlam, Linda, 138
Mee, Edith, 250
Meeker, Joyce, 124
Meeks, Noah, 189
Meigs, Van L., 109
Melone, Margie Ruth, 102
Mendoza, Yolanda, 289
Mericle, Amy, 288
Merrilees, Susanne, 162
Merrill, Erma Jean, 46
Merritt, Ruby M., 65
Meskill, James, 176
Messinger, G. R., 254
Meyer, Dagmar W., 133
Meyers, Wretha, 146
Michael, Keszeg, 202
Middleston, E., 104
Middleton, Janet, 57
Mided, Ann, 140
Mieras, Bonnie L., 184
Mierzejewski, Justin, 101
Mihal, Margareta G., 168
Mijares, Yvonne A., 59
Mijic, Mile, 178
Miles, Kelly M., 292
Millard, Wendy, 197
Miller, Chad, 111
Miller, Emily, 65
Miller, Janice, 178, 225
Miller, Mary A., 171
Miller, Patricia, 84
Millich, Daral N., 192
Milligan, Margaret M., 135
Miner, Theresa L., 103
Minnicks, Latise D., 279
Mirage, Amethyst, 299
Mirosevic, Ivan, 62
Misenhimer, Ann R., 112
Mistretta, Richard, 287
Miszta-Lane, Helena, 41
Mitchell, Gaylene, 246
Mitchell, Jeffrey L., 72
Mitchell, Jennifer, 300

Mizzi, Marje Kaena, 78
Moat, Chris, 17
Moindroti, P. C., 81
Molyneux, Victor, 139
Montgomery, Mary, 98
Montoya, Athena, 228
Moore, Deborah, 205
Moore, Patricia Ann, 214
Moore, Tammy A., 155
Morey, Marcella, 51
Morgan, Clara L., 61
Morlan, Dorothy, 253
Morris, Lisa, 208
Morris, Reg, 189
Morriss, Paula, 140
Morrow, Ramona D., 254
Morton, Janet, 164
Moser, Alexandra, 210
Mosier, Rachelle, 53
Motschenbacher, Anna, 196
Moussally, Lois, 53
Mowatt, Wanda, 266
Muer Tanner, Lisa, 15
Muffett, Amanda, 86
Muir Colligan, Margaret, 269
Mullins, D. F., 59
Mumpower, Shannon, 148
Murphy, Joan, 265
Musgrave, Meredith, 249
Myers, Alison C., 193

N

Nathan, Keith, 124
Nee, P. Vincent, 39
Neggers, Joey, 5
Negron, Rosene, 189
Neil, Bob, 16
Nelson, Beverly A., 158
Nelson, Deborah K., 250
Nelson, Hazel L., 279
Nelson, Lisa, 149
Nelson, Lynda Rae, 99
Nessel, Nelle, 191
Nettleton, Richard Lee, 175
Newell, Lisa G., 92
Newman, Eileen, 137
Newton, Norma Louise, 162
Nguyen, Tung T., 292
Nichols, Diane, 108
Nichols, Michelle, 271
Nielsen, Raymond E., 80
Niemi, Sandra, 58
Noice, Erin A., 132
Nolan, Joe, 95
Norderud, Jewel M., 32
Norman, Nassawanda, 217
Norris, Lorraine S., 78
Northover, Sue, 121
Notestine, Lawrence Edward, 97
Nuhfer, Shirley A., 182
Nyarady, Teresa A., 132
Nyffeler, Lois M., 54

O

O'Banyoun, Constance, 52
O'Brien Parker, Patricia, 161
O'Brien, Jean G., 82
O'Brien, Maureen, 79
O'Daniel, Millie, 48
O'Reilly, Colette M., 103
O'Reilly, Shirley, 118
O'Rourke Praria, Christine, 143
Oakes, Kristina, 49
Oakwood, Kevin L., 284
Ochoa, Rosa Maria, 198
Oesch, Kimberly, 181
Okorn, Lorna, 142
Old, J. C., 18
Oliva, Annette Mercedes, 202
Ondracek, Kayla, 252
Orr, Tom, 233
Ortiz, Erica, 86
Ortiz, Henry M., 63
Osenbaugh, Kristi, 290
Oshea, Helen, 272
Overton Bulger, Elaine, 73
Owens, Tom, 182

P

Paene, Andru, 264
Paeth, Mary Lynn, 263
Paige, Rilla, 81
Palmer, Charlotte L., 198
Palmer, N., 115
Palubinski, Faith, 117
Pankiw, Dee, 298
Panza, Barbara J., 278
Parker, Elizabeth, 132
Parker, Joseph, 11
Parker, Kim, 200
Parkin, Joy, 146
Parks, Jr., Robert R., 221
Parsons, Kevin B., 64
Pascoe, Erika, 212
Pathan, Nayab, 253
Patten, Gail Christie, 179
Patterson, Barbara A., 112
Paulhus, Jenny, 190
Payne, Elana, 36
Pearson, Wayne E., 104
Pederson, Anita L., 9
Peete, Jessica, 148
Pelengaris, Paul A., 135
Pennington, Shane, 227
Pequeno, Jenet G., 164
Perkins, Dave E., 151
Perkins, Juliet, 166
Perkins, Valerie, 272
Perkins, Wanda, 92
Perry, Jillian, 252
Perry, Nancy, 145
Persten, Geoffrey, 44
Petano, Eileen, 204
Peterson, Brenda L., 86
Peterson, Jan, 304

Peterson, Lia, 190
Petty, Jackie F., 286
Pfingstag, Alice L., 169
Pflugradt, Deanna, 268
Phang, Mabel W., 81
Phelan, Loraine A., 269
Phelps, Willena, 270
Philips, Marvin J., 49
Phillips O'Day, Gladys, 263
Phillips, Bernice, 65
Phinney, Kathleen E., 125
Pick, Jeremy C., 247
Pierre, Kathleen, 106
Pike, Alice, 40
Pinckney, Melissa, 158
Pinnock, Imogene, 252
Pinson, Rebecca Ann, 288
Plaus, Marion E., 94
Pleasance, Hilda C., 162
Plummer, David L., 173
Pollard, Revena M., 83
Pool, Bianca F., 143
Poppenga, Shirley, 97
Porterfield, M. L., 304
Post, Robin, 267
Postlethwaite, Rosemary, 105
Potters, Alberta D., 171
Poulsen, Melanie, 300
Powell, Alda R., 49
Powell, Geoff, 237
Powelson, Donna A., 153
Prall, Jessica, 289
Pratt, Cindy, 172
Pratt, D. C., 255
Prehart Fourcaud, Lorraine Helen, 237
Prentice, Richard C., 174
Prest, I., 141
Preston, Laura, 44
Price, James C., 115
Price, Marlene, 305
Prickett, Tony, 179
Provost, C. Antonio, 279
Pum Anders, Hilda, 149
Puttonen, Erin, 256

Q

Qualls, Ryan, 185

R

Radcliffe, Thomas E., 80
Radin, Cheryl Ann, 186
Raes, Resi Olimpia, 124
Rafuse, Patricia S., 255
Rains, Jr., Billy D., 88
Rainwater, Bill, 277
Rajkumar, Jenifer, 13
Ramirez, Nicholas, 137
Randall, S. M., 261
Rapport, Pamela L., 74
Rasmussen, Sarah, 215
Ratanavong, Kiton, 146
Ratcliff, Mandy, 139
Ratcliffe, Elizabeth, 251
Raus, Annie Mae, 268
Ravetto, Chris, 231

Ray, Louisa, 122
Read, Elizabeth, 181
Reber, Rebecka, 191
Reed, Isabel, 84
Reel, Daisy W., 129
Reese, Aaron, 54
Reeves, Veronica W., 15
Reid, Samantha, 161
Reinhart, Victoria, 153
Reisnour, Stephanie P., 211
Reissener, Briana, 221
Rempel, Susie, 69
Renata, Xina Michelle, 39
Rene, Cameo, 282
Retzer, Michael, 213
Reynolds II, William R., 109
Reynolds, Alfred, 114
Rice, Lori Wade, 43
Richards, Jill L., 226
Richards, Sandra L., 262
Richardson, Amy, 260
Richardson, Carol, 167
Richardson, H. E., 203
Richardson, Jodi A., 8
Richardson, Marcia, 264
Richardson, Robert M., 244
Richardson-Wilson, Tena, 302
Richens, Lesley, 282
Richman Colonna, Tracy L., 151
Richmond, Angus, 113
Richmond, C., 115
Ricketts, Joanne, 186
Rickwood, S. K., 15
Ridd, Brian, 73
Rieniets, Peggy R., 126
Rightmire, Wendy, 236
Riner, Debbie, 298
Ritchie, Patricia S., 248
Roberts, Chastity N., 103
Roberts, Jeadenia Ann, 285
Roberts, Shonette, 77
Robertson, Ben, 95
Robinson, G. R., 233
Robinson, Karen, 238
Rod, Justin, 139
Rodgers, Helen, 165
Rodney, Helen Rebecca, 24
Rodriguez, Terese, 199
Roebuck, Rita, 138
Rogers, Linda S., 290
Rogers, Sabrina, 19
Rogers, Tara Christine, 293
Rohan, Deborah, 87
Roller, Amanda I., 57
Rolli, Linda, 206
Romano, Francis J., 199
Romanyschyn, Kristen, 112
Romine, Mary, 252
Rorabaugh, Deanna, 306
Rosen, Larry, 128
Ross, Judith A., 92
Rotert, Patty, 59
Rothschild, Barry, 121
Rourke, Patricia G., 17

Rowbottom, Andrea, 295
Roy, C. V., 163
Rue, Tammy W., 95
Ruse, Jessica, 271
Russell, Leah Allen, 111
Russell, M. F., 91
Russell, Pauline, 66
Rutenberg, Mary Lou, 209
Ruth, Helen V., 48
Rutterbush, Bobbie Jo, 64
Ryan, Donna A., 254
Ryan, Stacy, 63
Rybeck, Coretta, 84
Rysdale, Brian, 39

S

Sabo, James, 90
Sagisi, Joseph A., 234
Sampley, Laura, 67
Sampson, Christopher, 98
Sanders, Jennifer, 50
Sandy, Jr., Vance, 160
Sangcap, Loriedel D., 242
Sapienza, Beverly, 157
Saracco, Scot, 77
Saunders, Gail Wilkerson, 29
Saunders, Steve, 163
Savage, Pearl, 306
Sawey, Doris A., 167
Sawtelle, Barbara R., 5
Saxby, Sheryl, 114
Saxby, Victor, 258
Saxton, F., 115
Sayers, G. B., 218
Schaffer, Christy Marie, 297
Scherling, Ellen, 236
Schick, Barbara, 165
Schilling, Paul R., 225
Schirrmacher, Marlene K., 74
Schmader, Kimberlee, 27
Schmeling, Manda, 243
Schmersal, Joanna L., 170
Schoppe, Linda, 12
Schowers, Bruce, 224
Schulze, Jon R., 270
Schumacher, Robert E., 193
Scott, K. A., 140
Scott, Lisa, 146
Scott, Ruth A., 14
Scott, Wednesday A., 17
Scourby, Maria, 237
Seabrook, Annie L., 152
Seado, James, 133
Sedor, Barbara J., 33
Semeniuk, Melissa A., 145
Sernotti, Craig, 94
Sessions, Mabel, 127
Setzer, Sheri, 46
Sewell, Ruth, 228
Sexton, Hannah, 79
Shaffer, Eric B., 282
Shah, Annoria Lynn, 60
Shah, Kiran, 48
Shareak, Joan J., 159
Sharp, Mary K., 200

Sharpton, Homer, 142
Shaulis, Bonnie, 106
Shaw, Amanda, 277
Sheetz, Kimberly A., 73
Sheila, Aunt, 174
Shelton, Martine L., 248
Shepherd, Jamey, 279
Shepherd, Jennifer Suzanne, 170
Sheridan, Christalyn, 270
Sherman, Helen, 62
Sherrard, Isobel, 40
Shew, N., 134
Shiffman, Rhonda, 105
Shindledecker, Todd, 35
Shlosberg, Kevin, 224
Short, Stacey, 150
Shoukri, Gina, 275
Shoup, Jennifer, 128
Simmonds, Rebecca, 129
Simms, Thomas J., 170
Simon Sears, Sebastian Darrel, 31
Simon, Gerri, 37
Simon, Linda L., 44
Sims, Ellen, 5
Sims, Kathy, 189
Sizemore, Walter M., 158
Skazinski, Eugene, 60
Skoog, Jan, 166
Skripochenko, Nicole, 230
Slater, Gertrude Ann, 207
Slater, Russell, 273
Smallwood, Tracy, 195
Smart, David, 193
Smathers, Linda, 80
Smith, Aldrema, 213
Smith, Andrea, 190
Smith, Audrey Nadine, 6
Smith, D. J., 112, 116
Smith, David, 278
Smith, David J., 141
Smith, Dorothy E., 35
Smith, Elinor, 130
Smith, Gary J., 283
Smith, Glenna, 301
Smith, Jenny, 307
Smith, Joanne, 272
Smith, Julie, 108
Smith, Laura K., 144
Smith, M. J., 125
Smith, Marilyn, 245
Smith, Maxine, 79
Smith, Rachel Ann, 113
Smith, Richard, 6
Smith, Robin M., 242
Smith, Sean, 255
Snead, Tammy L., 176
Snyder, Evelyn J., 249
Soares, Karen, 70
Solberg, Beverly, 185
Solley, Troyce, 7
Solverson, Samantha S., 286
Somerton, Carrie, 61

Somsen, Johanna, 257
Souder, Vicki L., 147
Southard, Carrie, 217
Sparrock, Jean H., 22
Spires, Marylou, 136
Sprecher, Julie, 240
Spry, Jack E., 107
Spunky,, 127
Squire, Eunice C., 261
Srbu, Georgeta, 118
St. Fort, Yolaine, 223
Stallard, Dawn Marie, 165
Stampone, Mary, 230
Standifer, Mary S., 246
Stanley, Eric, 111
Stanway, Joyce, 110
Stecco, Kristina, 7
Steeber, Doris, 153
Steel, P., 273
Steepy, Ruth E., 85
Steinhilber, Ruth, 265
Sternberg, Claudette, 147
Stevens, Andrew, 273
Stevens, J., 96
Stevens, Judy A., 159
Stevenson, Dawn, 199
Stevenson, Jean, 94
Stewart, Kira, 44
Stewart, Koleena, 194
Stigen, Diane R., 76
Stiles, Harold, 243
Still, Allison, 47
Still, Beverly A., 295
Stirn, Amanda Anne, 12
Stone, Jeannie, 56
Storer, Karissa, 182
Storms, Deedle, 51
Stough, Hoyt D., 125
Stout, Meleah, 82
Strackeljahn, Freyda E., 5
Strahler, Mary D., 7
Straniero, Gerard, 206
Stratton, Vivian, 87
Stratz, Teresa, 246
Strom, Helen L., 91
Strothers, Petrina, 290
Stubbs, G. J., 110
Sturm, Ethel M., 201
Sullivan, Anne Mary, 259
Supe, Mildred, 43
Surette, Barbara, 279
Surles, Kay, 60
Sussex, Jan, 189
Sutherland, Leon, 116
Swambo, P., 16
Swanbeck, C. Robert, 11
Swaney, Mary Alice, 291
Swank–Kolb, Marcie, 14
Sweeny, Janina, 294
Swift, Jonathan, 23
Symons, Mary, 120
Synowicz, Michael, 297

T

Tabb, Teresa A., 183
Taggard, Robert S., 262
Tally, Alice Jane, 93
Taormina, Marianne, 199
Tapp, Violet, 130
Tartaglia III, Joseph A., 34
Tate, Chris, 280
Taylor, Angel, 288
Taylor, Beckie, 18
Taylor, Lachlan, 100
Taylor, Sarah, 213
Taylor, Shirley, 51
Taylor, Troy E., 38
Tedder, Ann, 289
Tegge, Della H., 180
Tempel, Margaret A., 126
Tenny, Marie Ann, 4
Terrero Rivera, Jenny, 16
Terris, Nikki C., 187
Terry, Evelyn, 63
Thain, Agnes, 196
Thatcher, Charlotte, 177
Thomas Mulligan, Jaya, 115
Thomas, A., 55
Thomas, Denise, 294
Thomas, Juanita M., 186
Thomas, Laura, 49
Thompson, Beverly R., 26
Thompson, C. R., 218
Thompson, Christine, 93
Thompson, Kenneth Michael, 161
Thompson, Melissa S., 48
Thompson, R. F., 62
Thompson, Sheila K. A., 275
Thornton, Paul R., 54
Thurman, Steve, 298
Tiboldo, Geraldine, 121
Tich, Kim E., 244
Tiernan, Diana, 19
Tilley, Ryan, 291
Tingle, Angelia B., 71
Tioran, Karen, 86
Tocci, Carrie Anne, 142
Tolle, Bonnie L., 167
Tracey, Ian, 175
Traynor, James A., 72
Trelles, Guadalupe, 164
Triplett, Sheryl A., 296
Tripp, Richard E., 235
Troolines, Amanda, 188
Tuinstra, Tresa, 130
Turkel, Louise, 225
Turmeau, Gilly, 243
Turnbull, Georgette, 272
Turner Collins, Nancy, 276
Tyler, E. C., 92

V

Valand, Diane M., 22
Valentine, L. J., 287
Vallabh, Sonia, 89
Van De Voorde, G. A., 105
VanAllen, M. S., 141
Vanden Langenberg, D. J., 231
VanderFord, Sylvia, 117
Vanderlee, Jennifer, 281
Vasquez, William L., 114
Vassar, Angela, 31
Vaughn, Mark, 127
Venters, Eric D., 155
Vera, Jr., Rene, 216
Verma, Kamni, 103
Villarreal, Adriana, 23
Villena, Carlo J., 46
Viner, Miriam, 100
Vivian, Val, 173

W

Wachholz, Maxine A., 296
Wagstaff, Barbara, 140
Wakeland, Kathy, 104
Walker, James P., 215
Walker, Laurie Ann, 58
Walker, Patricia Elizabeth, 297
Wall, Ann–Marie, 175
Wallace, Stephanie L., 13
Walsh, Robert E., 263
Walters, Jacqueline, 134
Walulik, Janinka E., 30
Ward, Glenn Isaac, 246
Ward, Laurie A., 133
Ward, Lyndsey, 187
Ward, Mary R., 87
Wardle Bron, Tracey, 242
Warnek, Lucille, 196
Warren, Susan M., 157
Watson, Donnie, 209
Watt, Sally Ann, 243
Wawro, Joann, 136
Weaver, Jeffrey, 206
Weaver, Pamela J., 83
Webb, Jamilla, 247
Webb, Timothy, 162
Weber, Cecelia, 280
Weber, Isabelle F., 210
Weber, Rob S., 303
Webster, Lydia, 105
Weeks, Heather, 8
Weeks, Mary, 211
Weeks, Phyllis, 50
Weichert, Larry, 299
Weidman, Jill D., 30
Weiseman, Mary L., 197
Wellman, Jr., Timothy A., 201
Wennerstrom, Katie, 133
Werdebaugh, Patricia, 76
Wersyn, Andrea, 119
West, LaTonya Lynn, 156
Weybrecht, Ken R., 222
Wheeler Luby, Grace, 10
Wheeler, Brenda, 244
Wheeler, Mary Paula G., 27
Whelton, Marilyn, 176
Whirl, Jermaine, 204
Whitaker, Brenda G., 63
Whitcher, Betty, 259
White, Albert, 194
White, Betty, 190
White, Deborah, 208
White, Harold L., 212
White, Philip, 218
Whitehouse, Jean, 192
Whitehouse, June, 41
Whitlow, Jennifer, 158
Widdowson, Vivien, 239
Wietrick, Bill, 88
Wilbur, Pamela C., 96
Wilkinson, Joyce, 12
Williams, Deborah Christine, 144
Williams, Eddie M., 216
Williams, Gerald D., 14
Williams, Hubert D., 58
Williams, Jeremy D., 271
Williams, Monica, 79
Williams, N., 150
Williams, Patricia, 40
Williams, Ray, 289
Williams, Stanley, 220
Williams, T., 63
Williams, Wes, 183
Willis, Josie, 239
Willis, Katie, 25
Wilson, A. R., 259
Wilson, Barbara, 255
Wilson, Cheryl A., 50
Wilson, Eloise, 90
Wilson, Erica, 184
Wilson, Linda, 179
Wilson, Mike, 235
Wilson, Patricia N., 200
Wilson, Robert Earnest, 185
Wilson, Trina, 157
Windell, Brenda J., 288
Winebrenner, Lisa, 172
Wingfield, Rita, 195
Winsor, Marian, 280
Wisdom, Pauline, 236
Wise, K. L., 235
Wise, Stephanie Lynn, 209
Wiseman, Loring W., 289
Witherspoon, Amalean, 144
Wolfe, Vanessa, 182
Woman, Wolf, 71
Wong, Bradley, 235
Wong, Elaine, 12
Wood, Sheila Ann, 200
Woodall, Natalie Joy, 307
Woodall, Tammera S., 305
Woodard, Paulette, 47
Woodford, Carol L., 253
Woodhams, Keith, 245
Woodley, Patrica, 9
Woods, D., 220
Woods, Heidi R., 76
Woods, Pam, 227
Woodward, Lesley, 6
Woolums, Don, 82
Wright, B., 46
Wright, Barbara L., 154
Wright, Marian, 135
Wuest, Tracy A., 212
Wynn, Naomi, 75

Y

Yankee, Jessica, 126
Yarbrough, Kathy A., 26
Yates, Joan H., 122
Youe, F. K., 34

Young, Amanda, 101
Youngs, Patricia, 221

Z

Zamal, Andrew, 108
Zarzeczny, Matt D., 169
Zeiger, Perry, 170
Zimbrich, Charmane, 127
Zorrer Ley, Yvonne, 227
Zuk, Donna J., 24
Zumwalt, Steven, 181